Revolutionary Patriots

of

Washington County

Maryland

1776-1783

Henry C. Peden, Jr.

WILLOW BEND BOOKS
2005

WILLOW BEND BOOKS
AN IMPRINT OF HERITAGE BOOKS, INC.

Books, CDs, and more—Worldwide

For our listing of thousands of titles see our website
at
www.HeritageBooks.com

Published 2005 by
HERITAGE BOOKS, INC.
Publishing Division
65 East Main Street
Westminster, Maryland 21157-5026

COPYRIGHT © 1998 HENRY C. PEDEN, JR.

All rights reserved. No part of this book may be reproduced or transmitted in any form or by any means, electronic or mechanical, including photocopying, recording or by any information storage and retrieval system without written permission from the author, except for the inclusion of brief quotations in a review.

International Standard Book Number: 1-888265-80-9

INTRODUCTION

This book has been compiled for the purpose of serving as a research tool for locating the men and women of Washington County, Maryland (which at the time included the present day counties of Allegany and Garrett) who served in the military, rendered material aid to the army or navy, took the Oath of Allegiance and Fidelity, served in an office or on a committee at the town, county or state level, or in some fashion contributed and supported the fight for freedom by the American colonies from the rule of Great Britain during the Revolutionary War, 1775-1783.

It is hoped that this book, which is the eleventh in a series on Revolutionary War patriots and soldiers in Maryland, will encourage and enable interested persons to become members of such patriotic organizations as The Sons of the American Revolution, The Daughters of the American Revolution, The Sons of the Revolution, and The Society of the Cincinnati.

Information for this book has been gleaned from many primary and secondary sources, which makes this book far more than just a listing of names and ranks. Most of the approximately 4,000 persons named herein have genealogical data included with their respective entries, such as places of residence and dates of birth, death, and marriage, names of wives, husbands, children and other relatives, plus physical descriptions, occupations, and information gleaned from newspapers, church records, military lists, pension files, probate records, equity cases, and other court records.

Each entry in this book has been documented and a key to that documentation has been implemented within the text to enable the reader to review the cited source. A letter followed by a number is the code used for a source and the page within that source. For example, [Ref: D-555] would indicate that the information can be found on page 555 of Reference D, which is *Archives of Maryland, Volume 18*. The coded sources cited herein are as follows:

A = *Revolutionary War Military Collection, Manuscript MS.1146* (Baltimore: Maryland Historical Society, Manuscript Division)

B = *Archives of Maryland, Volume XII*. "Journal and Correspondence of the Maryland Council of Safety, July 7, 1776 - December 31, 1776" (Baltimore: Maryland Historical Society, 1893)

C = *Archives of Maryland, Volume XVI*. "Journal and Correspondence of the Council of Safety, January 1, 1777 - March 20, 1777" and "Journal and Correspondence of the State Council, March 20, 1777 - March 28, 1778" (Baltimore: Maryland Historical Society, 1897)

D = *Archives of Maryland, Volume XVIII*. "Muster Rolls and Other Records of Service of Maryland Troops in the American Revolution, 1775-1783" (Baltimore: Maryland Historical Society, 1900)

E = *Archives of Maryland, Volume XXI*. "Journal and Correspondence of the Council of Maryland, April 1, 1778 - October 26, 1779" (Baltimore: Maryland Historical Society, 1901)

F = *Archives of Maryland, Volume XLIII*. "Journal and Correspondence of the State Council of Maryland, 1779-1780" (Baltimore: Maryland Historical Society, 1924)

G = *Archives of Maryland, Volume XLV*. "Journal and Correspondence of the State Council of Maryland, 1780-1781" (Baltimore: Maryland Historical Society, 1927)

H = *Archives of Maryland, Volume XLVII*. "Journal and Correspondence of the State Council of Maryland, 1781" (Baltimore: Maryland Historical Society, 1930)

I = *Archives of Maryland, Volume XLVIII*. "Journal and Correspondence of the State Council of Maryland, 1781-1784" (Baltimore: Maryland Historical Society, 1931)

J = Clark, Raymond B. Jr. *Washington County, Maryland Records: Oaths of Allegiance, 1778, and Balance Books (Distributions) on Estates, 1778-1801* (St. Michaels, MD: Maryland and Delaware Genealogy, 1989).

K = *Revolutionary War Military Collection, Manuscript MS.1814* (Baltimore: Maryland Historical Society, Manuscript Division)

L = Carothers, Bettie. *9000 Men Who Took the Oath of Allegiance and*

Fidelity to the State of Maryland During the Revolution (Lutherville, Maryland: Privately Compiled by the Author, 1978)

M = Clements, S. Eugene and Wright, F. Edward. *The Maryland Militia in the Revolutionary War* (Silver Spring, Maryland: Family Line Publications, 1987)

N = Newman, Harry Wright. *Maryland Revolutionary Records* (Baltimore: Genealogical Publishing Company, 1980 reprint)

O = Hodges, Margaret Roberts. *Unpublished Revolutionary Records of Maryland, Volume 3*, Oaths of Allegiance and Fidelity taken in Washington County in 1778 (Compiled by the author circa 1939).

P = Papenfuse, Edward C., et al. *An Inventory of Maryland State Papers, Volume I*, "The Era of the American Revolution, 1775-1789" (Annapolis: Hall of Records Commission, 1977)

Q = "Proceedings of the Committee of Observation for Elizabeth Town District [Washington County]," *Maryland Historical Magazine*, Volume 12 (1917) and Volume 13 (1918)

R = *Maryland Pension Rolls of 1835: Report from the Secretary of War in Relation to the Pension Establishment of the United States* (Baltimore: Genealogical Publishing Company, Inc., 1968 reprint)

S = Scharf, J. Thomas. *History of Western Maryland, Volume II* (Baltimore: Regional Publishing Company, 1968 reprint)

T = Burns, Annie Walker. *Maryland Soldiers of the Revolutionary, 1812, and Indian Wars Who Drew Pensions While Residing in Kentucky* (Washington, DC: Privately Compiled by the Author, 1939)

U = *National Genealogical Society Quarterly* (as cited)

V = White, Virgil D. *Genealogical Abstracts of Revolutionary War Pension Files* (Waynesboro, Tennessee: The National Historical Publishing Company, 1990, 4 volumes)

W = Williams, Thomas J. C. *A History of Washington County, Maryland* (Baltimore: Regional Publishing Company, 1968 reprint)

X = "Some Little Known Data Regarding Maryland Signers of the Oath of Fidelity," by Richard B. Miller, *Maryland Genealogical Society Bulletin*, Volume 27, No. 1, pp. 101-124 (Winter, 1986)

Y = *Calendar of Maryland State Papers, The Red Books, No. 4, Part 1 and Part 2* (Annapolis: The Hall of Records Commission, 1950)

Z = Wright, F. Edward. *Marriages and Deaths from the Newspapers of Allegany and Washington Counties, Maryland, 1820-1830* (Silver Spring, Maryland: Family Line Publications, 1987).

AA = Brumbaugh, Gaius M. *Maryland Records: Colonial, Revolutionary, County and Church, Volume II* (Baltimore: Genealogical Publishing Company, Inc., 1985 reprint)

BB = *Directory of Maryland State Society, Daughters of the American Revolution and Their Revolutionary Ancestors, 1892-1965* (Published by Maryland Society, Daughters of the American Revolution, 1966)

CC = *Maryland Society, Sons of the American Revolution.* Approved and documented applications identified by Maryland State Society membership number (original records in the Langsdale Library at the University of Baltimore)

DD = Brown, Helen W. *Marriages and Deaths, 1830-1837, Washington County, Maryland, Recorded in The Republican Banner* (College Park, Maryland: Privately compiled by the author, 1962)

EE = *Maryland Genealogical Society Bulletin* (as cited)

FF = Saffell, W. T. R. *Records of the Revolutionary War* (Baltimore: Genealogical Publishing Company, 1969 reprint)

GG = Retzer, Henry J. *The German Regiment of Maryland and Pennsylvania in the Continental Army, 1776-1781* (Westminster, Maryland: Family Line Publications, 1991)

HH = *Red Books* (Original records at the Maryland State Archives, Annapolis, Maryland, Accession No. MdHR4590)

II = *The Minutes and Proceedings of Washington County Court Held in*

Elizabeth Town, 1776-1810 (Typescript by Gerald J. Sword in 1965, copied from the original books that were stored in the basement in the old part of the Washington County Court House in Hagerstown)

JJ = Morrow, Dale W., ed. *Washington County, Maryland, Cemetery Records*. Recorded by Samuel Webster Piper between 1935-1936 and typed and presented by the Conococheague Chapter, NSDAR, of Hagerstown in 1942 (Westminster, Maryland: Family Line Publications, 1992-1994), 7 volumes

KK = Papenfuse, Edward C., et al. *A Biographical Dictionary of the Maryland Legislature, 1635-1789* (Baltimore: The Johns Hopkins University Press, 1979), 2 volumes

LL = Wright, F. Edward. *Western Maryland Abstracts, 1786-1810* (Silver Spring, Maryland: Family Line Publications, 1985-1987), 3 volumes

MM = Russell, Donna Valley, ed. *Western Maryland Genealogy* (New Market, Maryland: Catoctin Press, Inc.)

It must be noted that it is not possible to know who all of the patriots were who served in or from Washington County during the entire Revolutionary War period. This is especially true for those who joined the Maryland Line and served in the Continental Army. Due to the constant reorganization of the Maryland troops during the war, it is not easily determinable which soldier served from which county. Also, some men from Washington County initially served in Frederick County until Washington was created in the latter part of 1776. At that time Washington County included the present day counties of Garrett and Allegany.

As may be the case in works such as this, it is possible that some patriots may have been inadvertently omitted and additional research may be necessary before drawing conclusions. Therefore, one should check the many lists found in the *Archives of Maryland, Volume 18*, for perhaps even more names of soldiers from Washington County, as well as articles in *Western Maryland Genealogy* and other genealogical publications.

Henry C. Peden, Jr.
Bel Air, Maryland
January 1, 1998

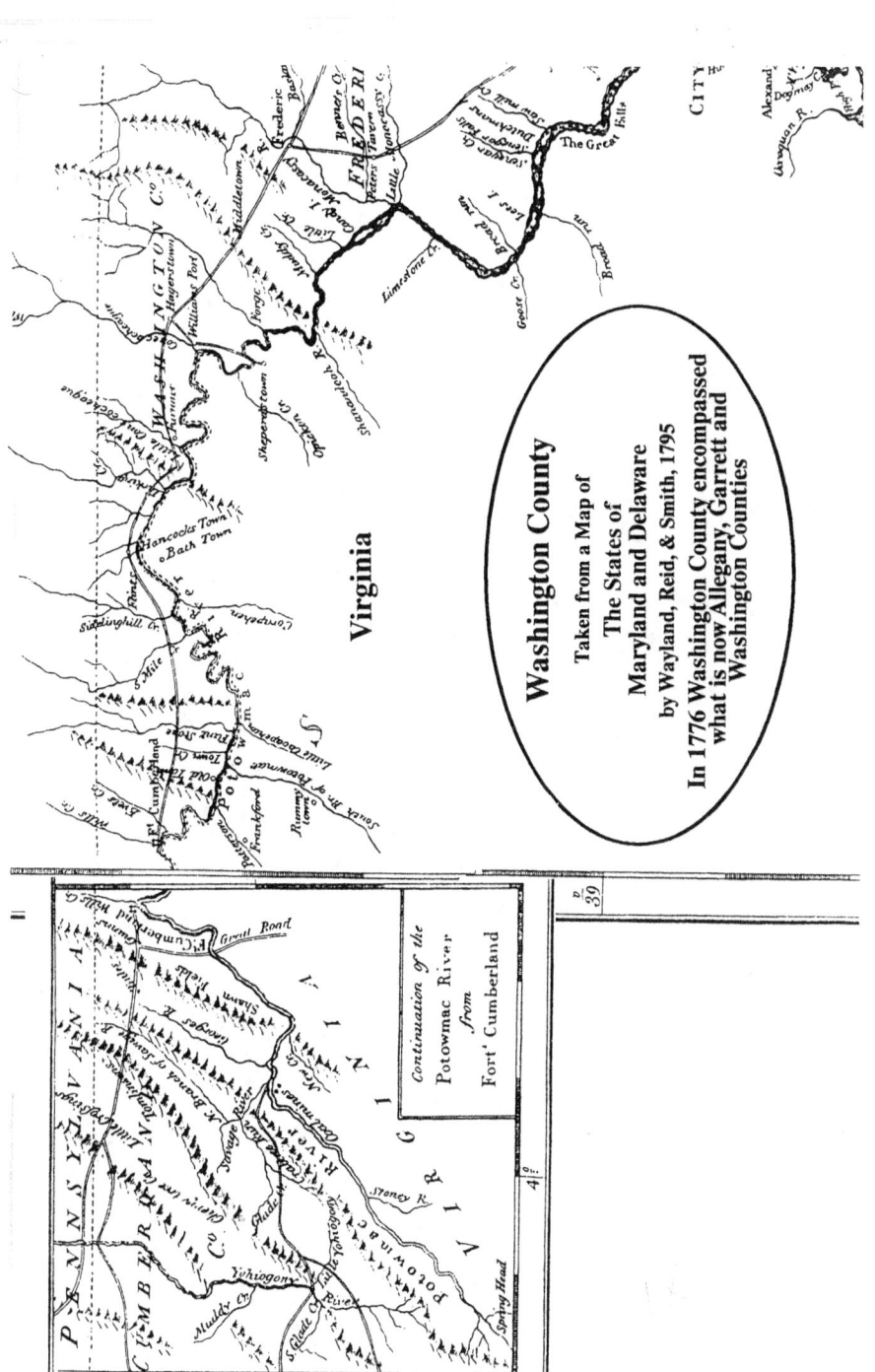

REVOLUTIONARY PATRIOTS
OF WASHINGTON COUNTY, MARYLAND
1776-1783

ABBONET, Hannah. See "Frederick Knockel," q.v.

ACKART, Henry. Assistant Commissary of Purchases under Col. Moses Rawlings, licensed to act in Washington County on October 16, 1779 by the Council of Maryland [Ref: E-557].

ACKENBERGER, Valentine. See "Matthias Ridenour," q.v.

ACKER, Casper. Took the Oath of Allegiance before the Hon. John Cellars in January, 1778 [Ref: K-1814, O-40, J-6].

ACKLIN, James. Private who was recruited and passed by County Lieutenant Thomas Sprigg on April 22, 1780 [Ref: D-336].

ACRE, Conomus. Private who was enrolled by Capt. Henry Hardman and passed on July 19, 1776 in Frederick (now Washington) County [Ref: D-51].

ACTON, John. See "John Fackler," q.v.

ACTON, Richard. Fourth Sergeant, Militia, Capt. Barnett Johnston's Company, 3rd Battalion, 1776/1777 [Ref: M-242]. On January 13, 1777 he and his company were compensated by the Committee of Observation for Elizabeth Town District (now the Hagerstown area of Washington County) "for their expense and trouble of apprehending and delivering John Marshall to the committee as they lived at a great distance." [Ref: Q-38]. Took the Oath of Allegiance before the Hon. William Yates in 1778 [Ref: O-48, J-11].

ADAIR, James. Private, Militia, 5th Class, Capt. Isaac Baker's Company, 1776/1777 [Ref: A-1146, M-247]. Took the Oath of Allegiance before the Hon. Samuel Hughes before March 1, 1778 [Ref: O-33, J-1].

ADAIR, John. One of several patriots appointed by the Committee of Observation on December 30, 1776 "to form the county into companies (after the militia had marched) for the purpose of relieving the distressed inhabitants of said county and also to compel the Dunkards and Mennonists to give their assistance." [Ref: Q-346]. Appointed to serve on the Committee of Observation for Elizabeth Town District (now the Hagerstown area of Washington County) on February 15, 1777 [Ref: Q-235]. Paid "10/6 for three buckets by him made for use of the Tory Goal" on March 1, 1777 [Ref: Q-239]. Took the Oath of Allegiance before the Hon. Samuel Hughes before March 1, 1778 [Ref: O-33, J-1].

ADAM, Jacob. Took the Oath of Allegiance before the Hon. Henry Schnebley in 1778 [Ref: O-50, J-14].

ADAM, John. One of several patriots appointed by the Committee of Observation on December 30, 1776 "to form the county into companies (after the militia had marched) for the purpose of relieving the distressed inhabitants of said county and also to compel the Dunkards and Mennonists to give their assistance." [Ref: Q-345].

ADAM, John Jr. Took the Oath of Allegiance before the Hon. Henry Schnebley in 1778 [Ref: O-49, J-13].

ADAM, Peter. Took the Oath of Allegiance before the Hon. Henry Schnebley in 1778 [Ref: O-49, J-13].

ADAM, William. Took the Oath of Allegiance before the Hon. John Barnes before February 28, 1778 [Ref: O-44, J-9].

ADAMS, Francis. Enrolled in the first militia company organized for the Revolutionary War in the Elizabeth Town District of Frederick County (now the Hagerstown area of Washington County) on January 6, 1776 [Ref: Q-270, W-1190].

ADAMS, Jacob. Private, Militia, 8th Class, Capt. John Cellars' Company, 1776/1777 [Ref: A-1146, M-246]. Private, Militia, Capt. John Kershner's Company, on duty guarding prisoners of war at Fort Frederick until discharged on June 6, 1778 [Ref: D-328].

ADAMS, John. Private, Militia, 2nd Class, Capt. John Cellars' Company, 1776/1777 [Ref: A-1146, M-246].

ADAMS, Jonathan. Private, Militia, 4th Class, Capt. Peter Swingle's (Swingley's) Company, 1776/1777 [Ref: A-1146, M-248].

ADAMS, Peter. Private, Militia, 3rd Class, Capt. John Cellars' Company, 1776/1777 [Ref: A-1146, M-246]. Private, Militia, Capt. John Kershner's Company, on duty guarding prisoners of war at Fort Frederick on June 27, 1778 [Ref: D-328].

ADAMS, William. Private, Militia, 6th Class, Capt. James Smith's Company, 2nd Battalion, 1776/1777 [Ref: M-240, A-1146].

ADAMS, William. Private, Militia, 6th Class, Capt. Barnett Johnston's Company, 3rd Battalion, 1776/1777 [Ref: M-242].

ADAMS, William. Private, Militia, by January 22, 1777 when ordered by the Committee of Observation "to march with some company of militia to the reinforcement of his Excellency General Washington" or appear before the Committee and state his reason for not marching. He apparently marched since he never appeared to the contrary [Ref: Q-48, which listed the name as "Wm. or Mr. Adams"].

ADULT, Margaret. See "Martin Ridenour (Reitenower)," q.v.

AIM, John. Private who was enrolled by Capt. Henry Hardman and passed on July 19, 1776 in Frederick (now Washington) County [Ref: D-51].

AIRHART, Philip. See "Philip Earhart," q.v.
AIRKOLT, Michael. Private, Militia, 1st Class, Capt. Peter Swingle's (Swingley's) Company, 1776/1777 [Ref: A-1146, M-248].
AKLEBARGER, Catherine and David. See "Michael Aklebarger," q.v.
AKLEBARGER, Elizabeth and Enoch. See "Michael Aklebarger," q.v.
AKLEBARGER, Jacob and John. See "Michael Aklebarger," q.v.
AKLEBARGER, Michael. Private, Militia, 3rd Class, Capt. Martin Kershner's Company, 1776/1777 [Ref: A-1146, M-247, which listed the name as "Michael Akcringbarger"]. One Michael Aklebarger died before July 29, 1785 (date of balance book entry in Washington County), leaving a widow (not named, but Catherine Aklebarger was the administratrix) and equal shares to Rebecca, John, Jacob, Michael, David, Elizabeth, Catherine and Enoch Aklebarger [Ref: J-26].
AKLEBARGER, Rebecca. See "Michael Aklebarger," q.v.
AKORD, Francis. Private, Militia, 5th Class, Capt. Basil Williams' Company, 1776/1777 [Ref: M-244, A-1146].
ALBERT, Elizabeth and Frederick. See "Jacob Albert," q.v.
ALBERT, Jacob (c1755-1830). Soldier who resided in Washington County and was granted a pension certificate in August, 1820, according to an Act of Congress of March 18, 1818, since he had proven that he was "in the enjoyment of a certain degree of poverty" as required by the Act as amended on May 1, 1820 [Ref: W-1190]. Private, Pennsylvania Line, died May 4, 1830 [Ref: R-42]. A Frederick Albert died before August 9, 1785 (date of balance book entry in Washington County), leaving a widow (not named, but Elizabeth Albert was the administratrix) and equal shares to John, Elizabeth and Jacob Albert [Ref: J-26].
ALBERT (ALDBERT), John. Took the Oath of Allegiance before September 1, 1780 [Ref: X-104]. See "Jacob Albert," q.v.
ALBRIGHT, Peter. Private, Militia, 4th Class, Capt. Isaac Baker's Company, 1776/1777 [Ref: A-1146, M-247]. Took the Oath of Allegiance before the Hon. Henry Schnebley in 1778 [Ref: O-50, J-14].
ALDER, Christopher. See "Christopher Alter," q.v.
ALDRIDGE, John Simpson. Private who was enrolled by Lieut. Clement Hollyday and passed by Col. William Luckett on August 8, 1776 [Ref: D-49].
ALEY, Isaac. See "Jacob Yakly," q.v.
ALEY, Peter. Private who enlisted in the militia on August 18, 1781 for service in the Continental Army [Ref: D-388].
ALINGER, Christian. See "Chr. Olinger," q.v.
ALLEN, James. Enrolled in the second militia company organized for the Revolutionary War in the Elizabeth Town District of Frederick County

(now the Hagerstown area of Washington County) on March 9, 1776 [Ref: Q-271]. Private, Militia, 5th Class, Capt. Henry Boteler's Company, 1776/1777 [Ref: M-237, A-1146]. Took the Oath of Allegiance before the Hon. Christopher Cruse in Lower Antietam Hundred before March 2, 1778 [Ref: J-3, O-35].

ALLEN, Jeremiah. Private, Militia, 7th Class, Capt. James Prather's Company, 3rd Battalion, 1776/1777 [Ref: M-243, which listed the name as "Jeramiah Allan"]. Took the Oath of Allegiance before the Hon. Lemuel Barritt before March 16, 1778 [Ref: O-43, J-8, which listed the name as "Jeremiah Allin"].

ALLEN, John. Took the Oath of Allegiance before the Hon. William Yates in 1778 [Ref: O-48, J-11].

ALLEN, Thomas. Fourth Sergeant, Militia, Capt. Griffin Johnson's Company, 3rd Battalion, 1776/1777 [Ref: M-243].

ALLEN, Thomas. Private, Militia, 5th Class, Capt. Griffin Johnson's Company, 3rd Battalion, 1776/1777 [Ref: M-243].

ALLEN, William. Private, Militia, 3rd Class, Capt. Samuel Hughes' Company, 2nd Battalion, 1776/1777 [Ref: M-238, A-1146]. Private who enlisted in the militia on August 17, 1781 for service in the Continental Army [Ref: D-388]. Substitute, Maryland Line, discharged on October 30, 1781 [Ref: G-656].

ALLEN, William. Private, Militia, Capt. John Kershner's Company, on duty guarding prisoners of war at Fort Frederick on June 27, 1778 [Ref: D-328, which listed the name as "William Allin"]. Private who was recruited and passed by County Lieutenant Thomas Sprigg on April 22, 1780 [Ref: D-336, which listed the name as "William Allin"]. Private who enlisted in the militia on August 15, 1781 for service in the Continental Army and reportedly "deserted." [Ref: D-388].

ALLENDER, Richard. First Sergeant, Militia, Capt. Conrad Hogmire's Company, 1776/1777 [Ref: M-244, A-1146]. Took the Oath of Allegiance before the Hon. Samuel Hughes before March 1, 1778 [Ref: O-33, J-1].

ALLER, George. Took the Oath of Allegiance before the Hon. Andrew Bruce before March 2, 1778 [Ref: O-41, J-6].

ALLISON, Robert. Private, Militia, 7th Class, Capt. Samuel Hughes' Company, 2nd Battalion, 1776/1777 [Ref: M-238, A-1146]. Took the Oath of Allegiance before the Hon. Joseph Sprigg before April 1, 1778 [Ref: O-54, J-16].

ALLSY, Richard. Private who was recruited and passed by County Lieutenant Thomas Sprigg on April 22, 1780 [Ref: D-336].

ALLUM, Thomas. Took the Oath of Allegiance before the Hon. William Yates in 1778 [Ref: O-48, J-11].

ALMOND, Nancy Lee. See "Joseph Lemaster," q.v.

ALTER (ALDER), Christian. Private, Militia, 7th Class, Capt. John Cellars' Company, 1776/1777 [Ref: A-1146, M-246].

ALTER (ALDER), Christopher (1744-1804). Took the Oath of Allegiance before the Hon. Henry Schnebley in 1778 [Ref: O-50, J-14, which listed the name as "Christopher Alder"]. "Christopher Alter" died testate in Elizabeth Town after a lingering illness on the Thursday before June 6, 1804, in his 60th year, leaving a wife Susanna and several children [Ref: LL-96, MM-13:38, 39].

ALTER (ALDER), Frederick. Took the Oath of Allegiance before the Hon. Joseph Sprigg before April 1, 1778 [Ref: O-53, J-16].

ALTER, Susannah. See "Christopher Alter (Alder)," q.v.

ALTIGH, Michael (c1758-1826). Private, Pennsylvania Line, who resided in Washington County and was granted a pension S34626 in August, 1820, according to an Act of Congress of March 18, 1818. He applied on March 31, 1818 and proved that he was "in the enjoyment of a certain degree of poverty" as required by the Act as amended on May 1, 1820. His wife (no name given) was aged 55 in 1820, Michael was aged 60, and he died on July 12, 1826 [Ref: R-42, V-I:48, W-1190].

ALTIZER, Emery (c1736-1819). Private, Virginia Line, who married Mary Pitzer in Hagerstown, Maryland in July, 1773, and died in Berkeley County, Virginia in September, 1819. His widow applied for and received pension W3720 in Montgomery County, Virginia on October 5, 1840, aged 81 [Ref: V-I:48]. "Emera Altizera" was born circa 1736 in Germany [Ref: Y-I:51].

ALTIZER, Mary. See "Emery Altizer," q.v.

ANCHONEY, Christian. See "Dewalt Ankeny," q.v.

ANDERSON, Charles. Private, Militia, 2nd Class, Capt. Barnett Johnston's Company, 3rd Battalion, 1776/1777 [Ref: M-242]. Took the Oath of Allegiance before the Hon. William Yates in 1778 [Ref: O-48, J-11].

ANDERSON, Daniel. Private, Militia, 3rd Class, Capt. Barnett Johnston's Company, 3rd Battalion, 1776/1777 [Ref: M-242].

ANDERSON, Jeremiah. Private, Militia, 2nd Class, Capt. Daniel Cresap's Company, 3rd Battalion, 1776/1777 [Ref: M-241]. Took the Oath of Allegiance before the Hon. Lemuel Barritt before March 16, 1778 [Ref: O-42, J-8].

ANDERSON, Josiah. Private, Militia, 7th Class, Capt. Daniel Cresap's Company, 3rd Battalion, 1776/1777 [Ref: M-241].

ANDERSON, Mary. See "Thomas Bissett," q.v.

ANDERSON, Richard. Private, Militia, 6th Class, Capt. Conrad Hogmire's Company, 1776/1777 [Ref: M-244, A-1146].

ANDERSON, William. Took the Oath of Allegiance before the Hon. Lemuel Barritt before March 16, 1778 [Ref: O-42, J-7].

ANDRE, Major. See "John Hughes," q.v.

ANDREW, Barbara and Christopher. See "John Andrews," q.v.

ANDREWS, John. Private, Militia, 6th Class, Capt. Peter Swingle's (Swingley's) Company, 1776/1777 [Ref: A-1146, M-248]. One John Andrews died before May 8, 1784 (date of balance book entry in Washington County), leaving Barbara and Christopher Andrew *[sic]* equal shares of his estate [Ref: J-25].

ANDREWS, Nicholas. Third Corporal, Militia, Capt. Peter Swingle's (Swingley's) Company, 2nd Battalion, 1776/1777 [Ref: M-248, A-1146].

ANDREWS, Robert. Private, Militia, by January 22, 1777 when ordered by the Committee of Observation "to march with some company of militia to the reinforcement of his Excellency General Washington" or appear before the Committee and state his reason for not marching. He apparently marched since he never appeared to the contrary [Ref: Q-48].

ANGEL, Sary. See "Joseph Wyand," q.v.

ANKENY (ANCHONEY), Dewalt (1728-1781). One of several patriots appointed by the Committee of Observation on December 30, 1776 "to form the county into companies (after the militia had marched) for the purpose of relieving the distressed inhabitants of said county and also to compel the Dunkards and Mennonists to give their assistance." [Ref: Q-345, which listed the name as "Devalt Anchony"]. Took the Oath of Allegiance before the Hon. John Barnes before February 28, 1778 [Ref: O-44, which listed the name as "Devolt Ankeny" and J-9, which listed the name as "Levolt (Dewalt) Ankeny"]. "Davolt Anchoney" died before April 9, 1782 (date of balance book entry in Washington County), leaving many children (no names were given in this account), with "Christian Anchoney" as executor [Ref: J-23]. "Dewalt Ankeny" was born in Germany in 1728, married Mrs. Margaret Frederick, and died before April 7, 1781 [Ref: Y-I:69]. The first of his name and founder of that family in America, Dewalt Ankeny (1728-1781) is buried in the cemetery at St. Paul's Lutheran Reformed Church on Route 40 near Clearspring in Washington County [Ref: JJ-V:88].

ANKENY (ANCHONEY), John. Took the Oath of Allegiance before the Hon. John Barnes before February 28, 1778 [Ref: O-44, J-9]. "Capt. John Ankeny" died at West Conococheague in Washington County on the Monday before February 28, 1799 [Ref: LL-2:39].

ANSWINGER, Christian. See "Christian Ensminger," q.v.

ANTHONY, John. Private, Militia, 6th Class, Capt. John Bennet's Company, 1776/1777 [Ref: M-246, A-1146].

ANTHONY, Philip. Private who enlisted in the militia on September 5, 1781 for service in the Continental Army [Ref: D-388].

ARMSTRONG, John. Private, Militia, Capt. William Heyser's Company, muster roll dated October 23, 1776, in continental service [Ref: D-264, W-1190, L-79]. Private, German Regiment, Lt. Col. Ludwick Weltner's Company, continental service, reenlisted July 27, 1778 and discharged on July 26, 1779 at Fort Wyoming, Pennsylvania [Ref: D-265, GG-96].

ARNOLD, George. Private, Militia, 4th Class, Capt. Peter Beall's Company, 1st Battalion, 1776/1777 [Ref: M-240].

ASBY, Jacob. See "Jacob Aspey," q.v.

ASH, Henry. Second Sergeant, Militia, Capt. John Bennet's Company, 1776/1777 [Ref: M-246, A-1146]. Took the Oath of Allegiance before the Hon. Richard Davis in 1778 [Ref: J-4, O-36].

ASHBY, William. Private, Militia, Capt. Charles Coulson's Company, enrolled August 28, 1776 [Ref: M-243, A-1146].

ASHER, Gabriel. Took the Oath of Allegiance before the Hon. John Stull in 1778 [Ref: O-46, J-10].

ASHLEY, James. Private, German Regiment, Lt. Col. Ludwick Weltner's Company, continental service, enlisted April 25, 1778 and transferred to 3rd Maryland Line in 1781 [Ref: D-265]. Corporal, 5th Company, 2nd Maryland Line, 1782 [Ref: GG-96, which listed the name as "James W. L. Ashley"].

ASPEY, Jacob. Took the Oath of Allegiance before the Hon. Henry Schnebley in 1778 [Ref: O-49, J-13]. Private, Militia, 4th Class, Capt. Martin Kershner's Company, 1776/1777 [Ref: A-1146, M-247, which listed the name as "Jacob Asby"].

ATHERTON, Aaron. Took the Oath of Allegiance before the Hon. Lemuel Barritt before March 16, 1778 [Ref: O-42, J-7].

ATHERTON, Aaron Jr. Took the Oath of Allegiance before the Hon. Lemuel Barritt before March 16, 1778 [Ref: O-42, J-8, which listed the name as "Aaron Atheron Jnr"].

ATHERTON, Benjamin. Took the Oath of Allegiance before the Hon. Lemuel Barritt before March 16, 1778 [Ref: O-42, J-7].

ATHERTON, John (c1740-c1816). Took the Oath of Allegiance before the Hon. Lemuel Barritt before March 16, 1778 [Ref: O-42, J-7]. John Atherton was born circa 1740 in Maryland, married Sarah ----, rendered patriotic service during the Revolution, and died in Kentucky after December 2, 1816 [Ref: Y-I::88].

ATHERTON, Joshua. Took the Oath of Allegiance before the Hon. Lemuel Barritt before March 16, 1778 [Ref: O-42, J-7].

ATHERTON, Sarah. See "John Atherton," q.v.

AUD (AUE?), Jacob. Private, Select Militia, Capt. Adam Ott's Company, 1781 [Ref: M-238, A-1146, M-238].

AUGLE, Henry. Private, Militia, 7th Class, Capt. Isaac Baker's Company, 1776/1777 [Ref: A-1146, M-247].

AUGUSTEEN, George. Private, Militia, 4th Class, Capt. Samuel Hughes' Company, 2nd Battalion, 1776/1777 [Ref: M-238, A-1146].

AUGUSTEEN, John. Private, Militia, Capt. John Kershner's Company, on duty guarding prisoners of war at Fort Frederick, 1778, and who reportedly "deserted" on May 26, 1778 [Ref: D-328].

AUGUSTEEN, John Jr. Private, Militia, 3rd Class, Capt. Samuel Hughes' Company, 2nd Battalion, 1776/1777 [Ref: M-238, A-1146].

AUGUSTINE, Catherine. See "Andrew Steffee," q.v.

AUGUSTUS, Joseph. Took the Oath of Allegiance before the Hon. John Barnes before February 28, 1778 [Ref: O-44, J-9].

AULT, Henry. Enrolled in the second militia company organized for the Revolutionary War in the Elizabeth Town District of Frederick County (now the Hagerstown area of Washington County) on March 9, 1776 [Ref: Q-272]. Private, Militia, 6th Class, Capt. Henry Boteler's Company, 1776/1777 [Ref: M-237, A-1146].

AULT, John. Enrolled in the second militia company organized for the Revolutionary War in the Elizabeth Town District of Frederick County (now the Hagerstown area of Washington County) on March 9, 1776 [Ref: Q-272].

AULT, William. Enrolled in the second militia company organized for the Revolutionary War in the Elizabeth Town District of Frederick County (now the Hagerstown area of Washington County) on March 9, 1776 [Ref: Q-272].

AUSTIN, James. Enrolled in the second militia company organized for the Revolutionary War in the Elizabeth Town District of Frederick County (now the Hagerstown area of Washington County) on March 9, 1776 [Ref: Q-271].

AUSTIN, John. Enrolled in the second militia company organized for the Revolutionary War in the Elizabeth Town District of Frederick County (now the Hagerstown area of Washington County) on March 9, 1776 [Ref: Q-272]. Private, Militia, 7th Class, Capt. Henry Boteler's Company, 1776/1777 [Ref: M-237, A-1146, which listed the name as "John Austain"].

AVERY, Jacob. Private, Militia, 6th Class, Capt. James Walling's Company, 2nd Battalion, 1776/1777 [Ref: M-239, A-1146].

AVEY, Christian. See "Christian Evey," q.v.

AYERS, Moses Jr. Took the Oath of Allegiance before the Hon. Lemuel Barritt before March 16, 1778 [Ref: O-42, J-7]. Private, Militia, 6th Class, Capt. Daniel Cresap's Company, 3rd Battalion, 1776/1777 [Ref: M-241, which listed the name as "Moses Ayres, Jr."]. On September 23, 1780, Col. Lemuel Barritt recommended to Governor Lee that "Moses Ayrs, Junr" be commissioned a first lieutenant in the militia at "Oper Old Town" since so many officers of the Western Battalion had moved out of Maryland to Kentucky and elsewhere [Ref: G-123].

AYERS, Moses Sr. Took the Oath of Allegiance before the Hon. Lemuel Barritt before March 16, 1778 [Ref: O-42, J-8].

BACHLEY, Martin. Private, Militia, 6th Class, Capt. John Cellars' Company, 1776/1777 [Ref: A-1146, M-246].

BACHTELL, Isaac. Private, Militia, 7th Class, Capt. Daniel Clapsaddle's Company, 1st Battalion, 1776/1777 [Ref: M-236, A-1146].

BACHTELL, Samuel Jr. Private, Militia, 1st Class, Capt. Daniel Clapsaddle's Company, 1st Battalion, 1776/1777 [Ref: M-236, A-1146].

BACHUS, Benjamin. Took the Oath of Allegiance before the Hon. John Barnes before February 28, 1778 [Ref: O-45, J-10].

BACKER, Peter. See "Peter Baker," q.v.

BACORN, John. Private, Militia, 2nd Class, Capt. Daniel Cresap's Company, 3rd Battalion, 1776/1777 [Ref: M-241].

BAGGS, Andrew. Third Sergeant, Militia, Capt. Michael Fackler's Company, 1776/1777 [Ref: M-245, A-1146]. Took the Oath of Allegiance before the Hon. Samuel Hughes before March 1, 1778 [Ref: O-33, J-1, which listed the name as "Andrew Beggs"].

BAGUN, Henry. Private, Maryland line. He was born February 27, 1761 in Buston Township, Lancaster County, Pennsylvania and lived in Washington County, Maryland at the time of his enlistment. In 1788 he moved to Huntington County, Pennsylvania, in 1803 to Fayette County, in 1806 to Westmoreland County, in 1811 to Wayne County, Ohio, and in 1822 to Stark County, Ohio. He applied for and received pension S5269 on August 8, 1832, aged 72 [Ref: V-I:112].

BAHN, Eva. See "Yost Harbaugh," q.v.

BAIRD, Nicholas. Private, Militia, Capt. William Heyser's Company, muster roll dated October 23, 1776, in continental service, and on duty in May, 1777 [Ref: D-264, W-1190, GG-96, L-79, which latter source listed the name as "Nicholas Biard"].

BAIRD, Phillip. Private, Militia, 1st Class, Capt. Conrad Hogmire's Company, 1776/1777 [Ref: M-244, A-1146].

BAIRD, William. There were several men with this name who rendered service during the Revolutionary War. Additional research may be necessary before drawing conclusions. (1) Elected to serve on the Committee of Observation for the Elizabeth Town District (now the Hagerstown area of Washington County) on September 12, 1775 [Ref: Q-142]. On February 15, 1777 the Committee reported "William Baird, Esq. has marched to camp, his seat in Committee being thereby vacated." [Ref: Q-235]. (2) Took the Oath of Allegiance before the Hon. Joseph Sprigg before April 1, 1778 [Ref: O-53, J-16]. (3) Private, Militia, 5th Class, Capt. Daniel Clapsaddle's Company, 1st Battalion, 1776/1777 [Ref: M-236, A-1146]. (4) Private, Militia, 6th Class, Capt. James Walling's Company, 2nd Battalion, 1776/1777 [Ref: M-239, A-1146]. See "William Beard," q.v.

BAIRD, William Jr. Private, Select Militia, Capt. Adam Ott's Company, 1781 [Ref: M-238, A-1146].

BAKEN, John. Private, Militia, 7th Class, Capt. Daniel Cresap's Company, 3rd Battalion, 1776/1777 [Ref: M-241].

BAKER, Abraham. First Lieutenant, Militia, Capt. John Rennolds' (Reynolds') Company, 2nd Battalion, 1776/1777 [Ref: M-240]. On January 18, 1777 the Committee of Observation resolved that "Capt. Abraham Baker obtain an order to press waggons, horses, gears, waggon cloaths, screws and blankets for the use of his company." [Ref: Q-42]. Took the Oath of Allegiance before the Hon. Christopher Cruse in Sharpsburg Hundred before March 2, 1778 [Ref: O-34, J-2]. See "Peter Baker," q.v.

BAKER, Andrew. See "Peter Baker," q.v.

BAKER, Anna Barbara and B. F. See "John Samuel Baker," q.v.

BAKER, Benjamin. Took the Oath of Allegiance before the Hon. Richard Davis in 1778 [Ref: J-4, O-37].

BAKER, Boston. Took the Oath of Allegiance before the Hon. John Stull in 1778 [Ref: O-46, J-10, which listed the name as "Bastin Baker"]. Third Sergeant, Militia, Capt. Jacob Sharer's Company, 1776/1777 [Ref: M-248, A-1146, which listed the name as "Baustin Baker"]. His account of "clothing due to be delivered to William Simkins" was reported to the State on November 29, 1779 [Ref: I-250, which listed the name as "Boston Baker"].

BAKER, Christina. See "Peter Baker," q.v.

BAKER, Elizabeth. See "Meshach Baker," q.v.

BAKER, Evan. Captain, Militia, 3rd Battalion, by February, 1777 and to at least June 22, 1778 [Ref: M-49, E-145, Q-232].
BAKER, Gabriel. Took the Oath of Allegiance before the Hon. Richard Davis in 1778 [Ref: J-4, O-37, which listed the name as "Gabrail Baker"]. Private, Militia, 1st Class, Capt. Jeremiah Spires' Company, 2nd Battalion, 1776/1777 [Ref: M-239, A-1146].
BAKER, George. Private, Militia, 6th Class, Capt. Daniel Clapsaddle's Company, 1st Battalion, 1776/1777 [Ref: M-236, A-1146].
BAKER, Henry. Private, Militia, 3rd Class, Capt. Conrad Nichodemus' Company, 2nd Battalion, 1776/1777 [Ref: M-237, A-1146].
BAKER, Isaac. Appointed to raise funds on January 24, 1775 for the Committee of Observation in Conococheague Hundred in Frederick (now Washington) County [Ref: L-75]. Appointed by the Committee of Observation to carry the Association of Freemen to male residents in Conococheague Hundred on September 14, 1775 "and require their subscription to the same and make an exact account of those who sign and those that refuse with their reasons for refusing." [Ref: Q-143]. One of several patriots appointed by the Committee of Observation on December 30, 1776 "to form the county into companies (after the militia had marched) for the purpose of relieving the distressed inhabitants of said county and also to compel the Dunkards and Mennonists to give their assistance." [Ref: Q-346, which listed him as "Capt. Isaac Baker"]. Took the Oath of Allegiance before the Hon. John Barnes before February 28, 1778 [Ref: O-44, J-9]. Captain, Militia, 1776, who "moved from the county" by November 17, 1780 [Ref: M-49, M-247, A-1146, Q-153].
BAKER, James. Private, Militia, 1st Class, Capt. James Prather's Company, 3rd Battalion, 1776/1777 [Ref: M-242].
BAKER, John. Private, Militia, 5th Class, Capt. Isaac Baker's Company, 1776/1777 [Ref: A-1146, M-247]. Took the Oath of Allegiance before the Hon. Joseph Sprigg before April 1, 1778 [Ref: O-53, J-16]. See "John Samuel Baker" and "Peter Baker," q.v.
BAKER, John Dorsey. Took the Oath of Allegiance before the Hon. Richard Davis in 1778 [Ref: J-5, O-37].
BAKER, John Samuel (1729-1819). "A soldier in the American Revolution," John Samuel Baker was born on May 12, 1729, died on April 12, 1819, and is buried next to his first wife Rosanna Baker (1741-1774) and second wife Anna Barbara Baker (1749-1816) in a graveyard on the B. F. Baker farm on Dog Street near Keedysville in Washington County [Ref: JJ-V:65]. It must be noted that John Samuel Baker is not listed in military rolls in Maryland, but John Baker and Samuel Baker

are mentioned; perhaps he was one or the other. Additional research will be necessary before drawing conclusions.

BAKER, Mark. Took the Oath of Allegiance before the Hon. Christopher Cruse in Sharpsburg Hundred before March 2, 1778 [Ref: O-34, J-1].

BAKER, Mary. See "Hugh McNamee," q.v.

BAKER, Meshach (1733-c1785). Took the Oath of Allegiance before the Hon. Richard Davis in 1778 [Ref: J-4, O-37]. Private, Militia, 2nd Class, Capt. Jeremiah Spires' Company, 2nd Battalion, 1776/1777 [Ref: M-239, A-1146, which listed the name as "Meshack Baker"]. "Mashack Baker" was born in Maryland on April 27, 1733, married Elizabeth ----, and died between 1778 and 1790 [Ref: Y-I:126].

BAKER, Morris (Maurice). There appears to have been several men with this name who rendered service during the Revolutionary War. Additional research will be necessary before drawing conclusions. (1) Private who was enrolled by Capt. Henry Hardman and passed on July 19, 1776 in Frederick (now Washington) County [Ref: D-51, which listed the name as "Maurice Baker"]. (2) Private, Militia, 6th Class, Capt. Jeremiah Spires' Company, 2nd Battalion, 1776/1777 [Ref: M-239, A-1146]. (3) Private, Militia, 7th Class, Capt. Conrad Hogmire's Company, 1776/1777 [Ref: M-244, A-1146]. (4) One took the Oath of Allegiance before the Hon. Richard Davis in 1778 [Ref: J-4, O-37].

BAKER, Peter. Ensign, Militia, Capt. Daniel Clapsaddle's Company, 1st Battalion, 1776/1777 [Ref: M-236, A-1146]. Second Lieutenant, Militia, Capt. John Kershner's Company, on duty guarding prisoners of war at Fort Frederick on June 27, 1778 [Ref: D-328, which listed the name as "Peter Backer"]. Took the Oath of Allegiance before the Hon. John Stull in 1778 [Ref: O-46, J-10]. Rendered patriotic service by supplying corn for the use of the military on March 30, 1780 [Ref: W-1190, HH-73]. Andrew Baker died by 1798 (exact date not given in balance book in Washington County) and Peter Baker was one of the administrators of his estate [Ref: J-36]. One Peter Baker died testate by December 22, 1804, leaving a wife Christian and among his heirs were sons Peter, John, and Abraham [Ref: MM-13:131]. See the other "Peter Baker," q.v.

BAKER, Peter. Private, Militia, 4th Class, Capt. Conrad Nichodemus' Company, 2nd Battalion, 1776/1777 [Ref: M-237, A-1146]. One Peter Baker was a private in the Third Vacant Company under Capt. Philip Graybill and Col. Lewis Weltner at Valley Forge in March, 1778 [Ref: FF-222]. See the other "Peter Baker," q.v.

BAKER, Rosanna. See "John Samuel Baker," q.v.

BAKER, Samuel. Private, Militia, 6th Class, Capt. Conrad Nichodemus' Company, 2nd Battalion, 1776/1777 [Ref: M-237, A-1146]. See "John Samuel Baker," q.v.

BAKER, William. One of several patriots appointed by the Committee of Observation on December 30, 1776 "to form the county into companies (after the militia had marched) for the purpose of relieving the distressed inhabitants of said county and also to compel the Dunkards and Mennonists to give their assistance." [Ref: Q-345].

BAKER, William. Private, Militia, 2nd Class, Capt. Isaac Baker's Company, 1776/1777 [Ref: A-1146, M-247].

BAKER, Zebediah. Private, Militia, 4th Class, Capt. Jeremiah Spires' Company, 2nd Battalion, 1776/1777 [Ref: M-239, A-1146]. Took the Oath of Allegiance before the Hon. Richard Davis in 1778 [Ref: J-5, O-37].

BALL, Nancy (Ann). See "George Miller," q.v.

BALL, Zepheniah. Took the Oath of Allegiance before the Hon. Lemuel Barritt before March 16, 1778 [Ref: O-42, J-8, which latter source listed the name as "Zaphemiah Ball"]. On September 23, 1780, Col. Lemuel Barritt recommended to Governor Lee that "Zepeniah Ball" be commissioned a first lieutenant in the militia at Willstown since so many officers of the Western Battalion had moved out of Maryland to Kentucky and elsewhere [Ref: G-123].

BALMER, Peter. See "Peter Palmer," q.v.

BALZAR (BELSOR), Anthony (c1754-1842). Soldier who resided in Washington County and was granted a pension certificate in August, 1820, according to an Act of Congress of March 18, 1818, since he had proven that he was "in the enjoyment of a certain degree of poverty" as required by the Act as amended on May 1, 1820 [Ref: W-1190, which listed the name as "Anthony Balzar"]. Private, Pennsylvania Line, who received a pension of $96 per year in Washington County, Maryland in October, 1818 [Ref: R-42, which listed the name as "Anthony Blazar"]. Resided in the household of George Hamilton in the 5th District of Washington County in 1840, aged 88 [Ref: EE-28:4 (p. 442), containing an article by Elba Anthony Dardeau, Jr.]. Soldier and pensioner of the Revolution who died near Boonsboro, Maryland on February 19, 1842 [Ref: Y-I:140, and EE-6:1 (p. 6), containing Robert W. Barnes' article citing the *Baltimore Sun*, February 26, 1842, which listed the name as "Anthony Bellsler"]. "Anthony Balzar or Balser or Baltser" applied for a pension in Washington County, Maryland on September 15, 1818, aged 64, stating that he had enlisted in Hagerstown, Maryland and served in the Pennsylvania Line. In 1820 his wife Elizabeth was aged 48, a daughter Milly was aged 10, and another daughter (not named) was aged 7 and "foolish." On June 13, 1843 Elizabeth Balzar, aged 76, applied for and received pension W3752, stating they were married on September 9, 1788 and he died on February 19, 1842. She died on September 1, 1847 [Ref: V-I:139].

BALZAR, Elizabeth and Milly. See "Anthony Balzar," q.v.

BAMBERGEN, John. Private, Militia, 7th Class, Capt. Conrad Nichodemus' Company, 2nd Battalion, 1776/1777 [Ref: M-237, A-1146].

BANAGER, Gasper. Third Corporal, Militia, Capt. Charles Coulson's Company, enrolled August 28, 1776 [Ref: M-243, A-1146].

BANDER, Daniel. Rendered patriotic service by supplying (selling) thirty bushels of salt to the military in June, 1776 [Ref: Q-275].

BANFIELD, Prudence. See "Zadock Williams," q.v.

BANHAM, Peter. See "Peter Bonham," q.v.

BANKS, John. Enrolled in the first militia company organized for the Revolutionary War in the Elizabeth Town District of Frederick County (now the Hagerstown area of Washington County) on January 6, 1776 [Ref: Q-270, W-1189]. Private, Militia, 1st Class, Capt. John Rennolds' (Reynolds') Company, 2nd Battalion, 1776/1777 [Ref: M-240]. Took the Oath of Allegiance before September 1, 1780 [Ref: X-105].

BANNISTER, Rebecca. See "William Davis," q.v.

BANY, Jeremiah. Private, Militia, 8th Class, Capt. Peter Swingle's (Swingley's) Company, 1776/1777 [Ref: A-1146, M-249].

BARDONA, Margaret. See "William Fleck," q.v.

BARE, Christian. See "Christian Bear," q.v.

BARGMAN, Frederick. Took the Oath of Allegiance before the Hon. Christopher Cruse in Lower Antietam Hundred before March 2, 1778 [Ref: J-2, O-35]. See "Frederick Barkman," q.v.

BARGMAN, Jacob. Took the Oath of Allegiance before the Hon. Christopher Cruse in Lower Antietam Hundred before March 2, 1778 [Ref: J-2, O-35]. See "Jacob Barkman," q.v.

BARK, John. Enrolled in the third militia company organized for the Revolutionary War in the Elizabeth Town District of Frederick County (now the Hagerstown area of Washington County), passed by the Committee of Observation on June 5, 1776, and assigned to Capt. John Reynolds' command [Ref: Q-273]. Private, Militia, 1st Class, Capt. John Rennolds' (Reynolds') Company, 2nd Battalion, 1776/1777 [Ref: M-240]. Took the Oath of Allegiance before September 1, 1780 [Ref: X-105].

BARKEN, Andrew. Private, Militia, 6th Class, Capt. Conrad Nichodemus' Company, 2nd Battalion, 1776/1777 [Ref: M-237, A-1146].

BARKEN, Peter. Private, Militia, 6th Class, Capt. Conrad Nichodemus' Company, 2nd Battalion, 1776/1777 [Ref: M-237, A-1146].

BARKMAN, Frederick. Second Sergeant, Militia, Capt. Conrad Nichodemus' Company, 2nd Battalion, 1776/1777 [Ref: M-237, A-1146]. Jacob Barkman died before June 16, 1798 (date of balance book entry in Washington County) and one of his sons was Frederick Barkman [Ref: J-36]. See "Frederick Bargman," q.v.

BARKMAN, Jacob. See "Frederick Barkman," q.v.

BARKMAN, John. Corporal, Select Militia, Capt. Adam Ott's Company, 1781 [Ref: M-238, A-1146]. See "John Bargman," q.v.

BARKMAN, Peter. See "Peter Barken" and "Jacob Russell, Jr.," q.v.

BARKSHIRE, Jessey. First Sergeant, Militia, Capt. Griffin Johnson's Company, 3rd Battalion, 1776/1777 [Ref: M-243].

BARKSHIRE, John. Private, Militia, 6th Class, Capt. Griffin Johnson's Company, 3rd Battalion, 1776/1777 [Ref: M-243, which listed the name as "John Burkshire"]. Took the Oath of Allegiance before the Hon. Andrew Bruce before March 2, 1778 [Ref: O-41, J-7, which listed the name as "Johnse Barkshire"].

BARKSHIRE, Richard. First Corporal, Militia, Capt. Griffin Johnson's Company, 3rd Battalion, 1776/1777 [Ref: M-243].

BARMAN, John. Took the Oath of Allegiance before the Hon. Lemuel Barritt before March 16, 1778 [Ref: O-43, J-8].

BARNES, Abraham. See "John Barnes," q.v.

BARNES, Able. Second Corporal, Militia, Capt. Basil Williams' Company, 1776/1777 [Ref: M-244, A-1146]. Took the Oath of Allegiance before the Hon. Richard Davis in 1778 [Ref: J-4, O-37, which listed the name as "Able Barns"].

BARNES, David. Private, Militia, 2nd Class, Capt. Jeremiah Spires' Company, 2nd Battalion, 1776/1777 [Ref: M-239, A-1146, which listed the name as "David Barns"].

BARNES, Deitrick. Took the Oath of Allegiance before the Hon. Henry Schnebley in 1778 [Ref: O-50, J-14, which listed the name as "Deitrick Barns"].

BARNES, Ezekiel. Private, Militia, 8th Class, Capt. Jeremiah Spires' Company, 2nd Battalion, 1776/1777 [Ref: M-239, A-1146, which listed the name as "Ezekiel Barns"]. Took the Oath of Allegiance before the Hon. Richard Davis in 1778 [Ref: J-4, O-37].

BARNES, Henry. Took the Oath of Allegiance before the Hon. Richard Davis in 1778 [Ref: J-4, O-37, which listed the name as "Henry Barns"].

BARNES, Henry Jr. Private, Militia, 1st Class, Capt. Jeremiah Spires' Company, 2nd Battalion, 1776/1777 [Ref: M-239, A-1146, which listed the name as "Henry Barns Junr"]. Took the Oath of Allegiance before the Hon. Richard Davis in 1778 [Ref: J-5, O-37, which listed the name as "Henry Barns"].

BARNES, Hezekiah. Private, Militia, 5th Class, Capt. Jeremiah Spires' Company, 2nd Battalion, 1776/1777 [Ref: M-239, A-1146]. Took the Oath of Allegiance before the Hon. Richard Davis in 1778 [Ref: J-4, O-37, which listed the name as "Ezekiah Barns"].

BARNES, John, of Abraham (c1743-1800). Took the Oath of Allegiance on May 31, 1777 [Ref: K-1814, Box 4]. Justice who administered the Oath of Allegiance before February 28, 1778 [Ref: O-45, O-45, J-9, J-10]. Justice of the County Court, June 20, 1778 [Ref: E-141]. Rendered patriotic service by supplying rye for the use of the military on January 18, 1780, and wheat on March 23, 1780 [Ref: W-1190, HH-72]. Served in the Maryland House of Delegates, 1777-1782. Justice of the Peace and Judge of the Orphans Court, January 30, 1781 [Ref: G-293, K-I:78-86, K-I:115-116, which contains more detailed information]. "Col. John Barnes" died at his plantation about 15 miles from Hagerstown on the Tuesday before June 26, 1800 "after a few days illness of a misplaced gout." [Ref: LL-2:54].

BARNES, John. Private, Militia, 2nd Class, Capt. Michael Fackler's Company, 1776/1777 [Ref: M-245, A-1146]. Took the Oath of Allegiance before the Hon. Richard Davis in 1778 [Ref: J-3, O-36, which listed the name as "John Barns"].

BARNES, Joshua. Appointed by the Committee of Observation to carry the Association of Freemen to male residents in his hundred (district) on March 4, 1776 "and present it for signing and make an exact account of those that sign and those that refuse with their reasons for refusing." [Ref: Q-153, L-82]. Private, Militia, 8th Class, Capt. Jeremiah Spires' Company, 2nd Battalion, 1776/1777 [Ref: M-239, A-1146, which listed the name as "Joshua Barns"]. Took the Oath of Allegiance before the Hon. Richard Davis in 1778 [Ref: J-3, O-36, which listed the name as "Joshua Barns"]. First Lieutenant, Militia, Capt. Basil Williams' Company, June 22, 1778 [Ref: M-50, M-244, E-145].

BARNES, Joshua Jr. Private, Militia, 7th Class, Capt. Jeremiah Spires' Company, 2nd Battalion, 1776/1777 [Ref: M-239, A-1146, which listed the name as "Joshua Barns Junr"].

BARNES, Joshua (of Henry). Took the Oath of Allegiance before the Hon. Richard Davis in 1778 [Ref: J-4, O-37, which listed the name as "Joshua Barns, son of Henry"].

BARNES, Joshua (of James). Took the Oath of Allegiance before the Hon. Richard Davis in 1778 [Ref: J-4, O-37, which listed the name as "Joshua Barns, son of James"].

BARNES, Nathan. Private, Militia, 4th Class, Capt. Jeremiah Spires' Company, 2nd Battalion, 1776/1777 [Ref: M-239, A-1146]. Rendered patriotic service by providing "a brown horse with star in forehead" for the use of the military in January, 1777, as recorded by the Committee of Observation on January 27, 1777 [Ref: Q-53]. Took the Oath of Allegiance before the Hon. Richard Davis in 1778 [Ref: J-3, O-36, which listed the name as "Nathan Barns"].

BARNES, Peter. Second Sergeant, Militia, Capt. Basil Williams' Company, 1776/1777 [Ref: M-244, A-1146]. Took the Oath of Allegiance before the Hon. Richard Davis in 1778 [Ref: J-4, O-37, which listed the name as "Peter Barns"].

BARNES, Robert W. See "Anthony Balzar" and "William Davis" and "Abraham Storms" and "John Wagoner" and "Elie Williams," q.v.

BARNES, Silvanus. Private, Militia, 2nd Class, Capt. Jeremiah Spires' Company, 2nd Battalion, 1776/1777 [Ref: M-239, A-1146, which listed the name as "Silvanus Barns"]. Took the Oath of Allegiance before the Hon. Richard Davis in 1778 [Ref: O-37, which listed the name as "Lilrannius Barns" and J-4, which listed the name as "Librannius Barns"]. Rendered patriotic service by supplying rye for the use of the military in January and April, 1780 [Ref: HH-74 and W-1190, which listed the name as "Selvanus Barnes"]. It is interesting to note that there was a Sylvanus Barnes (1751-1828) who served in Pennsylvania and died in Virginia [Ref: Y-I:159].

BARNES, Teaten. Private, Militia, 7th Class, Capt. John Cellars' Company, 1776/1777 [Ref: A-1146, M-246].

BARNES, Uz. Took the Oath of Allegiance before the Hon. John Stull in 1778 [Ref: O-46, J-10, which latter source listed the name as "U. Barns"].

BARNET, Isaac. Private who was enrolled by Capt. Henry Hardman and passed on July 19, 1776 in Frederick (now Washington) County [Ref: D-51].

BARNHART, George. Took the Oath of Allegiance before the Hon. William Yates [Ref: O-48, J-11]. George Barnhart died testate by March 13, 1804, leaving a wife Francisca Appolonica, and among his heirs was a son George [Ref: MM-13:40].

BARNHART, George. Private, Militia, 5th Class, Capt. Jacob Sharer's Company, 1776/1777 [Ref: A-1146, M-248]. Took the Oath of Allegiance before the Hon. Richard Davis [Ref: J-4, O-37]. See the other "George Barnhart," q.v.

BARNHEIZER (BARNHISER), John (c1753-1848). Soldier who resided in Washington County and was granted a pension certificate in August, 1820, according to an Act of Congress of March 18, 1818, since he had proven that he was "in the enjoyment of a certain degree of poverty" as required by the Act as amended on May 1, 1820 [Ref: W-1190]. Private, Pennsylvania Line, pensioned at $96 per year effective March 5, 1819, and died on June 2, 1848 [Ref: Y-I:153, and R-42, which listed the name as "John Barnheiser"].

BARNHEND, George. Took the Oath of Allegiance before the Hon. John Stull in 1778 [Ref: O-46, J-10]. See "George Benhard," q.v.

BARNT, Jacob. First Corporal, Militia, Capt. John Cellars' Company, 1776/1777 [Ref: M-246, A-1146]. Second Corporal, Militia, Capt. John Kershner's Company, on duty guarding prisoners of war at Fort Frederick on June 27, 1778 [Ref: D-328].

BARR, David. Rendered patriotic service by supplying wheat for the use of the military on February 4, 1780 [Ref: W-1190, HH-72].

BARRINGER, Adam. Took the Oath of Allegiance before the Hon. Henry Schnebley in 1778 [Ref: O-51, J-15].

BARRINGER, Andrew. Private who enlisted in the militia on August 24, 1781 for service in the Continental Army [Ref: D-388, which listed the name as "Andrew Barranger"]. Substitute, Maryland Line, discharged on October 26, 1781 upon the recommendation of Dr. James Murray [Ref: G-653].

BARRINGHART, George. Private, Militia, 2nd Class, Capt. Barnett Johnston's Company, 3rd Battalion, 1776/1777 [Ref: M-242].

BARRITT (BARRETT), Lemuel (1722-1814). Colonel, Militia, 3rd or Western Battalion, May 16, 1778 [Ref: M-50, E-86, which listed the name as "Lemuel Barritt"]. Justice of the County Court, June 20, 1778 [Ref: E-141, which listed the name as "Lemuel Barrett"]. Justice who administered the Oath of Allegiance in 1778 [Ref: K-1814]. Took the Oath of Allegiance before the Hon. Andrew Bruce before March 2, 1778 [Ref: O-41, J-6]. Justice of the Peace, January 30, 1781 [Ref: G-293, which listed the name as "Lemuel Barret"]. It must be noted that some have indicated "Samuel Barrits" or "Daniel Barrits" was the justice, but "Lemuel Barritt" (who was the colonel of militia) was one of those appointed and who took the oath on June 5, 1777 to administer the Oath of Allegiance in Washington County [Ref: Original list in Manuscript MS.1814 (Box 4) at the Maryland Historical Society]. Lemuel Barrett was born in England in 1722, married Sarah Tittle, rendered military, civil and patriotic service in Maryland during the Revolution, and died in Kentucky in 1814 [Ref: Y-I:167].

BARRITT (BARRETT), Thomas. Private who was enlisted by Lieut. Moses Chapline and passed on July 24, 1776 in Frederick (now Washington) County [Ref: D-50, which listed the name as "Thomas Barrett, D.S.T."].

BARRY, John. Private who was enrolled by Capt. Henry Hardman and passed on July 19, 1776 in Frederick (now Washington) County [Ref: D-51].

BARTLEY (BARTLETT), Thomas. Private, Gist's Regiment, Continental Line, who applied for pension (R591) in 1832, aged 78, in Monroe County, Kentucky, stating he was an apprentice to a butcher named John Houseman in Philadelphia and he enlisted in the regular army under Col. Shryhawk [Shryock]. He lost his discharge or left it in Hagerstown, Maryland where he lived for three years after the close of the war. He moved to Virginia for four years, fought in the Indian War, returned to Virginia for three years, and then moved to Kentucky and married Margaret ----. His widow applied for pension in Monroe County in 1855 [Ref: T-62]. One Thomas Barkley was born in England on April 9, 1759, married (name not given), rendered military and other patriotic services in Maryland during the Revolution, and died in South Carolina on September 16, 1854 [Ref: Y-I:176]. Additional research may be necessary before drawing conclusions.

BARTMAN, Adam. See "Adam Hartman," q.v.

BARTON, Jacob and Margaret. See "William Fleck," q.v.

BARTON, Martha. See "Adrian Hoblitzell," q.v.

BASEL, Frederick. Private, Militia, 5th Class, Capt. Martin Kershner's Company, 1776/1777 [Ref: A-1146, M-247].

BATEMAN, John Jr. Private, Militia, 7th Class, Capt. Basil Williams' Company, 1776/1777 [Ref: M-244, A-1146].

BATEMAN, John Sr. Private, Militia, 2nd Class, Capt. Basil Williams' Company, 1776/1777 [Ref: M-244, A-1146]. Took the Oath of Allegiance before the Hon. Richard Davis in 1778 [Ref: O-37, which listed the name as "John Batman" and J-4, which listed the name as "John Eatman"].

BATEMAN, Thomas. Private, Militia, 2nd Class, Capt. Basil Williams' Company, 1776/1777 [Ref: M-244, A-1146].

BATES, Phillip. Took the Oath of Allegiance before the Hon. Christopher Cruse in Sharpsburg Hundred before March 2, 1778 [Ref: O-34, J-2].

BAUGH, Andrew. Private, Militia, 8th Class, Capt. Conrad Hogmire's Company, 1776/1777 [Ref: M-244, A-1146].

BAUM, Bartolome. Took the Oath of Allegiance before the Hon. John Stull in 1778 [Ref: O-46, J-10].
BAUM, Catharine and George. See "Michael Weirick," q.v.
BAUMAN, Martin. Took the Oath of Allegiance before the Hon. Joseph Sprigg before April 1, 1778 [Ref: O-53, J-16].
BAUMGARTNER, Adam. See "Adam Bumgardner," q.v.
BAUR, Michael. Took the Oath of Allegiance before the Hon. John Stull in 1778 [Ref: O-46, J-10].
BAWARD, Henry. See "Henry Boward," q.v.
BEALL, Basil. Took the Oath of Allegiance before the Hon. Christopher Cruse in Sharpsburg Hundred before March 2, 1778 [Ref: O-34, J-2].
BEALL, Daniel (1740-1835). County Sheriff, May 13, 1777 [Ref: C-249]. Took the Oath of Allegiance on May 27, 1777 [Ref: K-1814, which listed the name as "Daniel Beall, sheriff"]. Daniel Beall was born in 1740, married Nancy ----, rendered patriotic service during the Revolution, and died on January 4, 1835 [Ref: Y-I:195].
BEALL, Daniel. Private, Militia, 1st Class, Capt. Joseph Chapline's Company, 2nd Battalion, 1776/1777 [Ref: M-241].
BEALL, Daniel. Private, Militia, 6th Class, Capt. Michael Fackler's Company, 1776/1777 [Ref: M-245, A-1146].
BEALL, Isaac. See "Thomas Beall, of Samuel," q.v.
BEALL, John. Private, Militia, 2nd Class, Capt. James Prather's Company, 3rd Battalion, 1776/1777 [Ref: M-242]. See "Samuel Beall," q.v.
BEALL, Nancy. See "Daniel Beall," q.v.
BEALL, Peter. Served on the Committee of Observation for the Elizabeth Town District (now the Hagerstown area of Washington County) in December, 1776 [Ref: Q-340]. Captain, Militia, 2nd Company, 1st Battalion, January 15, 1777 [Ref: C-42, C-50, M-240, which also listed the name as "Peter Bell"]. Took the Oath of Allegiance before the Hon. Andrew Rentch before March 7, 1778 [Ref: O-52, J-15, which listed the name as "Peter Beala"].
BEALL, Samuel (c1713/4-1778). Elected to serve on the Committee of Observation for the Elizabeth Town District (now the Hagerstown area of Washington County) on September 12, 1775 [Ref: Q-142, Q-154]. Appointed by the Committee of Observation to serve on a Committee for Licensing Suits on September 14, 1775 [Ref: Q-142]. Served on the Committee of Observation for the Elizabeth Town District (now the Hagerstown area of Washington County) in December, 1776 [Ref: Q-340]. Justice of the Orphans Court, June 4, 1777 [Ref: C-275]. Colonel Samuel Beall, son of John, was born circa 1713/4 in Maryland, married

Eleanor Brooke, rendered civil and patriotic services during the Revolution (including service in the Maryland House of Delegates in 1777), and died in January, 1778 [Ref: Y-I:197, KK-I:76, K-I:124-125, which contains more detailed information]. See "Thomas Bissett" and "Thomas Beall," q.v.

BEALL, Thomas, of Samuel (1743-1823). Captain, Maryland Line, died at an advanced age on November 16 (or 25?), 1823. "He participated in the struggles of the Revolution and was proprietor of the town of Cumberland." [Ref: Y-I:197, Z-1, Z-5, Z-17, citing an equity court case in Allegany County in 1827 (Cumberland Bank of Allegany, et al. vs. Isaac Beall, et al.) which listed numerous heirs living in and outside of Maryland].

BEALL, William. Private, Militia, 8th Class, Capt. James Prather's Company, 3rd Battalion, 1776/1777 [Ref: M-243].

BEALL, Zephaniah. Private, Militia, 5th Class, Capt. Daniel Cresap's Company, 3rd Battalion, 1776/1777 [Ref: M-241].

BEAN, Henry. Private, Militia, 8th Class, Capt. Barnett Johnston's Company, 3rd Battalion, 1776/1777 [Ref: M-242].

BEAN, Henry. Private, Militia, 2nd Class, Capt. Griffin Johnson's Company, 3rd Battalion, 1776/1777 [Ref: M-243].

BEAN, John. Private, Militia, 1st Class, Capt. Peter Swingle's (Swingley's) Company, 1776/1777 [Ref: A-1146, M-248]. Took the Oath of Allegiance before the Hon. John Barnes before February 28, 1778 [Ref: O-44, J-9].

BEAN, Leonard. Private, Militia, 4th Class, Capt. Barnett Johnston's Company, 3rd Battalion, 1776/1777 [Ref: M-242, which listed the name as "Leonard Beans"].

BEAN, Thomas. Private, Militia, 3rd Class, Capt. Griffin Johnson's Company, 3rd Battalion, 1776/1777 [Ref: M-243].

BEAN, Thomas. Private, Militia, 8th Class, Capt. Barnett Johnston's Company, 3rd Battalion, 1776/1777 [Ref: M-242].

BEANE, Henry. Took the Oath of Allegiance before the Hon. William Yates in 1778 [Ref: O-48, J-11].

BEANE, John. Took the Oath of Allegiance before the Hon. William Yates in 1778 [Ref: O-48, J-11].

BEANER, Lodwick. Private, Militia, 5th Class, Capt. Peter Swingle's (Swingley's) Company, 1776/1777 [Ref: A-1146, M-248].

BEAR, Christian. Private, Militia, 7th Class, Capt. Samuel Hughes' Company, 2nd Battalion, 1776/1777 [Ref: M-238, A-1146, which listed the name as "Christian Bare"]. See "Frederick Guiser," q.v.

BEAR, David. Private, Militia, 4th Class, Capt. James Walling's Company, 2nd Battalion, 1776/1777 [Ref: M-239, A-1146].

BEAR, John. Private, Militia, by January 22, 1777 when ordered by the Committee of Observation "to march with some company of militia to the reinforcement of his Excellency General Washington" or appear before the Committee and state his reason for not marching. He apparently marched since he never appeared to the contrary [Ref: Q-48].

BEAR, Mary. See "Jacob Martin," q.v.

BEARD, Andrew. Private, Militia, 6th Class, Capt. Samuel Hughes' Company, 2nd Battalion, 1776/1777 [Ref: M-238, A-1146].

BEARD, Anna Christina. See "John Beard," q.v.

BEARD, David. Took the Oath of Allegiance before the Hon. John Barnes before February 28, 1778 [Ref: O-44, J-9].

BEARD, John (c1755-1827). Private who enlisted in the militia on August 27, 1781 for service in the Continental Army [Ref: D-388]. John Beard died at his residence in Sharpsburg on March 27, 1827, at an advanced age [Ref: Z-89].

BEARD, John (1758-1817). "Major John Beard" was born on June 11, 1758, died on November 26, 1817, and is buried in Beard's Graveyard near Beard's Church at Chewsville in Washington County, Maryland. Anna Christina Geiser, wife of Major John Beard, was born on March 6, 1761 in Lancaster County, Pennsylvania, married on February 14, 1781 and "lived without inheritance during the life of social marriage, 27 years, 8 months and 19 days." Anna Christina Beard died on October 26, 1809, in her 49th year, after a short illness, and is buried beside her husband [Ref: JJ-IV:101, LL-3:80].

BEARD, William. Served on the Committee of Observation for the Elizabeth Town District (now the Hagerstown area of Washington County) in 1776 [Ref: Q-154, Q-155, Q-340, which listed the name as "William Beard, Esquire"]. Rendered patriotic service by supplying a blanket for the use of the military in March, 1776, as recorded by the Committee of Observation on April 12, 1776 [Ref: Q-156, L-82, which latter source listed the name as "William Baird"].

BEATTY, Mark. Private, Militia, 1st Class, Capt. James Walling's Company, 2nd Battalion, 1776/1777 [Ref: M-238, A-1146, which listed the name as "Mark Beaty"]. Took the Oath of Allegiance before the Hon. Joseph Sprigg before April 1, 1778 [Ref: O-53, J-15].

BEATTY, Walter. Private, Militia, 1st Class, Capt. Isaac Baker's Company, 1776/1777 [Ref: A-1146, M-247].

BEAVIS, Ezekiel. Private, Militia, 7th Class, Capt. Griffin Johnson's Company, 3rd Battalion, 1776/1777 [Ref: M-243].

BECKER, Anna Margaret. See "Yost Harbaugh," q.v.

BECHTEL, Philip. Private, Maryland and Pennsylvania Lines. He applied for and received pension S22637 in Schuylkill County, Pennsylvania on July 24, 1833, aged 73 to 74, stating that he lived in Hagerstown, Maryland for 4 or 5 years before moving to Dauphin County and then to Schuylkill County [Ref: V-I:207].

BECKLEHIMER, John. Private, Militia, 1st Class, Capt. Isaac Baker's Company, 1776/1777 [Ref: A-1146, M-247]. See "Jacob Picklehimer," q.v.

BEEDING, Henry. Private who was enrolled by Capt. Aeneas Campbell and passed by Major Francis Deakins on July 18, 1776 [Ref: D-49].

BEEDING, Joseph. Private who was enrolled by Lieut. Clement Hollyday and passed by Major Francis Deakins on July 25, 1776 [Ref: D-49].

BEEN, John. Private who was enlisted by Capt. John Reynolds and passed on July 18, 1776 in Frederick (now Washington) County [Ref: D-50]. Took the Oath of Allegiance before the Hon. Lemuel Barritt before March 16, 1778 [Ref: O-43, J-8].

BEEVER, Stuffle. See "Stuffle Reever," q.v.

BEGGS, Andrew. See "Andrew Baggs," q.v.

BELL, Anthony. Second Sergeant, Militia, Capt. Daniel Clapsaddle's Company, 1st Battalion, 1776/1777 [Ref: M-236, A-1146]. Took the Oath of Allegiance before the Hon. Andrew Rentch before March 7, 1778 [Ref: O-52, J-15].

BELL, Captain. See "Thomas Chenoweth," q.v.

BELL, Charles. Private, Militia, 7th Class, Capt. James Walling's Company, 2nd Battalion, 1776/1777 [Ref: M-239, A-1146]. Took the Oath of Allegiance before the Hon. John Stull in 1778 [Ref: O-46, J-10].

BELL, Daniel and Elizabeth. See "Peter Bell," q.v.

BELL, Frederick and J. Ulianna. See "Peter Bell," q.v.

BELL, John. Took the Oath of Allegiance before the Hon. Lemuel Barritt before March 16, 1778 [Ref: O-43, J-8].

BELL, Leonard. Private, Militia, 3rd Class, Capt. Conrad Nichodemus' Company, 2nd Battalion, 1776/1777 [Ref: M-237, A-1146].

BELL, Margaret. See "Peter Bell," q.v.

BELL, Peter. Rendered patriotic service by providing "rashons" for the use of the military in July, 1775, as recorded by the Committee of Observation at Elizabeth Town on November 4, 1775 [Ref: Q-150]. Rendered patriotic service in Hagerstown by providing sundries to Capt. John Nelson's Company, continental service, Maryland Line, April, 1776 [Ref: Q-162]. Private, Militia, 4th Class, Capt. Conrad Nichodemus'

Company, 2nd Battalion, 1776/1777 [Ref: A-1146, M-237, which listed the name as "Peter Bell (Bill?)"]. One Peter Bell died testate before July 14, 1792 (date of balance book entry in Washington County), leaving a widow (no name given in this account) and equal shares to J. Ulianna (Julianna?), Frederick, Elizabeth, Margaret, Peter, and Daniel Bell [Ref: J-31]. One Peter Bell was born in Germany circa 1744, married Elizabeth Leiter, served as a captain in Maryland during the Revolution, and died on May 15, 1778 [Ref: Y-I:219]. There appears to have been more then one Peter Bell. Additional research will be necessary before drawing conclusions.

BELSOR, Anthony. See "Anthony Balzar," q.v.

BELT, Benoni. Took the Oath of Allegiance before the Hon. Richard Davis in 1778 [Ref: J-4, O-37].

BELT, Thomas (1751-1823). He was appointed Register of Wills for Washington County on November 25, 1780 in the room of Thomas Sprigg who had resigned [Ref: G-224]. "Thomas Belt, Esq." died at the Globe Tavern in Hagerstown on December 3, 1823, in his 83rd year [Ref: Z-50].

BELTZHOOVER, Jacob. Private, Militia, Capt. William Heyser's Company, enlisted July 26, 1776 and on muster roll dated October 23, 1776, in continental service [Ref: D-264, which listed the name as "Jacob Belsoover" and W-1190, which listed the name as "Jacob Beltzhoover" and L-79, which listed the name as "Jacob Belshoover"]. Private, German Regiment, Lt. Col. Ludwick Weltner's Company, continental service, discharged on July 26, 1779 at Fort Wyoming, Pennsylvania [Ref: D-265, D-191, which latter source listed the name as "Jacob Betzhover" and GG-96, which listed the name as "Jacob Belzhoover"].

BELTZHOOVER, Melchor. Took the Oath of Allegiance before the Hon. Joseph Sprigg before April 1, 1778 [Ref: O-53, J-16]. Private, Militia, 6th Class, Capt. Peter Beall's Company, 1st Battalion, 1776/1777 [Ref: M-240, which listed the name as "Melchar Bellhover"].

BEMHART, John. Private who was enrolled by Capt. Henry Hardman and passed on July 19, 1776 in Frederick (now Washington) County [Ref: D-51].

BENEDICT, Bowman. See "Benedict Bowman," q.v.

BENHARD, George. Private, Militia, 1st Class, Capt. James Smith's Company, 2nd Battalion, 1776/1777 [Ref: M-239, A-1146]. See "George Barnhend," q.v.

BENNET, John. Captain, Militia, 1776 [Ref: M-246, A-1146]. Appointed by the Committee of Observation to carry the Association of Freemen to male residents in his hundred (district) on March 4, 1776 "and present it for signing and make an exact account of those that sign and those that refuse with their reasons for refusing." [Ref: Q-153, L-82, which latter source listed the name as "John Bonett"]. See "John Bonnet," q.v.

BENNET, John. Private, Militia, 6th Class, Capt. James Smith's Company, 2nd Battalion, 1776/1777 [Ref: M-240, A-1146, which listed the name as "John Bennit"].

BENNET, Rinear. Private who was enlisted by Lieut. Moses Chapline and passed on July 24, 1776 in Frederick (now Washington) County [Ref: D-50, which listed the name as "Rinear Bennett"].

BENNET, Robert. On March 1, 1777 the accounts of the Committee of Observation stated "to cash received from Robert Bennet advanced to him by Capt. Wallen in militia service, 15 shillings." [Ref: Q-247].

BENSON, Perry. Attained the rank of major general in the United States Army and distinguished himself in the campaign in the southern states during the Revolutionary War, and afterwards in the War of 1812. He was "another of the brave officers furnished by Washington County for the service of their native land in the struggle for freedom." [Ref: L-80]. There was a Perry Benson who was an officer in the militia of Talbot County in 1776 [Ref: D-67]. Additional research may be necessary before drawing conclusions.

BENTER, Henry (1748-   ). Private, Militia, Capt. William Heyser's Company, enlisted July 27, 1776 and on muster roll dated October 23, 1776, in continental service [Ref: D-264, W-1190, L-79, GG-96]. Private, German Regiment, Lt. Col. Ludwick Weltner's Company, continental service, discharged October 12, 1779 at Fort Wyoming, Pennsylvania [Ref: D-265, GG-96, which listed the name as "Henry Bender, Painter, Benter, Painther"]. See "Henry Painter," q.v.

BENTER, Mary. See "Melcher Benter," q.v.

BENTER, Melcher (c1739-   ). Private, Militia, Capt. William Heyser's Company, enlisted July 17, 1776, muster roll dated October 23, 1776, in continental service [Ref: GG-96, D-264, W-1190, L-79, which latter source listed the name as "Melcher Bender"]. Private, German Regiment, Lt. Col. Ludwick Weltner's Company, continental service, discharged on July 17, 1779 at Fort Wyoming, Pennsylvania [Ref: D-265, which listed the name as "Melcher Benner" and GG-96, which listed the name as "Melcher/Melchior/Michael Benter, Benner, Painter"]. Pension of half-pay of a private for life awarded to widow Mary in Washington, D. C. on April 1, 1838 [Ref: GG-96]. See "Melchoir Painter," q.v.

BENTZ, Jacob (1750-1827). Took the Oath of Allegiance before September 1, 1780 [Ref: X-105]. Jacob Bentz died on September 23,

1827, aged 87 years, 10 months, and is buried beside his wife Elizabeth Bentz (1758-1828) in the Funkstown Public Cemetery in Washington County, Maryland [Ref: JJ-IV:5].

BENWICK, William. See "William Renwick," q.v.

BEONTRER, Andrew. Private, Militia, 1st Class, Capt. James Smith's Company, 2nd Battalion, 1776/1777 [Ref: M-239, A-1146].

BERESFORD, John. Took the Oath of Allegiance before the Hon. John Stull in 1778 [Ref: O-46, J-10].

BERGD, Peter. Took the Oath of Allegiance before the Hon. John Stull in 1778 [Ref: O-46, J-10].

BERGER, George. Wagoner, Capt. William's Company, before February 1, 1777, when he reported to the Committee of Observation for Elizabeth Town District (now the Hagerstown area of Washington County) "that part of the team by him drove is become unfit for service and are now at Smizer's Tavern near York Town, therefore resolved that the respective owners thereof apply at said Smizer's for their respective properties." [Ref: Q-232].

BERGER, John. Enrolled in the first militia company organized for the Revolutionary War in the Elizabeth Town District of Frederick County (now the Hagerstown area of Washington County) on January 6, 1776 [Ref: Q-270, W-1189].

BERKSHIRE, Henry. Private, Militia, 4th Class, Capt. Griffin Johnson's Company, 3rd Battalion, 1776/1777 [Ref: M-243].

BERNTH, Jacob. Took the Oath of Allegiance before the Hon. Henry Schnebley in 1778 [Ref: O-51, J-14].

BERRINGER, Chn. Private who was enrolled by Capt. Henry Hardman and passed on July 19, 1776 in Frederick (now Washington) County [Ref: D-51].

BERRY, Bassel. Took the Oath of Allegiance before the Hon. Richard Davis in 1778 [Ref: J-5, O-37].

BERRY, John. Private who was enlisted by Lieut. Moses Chapline and passed on July 24, 1776 in Frederick (now Washington) County [Ref: D-50].

BERRY, Mary. See "Christopher Bruff," q.v.

BERRYHILL, William. Private, Militia, 2nd Class, Capt. John Cellars' Company, 1776/1777 [Ref: A-1146, M-246].

BESTY, William. Took the Oath of Allegiance before the Hon. John Stull in 1778 [Ref: O-46, J-10].

BEVEN, Leonard. Took the Oath of Allegiance before the Hon. John Barnes before February 28, 1778 [Ref: O-44, J-9].

BICKNELL, Esau (c1758-   ). Soldier who resided in Washington County and was granted a pension certificate in August, 1820, according to an Act of Congress of March 18, 1818, since he had proven that he was "in the enjoyment of a certain degree of poverty" as required by the Act as amended on May 1, 1820 [Ref: W-1190]. Private, Maryland Line, pensioned at $96 per year effective September 13, 1820 [Ref: R-42].

BIERLY, Joseph. Rendered patriotic service by supplying a blanket for the use of the military in March, 1776, as recorded by the Committee of Observation on April 12, 1776 [Ref: Q-156, L-82, which latter source listed the name as "Joseph Birely"].

BIGGLEMAN, George. See "George Riggleman," q.v.

BILMIRE (BELMIRE, BILLMYER), Leonard. Appeared before the Committee of Observation on June 28, 1776, having been accused of "expressing sentiments inimical to the liberties of America and advising Capt. Keller's Company to lay down their arms, [and] upon hearing the evidence the Committee was of the opinion they ought to be discharged, on promising good behaviour for the future." [Ref: Q-324, which listed the name as "Leonard Belmire"]. Ensign, Militia, Capt. Conrad Nichodemus' Company, 2nd Battalion, 1776/1777 [Ref: M-237, A-1146]. One of several patriots appointed by the Committee of Observation on January 19, 1777 "to form the county into companies (after the militia had marched) for the purpose of relieving the distressed inhabitants of said county and also to compel the Dunkards and Mennonists to give their assistance." [Ref: Q-43]. Took the Oath of Allegiance before the Hon. Christopher Cruse in Lower Antietam Hundred before March 2, 1778 [Ref: J-3, O-35, which listed the name as "Leonard Billmyer"]. Second Lieutenant, Capt. Martin Billmyer's Company, 2nd Battalion, November 21, 1780 [Ref: G-220].

BILMIRE (BELMIRE, BILLMYER), Martin (1746-1812, or 1756-1819). He appeared before the Committee of Observation on June 28, 1776, having been accused of "expressing sentiments inimical to the liberties of America and advising Capt. Keller's Company to lay down their arms, [and] upon hearing the evidence the Committee was of the opinion they ought to be discharged, on promising good behaviour for the future." [Ref: Q-324, which listed the name as "Martin Belmore"]. Apparently, his sentiments changed dramatically, based on his subsequent military service: Second Lieutenant, Militia, Capt. Conrad Nichodemus' Company, 2nd Battalion, 1776/1777 [Ref: M-237, A-1146, which listed the name as "Martain Bilmire"]. First Lieutenant, Militia, Capt. Conrad Nichodemus' Company, 2nd Battalion, June 22, 1778 [Ref: M-53, M-237, E-145, which listed the name as "Martin Billmire"]. On October 28, 1780,

Conrad Nichodemus resigned his captaincy and recommended "Martin Billmeyer" as his successor [Ref: G-165]. Captain, 2nd Battalion, November 21, 1780 [Ref: G-220, which listed the name as "Martin Billmyer"]. "Martin Billmyer or Billmire" was born in Pennsylvania on June 13, 1746, married Catherine Thomas, served as a captain in Maryland during the Revolution, and died in Maryland on April 12, 1812 [Ref: Y-I:255]. There is a discrepancy in the years of his birth and death. The tombstone of "Martin Billmeyer" states he died on April 12, 1819, aged 65 years, 10 months. He is buried in a graveyard at the Geeting Meeting House, 1st U. B. Church at Mt. Hebron, Eakle's Mill, in Washington County [Ref: JJ-V:64]. Additional research will be necessary before drawing conclusions.

BILMIRE (BELMIRE, BILLMYER), Michael. Private, Militia, 5th Class, Capt. Conrad Nichodemus' Company, 2nd Battalion, 1776/1777 [Ref: M-237, A-1146, which listed the name as "Michael Belmire"].

BILMORE, John. One of several patriots appointed by the Committee of Observation on December 30, 1776 "to form the county into companies (after the militia had marched) for the purpose of relieving the distressed inhabitants of said county and also to compel the Dunkards and Mennonists to give their assistance." [Ref: Q-345]. Rendered patriotic service by providing necessaries to Capt. John Reynolds' Company in the Flying Camp and belonging to the Maryland Service in July, 1776, as recorded by the Committee of Observation at Sharpsburg on August 6, 1776 [Ref: Q-332]. Took the Oath of Allegiance before the Hon. John Stull in 1778 [Ref: O-46, J-10, which latter source listed the name as "John Bilmone"].

BIMSON, Jacob. See "Jacob Brinson," q.v.

BINKLER, Jacob. Private, Militia, 3rd Class, Capt. Martin Kershner's Company, 1776/1777 [Ref: A-1146, M-247, which listed the name as "Jacob Bincklar"]. Private, Militia, Capt. John Kershner's Company, on duty guarding prisoners of war at Fort Frederick on June 27, 1778 [Ref: D-328].

BISHOP, Jacob (1758-1813). Private, Militia, Capt. William Heyser's Company, enlisted July 26, 1776, muster roll dated October 23, 1776, in continental service [Ref: GG-96, D-264, W-1190, L-79]. Private, German Regiment, Lt. Col. Ludwick Weltner's Company, continental service, discharged on July 26, 1779 at Fort Wyoming, Pennsylvania [Ref: GG-96, D-265]. Mary Bishop, widow of Jacob, applied for and received pension W3381 in Bedford County, Pennsylvania on January 30, 1839, age 74, stating she was Mary Powel when she married Jacob Bishop on December 25, 1781 (by Rev. Joseph Powel by license obtained in

Philadelphia). Jacob Bishop died on April 10, 1813, aged 54 years, 7 months, 4 days, and is buried in the Tonoloway Baptist Church Graveyard north of Hancock in Pennsylvania near the Maryland State Line. In 1839 a son William Bishop was mentioned. In 1855 Mary Bishop lived in Fulton County, Pennsylvania [Ref: V-I:269, GG-96, JJ-II:51]. One Jacob Bishop died testate in Washington County, Maryland before April, 1798 (date of balance book entry) and he had a son Jacob Bishop [Ref: J-35].

BISHOP, Mary. See "Jacob Bishop," q.v.

BISHOP, William. Private, Militia, 1st Class, Capt. Peter Beall's Company, 1st Battalion, 1776/1777 [Ref: M-240]. See "Jacob Bishop," q.v.

BISSETT, Thomas. Private who was enlisted by Capt. John Reynolds and passed on July 18, 1776 in Frederick (now Washington) County [Ref: D-50]. Thomas Bissett died testate in 1794 (exact date not indicated in balance book entry in Washington County), leaving equal shares to Thomas Bissett, Samuel Beal, Susannah Murphy, Elenor Mullen, and Mary Anderson's heirs [Ref: J-33].

BISSETT, Thomas Jr. Enrolled in the third militia company organized for the Revolutionary War in the Elizabeth Town District of Frederick County (now the Hagerstown area of Washington County), passed by the Committee of Observation on June 5, 1776, and assigned to Capt. John Reynolds' command [Ref: Q-273]. See "Thomas Bissett," q.v.

BLACHER, Frederick. See "Frederick Plecker," q.v.

BLACK, James. Enrolled in the first militia company organized for the Revolutionary War in the Elizabeth Town District of Frederick County (now the Hagerstown area of Washington County) on January 6, 1776 [Ref: Q-271, W-1190]. Private, Militia, 3rd Class, Capt. John Rennolds' (Reynolds') Company, 2nd Battalion, 1776/1777 [Ref: M-240].

BLACK, John. Private, Militia, 4th Class, Capt. John Rennolds' (Reynolds') Company, 2nd Battalion, 1776/1777 [Ref: M-240]. Took the Oath of Allegiance before the Hon. William Yates in 1778 [Ref: O-48, J-11]. Private, Maryland and Pennsylvania Lines. He applied for a pension (R887) on March 13, 1834, aged 70, in Highland County, Ohio, stating he was born in Lancaster County, Pennsylvania on March 13, 1763 and lived in Washington County, Maryland at the time of his enlistment. During the war he moved to Berkeley County, Virginia and lived there 5 years before moving to Fayette County, Pennsylvania for 13 years, then to Adams County, Ohio for 24 years, then to Highland County, and in 1839 to Clermont County, Ohio. In 1852 he lived in Union Township, Brown County, Ohio. His son, William H. Black, stated his father died prior to 1856 and he had two brothers (his uncles), Samuel and William, who also enlisted in Williamsport, Maryland [Ref: V-I:277].

BLACK, Samuel. Took the Oath of Allegiance before the Hon. Henry Schnebley in 1778 [Ref: O-49, J-13]. One Samuel Black applied for a pension (R892) in Adams County, Ohio on June 17, 1826, aged 64, with a wife aged 58 and children all of age (no names were given). He stated he served in the Maryland and Pennsylvania Lines and also in the sea service [Ref: V-I:278]. See "John Black," q.v.

BLACK, William. Private, Militia, 7th Class, Capt. John Bennet's Company, 1776/1777 [Ref: M-246, A-1146]. Took the Oath of Allegiance before the Hon. Henry Schnebley in 1778 [Ref: O-49, J-13]. See "John Black," q.v.

BLACK, William H. See "John Black," q.v.

BLACKBURN, Elizabeth. Rendered patriotic service in Hagerstown by making hunting shirts for Capt. John Nelson's Company, continental service (Maryland Line), April, 1776 [Ref: Q-161].

BLACKBURN, John. Private, Militia, 7th Class, Capt. Michael Fackler's Company, 1776/1777 [Ref: M-245, A-1146].

BLACKBURN, Thomas. Private, Militia, 6th Class, Capt. Isaac Baker's Company, 1776/1777 [Ref: A-1146, M-247]. Private, Select Militia, Capt. Adam Ott's Company, 1781 [Ref: M-238, A-1146].

BLACKBURN, William. Private, Militia, 2nd Class, Capt. John Bennet's Company, 1776/1777 [Ref: M-246, A-1146].

BLACKER, Lydia. See "Henry Franks," q.v.

BLACKMORE, Calep. Took the Oath of Allegiance before the Hon. John Barnes before February 28, 1778 [Ref: O-44, J-9].

BLACKMORE, William. Took the Oath of Allegiance before the Hon. John Barnes before February 28, 1778 [Ref: O-44, J-9].

BLACKWELL, Francis. Private, Militia, 5th Class, Capt. Peter Swingle's (Swingley's) Company, 1776/1777 [Ref: A-1146, M-248]. See "David Meek," q.v.

BLAIR, Andrew. Took the Oath of Allegiance before September 1, 1780 [Ref: X-105].

BLAIR, James (1735-1828). Private, Militia, 7th Class, Capt. Isaac Baker's Company, 1776/1777 [Ref: A-1146, M-247]. Took the Oath of Allegiance before September 1, 1780 [Ref: X-105]. James Blair died in Blair's Valley on March 15, 1828, in his 93rd year, "one among the first settlers of this part of Washington County, and bore a part in the many skirmishes with the Indians." [Ref: Z-98].

BLAIR, John. Took the Oath of Allegiance before September 1, 1780 [Ref: X-105].

BLAIR, William. Enrolled in the second militia company organized for the Revolutionary War in the Elizabeth Town District of Frederick County (now the Hagerstown area of Washington County) on March 9, 1776 [Ref: Q-272].
BLEACHY, ----. See "Henry Newcomer," q.v.
BLENY, Rudolph. Took the Oath of Allegiance before the Hon. Henry Schnebley in 1778 [Ref: O-49, J-13].
BLEW, Abraham. Private, Militia, 3rd Class, Capt. Daniel Cresap's Company, 3rd Battalion, 1776/1777 [Ref: M-241]. Took the Oath of Allegiance before the Hon. Lemuel Barritt before March 16, 1778 [Ref: O-42, J-8].
BLUME, Henry. Took the Oath of Allegiance before the Hon. John Stull in 1778 [Ref: O-46, J-10, which latter source listed the name as "Henry Plume"].
BOARDY, Peter. Private who was enrolled by Capt. Aeneas Campbell and passed by Major John Fulford on July 18, 1776 [Ref: D-49].
BOCKMAN, Abraham. See "Jacob Kuhn," q.v.
BOHRER, George. See "George Rohrer," q.v.
BOILL, Benjamin. Private, Militia, 8th Class, Capt. Conrad Nichodemus' Company, 2nd Battalion, 1776/1777 [Ref: M-237, A-1146].
BOMGARDNER, Margaret and William. See "William Bumgardner," q.v.
BOND, Ann and Edward. See "Walter Bond," q.v.
BOND, George Jr. Private, Militia, 2nd Class, Capt. James Walling's Company, 2nd Battalion, 1776/1777 [Ref: M-238, A-1146].
BOND, George Sr. Rendered patriotic service in Hagerstown by providing a rifle to Capt. John Nelson's Company, continental service (Maryland Line), April, 1776 [Ref: Q-161]. See "Walter Bond," q.v.
BOND, John. Private, Militia, 7th Class, Capt. James Walling's Company, 2nd Battalion, 1776/1777 [Ref: M-239, A-1146].
BOND, Joseph. See "Walter Bond," q.v.
BOND, Walter. Private, Militia, 8th Class, Capt. James Walling's Company, 2nd Battalion, 1776/1777 [Ref: M-239, A-1146]. Took the Oath of Allegiance before September 1, 1780 [Ref: X-105]. One Walter Bond died before November 12, 1785 (date of balance book entry in Washington County), leaving a widow (not named, but Lucy? Bond was the administratrix) and equal shares to George, Edward, Joseph and Ann Bond [Ref: J-26].
BONHAM, Peter. Took the Oath of Allegiance before the Hon. Lemuel Barritt before March 16, 1778 [Ref: O-42, J-7]. Private, Militia, 8th Class, Capt. Charles Clinton's Company, 1776/1777 [Ref: M-245, A-1146,

which listed the name as "Peter Banham"]. Third Corporal, Militia, Capt. Charles Clinton's Company, 1776/1777 [Ref: M-245, A-1146].

BONMAN, Simon. Took the Oath of Allegiance before the Hon. Henry Schnebley in 1778 [Ref: O-49, J-13, which latter source listed the name as "Simon Honman"].

BONNET, John. Captain, by June, 1776, at which time he and other officers were ordered by the Committee of Observation "to summons non-enrollers and non-associators to attend at Elisabeth Town the first Tuesday in July next to shew cause if any they have why they shall not be fined according to the Resolves of the Convention in July last." [Ref: Q-269]. See "John Bennet," q.v.

BONNETT, John. Fourth Corporal, Militia, Capt. John Bennet's Company, 1776/1777 [Ref: M-246, A-1146]. Took the Oath of Allegiance before the Hon. John Barnes before February 28, 1778 [Ref: O-44, J-9].

BOOKER, Casper. Private, Militia, 5th Class, Capt. Conrad Hogmire's Company, 1776/1777 [Ref: M-244, A-1146].

BOOKER, Daniel. Fourth Corporal, Militia, Capt. Samuel Hughes' Company, 1776/1777 [Ref: M-238, A-1146].

BOOKER, Daniel. Private, Militia, 5th Class, Capt. James Walling's Company, 2nd Battalion, 1776/1777 [Ref: M-239, A-1146].

BOOKER, Daniel. Took the Oath of Allegiance before September 1, 1780 [Ref: X-105].

BOOM, Jacob. Private, Select Militia, Capt. Adam Ott's Company, 1781 [Ref: M-238, A-1146].

BOOND, John. Took the Oath of Allegiance before the Hon. John Stull in 1778 [Ref: O-46, J-10].

BOONE, Nicholas. Private, Militia, 1st Class, Capt. Martin Kershner's Company, 1776/1777 [Ref: A-1146, M-247].

BOORT, Andrew. Enrolled in the first militia company organized for the Revolutionary War in the Elizabeth Town District of Frederick County (now the Hagerstown area of Washington County) on January 6, 1776 [Ref: Q-271, W-1190].

BOOT, Adam. Enrolled in the second militia company organized for the Revolutionary War in the Elizabeth Town District of Frederick County (now the Hagerstown area of Washington County) on March 9, 1776 [Ref: Q-272]. Private, Militia, 4th Class, Capt. Henry Boteler's Company, 1776/1777 [Ref: M-237, A-1146].

BOOT, George. Private, Militia, 4th Class, Capt. Henry Boteler's Company, 1776/1777 [Ref: M-237, A-1146].

BOOTH, John (1756-1840). Private, 1st Maryland Line, 1776-1777 [Ref: D-16, D-81]. John Booth died on November 27, 1840, aged 84, and is buried beside his wife Drusilla Swearingen (1759-1816) in a graveyard on the Joe Mullendore farm at Antietam Creek and Devil's Backbone in Washington County [Ref: JJ-V:49].

BOOTH, Reverend. See "John Ferguson," q.v.

BOOTH, Robert. Enrolled in the second militia company organized for the Revolutionary War in the Elizabeth Town District of Frederick County (now the Hagerstown area of Washington County) on March 9, 1776 [Ref: Q-272].

BOOTH, William. Enrolled in the second militia company organized for the Revolutionary War in the Elizabeth Town District of Frederick County (now the Hagerstown area of Washington County) on March 9, 1776 [Ref: Q-272]. Rendered patriotic service by supplying corn for the use of the military on March 4 and March 18, 1780 [Ref: W-1190, HH-74].

BOOZER, John. Rendered patriotic service by providing a rifle for Capt. Daniel Cresap's Company in July, 1775, as recorded by the Committee of Observation at Elizabeth Town on November 4, 1775 [Ref: Q-149].

BORDAM, Jacob. Took the Oath of Allegiance before the Hon. Henry Schnebley in 1778 [Ref: O-50, J-13, which latter source listed the name as "Jacob Bordam or Rordam"].

BORET, Peter. Private who enlisted in the militia on August 16, 1781 for service in the Continental Army [Ref: D-388]. Substitute, Maryland Line, discharged on October 30, 1781 [Ref: G-657, which listed the name as "Peter Borat"].

BORDENHEIMER, Anne. See "John Ringer," q.v.

BORETT, Balser. Private who was recruited and passed by County Lieutenant Thomas Sprigg on April 22, 1780 [Ref: D-336].

BOSSE, David. Took the Oath of Allegiance before the Hon. Richard Davis in 1778 [Ref: O-37, J-5, which latter source listed the name as "David Rosse"].

BOTELER, Henry (1728-1814). Captain, Militia, resigned by May 10, 1778 [Ref: M-54, M-237, A-1146]. Henry Boteler was born on October 15, 1728, married Sallie Elsby, and died in 1814 [Ref: Y-I:313]. See "Thomas Odel," q.v.

BOTELER, Henry Edward. Second Sergeant, Militia, Capt. Henry Boteler's Company, 1776/1777 [Ref: M-237, A-1146].

BOTTS, Andrew. Took the Oath of Allegiance before the Hon. John Stull in 1778 [Ref: O-46, J-10].

BOUGHMAN, George. Private, Militia, 5th Class, Capt. John Cellars' Company, 1776/1777 [Ref: A-1146, M-246].

BOUGHSLOUGH. Peter. See "Peter Roughslough," q.v.

BOUMAN, John. Private, Militia, 4th Class, Capt. James Walling's Company, 2nd Battalion, 1776/1777 [Ref: M-239, A-1146].

BOUSER, Henry. Private, Militia, 4th Class, Capt. Henry Boteler's Company, 1776/1777 [Ref: M-237, A-1146].

BOUSSER, John. Took the Oath of Allegiance before the Hon. Henry Schnebley in 1778 [Ref: O-50, J-14, which latter source listed the name as "John Rousser"].

BOUTTAUFF, Andrew. Took the Oath of Allegiance before the Hon. John Barnes before February 28, 1778 [Ref: O-44, J-9, which latter source listed the name as "Andrew Boutauff"].

BOUTTAUFF, Martin. Took the Oath of Allegiance before the Hon. John Barnes before February 28, 1778 [Ref: O-44, J-9, which latter source listed the name as "Martin Boutauff"].

BOVILL, John. Enrolled in the third militia company organized for the Revolutionary War in the Elizabeth Town District of Frederick County (now the Hagerstown area of Washington County), passed by the Committee of Observation on June 5, 1776, and assigned to Capt. John Reynolds' command [Ref: Q-272].

BOWARD, Henry. Took the Oath of Allegiance before the Hon. Henry Schnebley in 1778 [Ref: O-51, J-15, which listed the name as "Henry Baward"].

BOWARD, Leonard. Private, Maryland Line, who resided in Washington County and was listed as "defective" on May 7, 1781 [Ref: D-414].

BOWARD, Michael. Private, Militia, Capt. William Heyser's Company, enlisted in 1776, muster roll dated October 23, 1776, in continental service; discharged on July 16, 1779 at Fort Wyoming, Pennsylvania [Ref: GG-96, D-264, which latter source misspelled the name as "Micgael Boward"].

BOWARS, Leonard and Nancy Ann. See "Leonard Bowers," q.v.

BOWE, Michael. Private, Militia, 2nd Class, Capt. Martin Kershner's Company, 1776/1777 [Ref: A-1146, M-247].

BOWEN, Charles. Took the Oath of Allegiance before the Hon. John Cellars in January, 1778 [Ref: O-40, J-6, K-1814, which latter source listed the name as "Charels Bowen"].

BOWEN, Frederick. Took the Oath of Allegiance before the Hon. Henry Schnebley in 1778 [Ref: O-49, J-13].

BOWEN, Frederick. Took the Oath of Allegiance before the Hon. John Cellars in January, 1778 [Ref: O-40, J-6, K-1814].

BOWEN, James. Private who enlisted in the militia for service in the Continental Army and was discharged in 1781 [Ref: D-407].

BOWER, Abraham. Private, Militia, 3rd Class, Capt. Peter Beall's Company, 1st Battalion, 1776/1777 [Ref: M-240]. Private, Militia, Capt. John Kershner's Company, on duty guarding prisoners of war at Fort Frederick on June 27, 1778 [Ref: D-328]. Took the Oath of Allegiance before the Hon. Henry Schnebley in 1778 [Ref: O-51, J-15]. He died testate by October 12, 1802 [Ref: MM-12:81].
BOWER, Adam. Private, Select Militia, Capt. Adam Ott's Company, 1781 [Ref: M-238, A-1146].
BOWER, Anna and Barbara. See "Jacob Bower," q.v.
BOWER, Catharine and Christiana. See "Jacob Bower," q.v.
BOWER, Elizabeth. See "William Bower" and "Jacob Bower," q.v.
BOWER, Frederick. Private, Militia, 2nd Class, Capt. Basil Williams' Company, 1776/1777 [Ref: M-244, A-1146]. Took the Oath of Allegiance before the Hon. Richard Davis in 1778 [Ref: J-4, O-37]. See "Jacob Bower," q.v.
BOWER, George. Private, Militia, 3rd Class, Capt. Joseph Chapline's Company, 2nd Battalion, 1776/1777 [Ref: M-241]. See "George Bowers" and Jacob Bower," q.v.
BOWER, George. Private, Militia, 6th Class, Capt. Jacob Sharer's Company, 1776/1777 [Ref: A-1146, M-248]. One George Bower took the Oath of Allegiance before the Hon. John Stull in 1778 [Ref: O-46, J-10].
BOWER, Jacob (1754-1824). Took the Oath of Allegiance before the Hon. Joseph Sprigg before April 1, 1778 [Ref: O-53, J-16]. Private, Maryland and Pennsylvania Lines, who applied for a pension in Stark County, Ohio in April 13, 1818, age 69, and died in 1824. His widow applied for and received pension W5227 in September, 1839, aged 75, at Lake Township in Stark County, Ohio. Her maiden name was Anna Rohrer (daughter of John Rohrer) and she was born on January 1, 1764. She married Jacob Bower on February 14, 1782 in Washington County, Maryland. He was born in Lancaster County, Pennsylvania on October 11, 1754 and enlisted first in 1775 in Maryland. Their children were: Christiana Bower (born September 3, 1782), Jacob Bower (born April 1, 1784), Anna Bower (born March 26, 1789), Susannah Bower (born October 28, 1790), John Bower (born June 20, 1794), Catharine Bower (born March 10, 1797), Frederick Bower (born May 29, 1798), Barbara Bower (born February 13, 1801), Elizabeth Bower (born October 7, 1803), and Sarah Bower (born August 25, 1808). Around 1810 they moved from Bedford County, Pennsylvania to Stark County, Ohio [Ref: V-I:339]. One Jacob Bower died before March 29, 1783 (date of balance book entry in Washington County) and his heirs included Jacob Bower

and George Bower [Ref: J-24]. Additional research may be necessary before drawing conclusions.

BOWER, John. See "Jacob Bower" and "Jacob Kuhn," q.v.

BOWER, Mary Magdalena. See "Conrad Coffroth," q.v.

BOWER, Maurice. Took the Oath of Allegiance before the Hon. Henry Schnebley in 1778 [Ref: O-51, J-15].

BOWER, Morris. Took the Oath of Allegiance before the Hon. John Stull in 1778 [Ref: O-46, J-10].

BOWER, Sarah and Susannah. See "Jacob Bower," q.v.

BOWER, William (c1745/8-c1825). Soldier who resided in Washington County and applied for pension S34656 on July 7, 1818, aged 70, He was granted a pension certificate in August, 1820, according to an Act of Congress of March 18, 1818, since he had proven that he was "in the enjoyment of a certain degree of poverty" as required by the Act as amended on May 1, 1820. He stated he was aged 75 in 1820 with a wife (not named) aged 55 and a daughter Elizabeth, aged 20, living with them [Ref: V-I:340, W-1190]. Private, Maryland Line, pensioned effective March 5, 1819 at $96 per year [Ref: R-42].

BOWERS, Allen and Anna. See "Leonard Bowers," q.v.

BOWERS, David and Elizabeth. See "Leonard Bowers," q.v.

BOWERS, George. One George Bowers served in the Maryland Line, applied for and received pension S40017 on June 19, 1818, age 60, in Wheatfield Township, Indiana County, Pennsylvania, and died on December 15, 1847. His son George C. Bowers lived in Pittsburgh in 1857. Another George Bowers also served in the Maryland Line, applied for and received pension S40018 on June 5, 1819, aged 58, in the Western District of Pennsylvania at Pittsburgh. He enlisted in Frederick, Maryland in 1778 and had a wife (not named) with him in 1821 [Ref: V-I:340].

BOWERS, Henry. See "Leonard Bowers," q.v.

BOWERS, Jessey and John. See "Leonard Bowers," q.v.

BOWERS (BOWARS), Leonard. Private, Maryland Line. He applied for a pension in Carter County, Tennessee on September 18, 1832, aged 72, stating he had lived at Hagerstown, Maryland at the time of his enlistment in 1778. On November 9, 1844, his widow applied for and received pension W49, stating she was born on March 24, 1769 and Leonard was born in the fall of 1760. Her maiden name was Rebecca Nave and they were married on August 2, 1785. Their children were: William Bowers (born May 22, 1787), Valantine Bowers (born September 23, 1788), Henry Bowers (born August 23, 1790), John Bowers (born January 27, 1792), Elizabeth Bowers (born March 6,

1795), David Bowers (born December 2, 1799), Leonard Bowers (born October 30, 1801 and lived in Carter County, Tennessee in 1851), Rebakah Bowers (born September 22, 1803), Mary Bowers (born October 13, 1806), Anna Bowers (born October 10, 1808), Jessey Bowers (born October 30, 1809), and Margait Bowers (born September 14, 1812). Leonard (the soldier) died on October 5, 1840. In 1845 Elizabeth's brothers were Abraham Nave, aged 76, and John Nave, aged 74. She died on September 20, 1849 at which time a Mark W. Nave was mentioned. An illegitimate grandson named Allen Bowers, who was a son of the soldier's daughter Nancy Ann (Bowars) Hays, was named in her mother's will. Also mentioned was a David Bowers (born June 11, 1831), but no relationship was stated [Ref: V-I:336].

BOWERS, Margait and Mary. See "Leonard Bowers," q.v.

BOWERS, Rebakah and Valantine. See "Leonard Bowers," q.v.

BOWERSMITH, George. Private who was enlisted by Lieut. Christian Orndorff and passed on July 20, 1776 in Frederick (now Washington) County [Ref: D-50].

BOWERT, Henry. Private, Militia, 5th Class, Capt. Peter Beall's Company, 1st Battalion, 1776/1777 [Ref: M-240].

BOWLEN, John. Ensign, Militia, Capt. Jacob Sharer's Company, 1776/1777 [Ref: M-248, A-1146].

BOWLES, James H. See "Peter Swope," q.v.

BOWMAN, Aaron. Private, Militia, 2nd Class, Capt. James Smith's Company, 2nd Battalion, 1776/1777 [Ref: M-239, A-1146]. Private, Militia, Capt. Martin Kershner's Company, 32nd Battalion, December 27, 1776 [Ref: K-1814, Box 3]. Took the Oath of Allegiance before the Hon. Henry Schnebley in 1778 [Ref: O-49, J-12].

BOWMAN, Benedict. Private, Militia, 2nd Class, Capt. Samuel Hughes' Company, 2nd Battalion, 1776/1777 [Ref: M-238, A-1146]. Took the Oath of Allegiance before the Hon. Andrew Rentch before March 7, 1778 [Ref: O-52, J-15, which listed the name as "Bowman Benedict"].

BOWMAN, Benjamin. Private, Militia, 7th Class, Capt. James Walling's Company, 2nd Battalion, 1776/1777 [Ref: M-239, A-1146].

BOWMAN, Daniel. Private, Militia, 5th Class, Capt. James Smith's Company, 2nd Battalion, 1776/1777 [Ref: M-240, A-1146]. Took the Oath of Allegiance before the Hon. Richard Davis in 1778 [Ref: J-3, O-36].

BOWMAN, Jacob. Private, Select Militia, Capt. Adam Ott's Company, 1781 [Ref: M-238, A-1146]. Took the Oath of Allegiance before the Hon. Henry Schnebley in 1778 [Ref: O-49, J-13]. "Mrs. Bowman, widow of the late Jacob Bowman" died at an advanced age on January 13, 1829 in Hagerstown [Ref: Z-106].

BOWMAN, John. There were two men with this name who rendered service during the Revolutionary War. (1) Private, Militia, 5th Class, Capt. Martin Kershner's Company, 1776/1777 [Ref: A-1146, M-247]. (2) Fourth Sergeant, Militia, Capt. James Prather's Company, 3rd Battalion, 1776/1777 [Ref: M-242]. One John Bowman took the Oath of Allegiance before the Hon. Henry Schnebley in 1778 [Ref: O-49, J-12].

BOWMAN, Reynon. There appears to have been two men with this name who rendered service during the Revolutionary War. (1) Private, Militia, 6th Class, Capt. Daniel Cresap's Company, 3rd Battalion, 1776/1777 [Ref: M-241]. (2) Second Corporal, Militia, Capt. Daniel Cresap's Company, 3rd Battalion, 1776/1777 [Ref: M-241]. (3) Took the Oath of Allegiance before the Hon. Lemuel Barritt before March 16, 1778 [Ref: O-42, J-8, which latter source listed the name as "Reynon Roman"]. (4) On September 23, 1780, Col. Lemuel Barritt recommended to Governor Lee that "Bynon Bahman" be commissioned an ensign in the militia at "Oper Old Town" since so many officers of the Western Battalion had moved out of Maryland to Kentucky and elsewhere [Ref: G-123]. Additional research may be necessary before drawing conclusions.

BOWMAN, Simon. One of several patriots appointed by the Committee of Observation on December 30, 1776 "to form the county into companies (after the militia had marched) for the purpose of relieving the distressed inhabitants of said county and also to compel the Dunkards and Mennonists to give their assistance." [Ref: Q-345]. On January 23, 1777 the Committee of Observation ordered "that Capt. Andrew Lynck pay Simon Bowman 7/6 out of the publick money in his hands, it being for said Bowman's riding express to Denton Jacques." [Ref: Q-49].

BOWMAN, Sterling. Took the Oath of Allegiance before the Hon. Richard Davis in 1778 [Ref: J-3, O-36].

BOWMAN, Syar. Private, Militia, 2nd Class, Capt. Peter Swingle's (Swingley's) Company, 1776/1777 [Ref: A-1146, M-248].

BOWYER, Henry. Enrolled in the second militia company organized for the Revolutionary War in the Elizabeth Town District of Frederick County (now the Hagerstown area of Washington County) on March 9, 1776 [Ref: Q-272].

BOWYER, John Urick. Took the Oath of Allegiance before the Hon. Henry Schnebley in 1778 [Ref: J-14, O-51, which latter source listed the name as "John Urick Bawyer"].

BOYCE, Arthur. Private ("recruit for during the war") who enlisted in the militia on September 5, 1781 for service in the Continental Army [Ref: D-388, H-451, which latter source listed the name as "Arthur Boyes"].

BOYD, Joseph. Private, Militia, 2nd Class, Capt. John Bennet's Company, 1776/1777 [Ref: M-246, A-1146].

BOYD, Walter. Private, Militia, 2nd Class, Capt. Martin Kershner's Company, 1776/1777 [Ref: A-1146, M-247]. Took the Oath of Allegiance before the Hon. John Cellars in January, 1778 [Ref: K-1814, O-40, J-6]. "Walter Boyd, Esq." died on July 21, 1828 at his residence near Cavetown, an old inhabitant of this county [Washington] and for many years a practical surveyor of this section of the county [Ref: Z-101].

BOYD, William. Took the Oath of Allegiance before the Hon. John Cellars in January, 1778 [Ref: K-1814, O-40, J-6]. "William Boyd, Sr." took the Oath of Allegiance before the Hon. Joseph Sprigg before April 1, 1778 [Ref: O-53, J-16].

BOYD, William Jr. Private, Select Militia, Capt. Adam Ott's Company, 1781 [Ref: M-238, A-1146]. See "William Boyd," q.v.

BOYDS, William. See "John Stewart," q.v.

BOYER, Henry. Private, Militia, 6th Class, Capt. Joseph Chapline's Company, 2nd Battalion, 1776/1777 [Ref: M-241].

BRACKAUNIER, Peter. See "Peter Brockunier," q.v.

BRADDOCK, General. See "Yost Harbaugh," q.v.

BRADDON, Mary and William. See "Samuel Downey," q.v.

BRADFORD, William. Appointed by the Committee of Observation on July 7, 1776 "to take the number of inhabitants within Sharpsburg Hundred, both whites and blacks, distinguishing respectively the age and sex of each, to be transmitted to the Council of Safety immediately." [Ref: Q-331]. Rendered patriotic service by providing necessaries to Capt. John Reynolds' Company in the Flying Camp and belonging to the Maryland Service in July, 1776, as recorded by the Committee of Observation at Sharpsburg on August 6, 1776 [Ref: Q-333]. Took the Oath of Allegiance on July 26, 1777 [Ref: K-1814, Box 4].

BRADFORD, William. Private who was enlisted by Capt. John Reynolds and passed on July 18, 1776 in Frederick (now Washington) County [Ref: D-50]. Private, Militia, 3rd Class, Capt. Joseph Chapline's Company, 2nd Battalion, 1776/1777 [Ref: M-241]. Took the Oath of Allegiance before the Hon. Christopher Cruse in Sharpsburg Hundred before March 2, 1778 [Ref: O-34, J-2].

BRADLEY, Thomas. On January 9, 1777 he was brought before the Committee of Observation because "he neither had nor would enroll himself" and was ordered "kept under guard and then delivered to Capt.

James Wallen, marched to camp with his company, and pay all expenses of guard, etc." He later paid the charges, joined the continental service and was released from confinement on January 14, 1777 [Ref: Q-34, Q-35, Q-39].

BRADSHAW, George (1741-1826). Soldier who resided in Washington County and was granted a pension certificate in August, 1820, according to an Act of Congress of March 18, 1818, since he had proven that he was "in the enjoyment of a certain degree of poverty" as required by the Act as amended on May 1, 1820 [Ref: W-1190]. Private, Pennsylvania Line, died in Hagerstown on January 15, 1826, in the 85th year of his age [Ref: R-42, Z-79].

BRADY, Benjamin (1761-1839). Private, Virginia Militia, applied for and received pension S8107 in Allegany County, Maryland on October 16, 1832, aged 71, at $21.65 per year under the Act of June 7, 1832 retroactive to March 4, 1831. He was born on April 14, 1761 in York County, Pennsylvania and moved to Loudoun County, Virginia in 1765. About four years after his discharge he moved to Allegany County, Maryland. He married Barbara Miller and died in 1839 [Ref: V-I:362, R-45, Y-I:342].

BRAGONER, Peter. Private, Militia, 8th Class, Capt. Martin Kershner's Company, 1776/1777 [Ref: A-1146, M-248].

BRAMICK, Daniel. See "Daniel Bremick," q.v.

BRANCH, Daniel. Private, Militia, 8th Class, Capt. Joseph Chapline's Company, 2nd Battalion, 1776/1777 [Ref: M-242].

BRAND, James. Took the Oath of Allegiance before the Hon. Richard Davis in 1778 [Ref: J-3, O-36].

BRAND, James Jr. Private, Militia, 4th Class, Capt. Peter Swingle's (Swingley's) Company, 1776/1777 [Ref: A-1146, M-248]. Took the Oath of Allegiance before the Hon. Richard Davis in 1778 [Ref: J-3, O-36].

BRANDBUN, John. Private, Militia, 8th Class, Capt. Peter Swingle's (Swingley's) Company, 1776/1777 [Ref: A-1146, M-249].

BRANDENBAUGH (BRANDENBUGH), Christopher. Private, Militia, 1st Class, Capt. Daniel Clapsaddle's Company, 1st Battalion, 1776/1777 [Ref: M-236, A-1146]. Took the Oath of Allegiance before the Hon. Samuel Hughes before March 1, 1778 [Ref: O-33, J-1].

BRANDLINGER, Conrad. See "Conrad Brentlinger," q.v.

BRANDSTATTER, Andrew. Took the Oath of Allegiance before the Hon. Henry Schnebley in 1778 [Ref: O-51, J-15, which latter source listed the name as "Andrew Brandstetter"]. Private, Militia, 6th Class, Capt. Conrad Hogmire's Company, 1776/1777 [Ref: M-244, A-1146, which listed the name as "Andrew Branstreter"].

BRANNER, Philip. Took the Oath of Allegiance before the Hon. Henry Schnebley in 1778 [Ref: O-49, J-12, which latter source listed the name as "Philip Pranner"].

BRANON, Patrick. Took the Oath of Allegiance before the Hon. Joseph Sprigg before April 1, 1778 [Ref: O-54, J-16].

BRANT, George (attorney). Took the Oath of Allegiance on July 26, 1777 [Ref: K-1814, Box 4]. "George Brent" died on January 11, 1782, aged 38, and is buried in a graveyard on the Charles Locher farm, along Canal, west of Hancock, Maryland [Ref: JJ-II:48].

BRATHER, Rignal. See "Rignal Prather," q.v.

BRAY, Christena. See "Edward Roberts," q.v.

BRAY, Henry. Private who enlisted in the militia on September 5, 1781 for service in the Continental Army [Ref: D-388]. Took the Oath of Allegiance before the Hon. Lemuel Barritt before March 16, 1778 [Ref: O-42, J-7].

BREAD, David. Private, Militia, 4th Class, Capt. Isaac Baker's Company, 1776/1777 [Ref: A-1146, M-247].

BREECHER, John. Private, Militia, Capt. William Heyser's Company, enlisted July 17, 1776, muster roll dated October 23, 1776, and subsequently promoted to fourth corporal before May 22, 1777 [Ref: D-264, W-1190, L-79, GG-96]. Corporal, German Regiment, Lt. Col. Ludwick Weltner's Company, continental service, discharged on July 17, 1779 [Ref: D-264, which listed the name as "John Brucher" and GG-96, which listed the name as "John Brucher, Breecher"].

BREEMBAUGH, Jacob. See "Jacob Brumbaugh," q.v.

BREEZE, Andrew. Took the Oath of Allegiance before the Hon. Lemuel Barritt before March 16, 1778 [Ref: O-42, J-7].

BREMICK, Daniel. Took the Oath of Allegiance before the Hon. Christopher Cruse in Sharpsburg Hundred before March 2, 1778 [Ref: O-34, J-2, which latter source listed the name as "Daniel Bramick"].

BRENER, Philip. Private who was enrolled by Capt. Henry Hardman and passed on July 19, 1776 in Frederick (now Washington) County [Ref: D-51].

BRENT, George. See "George Brant," q.v.

BRENTLINGER, Conrad (1752-1829). Private, Militia, 4th Class, Capt. John Cellars' Company, 1776/1777 [Ref: A-1146, M-246, which listed the name as "Conrad Brandlinger"]. Took the Oath of Allegiance before the Hon. John Stull in 1778 [Ref: O-46, J-10, which listed the name as "Conrad Brendlinges"]. "Conrad Blentlinger" died suddenly on March 30, 1829 in his 77th year, an old inhabitant of Hagerstown [Ref: Z-107].

BRENTLINGER, Frederick (1753-1825). "Died at his residence near Mount Vernon, Ohio, in November, 1825, in his 73rd year, Frederick Brentlinger, formerly of this place [Hagerstown, Maryland], a revolutionary soldier." [Ref: Z-80, citing *The Torchlight and Public Advertiser* newspaper in Hagerstown on February 14, 1826].

BRESH, Philip. Took the Oath of Allegiance before the Hon. Henry Schnebley in 1778 [Ref: O-51, J-14].

BREWER, Anna Maria. See "Jacob Kershner," q.v.

BREWORE, Mary. See "Adam Troup," q.v.

BRIDENBAUGH, John. See "Felix Meyer," q.v.

BRIGH, Phillip. See "Philip Bruff," q.v.

BRIGHT, George. Took the Oath of Allegiance before the Hon. Richard Davis in 1778 [Ref: J-4, O-36].

BRINGMAN, Martin. Private who enlisted in the militia on August 22, 1781 for service in the Continental Army [Ref: D-388, D-406].

BRINSON (BIMSON?), Jacob. Private, Militia, 4th Class, Capt. John Rennolds' (Reynolds') Company, 2nd Battalion, 1776/1777 [Ref: M-240].

BRISON, Archibald. Private, Militia, 8th Class, Capt. Barnett Johnston's Company, 3rd Battalion, 1776/1777 [Ref: M-242].

BROCKLE, Richard. Private who was recruited and passed by County Lieutenant Thomas Sprigg on April 22, 1780 [Ref: D-336].

BROCKUNIER, Peter. Took the Oath of Allegiance before the Hon. Henry Schnebley in 1778 [Ref: O-51, J-15, which listed the name as "Peter Brackaunier"]. "Peter Brockener, farmer" died testate in 1804 and one of his heirs was a son Peter [Ref: MM-13:91, 92].

BROMBACH, Jacob. See "Jacob Brumbaugh," q.v.

BRONCE, Henry. Private, Militia, 7th Class, Capt. Conrad Hogmire's Company, 1776/1777 [Ref: M-244, A-1146].

BRONDS, John. Private, Militia, 6th Class, Capt. Conrad Nichodemus' Company, 2nd Battalion, 1776/1777 [Ref: M-237, A-1146].

BROOKE, Thomas. Elected to the Committee of Observation on January 9, 1777 in the room of Col. Andrew Rentch who had resigned [Ref: Q-36, Q-228]. Clerk to the Committee of Observation on February 5, 1776 [Ref: Q-152]. Appointed by the Committee of Observation to carry the Association of Freemen to male residents in his hundred (district) on March 4, 1776 "and present it for signing and make an exact account of those that sign and those that refuse with their reasons for refusing." [Ref: Q-153, L-82]. Served "in the chair" of the Committee of Observation on January 25, 1777 [Ref: Q-50, Q-51]. Took the Oath of Allegiance before the Hon. John Stull in 1778 [Ref: O-46, J-10, which latter source listed the name as "Thomas Brooks"].

BROOKE, Thomas Jr. Fourth Corporal, Militia, Capt. Jacob Sharer's Company, 1776/1777 [Ref: M-248, A-1146].

BROOKE, Thomas Sr. Private, Militia, 1st Class, Capt. Jacob Sharer's Company, 1776/1777 [Ref: A-1146, M-248].

BROTHERS, Tobias. Rendered patriotic service by supplying wheat for the use of the military on February 16, 1780 [Ref: W-1190, HH-74].

BROWN, Archibald. Private, Militia, by January 22, 1777 when ordered by the Committee of Observation "to march with some company of militia to the reinforcement of his Excellency General Washington" or appear before the Committee and state his reason for not marching. He apparently marched since he never appeared to the contrary [Ref: Q-48].

BROWN, Conrad. Private, Militia, 6th Class, Capt. Martin Kershner's Company, 1776/1777 [Ref: A-1146, M-248]. Took the Oath of Allegiance before the Hon. Henry Schnebley in 1778 [Ref: O-50, J-13].

BROWN, Edward. Private who was enlisted by Capt. John Reynolds and passed on July 18, 1776 in Frederick (now Washington) County [Ref: D-50]. Took the Oath of Allegiance before the Hon. Christopher Cruse in Sharpsburg Hundred before March 2, 1778 [Ref: O-34, J-2].

BROWN, George. Took the Oath of Allegiance before the Hon. Joseph Sprigg before April 1, 1778 [Ref: O-53, J-16]. One "George Brown, Sr. died on the morning of October 9, 1827 at the residence of his son (not named), 1 mile from Cumberland, in his 87th year. He was born in Philadelphia County, Pennsylvania, his parents were poor German emigrants, died when he was an infant. At the age of 16 he entered into the British Army where he remained 7 years, during which period he assisted as a provincial soldier in the taking of Canada from the French. After the cession of that province he returned to his native state and in a few years after settled at Pipe Creek, Frederick County, Maryland. He resided near this town [Cumberland] since autumn of 1795. He was bereft of his sight during the last three years." [Ref: Z-16].

BROWN, Jacob. Private, Militia, 3rd Class, Capt. James Smith's Company, 2nd Battalion, 1776/1777 [Ref: M-239, A-1146].

BROWN, James. Rendered patriotic service by providing a pair shoes for the use of the military in January, 1777, as recorded by the Committee of Observation on January 27, 1777 [Ref: Q-53]. Took the Oath of Allegiance before the Hon. Christopher Cruse in Sharpsburg Hundred before March 2, 1778 [Ref: O-35, J-2]. See "Thomas Hart," q.v.

BROWN, John. Private who was enrolled by Capt. Henry Hardman and passed on July 19, 1776 in Frederick (now Washington) County [Ref: D-51]. Private, Militia, 1st Class, Capt. Basil Williams' Company, 1776/1777

[Ref: M-244, A-1146]. Took the Oath of Allegiance before the Hon. Richard Davis in 1778 [Ref: J-4, O-36]. Private who was recruited and passed by County Lieutenant Thomas Sprigg on April 22, 1780 [Ref: D-336]. See "William Sutherland," q.v.

BROWN, John Rudolph. See "Posthumous Clagett," q.v.

BROWN, Lydia. See "Robert Compton," q.v.

BROWN, Rudolph (1740-1821). Private, Militia, 7th Class, Capt. Henry Boteler's Company, 1776/1777 [Ref: M-237, A-1146]. The widow (no name given) of Rudolph Brown died in Pleasant Valley on October 22, 1826, in her 82nd year. She had 86 grandchildren and 36 great-grandchildren [Ref: Z-86]. Rudolph Brown was born in 1740, died on June 28, 1821, and is buried beside his wife Abigail Brown (1744-1826) in a graveyard on the Wilbur Jennings farm at the north end of Brownsville in Washington County, Maryland [Ref: JJ-III:55].

BROWN, Simon. Took the Oath of Allegiance before the Hon. Samuel Hughes before March 1, 1778 [Ref: O-33, J-1].

BROWN, Susan. See "Joseph Wyand," q.v.

BROWN, William. Private, Militia, 5th Class, Capt. Michael Fackler's Company, 1776/1777 [Ref: M-245, A-1146].

BROWNER, Jacob. Private, Militia, 6th Class, Capt. Conrad Nichodemus' Company, 2nd Battalion, 1776/1777 [Ref: M-237, A-1146].

BRUCE, Andrew (c1740-1815). Lieutenant Colonel, Militia, 3rd or Western Battalion, by May 16, 1778 [Ref: M-57, E-86]. Took the Oath of Allegiance on June 5, 1777 [Ref: K-1814, Box 4]. Justice who administered the Oath of Allegiance before March 2, 1778 [Ref: O-41, J-7]. Justice of the County Court, June 20, 1778 [Ref: E-141]. Justice of the Peace, January 30, 1781 [Ref: G-293]. He married Barbara Murdock, raised a large family, and held many public offices in Frederick, Washington and Allegany Counties between 1775 and 1802 [Ref: KK-I:176-177, which contains more detailed information].

BRUFF, Christopher (1760-1805). Private, Maryland Line. He married Mary Berry and died on November 17, 1805 [Ref: Y-I:407].

BRUFF, Henrietta. See "James Bruff," q.v.

BRUFF, James (1734-1815). Captain, Maryland Line, who received bounty land #235-300-2 in November, 1791, and also received a disability pension, but his papers were destroyed when the British burned Washington, D.C. in 1814. He married Henrietta Bruff and died on November 15, 1815 [Ref: V-I:439, Y-I:407].

BRUFF, John (1740-1819). Private, Maryland Line. He was born on December 4, 1740, married Lucy Hopkins, and died on November 12, 1819 [Ref: Y-I:407].

BRUFF, Joseph. Private, Militia, 6th Class, Capt. John Bennet's Company, 1776/1777 [Ref: M-246, A-1146, which listed the name as "Joseph Brough"].

BRUFF, Peter. Ensign, Militia, Capt. John Bennet's Company, 1776 (date not given). [Ref: M-57, which listed the name as "Peter Brough"].

BRUFF, Philip. Private who was enrolled by Capt. Henry Hardman and passed on July 19, 1776 in Frederick (now Washington) County [Ref: D-51, which listed the name as "Philip Brugh"]. Private, Militia, 2nd Class, Capt. Jacob Sharer's Company, 1776/1777 [Ref: A-1146, M-248, which listed the name as "Phillip Brigh"].

BRUFF, William. Private, Maryland Line. On October 26, 1808 his widow Mary applied for an received bounty land warrant #433-100 in Washington County [Ref: V-I:439].

BRUIR, Joseph. Took the Oath of Allegiance before the Hon. John Barnes before February 28, 1778 [Ref: O-44, J-9].

BRUIR, Peter. Took the Oath of Allegiance before the Hon. John Barnes before February 28, 1778 [Ref: O-44, J-9].

BRUMBAUGH, Jacob. Rendered patriotic service by supplying two blankets for the use of the military in March, 1776, as recorded by the Committee of Observation on April 12, 1776 [Ref: L-82, Q-157, which latter source listed the name as "Jacob Breembaugh"]. Private, Militia, 8th Class, Capt. Daniel Clapsaddle's Company, 1st Battalion, 1776/1777 [Ref: M-236, A-1146, which listed the name as "Jacob Brumbock"]. Rendered patriotic service by supplying wheat and rye for the use of the military on March 8, 1780 [Ref: W-1190, HH-72, which listed the name as "Jacob Bromback"].

BRUMBAUGH, Jacob Jr. Private, Militia, 6th Class, Capt. John Cellars' Company, 1776/1777 [Ref: A-1146, M-246, which listed the name as "Jacob Brumbough, Jr."].

BRUMBAUGH, John. Private, Militia, 2nd Class, Capt. Daniel Clapsaddle's Company, 1st Battalion, 1776/1777 [Ref: M-236, A-1146, which listed the name as "John Brumboch"].

BRUNAR, Leonard. Rendered patriotic service in Hagerstown by providing two rifles to Capt. John Nelson's Company, continental service (Maryland Line), April, 1776 [Ref: Q-162].

BRUNER, Jacob. Private, Militia, 8th Class, Capt. Joseph Chapline's Company, 2nd Battalion, 1776/1777 [Ref: M-242].

BRUNER, Peter. Private, Militia, 1st Class, Capt. Isaac Baker's Company, 1776/1777 [Ref: A-1146, M-247].

BRUNNER, Jacob. Enrolled in the third militia company organized for the Revolutionary War in the Elizabeth Town District of Frederick

County (now the Hagerstown area of Washington County), passed by the Committee of Observation on June 5, 1776, and assigned to Capt. John Reynolds' command [Ref: Q-273]. Private who was enlisted by Lieut. Christian Orndorff and passed on July 20, 1776 in Frederick (now Washington) County [Ref: D-50].

BRUNNER, John. Took the Oath of Allegiance before the Hon. Christopher Cruse in Lower Antietam Hundred before March 2, 1778 [Ref: J-3, O-35].

BRYSON, Archibald. Took the Oath of Allegiance before the Hon. William Yates in 1778 [Ref: O-48, J-11].

BUCH, George. Private, Militia, Capt. William Heyser's Company, enlisted in 1776, muster roll dated October 23, 1776, in continental service, and on duty in May, 1777 [Ref: GG-96, D-264, W-1190, L-79, which also listed the name as "George Buck"].

BUCHANAN, John. See "Eli Williams," q.v.

BUCKER, Phillip. See "Philip Rucker," q.v.

BUGHMAN, George. Took the Oath of Allegiance before the Hon. John Cellars in January, 1778 [Ref: O-40, K-1814, which latter source indicated he had affirmed, and J-6, which listed the name as "George Hughman"].

BUMGARDNER, Adam. Private, Militia, 2nd Class, Capt. Peter Swingle's (Swingley's) Company, 1776/1777 [Ref: A-1146, M-248, which listed the name as "Adam Bamgardner"]. Took the Oath of Allegiance before the Hon. Henry Schnebley in 1778 [Ref: O-50, which listed the name as "Adam Bumgartner" J-14, which listed the name as "Adam Bumgarthner"].

BUMGARDNER, George. Private who was enlisted by Lieut. Moses Chapline and passed on July 24, 1776 in Frederick (now Washington) County [Ref: D-50, which listed the name as "George Baumgartner:"].

BUMGARDNER, Jacob. Private, Militia, 6th Class, Capt. Conrad Hogmire's Company, 1776/1777 [Ref: M-244, A-1146, which listed the name as "Jacob Bumgarner"]. Took the Oath of Allegiance before the Hon. John Stull in 1778 [Ref: J-10, O-46, which latter source listed the name as "Jacob Bungarner"].

BUMGARDNER, John. Private who enlisted in the militia on August 24, 1781 for service in the Continental Army [Ref: D-388]. Substitute, Maryland Line, discharged on October 30, 1781 [Ref: G-657, which listed the name as "John Bomgardner"].

BUMGARDNER, William (1751-1826). Private who was enlisted by Lieut. Moses Chapline and passed on July 24, 1776 in Frederick (now Washington) County [Ref: D-50, which listed the name as "William

Baumgartner"]. Private, Maryland Line, pensioned in Washington County on June 26, 1820 at $96 per year [Ref: R-42, which listed the name as "William Bomgardner"]. On February 16, 1820 the Treasurer of the Western Shore of Maryland was directed to pay to William Bomgardner, of Washington County, half pay of a private for his Revolutionary War services. On May 2, 1827 the Treasurer of the Western Shore of Maryland was directed to pay to Margaret Bomgardner, of Washington County, during life, half yearly, half pay of a private for her late husband's revolutionary services [Ref: AA-321]. "William Bomgardner" died in Hagerstown on April 8, 1826, in his 75th year, a soldier of the Revolution [Ref: Z-81].

BUMGARNER, M. See "Dewald Shaffer," q.v.

BUNCE, Margaret. See "Joseph Cresap," q.v.

BURCHAM, David. Enrolled in the first militia company organized for the Revolutionary War in the Elizabeth Town District of Frederick County (now the Hagerstown area of Washington County) on January 6, 1776 [Ref: Q-270, W-1190].

BURCKHART, George. Took the Oath of Allegiance before the Hon. Henry Schnebley in 1778 [Ref: O-50, J-13].

BURGARD, Crestoph. Rendered patriotic service by supplying a blanket for the use of the military in March, 1776, as recorded by the Committee of Observation on April 12, 1776 [Ref: Q-157, L-82, which latter source listed the name as "Christ'n Burgard"].

BURGESS, Francis. Took the Oath of Allegiance before the Hon. John Stull in 1778 [Ref: O-46, J-10, which listed the name as "Francis Burges"]. Private, Militia, 2nd Class, Capt. Michael Fackler's Company, 1776/1777 [Ref: M-245, A-1146, which listed the name as "Francis Burgiss"].

BURGESS, James. Took the Oath of Allegiance before the Hon. Richard Davis in 1778 [Ref: J-5, O-37].

BURGESS, Jane. See "Rezin Simpson," q.v.

BURGESS, John. Private, Militia, 2nd Class, Capt. Barnett Johnston's Company, 3rd Battalion, 1776/1777 [Ref: M-242].

BURK, Caty and David. See "John Burk," q.v.

BURK, John (1758-1840). Private, Militia, 2nd Class, Capt. Isaac Baker's Company, 1776/1777 [Ref: A-1146, M-247]. Took the Oath of Allegiance before the Hon. John Barnes before February 28, 1778 [Ref: O-45, J-10]. He applied for a pension on August 19, 1818, aged 60, stating he had enlisted in Hagerstown and served in the Maryland Line. He married Mary Stevens by bond dated May 1, 1786 and their children were: Lydia Burk (born January 11, 1788), John Burk (born January 15,

1790), Caty Burk (born March 15, 1792), Thomas Burk (born September 2, 1793), Robert Burk (born September 28, 1797), Lucy Burk (born August 9, 1800), and David Burk (born April 11, 1804). Also mentioned was James Stevens (born January 30, 1782). In 1821 Mary Burk was aged about 55. John Burk died in 1840 and his widow received pension W5952. Mary "Polly" Burk died in 1850 [Ref: V-I:471].

BURK, Lucy, Lydia, and Mary. See "John Burk," q.v.

BURK, Robert and Thomas. See "John Burk," q.v.

BURKETT, Christopher. Served on the Committee of Observation in February, 1777 [Ref: Q-228, which listed the name as "Christopher Burket"]. One "Christopher Burkhart" died testate before March 8, 1800 (date of balance book entry in Washington County) with the final account of his estate distributed to children George Burkhart, Christopher Burkhart, Elizabeth Burkhart, Mary Penn, Catherine Nigh, and Margaret Snell, and grandchildren Samuel and Daniel Burkhart [Ref: J-38].

BURKETT, George. Private, Militia, 7th Class, Capt. Conrad Hogmire's Company, 1776/1777 [Ref: M-244, A-1146].

BURKETT, Phillip. Private, Militia, 5th Class, Capt. Conrad Hogmire's Company, 1776/1777 [Ref: M-244, A-1146].

BURKETT, Stophel. One of several patriots appointed by the Committee of Observation on December 30, 1776 "to form the county into companies (after the militia had marched) for the purpose of relieving the distressed inhabitants of said county and also to compel the Dunkards and Mennonists to give their assistance." [Ref: Q-346, which listed the name as "Stophel Burket"].

BURKHART, Christopher, Daniel, Elizabeth, George, and Samuel. See "Christopher Burkett," q.v.

BURKMAN, Peter. Private, Militia, 5th Class, Capt. Conrad Nichodemus' Company, 2nd Battalion, 1776/1777 [Ref: M-237, A-1146].

BURKSHIRE, Richard. Private, Militia, 6th Class, Capt. Griffin Johnson's Company, 3rd Battalion, 1776/1777 [Ref: M-243].

BURLY, Joseph. Rendered patriotic service by supplying a coverlid for the use of the military in March, 1776, as recorded by the Committee of Observation on April 12, 1776 [Ref: Q-156, L-82].

BURN, Charles. See "Charles Byrne," q.v.

BURN, Christian. Took the Oath of Allegiance before the Hon. Henry Schnebley in 1778 [Ref: O-50, J-14].

BURNES, Michael. See "Michael Byrne," q.v.

BURNEY, Thomas. Private, Militia, Capt. William Heyser's Company, continental service, enlisted in 1776, muster roll dated October 23, 1776, which stated he had deserted, yet he was on duty in May, 1777 [Ref: GG-96, D-264, W-1190, L-79, which latter source listed the name as "Thomas Burney, Jr."].

BURNITT, Morress. Private, Militia, 3rd Class, Capt. Barnett Johnston's Company, 3rd Battalion, 1776/1777 [Ref: M-242].

BURNS, Jesse. Enrolled in the first militia company organized for the Revolutionary War in the Elizabeth Town District of Frederick County (now the Hagerstown area of Washington County) on January 6, 1776 [Ref: Q-271, W-1190].

BURNS, Robert and Ruth. See "Samuel Downey," q.v.

BURREL, Benjamin. Enrolled in the first militia company organized for the Revolutionary War in the Elizabeth Town District of Frederick County (now the Hagerstown area of Washington County) on January 6, 1776 [Ref: Q-270, W-1190].

BURREL, Peter. Enrolled in the first militia company organized for the Revolutionary War in the Elizabeth Town District of Frederick County (now the Hagerstown area of Washington County) on January 6, 1776 [Ref: Q-270, W-1190].

BURROUGHS, John. Private, Militia, 8th Class, Capt. Joseph Chapline's Company, 2nd Battalion, 1776/1777 [Ref: M-242]. Took the Oath of Allegiance before the Hon. William Yates in 1778 [Ref: O-48, J-11].

BUSHER, William. Took the Oath of Allegiance before the Hon. Lemuel Barritt before March 16, 1778 [Ref: J-7, O-42, which latter source listed the name as "William Rashr"].

BUSKIRK, Mary and Michael. See "John Chenoweth," q.v.

BUTLER, Henry. Appointed to raise funds on January 24, 1775 for the Committee of Observation in Lower Antietam Hundred in Frederick (now Washington) County [Ref: L-75]. Enrolled in the second militia company organized for the Revolutionary War in the Elizabeth Town District of Frederick County (now the Hagerstown area of Washington County) on March 9, 1776 [Ref: Q-271]. Captain, by June, 1776, at which time he presented an enrollment of a surplus company of militia to the Committee of Observation which was accepted and approved [Ref: Q-269, which listed the name as "Henry Butter"]. On January 18, 1777 the Committee of Observation resolved that "Capt. Henry Butler obtain an order to press waggons, horses, gears, baggs, waggon cloaths, screws and blankets for the use of his company." [Ref: Q-43]. See "Mrs. Mary Stull," q.v.

BUTLER, Henry Edward. Enrolled in the second militia company organized for the Revolutionary War in the Elizabeth Town District of

Frederick County (now the Hagerstown area of Washington County) on March 9, 1776 [Ref: Q-272].

BUTTERBAUGH, Henry. Private, Militia, 8th Class, Capt. Isaac Baker's Company, 1776/1777 [Ref: A-1146, M-247].

BYERLEY, Joseph. Private, Militia, 2nd Class, Capt. Peter Swingle's (Swingley's) Company, 1776/1777 [Ref: A-1146, M-248].

BYRNE, Anthony. Private who was recruited and passed by County Lieutenant Thomas Sprigg on April 22, 1780 [Ref: D-336].

BYRNE, Charles. Private who was enrolled by Capt. Aeneas Campbell and passed by Major Francis Deakins on July 18, 1776 [Ref: D-49, which listed the name as "Charles Byrn (Burn)"].

BYRNE, Michael. Private, Militia, by January 22, 1777 when ordered by the Committee of Observation "to march with some company of militia to the reinforcement of his Excellency General Washington" or appear before the Committee and state his reason for not marching. He apparently marched since he never appeared to the contrary [Ref: Q-48, which listed the name as "Michael Burnes"]. Took the Oath of Allegiance before the Hon. William Yates in 1778 [Ref: O-48, J-11].

BYRNES, Elizabeth and James. See "John Byrnes," q.v.

BYRNES (BYRNS), John (c1750-1836). Private, Pennsylvania and Virginia Lines. He applied for a pension in Harrison County, Virginia on April 13, 1818, aged 68, stating he had enlisted in Hagerstown, Maryland. He married Esther Cavalier on March 12, 1792 or 1793 in Fayette County, Pennsylvania and died on November 7, 1836 in Virginia. His widow Elizabeth Matson (name of second husband not given) applied for and received pension W6224 on November 16, 1850 in Harrison County, Virginia and mentioned these children: first child was a daughter (born in spring of 1794 and lived only a few days), Samuel Byrnes (born about 1803, married Elizabeth Wadsworth on January 6, 1822 in Virginia, and was killed by a falling tree on July 8, 1822), and James Byrnes (born about 1813); other children not named [Ref: V-I:507].

BYRNES, Samuel. See "John Byrnes," q.v.

CAHILL, Elisha (1762-   ). Private, Maryland Line, He applied for a pension (R1582) in Fentress County, Tennessee on July 21, 1834, aged 72, stating he was born on January 2, 1762 about 7 miles from Hagerstown in Washington County, Maryland and lived there at the time of his enlistment. In 1791 he moved to the western country, rambled through the country and finally settled in Pulaski County, Kentucky [Ref: V-I:510].

CAHILL, Ellender. See "James Cahill," q.v.

CAHILL, James (1749-1851). Private, Maryland Line. He was born in Maryland on January 27, 1749, married Ellender ----, and died in Ohio on February 5, 1851 [Ref: Y-I:467].

CAIN, Hugh. Enrolled in the first militia company organized for the Revolutionary War in the Elizabeth Town District of Frederick County (now the Hagerstown area of Washington County) on January 6, 1776 [Ref: Q-270, W-1189].

CAIRNS, Frederick. Private, Militia, 2nd Class, Capt. Joseph Chapline's Company, 2nd Battalion, 1776/1777 [Ref: M-241].

CALAMIN, John (1746-1830). Soldier of the Revolution who died in Pleasant Valley on Monday, October 25, 1830, aged 84 [Ref: DD-13, citing *The Republican Banner* on November 6, 1830, and Z-123, citing *The Torchlight and Public Advertiser* on November 4, 1830].

CALDWELL, Mary. See "Moses Chapline," q.v.

CALKLAZER, Henry. Private, Militia, 3rd Class, Capt. Martin Kershner's Company, 1776/1777 [Ref: A-1146, M-247].

CALLAR, George. See "George Cellars," q.v.

CALLARD, Joseph. Took the Oath of Allegiance before the Hon. Lemuel Barritt before March 16, 1778 [Ref: O-42, J-7].

CALLAY, George. Private, Militia, 7th Class, Capt. James Prather's Company, 3rd Battalion, 1776/1777 [Ref: M-243].

CALLER, ---- (blank). Private, Militia, 8th Class, Capt. Michael Fackler's Company, 1776/1777 [Ref: M-245, A-1146].

CALLY, Daniel. See "Daniel Kelly," q.v.

CALMES, George (1756-1834). Private, Virginia Line. He applied for and received pension S8172 in Allegany County, Maryland on May 1, 1834, aged 78, and died on November 20, 1834. His widow (not named) died prior to March 27, 1849 and was survived by only two children, Isabella Rogers (wife of John Rogers of Morgantown, Virginia) and Mary Hoye (of Cumberland, Maryland). George Calmes was a brother of Gen. Marquis Calmes, of Woodford County, Kentucky [Ref: V-I:517].

CALMES, Marquis. See "George Calmes," q.v.

CALSON, Charles. See "Charles Coulson," q.v.

CAMBLER, Michael. See "Michael Gambler," q.v.

CAMERON, Adam. Took the Oath of Allegiance before the Hon. Henry Schnebley in 1778 [Ref: O-51, J-15]. Second Corporal, Militia, Capt. John Cellars' Company, 1776/1777 [Ref: M-246, A-1146, which listed the name as "Adam Cammen"].

CAMERON, Elizabeth. See "John Miller," q.v.

CAMERON, Ludwick. Private, Militia, 4th Class, Capt. John Cellars' Company, 1776/1777 [Ref: A-1146, M-246]. One of several patriots appointed by the Committee of Observation on December 30, 1776 "to form the county into companies (after the militia had marched) for the purpose of relieving the distressed inhabitants of said county and also to compel the Dunkards and Mennonists to give their assistance." [Ref: Q-345, which listed the name as "Ludwick Cammerer"].

CAMERON, Ludwig. Rendered patriotic service by supplying wheat for the use of the military on February 7, 1780 and on April 13, 1780 for hauling wheat to the mill [Ref: W-1190, HH-72, which latter source is the original record and the named looked like "Ludwig Camerer" or possibly "Ludwig Cameren"]. Took the Oath of Allegiance before the Hon. Henry Schnebley in 1778 [Ref: O-50, J-14].

CAMMEL, Robert. Private, Militia, 2nd Class, Capt. Joseph Chapline's Company, 2nd Battalion, 1776/1777 [Ref: M-241].

CAMMER, Daniel. Private, Militia, 3rd Class, Capt. John Cellars' Company, 1776/1777 [Ref: A-1146, M-246]. Private, Militia, Capt. John Kershner's Company, on duty guarding prisoners of war at Fort Frederick on June 27, 1778 [Ref: D-328, which listed the name as "Daniel Kemmer"].

COON, Adam. Private, Militia, 3rd Class, Capt. John Cellars' Company, 1776/1777 [Ref: A-1146, M-246].

CAMPBELL, Aeneas. Captain, Upper District, Frederick County (now Washington County), July, 1776 [Ref: D-48].

CAMPBELL, Aeneas Jr. Cadet, enrolled by Capt. Aeneas Campbell and passed by Major Francis Deakins on July 18, 1776 [Ref: D-49].

CAMPBELL, Benjamin. Fourth Sergeant, Militia, Capt. Michael Fackler's Company, 1776/1777 [Ref: M-245, A-1146]. Took the Oath of Allegiance before the Hon. Samuel Hughes before March 1, 1778 [Ref: O-33, J-1].

CAMPBELL, Daniel. Private, Militia, 5th Class, Capt. Isaac Baker's Company, 1776/1777 [Ref: A-1146, M-247]. Took the Oath of Allegiance before the Hon. John Barnes before February 28, 1778 [Ref: O-44, J-9].

CAMPBELL, David. See "John Campbell," q.v.

CAMPBELL, Dugal. Second Sergeant, Militia, Capt. Barnett Johnston's Company, 3rd Battalion, 1776/1777 [Ref: M-242].

CAMPBELL, Francis. Third Corporal, Militia, Capt. Isaac Baker's Company, 1776/1777 [Ref: M-247, A-1146]. Took the Oath of Allegiance before the Hon. John Barnes before February 28, 1778 [Ref: O-44, J-9]. See "John Neff," q.v.

CAMPBELL, George. Took the Oath of Allegiance before the Hon. William Yates in 1778 [Ref: O-48, J-11].

CAMPBELL, James. Private, Militia, 6th Class, Capt. Griffin Johnson's Company, 3rd Battalion, 1776/1777 [Ref: M-243, which listed the name as "James Cambell"].

CAMPBELL, John. Private, Militia, 4th Class, Capt. Isaac Baker's Company, 1776/1777 [Ref: A-1146, M-247].

CAMPBELL, John (1761-c1840). Private, Maryland Line. He applied for and received pension S30915 in Scott County, Kentucky on April 18, 1833, aged 72, stating he was born in May, 1761 near Hagerstown, Maryland. His brother David signed an affidavit in 1833 [Ref: V-I:524, Y-I:478].

CAMPBELL, Robert. Private, Militia, 2nd Class, Capt. Isaac Baker's Company, 1776/1777 [Ref: A-1146, M-247]. Took the Oath of Allegiance before the Hon. Richard Davis in 1778 [Ref: J-5, O-38].

CAMPBLE, Francis. See "John Neff," q.v.

CAMPIAN, William. Private who was enrolled by Capt. Henry Hardman and passed on July 19, 1776 in Frederick (now Washington) County [Ref: D-51].

CANCANNON, Thomas. Private, Militia, Capt. Charles Coulson's Company, enrolled August 28, 1776 [Ref: M-243, A-1146].

CANE, Edward. Private who was enrolled by Lieut. Clement Hollyday and passed by Col. William Luckett on August 8, 1776 [Ref: D-49].

CANRAD, John. Took the Oath of Allegiance before the Hon. John Stull in 1778 [Ref: J-10]. See "John Conrad," q.v.

CAP, Michael. Private, Militia, 4th Class, Capt. Jeremiah Spires' Company, 2nd Battalion, 1776/1777 [Ref: M-239, A-1146].

CAPLINGER, Adam. Private, Militia, 1st Class, Capt. Henry Boteler's Company, 1776/1777 [Ref: M-237, A-1146].

CAPUT, John. Took the Oath of Allegiance before the Hon. John Barnes before February 28, 1778 [Ref: O-45, J-9].

CARE, Arthur. Took the Oath of Allegiance before the Hon. Henry Schnebley in 1778 [Ref: O-50, J-14].

CARE, Francis. Took the Oath of Allegiance before the Hon. Henry Schnebley in 1778 [Ref: O-50, J-14].

CAREPENY, John. Rendered patriotic service by providing a rifle for Capt. Daniel Cresap's Company in July, 1775, as recorded by the Committee of Observation at Elizabeth Town on November 4, 1775 [Ref: Q-149].

CARLOCK, Adam. Took the Oath of Allegiance before the Hon. John Barnes before February 28, 1778 [Ref: O-44, J-9].

CARN, Philip. Took the Oath of Allegiance before the Hon. John Barnes before February 28, 1778 [Ref: O-45, J-10].

CARNAN, Leonard. Enrolled in the second militia company organized for the Revolutionary War in the Elizabeth Town District of Frederick County (now the Hagerstown area of Washington County) on March 9, 1776 [Ref: Q-272, which listed the name as "Leonard Carner"]. Private, Militia, 6th Class, Capt. Henry Boteler's Company, 1776/1777 [Ref: M-237, A-1146, which listed the name as "Leonard Carnon"].

CARNAN, Michael. Private, Militia, 3rd Class, Capt. Isaac Baker's Company, 1776/1777 [Ref: A-1146, M-247].

CARNAN, Peter. Private, Militia, 8th Class, Capt. Isaac Baker's Company, 1776/1777 [Ref: A-1146, M-247].

CARNES, Michael. Private, Militia, 1st Class, Capt. John Rennolds' (Reynolds') Company, 2nd Battalion, 1776/1777 [Ref: M-240].

CARNIERA, Daniel. Private, Select Militia, Capt. Adam Ott's Company, 1781 [Ref: M-238, A-1146].

CARPENTER, Elizabeth. See "Michael Smith," q.v.

CARPENTER, John. Took the Oath of Allegiance before the Hon. Samuel Hughes before March 1, 1778 [Ref: O-33, J-1].

CARPENTER, Squire C. See "Michael Smith," q.v.

CARR, John (c1756-1819). Private, Militia, 2nd Class, Capt. Samuel Hughes' Company, 2nd Battalion, 1776/1777 [Ref: M-238, A-1146]. Lieutenant, Maryland Line, pensioned under Act of March 18, 1818 at $240 per year effective September 25, 1818 [Ref: R-42]. He applied for and received pension S35204 in Washington County on March 29, 1818, aged 62, and signed as "John Carr, Sr." He died on March 6, 1819 and was subsequently referred to as "Col. John Carr" in 1837 [Ref: V-I:550, Y-I:497].

CARRICK, Joseph. Private who was enlisted by Ensign Nathan Williams and passed on July 25, 1776 in Frederick (now Washington) County [Ref: D-51].

CARRICO, Bartholomew. Private, Militia, 3rd Class, Capt. Jeremiah Spires' Company, 2nd Battalion, 1776/1777 [Ref: M-239, A-1146].

CARRICO, Basil. Private, Militia, 8th Class, Capt. Jeremiah Spires' Company, 2nd Battalion, 1776/1777 [Ref: M-239, A-1146].

CARRICO, John. Private, Militia, 8th Class, Capt. Jeremiah Spires' Company, 2nd Battalion, 1776/1777 [Ref: M-239, A-1146]. Took the Oath of Allegiance before the Hon. Richard Davis in 1778 [Ref: J-5, O-37].

CARROLL, William. Private who was enrolled by Lieut. Clement Hollyday and passed by Col. William Luckett on August 8, 1776 [Ref: D-49].

CARTER, Dennis. Took the Oath of Allegiance before the Hon. Andrew Bruce before March 2, 1778 [Ref: O-41, J-6, which listed the name as

"Denis Carter"]. Private, Militia, Capt. Charles Coulson's Company, enrolled August 28, 1776 [Ref: M-244, A-1146]. Private, Militia, 5th Class, Capt. Charles Clinton's Company, 1776/1777 [Ref: M-245, A-1146].

CARTER, George. Private, Militia, 3rd Class, Capt. Daniel Clapsaddle's Company, 1st Battalion, 1776/1777 [Ref: M-236, A-1146]. Private, Militia, Capt. John Kershner's Company, on duty guarding prisoners of war at Fort Frederick on June 27, 1778 [Ref: D-328].

CARTER, Richard. One of the persons appointed by the Committee of Observation on January 9, 1777 "to appraise the several wagons, horses, wagon cloths and blankets that can be procured for the use of Col. Joseph Smith's Battalion." [Ref: Q-33]. Took the Oath of Allegiance before the Hon. Richard Davis in 1778 [Ref: J-3, O-36]. Rendered patriotic service by providing clothing for the use of the military on July 5, 1778 [Ref: CC-106].

CARTER, Richard Jr. Private, Militia, 2nd Class, Capt. Peter Swingle's (Swingley's) Company, 1776/1777 [Ref: A-1146, M-248].

CARTER, Thomas. Ensign, Militia, Capt. George Swingle's (Swingley's) Company, 2nd Battalion, June 22, 1778 [Ref: M-60, E-145, N-1142, M-248, which latter source indicated he was Second Sergeant in Capt. Peter Swingle's (Swingley's) Company, 2nd Battalion, but no date was given]. Took the Oath of Allegiance before the Hon. Richard Davis in 1778 [Ref: J-3, O-36].

CARTY, Daniel. Private who was enrolled by Capt. Henry Hardman and passed on July 19, 1776 in Frederick (now Washington) County [Ref: D-51].

CASEY, William. Private who was enrolled by Capt. Henry Hardman and passed on July 19, 1776 in Frederick (now Washington) County [Ref: D-51].

CASHERDY, John. Took the Oath of Allegiance before the Hon. Henry Schnebley in 1778 [Ref: O-51, J-15].

CASSART, Daniel. Took the Oath of Allegiance before the Hon. Lemuel Barritt before March 16, 1778 [Ref: O-43, J-8].

CASSART, William. Took the Oath of Allegiance before the Hon. Lemuel Barritt before March 16, 1778 [Ref: O-43, J-8].

CASTER, William. Private, Militia, 1st Class, Capt. Daniel Cresap's Company, 3rd Battalion, 1776/1777 [Ref: M-241].

CAULLIFLOWER, George and John. See "Michael Colleyflour," q.v.

CAULLIFLOWER, Michael. See "Michael Colleyflour," q.v.

CAVALIER, Elizabeth. See "John Byrnes," q.v.

CAVANNER, Patrick. Private, Militia, 4th Class, Capt. Griffin Johnson's Company, 3rd Battalion, 1776/1777 [Ref: M-243].

CAVIN, Francis. See "Francis Gavin," q.v.

CAW, Nicholas. See "Nicholas Cow," q.v.

CAYE, Michael. Private, Militia, 7th Class, Capt. James Smith's Company, 2nd Battalion, 1776/1777 [Ref: M-240, A-1146].

CELHOFFER, Dewalt. Private, Militia, 2nd Class, Capt. Peter Beall's Company, 1st Battalion, 1776/1777 [Ref: M-240].

CELLAR, Barbara. See "George Cellar," q.v.

CELLAR, George. Ensign, Militia, Capt. John Cellars' Company, 1776 (exact date not given). [Ref: M-61, A-1146, which listed the name as "George Cellar" and M-246, which listed the name as "George Callar"]. Took the Oath of Allegiance before the Hon. John Cellars in January, 1778 [Ref: K-1814, O-40, which listed the name as "George Cellar" and J-6, which listed the name as "George Celler"]. Barbara Cellar, wife of George, died on July 16, 1823 in her 65th year, after a lingering illness [Ref: Z-46].

CELLAR, Hannah. See "Michael Hager," q.v.

CELLAR, Henry. Appointed by the Committee of Observation to carry the Association of Freemen to male residents in Salisbury Hundred on September 14, 1775 "and require their subscription to the same and make an exact account of those who sign and those that refuse with their reasons for refusing." [Ref: Q-143].

CELLAR, Jacob. One of several patriots appointed by the Committee of Observation on December 30, 1776 "to form the county into companies (after the militia had marched) for the purpose of relieving the distressed inhabitants of said county and also to compel the Dunkards and Mennonists to give their assistance." [Ref: Q-345]. Appointed to raise funds on January 24, 1775 for the Committee of Observation in Salisbury Hundred in Frederick (now Washington) County [Ref: L-75, which listed the name as "Jacob Sellers"]. Took the Oath of Allegiance before the Hon. Henry Schnebley in 1778 [Ref: O-50, J-14, which listed the name as "Jacob Seller"]. See "Jacob Zeller," q.v.

CELLAR, John (c1747-1818). Elected to serve on the Committee of Observation for the Elizabeth Town District (now the Hagerstown area of Washington County) on September 12, 1775 [Ref: Q-142, Q-152, which referred to as "Capt. John Sellers" on February 19, 1776]. Appointed by the Committee of Observation to serve on a Committee for Licensing Suits on September 14, 1775 [Ref: Q-142, which listed the name as "John Cellar"]. Served on the Committee of Observation for the Elizabeth Town District in December, 1776 [Ref: Q-340, which referred to him as "Capt. John Cellar"]. Captain, Militia, 1776 [Ref: M-61, A-1146, M-246, which latter source listed the name as "John Collars" and Q-153, which listed the name as "Capt. Jno. Cellers" on February 19, 1776]. Took the Oath of Allegiance on May 20, 1777 [Ref: K-1814 (Box 4), which listed the name as "John Cellar"]. Justice who administered the Oath of Allegiance in January, 1778 [Ref: O-40, J-6, K-1814, which latter source listed the name as "John Cellar"]. Served on the Committee of Observation in April, 1776 [Ref: Q-154, Q-155, which listed the name as "John Celler" and "John Cellers"]. Appointed by the Committee of Observation to carry the Association of Freemen to male residents in his hundred (district) on March 4, 1776 "and present it for signing and make an exact account of those that sign and those that refuse with their reasons for refusing." [Ref: Q-153, L-82, which listed the name as "John Sellars" and "Sellers"]. Justice of the County Court, June 20, 1778 [Ref: E-141, which listed the name as "John Celler"]. Justice of the Peace and Judge of the Orphans Court, January 30, 1781, and served in the Maryland House of Delegates, 1784-1801 [Ref: KK-I:205, which contains more detailed information, and G-293, which listed the name as "John Celler"]. Margaret Cellar, widow of John Cellar and sister of the late Martin Kershner, Esq., died of a stroke of palsy in December, 1821, in her 70th year [Ref: Z-38; however, Source KK-I:205 states he married Susanna ---- in 1777]. See "Matthias Ridenour," q.v.

CELLAR, Margaret and Susanna. See "John Cellar," q.v.

CHAINEY, Nathan. See "Nathan Cheney," q.v.

CHAMBERS, John. Private who was recruited and passed by County Lieutenant Thomas Sprigg on April 22, 1780 [Ref: D-336].

CHAPLINE, Atlas and Cyrus. See "James Chapline," q.v.

CHAPLINE, Elizabeth. See "Jeremiah Chapline," q.v.

CHAPLINE, Heros. See "James Chapline," q.v.

CHAPLINE, James, of William (1750-c1825). Enrolled in the first militia company organized for the Revolutionary War in the Elizabeth Town District of Frederick County (now the Hagerstown area of Washington County) on January 6, 1776 [Ref: Q-270, W-1189]. First Lieutenant, Militia, Capt. Joseph Chapline's Company, 2nd Battalion, June 22, 1778, and Lieutenant, Select Militia, Capt. Joseph Chapline's Company, March 20, 1781 [Ref: M-61, M-241, E-145, G-368, H-271]. Took the Oath of Allegiance before the Hon. Christopher Cruse in Sharpsburg Hundred before March 2, 1778 [Ref: O-34, J-2]. Served in the Maryland House of Delegates, 1779-1783, and died before 1829 in Jefferson County, Ohio [Ref: KK-I:82-88, KK-II:209-210, which contains more detailed information]. An old Maryland chancery case (William Williams Chapline vs. James Chapline, et al.) dating back to 1790 and supplemented in 1809 (William Price, et al., vs. Henry Neighkirk, et al.) was noted in *The Farmers' Register and Maryland Herald* in Washington County on December 29, 1829. It stated, in part, that James Chapline died several years ago, intestate and insolvent, and his children and heirs were Alitha Wallace (wife of William Wallace), Romena Miser (wife of John Miser), Joseph Chapline, Heros Chapline, Atlas Chapline, and Cyrus Chapline, all of whom resided outside of Maryland [Ref: Z-125]. See "Walter Wilson," q.v.

CHAPLINE, James N. See "Jeremiah Chapline," q.v.

CHAPLINE, Jeremiah, of William (1756-1809). Enrolled in the first militia company organized for the Revolutionary War in the Elizabeth Town District of Frederick County (now the Hagerstown area of Washington County) on January 6, 1776 [Ref: Q-271, W-1190, Y-I:537, Y-I:537]. Took the Oath of Allegiance before the Hon. Christopher Cruse in Sharpsburg Hundred before March 2, 1778 [Ref: O-35, J-2]. By April, 1827, a bill of complaint was filed in Washington County court by his heirs (case of John Cravens and wife Ruhamah vs. Elizabeth Chapline, Jesse Roach and wife Mary Ann, James N. Chapline, Isaac C. White, and Adam Myers). It mentioned that Elizabeth Chapline and Jesse Roach and wife Mary Ann were non-residents of the state of Maryland [Ref: Z-90].

CHAPLINE, Joseph, of William (1746-1821). Appointed to raise funds on January 24, 1775 for the Committee of Observation in Sharpsburg Hundred in Frederick (now Washington) County [Ref: L-75]. Elected to serve on the Committee of Observation for the Elizabeth Town District on September 12, 1775 [Ref: Q-142, which listed the name as "Joseph Chaplain"]. Enrolled in the first militia company organized for the Revolutionary War in the Elizabeth Town District of Frederick County (now the Hagerstown area of Washington County) on January 6, 1776 [Ref: Q-270, W-1189]. Served on the Committee of Observation in April, 1776 [Ref: Q-154, Q-155]. Captain, Militia, Upper District, Frederick County, by July 4, 1776, and Captain, Militia, 2nd Battalion, Washington County, June 22, 1778, and Captain, Select Militia, March 20, 1781 [Ref: M-61, M-241, A-546, E-145, G-368]. Justice of the County Court, June 20, 1778 [Ref: E-141]. Justice who administered the Oath of Allegiance before April 17, 1779 (date of his returns). [Ref: J-5, O-39, which listed the name as "Joseph Chaplin"]. Assisted in the purchase of grains for the military in 1780 [Ref: P-280, HH-74]. Served in the Maryland House of Delegates, 1780, and Justice of the Peace and Judge of the Orphans Court, January 30, 1781 [Ref: G-293, KK-I:84, KK-II:211, which contains more detailed information]. "Died at Mount Pleasant, his seat, near

Sharpsburg, in this [Washington] county, Friday morning, August 31, 1821, Capt. Joseph Chapline, in the 75th year of his age. He was a soldier of the Revolution. He assembled an unusually large company of volunteers and led them on to the American Camp at the north." [Ref: Z-56]. Mary Ann Abigail Chapline, relict of Capt. Joseph Chapline, lately deceased, died near Sharpsburg on January 16, 1823, in her 74th year, an active member of St. Paul's Protestant Episcopal Church, for many years in a delicate state of health, her departure was sudden and unexpected [Ref: Z-61]. See "James Chapline," q.v.

CHAPLINE, Mary Ann Abigail. See "Joseph Chapline," q.v.

CHAPLINE, Moses, of William (1754-1812). Recommended by the Committee of Observation to the Continental Congress on February 19, 1776, that he was "a person fitting to take command of a company as captain in the service of his country." [Ref: Q-153]. First Lieutenant, Upper District, Frederick County (now Washington County), July, 1776 [Ref: D-48]. Took the Oath of Allegiance before the Hon. Christopher Cruse in Sharpsburg Hundred before March 2, 1778 [Ref: O-34, J-1]. Captain, Maryland Line, born on October 20, 1754, married Mary Caldwell, and died on February 10, 1812 in Virginia [Ref: Y-I:537].

CHAPLINE, Moses. Private, Militia, 8th Class, Capt. Joseph Chapline's Company, 2nd Battalion, 1776/1777 [Ref: M-242].

CHAPLINE, William Williams. See "James Chapline," q.v.

CHARLES, George. Private, Militia, 6th Class, Capt. John Cellars' Company, 1776/1777 [Ref: A-1146, M-246].

CHARLTON, John. First Lieutenant, Militia, Capt. Conrad Hogmire's Company, 1776/1777 [Ref: M-244, A-1146]. Appointed by the Committee of Observation to carry the Association of Freemen to male residents in his hundred (district) on March 4, 1776 "and present it for signing and make an exact account of those that sign and those that refuse with their reasons for refusing." [Ref: Q-153, L-82]. One John Charlton died testate before October, 1783 (date of balance book entry in Washington County), but balance and heirs were not given [Ref: J-25]. See "Thomas Charlton," q.v.

CHARLTON, Susannah. See "Thomas Charlton," q.v.

CHARLTON, Thomas. Private, Militia, 6th Class, Capt. Conrad Hogmire's Company, 1776/1777 [Ref: M-244, A-1146]. Took the Oath of Allegiance before the Hon. Samuel Hughes before March 1, 1778 [Ref: O-33, J-1]. One Thomas Charlton died testate before November 26, 1805, leaving a wife Susannah, and among his heirs were sons Thomas and John [Ref: MM-13:175].

CHARLTON, Thomas. Private, Militia, 1st Class, Capt. John Bennet's Company, 1776/1777 [Ref: M-246, A-1146]. Took the Oath of Allegiance before the Hon. John Barnes before February 28, 1778 [Ref: O-44, J-9]. See the other "Thomas Charlton," q.v.

CHARREY, Thomas. Took the Oath of Allegiance before the Hon. Lemuel Barritt before March 16, 1778 [Ref: O-43, J-8].

CHATTWELL, Thomas. Took the Oath of Allegiance before the Hon. William Yates in 1778 [Ref: O-48, J-11].

CHENEY, Ezekiel. Private, Militia, 2nd Class, Capt. James Smith's Company, 2nd Battalion, 1776/1777 [Ref: M-239, A-1146, which listed the name as "Ezekiel Chiney"]. "Ezekiel Cheyney" died testate before December 9, 1783 (date of balance book entry in Washington County), leaving a widow and five children, but names were not given [Ref: J-25].

CHENEY, Jeremiah (1720-1813). Rendered patriotic service by supplying wheat for the use of the military on March 6, 1780 [Ref: W-1190, HH-73, which latter source listed the name as "Jeremiah Chany"]. Jeremiah Cheney was born in 1720, died on June 1, 1813, and is buried beside Nancy Cheney (1734-1814) and other members of the Cheney family in a "graveyard on the Edison Groh farm near Death Curve, on State Penal Farm" in Washington County, Maryland [Ref: JJ-IV:20].

CHENEY, Jeremiah. Private, Militia, 6th Class, Capt. James Smith's Company, 2nd Battalion, 1776/1777 [Ref: M-240, A-1146, which listed the name as "Jeremiah Chiney"].

CHENEY, John. Private, Militia, 3rd Class, Capt. James Smith's Company, 2nd Battalion, 1776/1777 [Ref: M-239, A-1146, which listed the name as "John Chiney"].

CHENEY, Nancy. See "Jeremiah Cheney," q.v.

CHENEY, Nathan. Private, Militia, 8th Class, Capt. James Smith's Company, 2nd Battalion, 1776/1777 [Ref: M-240, A-1146, which listed the name as "Nathan Chiney" and Q-44, which listed the name as "Nathan Chainey"].

CHENEY, William. Private, Militia, 1st Class, Capt. James Smith's Company, 2nd Battalion, 1776/1777 [Ref: M-239, A-1146, which listed the name as "William Chiney"].

CHENOWETH, Benjamin and Cassandra. See "Thomas Chenoweth," q.v.

CHENOWETH, Isaac. See "John Chenoweth," q.v.

CHENOWETH, John (1751-1820). Sergeant, Maryland Line. He was born on May 15, 1751 and married first to Rachel Kerr and second to Mary Buskirk, daughter of Michael Buskirk, on March 13, 1792 in Shelby County, Kentucky. John died on March 3, 1820 and his widow Mary applied for and received pension W9787 in Vermillion County, Indiana on June 21, 1842. She stated that John had enlisted in Allegany County, Maryland [but it was actually Washington County since Allegany County was not created until 1789]. In 1843 a son Isaac was aged 43 and lived in Perryville, Indiana [Ref: V-I:618, Y-I:552].

CHENOWETH, Joseph. See "Thomas Chenoweth," q.v.

CHENOWETH, Mary. See "John Chenoweth" and "Thomas Chenoweth," q.v.

CHENOWETH, Thomas (1753-1814). Lieutenant, Maryland Line. His widow Cassandra applied for pension (R1906) in Taney County, Missouri on May 1, 1843, aged 80, stating her husband was born September 10, 1753, son of Thomas and Mary Chenoweth, and enlisted in 1782 in (now) Allegany County, Maryland under Captain Bell, Major Coulter and Colonel Crawford. Cassandra Foster married Thomas Chenoweth on March 17, 1785 in Allegany County, Maryland and he died on August 17, 1814. Their sons Benjamin (age 59) and Joseph lived in Taney County, Missouri in 1854. Her claim was disallowed as proof of service was not satisfactory [Ref: U-32:2 (1944), Y-I:552]. Thomas Chenoweth took the Oath of Allegiance before the Hon. Lemuel Barritt before March 16, 1778 [Ref: J-8, which listed the name as "Thomas Chinorath" and O-43, which listed the name as "Thomas Chinorsath"]. There was a Thomas Chenoweth who enlisted in the Maryland Line in Baltimore County in August, 1776 [Ref: D-52]. Additional research may be necessary before drawing conclusions.

CHEYNEY, Ezekiel. See "Ezekiel Cheney," q.v.

CHILLON, Mark. Private who was enrolled by Capt. Aeneas Campbell and passed by Major Francis Deakins on July 18, 1776 [Ref: D-49].

CHINEY, Jeremiah. See "Jeremiah Cheney," q.v.

CHINOTH, Richard. Fourth Corporal, Militia, Capt. James Prather's Company, 3rd Battalion, 1776/1777 [Ref: M-242, which listed the name as "Richard Chinsoth"]. Took the Oath of Allegiance before the Hon. Andrew Bruce before March 2, 1778 [Ref: O-41, J-6].

CHINOTH, Thomas. Took the Oath of Allegiance before the Hon. Andrew Bruce before March 2, 1778 [Ref: O-41, J-7].

CHINOTH, William. Private, Militia, 3rd Class, Capt. James Prather's Company, 3rd Battalion, 1776/1777 [Ref: M-242, which listed the name as "William Chinoath(?)"].

CHISTMAN, Paul. Private, Militia, 8th Class, Capt. Michael Fackler's Company, 1776/1777 [Ref: M-245, A-1146].

CHRISLIE, James. Took the Oath of Allegiance before the Hon. Richard Davis in 1778 [Ref: J-3, O-36].

CHRISTIAN, Daniel (1762-1847). Private, Pennsylvania Line, who pensioned in Washington County under the Act of June 7, 1832 at the annual allowance of $36.66 retroactive to March 4, 1831 [Ref: R-51]. He applied for and received pension S8201 in Washington County, Maryland on April 4, 1833, a resident of Boonsborough, and was referred to as Daniel Christian Sr. He stated he was born in November, 1762 in Berks County, Pennsylvania and lived at Reading, Pennsylvania at the time of his enlistment. He moved to Maryland about 4 or 5 years after the war and settled in Washington County [Ref: V-I:628]. He died on December 26, 1847 in Illinois [Ref: Y-I:561].

CHRISTMAN, Paul. Ensign, Militia, Capt. William Heyser's Company, muster roll dated October 23, 1776, in continental service [Ref: D-263]. Took the Oath of Allegiance before the Hon. Henry Schnebley in 1778 [Ref: O-49, J-13].

CHROSSEN, John. See "John Crossen," q.v.

CLAGETT, Alexander. County Sheriff, elected on October 13, 1779 [Ref: E-554]. Rendered patriotic service by supplying wheat and rye for the use of the military on March 21, 1780 [Ref: W-1190, HH-73].

CLAGETT, Elizabeth. See "Thomas Prather," q.v.

CLAGETT, Esther. See "Posthumous Clagett," q.v.

CLAGETT, Hezekiah. Sergeant, Select Militia, Capt. Adam Ott's Company, 1781 [Ref: M-238, A-1146].

CLAGETT, Posthumous (1738-1822). Took the Oath of Allegiance before the Hon. John Stull in 1778 [Ref: O-46, J-10, which listed the name as "Bothumas Claggett"]. Enrolled in the second militia company organized for the Revolutionary War in the Elizabeth Town District of Frederick County (now the Hagerstown area of Washington County) on March 9, 1776 [Ref: Q-271]. Rendered patriotic service by supplying wheat for the use of the military on February 16, 1780 [Ref: W-1190, HH-74]. "Posthumous Clagett" was born on April 19, 1738, died on January 24, 1822, and is buried beside his first wife Esther and second wife Mary in a graveyard on the John Rudolph Brown farm at Crampton near the Townsend War Monument in Washington County, Maryland [Ref: JJ-III:54].

CLAGETT, Mary. See "Posthumous Clagett," q.v.

CLAINLE(?), Michael. Private, Militia, 7th Class, Capt. John Rennolds' (Reynolds') Company, 2nd Battalion, 1776/1777 [Ref: M-240].

CLAIRCOMB, Henry. Took the Oath of Allegiance before the Hon. John Barnes before February 28, 1778 [Ref: O-44, J-9].

CLAM, Jacob. Private, Militia, 6th Class, Capt. John Rennolds' (Reynolds') Company, 2nd Battalion, 1776/1777 [Ref: M-240].

CLAPPER, John. See "John Clopper," q.v.

CLAPSADDLE, Daniel. Appointed by the Committee of Observation to carry the Association of Freemen to male residents in Elizabeth Town Hundred on September 14, 1775 "and require their subscription to the same and make an exact account of those who sign and those that refuse with their reasons for refusing." [Ref: Q-143, which listed the name as "Danl. Clapsadle"]. Took the Oath of Allegiance before the Hon. Andrew Rentch before March 7, 1778 [Ref: O-52, J-15, which listed the name as "Daniel Clapsadle"]. Captain, Militia, 1st Company, 1st Battalion, Flying Camp, commissioned September 26, 1776 [Ref: B-301, M-236, A-1146, D-73].

CLARK, Francis. Took the Oath of Allegiance before the Hon. John Barnes before February 28, 1778 [Ref: O-45, J-10].

CLARK, James. Served as clerk on the Committee of Observation for the Elizabeth Town District (now the Hagerstown area of Washington County) in December, 1776, and as chairman in February, 1777 [Ref: Q-228, Q-340]. Reimbursed on March 1, 1777 for a "sum advanced by him to Capt. Andrew Linck in behalf of the publick." [Ref: Q-239, Q-248]. Took the Oath of Allegiance before the Hon. Samuel Hughes before March 1, 1778 [Ref: O-33, J-1]. One "James Clark" was an heir to "Matthew Clarke" who died before August 13, 1782 (date of balance book entry in Washington County). [Ref: J-23].

CLARK, John. Took the Oath of Allegiance before the Hon. Lemuel Barritt before March 16, 1778 [Ref: O-43, J-8].

CLARK, Jonathan. Took the Oath of Allegiance before the Hon. Lemuel Barritt before March 16, 1778 [Ref: O-43, J-8].

CLARK, Joseph. Took the Oath of Allegiance before the Hon. Richard Davis in 1778 [Ref: J-3, O-36].

CLARK, Joseph Jr. Private, Militia, 1st Class, Capt. Basil Williams' Company, 1776/1777 [Ref: M-244, A-1146].

CLARK, Richard. Took the Oath of Allegiance before the Hon. Lemuel Barritt before March 16, 1778 [Ref: O-42, J-7].

CLARK, William. Private, Militia, 4th Class, Capt. Basil Williams' Company, 1776/1777 [Ref: M-244, A-1146, Q-48]. Took the Oath of Allegiance before the Hon. Richard Davis in 1778 [Ref: J-3, O-36].

CLARKE, Barzilla. Private, Militia, 2nd Class, Capt. James Prather's Company, 3rd Battalion, 1776/1777 [Ref: M-242].

CLARKE, Bazil. Took the Oath of Allegiance before the Hon. William Yates in 1778 [Ref: O-48, which listed the name as "Bazil Clarck" and J-12, which listed the name as "Basil Clark"].

CLARKE, Elisha. Drummer, Militia, Capt. James Prather's Company, 3rd Battalion, 1776/1777 [Ref: M-242].

CLARKE, John. Second Sergeant, Militia, Capt. James Prather's Company, 3rd Battalion, 1776/1777 [Ref: M-242]. Two men by this name Took the Oath of Allegiance before the Hon. William Yates in 1778 [Ref: O-48, which listed the name as "John Clarck" and J-12, which listed the name as "John Clark"].

CLARKE, Joseph. Rendered patriotic service by providing clothing for the use of the military on July 5, 1778 [Ref: CC-106].

CLARKE, Matthew. See "James Clark," q.v.

CLARKE, Robert. Private, Militia, 5th Class, Capt. Barnett Johnston's Company, 3rd Battalion, 1776/1777 [Ref: M-242]. Took the Oath of Allegiance before the Hon. William Yates in 1778 [Ref: O-48, which listed the name as "Robert Clarck" and J-12, which listed the name as "Robert Clark"].

CLASS, John. Private, Militia, 8th Class, Capt. John Cellars' Company, 1776/1777 [Ref: A-1146, M-246]. Private who was enlisted by Capt. John Reynolds and passed on July 18, 1776 in Frederick (now Washington) County [Ref: D-50].

CLAUBOUGH, Martin. Took the Oath of Allegiance before the Hon. John Stull in 1778 [Ref: O-46, J-10, which latter source listed the name as "Martin Clabaugh"]. Private, Militia, 3rd Class, Capt. Jacob Sharer's Company, 1776/1777 [Ref: A-1146, M-248, which listed the name as "Martin Clabback"].

CLAUNER, Daniel. Took the Oath of Allegiance before the Hon. Joseph Sprigg before April 1, 1778 [Ref: O-53, J-16].

CLAXTON, Samuel. Took the Oath of Allegiance before the Hon. Lemuel Barritt before March 16, 1778 [Ref: O-43, J-8].

CLAY, Henry. See "Thomas Hart," q.v.

CLAY, Joseph. Private who was recruited and passed by County Lieutenant Thomas Sprigg on April 22, 1780 [Ref: D-336].

CLAYCOMB, Henry. Private, Militia, 1st Class, Capt. John Bennet's Company, 1776/1777 [Ref: M-246, A-1146].

CLEM, David and Jacob. See "John Clem," q.v.

CLEM, John (1760-1827). Private, Maryland Line. He applied for a pension (R2040) in Warren County, Indiana on November 16, 1843, aged 83, stating he married Susannah ---- in February 11, 1778 about ten miles from Cumberland, Maryland. John died on April 18, 1827 and in 1842 his son John was then living, another son Jacob was aged 63, and their oldest sister (not named) was aged 63 on December 11, 1842. A grandson David Clem wrote a letter of inquiry on August 16, 1857 in

Vermillion County, Illinois, and his mother was deceased (no date given). [Ref: V-I:671].

CLEM, Susannah. See "John Clem," q.v.

CLEMENCE, Joseph. Private, Maryland Line. He applied for and received pension S30933 in Clarke County, Kentucky on June 17, 1834, aged 101, stating he was born in Bucks County, Pennsylvania on February 8, 1733, moved to Maryland when quite young, and enlisted from Washington County [Ref: V-I:671].

CLEMMONS, Ruth Ann. See "Jarratt Williams," q.v.

CLIFFORD, William. Private who enlisted in the militia on August 15, 1781 for service in the Continental Army [Ref: D-388]. Substitute, Maryland Line, discharged on October 30, 1781 [Ref: G-656].

CLIFTON, Samuel. Private, Militia, 3rd Class, Capt. Daniel Cresap's Company, 3rd Battalion, 1776/1777 [Ref: M-241].

CLIFTON, Thomas. Private, Militia, Capt. William Heyser's Company, enlisted on August 3, 1776, muster roll dated October 23, 1776, in continental service [Ref: GG-96, D-264, W-1190, L-79]. Private, German Regiment, Lt. Col. Ludwick Weltner's Company, continental service, discharged on July 26, 1779 at Fort Wyoming, Pennsylvania [Ref: D-265, GG-96]. Private, Maryland Line. He applied for and received pension S42125 in Ross County, Ohio on July 17, 1819, aged 74, stating he lived in Washington County, Maryland at the time of his enlistment. However, on April 18, 1821 he stated he was aged 66 with a wife (not named) and a son (not named, aged 15). Thomas died on September 30, 1832 [Ref: V-I:676].

CLINE, Conrad (c1759-1826). Private, Pennsylvania Line, pensioned under Act of March 18, 1818 in Washington County at $96 per year effective May 3, 1825, and died December 1, 1826 [Ref: R-42].

CLINE, Daniel. Private who was enrolled by Capt. Henry Hardman and passed on July 19, 1776 in Frederick (now Washington) County [Ref: D-51]. Private who was recruited and passed by County Lieutenant Thomas Sprigg on April 22, 1780 [Ref: D-336].

CLINE, Henry. Took the Oath of Allegiance before the Hon. Henry Schnebley in 1778 [Ref: O-50, J-13, which listed the name as "Henry Kleine"].

CLINE, Jacob. Private, Militia, Capt. William Heyser's Company, enlisted August 1, 1776, muster roll dated October 23, 1776, continental service [Ref: D-264, W-1190, L-79, which listed the name as "Jacob Klien"]. Private, German Regiment, Lt. Col. Ludwick Weltner's Company, discharged on July 26, 1779 or August 26, 1780 at Fort Wyoming,

Pennsylvania [Ref: D-223, D-265, which listed the name as "Jacob Kline" and GG-98, which listed the name as "Jacob Klein, Kline, Kleine"].

CLINE, John. Private, German Regiment, continental service, 1776, and discharged on October 12, 1779 [Ref: D-198, which listed the name as "John Cline or Kline"]. Took the Oath of Allegiance before the Hon. John Barnes before February 28, 1778 [Ref: O-44, J-9]. Private, Select Militia, Capt. Adam Ott's Company, 1781 [Ref: M-238, A-1146].

CLINE, Joseph. Private, Militia, 5th Class, Capt. Peter Beall's Company, 1st Battalion, 1776/1777 [Ref: M-240]. Took the Oath of Allegiance before the Hon. John Stull in 1778 [Ref: O-46, J-10].

CLINE, Nicholas. Private who enlisted in the militia on August 18, 1781 for service in the Continental Army [Ref: D-388, D-407]. Substitute, Maryland Line, discharged on October 30, 1781 [Ref: G-656, which listed the name as "Nicholas Clyne"].

CLINE, Phillip. Took the Oath of Allegiance before the Hon. Richard Davis in 1778 [Ref: J-5, O-37].

CLINE, Phillip Jr. Took the Oath of Allegiance before the Hon. Richard Davis in 1778 [Ref: J-5, O-37].

CLINESMITH, Andrew. Took the Oath of Allegiance before the Hon. Henry Schnebley in 1778 [Ref: O-50, J-13, which listed the name as "Andrew Kleinsmith"]. Sergeant, Select Militia, Capt. Adam Ott's Company, 1781 [Ref: A-1146, M-238, which latter source listed the name as "Andrew Clinesmith (Clieresmith)"].

CLINESMITH, Barbara. See "Matthias Nead," q.v.

CLINKENBEARD (CLINCKENBEARD), Isaac (1758-   ). Private, Maryland and Virginia Lines. He applied for and received pension S15380 in Bourbon County, Kentucky on November 1, 1833, aged 75, stating he was born on November 25, 1758 and first enlisted at Hancock, Maryland and later in Berkeley County, Virginia where he then lived. In 1779 he moved to Strode Station, Kentucky and enlisted again. He also mentioned a brother William Clinckenbeard who was a pensioner [Ref: V-I:677]. It must be noted, however, that no William Clinkenbeard or Clinckenbeard appears in this reference, although John Clinckenbeard (born 1755) does appear and mentions his two brothers William (aged 73 in 1834) and Isaac. Also, refer to pension S30930 of John Clinckenbeard who lived in Pennsylvania near the Maryland Line, moved to Berkeley County, Virginia with his father and brothers, and served in the North Carolina Line. He and his brothers were alive in 1834 [Ref: Y-I:597].

CLINKENBEARD, John and William. See "Isaac Clinkenbeard," q.v.

CLINTON, Charles. Captain, Militia, Upper District, Frederick County, by July 27, 1776. Captain, Militia, Washington County, 1776, "on frontier" by May 13, 1778. Captain, 3rd Battalion, June 22, 1778 [Ref: M-63, B-127, E-78, E-145, M-245, A-1146]. Took the Oath of Allegiance before the Hon. Andrew Bruce before March 2, 1778 [Ref: O-41, J-6].

CLINTON, Elizabeth. See "William Stewart," q.v.

CLINTON, Thomas (1760-1847). Private and fifer, Maryland Line. He applied for and received pension S34693 in Allegany County, Maryland on April 25, 1818, aged 58, stating he had enlisted in Monmouth County, New Jersey. In 1820 his wife [not named, but it was Catherine Michael] was aged about 50 and his children had all left home [Ref: V-I:678]. Soldier and pensioner of the Revolution who resided in the 2nd Division of Allegany County in 1840, aged 84, and died on January 7, 1847 [Ref: Y-I:597, and EE-28:4 (p. 442), containing an article by Elba Anthony Dardeau, Jr.].

CLOPPER, Catherine. See "Harmon Clopper," q.v.

CLOPPER, Charles. See "Henry Stotler," q.v.

CLOPPER, Elizabeth. See "Harmon Clopper," q.v.

CLOPPER (CLAPPER), Harmon. Private, Militia, 6th Class, Capt. Michael Fackler's Company, 1776/1777 [Ref: M-245, A-1146, which listed the name as "Harmon Claper"]. Took the Oath of Allegiance before the Hon. John Stull in 1778 [Ref: O-46, J-11, which listed the name as "Harmen Klapper"]. "Harmon Clopper" died before November 17, 1792 (date of balance book entry in Washington County), leaving a widow (no name given in this account) and equal shares to Catherine, John, Mary and Elizabeth Clopper [Ref: J-32].

CLOPPER (CLAPPER), Henry Jr. Private, Militia, 3rd Class, Capt. Daniel Clapsaddle's Company, 1st Battalion, 1776/1777 [Ref: M-236, A-1146].

CLOPPER (CLAPPER), John. Private, Militia, 6th Class, Capt. John Cellars' Company, 1776/1777 [Ref: A-1146, M-246]. See "Harmon Clopper," q.v.

CLOPPER (CLAPPER), John (stiller). Private, Militia, 4th Class, Capt. John Cellars' Company, 1776/1777 [Ref: A-1146, M-246].

CLOPPER (CLAPPER), John Henry. Private, Militia, 8th Class, Capt. John Cellars' Company, 1776/1777 [Ref: A-1146, M-247].

CLOPPER, Mary. See "Harmon Clopper," q.v.

CLOPPER (CLAPPER), Valentine. Private who was recruited and passed by County Lieutenant Thomas Sprigg on April 22, 1780 [Ref: D-336, which listed the name as "Volintine Claper"]. Took the Oath of

Allegiance before the Hon. John Stull in 1778 [Ref: O-46, J-10, which listed the name as "Wallingtine Klapper"].

CLOSS, John. Private who was enrolled by Capt. Henry Hardman and passed on July 19, 1776 in Frederick (now Washington) County [Ref: D-51].

CLOSSER, Michael. Second Lieutenant, Militia, Capt. Conrad Nichodemus' Company, June 22, 1778 [Ref: M-63, E-145]. See "Michael Glosser," q.v.

CLOSSON, Garrett. Private who was enlisted by Lieut. Christian Orndorff and passed on July 20, 1776 in Frederick (now Washington) County [Ref: D-50].

CLOWARD, Jacob. Private, Militia, by January 22, 1777 when ordered by the Committee of Observation "to march with some company of militia to the reinforcement of his Excellency General Washington" or appear before the Committee and state his reason for not marching. He apparently marched since he never appeared to the contrary [Ref: Q-48].

CLOWSE, William. Private, Militia, 2nd Class, Capt. James Prather's Company, 3rd Battalion, 1776/1777 [Ref: M-242]. Took the Oath of Allegiance before the Hon. Lemuel Barritt before March 16, 1778 [Ref: O-43, J-8, which listed the name as "William Clouge" or Clouze?].

CNADY(?), Isaac. Private, Militia, 5th Class, Capt. Peter Beall's Company, 1st Battalion, 1776/1777 [Ref: M-240].

COAL, Balser. Rendered patriotic service by providing dry goods for the use of the military in July, 1775, as recorded by the Committee of Observation at Elizabeth Town on November 4, 1775 [Ref: Q-150].

COALER, Conrad. Took the Oath of Allegiance before September 1, 1780 [Ref: X-107, which listed the name as "Conrad Cohler"].

COALER, George. One of several patriots appointed by the Committee of Observation on December 30, 1776 "to form the county into companies (after the militia had marched) for the purpose of relieving the distressed inhabitants of said county and also to compel the Dunkards and Mennonists to give their assistance." [Ref: Q-346].

COALER, George Jr. Private, Militia, 6th Class, Capt. Conrad Hogmire's Company, 1776/1777 [Ref: M-244, A-1146].

COALER, John. Fourth Corporal, Militia, Capt. Conrad Hogmire's Company, 1776/1777 [Ref: M-244, A-1146].

COCK, Cornelius. Private who enlisted in the militia on September 5, 1781 for service in the Continental Army [Ref: D-388].

COCKBURN, Robert. Enrolled in the first militia company organized for the Revolutionary War in the Elizabeth Town District of Frederick

County (now the Hagerstown area of Washington County) on January 6, 1776 [Ref: Q-270, W-1189].

COCKMAN, William. Took the Oath of Allegiance before the Hon. Henry Schnebley in 1778 [Ref: O-50, J-14].

CODD, William. Enrolled in the first militia company organized for the Revolutionary War in the Elizabeth Town District of Frederick County (now the Hagerstown area of Washington County) on January 6, 1776 [Ref: Q-270, W-1189]. Private, Militia, 8th Class, Capt. John Rennolds' (Reynolds') Company, 2nd Battalion, 1776/1777 [Ref: M-240].

CODDRINGTON, Benjamin. Private, Maryland Line, pensioned under Acts of July 5, 1812 and April 24, 1816, placed on the rolls on February 24, 1821 in Allegany County, and received an invalid's pension of $30 per year from April 25, 1812 and $48 per year from April 24, 1816 [Ref: R-2, AA-329].

COFFER, William. Private, Militia, 5th Class, Capt. Jeremiah Spires' Company, 2nd Battalion, 1776/1777 [Ref: M-239, A-1146, which listed the name as "William Coefer"]. Took the Oath of Allegiance before the Hon. Richard Davis in 1778 [Ref: J-4, O-37]. Rendered patriotic service by providing clothing for the use of the military on July 5, 1778 [Ref: CC-106].

COFFMAN, Jacob. Private, Maryland Line, who made affidavit in Mercer County, Kentucky on September 10, 1833, aged 70, stating that he was a fellow soldier of William Sutherland whom he knew in Washington County, Maryland during the war [Ref: T-21].

COFFROTH (COFFERATH), Conrad (1762-1831). Fifer, 7th Maryland Line, enlisted on March 20, 1777 and discharged in May, 1780 [Ref: D-196]. Fifer, Select Militia, Capt. Adam Ott's Company, 1781 [Ref: M-238, A-1146]. On March 8, 1826 the Treasurer of the Western Shore of Maryland was directed to pay to Conrad Coffroth, of Franklin County, Pennsylvania, half pay of a fifer, as a further remuneration for his services during the Revolutionary War. On February 28, 1832 the Treasurer of the Western Shore of Maryland was directed to pay to Magdalena Coffroth, of Washington County, Maryland, widow of Conrad Coffroth, a soldier of the Revolutionary War, during widowhood, half pay of a private, for the services rendered by her husband during said war [Ref: AA-330]. He was born on August 19, 1762, married Mary Magdalena Bower, and died on February 26, 1831 [Ref: Y-I:611].

COFFROTH, Magdalena. See "Conrad Coffroth (Cofferath)," q.v.

COFFROTH (COFFEROTH), William. Private who was enlisted by Capt. John Reynolds and passed on July 18, 1776 in Frederick (now Washington) County [Ref: D-50]. Fifer, 7th Maryland Line, enlisted on

December 26, 1777. Fife Major, January 27, 1778 and discharged on November 1, 1780 [Ref: D-196].

COFIELD, John. Private, Militia, 1st Class, Capt. James Smith's Company, 2nd Battalion, 1776/1777 [Ref: M-239, A-1146].

COHAN, Levy. Took the Oath of Allegiance before the Hon. Christopher Cruse in Sharpsburg Hundred before March 2, 1778 [Ref: O-34, J-1]. One of several patriots appointed by the Committee of Observation on January 7, 1777 "to form the county into companies (after the militia had marched) for the purpose of relieving the distressed inhabitants of said county and also to compel the Dunkards and Mennonists to give their assistance." [Ref: Q-31, which listed the name as "Levy Coharn"].

COLLARD, Joseph. Private, Militia, 4th Class, Capt. Daniel Cresap's Company, 3rd Battalion, 1776/1777 [Ref: M-241].

COLLARD, Joseph. Private, Militia, Capt. Charles Coulson's Company, enrolled August 28, 1776 [Ref: M-244, A-1146].

COLLARS, John. See "John Cellars," q.v.

COLLEY, George. Private who was enrolled by Capt. Henry Hardman and passed on July 19, 1776 in Frederick (now Washington) County [Ref: D-51].

COLLEY, Michael. On September 23, 1780, Col. Lemuel Barritt recommended to Governor Lee that "Michael Collye" be commissioned a second lieutenant in the militia at Keystone since so many officers of the Western Battalion had moved out of Maryland to Kentucky and elsewhere [Ref: G-123].

COLLEYFLOUR (COLLIFLOWER), George. Took the Oath of Allegiance before the Hon. Andrew Rentch before March 7, 1778 [Ref: O-52, J-15, which listed the name as "George Corrowflow"]. A "George Adam Colliflower" died testate by September 12, 1801 and among his heirs were sons George and Michael [Ref: MM-12:77].

COLLEYFLOUR (COLLIFLOWER), George Jr. (1756-1832). Second Corporal, Militia, Capt. Samuel Hughes' Company, 1776/1777 [Ref: M-238, A-1146, which listed the name as "George Colleyflour"]. Took the Oath of Allegiance before the Hon. Samuel Hughes before March 1, 1778 [Ref: J-1, O-33, which latter source listed the name as "George Coll_flower Jnr."]. "Georg Adam Colliflower" was born on January 12, 1756, died on March 1, 1832, and is buried beside Catherine Colliflower (1758-1852) in the Christ Reformed Church Graveyard at Cavetown in Washington County, Maryland [Ref: JJ-III:18]. See "Michael Colleyflour," q.v.

COLLEYFLOUR (COLLIFLOWER), Michael (1758-   ). Private, Militia, 7th Class, Capt. Samuel Hughes' Company, 2nd Battalion, 1776/1777

[Ref: M-238, A-1146]. Took the Oath of Allegiance before the Hon. Samuel Hughes before March 1, 1778 [Ref: J-1, O-33, which latter source listed the name as "Nicheal Coliflower"]. Private, Select Militia, Capt. Adam Ott's Company, 1781 [Ref: M-238, A-1146, which listed the name as "Michael Collyflower"]. "Michael Caulliflower" applied for a pension (R1817) in Frederick County, Maryland on March 3, 1835, aged 76, stating he was born on September 27, 1758 in Washington County, Maryland and moved to Frederick County in 1804. In 1835 he mentioned a deceased brother George Caulliflower and a John Caulliflower who signed an affidavit at that time [Ref: V-I:579]. See "George Colleyflour," q.v.

COLLIFLOWER, Catherine and George. See "George Colleyflour," q.v.

COLLINS, John. Private who was enrolled by Capt. Henry Hardman and passed on July 19, 1776 in Frederick (now Washington) County [Ref: D-51].

COLLINS, Patrick. Private who was recruited and passed by County Lieutenant Thomas Sprigg on April 22, 1780 [Ref: D-336].

COLLINS, Thomas. Private who was enrolled by Capt. Henry Hardman and passed on July 19, 1776 in Frederick (now Washington) County [Ref: D-51].

COLLYER (COLLIER), Isaac Jr. Took the Oath of Allegiance before the Hon. Lemuel Barritt before March 16, 1778 [Ref: O-43, J-8]. Private, Militia, 1st Class, Capt. James Prather's Company, 3rd Battalion, 1776/1777 [Ref: M-242, which listed the name as "Isaac Colliar"].

COLLYER (COLLIER), Isaac Sr. Took the Oath of Allegiance before the Hon. Lemuel Barritt before March 16, 1778 [Ref: O-43, J-8].

COLLYER (COLLIER), Michael. Private, Militia, 3rd Class, Capt. James Prather's Company, 3rd Battalion, 1776/1777 [Ref: M-242].

COLSON, Charles. Private, Militia, 7th Class, Capt. Charles Clinton's Company, 1776/1777 [Ref: M-245, A-1146].

COMAN, John. Took the Oath of Allegiance before the Hon. Lemuel Barritt before March 16, 1778 [Ref: O-42, J-8].

COMGROME, Ludwick. Private, Militia, 4th Class, Capt. James Smith's Company, 2nd Battalion, 1776/1777 [Ref: M-240, A-1146].

COMMINS, John. Private, Militia, 4th Class, Capt. James Prather's Company, 3rd Battalion, 1776/1777 [Ref: M-242, which listed the name as "John Commings"]. Took the Oath of Allegiance before the Hon. John Stull in 1778 [Ref: O-46, J-10].

COMMINS, William. Took the Oath of Allegiance before the Hon. John Stull in 1778 [Ref: O-46, J-10].

COMP, George Adam (c1761-   ). Private, Pennsylvania Militia, pensioned in Allegany County, Maryland at $36.66 per year under the Act of June 7, 1832 retroactive to March 4, 1831 [Ref: R-45].

COMPTON, Eliakim. See "Robert Compton," q.v.

COMPTON, John. Private who was enrolled by Capt. Aeneas Campbell and passed by Major John Fulford on July 18, 1776 [Ref: D-49].

COMPTON, Robert (1764-1857). Messenger for Gen. George Washington. Born on August 26, 1764 in Woodbridge, Middlesex County, New Jersey (son of Eliakim Compton), he married Lydia Brown on May 29, 1799 in New Brunswick, New Jersey, and died on February 13, 1857 in Grantsville, Garrett County, Maryland [Ref: S-3165, being the SAR application of Charles Edward Hafer, Sr., of LaVale, Maryland, approved on November 8, 1991 (National No. 137888) and citing DAR National No. 190116 as a reference].

CONESTRICK, Frederick. See "Frederick Kenistrick," q.v.

CONKRY, William. Took the Oath of Allegiance before the Hon. Andrew Rentch before March 7, 1778 [Ref: O-52, J-15].

CONN, John. Third Corporal, Militia, Capt. Peter Beall's Company, 1st Battalion, 1776/1777 [Ref: M-240]. Rendered patriotic service in Hagerstown by providing shoes and leather to Capt. John Nelson's Company, continental service (Maryland Line), April, 1776 [Ref: Q-161]. Also see pension S17890 for possible connection to this John Conn or the one listed below [Ref: V-I:735].

CONN, John. Private, Militia, 6th Class, Capt. Conrad Nichodemus' Company, 2nd Battalion, 1776/1777 [Ref: A-1146, M-237, which listed the name as "John Cou(?)"]. Took the Oath of Allegiance before the Hon. Samuel Hughes on March 1, 1778 [Ref: O-33, which listed the name as "John Con"]. Fourth Corporal, Militia, Capt. John Kershner's Company, on duty guarding prisoners of war at Fort Frederick in 1778, discharged on June 21, 1778 [Ref: D-328].

CONN, Peter. Private, Select Militia, Capt. Adam Ott's Company, 1781 [Ref: M-238, A-1146].

CONN, Peter. Private, Militia, 3rd Class, Capt. Michael Fackler's Company, 1776/1777 [Ref: M-245, A-1146, which listed the name as "Peter Con"]. Third Corporal, Militia, Capt. John Kershner's Company, on duty guarding prisoners of war at Fort Frederick on June 27, 1778 [Ref: D-328].

CONNELLY, Hugh. Private, Hazen's Regiment, who resided in Washington County and was granted a pension certificate in August, 1820, according to an Act of Congress of March 18, 1818, since he had proven that he was "in the enjoyment of a certain degree of poverty" as required by the Act as amended on May 1, 1820 [Ref: W-1190]. In December, 1816 the Treasurer of the Western Shore of Maryland was directed to pay to Hugh Connelly, Sr., of Washington County, late a private in the Revolutionary War, quarterly, during his life, the half pay of a private, as a further remuneration to him for his services during the struggle of his country for independence [Ref: AA-330].

CONNER, David. Private, Militia, 2nd Class, Capt. John Bennet's Company, 1776/1777 [Ref: M-246, A-1146].

CONNER, David. Private, Militia, 8th Class, Capt. John Cellars' Company, 1776/1777 [Ref: A-1146, M-247].

CONNER, David. Private, Militia, 4th Class, Capt. Martin Kershner's Company, 1776/1777 [Ref: A-1146, M-247].

CONNER, Timothy. Private, Militia, 3rd Class, Capt. Charles Clinton's Company, 1776/1777 [Ref: M-245, A-1146]. Private, Militia, Capt. Charles Coulson's Company, enrolled August 28, 1776 [Ref: M-244, A-1146]. Took the Oath of Allegiance before the Hon. Andrew Bruce before March 2, 1778 [Ref: O-41, J-6, which listed the name as "Timothy Connar"].

CONNER, William. Private, Militia, 1st Class, Capt. Henry Boteler's Company, 1776/1777 [Ref: M-237, A-1146]. Took the Oath of Allegiance before the Hon. Henry Schnebley in 1778 [Ref: O-49, J-13].

CONNER, William. Private, Militia, 3rd Class, Capt. Michael Fackler's Company, 1776/1777 [Ref: M-245, A-1146]. Took the Oath of Allegiance before the Hon. Henry Schnebley in 1778 [Ref: O-49, J-13].

CONRAD, Anna Maria. See "John Conrad," q.v.

CONRAD, Daniel. Third Corporal, Militia, Capt. James Walling's Company, 2nd Battalion, 1776/1777 [Ref: M-238, A-1146, which listed the name as "Daniel Conrod"]. Took the Oath of Allegiance before the Hon. John Stull in 1778 [Ref: O-46, J-10].

CONRAD, George. Private, Militia, 5th Class, Capt. Peter Swingle's (Swingley's) Company, 1776/1777 [Ref: A-1146, M-248, which listed the name as "George Conrod"].

CONRAD, Henry. Private, Militia, 8th Class, Capt. James Prather's Company, 3rd Battalion, 1776/1777 [Ref: M-243, which listed the name as "Henry Conrod"]. Took the Oath of Allegiance before the Hon. Lemuel Barritt before March 16, 1778 [Ref: O-43, J-8].

CONRAD, John (1729-1787). Took the Oath of Allegiance before the Hon. John Stull in 1778 [Ref: O-46]. "Johannes Conrad" was born on December 25, 1729, died on April 2, 1787, and is buried beside Anna Maria Conrad (1736-1817) in the Funkstown Public Cemetery in Washington County, Maryland [Ref: JJ-IV:6].

CONRAD, John. Took the Oath of Allegiance before the Hon. John Stull in 1778 [Ref: O-46, J-10, which latter source listed the name as "John Canrad"].

CONRAD, William. Ensign, Militia, Capt. Peter Beall's Company, 1st Battalion, January 15, 1777 [Ref: C-42, C-50, M-240, which latter two sources listed the name as "William Conrod"]. Ensign, Militia, Capt. John Kershner's Company, on duty guarding prisoners of war at Fort Frederick on June 27, 1778 [Ref: D-328, which listed the name as "Wm. Conrod"]. Took the Oath of Allegiance before the Hon. Joseph Sprigg before April 1, 1778 [Ref: O-53, J-16].

CONSELLA, Hermon. Private who was enlisted by Lieut. Christian Orndorff and passed on July 20, 1776 in Frederick (now Washington) County [Ref: D-50].

CONSTABLE, John. Private, Militia, 2nd Class, Capt. James Prather's Company, 3rd Battalion, 1776/1777 [Ref: M-242]. Took the Oath of Allegiance before the Hon. Andrew Bruce before March 2, 1778 [Ref: O-41, J-7].

CONSTABLE, Stephen. Private, Militia, 7th Class, Capt. James Prather's Company, 3rd Battalion, 1776/1777 [Ref: M-243]. Took the Oath of Allegiance before the Hon. Andrew Bruce before March 2, 1778 [Ref: O-41, J-6].

CONSTABLE, Thomas. Private, Militia, 5th Class, Capt. James Prather's Company, 3rd Battalion, 1776/1777 [Ref: M-243]. Took the Oath of Allegiance before the Hon. Andrew Bruce before March 2, 1778 [Ref: O-41, J-6].

CONSTABLE, Thomas. Private, Militia, 1st Class, Capt. Samuel Hughes' Company, 2nd Battalion, 1776/1777 [Ref: M-238, A-1146, which listed the name as "Thomas Cunstable"].

COOGLE, Christian. Rendered patriotic service by providing a rifle for Capt. Daniel Cresap's Company in July, 1775, as recorded by the Committee of Observation at Elizabeth Town on November 4, 1775 [Ref: Q-149]. Private, Militia, 6th Class, Capt. Peter Swingle's (Swingley's) Company, 1776/1777 [Ref: A-1146, M-248, which listed the name as "Christian Crugle"].

COOGLE, John. See "John Koogle," q.v.

COOKE, Susan F. See "Otho Holland Williams," q.v.

COON, Adam. Private, Militia, Capt. John Kershner's Company, on duty guarding prisoners of war at Fort Frederick until discharged on June 5, 1778 [Ref: D-328].

COON, Christian. Private, Maryland Line. He applied for and received pension S34712 in Washington County, Maryland on May 19, 1819, aged

68 or 69. In 1820 his wife (not named) was aged about 70 and they lived with one of their sons (not named). [Ref: V-I:756].

COONE, David. Second Corporal, Militia, Capt. Martin Kershner's Company, 1776/1777 [Ref: M-247, A-1146]. Took the Oath of Allegiance before the Hon. Henry Schnebley in 1778 [Ref: O-50, J-14].

COONSE, Henry. Private who was enlisted by Capt. John Reynolds and passed on July 18, 1776 in Frederick (now Washington) County [Ref: D-50].

COOPER, Isaac. One of several patriots appointed by the Committee of Observation on January 7, 1777 "to form the county into companies (after the militia had marched) for the purpose of relieving the distressed inhabitants of said county and also to compel the Dunkards and Mennonists to give their assistance." [Ref: Q-31]. Took the Oath of Allegiance before the Hon. John Stull in 1778 [Ref: O-46, J-10].

COPELAND, Elizabeth. See "David Lynn, Sr.," q.v.

COPLAR, Barnabas. Private, Pennsylvania Line, who received bounty land warrant #628-100 on March 8, 1814, with affidavits signed by Adam Ott of Washington County, Maryland on February 4, 1814 and Angus McDeaver of Berkeley County, Virginia on October 19, 1813 [Ref: V-I:763].

CORDRY, Thomas. Private, Militia, 8th Class, Capt. Charles Clinton's Company, 1776/1777 [Ref: M-245, A-1146]. Second Corporal, Militia, Capt. Charles Clinton's Company, 1776/1777 [Ref: M-245, A-1146]. Took the Oath of Allegiance before the Hon. Andrew Bruce before March 2, 1778 [Ref: O-41, J-7, which listed the name as "Thomas Cardry"].

CORE, Christian. One of several patriots appointed by the Committee of Observation on December 30, 1776 "to form the county into companies (after the militia had marched) for the purpose of relieving the distressed inhabitants of said county and also to compel the Dunkards and Mennonists to give their assistance." [Ref: Q-346, which listed the name as "Christian Kore"]. Took the Oath of Allegiance before the Hon. Henry Schnebley in 1778 [Ref: O-50, J-14]. Private, Militia, 2nd Class, Capt. Martin Kershner's Company, 1776/1777 [Ref: A-1146, M-247].

CORLEY, George (1747-). Private, Maryland Line. He applied for and received pension S9199 in Washington County, Maryland on August 11, 1835, aged 88, a resident of Franklin County, Pennsylvania. He stated he was born in Germany in 1747, lived in Washington County at the time of his enlistment, and moved to Franklin County in 1815 [Ref: V-I:768].

CORMAN, George. Private, Militia, 6th Class, Capt. Henry Boteler's Company, 1776/1777 [Ref: M-237, A-1146].

CORROWFLOW, George. See "George Colleyflour," q.v.

CORTS, Christopher. Private who was enlisted by Capt. John Reynolds and passed on July 18, 1776 in Frederick (now Washington) County [Ref: D-50, which listed the name as "Christopher Curts (Cortz)"].

CORTS, Michael. Private who was enlisted by Ensign Nathan Williams and passed on July 25, 1776 in Frederick (now Washington) County [Ref: D-51, which listed the name as "Michael Cortz"]. Private, Militia, 6th Class, Capt. Henry Boteler's Company, 1776/1777 [Ref: M-237, A-1146].

CORTS, Stophel. Private, Militia, 4th Class, Capt. Henry Boteler's Company, 1776/1777 [Ref: M-237, A-1146].

COSSART, David. Private, Militia, 4th Class, Capt. James Prather's Company, 3rd Battalion, 1776/1777 [Ref: M-242].

COSSERT, Daniel. Private, Militia, 5th Class, Capt. John Cellars' Company, 1776/1777 [Ref: A-1146, M-246].

COTZ, Mrs. See "Catharine Kotz," q.v.

COULSON, Charles. Captain, Militia, by December 3, 1776 [Ref: M-243, M-59, B-501, which latter source listed the name as "Charles Calson"]. Captain, Militia, "on frontier" by May 13, 1778 [Ref: M-65, E-80, which listed the name as "Charles Coulston"]. Took the Oath of Allegiance before the Hon. Andrew Bruce before March 2, 1778 [Ref: O-41, J-6].

COULTER, Major. See "Thomas Chenoweth," q.v.

COUNTRYMAN, Henry. See "Henry Guntryman," q.v.

COVE, John. Private who was enlisted by Ensign Nathan Williams and passed on July 25, 1776 in Frederick (now Washington) County [Ref: D-51, which listed the name as "John Eove (Cove?)"].

COW, Davoll. Private, Militia, 2nd Class, Capt. Daniel Clapsaddle's Company, 1st Battalion, 1776/1777 [Ref: M-236, A-1146].

COW, Frederick. Private, Militia, 4th Class, Capt. Daniel Clapsaddle's Company, 1st Battalion, 1776/1777 [Ref: M-236, A-1146].

COW, Henry. Private, Militia, 2nd Class, Capt. Isaac Baker's Company, 1776/1777 [Ref: A-1146, M-247]. Took the Oath of Allegiance before the Hon. John Barnes before February 28, 1778 [Ref: O-44, J-9].

COW, Jacob. Private, Militia, 8th Class, Capt. Isaac Baker's Company, 1776/1777 [Ref: A-1146, M-247].

COW, Nicholas. Private, Militia, 7th Class, Capt. John Cellars' Company, 1776/1777 [Ref: A-1146, M-246, which listed the name as "Nicholas Caw"].

COWEN, William. Private, Militia, 7th Class, Capt. James Prather's Company, 3rd Battalion, 1776/1777 [Ref: M-243].

COWMAN, Jacob. Private, Militia, 4th Class, Capt. Jacob Sharer's Company, 1776/1777 [Ref: A-1146, M-248].

COX, Abraham. Third Sergeant, Militia, Capt. Barnett Johnston's Company, 1776. Second Lieutenant, Militia, Capt. Philip Pindell's Company, 3rd or Western Battalion, May 16, 1778 [Ref: M-65, M-242, E-86]. "Abram Cox" took the Oath of Allegiance before the Hon. William Yates in 1778 [Ref: O-48, J-12]. See "Ezekiel Cox," q.v.

COX, Daniel and Elmer. See "Isaac Cox," q.v.

COX, Ezekiel. Appointed to raise funds on January 24, 1775 for the Committee of Observation in Fort Frederick Hundred in Frederick (now Washington) County [Ref: L-75]. Elected to serve on the Committee of Observation for the Elizabeth Town District (now the Hagerstown area of Washington County) on September 12, 1775 [Ref: Q-142, which listed the name as "Zekiel Cox"]. Took the Oath of Allegiance on June 7, 1777 [Ref: K-1814, Box 4]. One Ezekiel Cox died testate before August 12, 1783 (date of balance book entry in Washington County), leaving a widow and children (none named), with Abraham Cox as executor [Ref: J-25].

COX, Isaac. Private, Militia, 2nd Class, Capt. Barnett Johnston's Company, 3rd Battalion, 1776/1777 [Ref: M-242]. Took the Oath of Allegiance before the Hon. William Yates in 1778 [Ref: O-48, J-12]. Private, Maryland Line, who applied for and received pension S32186 in Rush County, Indiana on September 22, 1832, aged 77, a resident of Noble Township. He stated he enlisted in Washington County (the part that was formerly Frederick County) and since 1816 he had neither a wife nor children. Also mentioned were Jacob Cox (of Hamilton County, Ohio in 1826), Daniel Cox (postmaster at Pleasant Ridge in Rush County, Indiana in 1828), and Rev. Elmer H. Cox (of Rush County, Indiana in 1833), but no relationships were given [Ref: V-I:788].

COX, Jacob. Private, Militia, 4th Class, Capt. Barnett Johnston's Company, 3rd Battalion, 1776/1777 [Ref: M-242]. Took the Oath of Allegiance before the Hon. William Yates in 1778 [Ref: O-48, J-12]. See "Isaac Cox," q.v.

COX, John. One of several patriots appointed by the Committee of Observation on January 7, 1777 "to form the county into companies (after the militia had marched) for the purpose of relieving the distressed inhabitants of said county and also to compel the Dunkards and Mennonists to give their assistance." [Ref: Q-31].

COY, John Jr. Private, Militia, 6th Class, Capt. Daniel Cresap's Company, 3rd Battalion, 1776/1777 [Ref: M-241]. Took the Oath of Allegiance before the Hon. Lemuel Barritt before March 16, 1778 [Ref: O-43, J-8].

COY, John Sr. First Sergeant, Militia, Capt. Daniel Cresap's Company, 3rd Battalion, 1776/1777 [Ref: M-241]. Took the Oath of Allegiance before the Hon. Lemuel Barritt before March 16, 1778 [Ref: O-42, J-8].

COYLE, Mark (c1755-   ). Soldier who resided in Washington County and was granted a pension certificate in August, 1820, according to an Act of Congress of March 18, 1818, since he had proven that he was "in the enjoyment of a certain degree of poverty" as required by the Act as amended on May 1, 1820 [Ref: W-1190]. Private, Pennsylvania Line, pensioned at $96 per year effective November 4, 1818 [Ref: R-42]. Resided in the 4th District of Washington County in 1840, aged 85 [Ref: EE-28:4 (p. 442), containing an article by Elba Anthony Dardeau, Jr., which listed the name as "Mark Coil"].

CRABTREE, William. Private, Militia, 6th Class, Capt. Griffin Johnson's Company, 3rd Battalion, 1776/1777 [Ref: M-243].

CRAFORT, John. Took the Oath of Allegiance before the Hon. John Cellars in January, 1778 [Ref: K-1814, O-40, J-6].

CRAFT (CROFT), Frederick. Private, Militia, Capt. John Kershner's Company, on duty guarding prisoners of war at Fort Frederick on June 27, 1778 [Ref: D-328, which listed the name as "Frederick Craft"]. Private, Militia, 3rd Class, Capt. Peter Beall's Company, 1st Battalion, 1776/1777 [Ref: M-240, which listed the name as "Frederick Croft"]. Took the Oath of Allegiance before the Hon. Henry Schnebley in 1778 [Ref: O-51, which listed the name as "Frederick Grooft" and J-15, which listed the name as "Frederick Krooft"].

CRAFT (CROFT), John. Private, Militia, Capt. William Heyser's Company, enlisted July 27, 1776, muster roll dated October 23, 1776, in continental service [Ref: W-1190, L-79, D-264, which listed the name as "John Crafft"]. Private, German Regiment, Lt. Col. Ludwick Weltner's Company, discharged on July 24 or 26, 1779 at Fort Wyoming, Pennsylvania [Ref: D-265, W-1190, L-79, D-198, which listed the name as "John Croft" and GG-97, which listed the name as "John Crafft, Croft, Kroft, Kraft"].

CRAFT (CROFT), Peter. Private, Militia, 2nd Class, Capt. Peter Beall's Company, 1st Battalion, 1776/1777 [Ref: M-240].

CRAFT (CROFT), William. Corporal, German Regiment, continental service, 1776. Private, Third Vacant Company, under Capt. Philip Graybell and Col. Lewis Weltner at Valley Forge in March, 1778. Discharged on July 26, 1779 [Ref: D-198, which listed the name as "William Croft or Kraft" and FF-222, which listed the name as "William Craft"].

CRAGG, James. Private, Militia, 4th Class, Capt. James Prather's Company, 3rd Battalion, 1776/1777 [Ref: M-242]. Took the Oath of Allegiance before the Hon. Lemuel Barritt before March 16, 1778 [Ref: O-43, J-8, which listed the name as "James Crage"].

CRAIG, Philip (c1755-1824). Took the Oath of Allegiance before the Hon. John Barnes before February 28, 1778 [Ref: O-45, J-9]. Private, Militia, 3rd Class, Capt. Isaac Baker's Company, 1776/1777 [Ref: A-1146, M-247, which listed the name as "Phillip Creag"]. Private, Militia, Capt. John Kershner's Company, on duty guarding prisoners of war at Fort Frederick until discharged on June 14, 1778 [Ref: D-328, which listed the name as "Phillip Creigh"]. "Philip Kriegh, farmer" died in Washington County on February 19, 1824, at an advanced age [Ref: Z-66]. See "Philip Krick," q.v.

CRALE, James. Private who was enrolled by Capt. Henry Hardman and passed on July 19, 1776 in Frederick (now Washington) County [Ref: D-51].

CRALE, William. Private who was enrolled by Capt. Henry Hardman and passed on July 19, 1776 in Frederick (now Washington) County [Ref: D-51]. Took the Oath of Allegiance before the Hon. John Stull in 1778 [Ref: O-46, J-10, which latter source listed the name as "William Creal(?)"].

CRAMER, Peter. Private who enlisted in the militia on August 17, 1781 for service in the Continental Army [Ref: D-388]. Substitute, Maryland Line, discharged on October 30, 1781 [Ref: G-656].

CRAMPTON, Abraham and Ann. See "Thomas Crampton," q.v.

CRAMPTON, Elias, Elisha and Elizabeth. See "Thomas Crampton," q.v.

CRAMPTON, John, Josiah and Joshua. See "Thomas Crampton," q.v.

CRAMPTON, Ruth and Sarah Anne. See "Thomas Crampton," q.v.

CRAMPTON, Ozias (Hosias). Enrolled in the first militia company organized for the Revolutionary War in the Elizabeth Town District of Frederick County (now the Hagerstown area of Washington County) on January 6, 1776 [Ref: Q-270, W-1189, which listed the name as "Hosias Crampton"]. Private, Militia, 6th Class, Capt. Joseph Chapline's Company, 2nd Battalion, 1776/1777 [Ref: M-241, which listed the name as "Ozias Crampton"]. Took the Oath of Allegiance before the Hon. Joseph Chapline before April 17, 1779 [Ref: J-5, O-39, which listed the name as "Ozias Cramphin"].

CRAMPTON, Thomas (1735-1819). Appointed by the Committee of Observation to carry the Association of Freemen to male residents in Lower Antietam Hundred on September 14, 1775 "and require their subscription to the same and make an exact account of those who sign and those that refuse with their reasons for refusing." [Ref: Q-143]. Enrolled in the first militia company organized for the Revolutionary War in the Elizabeth Town District of Frederick County (now the Hagerstown area of Washington County) on January 6, 1776 [Ref: Q-270, W-1189]. Appointed to raise funds on January 24, 1775 for the Committee of Observation in Lower Antietam Hundred in Frederick (now Washington) County [Ref: L-75, which listed the name as "Thomas Cramphin"]. Took the Oath of Allegiance before the Hon. Joseph Chapline before April 17, 1779 [Ref: J-5, O-39]. Ensign, Select Militia, Capt. Joseph Chapline's Company, March 30, 1781 [Ref: M-66, G-368, which listed the name as "Thomas Cramplim"]. Second Lieutenant, Militia, Capt. Joseph Chapline's Company, 2nd Battalion, June 22, 1778. Lieutenant, Select Militia, Capt. Joseph Chapline's Company, June 4, 1781 [Ref: M-66, M-241, E-145, G-459]. The heirs of Thomas Crampton, late of Washington County, deceased in May, 1819, are listed in an equity court case in 1822. The children were: Elias Crampton, John Crampton, Josiah Crampton (all in Washington County, Maryland), Ruth Jackson (wife of Thomas Jackson) in Virginia, Mary Wood (widow of Joseph Wood) in Kentucky, and Elizabeth Keller (widow of Joseph Keller) in Washington County, Maryland. The grandchildren (children of Joshua Crampton, deceased) were: Elisha Crampton (in Ohio), Joseph Crampton, Mary Anne Rotrock (wife of Samuel Rotrock), Elizabeth Crampton, Sarah Anne Crampton (minor), Abraham Crampton (minor), John Crampton (minor), and Ruth Crampton (minor), all of Washington County, Maryland [Ref: Z-39, Z-40]. Ann Mary Maria Crampton, relict of the late Thomas Crampton, one of the earliest inhabitants of Pleasant Valley, died on August 28, 1825, in her 86th year. Elias Crampton, a resident of Pleasant Valley, died on October 6, 1825, in his 64th year [Ref: Z-76]. Thomas Crampton, the soldier, was born on July 4, 1735, married Maria Sabboth, and died on May 20, 1819 [Ref: Y-I:695].

CRAMPTON, Thomas (c1756-c1830). Private, Maryland Line, pensioned under Act of March 18, 1818 at $96 per year effective April 2, 1818 and "transferred from D. C. September 5, 1825 from September 4, 1825." [Ref: R-42].

CRAPP, John. See "John Cropp," q.v.

CRATON, James. Private, Militia, 6th Class, Capt. Jacob Sharer's Company, 1776/1777 [Ref: A-1146, M-248].

CRATON, Robert. Took the Oath of Allegiance before the Hon. John Stull in 1778 [Ref: O-46, J-10, which listed the name as "Robert Craturn"]. Ensign, Militia, Capt. Martin Billmyer's Company, 2nd Battalion, November 21, 1780 [Ref: G-220].

CRAUNER, Ernest. Took the Oath of Allegiance before the Hon. Joseph Sprigg before April 1, 1778 [Ref: O-53, J-16, which latter source listed the name as "Adam Craurer"].
CRAVENS, John and Ruhamah. See "Jeremiah Chapline," q.v.
CRAVER, Jacob. Private, Militia, 3rd Class, Capt. Peter Beall's Company, 1st Battalion, 1776/1777 [Ref: M-240]. Corporal, Select Militia, Capt. Adam Ott's Company, 1781 [Ref: M-238, A-1146].
CRAVER, John. First Corporal, Militia, Capt. John Kershner's Company, on duty guarding prisoners of war at Fort Frederick on June 27, 1778 [Ref: D-328].
CRAWFORD, Colonel. See "Thomas Chenoweth," q.v.
CREAGER, Christena. See "John Kausler," q.v.
CREAMER, Daniel. Fourth Sergeant, Militia, Capt. Peter Swingle's (Swingley's) Company, 2nd Battalion, 1776/1777 [Ref: M-248, A-1146].
CREAMER, Godfrey. First Corporal, Militia, Capt. Peter Swingle's (Swingley's) Company, 2nd Battalion, 1776/1777 [Ref: M-248, A-1146].
CREAMER, Peter. See "Peter Cramer," q.v.
CREEBUM, Adam. See "Philip Creekbaum," q.v.
CREEKBAUM, Philip (1758-1826). Private, Militia, 7th Class, Capt. Peter Beall's Company, 1st Battalion, 1776/1777 [Ref: M-240, which listed the name as "Phillip Creeybam(?)"]. Private, Militia, Capt. William Heyser's Company, muster roll dated October 23, 1776, in continental service and on duty in May, 1777 [Ref: GG-97, D-264, which listed the name as "Phillip Greechbaum" and W-1190, which listed the name as "Phillip Greekbawn" and L-79, which listed the name as "Phillip Greechbawm"]. Took the Oath of Allegiance before the Hon. Henry Schnebley in 1778 [Ref: O-51, which listed the name as "Philip Kreihbawm" and J-15, which listed the name as "Philip Kreibbaum"]. "Phillip Creekbaum" applied for and received pension S40860 in Fayette County, Pennsylvania on September 8, 1818, age 60, stating he enlisted in June or July, 1776 at Hagerstown, Maryland and served three years in the German Regiment. He participated in the Battles of Trenton, Princeton, Brandywine and Germantown. In 1820 he referred to his wife, two sons and four daughters (no names were given). Philip married Catherine Jolly (no date given) and died on March 2, 1826 [Ref: U-33:2 (1945), Y-I:704]. One "Adam Creebum" died before June 8, 1779 (date of balance book entry in Washington County) and one of his sons was "Philip Creebum." [Ref: J-22].
CREGER, Peter. Private, Militia, 1st Class, Capt. Jacob Sharer's Company, 1776/1777 [Ref: A-1146, M-248]. See "Peter Kreuger," q.v.
CREIGH, Phillip. See "Philip Craig," q.v.

CRESAP, Daniel (1728-1798). Took the Oath of Allegiance before the Hon. Lemuel Barritt before March 16, 1778 [Ref: O-42, J-7, which listed the name as "Daniel Cresop"]. Daniel Cresap, Sr., son of Thomas, was born on February 29, 1728 and died in July, 1798 [Ref: Y-I:705].

CRESAP, Daniel Jr. (1753-1794). Captain, Militia, Upper District, Frederick County, July 27, 1776. Captain, Militia, Washington County, "on frontier" by May 13, 1778. Captain, Militia, 3rd Battalion, June 22, 1778 [Ref: M-66, M-241, B-127, E-80, E-145]. Took the Oath of Allegiance before the Hon. Lemuel Barritt before March 16, 1778 [Ref: J-7, O-42, which listed the name as "Daniel Cresop Jnr"]. Daniel Cresap, Jr. was born in 1753, married Elizabeth Van Swearingen, and died on December 11, 1794 [Ref: Y-I:705, which listed his rank as lieutenant].

CRESAP, Elizabeth. See "Michael Cresap" and "Thomas Cresap," q.v.

CRESAP, Joseph (1755-1827). Private, Militia, 7th Class, Capt. Daniel Cresap's Company, 3rd Battalion, 1776/1777 [Ref: M-241, which listed the name as "Joseph Creysop"]. Took the Oath of Allegiance before the Hon. Lemuel Barritt before March 16, 1778 [Ref: O-42, J-7, which listed the name as "Joseph Cresop"]. On September 23, 1780, Col. Lemuel Barritt recommended to Governor Lee that "Joseph Crisop" be commissioned a captain in the militia at "Oper Old Town" since so many officers in the Western Battalion had moved out of Maryland to Kentucky and elsewhere [Ref: G-123]. On February 19, 1819 the Treasurer of the Western Shore of Maryland was directed to pay to Joseph Cresap, a sum of money equal to the half pay of a lieutenant, during his life, as a further remuneration for his services during the Revolutionary War. On February 23, 1822 it was recorded that Joseph Cresap, of Allegany County, a pensioner said to be wealthy, was living in affluence, therefore the resolution awarding him a pension was rescinded. On March 3, 1826, it was recorded that "whereas, from losses sustained by the said Joseph Cresap in consequence of endorsing for others in the Cumberland Bank of Allegany he is now greatly embarrassed, and has a large family to support" the Treasurer of the Western Shore of Maryland was directed to pay to Joseph Cresap, of Allegany County, half pay of a lieutenant, for life, as a further compensation for his services in the Revolutionary War [Ref: AA-331, AA-332]. The death notice of "Col. Joseph Cresap" appeared in the *Maryland Gazette* in Annapolis on January 24, 1827, noting his death on January 20, 1827 and his military services and his career in the Maryland Senate and House of Delegates. *The Torchlight and Public Advertiser* in Hagerstown on January 25, 1827 also reported the death of "Joseph Cresap, Esq., at an advanced age" at the residence of his daughter (not named, but stated she was the widow of the late James Scott) in Cumberland, but no date of death was given [Ref: Z-88]. Joseph Cresap married four times: (1) Deborah Whitehead; (2) Sarah Whitehead; (3) Sidney Sanford; (4) Margaret Bunce [Ref: Y-I:705, which stated he died on January 24, 1827]. See "John Jeremiah Jacob," q.v.

CRESAP, Mary. See "Michael Cresap," q.v.

CRESAP, Michael (1742-1775). Born in the part of Frederick County that later became Washington County, Michael was the youngest son of Col. Thomas Cresap. He served with his father in the French and Indian War in 1756, after which he established a colony on the Ohio River below Wheeling, (West) Virginia in 1774. Michael married Mary Whitehead, of Philadelphia and had five children. At the beginning of the Revolutionary War he was appointed captain of one of the two companies formed in the western part of Frederick (now Washington) County. He returned home to Maryland and led his riflemen to join Gen. George Washington at Boston. After a short period of active service there, he was taken ill and obtained sick leave. On his way home he died in New York and was buried in the old Trinity Churchyard [Ref: L-78]. The final account of the estate of Capt. Michael Cresap was entered in the balance book of Washington County on October 12, 1790 and mentioned his widow's thirds (name not given) and equal shares to Mary, Elizabeth and Sarah Cresap [Ref: J-30]. Michael Cresap was born on June 29, 1742 and died on October 18, 1775 [Ref: Y-I:705]. This latter source also lists a Michael Cresap who was born in 1750, served as a captain in Maryland and Virginia, married Elizabeth Whitehead, and died on September 30, 1788 [Ref: Y-I:706]. Additional research will be necessary before drawing conclusions. See "John Jeremiah Jacob," q.v.

CRESAP, Sarah. See "Michael Cresap" and "Thomas Cresap," q.v.

CRESAP, Thomas (1694-1788 or 1703-1790). Elected to serve on the Committee of Observation for the Elizabeth Town District (now the Hagerstown area of Washington County) on September 12, 1775 [Ref: Q-142]. On March 4, 1776 the Committee of Observation ordered an election to find replacements for "Coll. Thos. Cresap" and five others [Ref: Q-154]. Took the Oath of Allegiance before the Hon. Lemuel Barritt before March 16, 1778 [Ref: O-43, J-8, which listed the name as "Thomas Cresop"]. Sources differ as to his date of birth and date of death, but agree that he was born in Skipton, Yorkshire, England. He married first to Hannah Johnson and second to Mrs. Margaret Milburn. Thomas was extremely active on the western frontier and earned the respect of influential Maryland officials. The Pennsylvanians, however, viewed him as the "Maryland Monster." His children were Daniel, Thomas (killed by Indians in 1756), Michael (captain in the Revolutionary War), Elizabeth, and Sarah [Ref: Y-I:706, KK-I:244, which contains more detailed information].

CRETZEN, Leonard. Private, Militia, 5th Class, Capt. Conrad Nichodemus' Company, 2nd Battalion, 1776/1777 [Ref: M-237, A-1146].

CRILEY, Francis. Private, Militia, 1st Class, Capt. Peter Beall's Company, 1st Battalion, 1776/1777 [Ref: M-240, which listed the name as "Francis Cryley"].

CRILEY, Harmon. Private, Militia, 5th Class, Capt. Peter Beall's Company, 1st Battalion, 1776/1777 [Ref: M-240].

CRITES, George. Took the Oath of Allegiance before the Hon. Richard Davis in 1778 [Ref: J-4, O-37].

CROFT, John. See "John Craft (Croft)," q.v.

CROPP (GROOP), John. Private, Militia, Capt. William Heyser's Company, enlisted August 11, 1776, muster roll dated October 23, 1776, continental service. Private, German Regiment, Lt. Col. Ludwick Weltner's Company, discharged on July 26, 1779 at Fort Wyoming, Pennsylvania [Ref: D-264, W-1190, L-79, which latter source listed the name as "John Crapp" and GG-97, which listed the name as "John Cropp, Groop, Grupp" and D-265, which listed the name as "John Groop"].

CROSBY, James (1741-1835). Private, Maryland Line. He applied for and received pension S11339 in Perry County, Ohio on November 8, 1832, a resident of Clayton Township, stating he was born on July 25, 1741 in County Westmeath, Ireland and came to America at age 24 or 25. He lived about 2 miles from Hagerstown, Maryland at the time of his enlistment. In 1791 he moved to Bedford County, Pennsylvania where he lived for 25 years and then moved to Ohio in 1816. He died on June 3, 1835 [Ref: V-I:822].

CROSS, John. First Corporal, Militia, Capt. James Smith's Company, 2nd Battalion, 1776/1777 [Ref: M-239, A-1146].

CROSS, Thomas. Private, Militia, 1st Class, Capt. Daniel Clapsaddle's Company, 1st Battalion, 1776/1777 [Ref: M-236, A-1146].

CROSSEN, John. Took the Oath of Allegiance before the Hon. John Barnes before February 28, 1778 [Ref: J-9, O-44, which latter source listed the name as "John Chrossen"].

CROSSLEY, James (1741-   ). Private, Militia, 4th Class, Capt. James Smith's Company, 2nd Battalion, 1776/1777 [Ref: M-240, A-1146, N-17, which latter source listed the name as "James Crosley"]. Ensign, Capt.

Christopher Orendorff's Company, 2nd Battalion, November 21, 1780 [Ref: G-220].

CROSSLEY, Moses (1764-1843). Drummer and private in the militia; married Rachel Powell in Washington County on May 1, 1784 [Ref: N-17, N-112, which listed the name as "Moses Crosely"]. Moses Crosley or Crossley was born in Maryland on January 2, 1764 and died in Ohio on March 13, 1843 [Ref: Y-I:716].

CROSSLEY, Sarah. See "William Crossley," q.v.

CROSSLEY, William (1761-   ). Private, Militia, 2nd Class, Capt. James Smith's Company, 2nd Battalion, 1776/1777 [Ref: M-239, A-1146, N-17, which latter source listed the name as "William Crosley"]. One William Crosely or Crossley was a marine on the State Ship *Defence* in 1777 [Ref: D-655]. William Crosley or Crossley was born in Maryland on October 5, 1761, married Sarah ----, and died in Ohio on September 7, 1839 [Ref: Y-I:716].

CROW, Jacob. Private, Militia, 7th Class, Capt. Charles Clinton's Company, 1776/1777 [Ref: M-245, A-1146]. Private, Militia, Capt. Charles Coulson's Company, enrolled August 28, 1776 [Ref: M-244, A-1146].

CROW, John. Private, Militia, 3rd Class, Capt. Charles Clinton's Company, 1776/1777 [Ref: M-245, A-1146]. Private, Militia, Capt. Charles Coulson's Company, enrolled August 28, 1776 [Ref: M-244, A-1146].

CROW, Mathias. Private, Militia, 7th Class, Capt. Isaac Baker's Company, 1776/1777 [Ref: A-1146, M-247].

CROW, Philip. Private, Militia, Capt. Charles Coulson's Company, enrolled August 28, 1776 [Ref: M-244, A-1146]. Two men by this name took the Oath of Allegiance before the Hon. Lemuel Barritt before March 16, 1778 [Ref: O-42, O-43, J-7, J-8, which latter source listed the name as "Philop Crow"].

CROWLEY, William. Took the Oath of Allegiance before the Hon. Richard Davis in 1778 [Ref: J-4, O-36].

CRUGLE, Christian. See "Christian Coogle," q.v.

CRUMMY, Andrew. Enrolled in the first militia company organized for the Revolutionary War in the Elizabeth Town District of Frederick County (now the Hagerstown area of Washington County) on January 6, 1776 [Ref: Q-271, W-1190].

CRUMMY, Robert. Private, Militia, 1st Class, Capt. John Rennolds' (Reynolds') Company, 2nd Battalion, 1776/1777 [Ref: M-240].

CRUSE, Christopher (doctor). Justice who administered the Oath of Allegiance in Sharpsburg and Lower Antietam Hundreds in 1778 [Ref:

J-1, J-2, O-35, O-36, which listed the name as "Chrs. Cruso"]. One of several patriots appointed by the Committee of Observation on January 7, 1777 "to form the county into companies (after the militia had marched) for the purpose of relieving the distressed inhabitants of said county and also to compel the Dunkards and Mennonists to give their assistance." [Ref: Q-31, which listed the name as "Doctr. Cruss"]. Appointed by the Committee of Observation to carry the Association of Freemen to male residents in Lower Antietam Hundred on September 14, 1775 "and require their subscription to the same and make an exact account of those who sign and those that refuse with their reasons for refusing." [Ref: Q-143, which listed the name as "Dr. Cruse"]. Justice of the County Court, June 20, 1778 [Ref: E-141, which listed the name as "Christopher Cruse"]. Justice of the Peace, January 30, 1781 [Ref: G-293, which listed the name as "Christopher Cruise"].

CRUSE, Jacob. Fourth Corporal, Militia, Capt. John Cellars' Company, 1776/1777 [Ref: A-1146, M-246, which listed the name as "Jacob Crisse(?)"]. Private, Select Militia, Capt. Adam Ott's Company, 1781 [Ref: M-238, A-1146, which listed the name as "Jacob Cruiz"].

CRUSE, Peter. Private, German Regiment, continental service, 1776, and discharged on July 24, 1779 [Ref: D-222, which listed the name as "Peter Kruise"].

CRUTHERS, George. Private, Militia, 3rd Class, Capt. Isaac Baker's Company, 1776/1777 [Ref: A-1146, M-247].

CRUTSINGER, Jacob and Katherine. See "Solomon Crutsinger," q.v.

CRUTSINGER, Ludwick. See "Leonard Kretsinger," q.v.

CRUTSINGER (KRUTZINGER), Solomon (c1749-1837). Private, Maryland and Pennsylvania Lines; wounded (no date given). He applied for pension in Sullivan County, Tennessee circa 1833, aged 84, and died on May 17, 1837. His widow Katherine applied for and received pension W375 on April 11, 1844, aged 80 on June 21, 1844, stating she married Solomon on August 21, 1787. They had seven children, but only Jacob (born January 21, 1789) was mentioned and he stated his mother died on May 20, 1854 in Sullivan County [Ref: V-I:833, N-17].

CUGHS, Joseph. Private, Militia, 7th Class, Capt. Isaac Baker's Company, 1776/1777 [Ref: A-1146, M-247].

CULP, Henry. Private, Militia, 7th Class, Capt. John Cellars' Company, 1776/1777 [Ref: A-1146, M-246].

CULVER, Jonathan. Private, Militia, 8th Class, Capt. Daniel Cresap's Company, 3rd Battalion, 1776/1777 [Ref: M-241]. Took the Oath of Allegiance before the Hon. Lemuel Barritt before March 16, 1778 [Ref: O-42, J-7].

CUMMING, Robert (1753-1825). Obituary in Cumberland newspaper: "Revolutionary Hero gone! Died at his residence in Liberty-town, Monday evening November 14, 1825, Maj. General Robert Cumming, commander of the 2nd Division of Maryland Militia, in his 72nd year." [Ref: Z-7].

CUMMINGS, Juba. Took the Oath of Allegiance before the Hon. William Yates in 1778 [Ref: O-48, J-11].

CUMMINGS, William. Private, Militia, 7th Class, Capt. James Walling's Company, 2nd Battalion, 1776/1777 [Ref: M-239, A-1146].

CUNNINGHAM, James. Private who was enlisted by Lieut. Moses Chapline and passed on July 24, 1776 in Frederick (now Washington) County [Ref: D-50].

CURREN, John. Private, Militia, 1st Class, Capt. Samuel Hughes' Company, 2nd Battalion, 1776/1777 [Ref: M-238, A-1146].

CUSHWA, Benjamin and Elizabeth. See "John Cushwa," q.v.

CUSHWA, John (1731-1805). "Born in Burks County, Pennsylvania, 1731, he removed to and patented his homestead, "Cushwa's Establishment," in 1756; a Revolutionary patriot; assisted in forming Washington County, 1776." John Cushaw, his wife Elizabeth, and youngest son Benjamin Cushwa (1785-1848) are buried in a graveyard on the James Faith farm near Dry Run in Washington County, Maryland [Ref: JJ-II:22]. John Cushwa died testate by October 29, 1805 [Ref: MM-13:175].

CUSTER, George. Private, Militia, 5th Class, Capt. Jacob Sharer's Company, 1776/1777 [Ref: A-1146, M-248]. Took the Oath of Allegiance before the Hon. John Stull in 1778 [Ref: O-46, J-10, which listed the name as "George Custore"].

CYSTER, Daniel. Private, Militia, 2nd Class, Capt. Jacob Sharer's Company, 1776/1777 [Ref: A-1146, M-248]. Took the Oath of Allegiance before the Hon. John Stull in 1778 [Ref: O-47, J-11, which listed the name as "Daniel Syster"].

CYSTER, Henry (1757-c1840). Private, Militia, 4th Class, Capt. Jacob Sharer's Company, 1776/1777 [Ref: A-1146, M-248]. Private, Select Militia, Capt. Adam Ott's Company, 1781 [Ref: M-238, A-1146, which listed the name as "Henry Scyster"]. Private, Maryland Line, who applied for and received pension S8275 in Washington County on December 29, 1835, aged 78, a resident of Williamsport, Maryland. "Henry Cyester" stated he was born on August 28, 1757 at Reading in Berks County, Pennsylvania and when he was aged 9 his father moved to Frederick (now Washington) County, Maryland. After the war Henry moved to Pennsylvania for a few months, then to Virginia for a few months, and then returned to Williamsport, Maryland. In 1838 he made affidavit in Washington County that he was a fellow soldier of George Swingle during the war [Ref: V-I:859, T-39].

CYSTER, Jacob. Private, Militia, 8th Class, Capt. Jacob Sharer's Company, 1776/1777 [Ref: A-1146, M-248].

CYSTER, Michael. Took the Oath of Allegiance before the Hon. John Stull in 1778 [Ref: O-47, J-11, which listed the name as "Michael Syster"].

DAGER, Michael. Took the Oath of Allegiance before the Hon. Andrew Rentch before March 7, 1778 [Ref: J-15, O-52, which latter source listed the name as "Michal Dager"].

DAILING, Christian. Private, Militia, 1st Class, Capt. James Walling's Company, 2nd Battalion, 1776/1777 [Ref: M-238, A-1146].

DAMM, Conrad. Private, Militia, 4th Class, Capt. Henry Boteler's Company, 1776/1777 [Ref: M-237, A-1146].

DANNER, Jacob. Took the Oath of Allegiance before the Hon. Henry Schnebley in 1778 [Ref: J-13, O-49, which latter source listed the name as "Jacob Denner"].

DARBY, Henry. Private, Militia, 5th Class, Capt. Conrad Hogmire's Company, 1776/1777 [Ref: M-244, A-1146].

DARBY, John. Private, Militia, 6th Class, Capt. Conrad Hogmire's Company, 1776/1777 [Ref: M-244, A-1146].

DARDEAU, Elba Anthony Jr. See "Anthony Balzar" and "Thomas Clinton" and "Mark Coyle" and "Peter Figley" and "William Groves" and "George King" and "Francis Krick" and "Polly Lewis" and "Peter McMahon" and "James Skinner" and "Christian Smith," q.v.

DARLING, Lott. Private, Militia, 5th Class, Capt. James Walling's Company, 2nd Battalion, 1776/1777 [Ref: M-239, A-1146]. Took the Oath of Allegiance before the Hon. John Stull in 1778 [Ref: O-46, J-10].

DAUGHARTY, William. Took the Oath of Allegiance before the Hon. William Yates in 1778 [Ref: O-48, J-12].

DAVID, George. See "George Davis," q.v.

DAVIES, Richard. See "Richard Davis," q.v.

DAVINSLARY(?), William. Private, Militia, 3rd Class, Capt. Griffin Johnson's Company, 3rd Battalion, 1776/1777 [Ref: M-243].

DAVIS, Amos. First Lieutenant, Militia, 1776, Capt. Jeremiah Spires' Company, 2nd Battalion, June 22, 1778 [Ref: M-68, E-145, M-239]. One of several patriots appointed by the Committee of Observation on January 9, 1777 "to procure as many blankets as may be wanting to supply Col. Smith's Battalion." [Ref: Q-34, which listed the name as "Amos Davies"]. Took the Oath of Allegiance before the Hon. Richard Davis in 1778 [Ref: J-3, O-36]. Miss Sophia Davis, daughter of the late

Amos Davis, died at Springfield near Williams-Port in this county on October 4, 1825 [Ref: Z-76].

DAVIS, Boston. Private, Militia, 5th Class, Capt. Isaac Baker's Company, 1776/1777 [Ref: A-1146, M-247].

DAVIS, Caley. See "Joshua Davis," q.v.

DAVIS, Darius. Took the Oath of Allegiance before the Hon. Richard Davis in 1778 [Ref: J-3, O-36, which listed the name as "Daruis Davis" and "Darias Davis"].

DAVIS, Dennis. Fourth Sergeant, Militia, Capt. Jeremiah Spires' Company, 2nd Battalion, 1776/1777 [Ref: M-239, A-1146]. On January 20, 1777 the Committee of Observation resolved "that Dennis Davies, son of Col. Richard Davies, be exempted from marching with the militia of this county for the present campaign." [Ref: Q-44]. Took the Oath of Allegiance before the Hon. Richard Davis in 1778 [Ref: J-3, O-36].

DAVIS, Ebenezer. Private, Militia, 7th Class, Capt. Daniel Cresap's Company, 3rd Battalion, 1776/1777 [Ref: M-241].

DAVIS, Eleanor H. See "Rezin Davis," q.v.

DAVIS, George. Private, Militia, 4th Class, Capt. James Smith's Company, 2nd Battalion, 1776/1777 [Ref: M-240, A-1146].

DAVIS, George. Private, Militia, 7th Class, Capt. Peter Swingle's (Swingley's) Company, 1776/1777 [Ref: A-1146, M-249].

DAVIS, George. Took the Oath of Allegiance before the Hon. Richard Davis in 1778 [Ref: O-36, J-3, which latter source listed the name as "George David"].

DAVIS, John. Took the Oath of Allegiance before the Hon. Henry Schnebley in 1778 [Ref: O-50, J-14].

DAVIS, John Barton. Took the Oath of Allegiance before the Hon. John Barnes before February 28, 1778 [Ref: O-44, J-9, which latter source listed the name as "John Baryon Davis"].

DAVIS, Joseph. Private, Militia, 5th Class, Capt. Daniel Cresap's Company, 3rd Battalion, 1776/1777 [Ref: M-241]. Took the Oath of Allegiance before the Hon. Lemuel Barritt before March 16, 1778 [Ref: O-42, J-8, which listed the name as "Joseph Davies"].

DAVIS, Joshua. Private, Militia, 3rd Class, Capt. Charles Clinton's Company, 1776/1777 [Ref: M-245, A-1146]. Took the Oath of Allegiance before the Hon. Andrew Bruce before March 2, 1778 [Ref: O-41, J-6]. One Joshua Davis died before December 10, 1778 (date of balance book entry in Washington County) and equal shares were distributed to Ruth Davis, Joshua Davis, and Caley Davis [Ref: J-22].

DAVIS, Lewis. Private, Militia, 7th Class, Capt. Charles Clinton's Company, 1776/1777 [Ref: M-245, A-1146].

DAVIS, Mary. See "William Davis," q.v.

DAVIS, Phillip. Private, Militia, 3rd Class, Capt. Isaac Baker's Company, 1776/1777 [Ref: A-1146, M-247].

DAVIS, Rezin (1735-1800). Captain, Maryland Rifle Regiment, July 27, 1780, and declared a supernumerary on January 1, 1781 [Ref: D-365, D-519]. A notice appeared in the *Washington Spy* newspaper on May 21, 1794, stating "those desirous of serving in a troop of horse leave their names with Resin Davis." [Ref: LL-1:48]. Rezin Davis was born on April 29, 1735, died on March 17, 1800, was buried in Old St. John's Lutheran Churchyard beside his wife Eleanor H. Davis (1757-1815), and subsequently reinterred in Rose Hill Cemetery in Hagerstown [Ref: JJ-VII:110].

DAVIS, Richard. Appointed by the Committee of Observation to carry the Association of Freemen to male residents in Marsh Hundred on September 14, 1775 "and require their subscription to the same and make an exact account of those who sign and those that refuse with their reasons for refusing." [Ref: Q-143]. Rendered patriotic service by supplying a blanket for the use of the military in March, 1776, as recorded by the Committee of Observation on April 12, 1776 [Ref: Q-156, L-82]. One of several patriots appointed by the Committee of Observation on January 9, 1777 "to procure as many blankets as may be wanting to supply Col. Smith's Battalion." [Ref: Q-34, which listed the name as "Col. Richard Davies"]. Appointed "Collector of Cloathing" for Washington County on November 27, 1777 and an Agent for Purchasing Provisions for the Army of the United States on March 25, 1778 [Ref: C-426, C-551]. Justice who administered the Oath of Allegiance in 1778 [Ref: O-36, O-37, O-38, J-3, J-4, J-5, which latter source listed the name as "Richard David"]. Justice of the County Court, June 20, 1778 [Ref: E-141]. Reported his return (account) on the purchase of clothing for the use of the military on July 5, 1778 [Ref: CC-106]. Served as a Recruiting Officer in 1779-1780 [Ref: F-54]. Justice of the Peace, January 30, 1781 [Ref: G-293]. See "Dennis Davis," q.v.

DAVIS, Richard Jr. Lieutenant in Capt. Michael Cresap's Company in 1776 [Ref: L-78]. Took the Oath of Allegiance before the Hon. Richard Davis in 1778 [Ref: J-4, O-36]. Rendered patriotic service by supplying corn for the use of the military on March 31, 1780 [Ref: W-1190, HH-74].

DAVIS, Robert. Took the Oath of Allegiance before the Hon. John Stull in 1778 [Ref: O-46, J-10, which latter source listed the name as "Robert David"].

DAVIS, Ruth. See "Joshua Davis," q.v.

DAVIS, Samuel. Rendered patriotic service in Hagerstown by providing "a rifle gun & 20 yards of linen" to Capt. John Nelson's Company, continental service (Maryland Line), April, 1776 [Ref: Q-162, which listed the name as "Samuel Davies"]. Took the Oath of Allegiance before the Hon. Andrew Bruce before March 2, 1778 [Ref: O-41, J-6]. See "Jonathan Ray," q.v.

DAVIS, Sophia. See "Amos Davis," q.v.

DAVIS, William. Private who was enrolled by Capt. Aeneas Campbell and passed by Major Francis Deakins on July 18, 1776 [Ref: D-49].

DAVIS, William. Private who was enrolled by Capt. Henry Hardman and passed on July 19, 1776 in Frederick (now Washington) County [Ref: D-51].

DAVIS, William (1756-1843). Soldier and pensioner of the Revolution who "died at Cumberland, Maryland on April 17, 1843, upward of 90 years of age." [Ref: EE-6:2 (p. 14), containing Robert W. Barnes' article citing the *Baltimore Sun*, April 24, 1843]. William Davis was born on October 16, 1756, married first to Rebecca Bannister and second to Mary ----, and died in 1843 [Ref: Y-I:783]. See the other men named "William Davis," q.v.

DAVISON, Lewis. Took the Oath of Allegiance before the Hon. Andrew Bruce before March 2, 1778 [Ref: O-41, J-6].

DAWNEY, David. See "David Downey," q.v.

DAWNEY, William. See "William Downey," q.v.

DAWSON, Allom. Private, Militia, 5th Class, Capt. Daniel Cresap's Company, 3rd Battalion, 1776/1777 [Ref: M-241].

DAWSON, Edward. Private, Militia, 4th Class, Capt. Daniel Cresap's Company, 3rd Battalion, 1776/1777 [Ref: M-241]. Took the Oath of Allegiance before the Hon. Lemuel Barritt before March 16, 1778 [Ref: O-42, J-8].

DAWSON, Edward Jr. Private, Militia, 1st Class, Capt. Daniel Cresap's Company, 3rd Battalion, 1776/1777 [Ref: M-241].

DAWSON, James Sr. Private, Militia, 8th Class, Capt. Daniel Cresap's Company, 3rd Battalion, 1776/1777 [Ref: M-241].

DAWSON, Thomas. Private, Militia, 3rd Class, Capt. Daniel Cresap's Company, 3rd Battalion, 1776/1777 [Ref: M-241]. Took the Oath of Allegiance before the Hon. Lemuel Barritt before March 16, 1778 [Ref: O-42, J-8]. On September 23, 1780, Col. Lemuel Barritt recommended to Governor Lee that Thomas Dawson be commissioned a second lieutenant in the militia at "Oper Old Town" since so many officers of the Western Battalion had moved out of Maryland to Kentucky and elsewhere [Ref: G-123].

DAWSON, William Jr. Private, Militia, 4th Class, Capt. Daniel Cresap's Company, 3rd Battalion, 1776/1777 [Ref: M-241].

DAWSON, William Sr. Private, Militia, 3rd Class, Capt. Daniel Cresap's Company, 3rd Battalion, 1776/1777 [Ref: M-241].

DAY, John. Private, Militia, 2nd Class, Capt. Samuel Hughes' Company, 2nd Battalion, 1776/1777 [Ref: M-238, A-1146].

DEAKINS, Francis. Major who reviewed and passed troops enrolled in the Upper District of Frederick County (now Washington County) in July, 1776 [Ref: D-48, D-49].

DEAL, George. Enrolled in the third militia company organized for the Revolutionary War in the Elizabeth Town District of Frederick County (now the Hagerstown area of Washington County), passed by the Committee of Observation on June 5, 1776, and assigned to Capt. John Reynolds' command [Ref: Q-273]. Took the Oath of Allegiance before the Hon. Christopher Cruse in Sharpsburg Hundred before March 2, 1778 [Ref: O-34, J-2]. Private, Militia, 2nd Class, Capt. Joseph Chapline's Company, 2nd Battalion, 1776/1777 [Ref: M-241, which listed the name as "George Deale"]. Private who was enlisted by Capt. John Reynolds and passed on July 18, 1776 in Frederick (now Washington) County [Ref: D-50, which listed the name as "George Deale"].

DEAL, John. Private, Militia, 3rd Class, Capt. Peter Swingle's (Swingley's) Company, 1776/1777 [Ref: A-1146, M-248].

DEAL, Morris. Private, Militia, 4th Class, Capt. Peter Swingle's (Swingley's) Company, 1776/1777 [Ref: A-1146, M-248].

DEAL, Philip. Enrolled in the third militia company organized for the Revolutionary War in the Elizabeth Town District of Frederick County (now the Hagerstown area of Washington County), passed by the Committee of Observation on June 5, 1776, and assigned to Capt. John Reynolds' command [Ref: Q-273]. Took the Oath of Allegiance before the Hon. Christopher Cruse in Sharpsburg Hundred before March 2, 1778 [Ref: O-34, J-2]. Private, Militia, 6th Class, Capt. Joseph Chapline's Company, 2nd Battalion, 1776/1777 [Ref: M-241, which listed the name as "Philip Deale"].

DEAN, James. Enrolled in the first militia company organized for the Revolutionary War in the Elizabeth Town District of Frederick County (now the Hagerstown area of Washington County) on January 6, 1776 [Ref: Q-270, W-1189]. Private, Militia, 3rd Class, Capt. Henry Boteler's Company, 1776/1777 [Ref: M-237, A-1146].

DEAN, Massam. Enrolled in the first militia company organized for the Revolutionary War in the Elizabeth Town District of Frederick County (now the Hagerstown area of Washington County) on January 6, 1776

[Ref: Q-270, W-1189]. Private, Militia, 5th Class, Capt. Henry Boteler's Company, 1776/1777 [Ref: M-237, A-1146].

DEAN, Rodger. Private who was enlisted by Ensign Nathan Williams and passed on July 25, 1776 in Frederick (now Washington) County [Ref: D-51].

DEAN, Samuel. Enrolled in the first militia company organized for the Revolutionary War in the Elizabeth Town District of Frederick County (now the Hagerstown area of Washington County) on January 6, 1776 [Ref: Q-271, W-1190].

DEAN, Thomas. Enrolled in the first militia company organized for the Revolutionary War in the Elizabeth Town District of Frederick County (now the Hagerstown area of Washington County) on January 6, 1776 [Ref: Q-270, W-1190].

DEANOR, John. Enrolled in the third militia company organized for the Revolutionary War in the Elizabeth Town District of Frederick County (now the Hagerstown area of Washington County), passed by the Committee of Observation on June 5, 1776, and assigned to Capt. John Reynolds' command [Ref: Q-273].

DEBOY, John. Enrolled in the second militia company organized for the Revolutionary War in the Elizabeth Town District of Frederick County (now the Hagerstown area of Washington County) on March 9, 1776 [Ref: Q-272].

DEEDER, Abraham. See "Abraham Teeter," q.v.

DEEDS, Adam. Enrolled in the first militia company organized for the Revolutionary War in the Elizabeth Town District of Frederick County (now the Hagerstown area of Washington County) on January 6, 1776 [Ref: Q-270, W-1189].

DEEDS, Ernest. See "Ernst Deitz," q.v.

DEEFHEM, Frederick. Private, Militia, Capt. John Kershner's Company, on duty guarding prisoners of war at Fort Frederick on June 27, 1778 [Ref: D-328].

DEEMER, Catherine. See "Frederick Rohrer," q.v.

DEFENBAUGH, Reverend. See "Henry Young," q.v.

DEIBLY, Jacob. Took the Oath of Allegiance before the Hon. Henry Schnebley in 1778 [Ref: O-49, J-13].

DEITZ, Ernst. Took the Oath of Allegiance before the Hon. Henry Schnebley in 1778 [Ref: O-49, J-13]. Rendered patriotic service by providing gunsmith work for the military and by supplying a rifle for Capt. Daniel Cresap's Company in July, 1775, as recorded by the Committee of Observation at Elizabeth Town on November 4, 1775 [Ref: Q-148, Q-150, which listed the name as "Ernest Deeds"]. Private,

Militia, 7th Class, Capt. Peter Beall's Company, 1st Battalion, 1776/1777 [Ref: M-240, which listed the name as "Earnst Ditz"]. See "Francis Wagoner," q.v.

DELANG, John. Private, Militia, 1st Class, Capt. Charles Clinton's Company, 1776/1777 [Ref: M-245, A-1146].

DEMENT, George. Appointed by the Committee of Observation to carry the Association of Freemen to male residents in Upper Antietam Hundred on September 14, 1775 "and require their subscription to the same and make an exact account of those who sign and those that refuse with their reasons for refusing." [Ref: Q-143, L-82, which latter source listed the name as "George Demont"].

DENISON, Richard. See "Richard Dunnisin," q.v.

DENNER, Jacob. See "Jacob Danner," q.v.

DERR, George. Private, Militia, 4th Class, Capt. John Cellars' Company, 1776/1777 [Ref: A-1146, M-246].

DEVARN, Frederick. Private, Militia, 3rd Class, Capt. Isaac Baker's Company, 1776/1777 [Ref: A-1146, M-247].

DEVILBISS, Michael. On December 24, 1776 the Committee of Observation for Elizabeth Town District (now the Hagerstown area of Washington County) ordered Col. Stull to pay him compensation for the delivery of Samuel Finley to the Keeper of the Tory Goal (Jail) in Frederick Town [Ref: Q-343, which listed the name as "Michael Divelbiss"]. Took the Oath of Allegiance before the Hon. Henry Schnebley in 1778 [Ref: O-49, J-13, which listed the name as "Michael Dubilbis (Devilbise)"].

DEVOUR, Cornelious. Private, Militia, 5th Class, Capt. Charles Clinton's Company, 1776/1777 [Ref: M-245, A-1146].

DEW, Andrew. Second Lieutenant, Militia, Capt. Griffin Johnson's Company, by December 3, 1776 [Ref: M-69, M-243, B-501].

DEWARE, Isaac. Took the Oath of Allegiance before the Hon. Lemuel Barritt before March 16, 1778 [Ref: O-43, J-8].

DEWITT, Barney. Took the Oath of Allegiance before the Hon. Lemuel Barritt before March 16, 1778 [Ref: O-42, J-7].

DEWITT, Henry. Private, Militia, 7th Class, Capt. Daniel Cresap's Company, 3rd Battalion, 1776/1777 [Ref: M-241]. Took the Oath of Allegiance before the Hon. Lemuel Barritt before March 16, 1778 [Ref: O-42, J-8].

DEWITT, James. Took the Oath of Allegiance before the Hon. Lemuel Barritt before March 16, 1778 [Ref: O-43, J-8].

DEWITT, Martin. Took the Oath of Allegiance before the Hon. Lemuel Barritt before March 16, 1778 [Ref: O-42, J-7].

DEWITT, Peter. Third Corporal, Militia, Capt. Daniel Cresap's Company, 3rd Battalion, 1776/1777 [Ref: M-241, which listed the name as "Peter Duwitt"]. Took the Oath of Allegiance before the Hon. Lemuel Barritt before March 16, 1778 [Ref: O-42, J-8].

DIAL, Terrence. Private, Militia, 8th Class, Capt. Daniel Cresap's Company, 3rd Battalion, 1776/1777 [Ref: M-241]. Took the Oath of Allegiance before the Hon. Lemuel Barritt before March 16, 1778 [Ref: O-42, J-7, which listed the name as "Tarance Dial"].

DICE, Henry. Took the Oath of Allegiance before the Hon. John Cellars in January, 1778 [Ref: K-1814, O-40, J-5].

DICK, Elizabeth, John, and Mary. See "Peter Dick," q.v.

DICK, Peter. One of several patriots appointed by the Committee of Observation on January 7, 1777 "to form the county into companies (after the militia had marched) for the purpose of relieving the distressed inhabitants of said county and also to compel the Dunkards and Mennonists to give their assistance." [Ref: Q-31]. Took the Oath of Allegiance before the Hon. Christopher Cruse in Sharpsburg Hundred before March 2, 1778 [Ref: O-34, J-2]. Peter Dick died testate before May 9, 1798 (date of balance book entry in Washington County), leaving a widow (no name given in this account) and equal shares to George Kritzinger, John Dick, Elizabeth Dick, Mary Dick and Rebecca Dick [Ref: J-36].

DICK, Rebecca. See "Peter Dick," q.v.

DICKS, John. Private who was enrolled by Capt. Henry Hardman and passed on July 19, 1776 in Frederick (now Washington) County [Ref: D-51].

DICKSON, Andrew. Rendered patriotic service by providing a rifle for Capt. Daniel Cresap's Company in July, 1775, as recorded by the Committee of Observation at Elizabeth Town on November 4, 1775 [Ref: Q-149].

DICKSON, Nathaniel. Enrolled in the second militia company organized for the Revolutionary War in the Elizabeth Town District of Frederick County (now the Hagerstown area of Washington County) on March 9, 1776 [Ref: Q-272].

DIGMAN, Peter. Private who was enrolled by Capt. Henry Hardman and passed on July 19, 1776 in Frederick (now Washington) County [Ref: D-51].

DILE, Adam. Private, Militia, 1st Class, Capt. Peter Beall's Company, 1st Battalion, 1776/1777 [Ref: M-240]. Took the Oath of Allegiance before the Hon. Joseph Sprigg before April 1, 1778 [Ref: O-53, J-16, which listed the name as "Adam Diel"].

DILE, George. Rendered patriotic service by providing two rifles for the use of the military in July, 1775, as recorded by the Committee of Observation at Elizabeth Town on November 4, 1775 [Ref: Q-150]. Private, Militia, 8th Class, Capt. Peter Beall's Company, 1st Battalion, 1776/1777 [Ref: M-240, which listed the name as "George Dill"]. Took the Oath of Allegiance before the Hon. Henry Schnebley in 1778 [Ref: O-50, J-13, which listed the name as "George Deil"].

DILE, Phillip. Private, Militia, 2nd Class, Capt. Isaac Baker's Company, 1776/1777 [Ref: A-1146, M-247].

DILLON, R. S. See "John Slagle," q.v.

DILTS, John. Private, Militia, 6th Class, Capt. Daniel Clapsaddle's Company, 1st Battalion, 1776/1777 [Ref: M-236, A-1146]. Took the Oath of Allegiance before the Hon. Joseph Sprigg before April 1, 1778 [Ref: O-53, J-16].

DILTS, William. Private, Militia, 6th Class, Capt. Daniel Clapsaddle's Company, 1st Battalion, 1776/1777 [Ref: M-236, A-1146].

DIRELING, John. See "John Diverling," q.v.

DIREWORTH, John. Private, Militia, 7th Class, Capt. Jacob Sharer's Company, 1776/1777 [Ref: A-1146, M-248].

DITTO, E. W. See "Charles McColough," q.v.

DIVELLY, Martin. Private, Select Militia, Capt. Adam Ott's Company, 1781 [Ref: M-238, A-1146].

DIVERLING, John. Took the Oath of Allegiance before the Hon. John Stull in 1778 [Ref: O-46, J-10, which latter source listed the name as "John Diuerling"]. Private, Militia, 2nd Class, Capt. James Walling's Company, 2nd Battalion, 1776/1777 [Ref: M-238, A-1146, which listed the name as "John Direling"].

DIVERS, William. Private who was enrolled by Capt. Henry Hardman and passed on July 19, 1776 in Frederick (now Washington) County [Ref: D-51].

DIVLE, Michael. Second Sergeant, Militia, Capt. Michael Fackler's Company, 1776/1777 [Ref: M-245, A-1146].

DIXON, James. Private, Militia, 2nd Class, Capt. Isaac Baker's Company, 1776/1777 [Ref: A-1146, M-247].

DIXON, William. Private who was enrolled by Capt. Aeneas Campbell and passed by Major Francis Deakins on July 18, 1776 [Ref: D-49].

DODSON, Isaac. Private who enlisted in the militia on September 5, 1781 for service in the Continental Army [Ref: D-388].

DOLL, Adam. Private, Militia, 4th Class, Capt. Conrad Nichodemus' Company, 2nd Battalion, 1776/1777 [Ref: M-237, A-1146].

DOLL, John. Fourth Corporal, Militia, Capt. Henry Boteler's Company, 1776/1777 [Ref: M-237, A-1146].
DOMER, Michael. See "Michael Dorner," q.v.
DONALDSON, Aron. Private, Militia, 6th Class, Capt. James Walling's Company, 2nd Battalion, 1776/1777 [Ref: M-239, A-1146].
DONALDSON, Samuel. Enrolled in the first militia company organized for the Revolutionary War in the Elizabeth Town District of Frederick County (now the Hagerstown area of Washington County) on January 6, 1776 [Ref: Q-271, W-1190]. Private, Militia, 5th Class, Capt. John Rennolds' (Reynolds') Company, 2nd Battalion, 1776/1777 [Ref: M-240, which listed the name as "Samuel Donelson"]. On January 18, 1777 the Committee of Observation resolved that "whereas Samuel Donaldson who was charged with speaking inimical to the common cause, made appear to Committee that said charge was groundless, there ordered that said Donaldson be discharged from confinement and costs." [Ref: Q-43].
DONIEL, John O. See "John O'Doniel," q.v.
DONNEY, William. See "William Downey," q.v.
DONOVAN, Daniel. Private, Militia, by January 22, 1777 when ordered by the Committee of Observation "to march with some company of militia to the reinforcement of his Excellency General Washington" or appear before the Committee and state his reason for not marching. He apparently marched since he never appeared to the contrary [Ref: D-200, Q-48, which listed the name as "Danl. Donavan"]. Took the Oath of Allegiance before the Hon. William Yates in 1778 [Ref: O-48, J-12, which listed the name as "Daniel Dunnavan"].
DONOVAN, John (1740-1825). "Died on October 4, 1825, John Donovan, aged 85, for more than 60 years a resident of Hancock." [Ref: Z-76]. There were several men with this name in Maryland who served in the Revolutionary War [Ref: D-58, D-104, D-277, D-414, D-531, D-607, D-656]. Additional research will be necessary before drawing conclusions.
DORIER, Henry. See "John Thomas," q.v.
DORMINE, Michael. Took the Oath of Allegiance before the Hon. John Cellars in January, 1778 [Ref: K-1814, O-40, J-6].
DORNER, Michael. Ensign, Militia, Capt. Michael Fackler's Company, 1776/1777 (date not given). [Ref: M-70, A-1146, M-245, which latter source listed the name as "Michael Domer"]. Took the Oath of Allegiance before the Hon. Henry Schnebley in 1778 [Ref: O-49, J-13].
DORSEY, Lacon (Lakin). Ensign, Militia, 1776, Capt. Jeremiah Spires' Company, 2nd Battalion, June 22, 1778 [Ref: M-71, E-145, M-239, which latter source listed the name as "Laven Dorsey"]. Took the Oath of

Allegiance before the Hon. Richard Davis in 1778 [Ref: J-5, O-37, which listed the name as "Leakin Dorsey"].

DORSON, Allom. Took the Oath of Allegiance before the Hon. Lemuel Barritt before March 16, 1778 [Ref: O-42, J-8].

DORSON, Edward. Two men by this name took the Oath of Allegiance before the Hon. Lemuel Barritt before March 16, 1778 [Ref: O-42, J-7, J-8].

DORSON, James Jr. Took the Oath of Allegiance before the Hon. Lemuel Barritt before March 16, 1778 [Ref: O-42, J-7].

DORSON, James Sr. Took the Oath of Allegiance before the Hon. Lemuel Barritt before March 16, 1778 [Ref: O-42, J-7].

DORSON, William Sr. Took the Oath of Allegiance before the Hon. Lemuel Barritt before March 16, 1778 [Ref: O-42, J-7].

DOTSON, Mary. See "John Miller," q.v.

DOUGHERTY, Neel. Third Corporal, Militia, Capt. John Cellars' Company, 1776/1777 [Ref: M-246, A-1146].

DOUGLASS, John. Private, Militia, 1st Class, Capt. Samuel Hughes' Company, 2nd Battalion, 1776/1777 [Ref: M-238, A-1146].

DOUGLASS, Joseph. See "William Douglass," q.v.

DOUGLASS, Mary and Rachel. See "William Douglass," q.v.

DOUGLASS, Robert (1749-1834). Private, Sergeant, and Lieutenant, Maryland Militia, pensioned in Washington County under the Act of June 7, 1832 at the annual allowance of $85 retroactive to March 4, 1831 [Ref: R-51]. Second Lieutenant, Militia, Capt. Samuel Hughes' Company, 1st Battalion, June 23, 1778 [Ref: M-71, E-147, M-237, A-1146]. Took the Oath of Allegiance before the Hon. Joseph Sprigg before April 1, 1778 [Ref: O-53, J-16]. Applied for and received pension S8353 in Washington County on December 11, 1832, aged 83, a resident of Hagerstown, Maryland, stating he was born on April 15, 1749 in County Derry, Ireland and came to America in 1770 [Ref: V-I:1013]. He married Sarah ---- and died in Virginia in October, 1834 [Ref: Y-I:865].

DOUGLASS, Robert. Private, Select Militia, Capt. Adam Ott's Company, 1781 [Ref: M-238, A-1146]. See "William Douglass," q.v.

DOUGLASS, Samuel. Took the Oath of Allegiance before the Hon. Joseph Sprigg before April 1, 1778 [Ref: O-53, J-16]. See "William Douglass," q.v.

DOUGLASS, Sarah. See "Robert Douglass," q.v.

DOUGLASS (DOUGLAS), William. Took the Oath of Allegiance before the Hon. Joseph Sprigg before April 1, 1778 [Ref: O-53, J-16]. One of several patriots appointed by the Committee of Observation on December 30, 1776 "to form the county into companies (after the militia had marched) for the purpose of relieving the distressed inhabitants of said county and also to compel the Dunkards and Mennonists to give their assistance." [Ref: Q-345]. Rendered patriotic service by supplying a blanket for the use of the military in March, 1776, as recorded by the Committee of Observation on April 12, 1776 [Ref: Q-156, L-82]. One "William Douglas" died before June 19, 1790 (date of balance book entry in Washington County), leaving equal shares to Samuel, Robert, Joseph, William, Rachel, and Mary Douglas [Ref: J-28].

DOWDEN, Nancy. See "George Miller, Jr.," q.v.

DOWDLE, William (c1756-   ). Private, Maryland Line, pensioned under Act of March 18, 1818 at $96 per year effective October 8, 1818 [Ref: R-42].

DOWNEY, Ann and Basil. See "Samuel Downey," q.v.

DOWNEY, David. Private, Militia, 7th Class, Capt. Daniel Clapsaddle's Company, 1st Battalion, 1776/1777 [Ref: M-236, A-1146]. Took the Oath of Allegiance before the Hon. Joseph Sprigg before April 1, 1778 [Ref: J-16, O-53, which latter source listed the name as "David Dawney"].

DOWNEY, Edmond. See "Samuel Downey," q.v.

DOWNEY, Elizabeth. See "William Downey," q.v.

DOWNEY, Ezekiah. Private, Militia, 6th Class, Capt. Daniel Clapsaddle's Company, 1st Battalion, 1776/1777 [Ref: M-236, A-1146].

DOWNEY, Harriet. See "Samuel Downey," q.v.

DOWNEY, Isabella. See "William Downey," q.v.

DOWNEY, James. Took the Oath of Allegiance before the Hon. Joseph Sprigg before April 1, 1778 [Ref: O-53, J-16]. Rendered patriotic service by supplying wheat for the use of the military on March 8, 1780 [Ref: W-1190, HH-72]. See "William Downey," q.v.

DOWNEY, James Jr. Private, Militia, 8th Class, Capt. Daniel Clapsaddle's Company, 1st Battalion, 1776/1777 [Ref: M-236, A-1146].

DOWNEY, Jean. See "William Downey," q.v.

DOWNEY, John. Private, Militia, 8th Class, Capt. Daniel Clapsaddle's Company, 1st Battalion, 1776/1777 [Ref: M-236, A-1146]. Took the Oath of Allegiance before the Hon. Henry Schnebley in 1778 [Ref: O-50, J-13, which listed the name as "John Donney"]. See "Samuel Downey," q.v.

DOWNEY, Joseph. Private, Militia, 8th Class, Capt. Daniel Clapsaddle's Company, 1st Battalion, 1776/1777 [Ref: M-236, A-1146].

DOWNEY, Maria, Mary, and Polly. See "William Downey," q.v.

DOWNEY, Richard. Took the Oath of Allegiance before the Hon. John Barnes before February 28, 1778 [Ref: O-45, J-10].

DOWNEY, Ruth. See "Samuel Downey," q.v.

DOWNEY, Samuel. Private, Militia, 7th Class, Capt. Daniel Clapsaddle's Company, 1st Battalion, 1776/1777 [Ref: M-236, A-1146]. Rendered patriotic service by supplying corn for the use of the military on March 20, 1780 [Ref: W-1190, HH-72, which latter source listed the name as "Samuel Downy"]. Took the Oath of Allegiance before the Hon. Joseph Sprigg before April 1, 1778 [Ref: O-53, J-16]. A bill of complaint filed in Washington County in early 1829 stated that Samuel Downey died intestate in 1828, leaving real estate to Robert Downey, Mary Downey, William Braddon and wife Mary (non-resident), Ann Downey (non-resident), Samuel Downey (non-resident), John Downey, Rebecca Lyon (non-resident), Robert Burns and wife Ruth (non-residents), William Downey, Basil B. Downey, Harriet Downey, Maria Downey, and the following under age 21 and also non-residents: Susan Downey, Ruth Downey, Edmond Downey, and John Downey (listed twice). [Ref: Z-108].

DOWNEY, Susan. See "Samuel Downey," q.v.

DOWNEY, William. One of several patriots appointed by the Committee of Observation on December 30, 1776 "to form the county into companies (after the militia had marched) for the purpose of relieving the distressed inhabitants of said county and also to compel the Dunkards and Mennonists to give their assistance." [Ref: Q-345, which listed the name as "William Downy"]. Took the Oath of Allegiance before the Hon. Henry Schnebley in 1778 [Ref: O-51, J-15, which listed the name as "William Donney"]. One William Downey died testate before October 9, 1792 (date of balance book entry in Washington County), leaving a widow (no name given, but Jean Downey was one of the administrators, as was James Downey) and with equal shares to Polly Downey, Isabella Downey, and Elizabeth Downey [Ref: J-32]. Also see the other men named "William Downey," q.v.

DOWNEY, William. Private, Militia, 8th Class, Capt. Daniel Clapsaddle's Company, 1st Battalion, 1776/1777 [Ref: M-236, A-1146]. Took the Oath of Allegiance before the Hon. Joseph Sprigg before April 1, 1778 [Ref: J-16, O-53, which latter source listed the name as "William Dawney"]. See "Samuel Downey" and the other "William Downey," q.v.

DOWNEY, William Jr. Private, Militia, 6th Class, Capt. Daniel Clapsaddle's Company, 1st Battalion, 1776/1777 [Ref: M-236, A-1146].

DOWNEY, William (of James). Took the Oath of Allegiance before the Hon. Joseph Sprigg before April 1, 1778 [Ref: O-53, J-16]. See "William Downey," q.v.

DOWNEY, William (of William). Private, Militia, 2nd Class, Capt. Daniel Clapsaddle's Company, 1st Battalion, 1776/1777 [Ref: M-236, A-1146].

DOWNING, Ann, David, and Jane. See "Isaac Ellis," q.v.

DOWNING, John Jr. Private, Militia, 5th Class, Capt. Basil Williams' Company, 1776/1777 [Ref: M-244, A-1146].
DOWNING, John Sr. Private, Militia, 3rd Class, Capt. Basil Williams' Company, 1776/1777 [Ref: M-244, A-1146].
DOWNING, Joseph. Took the Oath of Allegiance before the Hon. Joseph Sprigg before April 1, 1778 [Ref: O-54, J-16].
DOWNING, Mister. See "Lawrence Williams," q.v.
DOWNING, Timothy. Private, Militia, 2nd Class, Capt. James Prather's Company, 3rd Battalion, 1776/1777 [Ref: M-242].
DOWNING, William. Took the Oath of Allegiance before the Hon. Joseph Sprigg before April 1, 1778 [Ref: O-54, J-16].
DOYLE, James. Took the Oath of Allegiance before the Hon. Richard Davis in 1778 [Ref: J-4, O-37].
DOYLE, Simon. Private, Militia, 3rd Class, Capt. Jeremiah Spires' Company, 2nd Battalion, 1776/1777 [Ref: M-239, A-1146]. Took the Oath of Allegiance before the Hon. Richard Davis in 1778 [Ref: J-5, O-37].
DRADEN, James. Private who was recruited and passed by County Lieutenant Thomas Sprigg on April 22, 1780 [Ref: D-336]. Took the Oath of Allegiance before the Hon. William Yates in 1778 [Ref: O-48, J-12, which listed the name as "James Draydon"].
DRAKE, Joseph (c1748-c1838). Second Sergeant, Militia, Capt. James Walling's Company, 2nd Battalion, 1776/1777 [Ref: M-238, A-1146]. Took the Oath of Allegiance before the Hon. John Stull in 1778 [Ref: O-46, J-10]. Recorded his animal brand in Washington County court on November 22, 1778 [Ref: II]. Second Lieutenant, Militia, Capt. James Patterson's Company, 2nd Battalion, November 21, 1780 [Ref: G-220, N-19]. He applied for and received pension S9387 in Warren County, Ohio on July 14, 1836, aged 88 or 89, stating he was born in Somerset County, New Jersey and lived within 6 miles of Hagerstown in Washington County, Maryland at the time of his enlistment. After the war he moved to Juniata, Pennsylvania and then moved to Ohio [Ref: V-I:1022].
DROMBACH, John. See "John Krombach," q.v.
DUBES, Oswald. Enrolled in the third militia company organized for the Revolutionary War in the Elizabeth Town District of Frederick County (now the Hagerstown area of Washington County), passed by the Committee of Observation on June 5, 1776, and assigned to Capt. John Reynolds' command [Ref: Q-273].
DUE, Andrew. Took the Oath of Allegiance before the Hon. Andrew Bruce before March 2, 1778 [Ref: O-41, J-7].

DUES, Christian. One of several patriots appointed by the Committee of Observation on December 30, 1776 "to form the county into companies (after the militia had marched) for the purpose of relieving the distressed inhabitants of said county and also to compel the Dunkards and Mennonists to give their assistance." [Ref: Q-345, which listed the name as "Christian Duss"].

DUES, Christopher. Took the Oath of Allegiance before the Hon. John Stull in 1778 [Ref: J-10, O-46, which latter source listed the name as "Christopher Duse"].

DUGGAN, Thomas. Took the Oath of Allegiance before the Hon. Samuel Hughes before March 1, 1778 [Ref: O-33, J-1].

DUMATT, Edward. Private who was enlisted by Capt. John Reynolds and passed on July 18, 1776 in Frederick (now Washington) County [Ref: D-50].

DUMEAGIN, Roger. Took the Oath of Allegiance before the Hon. Lemuel Barritt before March 16, 1778 [Ref: O-42, J-7].

DUNCAN, James. Private who was enrolled by Capt. Henry Hardman and passed on July 19, 1776 in Frederick (now Washington) County [Ref: D-51]. Private, Militia, Capt. William Heyser's Company, muster roll dated October 23, 1776, continental service [Ref: D-264, W-1190, L-79]. Private, German Regiment, Lt. Col. Ludwick Weltner's Company, discharged on July 16, 1779 at Fort Wyoming, Pennsylvania [Ref: GG-97, D-265, D-203, which latter source listed the name as "James Dunkin"].

DUNCAN, John. Enrolled in the first militia company organized for the Revolutionary War in the Elizabeth Town District of Frederick County (now the Hagerstown area of Washington County) on January 6, 1776 [Ref: Q-270, W-1189]. Private, Militia, 3rd Class, Capt. Joseph Chapline's Company, 2nd Battalion, 1776/1777 [Ref: M-241]. Took the Oath of Allegiance before the Hon. Joseph Chapline before April 17, 1779 [Ref: J-5, O-39, which listed the name as "John Dunkan"].

DUNKEN, John Miller. Private, Militia, 5th Class, Capt. John Cellars' Company, 1776/1777 [Ref: A-1146, M-246].

DUNKLE, Mathias. Private, Militia, Capt. William Heyser's Company, muster roll dated October 23, 1776, and in continental service in May, 1777 [Ref: D-264, W-1190, L-79, GG-97].

DUNN, George. Fourth Sergeant, Militia, Capt. John Cellars' Company, 1776/1777 [Ref: M-246, A-1146].

DUNN, Thomas. Private, Militia, 4th Class, Capt. Samuel Hughes' Company, 2nd Battalion, 1776/1777 [Ref: M-238, A-1146, which listed the name as "Thomas Dun"]. Took the Oath of Allegiance before the Hon. Samuel Hughes before March 1, 1778 [Ref: O-33, J-1].

DUNNISIN, Daniel. Private, Militia, 6th Class, Capt. Barnett Johnston's Company, 3rd Battalion, 1776/1777 [Ref: M-242].

DUNNISIN, John. Private, Militia, 7th Class, Capt. Barnett Johnston's Company, 3rd Battalion, 1776/1777 [Ref: M-242].

DUNWOODY, James. Private, Militia, 1st Class, Capt. James Walling's Company, 2nd Battalion, 1776/1777 [Ref: M-238, A-1146].

DUNWOODY, James. Private, Militia, 1st Class, Capt. Conrad Hogmire's Company, 1776/1777 [Ref: M-244, A-1146].

DURBIN, Edward. First Sergeant, Militia, Capt. Charles Coulson's Company, enrolled August 28, 1776 [Ref: M-243, A-1146, which listed the name as "Edward Derbin"]. Private, Militia, 1st Class, Capt. Charles Clinton's Company, 1776/1777 [Ref: A-1146, M-245, which listed the name as "Edward Dubin"]. Took the Oath of Allegiance before the Hon. Andrew Bruce before March 2, 1778 [Ref: O-41, J-6].

DURBIN, John. Private, Militia, 8th Class, Capt. Charles Clinton's Company, 1776/1777 [Ref: M-245, A-1146]. Second Sergeant, Militia, Capt. Charles Coulson's Company, enrolled August 28, 1776 [Ref: M-243, A-1146, which listed the name as "John Derbin"]. Took the Oath of Allegiance before the Hon. Andrew Bruce before March 2, 1778 [Ref: O-41, J-6].

DURBIN, Nicholas. Private, Militia, 2nd Class, Capt. Charles Clinton's Company, 1776/1777 [Ref: A-1146, M-245, which listed the name as "Nicholas Dubin"]. Took the Oath of Allegiance before the Hon. Andrew Bruce before March 2, 1778 [Ref: O-41, J-6].

DURBIN, Samuel. Took the Oath of Allegiance before the Hon. Andrew Bruce before March 2, 1778 [Ref: O-41, J-6].

DURBIN, William. Private, Militia, 8th Class, Capt. Charles Clinton's Company, 1776/1777 [Ref: M-245, A-1146]. First Corporal, Militia, Capt. Charles Coulson's Company, enrolled August 28, 1776 [Ref: M-243, A-1146, which listed the name as "William Derbin"]. Took the Oath of Allegiance before the Hon. Andrew Bruce before March 2, 1778 [Ref: O-41, J-6].

DURGLER, George. Took the Oath of Allegiance before the Hon. Henry Schnebley in 1778 [Ref: O-51, J-14].

DUSING, Amelia and John. See "Philip Dusing," q.v.

DUSING, Philip (c1748-1832). Private, Militia, 2nd Class, Capt. Michael Fackler's Company, 1776/1777 [Ref: A-1146, M-245, which listed the name as "Phillip Dusinger"]. Took the Oath of Allegiance before the Hon. Henry Schnebley in 1778 [Ref: O-51, J-14, which listed the name as "Philip Dussing"]. "Died in Hagerstown on April 26, 1832, Mr. Philip Dusing, in the 84th year of his age. The subject of this obituary was one of those patriots who raised the sword in defence of his country in times that tried men's souls." [Ref: DD-40, citing *The Republican Banner* on May 12, 1832]. "Phillip Dusing" was the administrator of John Dusing on July 25, 1789 (date of balance book entry in Washington County). [Ref: J-28]. Amelia Dusing, wife of Philip Dusing, of Hagerstown, died on April 15, 1827, in her 75th year [Ref: Z-90].

DUSS, Christian. See "Christian Dues," q.v.

DUST, Gaspert. Private, Militia, 3rd Class, Capt. Daniel Cresap's Company, 3rd Battalion, 1776/1777 [Ref: M-241].

DYALL, Edward. Private, Militia, 1st Class, Capt. Jeremiah Spires' Company, 2nd Battalion, 1776/1777 [Ref: M-239, A-1146].

DYE, Benjamin. Private who was enlisted by Ensign Nathan Williams and passed on July 25, 1776 in Frederick (now Washington) County [Ref: D-51].

EAKLE (EKELL, ECKLE), Christian. Second Lieutenant, Militia, 1776, Capt. James Smith's Company, 2nd Battalion, June 22, 1778 [Ref: M-239, A-1146, M-73, E-145, which latter two sources listed the name as "Christian Eckle"]. First Lieutenant, Capt. Robert Smith's Company, November 21, 1780 [Ref: G-220, which listed the name as "Christian Eakle"]. Took the Oath of Allegiance before the Hon. Samuel Hughes before March 1, 1778 [Ref: O-33, J-1, which listed the name as "Christian Ekell"]. "Christian Eakle" died testate by March 23, 1801 [Ref: MM-12:79].

EAKLE (EAKEL, EKILL), Harmon. "Harmon Ekill" took the Oath of Allegiance before the Hon. Joseph Chapline before April 17, 1779 [Ref: J-5, O-39]. "Harman Eakel" took the Oath of Allegiance before September 1, 1780 [Ref: X-110]. One "Harmon Eakle" died before September 12, 1801 (date of balance book entry in Washington County), leaving equal shares of his estate to Philip Eakle, Harmon Eakle, Peter Eakle, and Mary Grove [Ref: J-39].

EAKLE (EKILL), Henry (1751-1827). Took the Oath of Allegiance before the Hon. Joseph Chapline before April 17, 1779 [Ref: J-5, O-39]. Henry Eakle died in Pleasant Valley on February 27, 1827, in his 76th year [Ref: Z-89].

EAKLE (EKLE), Peter. Second Corporal, Militia, Capt. John Rennolds' (Reynolds') Company, 2nd Battalion, 1776/1777 [Ref: M-240, which listed the name as "Peter Ekle"]. Took the Oath of Allegiance before September 1, 1780 [Ref: X-110, which listed the name as "Peter Eakle"]. See "Harmon Eakle," q.v.

EAKLE, Philip. See "Harmon Eakle," q.v.

EAKLE (EAKEL), Stophel. Took the Oath of Allegiance before September 1, 1780 [Ref: X-110, which listed the name as "Stophel Eakel"].

EARHART, Jacob. Private, Militia, 3rd Class, Capt. Michael Fackler's Company, 1776/1777 [Ref: M-245, A-1146].

EARHART, Philip. Private, Militia, 8th Class, Capt. Jacob Sharer's Company, 1776/1777 [Ref: A-1146, M-248]. One of the persons appointed by the Committee of Observation for Elizabeth Town District (now the Hagerstown area of Washington County) on January 16, 1777 "to appraise the several wagons, horses, gears, wagon cloths, blankets, etc. that can be procured for the use of Col. Smith's Battalion." [Ref: Q-40, Q-41, which listed the name as "Philip Airhart"]. Took the Oath of Allegiance before the Hon. Andrew Rentch before March 7, 1778 [Ref: O-52, J-15]. See "Philip Erhard," q.v.

EARLEY, Abram. Took the Oath of Allegiance before the Hon. John Stull in 1778 [Ref: O-46, J-10].

EARLEYWINE, Abraham. Private, Militia, 8th Class, Capt. Jacob Sharer's Company, 1776/1777 [Ref: A-1146, M-248].

EASON, Ruth. See "William Eason," q.v.

EASON, William. Enrolled in the first militia company organized for the Revolutionary War in the Elizabeth Town District of Frederick County (now the Hagerstown area of Washington County) on January 6, 1776 [Ref: Q-270, W-1189]. "William Eason, Sr." died testate by June 1, 1805, leaving a wife Ruth and several children [Ref: MM-13:171].

EASTEN, William. Private, Militia, 5th Class, Capt. John Rennolds' (Reynolds') Company, 2nd Battalion, 1776/1777 [Ref: M-240].

EASTER, Adam. See "Peter Easter," q.v.

EASTER, George. Took the Oath of Allegiance before the Hon. John Barnes before February 28, 1778 [Ref: O-44, J-9].

EASTER, John (1760-c1835). Private, Select Militia, Capt. Adam Ott's Company, 1781 [Ref: M-238, A-1146]. He applied for and received pension S18389 in Morgan County, Virginia on November 26, 1832, stating he was born on January 17, 1760 in Washington County, Maryland and was drafted for three months near Big Spring in that county and guarded prisoners at Fort Frederick. He was drafted again for three months and served in the militia. He was drafted a third time for three months and served as a private in Rawlings' Regiment (no dates were given). He married Margaret Thomas and moved to Hampshire County (now Morgan County), Virginia about 30 years ago [Ref: U-32:4 (1944), Y-I:915, Y-I:915].

EASTER, Peter. Took the Oath of Allegiance before the Hon. John Barnes before February 28, 1778 [Ref: O-44, J-9]. Adam Easter died testate before April 22, 1783 (date of balance book entry in Washington County) and one of his children was Peter Easter [Ref: J-24].

EASTERN, William. Private, Militia, 3rd Class, Capt. Henry Boteler's Company, 1776/1777 [Ref: M-237, A-1146].

EASTON, Mary. See "John Kenistrick," q.v.

EATENIRON, Martin. See "Martin Etenier," q.v.

EATHERINGTON, Aaron. Private, Militia, 6th Class, Capt. Daniel Cresap's Company, 3rd Battalion, 1776/1777 [Ref: M-241].

EATHERINGTON, Benjamin. Private, Militia, 3rd Class, Capt. Daniel Cresap's Company, 3rd Battalion, 1776/1777 [Ref: M-241].

EATHERINGTON, John. First Corporal, Militia, Capt. Daniel Cresap's Company, 3rd Battalion, 1776/1777 [Ref: M-241].

EATHERINGTON, Joshua. Private, Militia, Capt. Daniel Cresap's Company, 3rd Battalion, 1776/1777 [Ref: M-241].

EATMAN, John. See "John Batman," q.v.

EBERT, Valentine. Rendered patriotic service by supplying rye and flour for the use of the military on February 11, 1780 [Ref: W-1190, and HH-72, which listed the name as "Vallentine Ebert"].

EBSBERGER, Wolgong. See "Wolfgang Ellsperger," q.v.

ECHELBERGER, Rosena. See "Matthias Ridenour," q.v.

ECKENBERGER, Jacob. Took the Oath of Allegiance before the Hon. Henry Schnebley in 1778 [Ref: O-51, J-14].

ECKERT, Elizabeth. See "John Tobias Stoyer," q.v.

ECKLE, Christian. See "Christian Ekill," q.v.

EDELMAN, Adam. Took the Oath of Allegiance before the Hon. Henry Schnebley in 1778 [Ref: O-49, J-12].

EDELMAN, Leonard (1761-c1845). Private, Select Militia, Capt. Adam Ott's Company, 1781 [Ref: M-238, A-1146, which listed the name as "Leonard Adleman"]. Substitute, Maryland Line, discharged on December 10, 1781 [Ref: N-20, I-17, which latter source listed the name as "Leonard Ettleman"]. "Leonard Edleman" applied for and received pension S30397 in Rush County, Indiana on September 22, 1832, aged 72, stating he was born in Hagerstown, Maryland in 1761 *[sic]* and enlisted there in March, 1781. After the war he moved to Green County, Tennessee and in 1817 to Bourbon County, Kentucky and in 1824 to Rush County, Indiana. On April 15, 1840 he applied for transfer from Indiana to Harrison County, Kentucky [Ref: T-46].

EDELMAN, Michael (1755-   ). Private who was enlisted by Lieut. Christian Orndorff and passed on July 20, 1776 in Frederick (now Washington) County [Ref: D-50]. Private, Maryland Line [Ref: N-20].

EDMONDSON, Archibald. Took the Oath of Allegiance before the Hon. Richard Davis in 1778 [Ref: J-3, O-36].

EDMONDSON, Nathan. Took the Oath of Allegiance before the Hon. Richard Davis in 1778 [Ref: J-5, O-37]. Private, Militia, 5th Class, Capt. Jeremiah Spires' Company, 2nd Battalion, 1776/1777 [Ref: M-239, A-1146].

EDMONSON, Thomas. Took the Oath of Allegiance before the Hon. John Barnes before February 28, 1778 [Ref: O-44, J-9].

EDWARDS, John. Rendered patriotic service by providing "rashons" for the use of the military in July, 1775, as recorded by the Committee of Observation at Elizabeth Town on November 4, 1775 [Ref: Q-150]. John Edwards died testate by August 3, 1805, leaving a wife Mary and the balance of his estate to his siblings [Ref: MM-13:172].

EICHELBERGER, Cathrin. See "John Eichelberger," q.v.

EICHELBERGER, Henry and Jacob. See "John Eichelberger," q.v.

EICHELBERGER (EIGLBERGER), John (1753-1822). Soldier who resided in Washington County and was granted a pension certificate in August, 1820, according to an Act of Congress of March 18, 1818, since he had proven that he was "in the enjoyment of a certain degree of poverty" as required by the Act as amended on May 1, 1820 [Ref: W-1190]. Private, Pennsylvania Line, pensioned at $96 per year effective March 5, 1819 and died April 27, 1823 [Ref: N-20, R-42, which listed the name as "John Eikelberger"]. Applied for pension in Washington County on March 30, 1818, aged 64 or 65, a resident of Booth's Hill, Maryland, stating he enlisted at Hagerstown and served in the Maryland and Pennsylvania Lines. He married Mary ---- in 1778 in Lebanon County, Pennsylvania and their children were: first child was a daughter (born in 1781 and lived only a short time), John (born October 13, 1783), Jacob (born March 9, 1785), Peter (born March 3, 1787 and still living in 1850), Henry (born April 30, 17889), Pollie (born August 7, 1792), and Cathrin (born August 14, 1798). The birth records gave the name as "Eiglberger" and John (the soldier) died on April 22, 1822 [aged 69]. His widow applied for and received pension W9424 at Hagerstown on January 1, 1839, aged 86, but later that year she stated she was aged 83 and gave her name as "Eichelberger." Theodore Eiglberger was mentioned in 1839, but no relationship was given [Ref: V-I:1094, Z-40].

EICHELBERGER, Mary. See "John Eichelberger," q.v.

EICHELBERGER, Michael. See "Michael Aklebarger," q.v.

EICHELBERGER, Peter and Pollie. See "John Eichelberger," q.v.

EICHELBERNER (EICHELBEANER), Conrad. Rendered patriotic service by supplying wheat for the use of the military on March 13, 1780 [Ref: W-1190, and HH-73, which latter source listed the name as "Cunrad Eichelberner"].

EIGENOR, Benedict. Enrolled in the third militia company organized for the Revolutionary War in the Elizabeth Town District of Frederick County (now the Hagerstown area of Washington County), passed by the Committee of Observation on June 5, 1776, and assigned to Capt. John Reynolds' command [Ref: Q-273, which listed the name as "Benedick Eigenor"]. Private who was enlisted by Capt. John Reynolds and passed on July 18, 1776 in Frederick (now Washington) County [Ref: D-50, which listed the name as "Benedict Elginor"]. Private, Militia, 4th Class, Capt. Joseph Chapline's Company, 2nd Battalion, 1776/1777 [Ref: M-241, which listed the name as "Benadict Igonder"].

EIGENOR, Henry. Enrolled in the third militia company organized for the Revolutionary War in the Elizabeth Town District of Frederick County (now the Hagerstown area of Washington County), passed by the Committee of Observation on June 5, 1776, and assigned to Capt. John Reynolds' command [Ref: Q-273]. Private, Militia, 5th Class, Capt. Joseph Chapline's Company, 2nd Battalion, 1776/1777 [Ref: M-241, which listed the name as "Henry Igonder"].

EIGENOR, John. Enrolled in the third militia company organized for the Revolutionary War in the Elizabeth Town District of Frederick County (now the Hagerstown area of Washington County), passed by the Committee of Observation on June 5, 1776, and assigned to Capt. John Reynolds' command [Ref: Q-273]. Private, Militia, 4th Class, Capt. Henry Boteler's Company, 1776/1777 [Ref: M-237, A-1146, which listed the name as "John Iginter"].

EIGLBERGER, Theodore. See "John Eickelberger," q.v.

EKILL, Harmon, and others. See "Harmon Eakle," q.v.

ELIE, William. Took the Oath of Allegiance before the Hon. John Stull in 1778 [Ref: O-47, J-11].

ELINGER, Eustatious. See "Eustatious Olinger," q.v.

ELKISON, William. Private who enlisted in the militia on August 18, 1781 for service in the Continental Army [Ref: D-388].

ELLIOTT, David. Private, Militia, 1st Class, Capt. Conrad Hogmire's Company, 1776/1777 [Ref: M-244, A-1146]. Took the Oath of Allegiance before the Hon. Joseph Sprigg before April 1, 1778 [Ref: O-53, J-16].

ELLIS, Ann and Duncan. See "Isaac Ellis," q.v.

ELLIS, Isaac (1752-1833). Private, Pennsylvania Line, who was born on October 29, 1752 in Frederick County (the part that later became part of Washington County), Maryland, and in 1775 moved with his father to Catfish Camp in Washington County, Pennsylvania, where he enlisted in the war. Isaac Ellis married Ann Downing on May 18, 1779 in Pennsylvania. She was born on October 18, 1762 in Virginia. Isaac later moved to Jefferson County, Kentucky and then to Owen County, Kentucky, where he died on May 14, 1833. His widow received pension W10013 in 1836 and in 1846 she moved to Lincoln County, Missouri with a son (not named). In 1837 her sister Jane Downing, aged 67, lived in Mason County, Kentucky. In 1846 Duncan Ellis witnessed Ann's signature, but no relationship was given. A Capt. Timothy Ellis and David Downing were also mentioned in 1833 [Ref: V-I:1104].

ELLIS, John. Private who was enrolled by Lieut. Clement Hollyday and passed by Major Francis Deakins on July 25, 1776 [Ref: D-49].

ELLIS, Timothy. See "Isaac Ellis," q.v.

ELLIT, Benjamin. Private who was enrolled by Lieut. Clement Hollyday and passed by Major Francis Deakins on July 25, 1776 [Ref: D-49].

ELLSPERGER, Wolfgang. Private, German Regiment, continental service, 1776. Private, Third Vacant Company, under Capt. Philip Graybell and Col. Lewis Weltner at Valley Forge in March, 1778. Discharged on July 16, 1779 [Ref: D-204, FF-222, which latter source listed the name as "Wolgong Ebsberger"].

ELSBY, Sallie. See "Henry Boteler," q.v.

EMERICK, Jonas. Private, Militia, 1st Class, Capt. Peter Beall's Company, 1st Battalion, 1776/1777 [Ref: M-240]. Took the Oath of Allegiance before the Hon. Henry Schnebley in 1778 [Ref: O-49, J-13].

EMMERSON, Thomas. Took the Oath of Allegiance before the Hon. Richard Davis in 1778 [Ref: J-5, O-37].

EMMERT, Benjamin. See "Yost Harbaugh," q.v.

EMRICH, Joseph. Private who was enlisted by Lieut. Christian Orndorff and passed on July 20, 1776 in Frederick (now Washington) County [Ref: D-50].

ENGLE, Martin. See "Owen Roby," q.v.

ENGLISH, Robert. Private who was enrolled by Capt. Henry Hardman and passed on July 19, 1776 in Frederick (now Washington) County [Ref: D-51].

ENGLISH, Uliana. See "Matthias Nead," q.v.

ENGLISH, William. Rendered patriotic service by providing a rifle for Capt. Daniel Cresap's Company in July, 1775, as recorded by the

Committee of Observation at Elizabeth Town on November 4, 1775 [Ref: Q-149].

ENSMINGER, Catherine. See "William Sutherland," q.v.

ENSMINGER, Christian. Private, Militia, 1st Class, Capt. Basil Williams' Company, 1776/1777 [Ref: M-244, A-1146, which listed the name as "Christian Answinger"].

ENT, Captain. See "Dr. Peter Woltz," q.v.

ENTIER, John. See "John Etenier," q.v.

ERHARD, Philip. Rendered patriotic service by providing a rifle for Capt. Daniel Cresap's Company in July, 1775, as recorded by the Committee of Observation at Elizabeth Town on November 4, 1775 [Ref: Q-149]. See "Philip Earhard," q.v.

ERNEST, Henry. See "Henry Ornest," q.c.

ERNEST, Michael. Private, Militia, 4th Class, Capt. Michael Fackler's Company, 1776/1777 [Ref: M-245, A-1146].

ERRET, Christophel. Private, Militia, 4th Class, Capt. John Bennet's Company, 1776/1777 [Ref: M-246, A-1146].

ERVIN, James. Took the Oath of Allegiance before the Hon. Richard Davis in 1778 [Ref: J-4, O-37].

ESSIX, Thomas. Private, Militia, 6th Class, Capt. Isaac Baker's Company, 1776/1777 [Ref: A-1146, M-247].

ESTELL, Daniel. Took the Oath of Allegiance before the Hon. Richard Davis in 1778 [Ref: J-4, O-37].

ESTLER, Thomas. Private, Militia, 2nd Class, Capt. Conrad Hogmire's Company, 1776/1777 [Ref: M-244, A-1146].

ETENIER, Daniel. See "Daniel Itnire (Itnise)," q.v.

ETENIER, John. Private, Militia, Capt. William Heyser's Company, enlisted July 16, 1776, muster roll dated October 23, 1776, in continental service [Ref: D-264, which listed the name as "John Itnier" and W-1190, L-79, which listed the name as "John Entier"]. Private, German Regiment, Lt. Col. Ludwick Weltner's Company, and discharged on July 26, 1779 at Fort Wyoming, Pennsylvania [Ref: D-265, D-204, which listed the name as "John Etnier" and GG-97, which listed the name as "John Etnier, Itnier"]. "John Itnire" died before November 19, 1791 (date of balance book entry in Washington County), leaving a widow (no name given in this account) and equal shares to John Itnire, Henry Itnire and George Itnire [Ref: J-32].

ETENIER, Martin. Private, Militia, 1st Class, Capt. Martin Kershner's Company, 1776/1777 [Ref: A-1146, M-247, which listed the name as "Martin Etenire"]. Took the Oath of Allegiance before the Hon. John

Cellars in January, 1778 [Ref: O-40, J-5, K-1814, which latter source listed the name as "Martain Eateniron"].

ETTLEMAN, Leonard. Se "Leonard Edelman," q.v.

EVANS, Elenor. See "Thomas Evans," q.v.

EVANS, John. Private, Militia, 4th Class, Capt. Griffin Johnson's Company, 3rd Battalion, 1776/1777 [Ref: M-243].

EVANS, Thomas (1754-1833). Private who was recruited and passed by County Lieutenant Thomas Sprigg on April 22, 1780 [Ref: D-336]. He applied for and received pension S34821 in Baltimore County, Maryland on October 2, 1818, aged 64, stating he had enlisted at Hagerstown, Maryland and served in the Maryland Line. In 1820 he had a wife Elenor, aged about 57, and in 1824 made an affidavit in Washington, D. C., but did not state his place of residence. Thomas Evans died on September 2, 1833 [Ref: V-I:1135].

EVERLY, John. Drummer, Select Militia, Capt. Adam Ott's Company, 1781 [Ref: M-238, A-1146].

EVERSOLE, Abraham. Private, Militia, 2nd Class, Capt. Jacob Sharer's Company, 1776/1777 [Ref: A-1146, M-248].

EVERSOLE, Catharine. See "Christian Eversole," q.v.

EVERSOLE, Christian. Rendered patriotic service by providing necessaries to Capt. John Reynolds' Company in the Flying Camp and belonging to the Maryland Service in July, 1776, as recorded by the Committee of Observation at Sharpsburg on August 6, 1776 [Ref: Q-333]. Rendered patriotic service by supplying a blanket, a quilt and a coverlid for the use of the military in March, 1776, as recorded by the Committee of Observation on April 12, 1776 [Ref: Q-156, which listed the name as "Christian Eversoles" and L-82, which listed the name as "Ch'n. Eversole"]. "Christian Eversole" died testate by February 23, 1805, leaving a wife Catharine, and among his heirs was a son Christian who received land in Kentucky [Ref: MM-13:133].

EVERSOLE, Peter. Private, Militia, 4th Class, Capt. Michael Fackler's Company, 1776/1777 [Ref: M-245, A-1146].

EVEY (AVEY), Christian (1761-1837). Private, Militia, 3rd Class, Capt. James Smith's Company, 2nd Battalion, 1776/1777 [Ref: M-239, A-1146]. "Christian Evey" died on March 17, 1837, aged 75 years, 2 months, 24 days, and is buried in the Benevola U. B. Church Graveyard at Benevola in Washington County, Maryland [Ref: JJ-II:89].

EVEY (AVEY), John. Private, Militia, 7th Class, Capt. James Walling's Company, 2nd Battalion, 1776/1777 [Ref: M-239, A-1146].

EVEY (EVY), Joseph. Private, Militia, 3rd Class, Capt. Jeremiah Spires' Company, 2nd Battalion, 1776/1777 [Ref: M-239, A-1146].

EVEY (EVIE), Peter. Private, Militia, 4th Class, Capt. James Smith's Company, 2nd Battalion, 1776/1777 [Ref: M-240, A-1146].

EWART, James. Took the Oath of Allegiance before the Hon. Christopher Cruse in Sharpsburg Hundred before March 2, 1778 [Ref: O-34, J-2].

FACKLER, John. Private, Militia, 8th Class, Capt. Michael Fackler's Company, 1776/1777 [Ref: M-245, A-1146]. Paid by the Committee of Observation on March 1, 1777 for "assisting to apprehend John Acton, etc., living at Green Spring Furnace." [Ref: Q-239, Q-248]. John Fackler, son of Michael, formerly of Elizabeth Town, died in Staunton, Virginia on February 16, 1804 [Ref: LL-2:93].

FACKLER, Michael. Served on the Committee of Observation for the Elizabeth Town District (now the Hagerstown area of Washington County) in December, 1776 [Ref: Q-340]. Captain, Militia, 1776 (succeeded, but date not given). [Ref: M-75, M-245, A-1146]. Took the Oath of Allegiance before the Hon. Henry Schnebley in 1778 [Ref: O-51, J-15]. See "John Fackler" and "Michael Fockler" and "Michael Fogler" and "Frederick Stydinger," q.v.

FAGUE, George. Private, Militia, 4th Class, Capt. Jacob Sharer's Company, 1776/1777 [Ref: A-1146, M-248].

FAGUE, John. Private, Militia, 4th Class, Capt. Jacob Sharer's Company, 1776/1777 [Ref: A-1146, M-248]. Took the Oath of Allegiance before the Hon. John Stull in 1778 [Ref: O-46, J-10, which listed the name as "John Fage"]. Rendered patriotic service by supplying a blanket for the use of the military in March, 1776, as recorded by the Committee of Observation on April 12, 1776 [Ref: Q-157, which listed the name as "John Fege" and L-82, which listed the name as "John Feagen"].

FAIR, Francis. Took the Oath of Allegiance before the Hon. John Stull in 1778 [Ref: O-46, J-10].

FAIRMAN, Henry. Private, Militia, 7th Class, Capt. Martin Kershner's Company, 1776/1777 [Ref: A-1146, M-248]. Private, Militia, Capt. Martin Kershner's Company, 32nd Battalion, December 27, 1776 [Ref: K-1814, Box 3]. Took the Oath of Allegiance before the Hon. Henry Schnebley in 1778 [Ref: O-50, J-14, which listed the name as "Henry Fahrman"].

FAITH, James. See "John Cushwa," q.v.

FAITS, John. Private, Militia, 3rd Class, Capt. James Prather's Company, 3rd Battalion, 1776/1777 [Ref: M-242].

FAKENBERGER, Michael. Took the Oath of Allegiance before the Hon. Henry Schnebley in 1778 [Ref: O-50, J-14].

FALLOWS, William. Took the Oath of Allegiance before the Hon. Samuel Hughes before March 1, 1778 [Ref: O-33, J-1, which latter source listed the name as "William Fullows"].

FANGLAR, George. Fourth Sergeant, Militia, Capt. John Kershner's Company, on duty guarding prisoners of war at Fort Frederick on June 27, 1778 [Ref: D-328].

FANNER, William. Private who was enlisted by Ensign Nathan Williams and passed on July 25, 1776 in Frederick (now Washington) County [Ref: D-51].

FANNING, James (c1744-). Soldier who resided in Washington County and was granted a pension certificate in August, 1820, according to an Act of Congress of March 18, 1818, since he had proven that he was "in the enjoyment of a certain degree of poverty" as required by the Act as amended on May 1, 1820 [Ref: W-1190]. Private, New Jersey Line, pensioned at $96 per year effective March 1, 1820 [Ref: R-42].

FARMER, Capt. See "Henry Knode" and Samuel Farmer," q.v.

FARMER, Henry. Private, Militia, 2nd Class, Capt. Jeremiah Spires' Company, 2nd Battalion, 1776/1777 [Ref: M-239, A-1146]. Took the Oath of Allegiance before the Hon. Richard Davis in 1778 [Ref: J-3, O-36].

FARMER, Phillinor. Private, Militia, 1st Class, Capt. Jeremiah Spires' Company, 2nd Battalion, 1776/1777 [Ref: M-239, A-1146].

FARMER, Samuel. Took the Oath of Allegiance before the Hon. Richard Davis in 1778 [Ref: J-4, O-36]. There was an Ensign Samuel Farmer in the 3rd Maryland Line in 1777 who became a lieutenant by August 16, 1780 when he was wounded and taken prisoner at the Battle of Camden in South Carolina. There was also a Capt. Samuel Farmer in the 3rd Maryland Line by March 2, 1780 when soldiers recruited in Baltimore were delivered to him. Additional research will be necessary before drawing conclusions. See "Henry Knode," q.v.

FARREL, Thomas. Took the Oath of Allegiance before the Hon. Richard Davis in 1778 [Ref: J-4, O-37].

FARROL, John. Private who was recruited and passed by County Lieutenant Thomas Sprigg on April 22, 1780 [Ref: D-336].

FASNIGHT, Adam. Private, Militia, 5th Class, Capt. Conrad Nichodemus' Company, 2nd Battalion, 1776/1777 [Ref: M-237, A-1146].

FASTNAUGHT, Jacob. Private, Militia, 3rd Class, Capt. Conrad Nichodemus' Company, 2nd Battalion, 1776/1777 [Ref: M-237, A-1146].

FAULKER, Robert. Private, Militia, 5th Class, Capt. Griffin Johnson's Company, 3rd Battalion, 1776/1777 [Ref: M-243].

FAUR, Henry. Took the Oath of Allegiance before the Hon. Andrew Rentch before March 7, 1778 [Ref: J-15, O-52, which latter source listed the name as "Henr (Henry) Faur"].

FAUR (FOWER), James. Took the Oath of Allegiance before the Hon. Lemuel Barritt before March 16, 1778 [Ref: O-43, J-8].

FAUSETT, Goodheart. Private, Militia, 3rd Class, Capt. Conrad Hogmire's Company, 1776/1777 [Ref: M-244, A-1146].

FAUT, Barnet (Bernhart). Private, Militia, Capt. Martin Kershner's Company, 32nd Battalion, December 27, 1776 [Ref: K-1814 (Box 3), which listed the name as "Bearnhard Faut"]. Fifer, Militia, Capt. Martin Kershner's Company, 1776/1777 [Ref: M-247, A-1146, which listed the name as "Bearnhard Tant"]. Took the Oath of Allegiance before the Hon. John Cellars in January, 1778 [Ref: K-1814, O-40, J-6, which latter sources listed the name as "Banet Faut"].

FEAGEN, John. See "John Fege," q.v.

FEAR, George. Took the Oath of Allegiance before the Hon. John Barnes before February 28, 1778 [Ref: O-45, J-10].

FEELY, Charles. Private who was enrolled by Capt. Henry Hardman and passed on July 19, 1776 in Frederick (now Washington) County [Ref: D-51].

FEETER, Abraham. See "Abraham Teeter," q.v.

FEGATE, John. Private, Militia, 7th Class, Capt. Conrad Hogmire's Company, 1776/1777 [Ref: M-244, A-1146].

FEIGLEY, Peter. See "Peter Figley," q.v.

FERGUSON, John. There were several men with this name who rendered service during the Revolutionary War. Additional research may be necessary before drawing conclusions. (1) "John Ferguson" was a private who was enlisted by Capt. John Reynolds and passed on July 18, 1776 in Frederick (now Washington) County [Ref: D-50]. (2) "John Ferguson, Jr." was a private, Militia, 5th Class, Capt. Joseph Chapline's Company, 2nd Battalion, 1776/1777 [Ref: M-241]. (3) "John Ferguson, Sr." took the Oath of Allegiance before the Hon. Joseph Chapline before April 17, 1779 [Ref: J-5, O-39, which listed the name as "John Furguson, Snr."]. (4) "John Ferguson, sub-sheriff" took the Oath of Allegiance on July 26, 1777 [Ref: K-1814, Box 4]. (5) Catharine, widow of "John Ferguson or Furguson," applied for and received pension W8808 in Hardin County, Kentucky on June 30, 1841, aged 86, stating she married John Ferguson in Frederick County, Maryland in the fall of 1776 or 1777 (by Rev. Booth) and she was Catharine Thomas, a great aunt of Gov. Thomas of Maryland. Her husband John Ferguson, while a resident of Frederick, enlisted in Hagerstown in 1776 and served one year as a private in Capt. Cresap's Maryland Riflemen. He later enlisted for 3 years in the spring of 1779, served in the 2nd Maryland Line, and was wounded in the arm (battle not named). They had children, the first born on January 4, 1780 (no name given), and the only one mentioned was Edney Strickler who was living in Elizabeth Town, Hardin County, Kentucky in 1840, aged 48. Catharine also mentioned a nephew, Col. John Thomas (born July 5, 1767), son of Francis Thomas and father of Gov. Thomas of Maryland [Ref: U-20:2 (1932)].

FERGUSON, Samuel. Private, Militia, 1st Class, Capt. Daniel Cresap's Company, 3rd Battalion, 1776/1777 [Ref: M-241, which listed the name as "Samuel Fergeston"]. Took the Oath of Allegiance before the Hon. Lemuel Barritt before March 16, 1778 [Ref: O-42, J-7, which listed the name as "Samuel Forgerson"].

FERRELL, John. Private who was enrolled by Lieut. Clement Hollyday and passed by Major Francis Deakins on July 25, 1776 [Ref: D-49].

FESLER, Michael. Private, Militia, 4th Class, Capt. Peter Beall's Company, 1st Battalion, 1776/1777 [Ref: M-240].

FETHWORTH, Isaac. Took the Oath of Allegiance before the Hon. Lemuel Barritt before March 16, 1778 [Ref: O-42, J-8].

FETZER, Philip. Took the Oath of Allegiance before the Hon. Henry Schnebley in 1778 [Ref: O-50, J-14]. Private, Militia, 5th Class, Capt. John Bennet's Company, 1776/1777 [Ref: M-246, A-1146, which listed the name as "Phillip Fetfer"]. Private, Militia, 6th Class, Capt. Basil Williams' Company, 1776/1777 [Ref: M-244, A-1146, which listed the name as "Phillip Fectar"].

FICHE, John. Private, Militia, Capt. John Kershner's Company, on duty guarding prisoners of war at Fort Frederick on June 27, 1778 [Ref: D-328].

FIELDS, Thomas. Private, Militia, 6th Class, Capt. Daniel Cresap's Company, 3rd Battalion, 1776/1777 [Ref: M-241]. Took the Oath of Allegiance before the Hon. Lemuel Barritt before March 16, 1778 [Ref: O-42, J-7, which listed the name as "Thomas Feaild"].

FIFER, Martin. See "Martin Pifer," q.v.

FIGHT, John. Took the Oath of Allegiance before the Hon. John Cellars in January, 1778 [Ref: K-1814, O-40, J-6].

FIGELY, George. Private who was enrolled by Capt. Henry Hardman and passed on July 19, 1776 in Frederick (now Washington) County [Ref: D-51, which listed the name as "George Feigley"].

FIGELY, John. Took the Oath of Allegiance before the Hon. Henry Schnebley in 1778 [Ref: O-49, J-13, which listed the name as "John Figeby"]. See "Peter Figely," q.v.

FIGLEY, Peter (1758-1845). Private who was enrolled by Capt. Henry Hardman and passed on July 19, 1776 in Frederick (now Washington) County [Ref: D-51, which listed the name as "Peter Fiegley"]. Private,

Flying Camp, born 1758 [Ref: N-21]. Took the Oath of Allegiance before the Hon. Henry Schnebley in 1778 [Ref: J-13, O-49, which latter source listed the name as "Peter Feigety"]. Private, Maryland Militia, pensioned in Washington County under the Act of June 7, 1832 at the annual allowance of $38.33 retroactive to March 4, 1831 [Ref: R-51, which listed the name as "Peter Figely"]. Resided in the 3rd District of Washington County in 1840, aged 86 [Ref: EE-28:4 (p. 442), containing an article by Elba Anthony Dardeau, Jr., which listed the name as "Peter Feighly, Sen."]. "Peter Figla or Figely" applied for and received pension S8468 in Washington County on November 27, 1832, age 74, a resident of Hagerstown and where he lived at the time of his enlistment. He died (date not given) leaving seven children (not named), of whom John and Samuel received final payment from his pension on September 17, 1853, retroactive to January 16, 1845 [Ref: V-II:1187]. "Peter Figeley, last Revolutionary soldier to die in Washington County" died on January 14, 1845, aged 96, was buried in Old St. John's Lutheran Churchyard, and subsequently reinterred in Rose Hill Cemetery in Hagerstown [Ref: JJ-VII:104].

FIGLEY, Samuel. See "Peter Figley," q.v.

FILLER, Frederick. Private, Militia, Capt. William Heyser's Company, enlisted in July, 1776, muster roll dated October 23, 1776, in continental service, and reenlisted in July 9, 1778 [Ref: GG-97, W-1190, L-79, D-264, which listed the name as "Frederick Filler"]. Private, German Regiment, Lt. Col. Ludwick Weltner's Company, and discharged on July 26, 1779 at Fort Wyoming [Ref: D-265, which listed the name as "Frederick Filter" and D-208, which listed the name as "Frederick Filler" and GG-97, which listed the name as "Frederick Filler, Filter"].

FILMAN, Mathias. Took the Oath of Allegiance before the Hon. John Stull in 1778 [Ref: O-46, J-10].

FINCH, Joseph. Private who was enlisted by Lieut. Moses Chapline and passed on July 24, 1776 in Frederick (now Washington) County [Ref: D-50].

FINGLESHARER, John. Rendered patriotic service in Hagerstown by dieting soldiers of Capt. John Nelson's Company, continental service (Maryland Line), April, 1776 [Ref: Q-161].

FINLEY, Samuel. See "Michael Devilbiss," q.v.

FIREY, Jacob. See "Henry Startzman," q.v.

FIREY, Joseph. Private, Militia, 5th Class, Capt. John Bennet's Company, 1776/1777 [Ref: M-246, A-1146]. Took the Oath of Allegiance before the Hon. John Barnes before February 28, 1778 [Ref: O-44, J-9, which listed the name as "Joseph Fiery"].

FISH, Thomas. Private who was enrolled by Capt. Henry Hardman and passed on July 19, 1776 in Frederick (now Washington) County [Ref: D-51].

FISHER, ---- (blank). Private, Militia, 7th Class, Capt. James Prather's Company, 3rd Battalion, 1776/1777 [Ref: M-243].

FISHER, Abraham. Took the Oath of Allegiance before the Hon. Henry Schnebley in 1778 [Ref: O-51, J-14].

FISHER, Adam. Private, Militia, 2nd Class, Capt. John Bennet's Company, 1776/1777 [Ref: M-246, A-1146]. Took the Oath of Allegiance before the Hon. John Barnes before February 28, 1778 [Ref: O-44, J-9]. See "Adam Ott," q.v.

FISHER, Balser. Private, Militia, Capt. William Heyser's Company, muster roll dated October 23, 1776, in continental service, and died March 15, 1777 [Ref: D-264, GG-97].

FISHER, Daniel. Private who was enrolled by Capt. Henry Hardman and passed on July 19, 1776 in Frederick (now Washington) County [Ref: D-51]. Took the Oath of Allegiance before the Hon. Henry Schnebley in 1778 [Ref: O-49, J-13]. See "Jacob Fisher," q.v.

FISHER, Elizabeth. See "Jacob Fisher," q.v.

FISHER, Jacob. Rendered patriotic service by providing shot bags for the use of the military in July, 1775, as recorded by the Committee of Observation at Elizabeth Town on November 4, 1775 [Ref: Q-150]. Rendered patriotic service by providing a leather line for the use of the military in January, 1777, as recorded by the Committee of Observation on January 27, 1777 [Ref: Q-53]. Took the Oath of Allegiance before the Hon. Joseph Sprigg before April 1, 1778 [Ref: O-53, J-16]. Jacob Fisher died before April 9, 1791 (date of balance book entry in Washington County), leaving a widow (no name given in this account) and equal shares to John Fisher, Molly Warble, Elizabeth Fisher, Mary Fisher, Jacob Fisher, and Daniel Fisher [Ref: J-30].

FISHER, Jacob Jr. Fourth Corporal, Militia, Capt. Peter Beall's Company, 1st Battalion, 1776/1777 [Ref: M-240]. Took the Oath of Allegiance before the Hon. Joseph Sprigg before April 1, 1778 [Ref: O-53, J-16, which listed the name without the "Jr."]. See "Jacob Fisher," q.v.

FISHER, John. Took the Oath of Allegiance before the Hon. Joseph Sprigg before April 1, 1778 [Ref: O-53, J-16]. Private, Select Militia, Capt. Adam Ott's Company, 1781 [Ref: M-238, A-1146]. Private who enlisted in the militia on August 24, 1781 for service in the Continental Army [Ref: D-387, H-451]. Substitute, Maryland Line, discharged on October 30, 1781 [Ref: G-657]. John Fisher applied for and received pension S2211 in Fairfield County, Ohio on November 5, 1832, age 70, stating he was born in Berks County, Pennsylvania in 1762 and later moved to Hagerstown, Maryland where he lived at the time of his enlistment [Ref: V-II:1199]. See "Jacob Fisher" and "John Miller," q.v.

FISHER, Mary. See "Jacob Fisher," q.v.

FISHER, Peter. See "Adam Ott," q.v.

FISHER, Philip. Private, Militia, Capt. William Heyser's Company, enlisted August 4, 1776, muster roll dated October 23, 1776, in continental service, and reenlisted August 9, 1778 [Ref: GG-97, D-264, W-1190, L-79]. Private, German Regiment, Lt. Col. Ludwick Weltner's Company, discharged on July 24 or 26, 1779 at Fort Wyoming, Pennsylvania [Ref: W-1190, L-79, D-265. GG-97].

FISHER, Walter. See "Yost Harbaugh," q.v.

FISTER, Luke. Private, Militia, 5th Class, Capt. Michael Fackler's Company, 1776/1777 [Ref: M-245, A-1146].

FITCH, James. Private, Militia, 2nd Class, Capt. Joseph Chapline's Company, 2nd Battalion, 1776/1777 [Ref: M-241]. Took the Oath of Allegiance before the Hon. Christopher Cruse in Sharpsburg Hundred before March 2, 1778 [Ref: O-34, J-2].

FITCH, Joseph. Private, Militia, 2nd Class, Capt. James Walling's Company, 2nd Battalion, 1776/1777 [Ref: M-238, A-1146]. Took the Oath of Allegiance before the Hon. John Stull in 1778 [Ref: O-46, J-10].

FITZGERALD, Nicholas (1757-1821). Private, Militia, 4th Class, Capt. Isaac Baker's Company, 1776/1777 [Ref: A-1146, M-247]. Resided in Washington County and was granted a pension certificate in August, 1820, according to an Act of Congress of March 18, 1818, since he had proven that he was "in the enjoyment of a certain degree of poverty" as required by the Act as amended on May 1, 1820 [Ref: W-1190]. Private, Maryland Line, applied for and received pension S34852 in Washington County on August 1, 1820, age 63, and received $96 per year effective September 13, 1820. He died on December 8, 1821 [Ref: R-42, N-21, V-II:1206, AA-341].

FITZHUGH, Peregrine. Cornet, Baylor's Regiment; captured and later exchanged on October 25, 1780 [Ref: D-616]. "Peregrine and William Fitzhugh also served with credit in the Revolutionary War. They were sons of Col. William Fitzhugh, a retired officer of the British Army, who removed to Washington County from the shores of the Patuxent at an early date." [Ref: L-79, L-80]. In November, 1791 Capt. William Fitzhugh, of Calvert County, received payment for his war services from Maryland's Treasurer of the Western Shore [Ref: AA-341].

FITZHUGH, William. See "Peregrine Fitzhugh," q.v.

FIVECOATS, Michael. Took the Oath of Allegiance before the Hon. John Barnes before February 28, 1778 [Ref: O-44, J-9]. Private, Militia, 6th Class, Capt. John Bennet's Company, 1776/1777 [Ref: M-246, A-1146, which listed the name as "Michael Fivicoat"].

FLACK, Andrew, and others. See "Andrew Fleck," q.v.

FLAKE, John, and others. See "John Fleck," q.v.

FLAKER, Frederick. See "Frederick Plecker," q.v.

FLAT, John. See "John Fleck (Fliet)," q.v.

FLECK (FLICK, FLACK), Andrew. Enrolled in the first militia company organized for the Revolutionary War in the Elizabeth Town District of Frederick County (now the Hagerstown area of Washington County) on January 6, 1776 [Ref: Q-271, W-1190]. Took the Oath of Allegiance before the Hon. Christopher Cruse in Sharpsburg Hundred before March 2, 1778 [Ref: O-35, J-2]. "Andrew Flack" was a private, Militia, 8th Class, Capt. John Rennolds' (Reynolds') Company, 2nd Battalion, 1776/1777 [Ref: M-240]. See "William Fleck," q.v.

FLECK (FLICK), Anna Christiana. See "Phillip Salladay," q.v.

FLECK (FLICK, FLAKE), George. Private who was enlisted by Lieut. Christian Orndorff and passed on July 20, 1776 in Frederick (now Washington) County [Ref: D-50]. Private, Militia, 2nd Class, Capt. John Rennolds' (Reynolds') Company, 2nd Battalion, 1776/1777 [Ref: M-240]. "George Flack" was a private who was recruited and passed by County Lieutenant Thomas Sprigg on April 22, 1780 [Ref: D-336]. "George Flake or Fleck or Flek" applied for an received pension S42625 in Washington County, Ohio on May 14, 1818, age 63, a resident of Union Township, stating he had lived in Hagerstown, Maryland at the time of his enlistment. In 1821 he had a wife aged 58 and no minor children (names not given). [Ref: V-II:1208].

FLECK (FLICK), Elizabeth. See "Jacob Piper (Pifer)," q.v.

FLECK (FLACK, FLAKE), Jacob. Took the Oath of Allegiance before the Hon. Lemuel Barritt before March 16, 1778 [Ref: O-43, J-8, which listed the name as "Jacob Flock"]. "Jacob Flake" was a private, Militia, 2nd Class, Capt. Griffin Johnson's Company, 3rd Battalion, 1776/1777 [Ref: M-243].

FLECK (FLACK), James. Private, Militia, 3rd Class, Capt. Conrad Hogmire's Company, 1776/1777 [Ref: M-244, A-1146]. Private, Militia, Capt. John Kershner's Company, on duty guarding prisoners of war at Fort Frederick on June 27, 1778 [Ref: D-328]. Took the Oath of Allegiance before the Hon. Joseph Sprigg before April 1, 1778 [Ref: O-53, J-16].

FLECK (FLIET, FLAT), John. Took the Oath of Allegiance before the Hon. Samuel Hughes before March 1, 1778 [Ref: O-33, J-1, which listed the name as "John Fleck"]. Private, German Regiment, Lt. Col. Ludwick Weltner's Company, continental service, discharged on July 26, 1779 [Ref: D-265, which listed the name as "John Fliet"]. Private who enlisted in the militia on September 5, 1781 for service in the Continental Army [Ref: D-388, which listed the name as "John Flat"].

FLECK (FLICK), John. Enrolled in the third militia company organized for the Revolutionary War in the Elizabeth Town District of Frederick County (now the Hagerstown area of Washington County), passed by the Committee of Observation on June 5, 1776, and assigned to Capt. John Reynolds' command [Ref: Q-272]. Private, Militia, Capt. William Heyser's Company, muster roll dated October 23, 1776, in continental service [Ref: D-264, W-1190, L-79]. Private, German Regiment, continental service, enlisted August 2, 1776 and discharged on July 26, 1779 at Fort Wyoming, Pennsylvania [Ref: D-208, GG-97, which latter source listed the name as "John Fleck, Fliet, Flick"]. Took the Oath of Allegiance before the Hon. Joseph Chapline before April 17, 1779 [Ref: J-5, O-39]. "John Flake" was a private, Militia, 1st Class, Capt. Daniel Clapsaddle's Company, 1st Battalion, 1776/1777 [Ref: M-236, A-1146].

FLECK (FLACK), Philip. Private who was enrolled by Capt. Henry Hardman and passed on July 19, 1776 in Frederick (now Washington) County [Ref: D-51].

FLECK (FLICK), William. Took the Oath of Allegiance before the Hon. Christopher Cruse in Sharpsburg Hundred before March 2, 1778 [Ref: O-34, J-2]. William Fleck died testate before June 20, 1801 (date of balance book entry in Washington County), leaving a widow (no name given in this account) and equal shares to Elizabeth Pifer or Piper (wife of Jacob Piper), Margaret Bardona or Barton (wife of Jacob Barton), Garttroat Hedrick or Hetrick (wife of Varner Hetrick), Catherine Miller (wife of David Miller), Christina Selety or Solladay ["Anna Christiana Flick" married "Philip Salladay," q.v.], and Andrew Fleck [Ref: J-39]. One William Flick died in 1790 and is buried in the Old Reformed Graveyard at Sharpsburg, Maryland beside his son Andrew (no dates given). [Ref: JJ-I:28]. See "Jacob Piper (Pifer)," q.v.

FLEGER, Peter. See "Peter Phleuger," q.v.

FLEMING, Patrick. Private, German Regiment, Lt. Col. Ludwick Weltner's Company, continental service, enlisted August 9, 1776 and discharged August 9, 1779 at Tioga, Pennsylvania [Ref: D-265, which listed the name as "Patrick Fliming" and GG-97, which listed the name as "Patrick Flemming, Flemon"].

FLENNARD, John. Took the Oath of Allegiance before the Hon. Henry Schnebley in 1778 [Ref: J-15, O-51, which latter source listed the name as "John Fleunard"].
FLENNARD, John Jr. Took the Oath of Allegiance before the Hon. Henry Schnebley in 1778 [Ref: O-49, J-13].
FLENNARD, Rudolph. Took the Oath of Allegiance before the Hon. Henry Schnebley in 1778 [Ref: O-50, J-14].
FLETCHER, Samuel. Private, Militia, 7th Class, Capt. Jeremiah Spires' Company, 2nd Battalion, 1776/1777 [Ref: M-239, A-1146].
FLICK, Andrew. See "Andrew Fleck (Flick)," q.v.
FLICK, Elizabeth. See "Jacob Piper (Pifer)," q.v.
FLICK, William. See "William Fleck" and "Jacob Piper," q.v.
FLINT, John. First Corporal, Militia, Capt. Barnett Johnston's Company, 3rd Battalion, 1776/1777 [Ref: M-242].
FLINT, John. Private, Militia, 5th Class, Capt. Barnett Johnston's Company, 3rd Battalion, 1776/1777 [Ref: M-242].
FLINT, John. Took the Oath of Allegiance before the Hon. William Yates in 1778 [Ref: O-48, J-12].
FLINT, Joseph. Took the Oath of Allegiance before the Hon. William Yates in 1778 [Ref: O-48, J-12].
FLORA, James. Took the Oath of Allegiance before the Hon. William Yates in 1778 [Ref: O-48, J-12].
FLORA, John. Took the Oath of Allegiance before the Hon. William Yates in 1778 [Ref: O-48, J-12].
FLORA, Richard Jr. Private, Militia, 6th Class, Capt. Barnett Johnston's Company, 3rd Battalion, 1776/1777 [Ref: M-242].
FLOWER, Robert. Took the Oath of Allegiance before the Hon. Lemuel Barritt before March 16, 1778 [Ref: O-43, J-8].
FLUKE, Henry and John. See "Jacob Russell, Jr.," q.v.
FOARD, James. See "James Ford (Foard)," q.v.
FOCEPEH, George. Took the Oath of Allegiance before the Hon. Lemuel Barritt before March 16, 1778 [Ref: J-8, O-43, which latter source listed the name as "George Foepeh"].
FOCKLER, Michael. Rendered patriotic service in Hagerstown by dieting soldiers of Capt. John Nelson's Company, continental service (Maryland Line), April, 1776 [Ref: Q-161]. Served on the Committee of Observation in April, 1776 [Ref: Q-154, Q-155]. See "Michael Fackler," q.v.
FOGELY, Christopher. Private who was enrolled by Capt. Henry Hardman and passed on July 19, 1776 in Frederick (now Washington) County [Ref: D-51].

FOGLE, George. Private, Militia, 4th Class, Capt. Basil Williams' Company, 1776/1777 [Ref: M-244, A-1146].

FOGLE, John. Private, Militia, Capt. William Heyser's Company, muster roll dated October 23, 1776, in continental service and on duty in May, 1777 [Ref: D-264, W-1190, L-79, GG-97].

FOGLER, Andrew. First Corporal, Militia, Capt. Daniel Clapsaddle's Company, 1st Battalion, 1776/1777 [Ref: M-236, A-1146]. The balance of the estate of Andrew Fogler was "paid to the widow only" (no name given) on April 9, 1782 in Washington County [Ref: J-23].

FOGLER, Christopher. Private, Militia, 5th Class, Capt. Daniel Clapsaddle's Company, 1st Battalion, 1776/1777 [Ref: M-236, A-1146].

FOGLER, Michael. Rendered patriotic service by providing "rashons" for the use of the military in July, 1775, as recorded by the Committee of Observation at Elizabeth Town on November 4, 1775 [Ref: Q-150]. See "Michael Fockler," q.v.

FOGLER, Simon. Private, Militia, Capt. William Heyser's Company, muster roll dated October 23, 1776, in continental service and on duty in May, 1777 [Ref: D-264]. Received a pension of $20 per year beginning September 4, 1793 [Ref: GG-97].

FOGLESONG, Barbara and Catherine. See "Christian Foglesong," q.v.

FOGLESONG, Christian. Took the Oath of Allegiance before the Hon. John Stull in 1778 [Ref: O-46, J-10, which listed the name as "Christian Forgresong"]. One Christian Foglesong died testate by March 24, 1792 (date of balance book entry in Washington County), leaving a widow (not named, but Barbara Foglesong was the executrix) and equal shares to Eve Yanders, Frederick Foglesong, Christian Foglesong, Catherine Foglesong, John Foglesong and David Foglesong [Ref: J-31]. Frederick Foglesong died before September 29, 1798 (date of balance book entry in Washington County) and one of his children was Christian Foglesong [Ref: J-37].

FOGLESONG, David, Frederick and John. See "Christian Foglesong," q.v.

FOLTZ, Daniel. See "Henry Schlosser," q.v.

FOLTZ, William. Private, Militia, 1st Class, Capt. Conrad Nichodemus' Company, 2nd Battalion, 1776/1777 [Ref: M-237, A-1146].

FONTER, John. Took the Oath of Allegiance before the Hon. Richard Davis in 1778 [Ref: J-3, O-36].

FORD (FOARD), Henry. Private, Militia, 3rd Class, Capt. John Cellars' Company, 1776/1777 [Ref: A-1146, M-246, Q-48, Q-227]. Took the Oath of Allegiance before the Hon. John Barnes before February 28, 1778 [Ref: O-44, J-9]. See "James Ford" and "Denton Jacques," q.v.

FORD (FOARD), James. Private, Militia, 4th Class, Capt. John Cellars' Company, 1776/1777 [Ref: A-1146, M-246, Q-48]. Took the Oath of Allegiance before the Hon. John Barnes before February 28, 1778 [Ref: O-44, J-9]. "James Ford" died testate by September 19, 1801 and among his heirs were sons James and Henry [Ref: MM-12:77].

FORD (FOARD), Robert. Private, Militia, 8th Class, Capt. John Cellars' Company, 1776/1777 [Ref: A-1146, M-247, Q-48, Q-227]. Took the Oath of Allegiance before the Hon. John Barnes before February 28, 1778 [Ref: O-44, J-9]. See "Denton Jacques," q.v.

FORD, Robert. Ensign, Militia, Capt. Barnett Johnston's Company, 3rd Battalion, 1776/1777 [Ref: M-242].

FORGERSON, Samuel. See "Samuel Ferguson," q.v.

FORKER, Robert. Private, Militia, 1st Class, Capt. James Walling's Company, 2nd Battalion, 1776/1777 [Ref: M-238, A-1146].

FORNEY (FURNEY), David. Private, Militia, 3rd Class, Capt. Michael Fackler's Company, 1776/1777 [Ref: M-245, A-1146, which listed the name as "David Furney"]. Private, Militia, Capt. John Kershner's Company, on duty guarding prisoners of war at Fort Frederick on June 27, 1778 [Ref: D-328, which listed the name as "David Fosney"].

FORNEY, Elizabeth. See "Joseph Wyand," q.v.

FORNEY (FURNIER), James. Private, German Regiment, Lt. Col. Ludwick Weltner's Company, continental service, enlisted in July, 1776, reenlisted on July 26, 1778, and discharged on July 26, 1779 at Fort Wyoming, Pennsylvania [Ref: D-265. GG-97, which listed the name as "James Furnier, Fournier, Forney"].

FORSHAY, Obadiah. See "George Miller," q.v.

FORSTER, Luke. Took the Oath of Allegiance before the Hon. Henry Schnebley in 1778 [Ref: O-49, J-12].

FORSYTHE, Jacob. Private who was enlisted by Ensign Nathan Williams and passed on July 25, 1776 in Frederick (now Washington) County [Ref: D-51].

FORSYTHE, Samuel. Private, Militia, by January 22, 1777 when ordered by the Committee of Observation "to march with some company of militia to the reinforcement of his Excellency General Washington" or appear before the Committee and state his reason for not marching. He apparently marched since he never appeared to the contrary [Ref: Q-48].

FOSE, Henry. Private, Militia, 8th Class, Capt. Conrad Hogmire's Company, 1776/1777 [Ref: M-244, A-1146].

FOSE, Jacob. Private, Militia, 3rd Class, Capt. Conrad Hogmire's Company, 1776/1777 [Ref: M-244, A-1146].

FOSE, Michael. Private, Militia, 8th Class, Capt. Conrad Hogmire's Company, 1776/1777 [Ref: M-244, A-1146].

FOSTER, Cassandra. See "Thomas Chenoweth," q.v.

FOSTER, Jeremiah. Private, Militia, 1st Class, Capt. John Rennolds' (Reynolds') Company, 2nd Battalion, 1776/1777 [Ref: M-240]. Jeremiah Foster died testate by Narch 23, 1805, leaving a wife Mary and a brother John Foster [Ref: MM-13:134].

FOSTER, John. Private, Militia, 1st Class, Capt. Jacob Sharer's Company, 1776/1777 [Ref: A-1146, M-248]. See "Jeremiah Foster," q.v.

FOSTER, Mary. See "Jeremiah Foster," q.v.

FOTH, Michael. See "Michael Poth," q.v.

FOWEE, Jacob. See "Jacob Lowre," q.v.

FOWER, James. See "James Faur," q.v.

FOWLER, John. Second Lieutenant, Militia, 1776, Capt. Jeremiah Spires' Company, 2nd Battalion, June 22, 1778 [Ref: M-76, E-145, M-239]. See "Joshua Fowler," q.v.

FOWLER, Joshua. Third Corporal, Militia, Capt. Jeremiah Spires' Company, 2nd Battalion, 1776/1777 [Ref: M-239, A-1146]. On January 20, 1777 John Fowler appeared before the Committee of Observation and "made evidence by Col. Davies that his son Joshua Fowler was uncapable at present to march with the militia by reason of an ulcer on his breast, ordered that said Joshua Fowler be exempted from that service." [Ref: Q-44].

FOWLER, Thomas. Enrolled in the third militia company organized for the Revolutionary War in the Elizabeth Town District of Frederick County (now the Hagerstown area of Washington County), passed by the Committee of Observation on June 5, 1776, and assigned to Capt. John Reynolds' command [Ref: Q-273]. Private who was enlisted by Capt. John Reynolds and passed on July 18, 1776 in Frederick (now Washington) County [Ref: D-50]. On December 24, 1776 the Committee of Observation for Elizabeth Town District ordered "that Col. Shryock have Thomas Fowler (a poor solder) interred, in a decent manner, and bring his account into this Committee at the next meeting." [Ref: Q-343].

FOX, Balser. Private who was recruited and passed by County Lieutenant Thomas Sprigg on April 22, 1780 [Ref: D-336].

FOX, Christopher. Private, Militia, 8th Class, Capt. Martin Kershner's Company, 1776/1777 [Ref: A-1146, M-248].

FOX, Frederick. Enrolled in the third militia company organized for the Revolutionary War in the Elizabeth Town District of Frederick County (now the Hagerstown area of Washington County), passed by the

Committee of Observation on June 5, 1776, and assigned to Capt. John Reynolds' command [Ref: Q-273]. Private, Militia, 4th Class, Capt. Joseph Chapline's Company, 2nd Battalion, 1776/1777 [Ref: M-241]. Took the Oath of Allegiance before the Hon. Christopher Cruse in Sharpsburg Hundred before March 2, 1778 [Ref: O-34, J-2].

FOX, George. Took the Oath of Allegiance before the Hon. Christopher Cruse in Sharpsburg Hundred before March 2, 1778 [Ref: O-34, J-2].

FOX, Michael. Enrolled in the first militia company organized for the Revolutionary War in the Elizabeth Town District of Frederick County (now the Hagerstown area of Washington County) on January 6, 1776 [Ref: Q-271, W-1190]. Private, Militia, 5th Class, Capt. Joseph Chapline's Company, 2nd Battalion, 1776/1777 [Ref: M-241].

FOYE, William. Private, Militia, 7th Class, Capt. Jacob Sharer's Company, 1776/1777 [Ref: A-1146, M-248].

FRANCE, Christian. Private who was enlisted by Lieut. Moses Chapline and passed on July 24, 1776 in Frederick (now Washington) County [Ref: D-50].

FRANCE, Nicholas. Private who was enlisted by Lieut. Christian Orndorff and passed on July 20, 1776 in Frederick (now Washington) County [Ref: D-50].

FRANK, Henry Sr. On January 16, 1777 the Committee of Observation for Elizabeth Town District (now the Hagerstown area of Washington County) reported "whereas Major Swearingen hath made complaint to this committee, that a wagon and horses etc. are wanting for the use of Capt. Swingley's Company, and can by no means be got, therefore ordered that Capt. Swingley apply to persons residing in his district (Henry Frank Sr. only excepted) for a wagon, four horses, gears, a wagon cloth etc. and in case of refusal, immediately to impress the same." [Ref: Q-41].

FRANKLIN, William. Private who was enrolled by Capt. Aeneas Campbell and passed by Major Francis Deakins on July 18, 1776 [Ref: D-49].

FRANKS, Christiana, and children. See "Henry Franks," q.v.

FRANKS, Henry. Private, Pennsylvania Line, who applied for pension in Wayne County, Ohio on September 3, 1832, stating he was born on June 26, 1763 or 1764 near Fredericktown in Washington County, Maryland and lived in Fayette County, Pennsylvania at the time of his enlistment. Henry died in Ohio on May 5, 1836 and his widow Christiana applied for and received pension W4956 on July 13, 1839, age 72. Henry Franks and Christiana Mason were married in April, 1786 and had these children: John Franks (born January 14, 1787 and married Polly Heckler or Leckler on February 14, 1814), Michael Franks (born September 4, 1788 and married Martha Thompson on January 14, 1813), Elizabeth Franks (born October 12, 1791 and married Samuel Higgins on the first Tuesday in December, 1810), Sarah Franks (born January 9, 1794 and married John Routzen on February 28, 1816), Henry Franks (born April 19, 1796), Abraham Franks (born February 9, 1798 and married Lydia Blacker on May 19, 1825), Uriah Franks (born October 21, 1799 and married Elizabeth Walls on January 30, 1823), Abigail Franks (born February 14, 1802), Christiana Franks (born March 15, 1804), Catharine Franks (born August 17, 1806), and Phebby Franks (born June 1, 1809). [Ref: V-II:1259].

FRANTZ, Abram. Private, German Regiment, continental service, 1776. Private, Third Vacant Company, under Capt. Philip Graybell and Col. Lewis Weltner at Valley Forge in March, 1778. Discharged on July 19, 1779 [Ref: D-208, FF-222, which latter source listed the name as "Abraham Frantz"].

FRANTZ, Stofel. Took the Oath of Allegiance before the Hon. Richard Davis in 1778 [Ref: J-5, O-38, which latter source listed the name as "Stofel Frants"].

FREELAND, Aaron. Private, Militia, 4th Class, Capt. Charles Clinton's Company, 1776/1777 [Ref: M-245, A-1146].

FRENCH, Catharine. See "Jacob Smith," q.v.

FRENCH, George. Private, Militia, 5th Class, Capt. James Prather's Company, 3rd Battalion, 1776/1777 [Ref: M-243]. George French was one of the heirs of John French who died testate in 1789 in Washington County [Ref: J-28].

FRENCH, John. See "George French," q.v.

FRENTLE, Michael. Private, Militia, 6th Class, Capt. Michael Fackler's Company, 1776/1777 [Ref: M-245, A-1146].

FRIEND, Eleanor. See "Jacob Friend," q.v.

FRIEND, Gabriel (1752-c1852). Private, Maryland Line, who applied for pension (R3805) in Allegany County, Maryland on December 12, 1849, age 90, stating he lived in Washington County (now Allegany) at the time of his enlistment. In 1850 he lived at Addison, Pennsylvania, in 1851 his wife was mentioned (name not given), and in 1852 he lived at Selbysport, Allegany County, Maryland. Justice of the Peace John P. Lowdermilk stated Gabriel's family record showed he was 100 years old on June 17, 1852 [Ref: V-II:1275]. See "Jacob Friend," q.v.

FRIEND, George. Private, Militia, 5th Class, Capt. Martin Kershner's Company, 1776/1777 [Ref: A-1146, M-247].

FRIEND, Jacob. Appointed to raise funds on January 24, 1775 for the Committee of Observation in Conococheague Hundred in Frederick (now

Washington) County [Ref: L-75]. Took the Oath of Allegiance on July 26, 1777 [Ref: K-1814, Box 4]. "Jacob Friend, Sr." died testate by February 16, 1802, leaving a wife Eleanor, and among his heirs were sons Jacob and Gabriel [Ref: MM-12:79, 80].

FRIEND, Jacob. Took the Oath of Allegiance before the Hon. John Stull in 1778 [Ref: O-46, J-10, O-46, which latter source listed the name as "Cacob Frend"]. See the other "Jacob Friend," q.v.

FRIEND, John. Private, Militia, Capt. Charles Coulson's Company, enrolled August 28, 1776 [Ref: M-243, A-1146].

FRIEND, Phillip Jr. Private, Militia, 6th Class, Capt. Martin Kershner's Company, 1776/1777 [Ref: A-1146, M-248].

FRIEND, Stophel. Private, Militia, 6th Class, Capt. Martin Kershner's Company, 1776/1777 [Ref: A-1146, M-248].

FRIEND, Tean. Private, Militia, Capt. Charles Coulson's Company, enrolled August 28, 1776 [Ref: M-243, A-1146].

FRIEND, Tobias. Private, Militia, Capt. William Heyser's Company, muster roll dated October 23, 1776, in continental service, which stated he had deserted, yet he was on duty in May, 1777 [Ref: D-264, W-1190, L-79, GG-97].

FRIGATE, Peter. One of several patriots appointed by the Committee of Observation on December 30, 1776 "to form the county into companies (after the militia had marched) for the purpose of relieving the distressed inhabitants of said county and also to compel the Dunkards and Mennonists to give their assistance." [Ref: Q-346].

FRIKE, John. Private, Militia, 3rd Class, Capt. John Cellars' Company, 1776/1777 [Ref: A-1146, M-246].

FRINCK, Thomas Sr. Appeared before the Committee of the Upper District of Frederick (now Washington) County on October 16, 1775 and reported that "he hath been often insulted by the residents of the upper part of Frederick County by refusing to pay their publick dues; it is the opinion and advice of this Committee that they ought to pay their levies and all their publick dues for the support of the civil government." [Ref: Q-146].

FRISEL, Jacob. Took the Oath of Allegiance before the Hon. Richard Davis in 1778 [Ref: J-5, O-38, which latter source listed the name as "Jacob Krisel"].

FROMAN, Jacob. Private, Militia, Capt. Charles Coulson's Company, enrolled August 28, 1776 [Ref: M-243, A-1146].

FRUMANTLE, Francis. Private who was enrolled by Capt. Henry Hardman and passed on July 19, 1776 in Frederick (now Washington) County [Ref: D-51].

FRUTH, Martin. Took the Oath of Allegiance before the Hon. Henry Schnebley in 1778 [Ref: O-49, J-13].

FRY, Bernard. Second Corporal, Militia, Capt. William Heyser's Company, muster roll dated October 23, 1776, in continental service [Ref: D-263, W-1190, L-79, which listed the name as "Bernard Frey"]. Corporal, German Regiment, Lt. Col. Ludwick Weltner's Company, continental service, 1776, and discharged on July 26, 1779 [Ref: D-264, W-1190, L-79, which listed the name as "Barnard Frey" and D-208, which listed the name as "Bernard Frey"].

FRY, George. Rendered patriotic service by supplying a blanket for the use of the military in March, 1776, as recorded by the Committee of Observation on April 12, 1776 [Ref: Q-156, L-82].

FRY, Peter. Private who enlisted in the militia on August 21, 1781 for service in the Continental Army [Ref: D-388]. See "Peter Pry," q.v.

FRY, William. Took the Oath of Allegiance before the Hon. John Stull in 1778 [Ref: J-10, O-46, which latter source listed the name as "William Fye"].

FULECONAR, Alexander. Took the Oath of Allegiance before the Hon. Richard Davis in 1778 [Ref: J-3, O-36].

FULFORD, John. Major who reviewed and passed troops enrolled by Capt. Aeneas Campbell in the Upper District of Frederick County (now Washington County) in July, 1776 [Ref: D-49].

FULLER, Andrew. Private, Militia, Capt. William Heyser's Company, muster roll dated October 23, 1776, in continental service, and subsequently promoted to First Corporal [Ref: W-1190, L-79, D-263, which latter source listed the name as "Andrew Filler"].

FULLOWS, William. See "William Fallows," q.v.

FULSOM, Jeremiah. Enrolled in the second militia company organized for the Revolutionary War in the Elizabeth Town District of Frederick County (now the Hagerstown area of Washington County) on March 9, 1776 [Ref: Q-272]. Private who was enrolled by Lieut. Clement Hollyday and passed by Col. William Luckett on August 8, 1776 [Ref: D-49, which listed the name as "Jeremiah Fulsome"].

FUNDAY, John. On February 1, 1777 he was brought before the Committee of Observation and "charged that he had spoke inimical to the United States. Upon examination of evidences it appeared that he had expressed such sentiments when excessive drunk, but before and since that time had spoken as a friend to the common cause." The committee ordered that he be discharged of the complaint upon paying the expense of his guards [Ref: Q-228].

FUNK, Andrew. See "Henry Funk," q.v.

FUNK, David. Private, Militia, 1st Class, Capt. James Smith's Company, 2nd Battalion, 1776/1777 [Ref: M-239, A-1146]. Took the Oath of Allegiance before September 1, 1780 [Ref: X-111, which listed the name as "David Funck"]. "Major David Funck" died after a short illness on August 25, 1799 [Ref: LL-2:44]. See "Henry Funk," q.v.

FUNK, George (1750-   ). Private, German Regiment [Ref: N-22].

FUNK, Henry ("at Bachtells"). Private, Militia, 6th Class, Capt. Daniel Clapsaddle's Company, 1st Battalion, 1776/1777 [Ref: M-236, A-1146].

FUNK, Henry. Private, Militia, 8th Class, Capt. James Walling's Company, 2nd Battalion, 1776/1777 [Ref: M-239, A-1146]. "Henry Funk, Sr." died testate before March 14, 1789 (date of balance book entry in Washington County), leaving equal shares to Andrew Funk, David Funk, Esther Stotler (wife of John Stotler), Catherine Winger (wife of John Winger), Jacob Funk, Henry Funk, and John Funk [Ref: J-29].

FUNK, Jacob (c1725-1794). Appointed to raise funds on January 24, 1775 for the Committee of Observation in Upper Antietam Hundred in Frederick (now Washington) County [Ref: L-75]. Rendered patriotic service by supplying wheat for the use of the military on March 14, 1780 [Ref: W-1190, HH-73, which listed the name as "Jacob Funck"]. Took the Oath of Allegiance before the Hon. Samuel Hughes before March 1, 1778 [Ref: O-33, J-1]. Founded the town of Jerusalem (later called Funkstown) in Washington County and served in the Maryland House of Delegates, 1785-1788. Migrated to Kentucky with a group of fifty people in 1791 and died in Jefferson County before May 6, 1794 [Ref: LL-1:30, KK-I:90, KK-I:334, which contains more detailed information]. See "Henry Funk," q.v.

FUNK, John. There was more then one man with this name during the Revolutionary War. Additional research will be necessary before drawing conclusions. (1) Private, Militia, 5th Class, Capt. Peter Beall's Company, 1st Battalion, 1776/1777 [Ref: M-240]. (2) Took the Oath of Allegiance before the Hon. Samuel Hughes before March 1, 1778 [Ref: O-33, J-1]. (3) Second Lieutenant, Militia, Capt. Jacob Sharer's Company, 1776. Captain, Militia, 2nd Battalion, June 22, 1778 through January 23, 1781 [Ref: M-76, E-145, H-34, M-248, A-1146]. One "Johannes Funck" died in 1783 (no age or birth date given) and is buried on the William Funk farm north of Mt. Lena, near Beaver Creek, in Washington County, Maryland [Ref: JJ-IV:97]. One John Funk (1750-c1818) was a son of "Jacob Funk," q.v. [Ref: KK-I:334, Y-I:1107]. See "Henry Funk," q.v.

FUNK, Joseph. Private, Militia, 5th Class, Capt. James Smith's Company, 2nd Battalion, 1776/1777 [Ref: M-240, A-1146]. "Died in this town Sat. evening last [in Hagerstown before November 7, 1820], Mrs. Susanna

Funk, relict of the late Joseph Funk, in the 58th year of her age; member of German Baptist Society." [Ref: Z-33].

FUNK, Maria. See "Samuel Funk," q.v.

FUNK, Martin. Private, Militia, 1st Class, Capt. Peter Beall's Company, 1st Battalion, 1776/1777 [Ref: M-240].

FUNK, Samuel (1750-1840). Private, Militia, 3rd Class, Capt. James Walling's Company, 2nd Battalion, 1776/1777 [Ref: M-238, A-1146]. "Samuel Funk, Sr." was born on January 10, 1750, died on August 15, 1840, and is buried beside his wife Maria Funk (1757-1829) and other members of the Funk family in a graveyard on the William Funk farm, north of Mt. Lena, near Beaver Creek, in Washington County, Maryland [Ref: JJ-IV:97].

FUNK, Susanna. See "Joseph Funk," q.v.

FUNK, William. See "Samuel Funk," q.v.

FURGUSON, John. See "John Ferguson," q.v.

FURNEY, David. See "David Forney," q.v.

FURNIER, James. Private, Militia, Capt. William Heyser's Company, muster roll dated October 23, 1776, in continental service [Ref: D-264, W-1190, L-79]. See "James Forney," q.v.

FYE, Christian. Private, Militia, 7th Class, Capt. Basil Williams' Company, 1776/1777 [Ref: M-244, A-1146].

FYE, William. See "William Fry," q.v.

GABBEY, John. Second Corporal, Militia, Capt. Daniel Clapsaddle's Company, 1st Battalion, 1776/1777 [Ref: M-236, A-1146]. One of several patriots appointed by the Committee of Observation on December 30, 1776 "to form the county into companies (after the militia had marched) for the purpose of relieving the distressed inhabitants of said county and also to compel the Dunkards and Mennonists to give their assistance." [Ref: Q-346, which listed the name as "John Gabby"]. Rendered patriotic service by supplying rye for the use of the military on March 30, 1780 [Ref: W-1190, and HH-73, which listed the name as "John Gaby"].

GABLE (GABRAL), Abraham. Took the Oath of Allegiance before the Hon. Henry Schnebley in 1778 [Ref: O-50, J-14, which listed the name as "Abraham Gabrel or Gabral"]. "Abraham Gable" died testate before November 12, 1785 (date of balance book entry in Washington County which mentioned three minor children, but no names were given) and the executors were Isabella Gable and John McGlocklan. On August 8, 1789 the final account filed by John McLaughlan named the three children as Ann, William, and Abraham Gable [Ref: J-26, J-28].

GABLE, Ann and Isabella. See "Abraham Gable," q.v.

GABLE (GABRAL), John. Private, Militia, Capt. John Kershner's Company, on duty guarding prisoners of war at Fort Frederick on June 27, 1778 [Ref: D-328, which listed the name as "John Gable"]. Took the Oath of Allegiance before the Hon. John Cellars in January, 1778 [Ref: O-40, J-6, K-1814, which latter source is the original record and the name looked like "Grabral"]. Rendered patriotic service by supplying wheat for the use of the military on March 4, 1780 [Ref: W-1190, HH-72, which both listed the name as "John Gabrall"].

GABLE, Phillip. Private, Militia, 6th Class, Capt. Jacob Sharer's Company, 1776/1777 [Ref: A-1146, M-248]. Took the Oath of Allegiance before the Hon. John Stull in 1778 [Ref: O-46, J-10, which listed the name as "Phillips Gable"].

GABLE, William. See "Abraham Gable," q.v.

GAHORT, Jacob. His account of "clothing due to be delivered to William Simpson" was reported to the State on November 29, 1779 [Ref: P-250].

GAIRING, Christopher. Took the Oath of Allegiance before the Hon. John Stull in 1778 [Ref: O-46, J-10].

GAITHER, Edward Sr. Took the Oath of Allegiance before the Hon. Richard Davis in 1778 [Ref: J-3, O-36]. See "Henry Gaither," q.v.

GAITHER, Henry. Private, Militia, 7th Class, Capt. Samuel Hughes' Company, 2nd Battalion, 1776/1777 [Ref: M-238, A-1146, which listed the name as "Henry Gathor"]. Ensign, Militia, by January 23, 1781 [Ref: M-77]. Took the Oath of Allegiance before the Hon. Samuel Hughes before March 1, 1778 [Ref: O-33, J-1]. Ensign, Capt. David Gillespie's Company, 1st Battalion, November 21, 1780 [Ref: G-220]. "Col. Henry Gaither, a captain in the Revolutionary War, was the father of H. H. and Edward Gaither, both at one time residents of Hagerstown. Major Gaither commanded a battalion from Hagerstown in the levies of 1791, in Darke's Regiment, under Maj. Gen. St. Clair against the Miami Indians. He was afterwards major in the Regular Army, 3rd Sub. Legion in 1792, lieutenant colonel in 1793, and left the service in 1802." [Ref: L-80[.

GAITHER, John. Private, Militia, 7th Class, Capt. Basil Williams' Company, 1776/1777 [Ref: M-244, A-1146]. Took the Oath of Allegiance before the Hon. Richard Davis in 1778 [Ref: J-3, O-36].

GAITHER, Richard. Took the Oath of Allegiance before the Hon. Samuel Hughes before March 1, 1778 [Ref: O-33, J-1].

GAITHER, Vachel. Private, Militia, 2nd Class, Capt. Basil Williams' Company, 1776/1777 [Ref: M-244, A-1146]. Took the Oath of Allegiance before the Hon. Richard Davis in 1778 [Ref: J-4, O-37, which latter source listed the name as "Vechal Gaither"].

GALL, George. Took the Oath of Allegiance before the Hon. John Barnes before February 28, 1778 [Ref: O-44, J-9].

GALLAGOUGH, John. Private, Militia, 1st Class, Capt. Barnett Johnston's Company, 3rd Battalion, 1776/1777 [Ref: M-242].

GALLOSPEY, John. Rendered patriotic service by supplying rye and wheat for the use of the military on April 10, 1780 [Ref: HH-72, W-1190, which latter source listed the name as "John Galloway"].

GALLOWAY, Mary. See "David Lynn, Jr.," q.v.

GAMBLER, Michael. Private, Militia, Capt. William Heyser's Company, enlisted July 26, 1776, muster roll dated October 23, 1776, in continental service [Ref: W-1190, L-79, D-264, which latter source listed the name as "Michael Cambler"]. Private, German Regiment, Lt. Col. Ludwick Weltner's Company, continental service, on duty in October, 1779 [Ref: D-265, GG-96, which latter source listed the name as "Michael Cambler, Camlee, Camler, Gambler"]. Private, recruited and passed by County Lieutenant Thomas Sprigg on April 22, 1780 and in the German Regiment on August 1, 1780 [Ref: D-336, D-198, which listed the name as "Michael Cambler or Gambler"].

GANSINGER, Abraham. Private, Militia, 2nd Class, Capt. John Cellars' Company, 1776/1777 [Ref: A-1146, M-246].

GANTZ, Catherine. See "Adam Miller," q.v.

GANTZ, George. Private, Militia, 6th Class, Capt. Jeremiah Spires' Company, 2nd Battalion, 1776/1777 [Ref: M-239, A-1146].

GANTZ, Sarah. See "Adam Miller," q.v.

GARAHTY, Patrick (1752-1834). "Died at his residence, one mile from Hancock, Patrick Garahty, a native of Ireland, in the 82nd year of his age. The deceased was a veteran of the Revolution." [Ref: DD-87, citing *The Republican Banner*, August 16, 1834].

GARDENER, Michael. Enrolled in the first militia company organized for the Revolutionary War in the Elizabeth Town District of Frederick County (now the Hagerstown area of Washington County) on January 6, 1776 [Ref: Q-271, W-1190].

GARDENOUR, Catherine, Jacob and John. See "Jacob Gardinour," q.v.

GARDINOUR, Jacob. Took the Oath of Allegiance before the Hon. Joseph Chapline before April 17, 1779 [Ref: J-5, O-39]. One "Jacob Gardenour" died before November 7, 1795 (date of balance book entry in Washington County), leaving equal shares to Jacob Gardenour, Mary McName, Catherine Gardenour, and John Gardenour [Ref: J-34].

GARDNER, Francis. Took the Oath of Allegiance before the Hon. John Stull in 1778 [Ref: O-46, J-10].

GARLOCK, John. Took the Oath of Allegiance before the Hon. William Yates in 1778 [Ref: O-48, J-12].

GARNER, Edward. Private who was enlisted by Ensign Nathan Williams and passed on July 25, 1776 in Frederick (now Washington) County [Ref: D-51, which listed the name as "Edward Garner, G.S.T."].

GARNER, Francis. Private, Militia, 3rd Class, Capt. James Walling's Company, 2nd Battalion, 1776/1777 [Ref: M-238, A-1146].

GARNER, Youst. Private, Militia, 1st Class, Capt. Henry Boteler's Company, 1776/1777 [Ref: M-237, A-1146].

GARRET, Bartin. Enrolled in the second militia company organized for the Revolutionary War in the Elizabeth Town District of Frederick County (now the Hagerstown area of Washington County) on March 9, 1776 [Ref: Q-271].

GATES, Horatio. See "Otho Holland Williams," q.v.

GATHY, William M. See "William McGathy," q.v.

GAVIN, Francis. Private, Militia, 7th Class, Capt. James Smith's Company, 2nd Battalion, 1776/1777 [Ref: M-240, A-1146, which listed the name as "Francis Gaven"]. Private, German Regiment, Lt. Col. Ludwick Weltner's Company, continental service, enlisted on August 4, 1778, and discharged on July 26, 1779 at Fort Wyoming, Pennsylvania [Ref: D-265, GG-96, which listed the name as "Francis Cavin, Gavin, Gavan"]. Private, enlisted in the militia on August 18, 1781 for service in the Continental Army [Ref: D-387].

GEARHART, Jacob. Private, Militia, Capt. John Kershner's Company, on duty guarding prisoners of war at Fort Frederick until discharged on June 5, 1778 [Ref: D-328, which listed the name as "Jacob Geerhert"].

GEARHART, John. Private, Militia, 1st Class, Capt. James Walling's Company, 2nd Battalion, 1776/1777 [Ref: M-238, A-1146].

GEARHART, John. Private, Militia, 2nd Class, Capt. Jeremiah Spires' Company, 2nd Battalion, 1776/1777 [Ref: M-239, A-1146, which listed the name as "John Garhart"]. Took the Oath of Allegiance before the Hon. Henry Schnebley in 1778 [Ref: O-51, J-14, which listed the name as "John Gayrherd"].

GEERHART, Elizabeth. See "Christian Trout," q.v.

GEETING, George. See "George Gitting," q.v.

GEETING, John. Private, 5th Maryland Line, enlisted March 1, 1778 and served through January 1, 1780 [Ref: D-209].

GEIGER, Johannes. See "John Gyer (Giger?)," q.v.

GELHART, Christopher. See "Christopher Gilhart," q.v.

GENSBERGER, Engell (Angle). Private, Militia, 1st Class, Capt. Martin Kershner's Company, 1776/1777 [Ref: A-1146, M-247, which listed the name as "Angle Gansburger"]. See "Peter Gensberger," q.v.

GENSBERGER, Peter (Petter). On several occasions in 1776 Engell and Peter Gensberger (Gansberger, Gainsberger) were brought before the Committee of Observation "for speaking and acting inimical to the common cause and speaking unbecoming words against the Association." On January 2, 1777, the Committee ordered them "kept under guard until the militia march, when they are to be taken with said militia to camp." [Ref: Q-30, Q-154, Q-346]. Private, Militia, 8th Class, Capt. Martin Kershner's Company, 1776/1777 [Ref: A-1146, M-248].

GENTILE, George. Private who was enrolled by Capt. Aeneas Campbell and passed by Major Francis Deakins on July 18, 1776 [Ref: D-49].

GENTILE, Stephen. Private who was enrolled by Lieut. Clement Hollyday and passed by Major Francis Deakins on July 25, 1776 [Ref: D-49].

GEORGE, Indian. Private who was recruited and passed by County Lieutenant Thomas Sprigg on April 22, 1780 [Ref: D-336].

GEORGE, Jacob. Private, Militia, 8th Class, Capt. James Smith's Company, 2nd Battalion, 1776/1777 [Ref: M-240, A-1146].

GEORGE, Joseph. Took the Oath of Allegiance before the Hon. Joseph Sprigg before April 1, 1778 [Ref: O-53, J-16].

GEORGE, Michael. Enrolled in the second militia company organized for the Revolutionary War in the Elizabeth Town District of Frederick County (now the Hagerstown area of Washington County) on March 9, 1776 [Ref: Q-272]. Private, Militia, 3rd Class, Capt. Henry Boteler's Company, 1776/1777 [Ref: M-237, A-1146].

GEORGE, Samuel. Took the Oath of Allegiance before the Hon. William Yates in 1778 [Ref: O-48, J-12].

GEORGE, Thomas. Took the Oath of Allegiance before the Hon. Andrew Rentch before March 7, 1778 [Ref: O-52, J-15].

GERBER, Michael. Private, Militia, 7th Class, Capt. Conrad Nichodemus' Company, 2nd Battalion, 1776/1777 [Ref: M-237, A-1146].

GERICK, George. Private, Militia, 8th Class, Capt. John Rennolds' (Reynolds') Company, 2nd Battalion, 1776/1777 [Ref: M-240].

GERLOCK, Henry. Took the Oath of Allegiance before the Hon. John Barnes before February 28, 1778 [Ref: O-44, J-9].

GESOTT, James. Private, Militia, 8th Class, Capt. James Prather's Company, 3rd Battalion, 1776/1777 [Ref: M-243].

GIBLER, Jacob. Took the Oath of Allegiance before the Hon. Henry Schnebley in 1778 [Ref: O-49, J-13].

GIESER, Frederick and Mathias. See "Mathias Guiser," q.v.

GILBERT, John. Private, Militia, 5th Class, Capt. John Bennet's Company, 1776/1777 [Ref: M-246, A-1146]. Took the Oath of Allegiance before the Hon. John Barnes before February 28, 1778 [Ref: O-44, J-9].

GILBERT, Michael. Private, Militia, 3rd Class, Capt. Barnett Johnston's Company, 3rd Battalion, 1776/1777 [Ref: M-242]. Took the Oath of Allegiance before the Hon. William Yates in 1778 [Ref: O-48, J-12].

GILHART, Christopher. Took the Oath of Allegiance before the Hon. John Stull in 1778 [Ref: O-47, J-11, which latter source listed the name as "Christopher Gelhart"].

GILLALAND, Hugh. Private, Militia, 2nd Class, Capt. John Bennet's Company, 1776/1777 [Ref: M-246, A-1146, Q-48, Q-227, which latter source listed the name as "Hugh Gilliland"]. See "Denton Jacques," q.v.

GILLAM, John. Private who was enrolled by Capt. Aeneas Campbell and passed by Major Francis Deakins on July 18, 1776 [Ref: D-49].

GILLEPIE (GILLIPIS), James. Took the Oath of Allegiance before the Hon. Samuel Hughes before March 1, 1778 [Ref: O-33].

GILLEPIE (GILLIPIS), John. Private, Militia, 5th Class, Capt. Barnett Johnston's Company, 3rd Battalion, 1776/1777 [Ref: M-242].

GILLEPIE (GELLIPSE), David. Took the Oath of Allegiance before the Hon. John Stull in 1778 [Ref: O-46, J-10].

GILLESPIE, David. First Lieutenant, Militia, Capt. Samuel Hughes' Company, 1776. Captain, Militia (date not given). [Ref: M-78, M-237, A-1146]. Took the Oath of Allegiance on June 21, 1777 [Ref: K-1814, Box 4]. Captain, 1st Battalion, November 21, 1778 [Ref: G-220].

GILLESPIE, Francis. Took the Oath of Allegiance before the Hon. Richard Davis in 1778 [Ref: J-5, O-37, which listed the name as "Francis Gilaspy"].

GILLESPIE, George. Took the Oath of Allegiance before the Hon. John Barnes before February 28, 1778 [Ref: O-44, J-9]. One of several patriots appointed by the Committee of Observation on December 30, 1776 "to form the county into companies (after the militia had marched) for the purpose of relieving the distressed inhabitants of said county and also to compel the Dunkards and Mennonists to give their assistance." [Ref: Q-346, which listed the name as "George Galaspy"].

GILLESPIE, James. On August 21, 1780 he wrote to Governor Lee and accepted a commission in the Extra Regiment, followed by his letter to Col. Thomas Stone regarding receipt of the appointment and troop movement in Washington County [Ref: G-56, P-311].

GILLESPIE, John. Second Sergeant, Militia, Capt. John Cellars' Company, 1776/1777 [Ref: M-246, A-1146]. Took the Oath of Allegiance before the Hon. William Yates in 1778 [Ref: O-48, J-12, which listed the name as "John Gillispye"].

GILLESPIE, Thomas. Private, Militia, 7th Class, Capt. John Bennet's Company, 1776/1777 [Ref: M-246, A-1146, which listed the name as "Thomas Gillispie"]. Took the Oath of Allegiance before the Hon. John Barnes before February 28, 1778 [Ref: O-44, J-9].

GILLHAM, Thomas. Private who was recruited and passed by County Lieutenant Thomas Sprigg on April 22, 1780 [Ref: D-336].

GILLIUM, Elizabeth. See "John Snyder," q.v.

GILLSAT, Michael. See "Michael Gilbert," q.v.

GILMOR, Anne. See "Otho Holland Williams," q.v.

GILPIN, Francis Green. Took the Oath of Allegiance before the Hon. Richard Davis in 1778 [Ref: J-4, O-37].

GILPIN, Green. Private, Militia, 4th Class, Capt. Jeremiah Spires' Company, 2nd Battalion, 1776/1777 [Ref: M-239, A-1146].

GILSON, William. Enrolled in the first militia company organized for the Revolutionary War in the Elizabeth Town District of Frederick County (now the Hagerstown area of Washington County) on January 6, 1776 [Ref: Q-270, W-1189]. Private, Militia, 1st Class, Capt. Henry Boteler's Company, 1776/1777 [Ref: M-237, A-1146].

GINES, Evan. Private, Militia, 2nd Class, Capt. Barnett Johnston's Company, 3rd Battalion, 1776/1777 [Ref: M-242].

GIRDLER, Charles. Private who was recruited and passed by County Lieutenant Thomas Sprigg on April 22, 1780 [Ref: D-336].

GIRTEY (GISTEY?), Thomas. Private, Militia, 8th Class, Capt. James Prather's Company, 3rd Battalion, 1776/1777 [Ref: M-243].

GITTING (GEETING), George. Private, Militia, and Drummer, Capt. William Heyser's Company, muster roll dated October 23, 1776, in continental service [Ref: W-1190, L-79, D-263, which latter source listed the name as "George Gittin"]. Private, German Regiment, Lt. Col. Ludwick Weltner's Company, continental service, discharged on July 26, 1779 [Ref: D-265, which listed the name as "George Getting"]. It is interesting to note that "Rev. George A. Geeting, Sr., born in Nassau, Siegerland, Neiderscheida, Germany, 6 Feb 1711, and ended his Master's Labours and his life 28 Jun 1812" is buried in the graveyard at Geeting Meeting House, 1st U. B. Church at Mt. Hebron, Eakle's Mill, in Washington County. Also buried there is "Rev. George A. Geeting, Minister of the Gospel for the last 34 years, born 27 Feb 1784, died 5 Feb 1842, aged 60 years, 11 months, 5 days." [Ref: JJ-V:64]. It appears that "Pvt. George Gitting" (no stone in this cemetery for him, however) may have been the son of Rev. George A. Geeting, Sr. and the father of the second Rev. George A. Geeting. Additional research will be necessary before drawing conclusions.

GITTING (GEETING), Jacob. Private, Militia, and Fifer, Capt. William Heyser's Company, muster roll dated October 23, 1776, in continental service [Ref: D-263].

GITTING (GEETING), Peter. Private, Militia, Capt. William Heyser's Company, enlisted July 28, 1776, muster roll dated October 23, 1776, in continental service, and died March 18, 1777 [Ref: GG-97, L-79, and W-1190, which listed the name as "Peter Getting" and D-264, which listed the name as "Peter Gittin"].

GIVENS, Daniel. Enrolled in the second militia company organized for the Revolutionary War in the Elizabeth Town District of Frederick County (now the Hagerstown area of Washington County) on March 9, 1776 [Ref: Q-271]. First Sergeant, Militia, Capt. Henry Boteler's Company, 1776/1777 [Ref: M-237, A-1146, which listed the name as "Daniel Giveings"].

GIZTEY, Thomas. See "Thomas Girtey," q.v.

GLADHILL, William. Enrolled in the second militia company organized for the Revolutionary War in the Elizabeth Town District of Frederick County (now the Hagerstown area of Washington County) on March 9, 1776 [Ref: Q-272]. Private, Militia, 4th Class, Capt. Henry Boteler's Company, 1776/1777 [Ref: M-237, A-1146]. Took the Oath of Allegiance before the Hon. Christopher Cruse in Lower Antietam Hundred before March 2, 1778 [Ref: J-3, O-35].

GLASS, Michael. Took the Oath of Allegiance before the Hon. Henry Schnebley in 1778 [Ref: O-51, J-14]. Private, Maryland and Virginia Lines, who applied for and received pension S16830 in Montgomery County, Missouri on February 5, 1833, age 69, stating he was born about 60 miles from Philadelphia, Pennsylvania and lived in Frederick County, Virginia at the time of his enlistment about five miles from Hagerstown, Maryland. After the war he lived in Fauquier County, Virginia for 30 years, then moved to Kentucky, and in 1815 or 1816 he moved to Missouri [Ref: V-II:1363].

GLASSNER, George. Fourth Corporal, Militia, Capt. Charles Clinton's Company, 1776/1777 [Ref: A-1146, M-245, which listed the name as "George Glasener"]. Private, Militia, Capt. Charles Coulson's Company, enrolled August 28, 1776 [Ref: M-244, A-1146]. Private, Militia, 5th Class, Capt. Charles Clinton's Company, 1776/1777 [Ref: M-245, A-1146, which listed the name as "George Glasner"].

GLASSNER, John. Private, Militia, Capt. Charles Coulson's Company, enrolled August 28, 1776 [Ref: M-244, A-1146]. Private, Militia, 8th

Class, Capt. Charles Clinton's Company, 1776/1777 [Ref: M-245, A-1146]. Took the Oath of Allegiance before the Hon. Andrew Bruce before March 2, 1778 [Ref: O-41, J-6, which listed the name as "John Glasner"].

GLASSON, Garret. On January 25, 1777 the Committee of Observation ordered Capt. Lynck to pay William Seitzler for attending Garret Glasson, a sick soldier. On February 1, 1777 the Committee ordered Capt. Linck to pay Dr. Peter Woltz for medicines given to Garret Glasson, a sick soldier belonging to the Flying Camp of this State [Ref: Q-51, Q-229].

GLISTER, David. Private, Militia, 7th Class, Capt. James Walling's Company, 2nd Battalion, 1776/1777 [Ref: M-239, A-1146].

GLOSSER, Michael. First Lieutenant, Militia, Capt. Conrad Nichodemus' Company, 2nd Battalion, 1776/1777 [Ref: M-237, A-1146, which listed the name as "Michael Glasser"]. First Lieutenant, Capt. Martin Billmyer's Company, 2nd Battalion, November 21, 1780 [Ref: G-220]. See "Michael Closser," q.v.

GODEY, Henry. Private, Militia, 2nd Class, Capt. Conrad Nichodemus' Company, 2nd Battalion, 1776/1777 [Ref: M-237, A-1146].

GONTZ, George. Private, Militia, 2nd Class, Capt. Conrad Hogmire's Company, 1776/1777 [Ref: M-244, A-1146].

GONTZ, Jacob Jr. Private, Militia, 2nd Class, Capt. Conrad Hogmire's Company, 1776/1777 [Ref: M-244, A-1146].

GONTZ, Joseph. Private, Militia, 6th Class, Capt. Conrad Hogmire's Company, 1776/1777 [Ref: M-244, A-1146].

GOOD, Abraham. Private, Militia, 6th Class, Capt. Conrad Hogmire's Company, 1776/1777 [Ref: M-244, A-1146].

GOOD, Christopher. Private, Militia, 4th Class, Capt. Conrad Hogmire's Company, 1776/1777 [Ref: M-244, A-1146].

GOOD, George. Rendered patriotic service in Hagerstown by providing "horse hire" to Capt. John Nelson's Company, continental service (Maryland Line), April, 1776 [Ref: Q-161].

GOOD, Jacob. Rendered patriotic service by supplying a rug for the use of the military in March, 1776, as recorded by the Committee of Observation on April 12, 1776 [Ref: L-82, Q-157, which latter source mistakenly listed the name as "Jacob Good Rugg"]. On January 10, 1777 the Committee of Observation for Elizabeth Town District (now the Hagerstown area of Washington County) ordered "that Jacob Good furnish one team to draw the cannon for the use of Col. Stull's Battalion and if he cannot furnish four horses [of] his own property, that he apply to some neighbor to assist him therein, who is hereby required to be assistive." [Ref: Q-35].

GOOD, John. Private, Militia, 1st Class, Capt. Conrad Hogmire's Company, 1776/1777 [Ref: M-244, A-1146].

GOOD, William. One of several patriots appointed by the Committee of Observation on January 19, 1777 "to form the county into companies (after the militia had marched) for the purpose of relieving the distressed inhabitants of said county and also to compel the Dunkards and Mennonists to give their assistance." [Ref: Q-43].

GOODING, Benjamin. Private, Militia, 6th Class, Capt. Charles Clinton's Company, 1776/1777 [Ref: M-245, A-1146].

GOODING, Joseph. Private, Militia, 6th Class, Capt. Charles Clinton's Company, 1776/1777 [Ref: M-245, A-1146].

GOODING, Moses. Private, Militia, 2nd Class, Capt. Charles Clinton's Company, 1776/1777 [Ref: M-245, A-1146].

GORDEN, Charles. Third Corporal, Militia, Capt. Samuel Hughes' Company, 1776/1777 [Ref: M-238, A-1146].

GORDEN, William. Private, Militia, 5th Class, Capt. James Prather's Company, 3rd Battalion, 1776/1777 [Ref: M-243]. Took the Oath of Allegiance before the Hon. Lemuel Barritt before March 16, 1778 [Ref: O-43, J-8, which listed the name as "William Gordon"]. On September 23, 1780, Col. Lemuel Barritt recommended to Governor Lee that "William Gordin" be commissioned a first lieutenant in the militia at Keystone since so many officers of the Western Battalion had moved out of Maryland to Kentucky and elsewhere [Ref: G-123]. One "William Gordon" died at an advanced age on the Tuesday before May 2, 1799, leaving a widow and two daughter, and was interred in the Protestant Episcopal burying ground in Elizabeth Town [Ref: LL-2:42].

GORMAN, Daniel. Private, Militia, 8th Class, Capt. Peter Swingle's (Swingley's) Company, 1776/1777 [Ref: A-1146, M-249]. Took the Oath of Allegiance before the Hon. Richard Davis in 1778 [Ref: J-3, O-36]. Rendered patriotic service by supplying wheat for the use of the military on January 27, 1780 [Ref: W-1190, HH-73].

GORMON, William. Private, Militia, 4th Class, Capt. Daniel Clapsaddle's Company, 1st Battalion, 1776/1777 [Ref: M-236, A-1146].

GORND, Adam. Private, Militia, 5th Class, Capt. Conrad Nichodemus' Company, 2nd Battalion, 1776/1777 [Ref: M-237, A-1146].

GRABLE, Peter. Took the Oath of Allegiance before September 1, 1780 [Ref: X-111]. See "Peter Graybill," q.v.

GRABRAL, John. Private, Militia, 3rd Class, Capt. John Cellars' Company, 1776/1777 [Ref: A-1146, M-246]. See "John Gabral," q.v.

GRACE, Adam. Private, Militia, 6th Class, Capt. Peter Swingle's (Swingley's) Company, 1776/1777 [Ref: A-1146, M-248].

GRADING, Isaac. Took the Oath of Allegiance before the Hon. Andrew Rentch before March 7, 1778 [Ref: O-52, J-15].

GRAHAM, James. Enrolled in the first militia company organized for the Revolutionary War in the Elizabeth Town District of Frederick County (now the Hagerstown area of Washington County) on January 6, 1776 [Ref: Q-270, W-1190]. Private, Militia, 4th Class, Capt. John Rennolds' (Reynolds') Company, 2nd Battalion, 1776/1777 [Ref: M-240]. Took the Oath of Allegiance before September 1, 1780 [Ref: X-111].

GRAHAM, Moses (1755-1833). Private, 6th Maryland Line, enlisted June 4, 1777 and served through 1780, including the southern campaign [Ref: D-210, D-348, D-354]. Moses Graham died on July 16, 1833, aged 78 years, 10 days, and is buried beside his wife Phebe Graham (1765-1821) in the Tonoloway Baptist Church Graveyard north of Hancock, Maryland in Pennsylvania near the Maryland State Line [Ref: JJ-II:50].

GRAHAM Phebe. See "Moses Graham," q.v.

GRANT, John. Private, Militia, 1st Class, Capt. Basil Williams' Company, 1776/1777 [Ref: M-244, A-1146]. Private who was enrolled by Capt. Henry Hardman and passed on July 19, 1776 in Frederick (now Washington) County [Ref: D-51]. Took the Oath of Allegiance before the Hon. Richard Davis in 1778 [Ref: J-3, O-36].

GRASS, Jacob. See "Jacob Gross," q.v.

GRAVER, George. Fourth Corporal, Militia, Capt. Peter Swingle's (Swingley's) Company, 2nd Battalion, 1776/1777 [Ref: M-248, A-1146].

GRAVER, Jacob. One of several patriots appointed by the Committee of Observation on December 30, 1776 "to form the county into companies (after the militia had marched) for the purpose of relieving the distressed inhabitants of said county and also to compel the Dunkards and Mennonists to give their assistance." [Ref: Q-345, which listed the name as Jacob Graves"]. On January 6, 1777 he was appointed to serve on the Committee of Observation for Elizabeth Town District (now the Hagerstown area of Washington County) in the room of Capt. Samuel Hughes who had resigned [Ref: Q-34]. Served on the Committee of Observation in February, 1777 [Ref: Q-228, which listed the name as "Jacob Grauer"].

GRAVEROD, ---- (blank). Private, Militia, 5th Class, Capt. James Prather's Company, 3rd Battalion, 1776/1777 [Ref: M-243].

GRAY, Robert. Took the Oath of Allegiance before the Hon. John Stull in 1778 [Ref: O-46, J-10].

GRAYBELL, Philip. Captain, German Regiment, 1776-1779, which included men from Baltimore, Frederick and Washington Counties. His "Third Vacant Company of the German Regiment of Pennsylvania stood at Valley Forge in March, 1778" under Col. Lewis Weltner [Ref: FF-222].

GRAYBILL, Peter. Enrolled in the first militia company organized for the Revolutionary War in the Elizabeth Town District of Frederick County (now the Hagerstown area of Washington County) on January 6, 1776 [Ref: Q-270, W-1190, which listed the name as "Peter Grabel"]. Private, Militia, 6th Class, Capt. John Rennolds' (Reynolds') Company, 2nd Battalion, 1776/1777 [Ref: M-240]. Took the Oath of Allegiance before the Hon. John Cellars in January, 1778 [Ref: K-1814, O-40, J-6, which listed the name as "Peter Graybail"].

GREATHOUSE, Jacob. Private, Militia, Capt. William Heyser's Company, muster roll dated October 23, 1776, in continental service, which stated he had deserted, yet he was on duty in May, 1777 [Ref: D-264, W-1190, L-79, GG-97].

GREECHBAUM, Phillip. See "Philip Creekbaum," q.v.

GREEN, General. See "Neale Peacock" and "Christian Orendorff" and "Otho Holland Williams," q.v.

GREEN, James. Private who was enrolled by Capt. Henry Hardman and passed on July 19, 1776 in Frederick (now Washington) County [Ref: D-51].

GREEN, Nathaniel. See "Otho Holland Williams," q.v.

GREGG, Robert Jr. Private, Militia, 7th Class, Capt. Charles Clinton's Company, 1776/1777 [Ref: M-245, A-1146]. Private, Militia, Capt. Charles Coulson's Company, enrolled August 28, 1776 [Ref: M-244, N-114]. Took the Oath of Allegiance before the Hon. Lemuel Barritt before March 16, 1778 [Ref: O-42, J-8, which listed the name as "Robert Gragg, Jr."].

GREGG, Robert Sr. Private, Militia, Capt. Charles Coulson's Company, enrolled August 28, 1776 [Ref: M-244, A-1146]. Private, Militia, 7th Class, Capt. Charles Clinton's Company, 1776/1777 [Ref: M-245, A-1146]. Took the Oath of Allegiance before the Hon. Andrew Bruce before March 2, 1778 [Ref: O-41, J-6, which listed the name without the "Sr."].

GREGORY, Jacob. Private who was recruited and passed by County Lieutenant Thomas Sprigg on April 22, 1780 [Ref: D-336].

GREYLISH, Francis. Took the Oath of Allegiance before the Hon. Henry Schnebley in 1778 [Ref: O-51, J-14].

GRIFFITHS, David. Took the Oath of Allegiance before the Hon. Richard Davis in 1778 [Ref: J-3, O-36].

GRIM, Jacob. First Corporal, Militia, Capt. Henry Boteler's Company, 1776/1777 [Ref: M-237, A-1146].

GRIME, Jacob. Enrolled in the second militia company organized for the Revolutionary War in the Elizabeth Town District of Frederick County (now the Hagerstown area of Washington County) on March 9, 1776 [Ref: Q-272].

GRIME, John Adam. Took the Oath of Allegiance before the Hon. Joseph Sprigg before April 1, 1778 [Ref: O-53, J-16, which listed the name as "John Adam Griem"]. A "John Adam Grimes" died testate in Shippensburgh, Cumberland County, Pennsylvania and his will was probated on May 21, 1790, naming only his son-in-law John Sailor and grandson Samuel Sailor (minor son of John Sailor). [Ref: Cumberland County Wills Book E, p. 179].

GRIMES, Adam. Rendered patriotic service by supplying two blankets for the use of the military in March, 1776, as recorded by the Committee of Observation on April 12, 1776 [Ref: Q-156, L-82].

GRIMES, Edward. Private, Militia, 5th Class, Capt. Charles Clinton's Company, 1776/1777 [Ref: M-245, A-1146]. Second Lieutenant, Militia, Capt. Charles Coulson's Company, by December 3, 1776 [Ref: M-243, M-81, B-501].

GRIMES, John. There appears to have been more than one man with this name who rendered service during the Revolutionary War. Additional research may be necessary before drawing conclusions. (1) Enrolled in the first militia company organized for the Revolutionary War in the Elizabeth Town District of Frederick County (now the Hagerstown area of Washington County) on January 6, 1776 [Ref: Q-270, W-1189]. (2) Private, Militia, 5th Class, Capt. James Prather's Company, 3rd Battalion, 1776/1777 [Ref: M-243]. (3) Private, Militia, 8th Class, Capt. Griffin Johnson's Company, 3rd Battalion, 1776/1777 [Ref: M-243]. See "John Adam Grime," q.v.

GRIMES, Martin. Private, Militia, 6th Class, Capt. Henry Boteler's Company, 1776/1777 [Ref: M-237, A-1146, which listed the name as "Marten Grims"].

GRIMES, William. Private, Militia, 2nd Class, Capt. James Prather's Company, 3rd Battalion, 1776/1777 [Ref: M-242]. Took the Oath of Allegiance before the Hon. Lemuel Barritt before March 16, 1778 [Ref: O-43, J-8].

GRINIM, Alexander. Enrolled in the second militia company organized for the Revolutionary War in the Elizabeth Town District of Frederick County (now the Hagerstown area of Washington County) on March 9, 1776 [Ref: Q-272].

GRIP, John. Rendered patriotic service by providing a rifle for Capt. Daniel Cresap's Company in July, 1775, as recorded by the Committee of Observation at Elizabeth Town on November 4, 1775 [Ref: Q-148].

GROFF, Jacob. Took the Oath of Allegiance before the Hon. Henry Schnebley in 1778 [Ref: O-50, J-14, which latter source listed the name as "Jacob Grooff"].

GROFF, Jacob Jr. Took the Oath of Allegiance before the Hon. Henry Schnebley in 1778 [Ref: O-51, J-15].

GROH, Edison. See "Jeremiah Cheney," q.v.

GROND, Phillip. Private, Militia, 8th Class, Capt. Conrad Nichodemus' Company, 2nd Battalion, 1776/1777 [Ref: M-237, A-1146].

GROOP, John. See "John Cropp (Groop)," q.v.

GROOFT, Frederick. See "Frederick Craft (Croft)," q.v.

GROSS, Jacob. Private, Militia, Capt. William Heyser's Company, muster roll dated October 23, 1776, in continental service [Ref: W-1190, L-79, D-264, GG-97, which latter two sources listed the name as "Jacob Grass"]. Took the Oath of Allegiance before September 1, 1780 [Ref: X-111].

GROVE, David (c1752-1831). Enrolled in the third militia company organized for the Revolutionary War in the Elizabeth Town District of Frederick County (now the Hagerstown area of Washington County), passed by the Committee of Observation on June 5, 1776, and assigned to Capt. John Reynolds' command [Ref: Q-273]. Private who was enlisted by Capt. John Reynolds and passed on July 18, 1776 in Frederick (now Washington) County [Ref: D-50]. Third Sergeant, Militia, Capt. John Rennolds' (Reynolds') Company, 2nd Battalion, 1778 [Ref: M-240]. Took the Oath of Allegiance before the Hon. Joseph Chapline before April 17, 1779 [Ref: J-5, O-39]. On February 17, 1820 the Treasurer of the Western Shore of Maryland was directed to pay to David Grove, of Washington County, half pay of a private for his Revolutionary War services [Ref: AA-349]. Private, Maryland Line, pensioned at $96 per year effective March 9, 1822 and died November 22, 1831 [Ref: R-42]. "Died at Pleasant Valley, at an advanced age, on Tuesday, November 22, 1831, Mr. Daniel *[sic]* Grove, Sr., a Revolutionary Soldier." [Ref: DD-30, citing *The Republican Banner*, December 3, 1831].

GROVE, Elizabeth. See "John Grove, Sr.," q.v.

GROVE, Jacob. Private, Militia, Capt. Martin Kershner's Company, 32nd Battalion, December 27, 1776 [Ref: K-1814, Box 3]. Private, Militia, 5th Class, Capt. Peter Swingle's (Swingley's) Company, 1776/1777 [Ref: A-

1146, M-248]. Took the Oath of Allegiance before the Hon. Richard Davis in 1778 [Ref: J-5, O-38].

GROVE, John. Took the Oath of Allegiance before the Hon. Richard Davis in 1778 [Ref: J-5, O-38].

GROVE, John Sr. (1721-1788). Took the Oath of Allegiance before September 1, 1780 [Ref: X-111]. John Grove died on March 14, 1788, aged 67, and is buried beside Elizabeth Grove (1725-1799) in a graveyard on the J. W. Vickers farm near Bakersville in Washington County [Ref: JJ-V:49].

GROVE, Mary. See "William Groves" and "Harmon Eakle," q.v.

GROVE, Philip. Enrolled in the first militia company organized for the Revolutionary War in the Elizabeth Town District of Frederick County (now the Hagerstown area of Washington County) on January 6, 1776 [Ref: Q-271, W-1190].

GROVE, William. See "William Groves," q.v.

GROVES, John. Enrolled in the third militia company organized for the Revolutionary War in the Elizabeth Town District of Frederick County (now the Hagerstown area of Washington County), passed by the Committee of Observation on June 5, 1776, and assigned to Capt. John Reynolds' command [Ref: Q-273]. Took the Oath of Allegiance before the Hon. Joseph Chapline before April 17, 1779 [Ref: J-5, O-39, which listed the name as "John Grove"]. See "John Grove," q.v.

GROVES, Joseph. Private, Militia, 1st Class, Capt. James Prather's Company, 3rd Battalion, 1776/1777 [Ref: M-242].

GROVES (GROVE), William (1755-1849). Private Maryland Line, who lived in Annapolis, Maryland at the time of his enlistment and after the war lived in Prince William County, Virginia. Around 1812 he moved to Allegany County, Maryland where he applied for pension on November 15, 1818, age 63. He married Mary Spencer (daughter of Elizabeth) in February, 1792 and she received pension W9461 in 1853. William died on February 27, 1849 (one source states January 1, 1849) and Mary died on September 5, 1856 [Ref: V-II:1452, Y-II:1248]. William Groves was a soldier and pensioner of the Revolution who resided in the 2nd Division of Allegany County in 1840, aged 83 [Ref: Y-II:1248, and EE-28:4 (p. 443), containing an article by Elba Anthony Dardeau, Jr.]. In January, 1820 "William Groves" was recorded as having been a private in the Maryland Line. On February 12, 1820 the Treasurer of the Western Shore of Maryland was directed to pay to "William Grover" of Allegany County, late a private in the Maryland Line during the Revolutionary War, during life, quarterly, half pay of a private. On March 1, 1850 the Treasurer of the Western Shore of Maryland was directed to pay to "Mary Grove, widow of William Grove, a revolutionary soldier, late of Allegany County, deceased" such sum of money, commencing January 1, 1850, during her life, as will equal the half pay of a private [Ref: AA-349].

GRUB, John. Enrolled in the first militia company organized for the Revolutionary War in the Elizabeth Town District of Frederick County (now the Hagerstown area of Washington County) on January 6, 1776 [Ref: Q-271, W-1190].

GRUNT, Adam. Took the Oath of Allegiance before the Hon. Christopher Cruse in Lower Antietam Hundred before March 2, 1778 [Ref: J-3, O-35].

GUEST, James. Took the Oath of Allegiance before the Hon. Andrew Bruce before March 2, 1778 [Ref: O-41, J-6].

GUILMAN, Samuel. Private who was recruited and passed by County Lieutenant Thomas Sprigg on April 22, 1780 [Ref: D-336].

GUIRE, Edmond. Private, Militia, by January 22, 1777 when ordered by the Committee of Observation "to march with some company of militia to the reinforcement of his Excellency General Washington" or appear before the Committee and state his reason for not marching. He apparently marched since he never appeared to the contrary [Ref: Q-48].

GUISER, Elizabeth. See "Frederick Guiser," q.v.

GUISER, Frederick. One of several patriots appointed by the Committee of Observation on December 30, 1776 "to form the county into companies (after the militia had marched) for the purpose of relieving the distressed inhabitants of said county and also to compel the Dunkards and Mennonists to give their assistance." [Ref: Q-346, which listed the name as "Frederick Gyzer"]. "Frederick Guiser" died testate before August 12, 1790 (date of balance book entry in Washington County), leaving equal shares to Mathias Guiser, Catherine Koler, Christian Bear, Rozana Hoover, Elizabeth Guiser, Mary Hoover, and Frederick Guiser [Ref: J-29]. See "Frederick Kiger (Kizer)" and "Frederick Keyser," q.v.

GUISER, Mathias. Private, Militia, Capt. William Heyser's Company, muster roll dated October 23, 1776, in continental service [Ref: D-264, W-1190, L-79, which listed the name as "Mathias Gieser"]. See "Frederick Guiser," q.v.

GULL, Baltzer. Private, Militia, 4th Class, Capt. Peter Beall's Company, 1st Battalion, 1776/1777 [Ref: M-240, which listed the name as "Balzer Gull"]. Rendered patriotic service by providing a black horse for the use of the military as noted in the minutes of the Committee of Observation on January 27, 1777 [Ref: Q-53]. Served on the Committee of Observation for Elizabeth Town District (now the Hagerstown area of Washington County) in 1777, "in whose hands the publick money is now deposited." [Ref: Q-228, Q-238].

GULL, George. Second Corporal, Militia, Capt. John Bennet's Company, 1776/1777 [Ref: M-246, A-1146].

GUNITY, William. Took the Oath of Allegiance before the Hon. John Stull in 1778 [Ref: O-46, J-10].

GUNTRYMAN (CUNTRYMAN, GUNERMAN), Henry. Private, Militia, 7th Class, Capt. Daniel Cresap's Company, 3rd Battalion, 1776/1777 [Ref: M-241, which listed the name as "Henry Cuntryman"]. Took the Oath of Allegiance before the Hon. Lemuel Barritt before March 16, 1778 [Ref: O-42, J-7, which listed the name as "Henry Gunerman"]. Took the Oath of Allegiance before the Hon. Henry Schnebley in 1778 [Ref: O-50, J-14, which listed the name as "Henry Guntryman"]. On September 23, 1780, Col. Lemuel Barritt recommended to Governor Lee that "Henry Gunteman" be commissioned a captain in the militia at Willstown since so many officers of the Western Battalion had moved out of Maryland to Kentucky and elsewhere [Ref: G-123].

GUNTRYMAN (COUNTRYMAN, GUNERMAN), Peter. Private, Militia, 8th Class, Capt. Daniel Cresap's Company, 3rd Battalion, 1776/1777 [Ref: M-241]. Took the Oath of Allegiance before the Hon. Lemuel Barritt before March 16, 1778 [Ref: O-42, J-8].

GUNTRYMAN (CUNTRYMAN, GUNERMAN), Henry Jr. Private, Militia, 6th Class, Capt. Martin Kershner's Company, 1776/1777 [Ref: A-1146, M-248, which listed the name as "Henry Cuntryman"]. Private, Militia, Capt. Martin Kershner's Company, 32nd Battalion, December 27, 1776 [Ref: K-1814, Box 3]. Took the Oath of Allegiance before the Hon. Lemuel Barritt before March 16, 1778 [Ref: O-42, J-8].

GUSELOR, Phillip. Took the Oath of Allegiance before the Hon. Christopher Cruse in Sharpsburg Hundred before March 2, 1778 [Ref: O-34, J-2, which latter source listed the name as "Phillip Guselor (prob. Kausler)"].

GUTHRIE, John. Took the Oath of Allegiance before the Hon. Richard Davis in 1778 [Ref: J-3, O-36].

GUTHRIE, John Jr. Private, Militia, 7th Class, Capt. Martin Kershner's Company, 1776/1777 [Ref: A-1146, M-248, which listed the name as "John Gutry, Jr."].

GUTHRIE, Robert. Rendered patriotic service by supplying a coverlid for the use of the military in March, 1776, as recorded by the Committee of Observation on April 12, 1776 [Ref: L-82, Q-156, which latter source listed the name as "Robert Guthry"]. Took the Oath of Allegiance before the Hon. Henry Schnebley in 1778 [Ref: O-49, J-13, which listed the name as "Robert Guthere"].

GUTSHALE, Lodwick. Took the Oath of Allegiance before the Hon. Joseph Sprigg before April 1, 1778 [Ref: O-54, J-16].

GYER (GIGER?), Frederick. Two men by this name took the Oath of Allegiance before the Hon. John Stull in 1778 [Ref: O-46, J-10].

GYER (GIGER?), John. Took the Oath of Allegiance before the Hon. John Stull in 1778 [Ref: O-46, J-10]. "Johannes Geiger" died on September 14, 1805, aged 55, was buried in Old St. John's Lutheran Churchyard, and subsequently reinterred in Rose Hill Cemetery [Ref: JJ-VII:105].

HAAGLAND, James. See "James Hoagland," q.v.

HAAZ(?), Henry. Private, Militia, 2nd Class, Capt. Peter Swingle's (Swingley's) Company, 1776/1777 [Ref: A-1146, M-248].

HACKAY, Nicholas. See "Nicholas Hockey," q.v.

HACKETT, John. Private who was recruited and passed by County Lieutenant Thomas Sprigg on April 22, 1780 [Ref: D-336].

HACKETT, Jonathan. Private, Militia, Capt. William Heyser's Company, enlisted July 18, 1776, muster roll dated October 23, 1776, in continental service [Ref: D-264, which listed the name as "Jonathan Hecket" and W-1190, L-79, which listed the name as "Jonathan Heckert"]. Private, German Regiment, Lt. Col. Ludwick Weltner's Company, discharged on July 26, 1779 at Tioga, Pennsylvania [Ref: D-265, which listed the name as "Jonathan Hackett" and GG-98, which listed the name as "Jonathan Hecket, Hacket, Hockett" and stated he deserted *[sic]* on August 25, 1779 at Tioga, Pennsylvania].

HACKLER, Martin. Private, Militia, 2nd Class, Capt. Samuel Hughes' Company, 2nd Battalion, 1776/1777 [Ref: M-238, A-1146].

HAFER, Charles E. See "Robert Compton," q.v.

HAFFE, George. See "George Naffe," q.v.

HAFLEBOWER, Sarah. See "Jacob Heflybower," q.v.

HAFNER, Johannes and Elizabeth. See "John Hefner," q.v.

HAGAN, Hugh. Private, Militia, 6th Class, Capt. Michael Fackler's Company, 1776/1777 [Ref: M-245, A-1146]. "Hugh Hagen, merchant of Creager's Town" died on the Monday before May 22, 1800 [Ref: LL-2:53].

HAGAN, John. Private, Militia, 7th Class, Capt. John Cellars' Company, 1776/1777 [Ref: A-1146, M-246].

HAGAN, Michael. Private who was enrolled by Capt. Aeneas Campbell and passed by Major Francis Deakins on July 18, 1776 [Ref: D-49].

HAGAN, Mr. See "Thomas Hart," q.v.

HAGER, Anna. See "Jonathan Hager," q.v.

HAGER, John. Private who was enrolled by Capt. Henry Hardman and passed on July 19, 1776 in Frederick (now Washington) County [Ref: D-51]. Took the Oath of Allegiance before the Hon. Henry Schnebley in 1778 [Ref: O-49, J-13, which listed the name as "John Hagger"].

HAGER, Jonathan (1717-1775). Appointed to raise funds on January 24, 1775 for the Committee of Observation in Salisbury Hundred in Frederick (now Washington) County [Ref: L-75]. Elected to serve on the Committee of Observation for the Elizabeth Town District (now the Hagerstown area of Washington County) on September 12, 1775, and appointed by the Committee of Observation "to receive all sums of money that may be voluntarily given for the publick good." [Ref: Q-142, Q-143]. "Captn. Hagar" was deceased by 1776 as noted in the minutes of the Committee of Observation in Elizabeth Town District on March 4, 1776 [Ref: Q-154]. "Captain Jonathan Hager, founder of Hagerstown, born in 1717, died November 6, 1775" and is buried in the cemetery at Zion Reformed Church in Hagerstown [Ref: JJ-VI:13].

HAGER, Jonathan (c1752-1823). Private, Militia, 4th Class, Capt. Peter Beall's Company, 1st Battalion, 1776/1777 [Ref: M-240, which listed the name as "Jonathan Hayer"]. Corporal, Select Militia, Capt. Adam Ott's Company, 1781 [Ref: M-238, A-1146, which listed the name as "Jonathan Hagar"]. Took the Oath of Allegiance before the Hon. Henry Schnebley in 1778 [Ref: O-49, J-13, which listed the name as "Jonathan Hagger"]. "Jonathan Hager, Sr." died on Sunday night, February 16, 1823, after a lingering illness in the 71st year of his age. "He resided in the neighborhood when the ground on which it stands was a howling wilderness. Soldier of the Revolution and participated in many of the hard fought battles." [Ref: Z-61, Z-62]. Anna Hager, relict of the late Jonathan Hager, died in Hagerstown on August 6, 1824, in her 68th year [Ref: Z-68]. See "Daniel Heister," q.v.

HAGER, Michael (1743-1781). Took the Oath of Allegiance before the Hon. Henry Schnebley in 1778 [Ref: O-49, J-13, which listed the name as "Michael Hagger"]. Michael Hager was born in 1743, married Hannah Cellar, and died in August, 1781 [Ref: Y-II:1263].

HAGISON, Thomas. Enrolled in the second militia company organized for the Revolutionary War in the Elizabeth Town District of Frederick County (now the Hagerstown area of Washington County) on March 9, 1776 [Ref: Q-272].

HAGLAND, James. See "James Hoagland," q.v.

HAHN, Adam. Private, Militia, 2nd Class, Capt. Conrad Hogmire's Company, 1776/1777 [Ref: M-244, A-1146].

HAHN, Henry. Enrolled in the first militia company organized for the Revolutionary War in the Elizabeth Town District of Frederick County (now the Hagerstown area of Washington County) on January 6, 1776 [Ref: Q-270, W-1189, which listed the name as "Henry Hann"].

HAHN, John. Ensign, Militia, Capt. George Swingle's (Swingley's) Company, 2nd Battalion, June 22, 1778 [Ref: M-82, E-145, A-1146, M-248, which latter source listed the name as "John Horne" in Capt. Peter Swingle's (Swingley's) Company, but no date was given]. First Lieutenant, Capt. Nicholas Mourer's Company, 2nd Battalion, November 21, 1780 [Ref: G-220, which listed the name as "John Hawn"].

HAINES, Jacob. Private, Militia, 6th Class, Capt. John Bennet's Company, 1776/1777 [Ref: M-246, A-1146].

HAINES, John. Took the Oath of Allegiance before the Hon. Richard Davis in 1778 [Ref: J-4, O-37, which listed the name as "John Hayns"].

HAINES, John. Took the Oath of Allegiance before the Hon. Andrew Bruce before March 2, 1778 [Ref: O-41, J-7, which listed the name as "John Hanes"].

HAINES, Joseph. Private, Militia, 6th Class, Capt. Jeremiah Spires' Company, 2nd Battalion, 1776/1777 [Ref: M-239, A-1146, which listed the name as "Joseph Hains"]. Rendered patriotic service by supplying corn for the use of the military on January 26, 1780 [Ref: W-1190, HH-74]. Took the Oath of Allegiance before the Hon. Richard Davis in 1778 [Ref: J-3, O-36, which listed the name as "Joseph Hains"].

HAINES, Michael. Took the Oath of Allegiance before the Hon. Richard Davis in 1778 [Ref: J-5, O-37, which listed the name as "Michael Hains"].

HAINES, Philip. Private, Militia, 8th Class, Capt. Jeremiah Spires' Company, 2nd Battalion, 1776/1777 [Ref: M-239, A-1146, which listed the name as "Phillip Hains"].

HALE, Joseph. Took the Oath of Allegiance before the Hon. William Yates in 1778 [Ref: O-48, J-12, which latter source listed the name as "Joseph Hall"].

HALE, Ruth S. See "Gabriel Williams," q.v.

HALL, Joseph. See "Joseph Hale," q.v.

HALLER, Daniel. Private, Militia, 6th Class, Capt. James Walling's Company, 2nd Battalion, 1776/1777 [Ref: M-239, A-1146].

HALLER, Frederick William. Private, German Regiment, continental service, 1776. Private, Third Vacant Company, under Capt. Philip Graybell and Col. Lewis Weltner at Valley Forge in March, 1778. Discharged on July 18, 1779 [Ref: FF-222, which listed the name as "Fred. Wm. Haller" and D-217, which listed the name as "F. William Haller"].

HALLETT, Richard. Private, Militia, 3rd Class, Capt. John Bennet's Company, 1776/1777 [Ref: M-246, A-1146].

HAM, Catharine and Elizabeth. See "Peter Ham," q.v.

HAM, John. Private, Militia, 1st Class, Capt. Barnett Johnston's Company, 3rd Battalion, 1776/1777 [Ref: M-242]. See "Peter Ham," q.v.

HAM, Joseph, Margaret, and Sarah. See "Peter Ham," q.v.

HAM, Peter. Enrolled in the third militia company organized for the Revolutionary War in the Elizabeth Town District of Frederick County (now the Hagerstown area of Washington County), passed by the Committee of Observation on June 5, 1776, and assigned to Capt. John Reynolds' command [Ref: Q-273]. Took the Oath of Allegiance before the Hon. Christopher Cruse in Sharpsburg Hundred before March 2, 1778 [Ref: O-34, J-2]. Peter Ham died testate before April, 1827, at which time an equity case in Washington County listed his heirs as wife Margaret Ham and children Peter, John, Joseph, Catharine, Sarah and Elizabeth (no surnames were given), and granddaughter Sarah Ham. It further stated that Peter Ham, John Ham, Joseph Ham, and Sarah Ham (now Sarah Rouner, wife of Michael Rouner) all resided outside of the state of Maryland [Ref: Z-89, Z-90].

HAMBLETON, Susannah. See "George King," q.v.

HAMILTON, George. See "Anthony Belsor," q.v.

HAMMON, George. Private, Militia, 6th Class, Capt. Samuel Hughes' Company, 2nd Battalion, 1776/1777 [Ref: M-238, A-1146].

HAMMON, Michael. Private who enlisted in the militia on August 18, 1781 for service in the Continental Army [Ref: D-388]. Private ("draught"), Maryland Line, discharged on November 12, 1781 [Ref: G-666, which listed the name as "Michael Hammond"].

HAMMON, Peter. One of several patriots appointed by the Committee of Observation on January 19, 1777 "to form the county into companies (after the militia had marched) for the purpose of relieving the distressed inhabitants of said county and also to compel the Dunkards and Mennonists to give their assistance." [Ref: Q-43, which listed the name as "Peter Hamon"].

HAMOR, William. Enrolled in the first militia company organized for the Revolutionary War in the Elizabeth Town District of Frederick County (now the Hagerstown area of Washington County) on January 6, 1776 [Ref: Q-271, W-1190].

HAMRICKHOUSE, Peter. See "Peter Humrichouse," q.v.

HANDLEN, Stephen. Took the Oath of Allegiance before the Hon. Henry Schnebley in 1778 [Ref: O-50, J-14].

HANDS, John. Private, Militia, 6th Class, Capt. Daniel Clapsaddle's Company, 1st Battalion, 1776/1777 [Ref: M-236, A-1146].

HANEY, William. Private who enlisted in the militia on August 27, 1781 for service in the Continental Army [Ref: D-388, D-408]. Substitute, Maryland Line, discharged on November 12, 1781 [Ref: G-666].

HANNAH, Samuel. Private, Militia, 4th Class, Capt. Daniel Cresap's Company, 3rd Battalion, 1776/1777 [Ref: M-241].

HANSON, John. On January 15, 1778 the Council of Maryland ordered the Western Shore Treasurer to issue money to John Hanson for him to deliver to Col. John Stull for the use of the marching militia of Washington County [Ref: C-467].

HANSON, Peter Contee. Second Lieutenant, Upper District, Frederick County (now Washington County), July, 1776; resigned by August 7, 1776 [Ref: D-48].

HANY, John. Private, Militia, 2nd Class, Capt. James Walling's Company, 2nd Battalion, 1776/1777 [Ref: M-238, A-1146].

HANY, Martin. One of several patriots appointed by the Committee of Observation on December 30, 1776 "to form the county into companies (after the militia had marched) for the purpose of relieving the distressed inhabitants of said county and also to compel the Dunkards and Mennonists to give their assistance." [Ref: Q-346].

HANY, Michael. Enrolled in the second militia company organized for the Revolutionary War in the Elizabeth Town District of Frederick County (now the Hagerstown area of Washington County) on March 9, 1776 [Ref: Q-272].

HARBAUGH, Anna, Eva, and Eve. See "Yost Harbaugh," q.v.

HARBAUGH, Jacob, John and Julianna. See "Yost Harbaugh," q.v.

HARBAUGH, Yost (1741-1831). Died at the residence of his son-in-law Benjamin Emmert on Antietam, near Hagerstown, in Washington County, Maryland on August 2, 1831, Mr. Yost Harbaugh, a soldier of the Revolution, a native of York County, Pennsylvania, in the 90th year of his age, another Revolutionary Hero gone." [Ref: DD-25, citing *The Republican Banner*, August 6, 1831]. Born on October 11, 1741 in York County, Pennsylvania, and served under Major General Braddock in an expedition against Fort Duquesne during the Indian Wars. He married Eva Bahn (December 23, 1742 - December 2, 1794) and was captain of the 7th Company, Second Battalion, York County Militia, in the Revolutionary War. Their children were: Julianna Johanne Harbaugh (born 1764, married John Knaub); Eve Harbaugh (born 1766, married Daniel Waeff); Anna Harbaugh (born 1768, married first to Walter Fisher and second to Casper Spengler); Jacob Harbaugh (no date of birth given); Anna Maria Harbaugh (born 1774, married Benjamin Emmert); and, John Harbaugh (born 1776, married Anna Margaret Becker). [Ref: BB-164].

HARBIN, Joshua (1755-   ). Private who was enrolled by Lieut. Clement Hollyday and passed by Major Francis Deakins on July 25, 1776 [Ref: D-49]. Private, Maryland Militia, and North Carolina service [Ref: N-28, which listed the name as "Joshua Horbin"].

HARBISON, David. Private, Militia, 2nd Class, Capt. Isaac Baker's Company, 1776/1777 [Ref: A-1146, M-247].

HARCKELL, Michael. Third Corporal, Militia, Capt. Daniel Clapsaddle's Company, 1st Battalion, 1776/1777 [Ref: M-236, A-1146].

HARDEY, Isaac. Private who was enrolled by Capt. Henry Hardman and passed on July 19, 1776 in Frederick (now Washington) County [Ref: D-51].

HARDIN, Larin. Took the Oath of Allegiance before the Hon. Andrew Bruce before March 2, 1778 [Ref: O-41, J-7, which latter source listed the name as "Larin Warden"].

HARDIN, Mark (1750-1835). Private, Pennsylvania Line, who lived on the Monongahela River in Pennsylvania at the time of his enlistment and moved to Washington County, Kentucky in 1781. He married Susannah Stull, daughter of Col. John Stull, of Hagerstown, Maryland on December 25, 1780. She died in 1846. For additional information see pension W423 [Ref: V-II:1515].

HARDMAN, Henry. Captain, Upper District, Frederick County (now Washington County), July, 1776 [Ref: D-48, D-51].

HARDWEIGH, George. Private, Militia, 8th Class, Capt. Conrad Hogmire's Company, 1776/1777 [Ref: M-244, A-1146].

HARGAN, Elizabeth, and others. See "Michael Hargan," q.v.

HARGAN, Michael (1755-1840). Private, Pennsylvania Line, who applied for pension in Hardin County, Kentucky on October 15, 1832, age 77, having originally applied there in 1820 with a wife Elizabeth, age 55, and daughter Prudence, age 17. He enlisted at Hagerstown, Maryland in 1776, married after August 3, 1791 but before January 1, 1794 in Berkeley County, Virginia (her maiden name being Wallingsford), and they moved to Kentucky in 1803. Michael died on December 15, 1840 and his widow applied for and received pension W8906 on May 31, 1843, age 76. Also mentioned were sons Joseph, Benjamin and Daniel Hargan [Ref: V-II:1519, T-45].

HARGIL, Michael. Private, Militia, 5th Class, Capt. Basil Williams' Company, 1776/1777 [Ref: M-244, A-1146].

HARKELL, Frederick. Private, Militia, 2nd Class, Capt. Daniel Clapsaddle's Company, 1st Battalion, 1776/1777 [Ref: M-236, A-1146].
HARKESHIMER, John (c1752-   ). Private, Virginia Line, pensioned under the Act of March 18, 1818 in Washington County at $96 per year effective October 16, 1827 [Ref: R-42].
HARLING, Cornelius. Private who was enrolled by Capt. Aeneas Campbell and passed by Major John Fulford on July 18, 1776 [Ref: D-49].
HARMAN, John. Private, Militia, 6th Class, Capt. Michael Fackler's Company, 1776/1777 [Ref: M-245, A-1146].
HARMONY, George. Private, Militia, Capt. William Heyser's Company, muster roll dated October 23, 1776, in continental service and on duty in May, 1777 [Ref: GG-97, D-264, W-1190, L-79, which latter source listed the name as "George Harmany"].
HARMUELL, John. Private, Militia, 5th Class, Capt. Isaac Baker's Company, 1776/1777 [Ref: A-1146, M-247].
HARNIDGE, Philip. Took the Oath of Allegiance before the Hon. Joseph Sprigg before April 1, 1778 [Ref: O-53, J-16].
HARR, Adam. Took the Oath of Allegiance before the Hon. Samuel Hughes before March 1, 1778 [Ref: O-33, J-1].
HARR, Jacob. Private, Militia, 7th Class, Capt. Martin Kershner's Company, 1776/1777 [Ref: A-1146, M-248, which listed the name as "Jacob Hur"].
HARRISON, James. Took the Oath of Allegiance before the Hon. William Yates in 1778 [Ref: O-48, J-12].
HARRISON, John. Took the Oath of Allegiance before the Hon. William Yates in 1778 [Ref: O-48, J-12].
HARRISON, William. Took the Oath of Allegiance before the Hon. William Yates in 1778 [Ref: O-48, J-12].
HARRISON, William Jr. (1736-1825). Private, Militia, 5th Class, Capt. Barnett Johnston's Company, 3rd Battalion, 1776/1777 [Ref: M-242]. Private, Maryland Line, by September, 1781 [Ref: H-473, H-474]. He applied for and received pension S38782 in Hawkins County, Tennessee on August 24, 1819, stating he was born on May 24, 1736 and enlisted in Hagerstown, Maryland. In 1820 he mentioned his wife and children (names not given) and died on August 4, 1825 [Ref: V-II:1541, which listed the name without the "Jr."].
HARRY, Andrew, Anna Maria, and Charles. See "Martin Harry," q.v.
HARRY, David (1750-1843). Private, Militia, 6th Class, Capt. Peter Beall's Company, 1st Battalion, 1776/1777 [Ref: M-240]. Rendered patriotic service by assisting in the apprehension of Isaac and Christian Shockey

[counterfeiters] for the Committee of Observation in February, 1777 [Ref: Q-234]. Took the Oath of Allegiance before the Hon. Henry Schnebley in 1778 [Ref: O-50, J-13]. David Harry was born on November 13, 1750, died on March 18, 1843, was buried in Old St. John's Lutheran Churchyard beside his wife Margaret (1755-1836), and they were subsequently reinterred in Rose Hill Cemetery in Hagerstown [Ref: JJ-VII:105, which source indicated he was a Revolutionary War soldier]. See "Martin Harry," q.v.

HARRY, Iona. See "Martin Harry," q.v.

HARRY, Jacob (1756-1806). Private, Militia, 4th Class, Capt. Peter Beall's Company, 1st Battalion, 1776/1777 [Ref: M-240]. Jacob Harry died on July 14, 1806, after a lingering illness, in the 50th year of his age, a merchant of Elizabeth Town (now Hagerstown). Mary E. Harry, widow of the late Jacob Harry, died in August, 1808, in her 50th year [Ref: LL-3:47, LL-3:70]. See "Martin Harry," q.v.

HARRY, John. Private, Militia, 5th Class, Capt. Michael Fackler's Company, 1776/1777 [Ref: M-245, A-1146]. Samuel Harry died at the residence of John Harry in Hagerstown on September 20, 1824 [ref: Z-69]. See "Martin Harry," q.v.

HARRY, Jonathan. Private, Militia, 4th Class, Capt. Peter Beall's Company, 1st Battalion, 1776/1777 [Ref: M-240]. Took the Oath of Allegiance before the Hon. Henry Schnebley in 1778 [Ref: O-50, J-13].

HARRY, Margaret. See "David Harry," q.v.

HARRY, Martin (1726-1788). Rendered patriotic service by providing "rashons" for the use of the military in July, 1775, as recorded by the Committee of Observation at Elizabeth Town on November 4, 1775 [Ref: Q-150]. Rendered patriotic service in Hagerstown by dieting soldiers of Capt. John Nelson's Company, continental service (Maryland Line), April, 1776 [Ref: Q-161]. Paid in February, 1777 for boarding services furnished to Capt. Daniel Clapsaddle's Company in the Flying Camp [Ref: Q-235, Q-236]. Rendered patriotic service by supplying corn for the use of the military on January 12, 1780 [Ref: W-1190, HH-73, which listed the name as "Martin Hary"]. Martin Harry was born in Germany on May 27, 1726, died on August 30, 1788, was buried in Old St. John's Lutheran Churchyard with his wife Anna Maria (1720-1780), and subsequently reinterred in Rose Hill Cemetery in Hagerstown [Ref: JJ-VII:104, which source indicates he was a Revolutionary War soldier]. Since Martin Harry, Jr. served in the militia, perhaps his father did also. One Martin Harry died testate before March 28, 1795 (date of balance book entry in Washington County), leaving a widow (not named in this account) and equal shares to Iona, David, Charles, Martin, Jacob, John, and Andrew Harry [Ref: J-34]. Additional research will be necessary before drawing conclusions.

HARRY, Martin Jr. Took the Oath of Allegiance before the Hon. Henry Schnebley in 1778 [Ref: O-51, J-14]. Private, Militia, 3rd Class, Capt. Peter Beall's Company, 1st Battalion, 1776/1777 [Ref: M-240, which listed the name without the "Jr."]. Private, Militia, Capt. John Kershner's Company, on duty guarding prisoners of war at Fort Frederick on June 27, 1778 [Ref: D-328, which listed the name as "Martain Harry (or Narry)"]. See "Martin Harry," q.v.

HARRY, Mary E. See "Jacob Harry," q.v.

HARRY, Samuel. See "John Harry," q.v.

HARSH, Frederick. Took the Oath of Allegiance before the Hon. Henry Schnebley in 1778 [Ref: O-50, J-13].

HARSHMAN, Mathias. Private, Militia, 8th Class, Capt. Jacob Sharer's Company, 1776/1777 [Ref: A-1146, M-248].

HART, Christopher (1753-c1840). Private who was enrolled by Capt. Henry Hardman and passed on July 19, 1776 in Frederick (now Washington) County [Ref: D-51, which listed the name as "Chr. Hart"]. Private, Maryland Line, who applied for and received pension S23684 in Bedford County, Pennsylvania on November 20, 1832, stating he was born on October 5, 1753 in Lancaster County, Pennsylvania and lived in Frederick County, Maryland at the time of his enlistment. He lived there for 10 or 12 years after the war, moved to Washington County, Maryland and later to Bedford County, Pennsylvania [Ref: V-II:1543].

HART, Ludwick. Private, Militia, 7th Class, Capt. Daniel Clapsaddle's Company, 1st Battalion, 1776/1777 [Ref: M-236, A-1146].

HART, Noah. Private, Militia, 4th Class, Capt. Michael Fackler's Company, 1776/1777 [Ref: M-245, A-1146]. Rendered patriotic service in Hagerstown by providing "doctor stuff" to Capt. John Nelson's Company, continental service (Maryland Line), April, 1776 [Ref: Q-161]. "Dr. Noah Hart" served on the Committee of Observation for the Elizabeth Town District (now the Hagerstown area of Washington County) in December, 1776 [Ref: Q-340]. "Doctor Hart" rendered patriotic service by providing a rifle for Capt. Daniel Cresap's Company in July, 1775, as recorded by the Committee of Observation at Elizabeth Town on November 4, 1775 [Ref: Q-149]. "Noah Hart" was appointed by the Maryland Convention on November 8, 1776 to be one of the three judges of elections for Washington County [Ref: CC-55].

HART, Thomas. His widow's obituary stated, in part, "died in Lexington, Kentucky on the 26th of August, in the 86th year of her age, Mrs. Susannah Hart, widow and relict of the late Col. Thomas Hart. Colonel

Hart and his family resided for several years in Washington County on the Long Meadow Farm, now owned by Mr. Hagan, where their daughter, Mrs. Henry Clay, was born; and also in this house now Mr. McIllhenny's Hotel. Mrs. Hart was a noble, virtuous woman; she was the mother of Mrs. Dr. Pindle [sic] formerly of Hagerstown, of Mrs. Brown, the lady of James Brown, minister to France, and the gallant Capt. Hart, who fell victim to Indian and British cruelty and barbarity at the massacre on the river Raisin during the late war. Of seven children, two only survive her.." [Ref: DD-46, citing *The Republican Banner*, September 15, 1832]. See "Richard Pindell," q.v.

HARTLE, Bostian and Eave. See "George Hartle," q.v.

HARTLE, Frederick. Took the Oath of Allegiance before the Hon. Andrew Rentch before March 7, 1778 [Ref: O-52, J-15]. See "George Hartle," q.v.

HARTLE, George (1722-1776). Rendered patriotic service by supplying a blanket for the use of the military in March, 1776, as recorded by the Committee of Observation on April 12, 1776 [Ref: Q-157, L-82]. "George Hartle" died before February 1, 1780 (date of balance book entry in Washington County), leaving a widow (no name given in this account) and equal shares to Martin, Frederick, Michael, Bostian, Eave, and Peggy Hartle [Ref: J-22]. "George Hertel" was born on May 10, 1722, died on September 13, 1776, and was buried about 100 yards from Antietam Creek at Beard's Church and near Trovinger's Mill. Jacob Hertel (died 1782) was also buried there. Their stones are now in the St. James Reformed Church Graveyard at Leitersburg in Washington County [Ref: JJ-V:1, 2].

HARTLE, Martin. Private, Militia, 8th Class, Capt. Samuel Hughes' Company, 2nd Battalion, 1776/1777 [Ref: M-238, A-1146, which listed the name as "Martin Hartell"]. See "George Hartle," q.v.

HARTLE, Michael. Took the Oath of Allegiance before the Hon. Henry Schnebley in 1778 [Ref: O-51, J-15, which listed the name as "Michael Hartel"]. See "George Martle," q.v.

HARTLE, Peggy. See "George Hartle," q.v.

HARTLEY, Homer. Took the Oath of Allegiance before the Hon. Lemuel Barritt before March 16, 1778 [Ref: J-8, O-43, which latter source listed the name as "Homes Hartely"].

HARTLEY, John. Private, Militia, 1st Class, Capt. James Prather's Company, 3rd Battalion, 1776/1777 [Ref: M-242]. Took the Oath of Allegiance before the Hon. Lemuel Barritt before March 16, 1778 [Ref: O-43, J-8, which listed the name as "John Hartely"].

HARTLEY, Michael. Private, Militia, Capt. John Kershner's Company, on duty guarding prisoners of war at Fort Frederick on June 27, 1778 [Ref: D-328, which listed the name as "Michael Hartly"].

HARTMAN, Adam. Private, Militia, 3rd Class, Capt. Martin Kershner's Company, 1776/1777 [Ref: A-1146, M-247]. Took the Oath of Allegiance before the Hon. John Cellars in January, 1778 [Ref: K-1814, O-40, J-6, which latter source listed the name as "Adam Bartman"].

HARTNESS, Robert. Private, Militia, Capt. William Heyser's Company, muster roll dated October 23, 1776, in continental service, which stated he had deserted, yet he was on duty in May, 1777 [Ref: D-264, W-1190, L-79, GG-97].

HARVEY, David. Second Lieutenant, Militia, Capt. Daniel Clapsaddle's Company, Flying Camp, commissioned September 26, 1776 [Ref: M-85, B-301, D-73, which listed the name as "David Harvy"].

HARVEY, James. Private who was recruited and passed by County Lieutenant Thomas Sprigg on April 22, 1780 [Ref: D-336].

HARVEY, Martin. Took the Oath of Allegiance before the Hon. Joseph Sprigg before April 1, 1778 [Ref: O-53, J-16].

HASE, James. Enrolled in the second militia company organized for the Revolutionary War in the Elizabeth Town District of Frederick County (now the Hagerstown area of Washington County) on March 9, 1776 [Ref: Q-271].

HASEN, Jacob. Substitute, Maryland Line, discharged on October 30, 1781 [Ref: G-657].

HASSE, Rudolph. Rendered patriotic service by supplying wheat for the use of the military on March 13, 1780 [Ref: W-1190, HH-73].

HASSELBACK, Nicholas. Private who was enlisted by Lieut. Christian Orndorff and passed on July 20, 1776 in Frederick (now Washington) County [Ref: D-50].

HASSEN, P. See "Dewald Shaffer," q.v.

HATFIELD, John. Private, Militia, Capt. William Heyser's Company, enlisted August 13, 1776, muster roll dated October 23, 1776, which mistakenly reported he had "deserted." [Ref: W-1190, L-79, D-264, which listed the name as "John Hattfield" and "John Hottfield"]. Private, German Regiment, Lt. Col. Ludwick Weltner's Company, continental service, and discharged on July 26, 1779 at Fort Wyoming, Pennsylvania [Ref: D-265, D-218, GG-98, which latter source listed the name as "John Hottfield, Hatfield"].

HATRICK, Charles. Rendered patriotic service in Hagerstown by providing sundries to Capt. John Nelson's Company, continental service (Maryland Line), April, 1776 [Ref: Q-161].

HAUCK, Jacob. Rendered patriotic service by supplying wheat for the use of the military on April 20, 1780 [Ref: HH-72].

HAUVER, Abraham. Rendered patriotic service by supplying corn for the use of the military on February 14, 1780 [Ref: W-1190, HH-74, which latter source listed the name as "Abraham Hauser"].

HAVER, Jacob. Private, German Regiment, Lt. Col. Ludwick Weltner's Company, continental service, discharged October 12, 1779 [Ref: D-265]. See "Jacob Hoover," q.v.

HAWKEN, Abraham. See "Jacob Kuhn," q.v.

HAWN, John. See "John Hahn," q.v.

HAYES, James. Private, Militia, 6th Class, Capt. Henry Boteler's Company, 1776/1777 [Ref: M-237, A-1146].

HAYES, Samuel. Private, Militia, 4th Class, Capt. Griffin Johnson's Company, 3rd Battalion, 1776/1777 [Ref: M-243].

HAYS, Nancy Ann. See "Leonard Bowers," q.v.

HAYS, William. First Corporal, Militia, Capt. Basil Williams' Company, 1776/1777 [Ref: M-244, A-1146]. Took the Oath of Allegiance before the Hon. Richard Davis in 1778 [Ref: J-3, O-36].

HAZELIP, Richard. On February 16, 1820 the Treasurer of the Western Shore of Maryland was directed to pay to Richard Hazelip, of Washington County, half pay of a private, for his services in the Revolutionary War [Ref: AA-353].

HEADLER, George. Private, Militia, 4th Class, Capt. Daniel Clapsaddle's Company, 1st Battalion, 1776/1777 [Ref: M-236, A-1146].

HEADRICKS, Charles. Private, Militia, 1st Class, Capt. Peter Swingle's (Swingley's) Company, 1776/1777 [Ref: A-1146, M-248].

HEAISKILL, Benjamin. Took the Oath of Allegiance before the Hon. John Stull in 1778 [Ref: O-46, J-10].

HEART, John. Private who was enrolled by Lieut. Clement Hollyday and passed by Col. William Luckett on August 8, 1776 [Ref: D-49].

HEASTER, Nicholas. Took the Oath of Allegiance before the Hon. Richard Davis in 1778 [Ref: J-4, O-37].

HEATHERINGTON, John. Private, Militia, 6th Class, Capt. Isaac Baker's Company, 1776/1777 [Ref: A-1146, M-247]. Took the Oath of Allegiance before the Hon. John Barnes before February 28, 1778 [Ref: J-9, O-44, which latter source listed the name as "John Heatherrington"].

HEATON, Michael. Took the Oath of Allegiance before the Hon. Lemuel Barritt before March 16, 1778 [Ref: O-42, J-8, which listed the name as "Michel Heaton"]. Private, Militia, 6th Class, Capt. Daniel Cresap's Company, 3rd Battalion, 1776/1777 [Ref: M-241, which listed the name as "Michael Heater"].

HECKERT, Jonathan. See "Jonathan Hackett," q.v.

HECKLER, Polly. See "Henry Franks," q.v.

HEDING, Ludwick. Enrolled in the third militia company organized for the Revolutionary War in the Elizabeth Town District of Frederick County (now the Hagerstown area of Washington County), passed by the Committee of Observation on June 5, 1776, and assigned to Capt. John Reynolds' command [Ref: Q-273].

HEDRICK, Werner. Enrolled in the third militia company organized for the Revolutionary War in the Elizabeth Town District of Frederick County (now the Hagerstown area of Washington County), passed by the Committee of Observation on June 5, 1776, and assigned to Capt. John Reynolds' command [Ref: Q-273]. Private, Militia, 8th Class, Capt. Joseph Chapline's Company, 2nd Battalion, 1776/1777 [Ref: M-242, which listed the name as "Varner Hatnick"]. See "William Fleck," q.v.

HEFLEY (HEFFLEY), Charles. Private, Militia, 2nd Class, Capt. John Cellars' Company, 1776/1777 [Ref: A-1146, M-246, which listed the name as "Charles Heffle"]. Took the Oath of Allegiance before the Hon. Henry Schnebley in 1778 [Ref: O-50, J-14, which listed the name as "Carte. Heoffety"].

HEFLEY (HEFFLICH), Peter (1742-1827). Private, Militia, 3rd Class, Capt. Peter Beall's Company, 1st Battalion, 1776/1777 [Ref: M-240, which listed the name as "Peter Hefley"]. Private, Militia, Capt. John Kershner's Company, on duty guarding prisoners of war at Fort Frederick on June 27, 1778 [Ref: D-328, which listed the name as "Peter Haflegh"]. Took the Oath of Allegiance before the Hon. Henry Schnebley in 1778 [Ref: O-50, J-13, which listed the name as "Peter Haofflick" and "Peter Heofflick"]. "Peter Hefflich" of Hagerstown died on June 17, 1827, in his 85th year [Ref: Z-92]. "Peter Heafibich" was a native of Germany and died on June 15, 1827, aged 84 years, 9 months, and 26 days. He was buried in Old St. John's Lutheran Cemetery and subsequently reinterred in Rose Hill Cemetery in Hagerstown [Ref: JJ-VII:105].

HEFNER, Baptist. Private, Militia, 7th Class, Capt. Daniel Clapsaddle's Company, 1st Battalion, 1776/1777 [Ref: M-236, A-1146, which listed the name as "Baptist Heafner"].

HEFNER, David, Elizabeth, and Felts. See "Jacob Hefner," q.v.

HEFNER, Jacob (1752/57-1848). Private, Militia, Capt. William Heyser's Company, enlisted August 18, 1776; muster roll dated October 23, 1776, mistakenly reported he had "deserted." [Ref: GG-97, W-1190, L-79, D-264, which listed the name as "Jacob Heefner"]. Private, German Regiment, Lt. Col. Ludwick Weltner's Company, continental service, discharged October 12, 1779 at Fort Wyoming, Pennsylvania [Ref: D-265]. Jacob was born in September, 1757, served in the Maryland Line, and resided in Richland County, Ohio when he applied for a pension on February 10, 1819; in 1834, he stated he was aged 77. He died on November 23, 1848 and his widow Elizabeth applied for and received pension W2546 in Ashland County, Ohio in 1853. She stated they were married in 1828 and that she and Jacob had been married previously. Three of his sons were David, Felts (or Fetts) and Valentine Heffner, and her son Hankey Priest was aged 30 in 1857 [Ref: V-II:1595, GG-98, which listed the name as "Jacob Heefner, Hefner, Heffner, Heiffner"]. Jacob Hefner was born on September 23, 1752 in Germany, married first to Elizabeth Miller and second to Mrs. Elizabeth Priest, and died on November 23, 1848 [Ref: Y-II:1384].

HEFNER, John. Private, Militia, 8th Class, Capt. Daniel Clapsaddle's Company, 1st Battalion, 1776/1777 [Ref: M-236, A-1146, which listed the name as "John Heafner"]. One "Johannes Hafner" was a son of Johannes and Elizabeth Hafner, born *"13 len 1728, in Dietland, Darlach ischenin Grahbein seine Eltin Yahein,"* married Barbara Mentzer, died on December 30, 1791, and was buried in the "Lutharan Church of Jacobs Graveyard" north of Leitersburg, near the Maryland-Pennsylvania line [Ref: JJ-V:20].

HEFNER, Valentine. See "Jacob Hefner," q.v.

HEFLYBOWER, Jacob. Private, Select Militia, Capt. Adam Ott's Company, 1781 [Ref: M-238, A-1146]. "Sarah Haflebower" was one of the heirs of Jacob Lug in Washington County in 1799 [Ref: J-35].

HEIBERGER, Conrat. See "Conrad Highbarger," q.v.

HEIMS, Andrew. See "Andrew Hymes," q.v.

HEIN, Jacob. Private, Militia, 5th Class, Capt. Conrad Nichodemus' Company, 2nd Battalion, 1776/1777 [Ref: M-237, A-1146].

HEISNIL, Frederick. On September 27, 1776 the Committee of Observation for Elizabeth Town District (now the Hagerstown area of Washington County) recorded that he had "delivered to Capt. Clapsadle's Company thirty-two tomyhocks with handles at 3 shilling each." [Ref: Q-337].

HEISTER, Daniel (1747-1804). "General Daniel Heister, the patriot, the soldier, and the Statesman" died testate on March 7, 1804, aged 57, and is buried beside his wife Rosanna Heister (1752-1810), daughter of Jonathan Hager, in the cemetery at Zion Reformed Church in Hagerstown [Ref: JJ-VI:9, LL-3:82, LL-2:93, MM-13:40, 41].

HELAME, Joseph. Took the Oath of Allegiance before the Hon. Richard Davis in 1778 [Ref: J-3, O-36].

HELFENSTONE, Nicholas. Took the Oath of Allegiance before the Hon. Christopher Cruse in Sharpsburg Hundred before March 2, 1778 [Ref: O-34, J-2].

HELLEN, David. See "William Massah," q.v.

HELMER, John William (c1742-1831). Soldier who resided in Washington County and was granted a pension certificate in August, 1820, according to an Act of Congress of March 18, 1818, since he had proven that he was "in the enjoyment of a certain degree of poverty" as required by the Act as amended on May 1, 1820 [Ref: W-1190]. Private, Pennsylvania Line, pensioned at $96 per year effective April 4, 1818 [Ref: R-42]. "Died at his residence in this county on Tuesday last, Mr. John W. Helmer, at an advanced age. He served during the Revolutionary War in the -- Regiment, commanded by --, and was one of those meritorious soldiers who has justly been entitled to and received a pension from his country, another Revolutionary Soldier gone." [Ref: DD-22, citing *The Republican Banner*, May 7, 1831].

HELSON, Godfree. Private, Militia, 6th Class, Capt. Isaac Baker's Company, 1776/1777 [Ref: A-1146, M-247].

HEMINDER, Andrew. Private, Militia, 5th Class, Capt. Samuel Hughes' Company, 2nd Battalion, 1776/1777 [Ref: M-238, A-1146].

HENBURN, John. Took the Oath of Allegiance before the Hon. Joseph Sprigg before April 1, 1778 [Ref: O-53, J-16].

HENCH, John. Second Lieutenant, Militia, Capt. Daniel Cresap's Company, 3rd Battalion, June 22, 1778 [Ref: M-86, M-241, E-145].

HENDERICK, Charles. Took the Oath of Allegiance before the Hon. Henry Schnebley in 1778 [Ref: O-49, J-12, which latter source listed the name as "Charles Hendrick"].

HENDERICK, John. Private, Militia, 1st Class, Capt. Conrad Nichodemus' Company, 2nd Battalion, 1776/1777 [Ref: M-237, A-1146, which listed the name as "John Hendderick"].

HENDERSON, Daniel. Private who was enrolled by Capt. Henry Hardman and passed on July 19, 1776 in Frederick (now Washington) County [Ref: D-51].

HENDERSON, John (c1759-1836). Born in Loudoun County, Virginia, served in the Revolution and engaged in the Battle of Yorktown, sustained through life the character of a good citizen and honest man, and died in Williamsport, Maryland on October 31, 1836, in the 77th year of his age [Ref: DD-119, citing *The Republican Banner*, November 5, 1836].

HENDRICKSON, William (1757-c1840). Private, Maryland Line, who applied for and received pension S2301 in Richland County, Ohio on

September 7, 1832, age 75 on December 3, 1832, stating he was born in 1757 in Middletown, New Jersey and enlisted at Frederickstown, Maryland. During the war he moved near Fort Cumberland, Maryland and lived there for 20 years after the war. He then moved to Knox County, Ohio for a short time and then moved to Richland County [Ref: V-II:1604].

HENRY, John. Private who was enrolled by Capt. Aeneas Campbell and passed by Major Francis Deakins on July 18, 1776 [Ref: D-49].

HENRY, Michael. Private, Militia, 1st Class, Capt. Henry Boteler's Company, 1776/1777 [Ref: M-237, A-1146].

HENRY, Nicholas. Took the Oath of Allegiance before the Hon. John Stull in 1778 [Ref: O-46, J-10].

HENS, Jacob. Took the Oath of Allegiance before the Hon. Henry Schnebley in 1778 [Ref: O-50, J-14].

HENTZ, John. Took the Oath of Allegiance before the Hon. Henry Schnebley in 1778 [Ref: O-50, J-14]. See "John Hench," q.v.

HEOFFLICK, Peter. See "Peter Hefley," q.v.

HEPWORTH, John. Took the Oath of Allegiance before the Hon. Richard Davis in 1778 [Ref: O-37, J-4, which latter source listed the name as "John Hipworth"].

HERALD, Michael. Took the Oath of Allegiance before the Hon. Richard Davis in 1778 [Ref: J-4, O-37].

HERRON, John. Took the Oath of Allegiance before the Hon. William Yates in 1778 [Ref: O-48, J-12].

HERSHMAN, Andrew. One of the persons appointed by the Committee of Observation for Elizabeth Town District (now the Hagerstown area of Washington County) on January 9, 1777 "to appraise the several wagons, horses, gears, wagon cloths, blankets, etc. that can be procured for the use of Col. Smith's Battalion." [Ref: Q-40, Q-41, which listed the name as "Andrew Hearshman"]. Took the Oath of Allegiance before the Hon. John Stull in 1778 [Ref: O-46, J-10, which latter source listed the name as "Andrew Harshman"].

HERSHMAN, Mathias. Took the Oath of Allegiance before the Hon. John Stull in 1778 [Ref: O-46, J-10].

HERSHMAN, Phillip. Took the Oath of Allegiance before the Hon. Christopher Cruse in Sharpsburg Hundred before March 2, 1778 [Ref: O-35, J-2].

HERTEL, George and Jacob. See "George Hartle," q.v.

HESS, Christian. Private, Militia, 6th Class, Capt. Conrad Nichodemus' Company, 2nd Battalion, 1776/1777 [Ref: M-237, A-1146].

HESS, Jacob. Private, Militia, 4th Class, Capt. Conrad Nichodemus' Company, 2nd Battalion, 1776/1777 [Ref: M-237, A-1146].

HESS, Joseph. Private, Militia, 2nd Class, Capt. Conrad Nichodemus' Company, 2nd Battalion, 1776/1777 [Ref: M-237, A-1146].

HESS, Peter. Private, Militia, 1st Class, Capt. Peter Beall's Company, 1st Battalion, 1776/1777 [Ref: M-240].

HESS, William. Took the Oath of Allegiance before the Hon. Henry Schnebley in 1778 [Ref: O-49, J-13].

HESTER, Phillip. Private, Militia, 3rd Class, Capt. Basil Williams' Company, 1776/1777 [Ref: M-244, A-1146].

HESTON, Jacob. Private, Militia, 7th Class, Capt. John Bennet's Company, 1776/1777 [Ref: M-246, A-1146].

HETHRICK, John. Took the Oath of Allegiance before the Hon. Christopher Cruse in Lower Antietam Hundred before March 2, 1778 [Ref: J-2, O-35].

HETHRICK, Vernon. Took the Oath of Allegiance before the Hon. Christopher Cruse in Sharpsburg Hundred before March 2, 1778 [Ref: O-34, J-2]. See "Werner Hedrick," q.v.

HETRICK, Garttroat and Varner. See "William Fleck," q.v.

HETRICK, Varner. See "Werner Hedrick," q.v.

HEWARD, Christian. Rendered patriotic service by providing a rifle for Capt. Daniel Cresap's Company in July, 1775, as recorded by the Committee of Observation at Elizabeth Town on November 4, 1775 [Ref: Q-149].

HEWETT, Christopher. Took the Oath of Allegiance before the Hon. John Stull in 1778 [Ref: O-46, J-10].

HEWITT, Robert. Soldier who resided in Washington County and was granted a pension certificate in August, 1820, according to an Act of Congress of March 18, 1818, since he had proven that he was "in the enjoyment of a certain degree of poverty" as required by the Act as amended on May 1, 1820 [Ref: W-1190].

HEYSER, Ann or Anna. See "William Heyser," q.v.

HEYSER, George. Enrolled in the third militia company organized for the Revolutionary War in the Elizabeth Town District of Frederick County (now the Hagerstown area of Washington County), passed by the Committee of Observation on June 5, 1776, and assigned to Capt. John Reynolds' command [Ref: Q-272].

HEYSER, William (c1745-c1790). Captain, Militia, muster roll dated October 23, 1776, in continental service [Ref: D-263, W-1190, L-79]. Rendered patriotic service by providing "rashons & drink" for the use of the military in July, 1775, as recorded by the Committee of Observation at Elizabeth Town on November 4, 1775 [Ref: Q-150]. Rendered patriotic service in Hagerstown by dieting soldiers of Capt. John Nelson's Company, continental service (Maryland Line), April, 1776 [Ref: Q-161, which listed the name as "Wm. Hyser"]. Served on the Committee of Observation in April, 1776 [Ref: Q-154, Q-155, which listed the name as "William Hisser" and "William Hizer"]. William Heyser or Heiser was born circa 1745, married Anna ----, and died before February 27, 1790 [Ref: Y-II:1385]. Ann Heyser (1748-1836) and son William Heyser (1769-1836) are buried in Zion Reformed Church cemetery in Hagerstown [Ref: JJ-VI:16].

HIATT, Elisha. First Sergeant, Militia, Capt. Basil Williams' Company, 1776/1777 [Ref: M-244, A-1146]. Took the Oath of Allegiance before the Hon. Richard Davis in 1778 [Ref: J-4, O-37].

HICK(?), George. First Corporal, Militia, Capt. John Rennolds' (Reynolds') Company, 2nd Battalion, 1776/1777 [Ref: M-240].

HICKMAN, Matthias. Ensign, Militia, Capt. Conrad Hogmire's Company, 1776. Ensign, Militia, Capt. Daniel Clapsaddle's Company, Flying Camp, commissioned September 26, 1776 [Ref: M-87, B-301, M-244, A-1146, D-73, Q-268].

HICSON, Joseph. Took the Oath of Allegiance before the Hon. Samuel Hughes before March 1, 1778 [Ref: J-1, O-33, which latter source listed the name as "Joseph Hieson"].

HIGGINS, Richard. Private who enlisted in the militia on August 24, 1781 for service in the Continental Army [Ref: D-388]. Substitute, Maryland Line, discharged on October 26, 1781 upon the recommendation of Dr. James Murray [Ref: G-653].

HIGGINS, Samuel. See "Henry Franks," q.v.

HIGGS, James. Took the Oath of Allegiance before the Hon. Richard Davis in 1778 [Ref: J-4, O-37].

HIGHAM, Moses. See "Moses Huffman," q.v.

HIGHBARGER, Abraham. Enrolled in the third militia company organized for the Revolutionary War in the Elizabeth Town District of Frederick County (now the Hagerstown area of Washington County), passed by the Committee of Observation on June 5, 1776, and assigned to Capt. John Reynolds' command [Ref: Q-273, which listed the name as "Abraham Hybarger"]. Private, Militia, 7th Class, Capt. Joseph Chapline's Company, 2nd Battalion, 1776/1777 [Ref: M-242]. Took the Oath of Allegiance before the Hon. Christopher Cruse in Sharpsburg Hundred before March 2, 1778 [Ref: O-34, which listed the name as "Abraham Hybarger"].

HIGHBARGER, Conrad. Enrolled in the third militia company organized for the Revolutionary War in the Elizabeth Town District of Frederick County (now the Hagerstown area of Washington County), passed by the Committee of Observation on June 5, 1776, and assigned to Capt. John Reynolds' command [Ref: Q-273, which listed the name as "Conrad Hybarger"]. Private, Militia, 6th Class, Capt. Joseph Chapline's Company, 2nd Battalion, 1776/1777 [Ref: M-241, which listed the name as "Conrad Highburger"]. Took the Oath of Allegiance before the Hon. Christopher Cruse in Sharpsburg Hundred before March 2, 1778 [Ref: O-34, which listed the name as "Conarad Hybarger"]. It is interesting to note that "Conrat Heiberger 1775 (n.o.i.)" is buried in the Old Reformed Graveyard at Sharpsburg, Maryland [Ref: JJ-I:27].

HILDERBRAND, David. Private, Militia, 3rd Class, Capt. Isaac Baker's Company, 1776/1777 [Ref: A-1146, M-247].

HILDERBRAND, John. Private, Militia, 2nd Class, Capt. Samuel Hughes' Company, 2nd Battalion, 1776/1777 [Ref: M-238, A-1146].

HILDERBRAND, Phillip. Private, Militia, 6th Class, Capt. Isaac Baker's Company, 1776/1777 [Ref: A-1146, M-247].

HILL, James. Private, Militia, 3rd Class, Capt. James Prather's Company, 3rd Battalion, 1776/1777 [Ref: M-242]. Two men by this name took the Oath of Allegiance before March 2, 1778: one before the Hon. Christopher Cruse in Sharpsburg Hundred [Ref: O-35, J-2], and one before the Hon. Andrew Bruce [Ref: O-41, J-6].

HILL, John. Enrolled in the first militia company organized for the Revolutionary War in the Elizabeth Town District of Frederick County (now the Hagerstown area of Washington County) on January 6, 1776 [Ref: Q-270, W-1189]. Private, Militia, 3rd Class, Capt. Henry Boteler's Company, 1776/1777 [Ref: M-237, A-1146].

HILL, Peter. Enrolled in the third militia company organized for the Revolutionary War in the Elizabeth Town District of Frederick County (now the Hagerstown area of Washington County), passed by the Committee of Observation on June 5, 1776, and assigned to Capt. John Reynolds' command [Ref: Q-273]. Private, Militia, 1st Class, Capt. Joseph Chapline's Company, 2nd Battalion, 1776/1777 [Ref: M-241]. Took the Oath of Allegiance before the Hon. Christopher Cruse in Sharpsburg Hundred before March 2, 1778 [Ref: O-34, J-2].

HILL, William. First Lieutenant, Militia, Capt. John Bennet's Company, 1776 (succeeded, but date not given). [Ref: M-87, M-246, A-1146]. Took the Oath of Allegiance before the Hon. John Barnes before February 28, 1778 [Ref: O-44, J-9].

HIMINGER, Andrew. See "Andrew Huninger," q.v.

HINDMAN, Joseph. Private, Militia, 8th Class, Capt. Peter Beall's Company, 1st Battalion, 1776/1777 [Ref: M-240]. Took the Oath of Allegiance before the Hon. Andrew Rentch before March 7, 1778 [Ref: O-52, J-15, which listed the name as "Joseph Hinsman"].

HINDS, John. Private, Militia, 2nd Class, Capt. Michael Fackler's Company, 1776/1777 [Ref: M-245, A-1146]. Took the Oath of Allegiance before the Hon. Joseph Sprigg before April 1, 1778 [Ref: O-53, J-16, which listed the name as "John Hinde"].

HINES, Thomas. See "Thomas Hynes," q.v.

HINKLE, Conrad. Private, Militia, 4th Class, Capt. John Rennolds' (Reynolds') Company, 2nd Battalion, 1776/1777 [Ref: M-240].

HINKLE, Leonard. Second Sergeant, Militia, Capt. John Rennolds' (Reynolds') Company, 2nd Battalion, 1776/1777 [Ref: M-240].

HINKLE, Mary. See "George Roush," q.v.

HINNYS, Peggy. See "Daniel Sampy," q.v.

HIPPENNLISER, John. See "John Hopponhizer," q.v.

HIRSH, Jacob. Private who was enrolled by Capt. Henry Hardman and passed on July 19, 1776 in Frederick (now Washington) County [Ref: D-51].

HIRSH, John. Took the Oath of Allegiance before the Hon. Lemuel Barritt before March 16, 1778 [Ref: O-43, J-8].

HISKELL, Frederick. Fourth Corporal, Militia, Capt. Michael Fackler's Company, 1776/1777 [Ref: M-245, A-1146]. Took the Oath of Allegiance before the Hon. Joseph Sprigg before April 1, 1778 [Ref: O-53, J-16, which listed the name as "Frederick Hieskell"]. Rendered patriotic service in Hagerstown by providing "tomhawks" to Capt. John Nelson's Company, continental service (Maryland Line), April, 1776 [Ref: Q-161, which listed the name as "Frederick Hyskill"]. Rendered patriotic service by providing necessaries to Capt. John Reynolds' Company in the Flying Camp and belonging to the Maryland Service in July, 1776, as recorded by the Committee of Observation at Sharpsburg on August 6, 1776 [Ref: Q-333, which listed the name as "Frederick Hyskill"].

HIX, Jacob. Second Sergeant, Militia, Capt. Martin Kershner's Company, 32nd Battalion, December 27, 1776 [Ref: K-1814, Box 3]. Ensign, Militia, Capt. Martin Kershner's Company, 1776/1777 [Ref: M-247, A-1146]. Took the Oath of Allegiance before the Hon. Henry Schnebley in 1778 [Ref: O-49, J-12].

HIX, Joshua. Private, Militia, 1st Class, Capt. Conrad Hogmire's Company, 1776/1777 [Ref: M-244, A-1146, which listed the name as "Joshua Hixs"].

HIXON, Joseph. Private, Militia, 8th Class, Capt. Martin Kershner's Company, 1776/1777 [Ref: A-1146, M-248]. Private, Militia, Capt. Martin Kershner's Company, 32nd Battalion, December 27, 1776 [Ref: K-1814 (Box 3), which listed the name as "Joseph Hixson"].

HIZER, William. See "William Heyser," q.v.

HO---- [sic], A. Took the Oath of Allegiance before the Hon. Henry Schnebley in 1778 [Ref: O-49, J-13].

HOAGLAND, James. Private, Militia, Capt. Charles Coulson's Company, enrolled August 28, 1776 [Ref: M-243, A-1146, which listed the name as "James Hogeland(?)"]. Took the Oath of Allegiance before the Hon. Andrew Bruce before March 2, 1778 [Ref: O-41, which listed the name as "James Haagland" and J-6, which listed the name as "James Hagland"].

HOBBINS, Moses. Enrolled in the third militia company organized for the Revolutionary War in the Elizabeth Town District of Frederick County (now the Hagerstown area of Washington County), passed by the Committee of Observation on June 5, 1776, and assigned to Capt. John Reynolds' command [Ref: Q-273]. Private, Militia, 6th Class, Capt. John Rennolds' (Reynolds') Company, 2nd Battalion, 1776/1777 [Ref: M-240, which listed the name as "Moses Hobins"]. Private who was enlisted by Capt. John Reynolds and passed on July 18, 1776 in Frederick (now Washington) County [Ref: D-50]. Took the Oath of Allegiance before the Hon. Richard Davis in 1778 [Ref: J-4, O-37].

HOBLITZELL, Adrian (1745-1802). Took the Oath of Allegiance before the Hon. Henry Schnebley in 1778 [Ref: O-49, J-13]. Adrian was born on February 6, 1745 in Germany, married first to Martha Barton and second to Christena ----, and died in 1802 [Ref: Y-II:1443]. One Adrian Hoblitzell was a son of John Hoblitzell who died intestate in 1818 [Ref: Z-1, citing an equity court case in 1823]. Additional research may be necessary before drawing conclusions.

HOCKEY, Christopher (Christian). Private, Militia, Capt. John Kershner's Company, on duty guarding prisoners of war at Fort Frederick on June 27, 1778 [Ref: D-328, which listed the name as "Christain Nockey (or Hockey)"]. Took the Oath of Allegiance before the Hon. Joseph Sprigg before April 1, 1778 [Ref: O-53, J-16, which listed the name as "Christopher Hockey"]. Private, Select Militia, Capt. Adam Ott's Company, 1781 [Ref: M-238, A-1146, which listed the name as "Christian Hockey"].

HOCKEY, Nicholas. First Sergeant, Militia, Capt. Michael Fackler's Company, 1776. Lieutenant, Select Militia, Capt. Adam Ott's Company, March 30, 1781 [Ref: M-88, M-245, A-1146, G-368, M-238, which latter source listed the name as "Nicholas Shockey"]. Rendered patriotic service in Hagerstown by providing sundries to Capt. John Nelson's Company, continental service (Maryland Line), April, 1776 [Ref: Q-162, which listed the name as "Nicholas Hackay"]. On September 17, 1776 he "delivered unto Col. Henry Shriock seven musketts with iron ramrods for the use of the flying camp made and delivered for John Uncel." [Ref: Q-336]. Took the Oath of Allegiance before the Hon. Joseph Sprigg before April 1, 1778 [Ref: O-53, J-16].

HOFFERD, Jacob. Rendered patriotic service by supplying wheat and rye for the use of the military on February 11, 1780 [Ref: W-1190, HH-72]. Jacob Hofferd died testate by February 12, 1805, leaving a wife Elizabeth and several children [Ref: MM-13:132, 133].

HOFFMAN, Casper. Took the Oath of Allegiance before the Hon. Henry Schnebley in 1778 [Ref: O-50, J-13].

HOFFMAN, Elizabeth. See "Christopher Orendorff," q.v.

HOFFMAN, George. Rendered patriotic service by supplying a blanket for the use of the military in March, 1776, as recorded by the Committee of Observation on April 12, 1776 [Ref: L-82, Q-157, which latter source listed the name as "George Hofman"]. Took the Oath of Allegiance before the Hon. Samuel Hughes before March 1, 1778 [Ref: O-33, J-1].

HOFFMAN, John. Private, Militia, 1st Class, Capt. John Rennolds' (Reynolds') Company, 2nd Battalion, 1776/1777 [Ref: M-240].

HOFFMAN, Michael. Private, Militia, 6th Class, Capt. John Rennolds' (Reynolds') Company, 2nd Battalion, 1776/1777 [Ref: M-240]. Took the Oath of Allegiance before the Hon. John Stull in 1778 [Ref: O-46, J-10, which latter source listed the name as "Michael Hofman"].

HOFFMAN, Richard. Took the Oath of Allegiance before the Hon. Christopher Cruse in Sharpsburg Hundred before March 2, 1778 [Ref: O-35, J-2].

HOFSTETH, Samuel. Private, Militia, 7th Class, Capt. Conrad Nichodemus' Company, 2nd Battalion, 1776/1777 [Ref: M-237, A-1146].

HOGG, Thomas. Appointed to raise funds on January 24, 1775 for the Committee of Observation in Lower Antietam Hundred in Frederick (now Washington) County [Ref: L-75, which listed the name as "Thomas Hogg"]. One of several patriots appointed by the Committee of Observation on January 7, 1777 "to form the county into companies (after the militia had marched) for the purpose of relieving the distressed inhabitants of said county and also to compel the Dunkards and Mennonists to give their assistance." [Ref: Q-31]. Took the Oath of Allegiance before the Hon. Joseph Chapline before April 17, 1779 [Ref: J-5, O-39].

HOGG, Zeb. Private, Militia, Capt. Charles Coulson's Company, enrolled August 28, 1776 [Ref: M-243, A-1146].

HOGHANOUR, Jacob. Private, Militia, 4th Class, Capt. Martin Kershner's Company, 1776/1777 [Ref: A-1146, M-247].

HOGMIRE, Conrad (1725-1797). Elected to serve on the Committee of Observation for the Elizabeth Town District (now the Hagerstown area of Washington County) on September 12, 1775 [Ref: Q-142]. Appointed by the Committee of Observation for Elizabeth Town District to serve on a Committee for Licensing Suits on September 14, 1775 [Ref: Q-142]. Appointed to raise funds on January 24, 1775 for the Committee of Observation in Upper Antietam Hundred in Frederick (now Washington) County [Ref: L-75]. Captain, Militia, 32nd Battalion, Frederick County, January 3, 1776. Captain, Militia, Washington County, resigned his commission on October 10, 1776 because of age [Ref: M-88, M-244, A-1146, P-61]. Referred to as Capt. Conrad Hogmire on February 19, 1776, and as Capt. Conrade Hogmire (chairman) on March 4, 1776 [Ref: Q-152, Q-153]. Served on the Committee of Observation in April, 1776 [Ref: Q-154, Q-155]. Took the Oath of Allegiance before the Hon. John Stull in 1778 [Ref: O-46, J-10]. Conrad Hogmire was born in Maryland on May 25, 1725, married first to Mary Magdalena ---- (second wife not named), died on December 20 or 26, 1797, was buried in Old St. John's Lutheran Churchyard, and subsequently reinterred in Rose Hill Cemetery in Hagerstown [Ref: Y-II:1451, JJ-VII:105, which latter source listed the name as "Conrad Hogmeyer"]. See "Patrick Owens," q.v.

HOGMIRE, Daniel. Fourth Sergeant, Militia, Capt. Samuel Hughes' Company, 1776/1777 [Ref: M-238, A-1146].

HOGMIRE, Samuel. Private, Militia, 2nd Class, Capt. Samuel Hughes' Company, 2nd Battalion, 1776/1777 [Ref: M-238, A-1146].

HOLLAND, Prudence. See "Otho Holland Williams," q.v.

HOLLAWAY, George. Private, Militia, 3rd Class, Capt. Griffin Johnson's Company, 3rd Battalion, 1776/1777 [Ref: M-243].

HOLLETT, John. Private, Militia, 2nd Class, Capt. James Prather's Company, 3rd Battalion, 1776/1777 [Ref: M-242].

HOLLETT, Thomas. Private, Militia, 1st Class, Capt. James Prather's Company, 3rd Battalion, 1776/1777 [Ref: M-242].

HOLLYDAY, Clement. First Lieutenant, Upper District, Frederick County (now Washington County), July, 1776 [Ref: D-48].

HOLMES, Barclay. Soldier who resided in Washington County and was granted a pension certificate in August, 1820, according to an Act of Congress of March 18, 1818, since he had proven that he was "in the enjoyment of a certain degree of poverty" as required by the Act as amended on May 1, 1820 [Ref: W-1190]. Private, Virginia Line, pensioned at $96 per year effective September 5, 1820 [Ref: R-42, which listed the name as "Barclay alias Bartlett Holmes"].

HONSAKER, Nicholas. Private, Militia, 3rd Class, Capt. Conrad Hogmire's Company, 1776/1777 [Ref: M-244, A-1146].

HOOD, John. Private who was enlisted by Lieut. Moses Chapline and passed on July 24, 1776 in Frederick (now Washington) County [Ref: D-50]. Private who was recruited and passed by County Lieutenant Thomas Sprigg on April 22, 1780 [Ref: D-336].

HOOF, Goddard. Third Corporal, Militia, Capt. Conrad Nichodemus' Company, 2nd Battalion, 1776/1777 [Ref: M-237, A-1146].

HOOFMAN, Casper. Private, Militia, 2nd Class, Capt. John Bennet's Company, 1776/1777 [Ref: M-246, A-1146].

HOOFMAN, Henry. Private, Militia, 4th Class, Capt. James Smith's Company, 2nd Battalion, 1776/1777 [Ref: M-240, A-1146].

HOOFMAN, Jacob. Private, Militia, 7th Class, Capt. John Rennolds' (Reynolds') Company, 2nd Battalion, 1776/1777 [Ref: M-240].

HOOFMAN, Jacob. Private, Militia, 3rd Class, Capt. Jacob Sharer's Company, 1776/1777 [Ref: A-1146, M-248].

HOOK, Peter. Took the Oath of Allegiance before the Hon. Henry Schnebley in 1778 [Ref: O-49, J-12].

HOOK (HOOKE), John Snowden. Private who was enrolled by Lieut. Clement Hollyday and passed by Col. William Luckett on August 8, 1776 [Ref: D-49]. Died in Cumberland on August 26, 1827, Mrs. Hook, relict of the late John S. Hook, aged upwards of 70 years, for more than 40 years a resident of this town [Ref: Z-16].

HOORAW(?), Adam. Private, Militia, 8th Class, Capt. John Cellars' Company, 1776/1777 [Ref: A-1146, M-247].

HOOVER, Adam. Private, Militia, 6th Class, Capt. Samuel Hughes' Company, 2nd Battalion, 1776/1777 [Ref: M-238, A-1146].

HOOVER, Adam Sr. Private, Militia, 1st Class, Capt. Samuel Hughes' Company, 2nd Battalion, 1776/1777 [Ref: M-238, A-1146].

HOOVER, Christopher. Took the Oath of Allegiance before the Hon. John Stull in 1778 [Ref: O-46, J-10].

HOOVER, Daniel. Private who enlisted in the militia on August 10, 1781 for service in the Continental Army [Ref: D-388, D-408, which listed the name as "Daniel Hover"]. Substitute, Maryland Line, discharged on October 30, 1781 [Ref: G-656, which listed the name as "Daniel Hover"].

HOOVER, Henry. Private, Militia, 4th Class, Capt. Conrad Hogmire's Company, 1776/1777 [Ref: M-244, A-1146].

HOOVER, Henry. Private, Militia, 4th Class, Capt. Basil Williams' Company, 1776/1777 [Ref: M-244, A-1146].

HOOVER, Jacob. Private, Militia, Capt. William Heyser's Company, enlisted in July, 1776, muster roll dated October 23, 1776, continental service, reenlisted July 16, 1778 for one year as a wagoner, and discharged October 12, 1779 at Fort Wyoming, Pennsylvania [Ref: D-264, W-1190, L-79, GG-98, which latter source listed the name as "Jacob Hoover, Haver"]. On January 15, 1778 the Council of Maryland ordered the Western Shore Treasurer to issue money to Jacob Hoover to be delivered to Daniel Hughes for defraying expenses of prisoners in Washington County [Ref: C-467, which also listed the name as "Jacob Hover"]. See "Jacob Hower" and "Jacob Haver," q.v.

HOOVER, Jacob Jr. Private, Militia, 2nd Class, Capt. Jacob Sharer's Company, 1776/1777 [Ref: A-1146, M-248].

HOOVER, Jacob Sr. Private, Militia, 5th Class, Capt. Jacob Sharer's Company, 1776/1777 [Ref: A-1146, M-248].

HOOVER, John. Private, Militia, 7th Class, Capt. Jacob Sharer's Company, 1776/1777 [Ref: A-1146, M-248].

HOOVER, John. Private, Militia, 7th Class, Capt. Peter Swingle's (Swingley's) Company, 1776/1777 [Ref: A-1146, M-249].

HOOVER, John Jr. Private, Militia, 5th Class, Capt. Conrad Hogmire's Company, 1776/1777 [Ref: M-244, A-1146].

HOOVER, Martin. Private, Militia, 3rd Class, Capt. Basil Williams' Company, 1776/1777 [Ref: M-244, A-1146].

HOOVER, Mary. See "Frederick Guiser," q.v.

HOOVER, Peter. Private, Militia, 5th Class, Capt. Samuel Hughes' Company, 2nd Battalion, 1776/1777 [Ref: M-238, A-1146].

HOOVER, Rozana. See "Frederick Guiser," q.v.

HOPEWELL, John and Milly. See "Abraham White," q.v.

HOPKINS, Lucy. See "John Bruff," q.v.

HOPPONHIZER, John. Took the Oath of Allegiance before the Hon. John Barnes before February 28, 1778 [Ref: J-9, O-45, which latter source listed the name as "John Hopponhiger"]. Private, Militia, 4th Class, Capt. Isaac Baker's Company, 1776/1777 [Ref: A-1146, M-247, which listed the name as "John Hippennliser"].

HORN, Vallentine. Took the Oath of Allegiance before the Hon. Lemuel Barritt before March 16, 1778 [Ref: O-43, J-8]. Fifer, Militia, Capt. James Prather's Company, 3rd Battalion, 1776/1777 [Ref: M-242, which listed the name as "Valentine Horne"].

HORNE, John. See "John Hahn," q.v.

HORNISH, Phillip. Private, Militia, 3rd Class, Capt. Peter Beall's Company, 1st Battalion, 1776/1777 [Ref: M-240].

HORST, Earl. See "Edmond Rutter," q.v.

HOSE, Jacob. Second Sergeant, Militia, Capt. William Heyser's Company, muster roll dated October 23, 1776, in continental service [Ref: D-263, W-1190, L-79]. Sergeant, German Regiment, Lt. Col. Ludwick Weltner's Company, continental service, 1776, and discharged on July 26, 1779 [Ref: D-264, W-1190, L-79, D-218].

HOSE, Peter (1745-1828). Private, Militia, 8th Class, Capt. Michael Fackler's Company, 1776/1777 [Ref: M-245, A-1146]. Took the Oath of Allegiance before the Hon. Joseph Sprigg before April 1, 1778 [Ref: O-54, J-16]. Peter Hose died in Hagerstown on January 26, 1828, in his 83rd year [Ref: Z-97].

HOSKINS, Charles. Private who was enrolled by Capt. Aeneas Campbell and passed by Major Francis Deakins on July 18, 1776 [Ref: D-49].

HOSKINS, George. Private who was enrolled by Capt. Aeneas Campbell and passed by Major Francis Deakins on July 18, 1776 [Ref: D-49].

HOSKINS, Joseph. Took the Oath of Allegiance before the Hon. Richard Davis in 1778 [Ref: O-37, J-4, which latter source listed the name as "Joseph Haskins"]. Private who enlisted in the militia on August 18, 1781 for service in the Continental Army [Ref: D-388, D-408]. Substitute, Maryland Line, discharged on October 30, 1781 [Ref: G-656].

HOSLER, Jacob. Enrolled in the third militia company organized for the Revolutionary War in the Elizabeth Town District of Frederick County (now the Hagerstown area of Washington County), passed by the Committee of Observation on June 5, 1776, and assigned to Capt. John Reynolds' command [Ref: Q-273]. Private who was enlisted by Capt. John Reynolds and passed on July 18, 1776 in Frederick (now Washington) County [Ref: D-50].

HOSS, Jeremiah. Private, Select Militia, Capt. Adam Ott's Company, 1781 [Ref: M-238, A-1146].

HOSS, John. Private, Militia, 2nd Class, Capt. Peter Swingle's (Swingley's) Company, 1776/1777 [Ref: A-1146, M-248].

HOUK, Adam. See "Jonathan Mayhew," q.v.

HOUK, Jacob. Private, Militia, 8th Class, Capt. Conrad Hogmire's Company, 1776/1777 [Ref: M-244, A-1146]. Took the Oath of Allegiance before the Hon. Andrew Rentch before March 7, 1778 [Ref: O-52, J-15, which latter source listed the name as "Jacob Houck"]. Rendered patriotic service by supplying grain for the use of the military in April, 1780 [Ref: W-1190, which listed the name as "Jacob Hauck"].

HOUK, Mathias. Private who was enrolled by Capt. Henry Hardman and passed on July 19, 1776 in Frederick (now Washington) County [Ref: D-51, which listed the name as "Mathias Houks"].

HOUK, Peter. Private, Militia, 2nd Class, Capt. Peter Beall's Company, 1st Battalion, 1776/1777 [Ref: M-240, which listed the name as "Peter Hoak"]. Took the Oath of Allegiance before the Hon. Joseph Sprigg before April 1, 1778 [Ref: O-53, which listed the name as "Peter Hawk" and J-16, which listed the name as "Peter Howk"].

HOUNTS, Joseph. Took the Oath of Allegiance before the Hon. Lemuel Barritt before March 16, 1778 [Ref: O-42, J-8].

HOUSE, Abraham Jr. Private, Militia, 3rd Class, Capt. James Walling's Company, 2nd Battalion, 1776/1777 [Ref: M-238, A-1146].

HOUSE, Andrew. Took the Oath of Allegiance before the Hon. Andrew Bruce before March 2, 1778 [Ref: O-41, J-7].

HOUSE, Christiana. See "Michael House," q.v.

HOUSE, John. Second Lieutenant, Militia, Capt. Charles Clinton's Company, 1776/1777 [Ref: M-245, A-1146]. Two men by this name took the Oath of Allegiance in 1778: one before the Hon. Lemuel Barritt before March 16, 1778 [Ref: O-43, J-8], and one before the Hon. Henry Schnebley [Ref: O-51, J-15]. Rendered patriotic service by providing wheat for the military in August, 1781 [Ref: P-424].

HOUSE, Michael (c1756-1827). Private, Pennsylvania Line, who resided in Washington County and was granted a pension certificate in August, 1820, according to an Act of Congress of March 18, 1818, since he had proven that he was "in the enjoyment of a certain degree of poverty" as required by the Act as amended on May 1, 1820 [Ref: W-1190]. Pensioned at $96 per year effective October 28, 1818. On February 23, 1822 the Treasurer of the Western Shore of Maryland was directed to pay to Michael House half pay of a private for his Revolutionary War services. He died February 1, 1827 [Ref: R-42, AA-356]. On March 12, 1827 the Treasurer of the Western Shore of Maryland was directed to pay to Christiana House, of Washington County, during life, half yearly, half pay of a private, for her husband Michael House's services during the war [Ref: AA-356]. Christiana House, relict of Michael House, died in Hagerstown on December 22, 1828, in her 76th year [Ref: Z-105].

HOUSE, William. Private, Militia, 1st Class, Capt. Griffin Johnson's Company, 3rd Battalion, 1776/1777 [Ref: M-243].

HOUSEHOLDER, Adam. Took the Oath of Allegiance before the Hon. Joseph Sprigg before April 1, 1778 [Ref: O-53, J-16]. Rendered patriotic service by providing clothing for the use of the military on July 5, 1778 [Ref: CC-106, which listed the name as "Adam Houshalter, Sr."].

HOUSEHOLDER, Adam Jr. Private, Militia, 2nd Class, Capt. Peter Swingle's (Swingley's) Company, 1776/1777 [Ref: A-1146, M-248]. Took the Oath of Allegiance before the Hon. Richard Davis in 1778 [Ref: J-4, O-37, which listed the name without the "Jr."]. Rendered patriotic service by providing clothing for the use of the military on July 5, 1778 [Ref: CC-106, which listed the name as "Adam Houshalter, Jr."].

HOUSEHOLDER, George. Took the Oath of Allegiance before the Hon. Henry Schnebley in 1778 [Ref: O-50, J-14, which listed the name as "George Houshatter"].

HOUSEHOLDER, Jacob. Took the Oath of Allegiance before the Hon. John Stull in 1778 [Ref: O-46, J-10, which listed the name as "John Housholler"].

HOUSEHOLDER, John. One of several patriots appointed by the Committee of Observation on January 9, 1777 "to procure as many blankets as may be wanting to supply Col. Smith's Battalion." [Ref: Q-34, which listed the name as "Mr. John Housholder"]. Took the Oath of Allegiance before the Hon. Henry Schnebley in 1778 [Ref: O-50, J-14, which listed the name as "John Houshatter"].

HOUSEHOLDER, Michael. Private, Militia, 7th Class, Capt. John Cellars' Company, 1776/1777 [Ref: A-1146, M-246]. Took the Oath of Allegiance before the Hon. Henry Schnebley in 1778 [Ref: O-50, J-14, which listed the name as "Michael Houshatter"].

HOUSEHOLDER, Simon. Took the Oath of Allegiance before the Hon. Henry Schnebley in 1778 [Ref: O-51, J-15, which listed the name as "Simon Housholder"]. First Corporal, Militia, Capt. Peter Beall's Company, 1st Battalion, 1776/1777 [Ref: M-240, which listed the name as "Simon Househalter"].

HOUSEMAN, Conrad. Private, German Regiment, continental service, 1776, and discharged on July 26, 1779 [Ref: D-218, which listed the name as "Conrad Hausman"].

HOUSEMAN, John. See "Thomas Bartley (Bartlett)," q.v.

HOUSER, Abraham, see "Abraham Hauser," q.v.

HOUSER, Henry. Private, Militia, 7th Class, Capt. John Cellars' Company, 1776/1777 [Ref: A-1146, M-246].

HOUSER, Isaac (c1755-1824). Private, Militia, 8th Class, Capt. James Walling's Company, 2nd Battalion, 1776/1777 [Ref: M-239, A-1146]. Isaac Houser, Sr. died at his residence in Washington County at an advanced age "about a fortnight since" as noted in *The Torchlight and Public Advertiser* newspaper in Hagerstown on March 9, 1824 [Ref: Z-66].

HOUSER, John. Private, Militia, 7th Class, Capt. Henry Boteler's Company, 1776/1777 [Ref: M-237, A-1146].
HOUSLEY, William. Private who was enrolled by Capt. Aeneas Campbell and passed by Major Francis Deakins on July 18, 1776 [Ref: D-49, which listed the name as "William Housley (Owsley)"].
HOUT, Peter. Second Corporal, Militia, Capt. Peter Beall's Company, 1st Battalion, 1776/1777 [Ref: M-240].
HOW, George. Private who was enrolled by Capt. Henry Hardman and passed on July 19, 1776 in Frederick (now Washington) County [Ref: D-51].
HOWE, General. See "John Marshall," q.v.
HOWARD, Benjamin. Private who enlisted in the militia on September 5, 1781 for service in the Continental Army and reportedly "deserted." [Ref: D-388].
HOWARD, Clement. Private, Militia, 3rd Class, Capt. Basil Williams' Company, 1776/1777 [Ref: M-244, A-1146]. Private who was enlisted by Ensign Nathan Williams and passed on July 25, 1776 in Frederick (now Washington) County [Ref: D-51]. Took the Oath of Allegiance before the Hon. Richard Davis in 1778 [Ref: J-4, O-36].
HOWARD, Colonel. See "Neale Peacock," q.v.
HOWARD, Frederick. Private, Militia, 5th Class, Capt. Conrad Hogmire's Company, 1776/1777 [Ref: M-244, A-1146].
HOWARD, Henry. Took the Oath of Allegiance before the Hon. Richard Davis in 1778 [Ref: J-3, O-36].
HOWARD, Jacob. Private, Militia, 1st Class, Capt. Samuel Hughes' Company, 2nd Battalion, 1776/1777 [Ref: M-238, A-1146].
HOWARD, John. Private, Militia, 6th Class, Capt. Peter Beall's Company, 1st Battalion, 1776/1777 [Ref: M-240]. Took the Oath of Allegiance before the Hon. John Stull in 1778 [Ref: O-46, J-10].
HOWARD, Philip. Took the Oath of Allegiance before the Hon. William Yates in 1778 [Ref: O-48, J-12]. Private, Militia, 2nd Class, Capt. Barnett Johnston's Company, 3rd Battalion, 1776/1777 [Ref: M-242].
HOWELL, William. Took the Oath of Allegiance before the Hon. Lemuel Barritt before March 16, 1778 [Ref: O-43, J-8].
HOWER, Anthony. Took the Oath of Allegiance before the Hon. John Cellars in January, 1778 [Ref: O-40, J-6, K-1814, which latter source listed the name as "Antoney Hower"].
HOWER, Anthony. Took the Oath of Allegiance before the Hon. Henry Schnebley in 1778 [Ref: O-49, J-12].
HOWER, Jacob. Private, Militia, Capt. Martin Kershner's Company, 32nd Battalion, December 27, 1776 [Ref: K-1814, Box 3]. Took the Oath of

Allegiance before the Hon. John Cellars in January, 1778 [Ref: K-1814, O-40, J-5]. See "Jacob Hoover or Hover," q.v.

HOWK, Peter. See "Peter Houk," q.v.

HOYE, Mary. See "George Calmes," q.v.

HOYLE, Conrad (c1760-1821). Private, Militia, Capt. William Heyser's Company, enlisted July 20, 1776, muster roll dated October 23, 1776, in continental service [Ref: D-264, W-1190, which listed the name as "Conrad Hoyt" and L-79, which listed the name as "Conrad Hoyl"]. Private, German Regiment, Lt. Col. Ludwick Weltner's Company, discharged on July 20, 1779 at Fort Wyoming, Pennsylvania [Ref: D-265]. Died on May 17, 1821 in Fayette County, Pennsylvania, age 61 [Ref: GG-98, which listed the name as "Conrad Hoyle, Hiles, Hogle, Stoyle"].

HOYNE, John. Took the Oath of Allegiance before the Hon. Richard Davis in 1778 [Ref: J-4, O-37].

HRABER, Jacob. Took the Oath of Allegiance before the Hon. Henry Schnebley in 1778 [Ref: O-49, J-12].

HUBART, John. Took the Oath of Allegiance before the Hon. Lemuel Barritt before March 16, 1778 [Ref: O-43, J-8].

HUBBS, Samuel. First Lieutenant, Militia, Capt. Daniel Cresap's Company, 3rd Battalion, June 22, 1778 [Ref: M-90, M-241, E-145]. Took the Oath of Allegiance before the Hon. Lemuel Barritt before March 16, 1778 [Ref: O-42, J-7].

HUBER, Henry. Took the Oath of Allegiance before September 1, 1780 [Ref: Z-113].

HUDGIN, Thomas. Private, Militia, 1st Class, Capt. Jeremiah Spires' Company, 2nd Battalion, 1776/1777 [Ref: M-239, A-1146].

HUDSON, George. Private, Militia, 3rd Class, Capt. Daniel Clapsaddle's Company, 1st Battalion, 1776/1777 [Ref: M-236, A-1146]. Private, Militia, Capt. John Kershner's Company, on duty guarding prisoners of war at Fort Frederick on June 27, 1778 [Ref: D-328].

HUERD, Ludwig. Took the Oath of Allegiance before the Hon. Henry Schnebley in 1778 [Ref: O-51, J-14].

HUET, Nicholas. Private, Select Militia, Capt. Adam Ott's Company, 1781 [Ref: M-238, A-1146]. Took the Oath of Allegiance before the Hon. Samuel Hughes before March 1, 1778 [Ref: O-33, J-1].

HUFFER, John. Private, Militia, 8th Class, Capt. Henry Boteler's Company, 1776/1777 [Ref: M-237, A-1146].

HUFFMAN, Aaron. Fourth Sergeant, Militia, Capt. Daniel Cresap's Company, 3rd Battalion, 1776/1777 [Ref: M-241]. Took the Oath of

Allegiance before the Hon. Lemuel Barritt before March 16, 1778 [Ref: O-42, J-7, which sources listed the name as "Aaron Hughnm"].

HUFFMAN, Henry. Fourth Sergeant, Militia, Capt. Conrad Nichodemus' Company, 2nd Battalion, 1776/1777 [Ref: M-237, A-1146, which listed the name as "Henry Hufman"].

HUFFMAN, Moses. Private, Militia, 5th Class, Capt. Daniel Cresap's Company, 3rd Battalion, 1776/1777 [Ref: M-241, which listed the name as "Moses Hufman"]. Took the Oath of Allegiance before the Hon. Lemuel Barritt before March 16, 1778 [Ref: O-43, which listed the name as "Moses Hugham" and J-8, which listed the name as "Moses Higham"].

HUFFMAN, Robert. Enrolled in the first militia company organized for the Revolutionary War in the Elizabeth Town District of Frederick County (now the Hagerstown area of Washington County) on January 6, 1776 [Ref: Q-271, W-1190]. Private, Militia, 3rd Class, Capt. Joseph Chapline's Company, 2nd Battalion, 1776/1777 [Ref: M-241, which listed the name as "Robert Huflman"].

HUGGET, Thomas. Took the Oath of Allegiance before the Hon. Richard Davis in 1778 [Ref: J-4, O-37].

HUGHAM, Moses. See "Moses Huffman," q.v.

HUGHES, Ann. See "Daniel Hughes," q.v.

HUGHES, Barnabas. See "John Hughes," q.v.

HUGHES, Daniel. Served on the Committee of Observation for the Elizabeth Town District (now the Hagerstown area of Washington County) in December, 1776 [Ref: Q-340]. Served on the Committee of Observation in February, 1777 [Ref: Q-228, C-467]. County Lieutenant from July 1, 1777 to December 21, 1779, having removed to Baltimore Town by that date [Ref: M-90, C-304, C-369, F-39]. Ann Hughes, widow of the late Col. Daniel Hughes, died at her residence in Hagerstown on August 29, 1825 [Ref: Z-76]. See "John Hughes," q.v.

HUGHES, James. Took the Oath of Allegiance before the Hon. John Barnes before February 28, 1778 [Ref: O-44, J-9]. This may be the James Hughes who received pension S39751 in Baltimore in 1820, aged 64, stating he served with the German Regiment in Frederick County, Maryland. Moses McKinsey, of Allegany County, made an affidavit on September 4, 1820 as to his military service with James Hughes [Ref: U-35:2 (1947)].

HUGHES, John. Son of Barnabas Hughes, a native of Ireland, who came to America circa 1750, John was a captain in the Revolutionary War and a prominent man in Washington County. He and Daniel Hughes built Mt. Aetna and other iron furnaces and cast many of the cannon used by the Continental Army at his Antietam Iron Works near Sharpsburg. He was an intimate friend of Major Andre during his confinement [Ref: L-79, L-80].

HUGHES, Samuel (c1741-c1821). Served on the Committee of Observation for the Elizabeth Town District (now the Hagerstown area of Washington County) in December, 1776 [Ref: Q-340, which referred to him as "Capt. Samuel Hughes"]. Appointed by the Committee of Observation to serve on a Committee for Licensing Suits on September 14, 1775 [Ref: Q-142]. Captain, Militia, 2nd Battalion, 1776 (succeeded, but date not given). [Ref: M-90, M-237, A-1146, Q-153]. Elected to serve on the Committee of Observation for the Elizabeth Town District on September 12, 1775 [Ref: Q-142]. Referred to as Capt. Samuel Hughes on March 4, 1776 [Ref: Q-153]. Justice who administered the Oath of Allegiance in 1778 [Ref: O-33, J-1]. Appointed by the Committee of Observation to carry the Association of Freemen to male residents in his hundred (district) on March 4, 1776 "and present it for signing and make an exact account of those that sign and those that refuse with their reasons for refusing." [Ref: Q-153, L-82]. Took the Oath of Allegiance on May 20, 1777 [Ref: K-1814, Box 4]. Justice of the Orphans Court, June 4, 1777 [Ref: C-275]. Justice of the County Court, June 20, 1778 [Ref: E-141]. Served in the Maryland House of Delegates, 1777-1779, and subsequently relocated to Harford County, Maryland where he held a number of offices, both public and private, including Associate Justice of the Harford County Circuit Court [Ref: KK-I:76-80, KK-I:470-471, which contains more detailed information].

HUGHES, Thomas. Took the Oath of Allegiance before the Hon. Henry Schnebley in 1778 [Ref: O-50, J-14].

HUGHETT, Ludwick. Private, Militia, 4th Class, Capt. Samuel Hughes' Company, 2nd Battalion, 1776/1777 [Ref: M-238, A-1146].

HUGHETT, Nicholas. Private, Militia, 5th Class, Capt. Samuel Hughes' Company, 2nd Battalion, 1776/1777 [Ref: M-238, A-1146].

HUGHETT, Stophel. Private, Militia, 4th Class, Capt. Samuel Hughes' Company, 2nd Battalion, 1776/1777 [Ref: M-238, A-1146].

HUGHMAN, George. See "George Bughman," q.v.

HULL, Benjamin. Took the Oath of Allegiance before the Hon. Lemuel Barritt before March 16, 1778 [Ref: O-42, J-8].

HULLOCK, Thomas. Second Sergeant, Militia, Capt. Griffin Johnson's Company, 3rd Battalion, 1776/1777 [Ref: M-243].

HUMPHREYS, Thomas. First Lieutenant, Militia, Capt. James Prather's Company, 3rd or Western Battalion, May 16, 1778 [Ref: M-90, E-86, M-242, which latter source listed the name as "Thomas Humphrys"]. Took the Oath of Allegiance before the Hon. Andrew Bruce before March 2, 1778 [Ref: O-41, J-6, which listed the name as "Thomas Humphry"].

HUMRICHOUSE, Peter (1753-1837). Private, ensign, and lieutenant, Pennsylvania Line, pensioned in Washington County under the Act of June 7, 1832 at the annual allowance of $93.32 retroactive to March 4, 1831 [Ref: R-51, which listed the name as "Peter Hamrickhouse"]. "Peter Humrichouse" died on February 18, 1837, aged 84, and is buried beside his wife Mary Ott (1756-1839) in the cemetery at Zion Reformed Church in Hagerstown [Ref: JJ-VI:11].

HUNINGER, Andrew. Took the Oath of Allegiance before the Hon. Andrew Rentch before March 7, 1778 [Ref: O-52, J-15, which latter source listed the name as "Andrew Himinger"].

HUNTER, Isaac and Joseph. See "John Hunter," q.v.

HUNTER, John (1762-c1854). Private, Virginia Line, who applied for pension (R5404) in Wabash County, Illinois on December 3, 1832, stating he was born on November 27, 1762 at Hagerstown, Maryland, a son of John Hunter, Sr. He also stated that Joseph Hunter, of Jonesborough in East Tennessee, had his father's family Bible. John stated he lived in Rockingham County, Virginia at the time of his enlistment and served as a substitute for his father. After the war he moved to East Tennessee for 10 years, then to Madison County, Kentucky for 12 years, to Montgomery County, Kentucky for 4 years, to Knox County (now Gibson County), Indiana in 1807, and afterwards lived in Lawrence and Wabash Counties, Illinois. A son Isaac Hunter signed a power of attorney in Wabash County on January 23, 1854 [Ref: V-II:1775].

HUR, Jacob. See "Jacob Harr," q.v.

HURDELL, James. Private, Militia, 3rd Class, Capt. Conrad Nichodemus' Company, 2nd Battalion, 1776/1777 [Ref: M-237, A-1146].

HURLEY, John. Private who was enlisted by Capt. John Reynolds and passed on July 18, 1776 in Frederick (now Washington) County [Ref: D-50].

HURST, Ann, Morgan, and Ruth. See "Joseph Hurst," q.v.

HURST, Joseph. Private, Militia, 5th Class, Capt. Barnett Johnston's Company, 3rd Battalion, 1776/1777 [Ref: Q-48, M-242, which latter source listed the name as "Joseph Hust"]. One Joseph Hurst was identified as a Quaker in February, 1777, and was fined for not enrolling [Ref: Q-229]. One Joseph Hurst died before September 16, 1786 (date of balance book entry in Washington County), leaving equal shares to Joseph, Ann, Morgan, and Ruth Hurst [Ref: J-27]. Additional research may be necessary before drawing conclusions.

HUSKINGS, Joseph. Private, Militia, 6th Class, Capt. James Smith's Company, 2nd Battalion, 1776/1777 [Ref: M-240, A-1146].

HUSTON, John. Private, Militia, 4th Class, Capt. Isaac Baker's Company, 1776/1777 [Ref: A-1146, M-247].

HUSTON, Paul. Private, Militia, 2nd Class, Capt. Isaac Baker's Company, 1776/1777 [Ref: A-1146, M-247].

HUTH, Richard. Took the Oath of Allegiance before the Hon. John Barnes before February 28, 1778 [Ref: O-44, J-9, which latter source listed the name as "Richard Ruth"].

HUTZEL, Adam and Edward. See "Martin Line," q.v.

HYATT, Hezekiah. Private, Militia, 4th Class, Capt. Griffin Johnson's Company, 3rd Battalion, 1776/1777 [Ref: M-243].

HYBARGER, Abraham. See "Abraham Highbarger," q.v.

HYBARGER, Conrad. See "Conrad Highbarger," q.v.

HYMAN, George. Private, Militia, 7th Class, Capt. James Walling's Company, 2nd Battalion, 1776/1777 [Ref: M-239, A-1146].

HYMES, Andrew. Private, Militia, 2nd Class, Capt. Joseph Chapline's Company, 2nd Battalion, 1776/1777 [Ref: M-241]. Took the Oath of Allegiance before the Hon. Christopher Cruse in Sharpsburg Hundred before March 2, 1778 [Ref: O-34, which listed the name as "Andrew Hyms" and J-2, which listed the name as "Andrew Hyons"]. Enrolled in the third militia company organized for the Revolutionary War in the Elizabeth Town District of Frederick County (now the Hagerstown area of Washington County), passed by the Committee of Observation on June 5, 1776, and assigned to Capt. John Reynolds' command [Ref: Q-273, which listed the name as "Andrew Heims"].

HYMES, John. Private, Militia, 1st Class, Capt. Joseph Chapline's Company, 2nd Battalion, 1776/1777 [Ref: M-241]. Took the Oath of Allegiance before the Hon. Christopher Cruse in Sharpsburg Hundred before March 2, 1778 [Ref: O-35, J-2, which listed the name as "John Hyms"]. Enrolled in the third militia company organized for the Revolutionary War in the Elizabeth Town District of Frederick County (now the Hagerstown area of Washington County), passed by the Committee of Observation on June 5, 1776, and assigned to Capt. John Reynolds' command [Ref: Q-272, which listed the name as "John Heimes"].

HYNES, Thomas. Appointed by the Committee of Observation to carry the Association of Freemen to male residents in Linton Hundred on September 14, 1775 "and require their subscription to the same and make an exact account of those who sign and those that refuse with their reasons for refusing." [Ref: Q-143]. Second Lieutenant, Militia,

Capt. Barnett Johnston's Company, 1776. First Lieutenant, Militia, Capt. Philip Pindell's Company, 3rd or Western Battalion, May 16, 1778 [Ref: M-91, E-86, M-242, which latter source listed the name as "Thomas Hines"]. Took the Oath of Allegiance before the Hon. William Yates in 1778 [Ref: O-48, J-12].

HYNES, William. Took the Oath of Allegiance before the Hon. William Yates in 1778 [Ref: O-48, J-12].

HYONS, Andrew. See "Andrew Hymes," q.v.

HYPLE, Christopher. Private, Militia, 1st Class, Capt. Conrad Hogmire's Company, 1776/1777 [Ref: M-244, A-1146].

HYSKILL, Frederick. See "Frederick Hiskell," q.v.

ICKELBERGER, Conrad. Took the Oath of Allegiance before the Hon. Joseph Sprigg before April 1, 1778 [Ref: J-16, O-53, which latter source listed the name as "Conrad Iclebarger"].

IDEN, John. Private who was enlisted by Ensign Nathan Williams and passed on July 25, 1776 in Frederick (now Washington) County [Ref: D-51].

IGONDER, Henry. See "Henry Eigenor," q.v.

INGHAM, John. Private, Militia, 5th Class, Capt. James Walling's Company, 2nd Battalion, 1776/1777 [Ref: M-239, A-1146]. Appointed to raise funds on January 24, 1775 for the Committee of Observation in Upper Antietam Hundred in Frederick (now Washington) County [Ref: L-75]. One of several patriots appointed by the Committee of Observation on January 7, 1777 "to form the county into companies (after the militia had marched) for the purpose of relieving the distressed inhabitants of said county and also to compel the Dunkards and Mennonists to give their assistance." [Ref: Q-31]. Rendered patriotic service by supplying a coverlid for the use of the military in March, 1776, as recorded by the Committee of Observation on April 12, 1776 [Ref: Q-156, L-82].

INGRAM, John. Took the Oath of Allegiance before September 1, 1780 [Ref: X-114].

INNES, Nicholas. Enrolled in the first militia company organized for the Revolutionary War in the Elizabeth Town District of Frederick County (now the Hagerstown area of Washington County) on January 6, 1776 [Ref: W-1190, Q-270, which latter source listed the name as "Nichl. Innas"].

INSLOW, Joseph. Ensign, Militia, Capt. Daniel Cresap's Company, 3rd or Western Battalion, May 16, 1778 [Ref: M-91, E-86, M-241, which latter source listed the name as "Joseph Inlow"]. Took the Oath of Allegiance before the Hon. Lemuel Barritt before March 16, 1778 [Ref: O-42, J-8].

IRONS, Jonathan. Private, Militia, 3rd Class, Capt. James Prather's Company, 3rd Battalion, 1776/1777 [Ref: M-242].

ISEMINGER, Christena. See "Jacob Smith," q.v.

ITNIER, John. See "John Etenier," q.v.

ITNIRE (ITNISE?), Daniel. Private, Maryland Militia, pensioned in Washington County under the Act of June 7, 1832 at the annual allowance of $30 retroactive to March 4, 1831 [Ref: R-51].

ITNIRE, George, Henry, and John. See "John Etenier," q.v.

ITNIRE, Martin. See "Martin Etenier," q.v.

JACK, Jeremiah. Third Sergeant, Militia, Capt. John Bennet's Company, 1776/1777 [Ref: M-246, A-1146]. Took the Oath of Allegiance before the Hon. Richard Davis in 1778 [Ref: J-3, O-36].

JACK, John. Private, Militia, 4th Class, Capt. John Bennet's Company, 1776/1777 [Ref: M-246, A-1146]. Took the Oath of Allegiance before the Hon. Richard Davis in 1778 [Ref: J-3, O-36].

JACKSON, David. Enrolled in the third militia company organized for the Revolutionary War in the Elizabeth Town District of Frederick County (now the Hagerstown area of Washington County), passed by the Committee of Observation on June 5, 1776, and assigned to Capt. John Reynolds' command [Ref: Q-272]. Private, Militia, 3rd Class, Capt. Joseph Chapline's Company, 2nd Battalion, 1776/1777 [Ref: M-241]. Took the Oath of Allegiance before the Hon. Joseph Chapline before April 17, 1779 [Ref: J-5, O-39].

JACKSON, Hugh. Took the Oath of Allegiance before the Hon. Christopher Cruse in Sharpsburg Hundred before March 2, 1778 [Ref: O-34, J-2].

JACKSON, Ruth. See "Thomas Crampton," q.v.

JACKSON, Thomas. Private, Militia, 1st Class, Capt. Joseph Chapline's Company, 2nd Battalion, 1776/1777 [Ref: M-241]. See "Thomas Crampton," q.v.

JACOB, John Jeremiah (1757-1839). Second Sergeant, Militia, Capt. Jeremiah Spires' Company, 2nd Battalion, 1776/1777 [Ref: M-239, A-1146]. Took the Oath of Allegiance before the Hon. Richard Davis in 1778 [Ref: J-3, O-36]. "John Jeremiah Jacob or Jacobs" applied for pension in Hampshire County, Virginia on May 27, 1818, age 61, and in 1820 lived in Allegany County, Maryland with his wife's son (not named) and stated his wife (not named) was very feeble. On July 4, 1821 he married second to Susan McDavitt at the home of Joseph Cresap in Allegany County, Maryland. He died on March 21, 1839 and his widow Susan applied for and received pension W11930 in Hampshire County, Virginia on September 26, 1853, age 58. Also mentioned was John W.

Vandiver, the widow's son-in-law [Ref: V-II:1815]. John Jeremiah Jacob resided with Capt. Michael Cresap and his family in Washington County from age 15 in 1772 until his military service was over in 1781, and he served in the Maryland House of Delegates in 1783 [Ref: KK-I:88, KK-II:480-481, which contains more detailed information].

JACOB, Martin. Private, Militia, 5th Class, Capt. Daniel Clapsaddle's Company, 1st Battalion, 1776/1777 [Ref: M-236, A-1146].

JACOB, Thomas. Private, Militia, 5th Class, Capt. Henry Boteler's Company, 1776/1777 [Ref: M-237, A-1146].

JACOBS, Gabriel. Private, Militia, 8th Class, Capt. James Prather's Company, 3rd Battalion, 1776/1777 [Ref: M-243]. Took the Oath of Allegiance before the Hon. William Yates in 1778 [Ref: O-48, J-12, which listed the name as "Gabrial Jacobs"].

JACOBY, Conrad. Rendered patriotic service by riding express for the Committee of Observation to the Maryland Assembly and was paid on March 6, 1777 [Ref: Q-248]. Took the Oath of Allegiance before the Hon. John Stull in 1778 [Ref: O-46, J-10].

JACQUES, Denton. On January 30, 1777 the Committee of Observation was informed by Robert Foard, Hugh Gilliland and Henry Foard that "the company of militia in which they had enrolled under Denton Jacques was making no preparations to march agreeable to orders for that purpose, etc." Therefore, the Committee ordered them to enroll said company, choose officers to command the,, and make a return to the Committee, noting delinquents [Ref: Q-227, Q-228]. See "Simon Bowman," q.v.

JACQUES, Lancelot (c1755-1827). "Died at his residence near Hancock in this county [Washington], after a short illness, on Monday morning October 29th [1827], Dr. Lancelot Jacques, aged about 72 years; native of England, migrated to this country early in life, educated at New Ark School. He served a short time as a surgeon in the American Army during the Revolutionary War and three times elected to the Legislature of Maryland; also filled several other public situations." [Ref: Z-95].

JACQUES, Thomas. Private, Militia, 7th Class, Capt. Barnett Johnston's Company, 3rd Battalion, 1776/1777 [Ref: M-242]. Took the Oath of Allegiance before the Hon. John Barnes before February 28, 1778 [Ref: O-45, J-10, which listed the name as "Thomas Jarques"]. One Thomas Jacques died near Jacques Forge on Licking Creek in Washington County on March 17, 1798, after a lingering illness [Ref: LL-1:74].

JACQUET, Daniel. Private, Militia, Capt. William Heyser's Company, 1776/1777 [Ref: W-1190, L-79, which listed the name as "Daniel Jaquet"]. Sergeant, German Regiment, continental service, 1777, and discharged on July 26, 1779 [Ref: D-220, which listed the name as "Daniel Jacquett"]. See "John Daniel Jacquet," q.v.

JACQUET, John Daniel. Third Sergeant, Militia, Capt. William Heyser's Company, muster roll dated October 23, 1776, in continental service [Ref: D-263, which listed the name as "Daniel Taquet (or Jaques)" and W-1190, L-79, which listed the name as "John Jaquet"]. Sergeant, German Regiment, Lt. Col. Ludwick Weltner's Company, continental service, discharged on July 26, 1779 [Ref: D-264].

JAMES, Abraham Jr. Took the Oath of Allegiance before the Hon. Richard Davis in 1778 [Ref: J-5, O-37, which listed the name as "Abraham Jemes, Jr."].

JAMES, Benjamin. Private, Militia, 3rd Class, Capt. Daniel Cresap's Company, 3rd Battalion, 1776/1777 [Ref: M-241].

JAMES, Evan. Private, Militia, 5th Class, Capt. Daniel Cresap's Company, 3rd Battalion, 1776/1777 [Ref: M-241]. Took the Oath of Allegiance before the Hon. Lemuel Barritt before March 16, 1778 [Ref: O-42, J-7, which listed the name as "Eran James"].

JAMES, George. Private, Militia, 7th Class, Capt. Barnett Johnston's Company, 3rd Battalion, 1776/1777 [Ref: M-242, Q-48]. Took the Oath of Allegiance before the Hon. John Barnes before February 28, 1778 [Ref: O-44, J-9].

JAMES, Grifet (Griffith). Took the Oath of Allegiance before the Hon. Christopher Cruse in Lower Antietam Hundred before March 2, 1778 [Ref: J-3, O-35].

JAMES, Joseph. Private, Militia, 6th Class, Capt. John Rennolds' (Reynolds') Company, 2nd Battalion, 1776/1777 [Ref: M-240].

JAMES, Richard. Private, Militia, 5th Class, Capt. Jeremiah Spires' Company, 2nd Battalion, 1776/1777 [Ref: M-239, A-1146]. Took the Oath of Allegiance before the Hon. Richard Davis in 1778 [Ref: J-3, O-36, which listed the name as "Richard Jeams"].

JAMES, Richard Jr. Private, Militia, 2nd Class, Capt. Basil Williams' Company, 1776/1777 [Ref: M-244, A-1146, which listed the name without the "Jr."]. Took the Oath of Allegiance before the Hon. Richard Davis in 1778 [Ref: J-4, O-37, which listed the name as "Richard Jeams, Jr."].

JARRETT (JARVETT?), Truman. Private, Militia, 7th Class, Capt. Griffin Johnson's Company, 3rd Battalion, 1776/1777 [Ref: M-243].

JECONS, Edward. Private, Militia, 6th Class, Capt. Charles Clinton's Company, 1776/1777 [Ref: M-245, A-1146].

JEFFERSON, Thomas. See "Adam Ott," q.v.

JENNINGS, Wilbur. See "Rudolph Brown" and "Peter Yertee," q.v.

JENNINGS, William. Private, Militia, 1st Class, Capt. Jacob Sharer's Company, 1776/1777 [Ref: A-1146, M-248].
JERKEL, George. Took the Oath of Allegiance before the Hon. Henry Schnebley in 1778 [Ref: O-50, J-14].
JILANARD, John. Private, Militia, 7th Class, Capt. John Cellars' Company, 1776/1777 [Ref: A-1146, M-246].
JILANARD, Rudolph. Private, Militia, 8th Class, Capt. John Cellars' Company, 1776/1777 [Ref: A-1146, M-246].
JINKISON, Matthew. Took the Oath of Allegiance before the Hon. William Yates in 1778 [Ref: O-48, J-12, which latter source listed the name as "Matthew Jinkinson"].
JOENS, David. See "David Poens," q.v.
JOHN, Joel. Private, Militia, 3rd Class, Capt. Barnett Johnston's Company, 3rd Battalion, 1776/1777 [Ref: M-242].
JOHNSON, Barney. Took the Oath of Allegiance before the Hon. John Stull in 1778 [Ref: O-46, J-10]. A "Barnet Johnson" died testate by February 11, 1794 (date of balance book entry in Washington County). [Ref: J-33].
JOHNSON, Benjamin. Private, Militia, 3rd Class, Capt. Barnett Johnston's Company, 3rd Battalion, 1776/1777 [Ref: M-242]. Took the Oath of Allegiance before the Hon. William Yates in 1778 [Ref: O-48, J-12].
JOHNSON, Benjamin (of William). Took the Oath of Allegiance before the Hon. Lemuel Barritt before March 16, 1778 [Ref: O-43, J-8, which listed the name as "Benjamin Johnson, Sr., of Wm. Johnson"].
JOHNSON, Griffin (Griffith). Captain, Militia, by December 3, 1776. Captain, 3rd Battalion, June 22, 1778 [Ref: M-92, B-501, E-145, M-243, which also listed the name as "Griffith Johnston"]. "Griffith Johnson, Sr." was born in Virginia in 1739, married Elizabeth Thomas circa 1759 in (now) Montgomery County, Maryland, served as a captain in the Maryland Militia, and died before May 18, 1805 in Allegany County, Maryland. A daughter, Jane Johnson, was born on June 24, 1772 in Washington County, Maryland and married Charles Twigg, son of John, circa 1789 in Allegany County, Maryland [Ref: S-3124, being the SAR application of Lewis Markwood Ward Twigg, of LaVale, Maryland, approved on May 24, 1991 (National No. 137067) and citing DAR National No. 679762 as a reference].
JOHNSON, Hannah. See "Thomas Cresap," q.v.
JOHNSON, Jane. See "Griffin (Griffith) Johnson," q.v.
JOHNSON, John. Soldier who married Elizabeth Whelan in Washington County in 1785 [Ref: N-116]. There were several men with this name

who served in the Maryland Line [Ref: D-126, D-228, D-218, D-219, D-310, D-318, D-394]. Additional research will be necessary before drawing conclusions.

JOHNSON, Thomas. Private, Militia, 4th Class, Capt. James Prather's Company, 3rd Battalion, 1776/1777 [Ref: M-242].

JOHNSON, William. Private, Militia, 2nd Class, Capt. Barnett Johnston's Company, 3rd Battalion, 1776/1777 [Ref: M-242]. Two men by this name took the Oath of Allegiance: one before the Hon. Lemuel Barritt before March 16, 1778 [Ref: O-43, J-8], and one before the Hon. William Yates [Ref: O-48, J-12].

JOHNSTON, Barnett. Captain, Militia, 3rd Battalion, 1776/1777 [Ref: M-242].

JOHNSTON, Benjamin. Appointed by the Committee of Observation to carry the Association of Freemen to male residents in Fort Frederick Hundred on September 14, 1775 "and require their subscription to the same and make an exact account of those who sign and those that refuse with their reasons for refusing." [Ref: Q-143, which listed the name as "Benjn. Jonston"].

JOHNSTON, Sarah. Rendered patriotic service in Hagerstown by providing sundries to Capt. John Nelson's Company, continental service (Maryland Line), April, 1776 [Ref: Q-161].

JOHNSTON, Thomas. Private, Militia, 6th Class, Capt. Charles Clinton's Company, 1776/1777 [Ref: M-245, A-1146]. Took the Oath of Allegiance before the Hon. Richard Davis in 1778 [Ref: J-4, O-37].

JOICE, George. Private, Militia, 8th Class, Capt. Henry Boteler's Company, 1776/1777 [Ref: A-1146, M-237, which listed the name as "George Toice"].

JOLLY, Catherine. See "Philip Creekbaum," q.v.

JOLLY, Peter. Private, Militia, 8th Class, Capt. John Rennolds' (Reynolds') Company, 2nd Battalion, 1776/1777 [Ref: M-240].

JONAS, John. Private, Maryland Line, pensioned under Act of June 7, 1785, placed on the rolls on February 24, 1821 in Allegany County, and received an invalid's pension of $60 per year from September 4, 1794 [Ref: R-2, AA-369]. The heirs of one John Jonas who died in 1813 or 1815 included a son John Jonas [Ref: Z-6, citing an equity court case in Cumberland in 1825].

JONES, David. Appointed to raise funds on January 24, 1775 for the Committee of Observation in Conococheague Hundred in Frederick (now Washington) County [Ref: L-75]. Appointed by the Committee of Observation to carry the Association of Freemen to male residents in his hundred (district) on March 4, 1776 "and present it for signing and make an exact account of those that sign and those that refuse with their reasons for refusing." [Ref: Q-153, L-82]. Appointed by the Committee of Observation to carry the Association of Freemen to male residents in Conococheague Hundred on September 14, 1775 "and require their subscription to the same and make an exact account of those who sign and those that refuse with their reasons for refusing." [Ref: Q-143]. Second Lieutenant, Militia, Capt. John Bennet's Company, 1776 (resigned, but date not given). [Ref: M-93, M-246, A-1146].

JONES, David Jr. Took the Oath of Allegiance before the Hon. Henry Schnebley in 1778 [Ref: O-49, J-13].

JONES, Jacob. First Sergeant, Militia, Capt. Barnett Johnston's Company, 3rd Battalion, 1776/1777 [Ref: M-242].

JONES, Jacob. Private, Militia, 7th Class, Capt. Martin Kershner's Company, 1776/1777 [Ref: A-1146, M-248].

JONES, John. Private, Militia, 4th Class, Capt. James Prather's Company, 3rd Battalion, 1776/1777 [Ref: M-242]. Took the Oath of Allegiance before the Hon. Henry Schnebley in 1778 [Ref: O-49, J-13]. See "Bazzell Wright," q.v.

JONES, John Court. Second Lieutenant, Upper District, Frederick County (now Washington County), July, 1776 [Ref: D-48].

JONES, Jonathan. Private, Militia, 6th Class, Capt. Martin Kershner's Company, 1776/1777 [Ref: A-1146, M-248].

JONES, Livie. Private who was enrolled by Capt. Henry Hardman and passed on July 19, 1776 in Frederick (now Washington) County [Ref: D-51].

JONES, Nancy. See "Bazzell Wright," q.v.

JONES, Samuel. Private, Militia, 5th Class, Capt. Barnett Johnston's Company, 3rd Battalion, 1776/1777 [Ref: M-242]. Took the Oath of Allegiance before the Hon. William Yates in 1778 [Ref: O-48, J-12].

JONES, Thomas. There were several men with this name who served in the Revolutionary War. (1) Private, Militia, 3rd Class, Capt. Joseph Chapline's Company, 2nd Battalion, 1776/1777 [Ref: M-241]. (2) Private, Militia, Capt. Charles Coulson's Company, enrolled August 28, 1776 [Ref: M-244, A-1146]. (3) Private, Militia, 5th Class, Capt. Martin Kershner's Company, 1776/1777 [Ref: A-1146, M-247]. (4) Private who was enrolled by Capt. Henry Hardman and passed on July 19, 1776 in Frederick (now Washington) County [Ref: D-51]. One Thomas Jones applied for and received pension S2655 in Clermont County, Ohio on November 5, 1832, stating he was born on January 26, 1756 in Washington County, Maryland and lived there at the time of his enlistment. After the war he moved to Westmoreland County,

Pennsylvania for 16 years, to Mason County, Kentucky for 3 years, and then to Clermont County, Ohio [Ref: V-II:1882].

JONES, William. Private, Militia, 2nd Class, Capt. Isaac Baker's Company, 1776/1777 [Ref: A-1146, M-247].

JONES, William. Private, Militia, 7th Class, Capt. John Bennet's Company, 1776/1777 [Ref: M-246, A-1146].

JORDON, James. Private who was enrolled by Capt. Henry Hardman and passed on July 19, 1776 in Frederick (now Washington) County [Ref: D-51].

JUPIN, John. Took the Oath of Allegiance before the Hon. Richard Davis in 1778 [Ref: J-4, O-37].

JUPIN, Mary. See "Hugh Lemaster," q.v.

JUSHEY, Obediah. Private, Militia, 1st Class, Capt. Griffin Johnson's Company, 3rd Battalion, 1776/1777 [Ref: M-243].

KAGY, Michael. See "Lodwick Keidy," q.v.

KALEHOFER, Devalt. Took the Oath of Allegiance before the Hon. Joseph Sprigg before April 1, 1778 [Ref: O-53, J-16, which latter source listed the name as "Devalt Keleofer"].

KALER, Daniel. Took the Oath of Allegiance before the Hon. John Stull in 1778 [Ref: O-46, J-10].

KALER, Frederick. Took the Oath of Allegiance before the Hon. John Stull in 1778 [Ref: O-46, J-10].

KAP, Michael. Took the Oath of Allegiance before September 1, 1780 [Ref: X-114]. "Michael Kapp, for many years an inn-keeper in Elizabeth Town," died after a short illness on the Monday before September 19, 1804 [Ref: LL-2:99].

KARNS, John. Took the Oath of Allegiance before the Hon. Christopher Cruse in Lower Antietam Hundred before March 2, 1778 [Ref: J-3, O-35].

KARSHNOR, Jonathan. See "Jonathan Kershner," q.v.

KAUFMAN, Adam. Took the Oath of Allegiance before the Hon. Henry Schnebley in 1778 [Ref: O-50, J-14].

KAUFMAN, Jacob. See "Jacob Kuhn," q.v.

KAUSLER, Jacob. See "George Shall," q.v.

KAUSLER, John (1753-1837). Private, Maryland Militia, pensioned in Washington County under the Act of June 7, 1832 at the annual allowance of $20 retroactive to March 4, 1831 [Ref: R-51]. John Kausler was born in Pennsylvania on March 22, 1753, served in the Maryland and Pennsylvania troops, married Christiana Creager, and died before June 22, 1837 in Maryland [Ref: Y-II:1639].

KAUSLER, Philip. See "Philip Guselor," q.v.

KEBBLER, John. See "John Kibler," q.v.

KEE, William. See "William Lee," q.v.

KEEDY (KEIDY), Lodwick. Private, Militia, 4th Class, Capt. James Walling's Company, 2nd Battalion, 1776/1777 [Ref: M-239, A-1146, which listed the name as "Lodwick Keidy"]. "Ludwick Keyday" and his wife were two of the executors of the estate of Michael Kagy in Washington County on February 19, 1786 [Ref: J-26].

KEENE, Daniel. Took the Oath of Allegiance before the Hon. Joseph Sprigg before April 1, 1778 [Ref: O-53, J-16].

KEEPERS, Isaac. Enrolled in the first militia company organized for the Revolutionary War in the Elizabeth Town District of Frederick County (now the Hagerstown area of Washington County) on January 6, 1776 [Ref: Q-270, W-1189].

KEESON, Jacob. Private who enlisted in the militia on August 14, 1781 for service in the Continental Army [Ref: D-387].

KEISSEKER, Philip. Private, Militia, 6th Class, Capt. John Cellars' Company, 1776/1777 [Ref: A-1146, M-246, which listed the name as "Phillip Kessaken"]. Took the Oath of Allegiance before the Hon. Henry Schnebley in 1778 [Ref: O-50, J-14, O-50].

KEISSEKER, Simon. Took the Oath of Allegiance before the Hon. Henry Schnebley in 1778 [Ref: J-14, O-50, which latter source listed the name as "Simon Kersseker"]. "Elizabeth Kiesecker, relict of the late Simon Kiesecker" died at her residence about 3 miles from Hagerstown on March 29, 1821, in her 67th year [Ref: Z-35].

KELLER, Casper. Captain, by June, 1776, at which time he and other officers were ordered by the Committee of Observation "to summons non-enrollers and non-associators to attend at Elisabeth Town the first Tuesday in July next to shew cause if any they have why they shall not be fined according to the Resolves of the Convention in July last." [Ref: Q-269].

KELLER, Elizabeth and Joseph. See "Thomas Crampton," q.v.

KELEOFER, Devalt. See "Devalt Kalehofer," q.v.

KELLOGH, Allen. See "Allen Killough," q.v.

KELLY, Daniel. Private, Militia, 3rd Class, Capt. Jeremiah Spires' Company, 2nd Battalion, 1776/1777 [Ref: M-239, A-1146, which listed the name as "Daniel Cally"]. Took the Oath of Allegiance before the Hon. Richard Davis in 1778 [Ref: J-3, O-36].

KELLY, George. Took the Oath of Allegiance before the Hon. Andrew Bruce before March 2, 1778 [Ref: O-41, J-6].

KELLY, James. Soldier from Washington County, discharged on June 22, 1778 [Ref: E-144, which listed the name as "John Kelley"].

KELLY, Patrick. Private, Militia, by January 22, 1777 when ordered by the Committee of Observation "to march with some company of militia to the reinforcement of his Excellency General Washington" or appear before the Committee and state his reason for not marching. He apparently marched since he never appeared to the contrary [Ref: Q-48, which listed the name as "Patk. Kelley"]. Took the Oath of Allegiance before the Hon. John Barnes before February 28, 1778 [Ref: O-45, J-10].

KELLY, Samuel. Private, Militia, 2nd Class, Capt. Jeremiah Spires' Company, 2nd Battalion, 1776/1777 [Ref: M-239, A-1146].

KELLY, William. Took the Oath of Allegiance before the Hon. John Stull in 1778 [Ref: O-46, J-10].

KEMMER, Daniel. See "Daniel Cammer," q.v.

KENDALL, William. Private, Militia, 8th Class, Capt. Jeremiah Spires' Company, 2nd Battalion, 1776/1777 [Ref: M-239, A-1146, which listed the name as "William Kendell"]. Took the Oath of Allegiance before the Hon. Richard Davis in 1778 [Ref: J-3, O-36]. In December, 1817 the Treasurer of the Western Shore of Maryland was directed to pay to "William Kindle" of Washington County, a private in the Revolutionary War, quarterly, the half pay of a private "as a further remuneration to him for those services by which his country has been so essentially benefitted." [Ref: AA-362].

KENDALL, William, Jr. Took the Oath of Allegiance before the Hon. Richard Davis in 1778 [Ref: J-4, O-36].

KENDLE, John Baptist. Private, Militia, 6th Class, Capt. Basil Williams' Company, 1776/1777 [Ref: M-244, A-1146].

KENISTRICK (KINSTRY), Frederick. First Sergeant, Militia, Capt. John Rennolds' (Reynolds') Company, 2nd Battalion, 1776/1777 [Ref: M-240, which listed the name as "Frederick Knisterick"]. Took the Oath of Allegiance before the Hon. Joseph Chapline before April 17, 1779 [Ref: J-5, O-39, which listed the name as "Frederick Conestrick"]. Private (draught) who enlisted in the militia on August 18, 1781 for service in the Continental Army [Ref: D-388, which listed the name as "Frederick Kinstry"]. See "John Kenistrick," q.v.

KENISTRICK (KENISTER), Henry. Private, Militia, 3rd Class, Capt. James Walling's Company, 2nd Battalion, 1776/1777 [Ref: M-238, A-1146]. See "John Kenistrick," q.v.

KENISTRICK, John. One of several patriots appointed by the Committee of Observation on January 19, 1777 "to form the county into companies (after the militia had marched) for the purpose of relieving the distressed inhabitants of said county and also to compel the Dunkards and Mennonists to give their assistance." [Ref: Q-43, which listed the name as "John Bennestrick"]. One John Kenistrick died testate before October 1, 1785 (date of balance book entry in Washington County), leaving equal shares to John Kenistrick, Henry Kenistrick, Catherine Tetwiler, Margarete Shafler, and Mary Easton, and also mentioning Frederick Kenistrick who received a lesser amount then the others [Ref: J-26].

KENNEAR, John. Private who was recruited and passed by County Lieutenant Thomas Sprigg on April 22, 1780 [Ref: D-336].

KENNEDY, David. Fourth Corporal, Militia, Capt. Isaac Baker's Company, 1776/1777 [Ref: M-247, A-1146]. Took the Oath of Allegiance before the Hon. John Barnes before February 28, 1778 [Ref: O-45, J-10].

KENNEDY, John. Second Sergeant, Militia, Capt. Daniel Cresap's Company, 3rd Battalion, 1776/1777 [Ref: M-241, which listed the name as "John Kennady"]. Took the Oath of Allegiance before the Hon. Andrew Bruce before March 2, 1778 [Ref: O-41, J-6].

KENNY, John. Private who was recruited and passed by County Lieutenant Thomas Sprigg on April 22, 1780 [Ref: D-336].

KEPHART, Jacob. Enrolled in the third militia company organized for the Revolutionary War in the Elizabeth Town District of Frederick County (now the Hagerstown area of Washington County), passed by the Committee of Observation on June 5, 1776, and assigned to Capt. John Reynolds' command [Ref: Q-273].

KEPHART, John. Enrolled in the third militia company organized for the Revolutionary War in the Elizabeth Town District of Frederick County (now the Hagerstown area of Washington County), passed by the Committee of Observation on June 5, 1776, and assigned to Capt. John Reynolds' command [Ref: Q-273]. Private, Militia, 7th Class, Capt. Isaac Baker's Company, 1776/1777 [Ref: A-1146, M-247]. Took the Oath of Allegiance before the Hon. Christopher Cruse in Sharpsburg Hundred before March 2, 1778 [Ref: O-34, J-2, which listed the name as "John Kiphart"].

KERENENKAN, Ludwig. Took the Oath of Allegiance before the Hon. Henry Schnebley in 1778 [Ref: O-49, J-13].

KERNAM, Michael. Private, Militia, Capt. John Kershner's Company, on duty guarding prisoners of war at Fort Frederick until discharged on May 17, 1778 [Ref: D-328].

KERNECOME, John. Took the Oath of Allegiance before the Hon. Joseph Sprigg before April 1, 1778 [Ref: O-53, J-16, which latter source listed the name as "John Kerecome"].

KERNEY, Edward. Private who was enlisted by Lieut. Christian Orndorff and passed on July 20, 1776 in Frederick (now Washington) County [Ref: D-50].

KERNEY, William. Private who was enlisted by Ensign Nathan Williams and passed on July 25, 1776 in Frederick (now Washington) County [Ref: D-51].

KERR, Mary. Rendered patriotic service by making caps for the use of the military in July, 1775, as recorded by the Committee of Observation at Elizabeth Town on November 4, 1775 [Ref: Q-150].

KERR, Rachel. See "John Chenoweth," q.v.

KERSHNER, Christiana. See "Philip Kershner," q.v.

KERSHNER, David. First Sergeant, Militia, Capt. Martin Kershner's Company, 32nd Battalion, December 27, 1776 [Ref: K-1814, Box 3]. Took the Oath of Allegiance before the Hon. Henry Schnebley in 1778 [Ref: J-12, O-49, which latter source listed the name as "David Kirshner"]. Second Lieutenant, Militia, Capt. Martin Kershner's Company, 1776/1777 [Ref: M-247, A-1146].

KERSHNER, George. One of several patriots appointed by the Committee of Observation on December 30, 1776 "to form the county into companies (after the militia had marched) for the purpose of relieving the distressed inhabitants of said county and also to compel the Dunkards and Mennonists to give their assistance." [Ref: Q-346]. Took the Oath of Allegiance before the Hon. John Cellars in January, 1778 [Ref: K-1814, O-40, J-5, which listed the name as "George Keshnor"]. Private, Select Militia, Capt. Adam Ott's Company, 1781 [Ref: M-238, A-1146]. Mary Kershner, a native of Washington County, Maryland, and widow of the late George Kershner, of Washington County, died in Bedford County, Pennsylvania on July 30, 1839 in her 85th year [Ref: Z-122].

KERSHNER, Isaac. See "Philip Kershner," q.v.

KERSHNER, Jacob (c1751-1815). Private, Militia, Capt. Martin Kershner's Company, 32nd Battalion, December 27, 1776 [Ref: K-1814, Box 3]. Took the Oath of Allegiance before the Hon. John Cellars in January, 1778 [Ref: K-1814, O-40, J-6, which listed the name as "Jacob Kershnor"]. Ensign, Militia (date not given). [Ref: M-95]. Jacob Kershner died on February 26, 1815, aged 64, and is buried beside his wife Anna Maria Brewer (1761-1835) in St. Paul's Lutheran Reformed Church cemetery on Route 40 near Clearspring in Washington County [Ref: JJ-V:92].

KERSHNER, John. First Lieutenant, Militia, Capt. Martin Kershner's Company, 1776. Captain, Militia, on duty guarding prisoners of war at

Fort Frederick by June 27, 1778 and through at least March 20, 1779 [Ref: M-95, E-325, M-247, N-146, D-328]. Second Lieutenant, Militia, Capt. Martin Kershner's Company, 32nd Battalion, December 27, 1776 [Ref: K-1814, Box 3]. Served on the Committee of Observation for the Elizabeth Town District (now the Hagerstown area of Washington County) in December, 1776 and January, 1777 (resigned). [Ref: Q-40, Q-340]. Took the Oath of Allegiance before the Hon. John Cellars in January, 1778 [Ref: K-1814, O-40, J-5, which listed the name as "John Kershnor"].

KERSHNER, Jonathan. Fourth Sergeant, Militia, Capt. Martin Kershner's Company, 32nd Battalion, December 27, 1776 [Ref: K-1814, Box 3]. Took the Oath of Allegiance before the Hon. Andrew Rentch before March 7, 1778 [Ref: J-15, O-52, which latter source listed the name as "Jonathan Karshnor"].

KERSHNER, Martin. Took the Oath of Allegiance on June 21, 1777 [Ref: K-1814, Box 4]. Captain, Militia, 32nd Battalion, by December 27, 1776 when his company entered service [Ref: K-1814, Box 3]. Rendered patriotic service by supplying flour for the use of the military on January 18 and April 12, 1780 [Ref: W-1190, HH-72, HH-73]. Rendered patriotic service in Hagerstown by providing a rifle to Capt. John Nelson's Company, continental service (Maryland Line), April, 1776 [Ref: Q-161]. Took the Oath of Allegiance before the Hon. John Stull in 1778 [Ref: J-10, O-40]. Qualified as an Associate Justice of Washington County in August, 1804 [Ref: II-44]. See "John Cellar," q.v.

KERSHNER, Mary. See "Michael Kershner" and "George Kershner," q.v.

KERSHNER, Michael (1752-1826). Private, German Regiment, continental service, 1776. Private, Third Vacant Company, under Capt. Philip Graybell and Col. Lewis Weltner at Valley Forge in March, 1778. Discharged on July 16, 1779 [Ref: D-223, FF-222, N-32, which latter source listed the name as "Michael Kirshner"]. "Michael Kirshner or Kershner or Kerchner" applied for and received pension S34947 in Allegany County, Maryland on April 20, 1818, age 67, but on October 12, 1820 he gave his age again as 67 with a wife (age 57) and a widowed daughter with her children living with him (names not given: granddaughters age 10 and 4, and grandson age 6). He stated he enlisted in the Maryland Line in Baltimore [Ref: V-II:1967]. In December, 1815 the Treasurer of the Western Shore of Maryland was directed to pay to Michael Kershner, of Allegany County, a private in the Revolutionary War, quarterly, the half pay of a private, "as a further remuneration to him for those services by which his country has been so essentially benefitted." On March 2, 1827 the Treasurer of the

Western Shore of Maryland was directed to pay to Mary Ann Kershner, of Allegany County, during life, half yearly, half pay of a private, for her late husband's services during the war. On March 6, 1832 the Treasurer of the Western Shore of Maryland was directed to pay to Jacob Lantz "for the use of Mrs. Mary C. Shryer, of Allegany County, next and near friend of Mrs. Mary A. Kershner, deceased, late a pensioner of the state, $14.55, balance due up to her deceased." [Ref: AA-362]. "Michael Kershner, a soldier of the Revolution, died in this town on Thursday last, after an illness of about one hour." [Ref: Z-9, citing the *Maryland Advocate* in Cumberland on April 17, 1826].

KERSHNER, Philip. Took the Oath of Allegiance before the Hon. Henry Schnebley in 1778 [Ref: O-50, J-14]. Private, Militia, 2nd Class, Capt. Martin Kershner's Company, 1776/1777 [Ref: A-1146, M-247]. Private, Militia, Capt. Martin Kershner's Company, 32nd Battalion, December 27, 1776 [Ref: K-1814, Box 3]. Christiana Kershner, wife of Philip, died at the residence of her son Isaac Kershner, about 3 miles from Hagerstown, on December 22, 1825, age 69 [Ref: Z-79].

KERSLEY, John. Rendered patriotic service by providing necessaries to Capt. John Reynolds' Company in the Flying Camp and belonging to the Maryland Service in July, 1776, as recorded by the Committee of Observation at Sharpsburg on August 6, 1776 [Ref: Q-333].

KESSINGER, George. Private, Militia, 5th Class, Capt. James Walling's Company, 2nd Battalion, 1776/1777 [Ref: M-239, A-1146].

KETCHAM, Daniel. Took the Oath of Allegiance before the Hon. Richard Davis in 1778 [Ref: O-36, J-4, which latter source listed the name as "Daniel Ketchem"].

KEVABLE (KSWABLE?), George. Private, Militia, 8th Class, Capt. Isaac Baker's Company, 1776/1777 [Ref: A-1146, M-247].

KEYDAY, Ludwick. See "Lodwick Keidy," q.v.

KEYKINDELL, Elijah. Private, Militia, 3rd Class, Capt. Daniel Cresap's Company, 3rd Battalion, 1776/1777 [Ref: M-241].

KEYSER, Frederick (1761-   ). Private, Maryland Militia, with Virginia and Kentucky service [Ref: N-32, which listed the name as "Frederick Kyzer"]. See "Frederick Kiger, Jr.," q.v.

KEYSER, Jacob (1750-   ). Private, German Regiment, continental service, enlisted February 13, 1779 and still in service on August 1, 1780 [Ref: D-223, N-31].

KEYSER, Martin. Private who was enrolled by Capt. Aeneas Campbell and passed by Major Francis Deakins on July 18, 1776 [Ref: D-49, which listed the name as "Martin Kiezer"].

KEYSER, Mathias. Private, German Regiment, Lt. Col. Ludwick Weltner's Company, continental service, enlisted August 10, 1776, and discharged on July 26, 1779 at Fort Wyoming, Pennsylvania [Ref: D-222, D-265, GG-98, which listed the name as "Mathias Keyser, Gieser, Keyer"].

KEYSER, Michael. Private, Militia, 2nd Class, Capt. Conrad Hogmire's Company, 1776/1777 [Ref: M-244, A-1146, which listed the name as "Michael Kaiser"].

KEYSER, Nicholas. Private, Third Vacant Company, under Capt. Philip Graybell and Col. Lewis Weltner at Valley Forge in March, 1778 [Ref: FF-222, which listed the name as "Nicholas Keiser"].

KEYSER, Peter. Private, Militia, 1st Class, Capt. Conrad Hogmire's Company, 1776/1777 [Ref: M-244, A-1146, which listed the name as "Peter Kaiser"].

KIBLER, Elizabeth and George. See "John Kibler," q.v.

KIBLER, Jacob. First Corporal, Militia, Capt. Martin Kershner's Company, 32nd Battalion, December 27, 1776 [Ref: K-1814 (Box 3), which listed the name as "Jacob Kebbler"]. Second Sergeant, Militia, Capt. Martin Kershner's Company, 1776/1777 [Ref: M-247, A-1146]. Took the Oath of Allegiance before the Hon. Henry Schnebley in 1778 [Ref: O-50, J-13, which listed the name as "Jacob Keibler"].

KIBLER, John (1760-1827). Private, Militia, Capt. William Heyser's Company, enlisted July 27, 1776, muster roll dated October 23, 1776, in continental service [Ref: D-264, GG-98, W-1190, L-79]. Private, German Regiment, Lt. Col. Ludwick Weltner's Company, continental service, discharged on July 26, 1779 at Fort Wyoming, Pennsylvania [Ref: D-265, which listed the name as "John Kebler"]. Private, Maryland Line, who applied for pension in Berkeley County, Virginia on April 28, 1818, age 58, but on December 11, 1820 he gave his age as 64 with a wife Mary (age 46) and these children: John Kibler (age 24), Jacob Kibler (age 22), Margaret Kibler (age 19), Elizabeth Kibler (age 17), George Kibler (age 12), Nancy Kibler (age 9), and Mary Ann Kibler (age 4). John stated he had enlisted in Hagerstown, Maryland and married Mary Shunford in Berkeley County, Virginia on April 9, 1781. His widow applied for and received pension W5014 in Wayne County, Ohio on September 3, 1832, age 84, stating John died on June 22, 1827. When she applied for bounty land #30753-160-55 in 1855 she stated her name before their marriage was Resse (Reffe?), although the Berkeley County court records show Shunford on the marriage license issued April 2, 1781 in Virginia [Ref: V-II:1938, N-31, GG-98, which latter source listed the name as "John Kibler, Kebler, Kibber"].

KIBLER, Mary, Margaret, and Nancy. See "John Kibler," q.v.

KIDING, Ludowick. Private who was enlisted by Capt. John Reynolds and passed on July 18, 1776 in Frederick (now Washington) County [Ref: D-50].

KIESECKER, Elizabeth. See "Simon Keisseker," q.v.

KIERNAN, Michael. Took the Oath of Allegiance before the Hon. John Barnes before February 28, 1778 [Ref: O-44, J-9, which latter source listed the name as "Michael Kiernen"].

KIFER, George. Took the Oath of Allegiance before the Hon. Christopher Cruse in Sharpsburg Hundred before March 2, 1778 [Ref: O-34, J-2]. Rendered patriotic service by providing necessaries to Capt. John Reynolds' Company in the Flying Camp and belonging to the Maryland Service in July, 1776, as recorded by the Committee of Observation at Sharpsburg on August 6, 1776 [Ref: Q-333, which listed the name as "George Kiffer"].

KIGER (KIZER), Frederick. One of several patriots appointed by the Committee of Observation on January 7, 1777 "to form the county into companies (after the militia had marched) for the purpose of relieving the distressed inhabitants of said county and also to compel the Dunkards and Mennonists to give their assistance." [Ref: Q-31]. Empowered by the Committee of Observation on January 16, 1777 "to examine any place that he may suspect there is any salt more than necessary for family use, see the salt measured, not exceeding two bushels, and the owner paid thirty shillings per bushel." Salt is needed for the companies of Capt. Jacob Sharer and Capt. James Wallen now in Jerusalem Town who "believe there is a quantity of salt concealed in said town." [Ref: Q-41, which listed the name as "Frederick Kiger Senr."]. See "Frederick Guiser," q.v.

KIGER (KIZER), Frederick Jr. Private, Militia, 1st Class, Capt. Jacob Sharer's Company, 1776/1777 [Ref: A-1146, M-248, which listed the name as "Frederick Keger, Jr."]. See "Frederick Keyser" and "Frederick Guiser," q.v.

KILLOUGH, Allen. Took the Oath of Allegiance before the Hon. John Barnes before February 28, 1778 [Ref: O-44, which listed the name as "Allen Killogh" and J-9, which listed the name as "Allen Kellogh"].

KILLOUGH, Francis. Private, Militia, 8th Class, Capt. Isaac Baker's Company, 1776/1777 [Ref: A-1146, M-247].

KIMBELAN, Jacob. Took the Oath of Allegiance before the Hon. Lemuel Barritt before March 16, 1778 [Ref: O-42, J-7].

KIMBERLIN, John. Took the Oath of Allegiance before the Hon. Lemuel Barritt before March 16, 1778 [Ref: O-43, J-8].

KIMBOL, William. Took the Oath of Allegiance before the Hon. Christopher Cruse in Lower Antietam Hundred before March 2, 1778 [Ref: J-3, O-35].

KIMMEL, Barbara. See "Christopher Trovinger," q.v.

KINCANNON, Thomas. Private, Militia, 2nd Class, Capt. Charles Clinton's Company, 1776/1777 [Ref: M-245, A-1146].

KINDLE, William. See "William Kendall," q.v.

KINETS, William. Private, Militia, 7th Class, Capt. Jacob Sharer's Company, 1776/1777 [Ref: A-1146, M-248].

KING, Francis. Private, Maryland Line, who resided in Washington County and was listed as "defective" in June, 1780 [Ref: D-414].

KING, George (1762-1848). Private, Maryland Line, pensioned in Allegany County at $80 per year under the Act of June 7, 1832 retroactive to March 4, 1831, aged 70 [Ref: R-45]. Resided in the 2nd Division of Allegany County in 1840, aged 78 [Ref: EE-28:4 (p. 443), containing an article by Elba Anthony Dardeau, Jr.]. Susannah King, widow of George, applied for and received pension W7980 in Allegany County on June 7, 1853, age 71, stating her name was Susannah Hambleton when she married George in July 9, 1808, and he died on August 30, 1848. She also applied for and received bounty land #38515-160-55 on March 31, 1855 [Ref: V-II:1951].

KING, James. Private, Militia, 3rd Class, Capt. Barnett Johnston's Company, 3rd Battalion, 1776/1777 [Ref: M-242].

KING, John. Private, Militia, 4th Class, Capt. Barnett Johnston's Company, 3rd Battalion, 1776/1777 [Ref: M-242]. Took the Oath of Allegiance before the Hon. William Yates in 1778 [Ref: O-48, J-12].

KING, John. Private, Militia, 4th Class, Capt. John Bennet's Company, 1776/1777 [Ref: M-246, A-1146]. Took the Oath of Allegiance before the Hon. Lemuel Barritt before March 16, 1778 [Ref: O-42, J-8].

KING, Richard. Enrolled in the first militia company organized for the Revolutionary War in the Elizabeth Town District of Frederick County (now the Hagerstown area of Washington County) on January 6, 1776 [Ref: Q-270, W-1189].

KING, Susannah. See "George King," q.v.

KINGREY, Christian. Private, Militia, 3rd Class, Capt. Conrad Hogmire's Company, 1776/1777 [Ref: A-1146, M-244, which listed the name as "Christian Kingreigh(?)"]. Private, Militia, Capt. John Kershner's Company, on duty guarding prisoners of war at Fort Frederick on June 27, 1778 [Ref: D-328, which listed the name as "Christian Kirgery"].

KINGSTON, George. Private who was enrolled by Lieut. Clement Hollyday and passed by Col. William Luckett on August 8, 1776 [Ref: D-49].

KINKLE, Jacob (1745-1828). Took the Oath of Allegiance before the Hon. Andrew Rentch before March 7, 1778 [Ref: J-15, which listed the name as "Jacob Kinkley" and O-52, which mistakenly listed the name as "Jacob Pinkley"]. "Jacob Kinkle" died in July, 1828, aged 83, was buried in Old St. John's Lutheran Churchyard, and subsequently reinterred in Rose Hill Cemetery in Hagerstown [Ref: JJ-VII:106]. "Jacob Kinkle, Sr." died at an advanced age on August 3, 1821 in Hagerstown [Ref: Z-55].

KINNELY, John. First Corporal, Militia, Capt. James Prather's Company, 3rd Battalion, 1776/1777 [Ref: M-242].

KINNOAD, Henry. See "Henry Knode," q.v.

KINSTRY, Frederick. See "Frederick Kenistrick," q.v.

KIRK, John. Private who was enrolled by Capt. Henry Hardman and passed on July 19, 1776 in Frederick (now Washington) County [Ref: D-51].

KIRKPATRICK, James. Private, Militia, 2nd Class, Capt. James Smith's Company, 2nd Battalion, 1776/1777 [Ref: M-239, A-1146]. Took the Oath of Allegiance before the Hon. John Stull in 1778 [Ref: O-46, J-11].

KIRKPATRICK, Michael. Took the Oath of Allegiance before the Hon. John Stull in 1778 [Ref: O-46, J-11].

KIRKPATRICK, William. Private, Militia, 6th Class, Capt. James Smith's Company, 2nd Battalion, 1776/1777 [Ref: M-240, A-1146]. Took the Oath of Allegiance before the Hon. John Stull in 1778 [Ref: O-46, J-10].

KISHMAN, George. Private, Militia, 2nd Class, Capt. James Smith's Company, 2nd Battalion, 1776/1777 [Ref: M-239, A-1146].

KISHMAN, Martin. Private, Militia, 7th Class, Capt. James Smith's Company, 2nd Battalion, 1776/1777 [Ref: M-240, A-1146]. Took the Oath of Allegiance before the Hon. Henry Schnebley in 1778 [Ref: O-50, J-13, which listed the name as "Martin Kirshman"].

KISSINGER, George. Third Corporal, Militia, Capt. John Bennet's Company, 1776/1777 [Ref: M-246, A-1146, which listed the name as "George Kisinger"]. Took the Oath of Allegiance before the Hon. Henry Schnebley in 1778 [Ref: O-50, J-14, which listed the name as "George Keissinger"].

KISSINGER, Simon. Private, Militia, 1st Class, Capt. John Cellars' Company, 1776/1777 [Ref: A-1146, M-246, which listed the name as "Simon Kesinger"].

KITZMILLER, Casper. Took the Oath of Allegiance before the Hon. Henry Schnebley in 1778 [Ref: O-50, J-14, which listed the name as

"Casper Keitzmiller"]. Private, Militia, 6th Class, Capt. Peter Swingle's (Swingley's) Company, 1776/1777 [Ref: A-1146, M-248, which listed the name as "Casper Kotchmiller" or Ketchmiller?].

KLAPPER, Wallingtine. See "Valentine Clapper," q.v.

KLEIN, Jacob. See "Jacob Cline," q.v.

KLEINSMITH, Andrew. See "Andrew Clinesmith," q.v.

KLOSNER, George. Took the Oath of Allegiance before the Hon. John Stull in 1778 [Ref: O-46, J-10].

KNAUB, John. See "Yost Harbaugh," q.v.

KNAVE, Abraham, and others. See "Abraham Neff," q.v.

KNAVE, Leonard. See "Jacob Yakly," q.v.

KNEEBELL, George. Private, Militia, 8th Class, Capt. Conrad Nichodemus' Company, 2nd Battalion, 1776/1777 [Ref: M-237, A-1146].

KNEFF, Abraham, and others. See "Abraham Neff," q.v.

KNISTERICK, Frederick. See "Frederick Kenistrick," q.v.

KNOCKEL, Frederick. Took the Oath of Allegiance before the Hon. Christopher Cruse in Lower Antietam Hundred before March 2, 1778 [Ref: J-2, O-35]. "Frederick Knokel" died before June 6, 1795 (date of balance book entry in Washington County), leaving equal shares to Hannah Abbonet and Catey Shilling, with Phillip Shilling as the administrator [Ref: J-34]. It is interesting to note that "Fredrick Knochelsingibo" was born in 1722, died on September 12, 1788, and is buried beside "Evalisabeth Knochelsingebo" (1762-1779) in the Shang Graveyard near Boonsboro, Maryland [Ref: JJ-II:91].

KNODE, Henry. On January 23, 1777 the Committee of Observation "upon reconsidering the resolution of this Committee on the 21st instant with respect to Henry Kinnoad, Sr., the committee do resolve that said Kinnoad be released from confinement, giving bond and sufficient security in the penalty of 1000 pounds conditioned that he shall well and truly deliver up his son Henry Kinnoad, deserted from Capt. Farmer's Company, to this Committee on Saturday the 8th day of February next, or on failure thereof, deliver up himself in lieu of said son that further order may be taken therein, and pay all expence of guards." [Ref: Q-49, Q-46]. A later entry by the Committee on February 8, 1777 indicated "that Henry Knode, Sr. appeared before Committee agreeable to the condition of his bond, upon making it appear to Committee that he had used his utmost endeavours to apprehend his son Henry Knode, Jr., a deserter from Capt. Farmer's Company, but could not possibly perform the same." The Committee ordered him, under penalty, to continue to "use all possible means to apprehend his said son." [Ref: Q-233].

KNODE, Jacob (1751-1828). Private, Militia, 1st Class, Capt. James Smith's Company, 2nd Battalion, 1776/1777 [Ref: A-1146, M-230, which latter source listed the name as "Jacob Knode (Knoe?)"]. Jacob Knode, Sr. was born on September 26, 1751, died on February 2, 1828, and is buried beside his wife Margaret (April 10, 1750 - July 15, 1828) in the cemetery at Zion Reformed Church in Hagerstown [Ref: JJ-VI:11]. It must be noted, however, that she died in 1824 (not 1828) as stated in her obituary: "Margaret Knode, wife of Jacob Knode, of Hagerstown, died on July 15, 1824, in her 75th year." [Ref: Z-67].

KNODE, John. Took the Oath of Allegiance before the Hon. Christopher Cruse in Sharpsburg Hundred before March 2, 1778 [Ref: O-34, J-2, which listed the name as "John Knote"].

KNODE, John Jr. Private, Militia, 3rd Class, Capt. Jeremiah Spires' Company, 2nd Battalion, 1776/1777 [Ref: M-239, A-1146].

KNODE, Margaret. See "Jacob Knode" and "John Seibert," q.v.

KNODE, Mathias. Private, Militia, 7th Class, Capt. James Smith's Company, 2nd Battalion, 1776/1777 [Ref: M-240, A-1146].

KNOTE, John. See "John Knode," q.v.

KNOTT, Ignatius (1747-   ). Private, Militia, 2nd Class, Capt. James Smith's Company, 2nd Battalion, 1776/1777 [Ref: M-239, A-1146]. Private, Maryland Line, who applied for pension in Clermont County, Ohio in November, 1832, age 85, stating he was born on April 17, 1747 in St. Mary's County, Maryland. At the age of 21 he moved to Washington County, Maryland and lived in Hagerstown, Maryland at the time of his enlistment. In 1799 he moved to Ohio [Ref: V-II:1978].

KNOW, John. Took the Oath of Allegiance before the Hon. John Barnes before February 28, 1778 [Ref: O-44, J-9].

KNOX, Mrs. Rendered patriotic service in Hagerstown by providing sundries to Capt. John Nelson's Company, Maryland Line, in April, 1776 [Ref: Q-161].

KOLER, Catherine. See "Frederick Guiser," q.v.

KONHN, George. Took the Oath of Allegiance before the Hon. Henry Schnebley in 1778 [Ref: O-51, J-14, which latter source listed the name as "George ----"].

KOOGLE, Christian. See "Christian Coogle," q.v.

KOOGLE, Dorothy. See "Martin Ridenour," q.v.

KOOGLE, John (1757-   ). Took the Oath of Allegiance before the Hon. Richard Davis in 1778 [Ref: J-5, O-38]. "John Kugel" was a private, Maryland Line, who applied for and received pension S15190 in Owen County, Kentucky on March 4, 1833, aged 75, stating he was born on November 20, 1757 in Lancaster County, Pennsylvania and moved with his father (not named) to Maryland when he was quite small. He enlisted in Washington County in July, 1776, lived in Maryland until 1801 when he moved to Fayette County, Kentucky, and 16 years later he moved to Owen County [Ref: T-60]. "John Coogle or Cugle" was a private in the militia, 6th Class, Capt. Peter Swingle's (Swingley's) Company, 1776/1777 [Ref: A-1146, M-248].

KORE, Christian. See "Christian Core," q.v.

KOTZ, Jacob. First Lieutenant, Militia, Capt. William Heyser's Company, muster roll dated October 23, 1776, in continental service [Ref: D-263, L-79, W-1190, which also listed the name as "Jacob Kottz"].

KOTZ, Catharine. Rendered patriotic service by providing a blanket for the use of the military in January, 1777, as recorded by the Committee of Observation on January 27, 1777 [Ref: Q-53]. "Mrs. Cotz was paid on March 1, 1777 for a blanket for the use of Capt. Williams' Company." [Ref: Q-248].

KOVNEE, Matthias. Enrolled in the third militia company organized for the Revolutionary War in the Elizabeth Town District of Frederick County (now the Hagerstown area of Washington County), passed by the Committee of Observation on June 5, 1776, and assigned to Capt. John Reynolds' command [Ref: Q-273].

KRAFT, William. See "William Croft," q.v.

KREAK (KRICK), Ellen. See "Jacob Krick," q.v.

KREICH, Catharina and Philip. See "Philip Krick," q.v.

KREIHBAWM, Philip. See "Philip Creekbaum," q.v.

KRETSINGER, Ludwick. Enrolled in the third militia company organized for the Revolutionary War in the Elizabeth Town District of Frederick County (now the Hagerstown area of Washington County), passed by the Committee of Observation on June 5, 1776, and assigned to Capt. John Reynolds' command [Ref: Q-273]. Private, Militia, 7th Class, Capt. Joseph Chapline's Company, 2nd Battalion, 1776/1777 [Ref: M-242, which listed the name as "Ludwick Crotzinger"].

KRETZER, Leonard (c1736-1821). Took the Oath of Allegiance before the Hon. Christopher Cruse in Sharpsburg Hundred before March 2, 1778 [Ref: O-35, J-2, which listed the name as "Leonard Kretcer"]. Leonard Kretzer died at his residence near Sharpsburg on July 15, 1821, in his 85th year [Ref: Z-55].

KREUGER, Peter. Took the Oath of Allegiance before the Hon. John Stull in 1778 [Ref: O-46, J-10]. See "Peter Creger," q.v.

KRICK (KREAK), Ellen. See "Jacob Krick," q.v.

KRICK, Francis. Soldier and pensioner of the Revolution who resided in the 4th District of Washington County in 1840, aged 80 [Ref: EE-28:4

(p. 444), containing an article by Elba Anthony Dardeau, Jr.]. However, it must be noted that Francis Krick is not listed in Sources V-II:1986 and Y-II:1718, but Jacob Krick is mentioned.

KRICK, George. See "Jacob Krick," q.v.

KRICK, Jacob (1760-1841). Private, Pennsylvania Line, who applied for pension (R6058) in Washington County, Maryland on April 23, 1839, aged 78, stating that he lived with his father (not named) in Berks County, Pennsylvania at the time of his enlistment. His brother George was aged 74 in 1839 and had lived at home during the war. In 1855 a Mrs. Ellen Kreak was mentioned and it was also stated that Jacob Krick had served under a Capt. Phillip Krick, but no relationships were given [Ref: V-II:1986]. Jacob Krick was born in Pennsylvania in 1760, married (name not given), and died in Maryland on December 15, 1842 [Ref: Y-II:1718]. See "Francis Krick," q.v.

KRICK, Philip. Rendered patriotic service by supplying wheat for the use of the military on April 8, 1780 [Ref: HH-72, and W-1190, which latter source listed the name as "Phyllin Krick"]. One "Philip Kreich" died testate by February 6, 1805, leaving a wife Catharina and among his heirs a son Philip [Ref: MM-13:132]. See "Philip Craig" and "Jacob Krick," q.v.

KRIEGH, Philip. See "Philip Craig," q.v.

KRISEL, Jacob. See "Jacob Frisel," q.v.

KRITZINGER, George. See "Peter Dick," q.v.

KROFT, John. See "John Craft (Croft)," q.v.

KROMBACH, John. Took the Oath of Allegiance before the Hon. Henry Schnebley in 1778 [Ref: O-49, J-13, which latter source listed the name as "John Drombach"].

KROOFT, Frederick. See "Frederick Grooft," q.v.

KROUT, Peter. Took the Oath of Allegiance before the Hon. Henry Schnebley in 1778 [Ref: O-50, J-14].

KUGEL, John. See "John Koogle," q.v.

KUHN, Amelia, Anna, and Abraham. See "Jacob Kuhn," q.v.

KUHN, Catharine and Christiana. See "Jacob Kuhn," q.v.

KUHN (KUHNE), Frederick. Took the Oath of Allegiance before the Hon. Christopher Cruse in Sharpsburg Hundred before March 2, 1778 [Ref: O-34, J-2, which listed the name as "Frederick Kuhno"].

KUHN (KUHNS), Jacob. Took the Oath of Allegiance before the Hon. Henry Schnebley in 1778 [Ref: O-51, J-14]. Jacob Kuhn died intestate before December, 1827, when an equity case was filed in Washington County Court, naming his heirs and representatives: John Kuhn (who died since the death of said Jacob Kuhn), Elizabeth Kuhn (who married

Daniel Sheets), Moddalena Kuhn, Judith Kuhn (who married Abraham Bockman and he is since dead), Sarah Kuhn (who married John Bower), Jacob Kuhn, Christiana Kuhn (who died without leaving any legitimate children), Anna Kuhn (who married Abraham Hawken), Catharine Kuhn (who married Joshua Smith, of Virginia), and Amelia Kuhn (who married Jacob Kauffman, of Pennsylvania). [Ref: Z-96].

KUHN, John, Joshua, and Judith. See "Jacob Kuhn," q.v.

KUHN (KUHNS), Mathias. Took the Oath of Allegiance before the Hon. Christopher Cruse in Sharpsburg Hundred before March 2, 1778 [Ref: O-34, J-2].

KUHN, Moddalena and Sarah. See "Jacob Kuhn," q.v.

KUPRO, Philip. Took the Oath of Allegiance before the Hon. Christopher Cruse in Sharpsburg Hundred before March 2, 1778 [Ref: O-34, J-1].

KURTS, Christopher Jr. Took the Oath of Allegiance before the Hon. Christopher Cruse in Lower Antietam Hundred before March 2, 1778 [Ref: J-3, O-35].

KURTZ, Reverend. See "Nicholas Ridenour," q.v.

KYZER, John. Second Lieutenant, Militia, Capt. John Funk's Company, 2nd Battalion, March 30, 1781 [Ref: M-96, G-368, which listed the name as "John Kyger"].

LACKLAND, Aaron. Third Sergeant, Militia, Capt. Jeremiah Spires' Company, 2nd Battalion, 1776/1777 [Ref: M-239, A-1146, which listed the name as "Aron Lacklan"]. Took the Oath of Allegiance before the Hon. Richard Davis in 1778 [Ref: J-5, O-37].

LACKLAND, Elisha. Third Sergeant, Militia, Capt. Basil Williams' Company, 1776/1777 [Ref: M-244, A-1146]. Took the Oath of Allegiance before the Hon. Richard Davis in 1778 [Ref: J-3, O-36]. "Elisha Lacklin" rendered patriotic service by supplying corn for the use of the military on January 26, 1780 [Ref: HH-74, and W-1190, which latter source listed the name as "Elisha Larkin"].

LACKLAND, Jeremiah. Took the Oath of Allegiance before the Hon. Richard Davis in 1778 [Ref: J-3, O-36, which listed the name as "Jeremiah Lacklen" and "Jeremiah Lacklin"].

LAISHER, John. See "John Leisher," q.v.

LAKIN, Basil. Private who enlisted in the militia on August 20, 1781 for service in the Continental Army [Ref: D-388].

LAMAR, William. Captain, 7th Maryland Line, pensioned in Washington County at $480 per year under the Act of May 15, 1828 [Ref: R-53].

LAMBERT, Eve. See "George Lambert," q.v.

LAMBERT, George (1746-1823). One of several patriots appointed by the Committee of Observation on December 30, 1776 "to form the county into companies (after the militia had marched) for the purpose of relieving the distressed inhabitants of said county and also to compel the Dunkards and Mennonists to give their assistance." [Ref: Q-346]. George Lambert was born on October 15, 1746, married Eve ----, died on July 10, 1823, and is buried in a graveyard on the William Leatherman farm near Bowman's Mill, near Leitersburg, in Washington County [Ref: JJ-V:24].

LAMBERT, George Jr. Private, Militia, 2nd Class, Capt. Conrad Hogmire's Company, 1776/1777 [Ref: M-244, A-1146].

LAMSTER, Thomas. See "Thomas Lemaster," q.v.

LANCY, Jeremiah. Took the Oath of Allegiance before the Hon. Richard Davis in 1778 [Ref: J-4, O-36].

LANDERS, Samuel. Private, Militia, 7th Class, Capt. Samuel Hughes' Company, 2nd Battalion, 1776/1777 [Ref: M-238, A-1146].

LANDREY, John Jr. Private, Militia, 1st Class, Capt. Charles Clinton's Company, 1776/1777 [Ref: M-245, A-1146].

LANE, Ja [sic]. First Lieutenant, Militia, by November 17, 1780 [Ref: M-96].

LANE, Jeremiah. Private, Militia, Capt. Martin Kershner's Company, 32nd Battalion, December 27, 1776 [Ref: K-1814 (Box 3), which listed the name as "Jarimiah Lane"].

LANG, Thomas. Took the Oath of Allegiance before the Hon. Andrew Rentch before March 7, 1778 [Ref: O-52, J-15, which latter source listed the name as "Thomas Long"].

LANSDALE, Major. See "Thomas McQuinny," q.v.

LANTZ (LANCE), Christian. Appointed by the Committee of Observation to carry the Association of Freemen to male residents in Upper Antietam Hundred on September 14, 1775 "and require their subscription to the same and make an exact account of those who sign and those that refuse with their reasons for refusing." [Ref: Q-143, which listed the name as "Christ. Lance"]. Second Lieutenant, Militia, Capt. Daniel Clapsaddle's Company, 1st Battalion, 1776/1777 [Ref: M-236, A-1146]. Served on the Committee of Observation in April, 1776 [Ref: Q-154, Q-155, which also listed the name as "Cn. Lentz"].

LANTZ, Christian. Private, Militia, 7th Class, Capt. Conrad Hogmire's Company, 1776/1777 [Ref: M-244, A-1146].

LANTZ (LANCE), Christian Jr. Private, Militia, 7th Class, Capt. Daniel Clapsaddle's Company, 1st Battalion, 1776/1777 [Ref: M-236, A-1146].

LANTZ, Daniel and Elizabeth. See "Jacob Lantz," q.v.

LANTZ (LANCE), Jacob. Private, Militia, 8th Class, Capt. Henry Boteler's Company, 1776/1777 [Ref: M-237, A-1146]. "Jacob Lantz" died testate by July 25, 1801, leaving a wife Elizabeth, and among his heirs was a son Jacob [Ref: MM-12:77, 78]. An equity court case in Cumberland in 1824 mentions Jacob Lantz as the administrator of Daniel Lantz and lists many of his heirs [Ref: Z-1]. See "Michael Kershner," q.v.

LAPEAR, William. Took the Oath of Allegiance before the Hon. Lemuel Barritt before March 16, 1778 [Ref: O-43, J-8, which latter source listed the name as "William Lepear"].

LAPORT, George. Private, Militia, 8th Class, Capt. Daniel Cresap's Company, 3rd Battalion, 1776/1777 [Ref: M-241, which listed the name as "George Saport(?)"].

LAPPIN, Paul. Private who was recruited and passed by County Lieutenant Thomas Sprigg on April 22, 1780 [Ref: D-336].

LARKIN, Elisha. See "Elisha Lackland," q.v.

LARRYMOR (LARMAR), Samuel. Private who enlisted in the militia on August 15, 1781 for service in the Continental Army [Ref: D-388]. Substitute, Maryland Line, discharged on October 30, 1781 [Ref: G-657, which listed the name as "Samuel Larmar"].

LASHER, John. Private, Militia, 6th Class, Capt. Griffin Johnson's Company, 3rd Battalion, 1776/1777 [Ref: M-243].

LASHER, Joseph. Private, Militia, 1st Class, Capt. Griffin Johnson's Company, 3rd Battalion, 1776/1777 [Ref: M-243].

LASHER, Joseph Jr. Private, Militia, 6th Class, Capt. Griffin Johnson's Company, 3rd Battalion, 1776/1777 [Ref: M-243].

LAURANCE, Richard. Private, Militia, 8th Class, Capt. Jacob Sharer's Company, 1776/1777 [Ref: A-1146, M-248].

LAYCOCK, Isaac. Private, Militia, 8th Class, Capt. Charles Clinton's Company, 1776/1777 [Ref: M-245, A-1146]. Took the Oath of Allegiance before the Hon. Lemuel Barritt on February 5, 1778 [Ref: O-42, J-7, which listed the name as "Isaac Laycok"].

LAYPORT, George. Took the Oath of Allegiance before the Hon. Lemuel Barritt before March 16, 1778 [Ref: O-42, J-8].

LAZER, Jacob. Rendered patriotic service by supplying a blanket for the use of the military in March, 1776, as recorded by the Committee of Observation on April 12, 1776 [Ref: Q-156, L-82].

LAZIER, John (1756-   ). Took the Oath of Allegiance before the Hon. Andrew Bruce before March 2, 1778 [Ref: O-41, J-6]. "John Lazer or Lazeir or Lazier" applied for and received pension S40075 in Allegany County, Maryland on October 15, 1818, age 62, stating he enlisted there in the Maryland Line [area was then Washington County]. In 1820 he was living in Bedford County, Pennsylvania with a wife (age 63), a daughter (age 24), and a granddaughter (age 2 years and 7 months), but no names were given [Ref: V-II:2034].

LAZIER, Joseph. Took the Oath of Allegiance before the Hon. Andrew Bruce before March 2, 1778 [Ref: O-41, J-6].

LAZIER, Thomas. Private, Militia, 8th Class, Capt. James Smith's Company, 2nd Battalion, 1776/1777 [Ref: M-240, A-1146].

LEANE, Henry. Took the Oath of Allegiance before the Hon. Andrew Bruce before March 2, 1778 [Ref: O-41, J-6].

LEAR, Philip. Rendered patriotic service by providing a rifle for Capt. Daniel Cresap's Company in July, 1775, as recorded by the Committee of Observation at Elizabeth Town on November 4, 1775 [Ref: Q-148].

LEASURE, Mary. See "Francis Twigg," q.v.

LEATHERMAN, Michael. Took the Oath of Allegiance before the Hon. John Stull in 1778 [Ref: O-46, J-11, which listed the name as "Michael Litherman"]. Private who enlisted in the militia on August 14, 1781 for service in the Continental Army [Ref: D-388, D-409]. Substitute, Maryland Line, discharged on October 30, 1781 [Ref: G-656, which listed the name as "Michael Letherman"].

LEATHERMAN, William. See "George Lambert," q.v.

LECKLER, Polly. See "Henry Franks," q.v.

LEE, John. Private, Militia, 3rd Class, Capt. Jacob Sharer's Company, 1776/1777 [Ref: A-1146, M-248]. Rendered patriotic service in Hagerstown by providing goods and a rifle to Capt. John Nelson's Company, continental service (Maryland Line), April, 1776 [Ref: Q-161].

LEE, Joseph. Took the Oath of Allegiance before the Hon. Lemuel Barritt before March 16, 1778 [Ref: O-42, J-8].

LEE, Joseph Jr. Took the Oath of Allegiance before the Hon. Lemuel Barritt before March 16, 1778 [Ref: O-42, J-8].

LEE, Josiah Jr. Private, Militia, 7th Class, Capt. Daniel Cresap's Company, 3rd Battalion, 1776/1777 [Ref: M-241].

LEE, Samuel. Private, Militia, 2nd Class, Capt. Daniel Cresap's Company, 3rd Battalion, 1776/1777 [Ref: M-241]. Took the Oath of Allegiance before the Hon. Lemuel Barritt before March 16, 1778 [Ref: O-42, J-8].

LEE, William. Private, Militia, 1st Class, Capt. Daniel Cresap's Company, 3rd Battalion, 1776/1777 [Ref: M-241]. Took the Oath of Allegiance before the Hon. Samuel Hughes before March 1, 1778 [Ref: O-33, J-1].

LEE, William. Private, Militia, 5th Class, Capt. Jacob Sharer's Company, 1776/1777 [Ref: A-1146, M-248]. Took the Oath of Allegiance before the Hon. Lemuel Barritt on January 27, 1778 [Ref: O-42, J-7, which latter source listed the name as "William Kee"].

LEE, William. Rendered patriotic service in Hagerstown by providing goods and a rifle to Capt. John Nelson's Company, continental service (Maryland Line), April, 1776 [Ref: Q-161].

LEER, Felix. Private, Militia, 5th Class, Capt. Isaac Baker's Company, 1776/1777 [Ref: A-1146, M-247]. Private, Militia, 8th Class, Capt. John Bennet's Company, 1776/1777 [Ref: A-1146, M-246, which listed the name as "Felix Leer(?)"].

LEFLER, George. Second Corporal, Militia, Capt. James Walling's Company, 2nd Battalion, 1776/1777 [Ref: M-238, A-1146].

LEIDY, Abraham. Private, Militia, 3rd Class, Capt. John Cellars' Company, 1776/1777 [Ref: A-1146, M-246, which listed the name as "Abraham Lidey"]. Private, Militia, Capt. John Kershner's Company, on duty guarding prisoners of war at Fort Frederick on June 27, 1778 [Ref: D-328, which listed the name as "Abraham Leedy"].

LEIDY, Adam. Private, Militia, 3rd Class, Capt. Martin Kershner's Company, 1776/1777 [Ref: A-1146, M-247, which listed the name as "Adam Lidy"]. Private, Militia, Capt. Martin Kershner's Company, 32nd Battalion, December 27, 1776 [Ref: K-1814 (Box 3); page was partially torn and soiled, making the name unclear]. Took the Oath of Allegiance before the Hon. Henry Schnebley in 1778 [Ref: O-49, J-13]. Private, Militia, Capt. John Kershner's Company, on duty guarding prisoners of war at Fort Frederick on June 27, 1778 [Ref: D-328, which misspelled the name as "Adam Sydey" when it was actually "Adam Lydey"]. "Adam Lyday" died testate by March 23, 1805, leaving a wife Rosina and sons George and Henry [Ref: MM-13:135].

LEIDY, George and Henry. See "Adam Leidy," q.v.

LEIDY, John. First Corporal, Militia, Capt. Michael Fackler's Company, 1776/1777 [Ref: M-245, A-1146, which listed the name as "John Leydia"]. On January 13, 1777 he contracted to furnish the Committee of Observation with sufficient quantities of bread (one and a half pounds per day per prisoner) to feed the Tories in custody in Elizabeth Town [Ref: Q-38, which listed the name as "John Leidey"]. Furnished rations for the use of Col. Stull's Battalion and was paid by Capt. Andrew Linck out of public money on January 27, 1777 [Ref: Q-53]. Took the Oath of Allegiance before the Hon. Joseph Sprigg before April 1, 1778 [Ref: O-53, J-16].

LEIDY, Michael. Took the Oath of Allegiance before the Hon. John Stull in 1778 [Ref: O-46, J-11, which listed the name as "Michael Lidac" (or Lidae?)].

LEIDY, Rosanna. See "Adam Leidy," q.v.

LEIDY, Simon. Private who enlisted in the militia on August 12, 1781 for service in the Continental Army [Ref: D-388, D-409, which listed the name as "Simon Lyday"]. Substitute, Maryland Line, discharged on October 30, 1781 [Ref: G-656, which listed the name as "Simon Lyday"].

LEIMBACH, John. Took the Oath of Allegiance before the Hon. Henry Schnebley in 1778 [Ref: O-51, J-15].

LEISHER, Adam. Private, Militia, Capt. William Heyser's Company, muster roll dated October 23, 1776, in continental service, which stated he had deserted, yet he was on duty in May, 1777 [Ref: D-264, W-1190, L-79, which listed the name as "Adam Lieser" and GG-98, which listed the name as "Adam Lieser, Leiser"]. Took the Oath of Allegiance before the Hon. Henry Schnebley in 1778 [Ref: O-51, J-15].

LEISHER, John. Private, Militia, 4th Class, Capt. Charles Clinton's Company, 1776/1777 [Ref: M-245, A-1146, which listed the name as "John Laisher"].

LEISHER, Peter. One of several patriots appointed by the Committee of Observation on December 30, 1776 "to form the county into companies (after the militia had marched) for the purpose of relieving the distressed inhabitants of said county and also to compel the Dunkards and Mennonists to give their assistance." [Ref: Q-345].

LEITER (LIGHTER), Abraham. Fourth Sergeant, Militia, Capt. Daniel Clapsaddle's Company, 1st Battalion, 1776/1777 [Ref: M-236, A-1146]. Took the Oath of Allegiance before the Hon. Andrew Rentch before March 7, 1778 [Ref: O-52, J-15].

LEITER (LIGHTER), Adam ("at Jacob Lighter's"). Private, Militia, 8th Class, Capt. Daniel Clapsaddle's Company, 1st Battalion, 1776/1777 [Ref: M-236, A-1146].

LEITER (LIGHTER), Christopher. Private, Militia, 7th Class, Capt. Daniel Clapsaddle's Company, 1st Battalion, 1776/1777 [Ref: M-236, A-1146].

LEITER (LIGHTER), Elizabeth. See "Peter Bell" and Philip Oster," q.v.

LEITER (LIGHTER), Jacob. Third Sergeant, Militia, Capt. Daniel Clapsaddle's Company, 1st Battalion, 1776/1777 [Ref: M-236, A-1146]. Took the Oath of Allegiance before the Hon. Andrew Rentch before March 7, 1778 [Ref: O-52, J-15]. See "Adam Leiter," q.v.

LEITER (LIGHTER), John. Private, Militia, 2nd Class, Capt. James Smith's Company, 2nd Battalion, 1776/1777 [Ref: M-239, A-1146, which listed the name as "John Lieter"]. On January 18, 1777 the Committee of Observation resolved that "John Lighter be excused from marching with the militia at this time, and that he take charge of Capt. James Smith's affairs until he returns from camp." [Ref: Q-42].

LEITER (LIGHTER), Peter. There appears to have been more then one man with this name. Additional research will be necessary before drawing conclusions. (1) Private, Militia, 1st Class, Capt. Conrad Hogmire's Company, 1776/1777 [Ref: M-244, A-1146]. (2) Private, Militia, 3rd Class, Capt. Daniel Clapsaddle's Company, 1st Battalion, 1776/1777 [Ref: M-236, A-1146]. (3) Fifer, Militia, Capt. John Kershner's Company, on duty guarding prisoners of war at Fort Frederick on June 27, 1778 [Ref: D-328].

LEMASTER, Abraham (1742-1820). Associator in Frederick County in 1775 who took the Oath of Allegiance in 1778 [Ref: *Revolutionary Patriots of Frederick County, Maryland, 1775-1783*, by Henry C. Peden, Jr. (1995), p. 223]. Abraham Lemaster was born on February 10, 1742, died on May 13, 1820, and is buried in a graveyard at the rear of Bast & Company, Undertakers, at Boonsboro in Washington County, Maryland [Ref: JJ-II:92].

LEMASTER, Benjamin. See "Joseph Lemaster," q.v.

LEMASTER, Catharyne and Charity. See "Joseph Lemaster," q.v.

LEMASTER, Hugh (1750-1837). Private, Militia, 6th Class, Capt. Basil Williams' Company, 1776/1777 [Ref: A-1146, N-33, M-244, which latter source listed the name as "Hugh Lamaster"]. Took the Oath of Allegiance before the Hon. Richard Davis in 1778 [Ref: J-4, O-37]. Hugh Lemaster applied for pension in Shelby County, Kentucky on January 16, 1834, age 83, stating he was born on May 27, 1750 in Charles County, Maryland and lived in Washington County, Maryland at the time of his enlistment. He married Mary Jupin on February 20, 1792 and they moved to Kentucky in 1796. Hugh died on May 9, 1837 and his widow applied for and received pension W2951 in Shelby County, Kentucky on July 3, 1845, age 78 [Ref: V-II:2053, N-117].

LEMASTER, Isaac. Private, Militia, 6th Class, Capt. James Prather's Company, 3rd Battalion, 1776/1777 [Ref: M-243, which listed the name as "Isaac Lamaster"]. Took the Oath of Allegiance before the Hon. Andrew Bruce before March 2, 1778 [Ref: O-41, J-7]. See "Joseph Lemaster," q.v.

LEMASTER, John Waddell. See "Joseph Lemaster," q.v.

LEMASTER, Joseph (1758-1826). Private, Virginia Line, who lived in Washington County, Maryland when he enlisted in Morgantown, Virginia, was a son of Isaac Lemaster. Joseph moved to Abbeville District, South Carolina after the war, married Mary Waddell in 1791 or 1792, and later moved to Maury County, Tennessee. He died in Williamson County, Tennessee in August, 1826 and Mary died in Maury County, Tennessee on April 16, 1845. Her widow's pension (W2951) gives the names of only 3 of their 7 children: John Waddell Lemaster (born October 21, 1793 and married Nancy Lee Almond on October 21, 1821); Mary Lemaster (age 24 in 1823); and, Elizabeth Lemaster (age 16 in 1823). It also mentioned Joseph's brothers and sisters Isaac, Richard, Benjamin and Thomas Lemaster, and Mary, Charity and Cathryne. His widow's brothers and sisters were John, William, George and James Waddell, and Jane and Elizabeth. Rebecca McKay, age 55, of Maury County, Tennessee in 1839, stated she was a daughter of Joseph Lemaster by his first wife (not named) and she was 8 years old when her father married Mary Waddell [Ref: V-II:2053].

LEMASTER, Mary and Richard. See "Joseph Lemaster," q.v.

LEMASTER, Thomas. Private, Militia, 5th Class, Capt. Barnett Johnston's Company, 3rd Battalion, 1776/1777 [Ref: M-242, which listed the name as "Thomas Lamster"]. See "Joseph Lemaster," q.v.

LENOX, John. Private, Maryland Line, who resided in Washington County and was listed as "defective" in October, 1780 [Ref: D-414].

LENTZ, Christian. Served on the Committee of Observation for the Elizabeth Town District (now the Hagerstown area of Washington County) in December, 1776 [Ref: Q-340]. See "Christian Lance," q.v.

LEONARD, James. Private, Maryland Line, pensioned under the Act of March 18, 1818 at $96 per year effective March 31, 1818 and "transferred from New York April 30, 1828, from March 4, 1828." [Ref: R-42].

LEONARD, Nicholas. Rendered patriotic service by providing clothing for the use of the military on July 5, 1778 [Ref: CC-106, which listed the name as "Nicholas Lennard"].

LEONARD, Thomas. Enrolled in the first militia company organized for the Revolutionary War in the Elizabeth Town District of Frederick County (now the Hagerstown area of Washington County) on January 6, 1776 [Ref: Q-270, W-1189].

LETHWORTH, Lanord. Took the Oath of Allegiance before the Hon. Lemuel Barritt before March 16, 1778 [Ref: O-42, J-8].

LEVEINGS(?), Thomas. Private, Militia, 2nd Class, Capt. Peter Beall's Company, 1st Battalion, 1776/1777 [Ref: M-240].

LEVITE, Nancy. See "Michael Smith," q.v.

LEWIS, Elizabeth. See "William Lewis," q.v.

LEWIS, Even. Private, Militia, 6th Class, Capt. Martin Kershner's Company, 1776/1777 [Ref: A-1146, M-248]. Took the Oath of Allegiance before the Hon. John Cellars in January, 1778 [Ref: K-1814, O-40, J-6].

LEWIS, George. Enrolled in the second militia company organized for the Revolutionary War in the Elizabeth Town District of Frederick County (now the Hagerstown area of Washington County) on March 9, 1776 [Ref: Q-272]. Private, Militia, 6th Class, Capt. Henry Boteler's Company, 1776/1777 [Ref: M-237, A-1146].

LEWIS, Henry. See "William Lewis," q.v.

LEWIS, John. Took the Oath of Allegiance before the Hon. Richard Davis in 1778 [Ref: J-4, O-36].

LEWIS, Mary. See "William Lewis," q.v.

LEWIS, Polly. Pensioner of the Revolution (husband's name not stated) who resided in the household of George Shryock in the 3rd District of Washington County in 1840, aged 82 [Ref: EE-28:4 (p. 444), containing an article by Elba Anthony Dardeau, Jr.]. This is probably Mary Lewis, widow of "William Lewis," q.v.

LEWIS, Richard. Private who was enrolled by Capt. Aeneas Campbell and passed by Major Francis Deakins on July 18, 1776 [Ref: D-49].

LEWIS, William (1755-1827). Private, Militia, 8th Class, Capt. Henry Boteler's Company, 1776/1777 [Ref: M-237, A-1146]. Private who enlisted in the militia on August 21, 1781 for service in the Continental Army [Ref: D-388, D-410, H-451]. Private, Maryland Line, 1776-1781, and Captain under Gen. Wayne in the Indian Wars, 1793, pensioned under the Act of March 18, 1818 at $96 per year effective October 8, 1818 and died May 20, 1827 [Ref: R-42, Z-92]. He applied for pension in Washington County on March 26, 1818, age 62, stating he enlisted at Hagerstown and also served under General Wayne in the Indian Wars. His widow Mary applied for and received pension W4263 at Hagerstown, Maryland on January 29, 1839, age 81, stating they were married on October 24, 1783 at Georgetown, D.C. and had 6 children, but only mentioned Henry and Elizabeth (born on August 5, 1784 and married George Shurock). [Ref: V-II:2074]. On February 25, 1826 the Treasurer of the Western Shore of Maryland was directed to pay to William Lewis, of Washington County, or order, during life, in quarterly payments in lieu of his present pension, the half pay of a captain, in consideration of his valuable military services, both in the Revolutionary War and in the war against the Indians. On March 14, 1828 the Treasurer of the Western Shore of Maryland was directed to pay to Mary Lewis, of Washington County, during life, half yearly, half pay of a captain, as further remuneration for her husband Capt. William Lewis' services during the Revolutionary War [Ref: AA-365, AA-366]. William Lewis died in Hagerstown on May 20, 1827 "in his 72nd year, and his remains were interred in the Lutheran burial ground. He was the late crier of Washington County Court; served at the battles of Trenton, Princeton, Brandywine, Germantown, Monmouth, and numerous skirmishes. When

General Wayne organized the U. S. Army and proceeded against the Indians in 1793, Lewis was promoted to captain and fought at the Miami. He was deprived of sight for 2 years before his death." [Ref: Z-13, Z-14, Z-92]. William Lewis was born on December 25, 1755, died on May 20, 1827, was buried in Old St. John's Lutheran Churchyard and subsequently reinterred in Rose Hill Cemetery in Hagerstown [Ref: JJ-VII:105]. See the other "William Lewis," q.v.

LEWIS, William. Private, Militia, Capt. William Heyser's Company, 1776, in continental service [Ref: W-1190, L-79]. Third Corporal, Militia, Capt. William Heyser's Company, muster roll dated October 23, 1776, in continental service [Ref: D-263, W-1190, L-79]. Sergeant, German Regiment, Lt. Col. Ludwick Weltner's Company, discharged on July 16, 1779 [Ref: D-264]. On February 17, 1820 the Treasurer of the Western Shore of Maryland was directed to pay to William Lewis, of Washington County, an old soldier in the Revolutionary War, for life, half pay of a sergeant, for his war services [Ref: AA-365]. One William Lewis died testate in 1805 and part of his estate was left "to William Lewis that is called my son." [Ref: MM-13:174]. Additional research may be necessry before drawing conclusions.

LEZIN, Jacob. Private, Militia, 3rd Class, Capt. Peter Swingle's (Swingley's) Company, 1776/1777 [Ref: A-1146, M-248].

LIGHT, Benjamin. On September 12, 1781 ten county justices sent a petition to Governor Lee in behalf of Benjamin Light who had been imprisoned since November 9, 1780, in heavy irons, on suspicion of passing counterfeit money. They requested that Benjamin be granted a pardon and allowed to enlist in the American Army for three years "as he is an extraordinary blacksmith and would be a valuable man in the army and might be kept with the travelling forages at his trade." The pardon was granted on September 12, 1781 under the conditions stated [Ref: H-488, H-489]. However, it must be noted that Benjamin Light is not listed in the muster rolls of Maryland troops in *Archives of Maryland, Volume 18*.

LIGHTER, Christian and Elizabeth. See "Philip Oster," q.v.

LIGHTER, Peter. See "Peter Leiter," q.v.

LINDER, Jacob. Private who was enlisted by Ensign Nathan Williams and passed on July 25, 1776 in Frederick (now Washington) County [Ref: D-51].

LINDER, Nathaniel. Private who was enlisted by Lieut. Christian Orndorff and passed on July 20, 1776 in Frederick (now Washington) County [Ref: D-50].

LINDSAY, John Sr. Took the Oath of Allegiance before the Hon. Lemuel Barritt before March 16, 1778 [Ref: J-7, which listed the name as "John Lindsay, Sr." and O-42, which listed the name as "John Lindsey Snr"].

LINDSEY, John. Private who was enrolled by Capt. Henry Hardman and passed on July 19, 1776 in Frederick (now Washington) County [Ref: D-51]. Private, Militia, Capt. Charles Coulson's Company, enrolled August 28, 1776 [Ref: M-244, A-1146]. Took the Oath of Allegiance before the Hon. Lemuel Barritt before March 16, 1778 [Ref: O-43, J-8, which listed the name as "John Lindsey, Jr."].

LINE, Catherin (Catharine). See "Martin Line," q.v.

LINE, Jacob. Private, Militia, 2nd Class, Capt. Conrad Nichodemus' Company, 2nd Battalion, 1776/1777 [Ref: M-237, A-1146]. See "Martin Line," q.v.

LINE, Martin (1712-1804). One of several patriots appointed by the Committee of Observation on January 19, 1777 "to form the county into companies (after the militia had marched) for the purpose of relieving the distressed inhabitants of said county and also to compel the Dunkards and Mennonists to give their assistance." [Ref: Q-43]. Took the Oath of Allegiance before the Hon. Christopher Cruse in Lower Antietam Hundred before March 2, 1778 [Ref: J-3, O-35, which listed the name as "Martin Loin"]. "Martin Line" was born in 1712, died in 1804, and was buried in a graveyard on the Edward Hutzel farm near Keedysville in Washington County, Maryland. His wife Catherine Line died in 1806. Their stones were later moved to a churchyard in Shepherdstown, West Virginia (iron fence enclosure) and the original burial ground was plowed over in 1890 by Adam Hutzel [Ref: JJ-III:92]. "Martin Lyon" died testate by December 7, 1804, leaving a wife Catharine, and among his heirs was a son Jacob Lyon [Ref: MM-13:92].

LINGENFELTER, Abraham. Took the Oath of Allegiance before the Hon. Christopher Cruse in Sharpsburg Hundred before March 2, 1778 [Ref: O-34, J-2].

LINGENFELTER, George. Enrolled in the third militia company organized for the Revolutionary War in the Elizabeth Town District of Frederick County (now the Hagerstown area of Washington County), passed by the Committee of Observation on June 5, 1776, and assigned to Capt. John Reynolds' command [Ref: Q-273]. Private, Militia, 1st Class, Capt. Joseph Chapline's Company, 2nd Battalion, 1776/1777 [Ref: M-241, which listed the name as "George Linganfelder"].

LINGO, Thomas. Private, 7th Maryland Line, mustered in June, 1778 and died in August, 1778 [Ref: D-225]. He may have been related to Samuel Lingo who died in Cumberland in 1827 [Ref: Z-18].

LINK, Andrew (died between February 15 and February 24, 1777). Appointed by the Committee of Observation to carry the Association of Freemen to male residents in Elizabeth Town Hundred on September 14, 1775 "and require their subscription to the same and make an exact account of those who sign and those that refuse with their reasons for refusing." [Ref: Q-143]. One of several patriots appointed by the Committee of Observation on December 30, 1776 "to form the county into companies (after the militia had marched) for the purpose of relieving the distressed inhabitants of said county and also to compel the Dunkards and Mennonists to give their assistance." [Ref: Q-345, which listed the name as "Andrew Lynch"]. Appointed by the Committee of Observation on January 2, 1777 as one of the persons authorized "to appraise all the arms that Col. Stull's Battalion may take with them to camp." [Ref: Q-29, Q-30]. On January 5, 1777 he was appointed to serve on the Committee of Observation for Elizabeth Town District in the room of Col. Joseph Smith [Ref: Q-31, which listed the name as "Andrew Linck"]. Served on the Committee of Observation in 1777 and reported deceased in the minutes of February 24, 1777, having attended the meeting of February 15, 1777 [Ref: Q-235, Q-237, which listed the name as "Capt. Andrew Linck" and Q-228, which listed the name as "Capt. Andrew Lynck"]. See "Simon Bowman," q.v.

LINN, George. Private, Militia, 8th Class, Capt. Michael Fackler's Company, 1776/1777 [Ref: M-245, A-1146]. Private, Militia, 4th Class, Capt. Conrad Nichodemus' Company, 2nd Battalion, 1776/1777 [Ref: M-237, A-1146, which listed the name as "George Lin"].

LINN, Peter. Private, Militia, 7th Class, Capt. Michael Fackler's Company, 1776/1777 [Ref: M-245, A-1146].

LINSLEY, John. Private, Militia, 1st Class, Capt. Henry Boteler's Company, 1776/1777 [Ref: M-237, A-1146].

LINTRIDGE, Samuel. Private who was enrolled by Capt. Aeneas Campbell and passed by Major Francis Deakins on July 18, 1776 [Ref: D-49].

LITTLE, Jessa. Took the Oath of Allegiance before the Hon. William Yates in 1778 [Ref: O-48, J-12].

LITTLE, Peter. Took the Oath of Allegiance before the Hon. Lemuel Barritt before March 16, 1778 [Ref: O-42, J-7].

LIVINGSTON, John. Took the Oath of Allegiance before the Hon. John Stull in 1778 [Ref: O-46, J-11].

LIZER, Mathias. Private, Militia, 4th Class, Capt. Daniel Clapsaddle's Company, 1st Battalion, 1776/1777 [Ref: M-236, A-1146]. Took the Oath of Allegiance before the Hon. John Stull in 1778 [Ref: O-46, J-11].

LOAR, Peter. See "Peter Lorr," q.v.

LOCKER, Barabar. See "Frederick Locker," q.v.

LOCKER, Frederick. Private, Militia, Capt. William Heyser's Company, enlisted August 5, 1776, muster roll dated October 23, 1776, in continental service [Ref: W-1190, L-79, D-264, which listed the name as "Frederick Locher"]. Private, German Regiment, Lt. Col. Ludwick Weltner's Company, discharged August 9, 1779 at Tioga, Pennsylvania [Ref: D-265, GG-98]. "Frederick Locker of Jerusalem Town" died testate by October 26, 1805, leaving a wife Barbara and sons John, Henry, and Jacob [Ref: MM-13:174, 175].

LOCKER, Henry, Jacob, and John. See "Frederick Locker," q.v.

LOCKER, Michael. Took the Oath of Allegiance before the Hon. Christopher Cruse in Lower Antietam Hundred before March 2, 1778 [Ref: J-3, O-35, which listed the name as "Michael Loker"].

LOCKER, Peter. Took the Oath of Allegiance before the Hon. Christopher Cruse in Lower Antietam Hundred before March 2, 1778 [Ref: J-3, O-35, which listed the name as "Peter Loker"].

LOCKER, Shederick. Private who was enrolled by Capt. Aeneas Campbell and passed by Major Francis Deakins on July 18, 1776 [Ref: D-49].

LOGSDON (LOGSDEN), Edward (1752-1834). Private, Maryland Militia, pensioned in Allegany County at $26.66 per year under the Act of June 7, 1832 retroactive to March 4, 1831 [Ref: R-45]. He was born on August 15, 1752 in Frederick County (where he had enlisted), applied for and received pension S8320 in Allegany County on June 12, 1833, and died on September 27, 1834 [Ref: V-II:2107].

LOGSDON (LOGSTON), Joseph. Private, Militia, Capt. Charles Coulson's Company, enrolled August 28, 1776 [Ref: M-244, A-1146].

LOGSDON (LOGSTON), Thomas. Private, Militia, Capt. Charles Coulson's Company, enrolled August 28, 1776 [Ref: M-244, A-1146, which listed the name as "Thomas Logston"]. Private, Militia, 4th Class, Capt. Charles Clinton's Company, 1776/1777 [Ref: M-245, A-1146]. Took the Oath of Allegiance before the Hon. Lemuel Barritt before March 16, 1778 [Ref: O-43, J-8, which latter source mistakenly listed the name as "Thomas Pogston"].

LOGSDON (LOGSTON), William. Private, Militia, Capt. Charles Coulson's Company, enrolled August 28, 1776 [Ref: M-244, A-1146, which listed the name as "William Logston"]. Took the Oath of Allegiance before the Hon. Andrew Bruce before March 2, 1778 [Ref: O-41, J-6, which listed the name as "William Logsdon"]. Private, Militia, 5th Class, Capt. Charles Clinton's Company, 1776/1777 [Ref: M-245, A-1146, which listed the name as "William Longston"]. "William Logsdon,

Sr." died before April, 1827 in Allegany County [Ref: Z-13, citing a chancery court case in 1827 which named many of his heirs, including several who resided outside of Maryland].

LOHR, Peter. See "Peter Lorr," q.v.

LOIN, Martin. See "Martin Line," q.v.

LONG, Jacob. Enrolled in the third militia company organized for the Revolutionary War in the Elizabeth Town District of Frederick County (now the Hagerstown area of Washington County), passed by the Committee of Observation on June 5, 1776, and assigned to Capt. John Reynolds' command [Ref: Q-273, D-50]. Private, Militia, 1st Class, Capt. Henry Boteler's Company, 1776/1777 [Ref: M-237, A-1146].

LONG, John (c1758-1823) Private, Militia, 6th Class, Capt. Martin Kershner's Company, 1776/1777 [Ref: A-1146, M-248, which listed the name as "John Long, Jr."]. Private who enlisted in the militia on August 24, 1781 for service in the Continental Army [Ref: D-388, which listed the name as "John Long"]. "John Long" died at his residence in Washington County on July 27, 1823, in his 64th year, for many years an inhabitant of this county [Ref: Z-63].

LONG, Jonathan. Private ("draught"), Maryland Line, discharged on November 10, 1781 [Ref: G-664].

LONG, Nicholas. Private, Militia, 6th Class, Capt. Martin Kershner's Company, 1776/1777 [Ref: A-1146, M-248]. Private, Militia, Capt. Martin Kershner's Company, 32nd Battalion, December 27, 1776 [Ref: K-1814, Box 3]. Took the Oath of Allegiance before the Hon. Henry Schnebley in 1778 [Ref: O-50, J-14].

LONG, Thomas. Private, Militia, 2nd Class, Capt. Michael Fackler's Company, 1776/1777 [Ref: M-245, A-1146]. Rendered patriotic service in Hagerstown by dieting soldiers of Capt. John Nelson's Company, continental service (Maryland Line), April, 1776 [Ref: Q-161]. One of several patriots appointed by the Committee of Observation on December 30, 1776 "to form the county into companies (after the militia had marched) for the purpose of relieving the distressed inhabitants of said county and also to compel the Dunkards and Mennonists to give their assistance." [Ref: Q-346]. Rendered patriotic service by providing meals and drink for the companies of Captains Clapsadle and Reynolds in January, 1777 [Ref: Q-51]. See "Thomas Lang," q.v.

LONGDON, Thomas. Private, Maryland Line, who resided in Washington County and was listed as "defective" in October, 1780 [Ref: D-414].

LONGNAKER, John. Private, Militia, 4th Class, Capt. Barnett Johnston's Company, 3rd Battalion, 1776/1777 [Ref: M-242].

LORE (LORD?), John. Private, Militia, 5th Class, Capt. Henry Boteler's Company, 1776/1777 [Ref: A-1146, M-237].

LORR, John. Enrolled in the third militia company organized for the Revolutionary War in the Elizabeth Town District of Frederick County (now the Hagerstown area of Washington County), passed by the Committee of Observation on June 5, 1776, and assigned to Capt. John Reynolds' command [Ref: Q-272].

LORR, Michael. Enrolled in the third militia company organized for the Revolutionary War in the Elizabeth Town District of Frederick County (now the Hagerstown area of Washington County), passed by the Committee of Observation on June 5, 1776, and assigned to Capt. John Reynolds' command [Ref: Q-273].

LORR, Peter (1757-   ). Enrolled in the third militia company organized for the Revolutionary War in the Elizabeth Town District of Frederick County (now the Hagerstown area of Washington County), passed by the Committee of Observation on June 5, 1776, and assigned to Capt. John Reynolds' command [Ref: Q-272]. Private who was enlisted by Lieut. Christian Orndorff and passed on July 20, 1776 in Frederick (now Washington) County [Ref: D-50, which listed the name as "Peter Loar"]. "Peter Lohr" applied for and received pension S5699 in Augusta County, Virginia on September 24, 1832, stating he was born in 1757 within seven miles of Little York, Pennsylvania. When very young he moved to Maryland where he enlisted at Hagerstown, and later moved to Virginia around 1790 [Ref: V-II:2107].

LORR, Philip. Private who was enlisted by Lieut. Christian Orndorff and passed on July 20, 1776 in Frederick (now Washington) County [Ref: D-50, which listed the name as "Philip Loar"].

LORRY, Henry. Took the Oath of Allegiance before the Hon. John Stull in 1778 [Ref: O-46, J-11].

LOUELE, Thomas. Took the Oath of Allegiance before the Hon. John Stull in 1778 [Ref: O-46, J-11].

LOUGHMAN, Gasper. Private, Militia, 4th Class, Capt. James Walling's Company, 2nd Battalion, 1776/1777 [Ref: M-239, A-1146].

LOURIE, Henry. First Corporal, Militia, Capt. James Walling's Company, 2nd Battalion, 1776/1777 [Ref: M-238, A-1146].

LOVELASS, Barton. Private who was enrolled by Capt. Aeneas Campbell and passed by Major Francis Deakins on July 18, 1776 [Ref: D-49].

LOVENS, John. Private, Militia, 5th Class, Capt. James Smith's Company, 2nd Battalion, 1776/1777 [Ref: M-240, A-1146].

LOVER, Jacob. Private, Militia, 8th Class, Capt. Barnett Johnston's Company, 3rd Battalion, 1776/1777 [Ref: M-242].

LOVETT, Barton. Private, Militia, 5th Class, Capt. Daniel Cresap's Company, 3rd Battalion, 1776/1777 [Ref: M-241].

LOVETT, Britten (Britton). Private, Militia, Capt. Charles Coulson's Company, enrolled August 28, 1776 [Ref: M-244, A-1146]. Took the Oath of Allegiance before the Hon. Lemuel Barritt before March 16, 1778 [Ref: J-7, O-42, which latter source mistakenly listed the name as "Bruttib Kivutt"].

LOVITT, Daniel. Took the Oath of Allegiance before the Hon. Lemuel Barritt before March 16, 1778 [Ref: O-42, J-7].

LOWDERMILK, John P. See "Gabriel Friend," q.v.

LOWER, George. Private, Militia, 2nd Class, Capt. James Smith's Company, 2nd Battalion, 1776/1777 [Ref: M-239, A-1146].

LOWER, Michael. Took the Oath of Allegiance before the Hon. Henry Schnebley in 1778 [Ref: O-49, J-13].

LOWMAN, John. Private, Militia, 1st Class, Capt. James Smith's Company, 2nd Battalion, 1776/1777 [Ref: M-239, A-1146].

LOWMAN, John. Private, Militia, 2nd Class, Capt. Charles Clinton's Company, 1776/1777 [Ref: M-245, A-1146].

LOWMAN, Martin. Private, Militia, 5th Class, Capt. Daniel Clapsaddle's Company, 1st Battalion, 1776/1777 [Ref: M-236, A-1146].

LOWREY, Jacob. Private, Militia, 6th Class, Capt. Michael Fackler's Company, 1776/1777 [Ref: M-245, A-1146]. Private, Militia, Capt. William Heyser's Company, muster roll dated October 23, 1776, continental service, and reportedly "deserted." [Ref: W-1190, L-79, which listed the name as "Jacob Lowre" and D-264, GG-97, which listed the name as "Jacob Fowee"]. Took the Oath of Allegiance before the Hon. Henry Schnebley in 1778 [Ref: O-51, J-15, which listed the name as "Jacob Lowry"]. "Jacob Lowry" applied for and received pension S13765 in Somerset County, Pennsylvania on September 3, 1832, stating he was born on October 12, 1758 in Lancaster County, Pennsylvania and in 1762 moved with his father [not named, but it may have been Michael] to Lebanon, Pennsylvania and lived there at enlistment. In April, 1777 he moved with his father to Hagerstown, Maryland and also enlisted there. In 1792 he moved to Cumberland, Maryland and about 1794 he moved to Somerset County, Pennsylvania. He was referred to as John Lowry, Sr., but no other family data was given [Ref: V-II:2134]. See "Michael Lowry, Jr.," q.v.

LOWREY, Michael Jr. Private, Militia, 7th Class, Capt. Michael Fackler's Company, 1776/1777 [Ref: M-245, A-1146]. He was a brother of Jacob Lowrey who also served in the war, and Michael served in the Whiskey Rebellion in 1794. He also moved along with his father [name not given, but possibly Michael Sr.] to Maryland and applied for and received pension S22373 in Somerset County, Pennsylvania on September 5, 1832. He signed as Michael Lowry, Sr., but no other family data was given [Ref: V-II:2134]. See "Jacob Lowrey," q.v.

LUCAS, Charles. Private who was enrolled by Lieut. Clement Hollyday and passed by Major Francis Deakins on July 25, 1776 [Ref: D-49].

LUCAS, William. Private who was enrolled by Capt. Aeneas Campbell and passed by Major Francis Deakins on July 18, 1776 [Ref: D-49].

LUCKETT, James. First Sergeant, Militia, Capt. Jeremiah Spires' Company, 2nd Battalion, 1776/1777 [Ref: M-239, A-1146]. Took the Oath of Allegiance before the Hon. Richard Davis in 1778 [Ref: J-3, O-36].

LUCKETT, Samuel. First Corporal, Militia, Capt. Jeremiah Spires' Company, 2nd Battalion, 1776/1777 [Ref: M-239, A-1146]. Took the Oath of Allegiance before the Hon. Richard Davis in 1778 [Ref: J-5, O-37].

LUCKETT, Thomas H. Private, Militia, 5th Class, Capt. Jeremiah Spires' Company, 2nd Battalion, 1776/1777 [Ref: M-239, A-1146, which listed the name as "Thomas Hez. Luckett"]. Took the Oath of Allegiance before the Hon. Richard Davis in 1778 [Ref: J-3, O-36, which listed the name as "Thomas Huz. Luckett"].

LUCKETT, William. Colonel who reviewed and passed troops enrolled in the Upper District of Frederick County (now Washington County) in July and August, 1776 [Ref: D-49, which listed the name as "William Lucket"].

LUDWICK, Leonard. Enrolled in the second militia company organized for the Revolutionary War in the Elizabeth Town District of Frederick County (now the Hagerstown area of Washington County) on March 9, 1776 [Ref: Q-272].

LUG, Jacob. See "Jacob Heflybower," q.v.

LUMAN, Barton. Private, Militia, 1st Class, Capt. Charles Clinton's Company, 1776/1777 [Ref: A-1146, M-245, which listed the name as "Bartin Laman"]. Took the Oath of Allegiance before the Hon. Andrew Bruce before March 2, 1778 [Ref: O-41, J-6].

LUMAN, Caleb. Took the Oath of Allegiance before the Hon. Andrew Bruce before March 2, 1778 [Ref: O-41, J-7]. Private, Militia, 5th Class, Capt. Charles Clinton's Company, 1776/1777 [Ref: M-245, A-1146, which listed the name as "Calip Luman"].

LUMAN, John. Took the Oath of Allegiance before the Hon. Andrew Bruce before March 2, 1778 [Ref: O-41, J-7].

LUMAN, Joshua. Private, Militia, 8th Class, Capt. Charles Clinton's Company, 1776/1777 [Ref: M-245, A-1146]. Took the Oath of Allegiance before the Hon. Andrew Bruce before March 2, 1778 [Ref: O-41, J-6].

LUMAN, Moses. Took the Oath of Allegiance before the Hon. Andrew Bruce before March 2, 1778 [Ref: O-41, J-7].

LUTRODE, John. Took the Oath of Allegiance before the Hon. Joseph Sprigg before April 1, 1778 [Ref: O-53, J-16].

LYNCH, Andrew. See "Andrew Link," q.v.

LYNCH, Samuel (c1745-1834). "Departed this life on the 8th instant at his residence in this place, Mr. Samuel Lynch, in the 89th year of his age, after a few days illness.. He was one of the last of the Revolutionary worthies of this [Washington] county.. His remains were interred on his farm about six miles below this place on Sunday last, attended by the Williamsport Rifle Company." [Ref: DD-91, citing *The Republican Banner*, November 15, 1834].

LYNN, Abigal and Clark. See "John Lynn," q.v.

LYNN, David Jr. (1758-1835). Ensign, Upper District, Frederick County (now Washington County), July, 1776 [Ref: D-48]. Captain, 7th Maryland Line, pensioned in Washington County at $480 per year under the Act of May 15, 1828, and died April 11, 1835 [Ref: R-53]. "Died at his residence in Cumberland after a short illness on April 11, 1835, in the 78th year of his age, David Lynn, a soldier of the Revolution." [Ref: DD-97, citing *The Republican Banner*, April 18, 1835]. The pension application of Harriet Williams, widow of Elisha Williams (W26019), stated that David Lynn, of Allegany County, served with her husband during the war [Ref: U-34:2 (1946)]. David Lynn, Jr. was born in Maryland on July 15, 1758, married Mary Galloway, and died on April 6, 1835 [Ref: Y-II:1867]. See "Thomas McQuinny," q.v.

LYNN, David Sr. (c1725/1730-1779). He was born in Ireland, married Elizabeth Copeland, rendered civil service during the Revolution, and died before December, 1779 in Maryland [Ref: Y-II:1867].

LYNN, Edmond and Elijah. See "John Lynn," q.v.

LYNN, John. Private, Militia, by January 22, 1777 when ordered by the Committee of Observation "to march with some company of militia to the reinforcement of his Excellency General Washington" or appear before the Committee and state his reason for not marching. He apparently marched since he never appeared to the contrary [Ref: Q-48, which listed the name as "John Lyn"]. Took the Oath of Allegiance before the Hon. William Yates in 1778 [Ref: O-48, J-12]. One John Lynn died before December 21, 1793 (date of balance book entry in Washington County), leaving a widow (not named, but Abigal Lynn was the administratrix) and equal shares to Edmond Lynn, Elijah Lynn, Clark Lynn, Dianah Lance, and Mary Lynn [Ref: J-33].

LYNN, Mary. See "John Lynn," q.v.

LYON, Martin. See "Martin Line," q.v.

LYON, Rebecca. See "Samuel Downey," q.v.

LYTTON, Margaret. See "Gabriel Williams," q.v.

MACAGEMER, John. Took the Oath of Allegiance before the Hon. Christopher Cruse in Sharpsburg Hundred before March 2, 1778 [Ref: J-2, O-34, which latter source listed the name as "John Macsgemer"].

MACK, Jacob. Took the Oath of Allegiance before the Hon. Christopher Cruse in Lower Antietam Hundred before March 2, 1778 [Ref: J-2, O-35].

MACKELFISH, Richard. Private, Militia, 6th Class, Capt. Jacob Sharer's Company, 1776/1777 [Ref: A-1146, M-248].

MACKELFISH, Thomas. Rendered patriotic service in Hagerstown by providing a rifle to Capt. John Nelson's Company, continental service (Maryland Line), April, 1776 [Ref: Q-162, which listed the name as "Thomas Macklefish"]. Private, Militia, 2nd Class, Capt. Jacob Sharer's Company, 1776/1777 [Ref: A-1146, M-248, which listed the name as "Thomas Meckelfish"].

MACKENZIE, Aaron. Took the Oath of Allegiance before the Hon. Andrew Bruce before March 2, 1778 [Ref: O-41, J-6].

MACKENZIE, Daniel. Took the Oath of Allegiance before the Hon. Andrew Bruce before March 2, 1778 [Ref: O-41, J-6].

MACKENZIE, Gabriel. Took the Oath of Allegiance before the Hon. Andrew Bruce before March 2, 1778 [Ref: O-41, J-6].

MACKENZIE, Samuel. Took the Oath of Allegiance before the Hon. Andrew Bruce before March 2, 1778 [Ref: O-41, J-6].

MACKEY, William. Private, Militia, 8th Class, Capt. Isaac Baker's Company, 1776/1777 [Ref: A-1146, M-247].

MACKMANS, David. Private, Militia, 1st Class, Capt. Barnett Johnston's Company, 3rd Battalion, 1776/1777 [Ref: M-242].

MACNABB, John. Took the Oath of Allegiance before the Hon. Samuel Hughes before March 1, 1778 [Ref: O-33, J-1, which latter source listed the name as "John MacNabo"].

MACONKEY, Jacob. Took the Oath of Allegiance before the Hon. Henry Schnebley in 1778 [Ref: O-49, J-13].

MACONKEY, John. Took the Oath of Allegiance before the Hon. Henry Schnebley in 1778 [Ref: O-49, J-13].

MADDEN, Mordica. First Sergeant, Militia, Capt. John Bennet's Company, 1776/1777 [Ref: M-246, A-1146]. Took the Oath of Allegiance before the Hon. Joseph Sprigg before April 1, 1778 [Ref: O-53, J-16, which listed the name as "Mordica Maddin"].

MADDORS, Thomas. Enrolled in the first militia company organized for the Revolutionary War in the Elizabeth Town District of Frederick County (now the Hagerstown area of Washington County) on January 6, 1776 [Ref: Q-270, W-1189].

MADDOX, Ignatius. Private who was enrolled by Lieut. Clement Hollyday and passed by Col. William Luckett on August 8, 1776 [Ref: D-49].

MAGAW, William. "Died at Meadville, at the house of his son Jesse Magaw, on May 1, 1829, Dr. William Magaw, formerly of Franklin County, Pennsylvania, aged about 89 years, patriot of the Revolution; served as surgeon in the Pennsylvania Line during the whole of the war." [Ref: Z-110, citing *The Torchlight and Public Advertiser* newspaper in Hagerstown, Maryland on May 28, 1829].

MAGEE, John. Private, Militia, 7th Class, Capt. John Bennet's Company, 1776/1777 [Ref: M-246, A-1146].

MAGEMER, Lodowick. Took the Oath of Allegiance before the Hon. Christopher Cruse in Lower Antietam Hundred before March 2, 1778 [Ref: J-3, O-35, which latter source listed the name as "Lodowick Mogemer"].

MAGER, Charles. Enrolled in the first militia company organized for the Revolutionary War in the Elizabeth Town District of Frederick County (now the Hagerstown area of Washington County) on January 6, 1776 [Ref: Q-270, W-1190].

MAGRUDER, Nathaniel Beale (1758-1821). Private, Maryland Line, who applied for and received pension S34973 in Allegany County on April 24, 1818, age 60. In 1820 he had a daughter aged 24 and sons aged 20, 15, and 13 living with him (no names given). Nathaniel died on November 25, 1821 [Ref: V-II:2166].

MAHAMAN, John. Private, Militia, 7th Class, Capt. Joseph Chapline's Company, 2nd Battalion, 1776/1777 [Ref: M-242].

MAHNIGER, Henry. Took the Oath of Allegiance before the Hon. Henry Schnebley in 1778 [Ref: O-51, J-14].

MAHONEY, Henry. Private, Militia, 1st Class, Capt. Jeremiah Spires' Company, 2nd Battalion, 1776/1777 [Ref: M-239, A-1146]. Took the Oath of Allegiance before the Hon. Richard Davis in 1778 [Ref: J-4, O-36].

MAHONEY, Thomas. Took the Oath of Allegiance before the Hon. Joseph Chapline before April 17, 1779 [Ref: J-5, O-39].

MAHORNEY, Henry. Second Corporal, Militia, Capt. Peter Swingle's (Swingley's) Company, 2nd Battalion, 1776/1777 [Ref: M-248, A-1146].

MAICHAL, John. Took the Oath of Allegiance before the Hon. Lemuel Barritt before March 16, 1778 [Ref: O-42, J-7].
MAKILLIP, Henry. See "Henry McKillip," q.v.
MALCOMB, James. Private, Militia, 7th Class, Capt. Barnett Johnston's Company, 3rd Battalion, 1776/1777 [Ref: M-242]. Took the Oath of Allegiance before the Hon. John Barnes before February 28, 1778 [Ref: O-45, which listed the name as "James Malcome" and J-10, which listed the name as "James Maloome"].
MALOTT, Daniel. See "Thomas McQuinny," q.v.
MALLOTT, John. See "John Melott," q.v.
MALOOME, James. See "James Malcome," q.v.
MALOTT, Thomas. See "Thomas Melott," q.v.
MANCE, John. Private, Militia, 3rd Class, Capt. Jeremiah Spires' Company, 2nd Battalion, 1776/1777 [Ref: M-239, A-1146].
MANDEL, Christian. Took the Oath of Allegiance before the Hon. Joseph Sprigg before April 1, 1778 [Ref: O-53, J-16].
MANDEY, Balthosar. Took the Oath of Allegiance before the Hon. Henry Schnebley in 1778 [Ref: O-50, J-13].
MANK, Davalt. See "Davolt Mong," q.v.
MARDIS, Nancy. See "Robert Marshall," q.v.
MARIATY, Jacob. Private, Militia, 1st Class, Capt. Henry Boteler's Company, 1776/1777 [Ref: M-237, A-1146].
MARKER, Michael. Private, Militia, 7th Class, Capt. Joseph Chapline's Company, 2nd Battalion, 1776/1777 [Ref: M-242]. Took the Oath of Allegiance before the Hon. Christopher Cruse in Sharpsburg Hundred before March 2, 1778 [Ref: O-34, J-2].
MARKER, William. Enrolled in the first militia company organized for the Revolutionary War in the Elizabeth Town District of Frederick County (now the Hagerstown area of Washington County) on January 6, 1776 [Ref: Q-270, W-1190].
MARKWELL, George. Took the Oath of Allegiance before the Hon. Lemuel Barritt before March 16, 1778 [Ref: O-42, J-8].
MARKWELL, William. Private, Militia, 8th Class, Capt. Daniel Cresap's Company, 3rd Battalion, 1776/1777 [Ref: M-241].
MARSHALL, John. Private, Militia, 2nd Class, Capt. Daniel Cresap's Company, 3rd Battalion, 1776/1777 [Ref: M-241]. On January 13, 1777 he was brought before the Committee of Observation and charged with "drinking the King's health, success to Lord and General Howe, and the British Army, saying that the King would have the country before the middle of June next, that if he should be put in confinement at Elizabeth Town, he valued it not, for Lord Howe would soon release

him." John Marshall acknowledged the charge and was ordered "kept in safe custody until he could give sufficient security that he shall neither say nor do anything inimical to the United States of America." The next day he joined the continental service and was released from confinement [Ref: Q-37, Q-39]. See "Richard Acton," q.v.

MARSHALL, Robert (1763-1837). Private, Maryland, who applied for pension in Campbell County, Kentucky on February 24, 1834, stating he was born on March 11, 1763, enlisted in the Revolutionary War about 7 miles from Hagerstown, Maryland, and also served under General Wayne in the Indian Wars. He married Nancy Mardis on October 24, 1797 and moved to Kentucky. His widow applied for and received pension W2141 in Kenton County (formerly part of Campbell County), Kentucky on March 18, 1850, age 69, stating Robert had died on July 1, 1837. She also received bounty land #38531-160-55 [Ref: V-II:2198].

MARSNER, Joseph. Took the Oath of Allegiance before the Hon. Andrew Bruce before March 2, 1778 [Ref: O-41, J-7].

MARTIN, Christian and David. See "Jacob Martin," q.v.

MARTIN, Elizabeth and Henry. See "Jacob Martin," q.v.

MARTIN, Jacob (1759-   ). Private, Militia, 6th Class, Capt. James Walling's Company, 2nd Battalion, 1776/1777 [Ref: N-37, A-1146, M-239, which latter source listed the name as "Jacob Martain"]. Rendered patriotic service by supplying wheat for the use of the military on January 31, 1780 [Ref: W-1190, HH-73]. One Jacob Martin died testate before October 24, 1789 (date of balance book entry in Washington County), leaving a widow (no name given in this account) and equal shares to Henry Martin, Jacob Martin, Christian Martin, John Martin, David Martin, Barbara Rodes, Mary Bear, and Elizabeth Martin [Ref: J-28].

MARTIN, James. Private who was enrolled by Capt. Henry Hardman and passed on July 19, 1776 in Frederick (now Washington) County [Ref: D-51]. Took the Oath of Allegiance before the Hon. Joseph Chapline before April 17, 1779 [Ref: J-5, O-39].

MARTIN, John. Private who was enrolled by Capt. Aeneas Campbell and passed by Major Francis Deakins on July 18, 1776 [Ref: D-49]. See "Jacob Martin," q.v.

MARTIN, Joseph. Private, Militia, 5th Class, Capt. Barnett Johnston's Company, 3rd Battalion, 1776/1777 [Ref: M-242]. Took the Oath of Allegiance before the Hon. William Yates in 1778 [Ref: O-48, J-12]. Private who enlisted in the militia on August 20, 1781 for service in the Continental Army [Ref: D-388]. Substitute, Maryland Line, discharged on October 26, 1781 upon the recommendation of Dr. James Murray [Ref: G-653].

MARTIN, Nehemiah. Private, Militia, 6th Class, Capt. Daniel Cresap's Company, 3rd Battalion, 1776/1777 [Ref: M-241]. Took the Oath of Allegiance before the Hon. Lemuel Barritt before March 16, 1778 [Ref: O-42, J-7].

MARTIN, Nicholas. Private, Militia, 4th Class, Capt. Martin Kershner's Company, 1776/1777 [Ref: A-1146, M-247]. Rendered patriotic service by supplying wheat for the use of the military on March 20, 1780 [Ref: W-1190, HH-72, which latter source listed the name as "Nicolaus Martin"]. See "Joseph Rentch," q.v.

MARTIN, Robert. Private, Militia, 2nd Class, Capt. Jacob Sharer's Company, 1776/1777 [Ref: A-1146, M-248]. Took the Oath of Allegiance before the Hon. John Stull in 1778 [Ref: O-46, J-11, which listed the name as "Robert Martain"].

MARTIN, William. Private, Militia, 6th Class, Capt. Barnett Johnston's Company, 3rd Battalion, 1776/1777 [Ref: M-242]. Took the Oath of Allegiance before the Hon. William Yates in 1778 [Ref: O-48, J-12].

MARTIN, William Jr. Took the Oath of Allegiance before the Hon. William Yates in 1778 [Ref: O-48, J-12, which latter source listed the name without the "Jr."]. Private, Militia, 5th Class, Capt. Barnett Johnston's Company, 3rd Battalion, 1776/1777 [Ref: M-242, which listed the name without the "Jr."].

MASON, Christiana. See "Henry Franks," q.v.

MASSAH, William. On January 14, 1777 David Hellen was brought before the Committee of Observation and "accused with speaking and acting inimical to the United States of America." The Committee ordered that he "provide himself with necessaries in order to march with Capt. Baker's Company, and pay expenses of guard." However, his apprentice, William Massah, appeared and voluntarily (with the consent of his master) "enlisted in the continental service, which exempted David Hellen from marching with the militia, paying expence of guard, and behaving as a friend to the United States." [Ref: Q-39].

MASSEY, Jesse. Soldier who resided in Washington County and was granted a pension certificate in August, 1820, according to an Act of Congress of March 18, 1818, since he had proven that he was "in the enjoyment of a certain degree of poverty" as required by the Act as amended on May 1, 1820 [Ref: W-1190]. Private, Delaware Line, pensioned at $96 per year effective March 26, 1819 [Ref: R-42].

MATLEY, Henry. Private, Militia, 4th Class, Capt. Charles Clinton's Company, 1776/1777 [Ref: M-245, A-1146]. Private, Militia, Capt.

Charles Coulson's Company, enrolled August 28, 1776 [Ref: M-244, A-1146].

MATSON, Elizabeth. See "John Byrnes," q.v.

MATTHEWS, Daniel. Private who was enrolled by Capt. Henry Hardman and passed on July 19, 1776 in Frederick (now Washington) County [Ref: D-51].

MATTHEWS, William. Private, Militia, 8th Class, Capt. Barnett Johnston's Company, 3rd Battalion, 1776/1777 [Ref: M-242, which listed the name as "William Mathews"]. Private, Militia, on January 22, 1777 when ordered by the Committee of Observation "to march with some company of militia to the reinforcement of his Excellency General Washington" or appear before the Committee and state his reason for not marching. He apparently marched since he never appeared to the contrary [Ref: Q-48]. Took the Oath of Allegiance before the Hon. John Barnes before February 28, 1778 [Ref: O-45, J-10].

MATTINGLY, Barnet. Took the Oath of Allegiance before the Hon. Andrew Bruce before March 2, 1778 [Ref: O-41, J-6].

MATTINGLY, Henry. Took the Oath of Allegiance before the Hon. Andrew Bruce before March 2, 1778 [Ref: O-41, J-7].

MATTINGLY, Richard. Private, Militia, 1st Class, Capt. James Prather's Company, 3rd Battalion, 1776/1777 [Ref: M-242, which listed the name as "Richard Matinlee"]. Took the Oath of Allegiance before the Hon. Andrew Bruce before March 2, 1778 [Ref: O-41, J-6].

MAXWELL, James. Private, Militia, 7th Class, Capt. Isaac Baker's Company, 1776/1777 [Ref: A-1146, M-247].

MAY, George. Private, Militia, 3rd Class, Capt. Conrad Hogmire's Company, 1776/1777 [Ref: M-244, A-1146]. Private, Militia, Capt. John Kershner's Company, on duty guarding prisoners of war at Fort Frederick, 1778, and who reportedly "deserted" on June 2, 1778 [Ref: D-328].

MAYER, Felix. See "Felix Meyer," q.v.

MAYER (MOYER), John (1759-   ). Private, Maryland Line, who applied for pension (R7476) in Washington County on April 4, 1821, age 62 [Ref: V-II:2234]. See "Jonathan Moyer," q.v.

MAYES, Andrew. Took the Oath of Allegiance before the Hon. John Barnes before February 28, 1778 [Ref: O-45, J-10, which latter source listed as "Andrew Wayes"].

MAYHEW (MAYHUGH), Jonathan (c1756-c1834). Soldier who resided in Washington County and was granted a pension certificate in August, 1820, according to an Act of Congress of March 18, 1818, since he had proven that he was "in the enjoyment of a certain degree of poverty" as required by the Act as amended on May 1, 1820 [Ref: W-1190]. Private, Maryland Line, who applied for and received pension S36054 in Washington County on April 9, 1818, aged about 62, stating he lived in Prince George's County at the time of his enlistment. In 1820 he had a wife aged 59 (no name given) and a daughter Sara Matilda (aged 16). On July 3, 1828 he moved to Washington, D.C. [Ref: V-II:2235]. On February 19, 1819 the Treasurer of the Western Shore of Maryland was directed to pay to Jonathan Mayhew, late a revolutionary soldier, during life, half pay of a private. On March 4, 1834 the Treasurer of the Western Shore of Maryland was directed to pay to Eleanor L. Mayhugh, widow of Jonathan Mayhugh, of Washington County, during life, quarterly, half pay of a private, for the services rendered by her husband during the Revolutionary War. On January 24, 1838 the Treasurer of the Western Shore of Maryland was directed to pay to Adam Houk, son-in-law of the late Eleanor L. Mayhugh, $8.00 for two months and twelve days pension due the said Eleanor L. Mayhugh on December 12, 1837, the day of her death [Ref: AA-373, AA-374].

MAYHUGH, Eleanor L. See "Jonathan Mayhew," q.v.

MAZE, James. Private, Militia, 1st Class, Capt. Isaac Baker's Company, 1776/1777 [Ref: A-1146, M-247].

McALLISTER, Archibald. Enrolled in the second militia company organized for the Revolutionary War in the Elizabeth Town District of Frederick County (now the Hagerstown area of Washington County) on March 9, 1776 [Ref: Q-271].

McALLISTER, John. Enrolled in the second militia company organized for the Revolutionary War in the Elizabeth Town District of Frederick County (now the Hagerstown area of Washington County) on March 9, 1776 [Ref: Q-271].

McCACKIN, Thomas. See "Thomas McMackin," q.v.

McCACKLIN, Bonsby. See "Banaby McMackin," q.v.

McCALLAM, Thomas. See "Thomas McCollam," q.v.

McCARDELL, Margaret. See "Patrick McCardle," q.v.

McCARDLE (MACKARDELL), Hugh. Private, Militia, 3rd Class, Capt. Michael Fackler's Company, 1776/1777 [Ref: M-245, A-1146].

McCARDLE (McCARDELL), Patrick. One of several patriots appointed by the Committee of Observation on December 30, 1776 "to form the county into companies (after the militia had marched) for the purpose of relieving the distressed inhabitants of said county and also to compel the Dunkards and Mennonists to give their assistance." [Ref: Q-346, which listed the name as "Patrick McCardal"]. Took the Oath of Allegiance before the Hon. Samuel Hughes before March 1, 1778 [Ref:

O-33, J-1, which listed the name as "Patrick McAdele"]. "Margaret M'Cardell, widow of Patrick M'Cardell," formerly of Elizabeth Town, died on the Saturday before July 25, 1804, in her 86th year, and was interred in the Catholic burying ground [Ref: LL-2:97].

McCAULEY, Charles and Hanna. See "Charles McColough," q.v.

McCLAIN, James. Took the Oath of Allegiance before the Hon. John Barnes before February 28, 1778 [Ref: O-44, J-9]. Private who was recruited and passed by County Lieutenant Thomas Sprigg on April 22, 1780 [Ref: D-336].

McCLANAHAN, Alexander. Third Corporal, Militia, Capt. Martin Kershner's Company, 1776/1777 [Ref: M-247, A-1146].

McCLANE, George. Private, Militia, 7th Class, Capt. Martin Kershner's Company, 1776/1777 [Ref: A-1146, M-248].

McCLANE, James. Private, Militia, 7th Class, Capt. John Bennet's Company, 1776/1777 [Ref: M-246, A-1146]. Took the Oath of Allegiance before the Hon. Richard Davis in 1778 [Ref: J-3, O-36, which listed the name as "James McLain"].

McCLANE, John. Private, Militia, 1st Class, Capt. Jeremiah Spires' Company, 2nd Battalion, 1776/1777 [Ref: M-239, A-1146]. Took the Oath of Allegiance before the Hon. Richard Davis in 1778 [Ref: J-3, O-36, which listed the name as "John McLain"].

McCLANE, Samuel. Private who was enlisted by Ensign Nathan Williams and passed on July 25, 1776 in Frederick (now Washington) County [Ref: D-51].

McCLARY (MALARRY), Patrick. Private, Militia, 1st Class, Capt. Isaac Baker's Company, 1776/1777 [Ref: A-1146, M-247].

McCLELLAN, Robert. Took the Oath of Allegiance before the Hon. Samuel Hughes before March 1, 1778 [Ref: O-33, J-1].

McCLOSKEY, Stephen. One of several patriots appointed by the Committee of Observation on December 30, 1776 "to form the county into companies (after the militia had marched) for the purpose of relieving the distressed inhabitants of said county and also to compel the Dunkards and Mennonists to give their assistance." [Ref: Q-346]. Rendered patriotic service in Hagerstown by providing shoes to Capt. John Nelson's Company, continental service (Maryland Line), April, 1776 [Ref: Q-161]. Took the Oath of Allegiance before the Hon. Samuel Hughes before March 1, 1778 [Ref: O-33, J-1, which listed the name as "Stephen McClosker"].

McCOLL, Thomas. Enrolled in the second militia company organized for the Revolutionary War in the Elizabeth Town District of Frederick

County (now the Hagerstown area of Washington County) on March 9, 1776 [Ref: Q-271].

McCOLOUGH, Charles. Private, Militia, by January 22, 1777 when ordered by the Committee of Observation "to march with some company of militia to the reinforcement of his Excellency General Washington or appear before the Committee and state his reason for not marching." He apparently marched since he never appeared before the Committee [Ref: Q-48, which listed the name as "Chars. McCullough"]. It is interesting to note that a "Charles McCauley" was born on May 15, 1754, died on April 10, 1817, and is buried beside his wife Hanna H. McCauley (1757-1835) and son Charles McCauley, Jr. (1799-1830) in a graveyard on the E. W. Ditto, Jr. farm on Mt. Atna Road, four miles east of Hagerstown, Maryland [Ref: JJ-IV:97]. Obviously, Charles McColough and Charles McCauley may well be two different people, so additional research will be necessary before drawing conclusions.

McCOLOUGH, Samuel. Took the Oath of Allegiance before the Hon. Christopher Cruse in Sharpsburg Hundred before March 2, 1778 [Ref: O-34, J-2].

McCOLOUGH, William. Private, German Regiment, continental service, 1776, and discharged on July 24, 1779 [Ref: D-234]. Took the Oath of Allegiance before the Hon. John Stull in 1778 [Ref: O-47, J-11].

McCOLLUM, Thomas. See "Thomas McCullam," q.v.

McCONNELL, Amanda and James. See "Michael Smith," q.v.

McCORGAN, David. First Sergeant, Militia, Capt. William Heyser's Company, muster roll dated October 23, 1776, in continental service [Ref: D-263, W-1190, L-79, which latter source listed the name as "David Morgan"].

McCORMICK, James. Rendered patriotic service by providing necessaries to Capt. John Reynolds' Company in the Flying Camp and belonging to the Maryland Service in July, 1776, as recorded by the Committee of Observation at Sharpsburg on August 6, 1776 [Ref: Q-333].

McCORMICK, John (1750-c1840). Private, Maryland and Pennsylvania Lines, who applied for pension (R6651) in Richland County, Ohio on February 20, 1834, stating he was born on September 22, 1750 in Kent County, Maryland, lived in Washington County, Maryland when he first enlisted, and then enlisted again in what is now Franklin County, Pennsylvania [Ref: V-II:2255].

McCOY, Archabald. Took the Oath of Allegiance before the Hon. John Stull in 1778 [Ref: O-47, J-11]. Private, Militia, 4th Class, Capt. James Walling's Company, 2nd Battalion, 1776/1777 [Ref: M-239, A-1146].

McCOY, Daniel. Private, Militia, 8th Class, Capt. James Walling's Company, 2nd Battalion, 1776/1777 [Ref: M-239, A-1146]. Took the Oath of Allegiance before September 1, 1780 [Ref: X-116].

McCOY, Hugh. Enrolled in the second militia company organized for the Revolutionary War in the Elizabeth Town District of Frederick County (now the Hagerstown area of Washington County) on March 9, 1776 [Ref: Q-272].

McCOY, James. Private, Militia, 5th Class, Capt. James Walling's Company, 2nd Battalion, 1776/1777 [Ref: M-239, A-1146].

McCOY, James Sr. Took the Oath of Allegiance before the Hon. Joseph Chapline before April 17, 1779 [Ref: J-5, O-39].

McCOY, John. Took the Oath of Allegiance before the Hon. Joseph Chapline before April 17, 1779 [Ref: J-5, O-39].

McCOY, John (of Archibald). Private, Militia, 8th Class, Capt. James Walling's Company, 2nd Battalion, 1776/1777 [Ref: M-239, A-1146].

McCOY, John (of Daniel). Private, Militia, 2nd Class, Capt. James Walling's Company, 2nd Battalion, 1776/1777 [Ref: M-238, A-1146].

McCOY, Joseph. Private, Militia, 1st Class, Capt. James Walling's Company, 2nd Battalion, 1776/1777 [Ref: M-238, A-1146]. Took the Oath of Allegiance before September 1, 1780 [Ref: X-116].

McCOY, Perry. First Sergeant, Militia, Capt. James Walling's Company, 2nd Battalion, 1776/1777 [Ref: M-238, A-1146]. First Lieutenant, Capt. Martin Billmyer's Company, November 21, 1780 [Ref: G-220].

McCULLAM, Alexander. Took the Oath of Allegiance before the Hon. John Barnes before February 28, 1778 [Ref: O-44, J-9].

McCULLAM, Archibald. Rendered patriotic service in Hagerstown by providing a rifle to Capt. John Nelson's Company, continental service (Maryland Line), April, 1776 [Ref: Q-162].

McCULLAM, Thomas. Rendered patriotic service in Hagerstown by providing a rifle to Capt. John Nelson's Company, continental service (Maryland Line), April, 1776 [Ref: Q-162]. Private, Militia, 3rd Class, Capt. John Bennet's Company, 1776/1777 [Ref: M-246, A-1146, which listed the name as "Thomas McCollum"]. Took the Oath of Allegiance before the Hon. John Barnes before February 28, 1778 [Ref: O-44, which listed the name as "Thomas McCollam" and J-9, which listed the name as "Thomas McCallam"]. Private, Militia, Capt. John Kershner's Company, on duty guarding prisoners of war at Fort Frederick on June 27, 1778 [Ref: D-328, which listed the name as "Thomas McCullim"].

McDANIEL, Thomas. Private who was recruited and passed by County Lieutenant Thomas Sprigg on April 22, 1780 [Ref: D-336].

McDAVITT, Susan. See "John Jeremiah Jacob," q.v.

McDEAVER, Angus. See "Barnabas Coplar," q.v.

McDONALD, Allen. Private, Militia, 5th Class, Capt. Conrad Hogmire's Company, 1776/1777 [Ref: M-244, A-1146, which listed the name as "Allen McDonneld"].

McDONALD, George. Private, Militia, by January 22, 1777 when ordered by the Committee of Observation "to march with some company of militia to the reinforcement of his Excellency General Washington" or appear before the Committee and state his reason for not marching. He apparently marched since he never appeared to the contrary [Ref: Q-48, which listed the name as "Geo. McDonnald"].

McDONALD, William (c1759-1821). Private who was recruited and passed by County Lieutenant Thomas Sprigg on April 22, 1780 [Ref: D-336]. Private, Maryland Line, pensioned under the Act of March 18, 1818 at $96 per year effective April 4, 1818 and died March 9, 1821 [Ref: R-42].

McFADDEN, Isaac. Private, Select Militia, Capt. Adam Ott's Company, 1781 [Ref: M-238, A-1146, which listed the name as "Isaac McFaddin"].

McFADDEN, James. See "John McFadden," q.v.

McFADDEN, John (1760-   ). Private, Maryland Line, who applied for and received pension S7193 in Augusta County, Virginia on August 21, 1832, stating he was born on September 15, 1760 about 9 miles from Hagerstown, Maryland and lived there at the time of his enlistment. In 1784 he moved to 16 miles southwest of Staunton, Virginia and some of his family (names not given) moved on to Kentucky. In 1832 James McFadden stated he was six years younger than his brother John [Ref: V-II:2272].

McFALL, John. First Corporal, Militia, Capt. Isaac Baker's Company, 1776/1777 [Ref: M-247, A-1146]. Took the Oath of Allegiance before the Hon. John Barnes before February 28, 1778 [Ref: O-44, J-9].

McFALL, Neal. Took the Oath of Allegiance before the Hon. John Barnes before February 28, 1778 [Ref: O-44, J-9].

McFARON, William. Private who was recruited and passed by County Lieutenant Thomas Sprigg on April 22, 1780 [Ref: D-336].

McFEELY, Edward. Took the Oath of Allegiance before the Hon. Joseph Sprigg before April 1, 1778 [Ref: O-53, J-16].

McGATHY, William. Enrolled in the first militia company organized for the Revolutionary War in the Elizabeth Town District of Frederick County (now the Hagerstown area of Washington County) on January 6, 1776 [Ref: Q-270, W-1189, which latter source listed the name as "William M. Gathy"].

McGILL, Charles. Private, Militia, 2nd Class, Capt. James Walling's Company, 2nd Battalion, 1776/1777 [Ref: M-238, A-1146].

McGLAUGHLIN, John. See "John McLaughlin," q.v.

McGLOCKLAN, John. See "Abraham Gable," q.v.

McGLOCKLIN, Charles. See "Charles McLaughlin," q.v.

McGUYER, Thomas. Private who was enrolled by Capt. Henry Hardman and passed on July 19, 1776 in Frederick (now Washington) County [Ref: D-51].

McHEIL, John. See "John McNeil," q.v.

McILLHENNY, Mr. See "Thomas Hart," q.v.

McKAY, Rebecca. See "Joseph Lemaster," q.v.

McKEAN, Governor. See "Frederick Rohrer," q.v.

McKEE, John. See "John McKey," q.v.

McKENNY, John. Private who was enlisted by Ensign Nathan Williams and passed on July 25, 1776 in Frederick (now Washington) County [Ref: D-51].

McKENSLEY, Charles. Private who was recruited and passed by County Lieutenant Thomas Sprigg on April 22, 1780 [Ref: D-336].

McKERN, Michael. On January 6, 1777 the Committee of Observation for Elizabeth Town District (now the Hagerstown area of Washington County) ordered that he "be kept under guard until the next company of militia may march, when he is to be delivered to the captain and marched with his company to camp." [Ref: Q-32].

McKEY, James Jr. Enrolled in the first militia company organized for the Revolutionary War in the Elizabeth Town District of Frederick County (now the Hagerstown area of Washington County) on January 6, 1776 [Ref: Q-270, W-1189].

McKEY, John. Enrolled in the first militia company organized for the Revolutionary War in the Elizabeth Town District of Frederick County (now the Hagerstown area of Washington County) on January 6, 1776 [Ref: Q-270, W-1190]. On January 27, 1777 the Committee of Observation acknowledged that "John McKee had turned out voluntarily in Capt. James Smith's Company on Battalion Day prior to any engagement made with Ignatius Simms relative to marching in his room, [and] therefore ordered that said McKee march on his own behalf and not in lieu of said Simms." [Ref: Q-53].

McKILLIP, Henry. Private, Militia, Capt. Martin Kershner's Company, 32nd Battalion, December 27, 1776 [Ref: K-1814, Box 3]. Took the Oath of Allegiance before the Hon. Henry Schnebley in 1778 [Ref: O-49, J-13, which listed the name as "Henry Makillip"].

McKINLEY, Archibald. Private, Militia, 6th Class, Capt. Jeremiah Spires' Company, 2nd Battalion, 1776/1777 [Ref: M-239, A-1146]. Took the

Oath of Allegiance before the Hon. Richard Davis in 1778 [Ref: J-5, O-37].

McKINLEY, Patrick. Took the Oath of Allegiance before the Hon. Richard Davis in 1778 [Ref: J-4, O-37, which latter source listed the name as "Patrick MacKinly"].

McKINNAN, Michael. Took the Oath of Allegiance before the Hon. John Barnes before February 28, 1778 [Ref: O-44, J-9].

McKINSEY, Aaron. Private, Militia, 7th Class, Capt. Charles Clinton's Company, 1776/1777 [Ref: M-245, A-1146].

McKINSEY, Daniel. Private, Militia, 7th Class, Capt. Charles Clinton's Company, 1776/1777 [Ref: M-245, A-1146].

McKINSEY, Gabriel. Private, Militia, 4th Class, Capt. Charles Clinton's Company, 1776/1777 [Ref: M-245, A-1146].

McKINSEY, Joshua. Drummer, German Regiment, Lt. Col. Ludwick Weltner's Company, continental service, 1779 [Ref: D-264].

McKINSEY, Moses. Drummer, German Regiment, Lt. Col. Ludwick Weltner's Company, continental service, 1779 [Ref: D-264]. In December, 1815 the Treasurer of the Western Shore of Maryland was directed to pay to Moses McKinsey, of Allegany County, a sum of money annually during life, quarterly, equal to half pay of a drummer in the Revolutionary War. On March 9, 1827 the Treasurer of the Western Shore of Maryland was directed to pay to Sarah McKinsey, of Allegany County, during life, half yearly, half pay of a private, for her husband Moses McKinsey's services during the war [Ref: AA-370]. See "James Hughes," q.v.

McKINSEY, Samuel. Private, Militia, 2nd Class, Capt. Charles Clinton's Company, 1776/1777 [Ref: M-245, A-1146].

McKINSEY, Sarah. See "Moses McKinsey," q.v.

McKISSICK, James (c1761-1826). Soldier who resided in Washington County and was granted a pension certificate in August, 1820, according to an Act of Congress of March 18, 1818, since he had proven that he was "in the enjoyment of a certain degree of poverty" as required by the Act as amended on May 1, 1820 [Ref: W-1190, which listed the name as "James McIssick"]. Private, Pennsylvania Line, pensioned at $96 per year effective October 31, 1818 and died December 23, 1826 [Ref: R-42, AA-370]. "James M'Kissick, an old inhabitant, died at his residence near Smithsburg on Friday, 22nd ult. [December 22, 1826] in his 65th year." [Ref: Z-87, citing *The Torchlight and Public Advertiser* newspaper in Hagerstown on January 11, 1827].

McKOY, James Jr. Private, Militia, 5th Class, Capt. Joseph Chapline's Company, 2nd Battalion, 1776/1777 [Ref: M-241].

McKOY, John. Private, Militia, 8th Class, Capt. Joseph Chapline's Company, 2nd Battalion, 1776/1777 [Ref: M-242].

McKOY, Thomas. Private who was enlisted by Capt. John Reynolds and passed on July 18, 1776 in Frederick (now Washington) County [Ref: D-50, which listed the name as "Thomas McKoy, D.S.T."]. Private, Militia, 1st Class, Capt. Joseph Chapline's Company, 2nd Battalion, 1776/1777 [Ref: M-241]. Took the Oath of Allegiance before the Hon. Christopher Cruse in Sharpsburg Hundred before March 2, 1778 [Ref: O-34, J-2].

McLAUGHLIN, Charles. Enrolled in the second militia company organized for the Revolutionary War in the Elizabeth Town District of Frederick County (now the Hagerstown area of Washington County) on March 9, 1776 [Ref: Q-271]. Took the Oath of Allegiance before the Hon. Richard Davis in 1778 [Ref: J-3, O-36, which listed the name as "Charles McGlocklin"].

McLAUGHLIN, Hugh. Private, Militia, 8th Class, Capt. Samuel Hughes' Company, 2nd Battalion, 1776/1777 [Ref: M-238, A-1146, which listed the name as "Hugh McGlocklan"]. Private who enlisted in the militia on August 25, 1781 for service in the Continental Army [Ref: D-410, D-388, which listed the name as "Hugh McGlaughlan"]. Substitute, Maryland Line, discharged on November 12, 1781 [Ref: G-666, which listed the name as "Hugh McLaughlin"].

McLAUGHLIN, James. Appointed by the Committee of Observation on July 7, 1776 "to take the number of inhabitants within Conococheague Hundred, both whites and blacks, distinguishing respectively the age and sex of each, to be transmitted to the Council of Safety immediately." [Ref: Q-331]. Private, Militia, 4th Class, Capt. Isaac Baker's Company, 1776/1777 [Ref: A-1146, M-247, which listed the name as "James McGlanglen"]. Took the Oath of Allegiance before the Hon. John Cellars in January, 1778 [Ref: K-1814, O-40, J-6].

McLAUGHLIN, John. First Lieutenant, Militia, Capt. John Cellars' Company, 1776/1777 [Ref: A-1146, M-246, which listed the name as "John McLaughlin" and Q-153, which listed the name as "Leutennt. McGlaughlin" on February 19, 1776]. First Lieutenant, Militia, Capt. John Kershner's Company, on duty guarding prisoners of war at Fort Frederick, June 27, 1778 [Ref: D-328]. Took the Oath of Allegiance before the Hon. John Cellars in January, 1778 [Ref: K-1814, O-40, J-6]. "John M'Laughlin," husband and father, died September 13, 1804, at an advanced age, after a short illness, and was interred in the Protestant Episcopal burial ground in Hagerstown [Ref: LL-2:99]. See "Abraham Gable," q.v.

McLONEY, Alexander. Took the Oath of Allegiance before the Hon. Andrew Bruce before March 2, 1778 [Ref: O-41, J-7].

McMACKIN, Barnaby. Private, Militia, by January 22, 1777 when ordered by the Committee of Observation "to march with some company of militia to the reinforcement of his Excellency General Washington" or appear before the Committee and state his reason for not marching. He apparently marched since he never appeared to the contrary [Ref: Q-48, which listed the name as "Barnabas McMachan"]. Took the Oath of Allegiance before the Hon. John Barnes before February 28, 1778 [Ref: O-45, which listed the name as "Banaby McMackin" and J-9, which listed the name as "Bonsby McCacklin"].

McMACKIN, Thomas. Private, Militia, 6th Class, Capt. John Bennet's Company, 1776/1777 [Ref: M-246, A-1146, which listed the name as "Thomas McMacken"]. Took the Oath of Allegiance before the Hon. John Barnes before February 28, 1778 [Ref: O-44, J-9, which latter source listed the name as "Thomas McCackin"].

McMAHON, Elizabeth. See "Moses Rawlings," q.v.

McMAHON, Peter (1754-c1844). Soldier and pensioner of the Revolution who resided in the 2nd Division of Allegany County in 1840, aged 86 [Ref: EE-28:4 (p. 444), containing an article by Elba Anthony Dardeau, Jr.].

McNAME, Mary. See "Jacob Gardinour," q.v.

McNAMEE, Adam and Alice. See "Hugh McNamee," q.v.

NcNAMEE, George, Gettee, and Hannah. See "Hugh McNamee," q.v.

McNAMEE, Hugh. Private, Militia, 3rd Class, Capt. Henry Boteler's Company, 1776/1777 [Ref: M-237, A-1146, which listed the name as "Hugh McMeme"]. "Hugh McNamee" died before June 22, 1805 (date of balance book entry in Washington County), leaving a widow (no name given in this account) and equal shares to Job, Thomas, Hannah, Adam, George, Gettee, Moses and Alice McNamee, and Mary Baker [Ref: J-39]. "Mary Macnamee, wife of Moses Macnamee" died in Cumberland at the end of July, 1828, in her 49th year [Ref: Z-20].

McNAMEE, Job. See "Hugh McNamee," q.v.

McNAMEE, Mary and Moses. See "Hugh McNamee," q.v.

McNAMEE, Robert. Enrolled in the first militia company organized for the Revolutionary War in the Elizabeth Town District of Frederick County (now the Hagerstown area of Washington County) on January 6, 1776 [Ref: Q-271, W-1190].

McNAMEE, Thomas. See "Hugh McNamee," q.v.

McNIEL, John. Private who enlisted in the militia on September 5, 1781 for service in the Continental Army [Ref: D-388]. Took the Oath of

Allegiance before the Hon. William Yates in 1778 [Ref: O-48, J-12, which listed the name as "John McHeil"].

McNUTT, Alexander Jr. Enrolled in the first militia company organized for the Revolutionary War in the Elizabeth Town District of Frederick County (now the Hagerstown area of Washington County) on January 6, 1776 [Ref: Q-271, W-1190]. Private, Militia, 5th Class, Capt. Joseph Chapline's Company, 2nd Battalion, 1776/1777 [Ref: M-241, which listed the name without the "Jr."]. Took the Oath of Allegiance before the Hon. Joseph Chapline before April 17, 1779 [Ref: J-5, O-39].

McNUTT, Alexander Sr. Took the Oath of Allegiance before the Hon. Joseph Chapline before April 17, 1779 [Ref: J-5, O-39].

McNUTT, Barnett (Barnard). Enrolled in the first militia company organized for the Revolutionary War in the Elizabeth Town District of Frederick County (now the Hagerstown area of Washington County) on January 6, 1776 [Ref: Q-270, W-1190]. Private, Militia, 3rd Class, Capt. Joseph Chapline's Company, 2nd Battalion, 1776/1777 [Ref: M-241, which listed the name as "Barnard McNutt"]. Took the Oath of Allegiance before the Hon. Joseph Chapline before April 17, 1779 [Ref: J-5, O-39].

McNUTT, James. Enrolled in the first militia company organized for the Revolutionary War in the Elizabeth Town District of Frederick County (now the Hagerstown area of Washington County) on January 6, 1776 [Ref: Q-270, W-1190]. Private, Militia, 2nd Class, Capt. Joseph Chapline's Company, 2nd Battalion, 1776/1777 [Ref: M-241]. Took the Oath of Allegiance before the Hon. Joseph Chapline before April 17, 1779 [Ref: J-5, O-39].

McNUTT, Robert. Enrolled in the first militia company organized for the Revolutionary War in the Elizabeth Town District of Frederick County (now the Hagerstown area of Washington County) on January 6, 1776 [Ref: Q-270, W-1190]. Private, Militia, 4th Class, Capt. Joseph Chapline's Company, 2nd Battalion, 1776/1777 [Ref: M-241]. Took the Oath of Allegiance before the Hon. Joseph Chapline before April 17, 1779 [Ref: J-5, O-39].

McNUTT, William. Private, Militia, 2nd Class, Capt. Joseph Chapline's Company, 2nd Battalion, 1776/1777 [Ref: M-241].

McPHERRIN, Thomas. Took the Oath of Allegiance before the Hon. Joseph Sprigg before April 1, 1778 [Ref: O-54, J-16].

McQUINNY, Thomas (c1738-1827). Soldier who resided in Washington County and was granted a pension certificate in August, 1820, according to an Act of Congress of March 18, 1818, since he had proven that he was "in the enjoyment of a certain degree of poverty" as required by the

Act as amended on May 1, 1820 [Ref: W-1190]. Private, Maryland Line, pensioned at $96 per year effective September 6, 1818. He died on November 15 (or 17), 1827, in his 89th year, at the residence of Col. Daniel Malott in Washington County. Thomas was a native of Ireland and enlisted at Elkton, Maryland during the Revolutionary War. He served in the 5th Maryland Line under Major Lansdale, Captain Muse, and Captain Lynn, of (now) Allegany County. Some time after the war he moved to Washington County and is buried at the Stone Church near Major Baker's store [Ref: Z-95, D-464, R-42, which latter source mistakenly listed the name as "James McQuinney"].

McTARDEN, John. Private, Militia, 1st Class, Capt. Martin Kershner's Company, 1776/1777 [Ref: A-1146, M-247].

McWILLIAMS, George. Private, Militia, 1st Class, Capt. Samuel Hughes' Company, 2nd Battalion, 1776/1777 [Ref: M-238, A-1146].

McWILLIAMS, John. Private, Militia, 5th Class, Capt. Samuel Hughes' Company, 2nd Battalion, 1776/1777 [Ref: M-238, A-1146].

MEDCALF, Bennett. Private who was enlisted by Ensign Nathan Williams and passed on July 25, 1776 in Frederick (now Washington) County [Ref: D-51, which listed the name as "Bennett Madcalf"].

MEDCALF, William. Took the Oath of Allegiance before the Hon. Richard Davis in 1778 [Ref: J-4, O-36].

MEEK, David. Enrolled in the first militia company organized for the Revolutionary War in the Elizabeth Town District of Frederick County (now the Hagerstown area of Washington County) on January 6, 1776 [Ref: Q-270, W-1190]. Private, Militia, 1st Class, Capt. John Rennolds' (Reynolds') Company, 2nd Battalion, 1776/1777 [Ref: M-240]. In December, 1776, Frances Blackwell informed the Committee of Observation that David Meek had "expressed sentiments in his presence on December 10, 1776 and in the presence of Walter Wilson, inimical to the United States of America." On December 24, 1776 David Meek "was brought before the Committee agreeable to their order, and upon his voluntarily taking the Oath of Fidelity to this State, was discharged upon paying cost." [Ref: Q-343]. Private, Militia, 7th Class, Capt. Martin Kershner's Company, 1776/1777 [Ref: A-1146, M-248]. Took the Oath of Allegiance before the Hon. John Cellars in January, 1778 [Ref: K-1814, O-40, J-6].

MEEK, Thomas. Private, Militia, 1st Class, Capt. Martin Kershner's Company, 1776/1777 [Ref: A-1146, M-247]. Took the Oath of Allegiance before the Hon. Henry Schnebley in 1778 [Ref: O-50, J-14].

MEHANEY, Thomas. Private, Militia, 5th Class, Capt. Conrad Nichodemus' Company, 2nd Battalion, 1776/1777 [Ref: M-237, A-1146].

MELLAN, Patrick. Private who was recruited and passed by County Lieutenant Thomas Sprigg on April 22, 1780 [Ref: D-336].
MELON, James. Third Corporal, Militia, Capt. John Rennolds' (Reynolds') Company, 2nd Battalion, 1776/1777 [Ref: M-240].
MELONE, James. Private, Militia, 8th Class, Capt. John Rennolds' (Reynolds') Company, 2nd Battalion, 1776/1777 [Ref: M-240].
MELONE, John Jr. Private, Militia, 3rd Class, Capt. John Rennolds' (Reynolds') Company, 2nd Battalion, 1776/1777 [Ref: M-240].
MELONEY, Alexander. Private, Militia, 5th Class, Capt. Charles Clinton's Company, 1776/1777 [Ref: M-245, A-1146].
MELONEY, John. Private, Militia, 6th Class, Capt. Barnett Johnston's Company, 3rd Battalion, 1776/1777 [Ref: M-242].
MELOTT, Benjamin. Private, Militia, 3rd Class, Capt. James Smith's Company, 2nd Battalion, 1776/1777 [Ref: M-239, A-1146]. Took the Oath of Allegiance before the Hon. Richard Davis in 1778 [Ref: J-5, O-37, which latter source listed the name as "Benjamin Melot"].
MELOTT, John. Took the Oath of Allegiance before the Hon. Richard Davis in 1778 [Ref: J-4, which listed the name as "John Molett" and O-37, which listed the name as "John Mallott"].
MELOTT, Joseph. Private, Militia, 2nd Class, Capt. Peter Swingle's (Swingley's) Company, 1776/1777 [Ref: A-1146, M-248]. Took the Oath of Allegiance before the Hon. Richard Davis in 1778 [Ref: J-3, O-36].
MELOTT, Peter. Ensign, Militia, Capt. James Smith's Company, 2nd Battalion, June 22, 1778 [Ref: M-103, E-145]. Ensign, Militia, Capt. James Smith's Company, 2nd Battalion; "not fit" (date not given), but subsequently returned to service [Ref: M-239, A-1146]. Took the Oath of Allegiance before the Hon. Richard Davis in 1778 [Ref: J-4, O-37, which latter source listed the name as "Peter Molett"]. Second Lieutenant, Capt. Robert Smith's Company, 2nd Battalion, November 21, 1778 [Ref: G-220].
MELOTT, Theodores. Took the Oath of Allegiance before the Hon. Richard Davis in 1778 [Ref: J-4, O-37, which latter source listed the name as "Theodores Molett"]. Private, Militia, 5th Class, Capt. James Smith's Company, 2nd Battalion, 1776/1777 [Ref: M-240, A-1146, which listed the name as "Theodotious Melott"].
MELOTT, Thomas. Second Sergeant, Militia, Capt. James Smith's Company, 2nd Battalion, 1776, noting he was "fit for a officer" (date not given). [Ref: M-239, A-1146]. Took the Oath of Allegiance before the Hon. Richard Davis in 1778 [Ref: J-4, O-37, which latter source listed the name as "Thomas Malott"].

MENGENNER, John. Took the Oath of Allegiance before the Hon. John Stull in 1778 [Ref: O-46, J-11].
MENSON, Richard. Private, Militia, 3rd Class, Capt. John Bennet's Company, 1776/1777 [Ref: M-246, A-1146]. Private, Militia, Capt. John Kershner's Company, on duty guarding prisoners of war at Fort Frederick on June 27, 1778 [Ref: D-328].
MENTZER, Barbara. See "John Hefner," q.v.
MENTZER (MENCER), Michael. Private, Militia, 4th Class, Capt. Conrad Hogmire's Company, 1776/1777 [Ref: M-244, A-1146].
MERRIWEATHER, Frances. See "Basil Prather," q.v.
MERSER, John Casper. Private who was recruited and passed by County Lieutenant Thomas Sprigg on April 22, 1780 [Ref: D-336].
MESSERSMITH, Andrew. Took the Oath of Allegiance before the Hon. Richard Davis in 1778 [Ref: J-4, O-37].
MESSERSMITH, Valentine. Private, Militia, 5th Class, Capt. James Walling's Company, 2nd Battalion, 1776/1777 [Ref: M-239, A-1146]. Took the Oath of Allegiance before the Hon. John Stull in 1778 [Ref: O-46, J-11, which listed the name as "Wallintine Messersmith"].
MESSERSMITH, William. Private who was enlisted by Capt. John Reynolds and passed on July 18, 1776 in Frederick (now Washington) County [Ref: D-50]. See "William Mercer Smith," q.v.
METTS, Christian. Private, Militia, 5th Class, Capt. Daniel Clapsaddle's Company, 1st Battalion, 1776/1777 [Ref: M-236, A-1146]. Private who was enrolled by Capt. Henry Hardman and passed on July 19, 1776 in Frederick (now Washington) County [Ref: D-51, which listed the name as "Chr. Metts"].
METTS, John. Private, Militia, Capt. William Heyser's Company, muster roll dated October 23, 1776, in continental service, which stated he had deserted, yet he was on duty in May, 1777 [Ref: L-79, W-1190, D-264, which latter sources listed the name as "John Mettz" and GG-98, which listed the name as "John Metz, Mettz"].
MEYER, Adam. Took the Oath of Allegiance before the Hon. Christopher Cruse in Sharpsburg Hundred before March 2, 1778 [Ref: O-35, J-2]. Enrolled in the third militia company organized for the Revolutionary War in the Elizabeth Town District of Frederick County (now the Hagerstown area of Washington County), passed by the Committee of Observation on June 5, 1776, and assigned to Capt. John Reynolds' command [Ref: Q-273, which listed the name as "Adam Myer"]. Private, Militia, 8th Class, Capt. Basil Williams' Company, 1776/1777 [Ref: M-244, A-1146]. Appeared before the Committee on February 22, 1777 and

"forthwith marched to the reinforcement of General Washington." [Ref: Q-236]. See "Jeremiah Chapline," q.v.

MEYER, Felix. Took the Oath of Allegiance before the Hon. Henry Schnebley in 1778 [Ref: O-51, J-14, which listed the name as "Felia Meyer"]. One "Felix Mayer" died testate by February 3, 1798 (date of balance book entry in Washington County) with the "whole balance to John Bridenbaugh." [Ref: J-35]. See "Phelix Moyer," q.v.

MEYER, George. Took the Oath of Allegiance before the Hon. Christopher Cruse in Sharpsburg Hundred before March 2, 1778 [Ref: O-35, J-2]. See "George Miers," q.v.

MEYER (MYERS), Jacob (c1745-1821). Took the Oath of Allegiance before the Hon. Christopher Cruse in Sharpsburg Hundred before March 2, 1778 [Ref: O-35, J-2]. "Jacob Myers" died at his residence near Sharpsburg on July 8, 1821, in his 76th year, after a short illness [Ref: Z-55].

MEYER, Lodowick. Took the Oath of Allegiance before the Hon. Christopher Cruse in Sharpsburg Hundred before March 2, 1778 [Ref: O-34, J-2].

MEYER, Michael Sr. Took the Oath of Allegiance before the Hon. Christopher Cruse in Sharpsburg Hundred before March 2, 1778 [Ref: O-34, J-2].

MEYER, Peter. Took the Oath of Allegiance before the Hon. Christopher Cruse in Sharpsburg Hundred before March 2, 1778 [Ref: O-35, J-2].

MEYER, Simon. Rendered patriotic service by supplying a blanket for the use of the military in March, 1776, as recorded by the Committee of Observation on April 12, 1776 [Ref: L-82, Q-156, which latter source listed the name as "Simon Myre"]. Rendered patriotic service by providing a wagon cloth for the use of the military in January, 1777, as recorded by the Committee of Observation on January 27, 1777 [Ref: Q-53, which listed the name as Simon Myer"].

MICHAEL, Henry. Private, Militia, Capt. William Heyser's Company, enlisted August 22, 1776, muster roll dated October 23, 1776, in continental service [Ref: D-264, W-1190, L-79]. Private, German Regiment, Lt. Col. Ludwick Weltner's Company, discharged on July 26, 1779 at Fort Wyoming, Pennsylvania [Ref: D-265, GG-98].

MICHAEL, John. Private, Militia, Capt. William Heyser's Company, enlisted July 16, 1776, muster roll dated October 23, 1776, in continental service [Ref: D-264, W-1190, L-79, GG-98]. Corporal, German Regiment, Lt. Col. Ludwick Weltner's Company, after May 22, 1777, and discharged on July 16, 1779 [Ref: D-264, GG-98].

MICHAEL, Ludwick. Enrolled in the third militia company organized for the Revolutionary War in the Elizabeth Town District of Frederick County (now the Hagerstown area of Washington County), passed by the Committee of Observation on June 5, 1776, and assigned to Capt. John Reynolds' command [Ref: Q-273]. Private, Militia, 4th Class, Capt. John Rennolds' (Reynolds') Company, 2nd Battalion, 1776/1777 [Ref: M-240]. Took the Oath of Allegiance before the Hon. Joseph Chapline before April 17, 1779 [Ref: O-39, J-5, which latter source listed the name as "Ludrick Michael"].

MICHEL, John Everhart. Took the Oath of Allegiance before the Hon. John Cellars in January, 1778 [Ref: K-1814, O-40, J-5].

MIDDLECALF, John. Enrolled in the third militia company organized for the Revolutionary War in the Elizabeth Town District of Frederick County (now the Hagerstown area of Washington County), passed by the Committee of Observation on June 5, 1776, and assigned to Capt. John Reynolds' command [Ref: Q-273, which listed the name as "John Mittlecalf"]. On July 2, 1776, Capt. John Reynolds reported to the Committee of Observation for Elizabeth Town District that "John Middlecoff, non effective, has signed the Association." [Ref: Q-325]. One of several patriots appointed by the Committee of Observation on January 19, 1777 "to form the county into companies (after the militia had marched) for the purpose of relieving the distressed inhabitants of said county and also to compel the Dunkards and Mennonists to give their assistance." [Ref: Q-43, which listed the name as "John Middlecalf"]. Took the Oath of Allegiance before the Hon. Christopher Cruse in Lower Antietam Hundred before March 2, 1778 [Ref: J-3, O-35, which listed the name as "John Midolealf"].

MIDDLECALF, John Jr. (1758-1834). Private, Militia, 3rd Class, Capt. John Rennolds' (Reynolds') Company, 2nd Battalion, 1776/1777 [Ref: M-240, which listed the name as "John Middcalf(?), Jr."]. "John Middlekauff, Sr." died on January 25, 1834, aged 75 years, 9 months, 15 days, and is buried in the Old Reformed Graveyard at Sharpsburg, Maryland [Ref: JJ-I:27].

MIDDLECOF, Christian. See "Jacob Russell, Jr.," q.v.

MIERS, George. Private, Militia, 3rd Class, Capt. James Smith's Company, 2nd Battalion, 1776/1777 [Ref: A-1146, M-239, which listed the name as "George Miers"]. See "George Meyer" and "George Myers," q.v.

MIERS, George Jr. Took the Oath of Allegiance before the Hon. Richard Davis in 1778 [Ref: J-4, O-37].

MIGSOVE, Adam. Private, Militia, 5th Class, Capt. James Smith's Company, 2nd Battalion, 1776/1777 [Ref: M-240, A-1146].

MILBURN, Margaret. See "Thomas Cresap," q.v.

MILLER, Abraham. There appears to have been three men with this name who rendered service during the Revolutionary War. Additional research may be necessary before drawing conclusions. (1) Private, Militia, 2nd Class, Capt. Basil Williams' Company, 1776/1777 [Ref: A-1146, M-244]. (2) Private, Militia, 2nd Class, Capt. John Cellars' Company, 1776/1777 [Ref: A-1146, M-246]. (3) Private who was enrolled by Capt. Henry Hardman and passed on July 19, 1776 in Frederick (now Washington) County [Ref: D-51]. See "Christian Miller" and "John Miller," q.v.

MILLER, Adam. Third Sergeant, Militia, Capt. Martin Kershner's Company, 1776/1777 [Ref: M-247, A-1146]. Took the Oath of Allegiance before the Hon. John Barnes before February 28, 1778 [Ref: O-44, J-9]. Substitute, Maryland Line, enlisted on August 24, 1781 and discharged on October 26, 1781 upon the recommendation of Dr. James Murray [Ref: G-653, D-388]. One Adam Miller died before February 26, 1783 (date of balance book entry in Washington County), leaving a widow (not named, but Mary Miller was the administratrix) and equal shares to Philip Miller, Catherine Gantz, Sarah Gantz, Barnet Swop, and Barbara Miller [Ref: J-24].

MILLER, Allen (Allan). Private, Militia, 3rd Class, Capt. Basil Williams' Company, 1776/1777 [Ref: M-244, A-1146]. Rendered patriotic service by providing "a bay gelding with gears" for the use of the military in January, 1777, as recorded by the Committee of Observation on January 27, 1777 [Ref: Q-53].

MILLER, Andrew. Private, Militia, 3rd Class, Capt. Peter Beall's Company, 1st Battalion, 1776/1777 [Ref: M-240]. Private, Militia, Capt. John Kershner's Company, on duty guarding prisoners of war at Fort Frederick until discharged on June 8, 1778 [Ref: D-328].

MILLER, Ann Mary. See "Melchoir Painter," q.v.

MILLER, Barbara. See "Christian Miller" and "Adam Miller" and "Benjamin Brady," q.v.

MILLER, Catherine. See "John Miller" and "William Fleck," q.v.

MILLER, Christian (1748-1828). Private, Militia, 8th Class, Capt. Conrad Nichodemus' Company, 2nd Battalion, 1776/1777 [Ref: M-237, A-1146]. Christian Miller died on July 17, 1828 at his residence three miles north of Hagerstown, aged 80 years, 6 months, and 22 days [Ref: Z-101].

MILLER, Christian (c1720-c1782). Rendered patriotic service by supplying a coverlid for the use of the military in March, 1776, as recorded by the

Committee of Observation on April 12, 1776 [Ref: Q-156, L-82]. Took the Oath of Allegiance before the Hon. Christopher Cruse in Lower Antietam Hundred before March 2, 1778 [Ref: J-3, O-35]. Rendered patriotic service by supplying corn for the use of the military on March 13, 1780 [Ref: W-1190, HH-73, which latter source listed the name as "Cristian Miller"]. One Christian Miller died before June 11, 1782 (date of balance book entry in Washington County), leaving equal shares to Abraham, Fronia, Henry, Samuel, Barbara, Esther, Mary, and Christianna Miller [Ref: J-23]. Since there were two men with this name, additional research may be necessary before drawing conclusions.

MILLER, Christianna. See "Christian Miller," q.v.

MILLER, Conrad (c1710-1783). Took the Oath of Allegiance before the Hon. John Cellars in January, 1778 [Ref: K-1814, O-40, J-6]. Conrad Miller was born circa 1710 in Germany, married Hannah ----, rendered patriotic service in Maryland, and died before June 9, 1783 in Pennsylvania [Ref: Y-II:2023].

MILLER, Daniel. There were several men with this name who served in the Revolutionary War. Additional research may be necessary before drawing conclusions. (1) Private, Militia, 3rd Class, Capt. Isaac Baker's Company, 1776/1777 [Ref: A-1146, M-247]. (2) Private, Militia, 1st Class, Capt. John Cellars' Company, 1776/1777 [Ref: A-1146, M-246]. (3) Private, Select Militia, Capt. Adam Ott's Company, 1781 [Ref: M-238, A-1146]. (4) Rendered patriotic service by providing a rifle for Capt. Daniel Cresap's Company in July, 1775, as recorded by the Committee of Observation at Elizabeth Town on November 4, 1775 [Ref: Q-149]. (5) Took the Oath of Allegiance before the Hon. John Cellars in January, 1778 [Ref: K-1814, O-40, J-6]. See "John Miller," q.v.

MILLER, David. There were several men with this name who served in the Revolutionary War. Additional research may be necessary before drawing conclusions. (1) Enrolled in the first militia company organized for the Revolutionary War in the Elizabeth Town District of Frederick County (now the Hagerstown area of Washington County) on January 6, 1776 [Ref: Q-271, W-1190]. (2) Private, Militia, 4th Class, Capt. Joseph Chapline's Company, 2nd Battalion, 1776/1777 [Ref: M-241]. (3) Private, Militia, 4th Class, Capt. John Cellars' Company, 1776/1777 [Ref: A-1146, M-246]. (4) Private, Militia, 1st Class, Capt. Martin Kershner's Company, 1776/1777 [Ref: A-1146, M-247]. (5) Took the Oath of Allegiance before the Hon. Christopher Cruse in Sharpsburg Hundred before March 2, 1778 [Ref: O-35, J-2]. See "John Miller" and "William Fleck," q.v.

MILLER, Elizabeth. See "Jacob Hefner," q.v.

MILLER, Ellen. Rendered patriotic service by supplying a blanket for the use of the military in March, 1776, as recorded by the Committee of Observation on April 12, 1776 [Ref: L-82, Q-156, which latter source listed the name as "Ellon Miller"].

MILLER, Esther. See "Christian Miller," q.v.

MILLER, Frederick. Took the Oath of Allegiance before the Hon. John Stull in 1778 [Ref: O-46, J-11].

MILLER, Fronia. See "Christian Miller," q.v.

MILLER, George. There were several men with this name who served in the Revolutionary War. Additional research will be necessary before drawing conclusions. (1) Private, Militia, 5th Class, Capt. James Prather's Company, 3rd Battalion, 1776/1777 [Ref: M-243]. (2) Private, Militia, 6th Class, Capt. Griffin Johnson's Company, 3rd Battalion, 1776/1777 [Ref: M-243]. (3) Private, Militia, 4th Class, Capt. John Bennet's Company, 1776, "deserted" and returned to duty in Capt. Bonnet's *[sic]* Company by order of the Committee of Observation on February 8, 1777 [Ref: M-246, A-1146, Q-232, Q-234]. (4) Private, Capt. William Heyser's Company, muster roll dated October 23, 1776, in continental service, and on duty in May, 1777 [Ref: D-264, W-1190, L-79, GG-98]. (6) Two men by this name took the Oath of Allegiance in 1778: one before the Hon. John Stull [Ref: O-46, J-11], and one before the Hon. Henry Schnebley [Ref: O-50, J-14]. (7) One George Miller died at his residence in Washington County on Sunday night, November 29, 1835, aged upwards of 80 years, "an active soldier in our Revolutionary Army for 5 years, and engaged in several important battles." [Ref: DD-107, citing *The Republican Banner*, December 5, 1835]. (8) One George Miller married Judith Wisner in 1777 at Hagerstown, Maryland and moved to Philadelphia. He served in the Maryland and Pennsylvania Lines and died on June 15, 1830. His widow received pension W9570 in Franklin County, Missouri in 1836. (9) One George Miller was born in Hagerstown, Maryland in 1764 and lived in Washington County, Pennsylvania at enlistment. He moved to Monroe County, Ohio and applied for a pension (R7190) in 1832. (10) One George Miller was born in February, 1760 in Washington County, Maryland about 6 or 8 miles south of Hagerstown and at age 5 moved with his father (not named) to what now Washington County, Pennsylvania. He applied for a pension (R7191) in Monroe County, Ohio in 1834 [Ref: V-II:2352, V-II:2353, N-119]. (11) One George Miller died at his residence adjoining Hagerstown on September 6, 1823, aged about 65 [Ref: Z-48].

MILLER, Hannah. See "Conrad Miller," q.v.

MILLER, Hans. Took the Oath of Allegiance before the Hon. Henry Schnebley in 1778 [Ref: O-49, J-13].

MILLER, Henry. There were several men with this name who rendered service during the war. Additional research may be necessary before drawing conclusions. (1) Private, Militia, 7th Class, Capt. Michael Fackler's Company, 1776/1777 [Ref: M-245, A-1146]. (2) Private, Militia, Capt. Martin Kershner's Company, 32nd Battalion, December 27, 1776 [Ref: K-1814, Box 3]. (3) Third Sergeant, Militia, Capt. John Cellars' Company, 1776/1777 [Ref: M-246, A-1146]. (4) Took the Oath of Allegiance before the Hon. Henry Schnebley in 1778 [Ref: O-49, J-13]. See "Christian Miller," q.v.

MILLER, Henry (of Conrad). Took the Oath of Allegiance before the Hon. Henry Schnebley in 1778 [Ref: O-51, J-14].

MILLER, Henry (of Hance). Private, Militia, 2nd Class, Capt. John Cellars' Company, 1776/1777 [Ref: A-1146, M-246, which listed the name as "Henry Miller, son of Hance"]. Took the Oath of Allegiance before the Hon. Henry Schnebley in 1778 [Ref: O-51, J-14, which listed the name as "Henry Miller, son of Hans"].

MILLER, Jacob. There were several men with this name who served in the Revolutionary War. Additional research will be necessary before drawing conclusions. (1) Fourth Sergeant, Militia, Capt. William Heyser's Company, muster roll dated October 23, 1776, continental service [Ref: D-263, W-1190, L-79]. (2) Private, Militia, Capt. William Heyser's Company, 1776, in continental service [Ref: W-1190, L-79]. (3) Private, Militia, 8th Class, Capt. Peter Swingle's (Swingley's) Company, 1776/1777 [Ref: A-1146, M-249]. (4) One Jacob Miller was one of several patriots appointed by the Committee of Observation on December 30, 1776 "to form the county into companies (after the militia had marched) for the purpose of relieving the distressed inhabitants of said county and also to compel the Dunkards and Mennonists to give their assistance." [Ref: Q-346]. (5) One Jacob Miller took the Oath of Allegiance before the Hon. John Cellars in January, 1778 [Ref: K-1814, O-40, J-6].

MILLER, Jacob (of Conrad). Private, Militia, 5th Class, Capt. John Cellars' Company, 1776/1777 [Ref: A-1146, M-246].

MILLER, Jacob (of Jacob). Private, Militia, 8th Class, Capt. John Cellars' Company, 1776/1777 [Ref: A-1146, M-246].

MILLER, John. There were several men named John Miller who rendered patriotic service during the Revolutionary War. Additional research will be necessary before drawing conclusions. (1) Appointed by the Committee of Observation for Elizabeth Town District (now the Hagerstown area of Washington County) on July 7, 1776 "to take the number of inhabitants within Elizabeth Hundred, both whites and blacks, distinguishing respectively the age and sex of each, to be transmitted to the Council of Safety immediately." [Ref: Q-331]. (2) Rendered patriotic service by providing a rifle for Capt. Daniel Cresap's Company in July, 1775, as recorded by the Committee of Observation at Elizabeth Town on November 4, 1775 [Ref: Q-148]. (3) Rendered patriotic service in Hagerstown by providing "a rifle gun" to Capt. John Nelson's Company, continental service (Maryland Line), April, 1776 [Ref: Q-162]. (4) Private, Militia, 5th Class, Capt. Martin Kershner's Company, 1776/1777 [Ref: A-1146, M-247]. (5) Constable in Elizabeth Town District in 1776 [Ref: Q-268]. (6) Four men by this name took the Oath of Allegiance in 1778: one before the Hon. Richard Davis, one before the Hon. John Stull, and two before the Hon. Henry Schnebley [Ref: O-37, O-47, O-50, O-51, J-4, J-11, J-14, J-15]. (7) John Miller served in the Maryland Line and lived in Washington County, Maryland at the time of his enlistment. Soon after the war he moved with his father (not named) to Pennsylvania and then to the Shenandoah Valley in Virginia where he married Mary Dotson on July 5, 1787. They moved to Botetourt County, Virginia and then to Grainger County, Tennessee and then to White County, Tennessee where he applied for pension in 1834. He died there on November 4, 1846 and his wife applied for and received pension W47 on August 14, 1849, age 81 [Ref: V-II:2356]. (8) One John Miller died before February 26, 1783 (date of balance book entry in Washington County), leaving a widow (no name given in this account) and daughter Catherine Miller [Ref: J-24]. (9) One John Miller died testate before April 9, 1799 (date of balance book entry in Washington County), leaving equal shares to Daniel Miller, John Fisher, John Miller, Susannah Wissinger, Mary Studanbaker, Elizabeth Cameron, Jacob Miller, Abraham Miller, Lodwick Miller, and David Miller [Ref: J-37]. (10) One John Miller died on October 20, 1825, aged 77, was buried in Old St. John's Lutheran Churchyard, and subsequently reinterred in Rose Hill Cemetery in Hagerstown [Ref: JJ-VII:105]. Several more men named John Miller served in the military as indicated separately below. Also see "Michael Ott," q.v.

MILLER, John (cooper). Private, Militia, 3rd Class, Capt. Peter Swingle's (Swingley's) Company, 1776/1777 [Ref: A-1146, M-248].

MILLER, John (weaver). Private, Militia, 7th Class, Capt. Peter Swingle's (Swingley's) Company, 1776/1777 [Ref: A-1146, M-249].

MILLER, John (of Conrad). Private, Militia, 1st Class, Capt. John Cellars' Company, 1776/1777 [Ref: A-1146, M-246].

MILLER, John (of Hance). Private, Militia, 1st Class, Capt. John Cellars' Company, 1776/1777 [Ref: A-1146, M-246].
MILLER, John (of Jacob). Private, Militia, 6th Class, Capt. John Cellars' Company, 1776/1777 [Ref: A-1146, M-246].
MILLER, John Solomon. Private, Militia, 6th Class, Capt. John Bennet's Company, 1776/1777 [Ref: A-1146, M-246, which listed the name as "John Sollomon Miller"]. Absconded (delinquent) and returned to duty in Capt. Bonnet's [sic] Company by order of the Committee of Observation on February 8, 1776 [Ref: Q-232, Q-234]. Took the Oath of Allegiance before the Hon. Richard Davis in 1778 [Ref: J-4, O-36].
MILLER, Lodwick. See "John Miller," q.v.
MILLER, Martin. Private, Militia, Capt. Charles Coulson's Company, enrolled August 28, 1776 [Ref: M-243, A-1146].
MILLER, Mary. See "Christian Miller" and "Adam Miller," q.v.
MILLER, Michael. There were several men with this name who served in the Revolutionary War. Additional research will be necessary before drawing conclusions. (1) Private, Militia, 4th Class, Capt. Jeremiah Spires' Company, 2nd Battalion, 1776/1777 [Ref: M-239, A-1146]. (2) Private, Militia, 1st Class, Capt. Peter Swingle's (Swingley's) Company, 1776/1777 [Ref: A-1146, M-248]. (3) One rendered patriotic service by supplying four blankets for the use of the military in March, 1776, as recorded by the Committee of Observation on April 12, 1776 [Ref: Q-157, L-82]. (4) One took the Oath of Allegiance before the Hon. Henry Schnebley in 1778 [Ref: O-50, J-14].
MILLER, Philip. See "Adam Miller," q.v.
MILLER, Samuel. See "Christian Miller," q.v.
MILLER, Solomon. One of several patriots appointed by the Committee of Observation on December 30, 1776 "to form the county into companies (after the militia had marched) for the purpose of relieving the distressed inhabitants of said county and also to compel the Dunkards and Mennonists to give their assistance." [Ref: Q-345]. Took the Oath of Allegiance before the Hon. John Stull in 1778 [Ref: O-46, J-11].
MILLER, Stephen. Private, Militia, 4th Class, Capt. John Cellars' Company, 1776/1777 [Ref: A-1146, M-246].
MILLER, Ulrick. Took the Oath of Allegiance before the Hon. John Stull in 1778 [Ref: O-46, J-11].
MILLER, William. Took the Oath of Allegiance before the Hon. Richard Davis in 1778 [Ref: J-4, O-36].
MILLER, William. Took the Oath of Allegiance before the Hon. Joseph Sprigg before April 1, 1778 [Ref: O-53, J-16].

MILLHOUSE, John. Third Sergeant, Militia, Capt. Isaac Baker's Company, 1776/1777 [Ref: M-247, A-1146]. Took the Oath of Allegiance before the Hon. John Barnes before February 28, 1778 [Ref: O-44, J-9].

MILLME, John. Took the Oath of Allegiance before the Hon. William Yates in 1778 [Ref: O-48, J-12].

MILLS, Elijah. Private, Militia, by January 22, 1777 when ordered by the Committee of Observation "to march with some company of militia to the reinforcement of his Excellency General Washington" or appear before the Committee and state his reason for not marching. He apparently marched since he never appeared to the contrary [Ref: Q-48].

MILLS, Jacob (constable). Appointed by the Committee of Observation on July 7, 1776 "to take the number of inhabitants within Fort Frederick Hundred, both whites and blacks, distinguishing respectively the age and sex of each, to be transmitted to the Council of Safety immediately." [Ref: Q-331]. Took the Oath of Allegiance before the Hon. William Yates in 1778 [Ref: O-48, J-12].

MILLS, Jacob. Private, Militia, by January 22, 1777 when ordered by the Committee of Observation "to march with some company of militia to the reinforcement of his Excellency General Washington" or appear before the Committee and state his reason for not marching. He apparently marched since he never appeared to the contrary [Ref: Q-48].

MILLS, James. Private, Militia, 3rd Class, Capt. Barnett Johnston's Company, 3rd Battalion, 1776/1777 [Ref: M-242]. Took the Oath of Allegiance before the Hon. William Yates in 1778 [Ref: O-48, J-12].

MILLS, Michael. Private, Militia, by January 22, 1777 when ordered by the Committee of Observation "to march with some company of militia to the reinforcement of his Excellency General Washington" or appear before the Committee and state his reason for not marching. He apparently marched since he never appeared to the contrary [Ref: Q-48].

MIRES, Even. Private, Militia, 6th Class, Capt. Barnett Johnston's Company, 3rd Battalion, 1776/1777 [Ref: M-242].

MIRS (MOSS?), Frederick. Private, Militia, 4th Class, Capt. Joseph Chapline's Company, 2nd Battalion, 1776/1777 [Ref: M-241].

MISER, John and Romena. See "James Chapline," q.v.

MISHLAR, Lawrence. Private, Select Militia, Capt. Adam Ott's Company, 1781 [Ref: M-238, A-1146].

MITTAG, Frederick (1734-1821). Soldier who enlisted in Frederick, Maryland, resided in Washington County, and was granted a pension certificate in August, 1820, according to an Act of Congress of March 18, 1818, since he had proven that he was "in the enjoyment of a certain degree of poverty" as required by the Act as amended on May 1, 1820 [Ref: W-1190]. Private, German Regiment, Maryland Line, pensioned (S34999) at $96 per year effective September 14, 1818 and died by November, 1821 [Ref: N-38, R-43, V-II:2383, which latter sources listed the name as "Frederick Mittag or Meddack"]. "Died on October 31, 1821, Mr. Mittoe(?), aged 87, soldier of the Revolution." [Ref: Z-56].

MOCK, Peter. Private, Militia, 5th Class, Capt. Jacob Sharer's Company, 1776/1777 [Ref: A-1146, M-248]. Took the Oath of Allegiance before the Hon. John Stull in 1778 [Ref: O-46, J-11].

MOCK, William. Private, Militia, 4th Class, Capt. Conrad Hogmire's Company, 1776/1777 [Ref: M-244, A-1146].

MOCOMAN, Ludwick. Private, Militia, 5th Class, Capt. Henry Boteler's Company, 1776/1777 [Ref: M-237, A-1146].

MOFFET, William. Took the Oath of Allegiance before the Hon. John Stull in 1778 [Ref: O-46, J-11].

MOLETT, Peter. See "Peter Melott," q.v.

MOLLEY, Peter. See "Peter Sholley," q.v.

MONDLE, George. See "George Mundle," q.v.

MONDY, Balser. Fourth Sergeant, Militia, Capt. John Bennet's Company, 1776/1777 [Ref: M-246, A-1146]. See "Balser Moody," q.v.

MONDY, John (1757-1849). Private, Militia, 5th Class, Capt. John Bennet's Company, 1776/1777 [Ref: M-246, A-1146]. Private, Maryland Line, who applied for pension (R7296) in Richland County, Ohio on April 14, 1836, stating he was born in 1757 in Washington County, Maryland and lived there at the time of his enlistment. After the war he moved to Bedford County, Pennsylvania and in the winter of 1819 he moved to Wayne County, Ohio. In 1824 he moved to Richland County, Ohio and died on February 4, 1849 in Ashland County, Ohio. His widow Rosannah applied for pension on January 27, 1852, stating they were married in February, 1790 in Williamsport, Maryland. Another source indicates John Mondy or Monday married Rosannah Huffman in Washington County on March 16, 1788 [Ref: N-38, N-119, V-II:2387].

MONEY, Adam. Enrolled in the third militia company organized for the Revolutionary War in the Elizabeth Town District of Frederick County (now the Hagerstown area of Washington County), passed by the Committee of Observation on June 5, 1776, and assigned to Capt. John Reynolds' command [Ref: Q-273].

MONG, Adam Jr. First Corporal, Militia, Capt. Samuel Hughes' Company, 1776/1777 [Ref: M-238, A-1146]. Took the Oath of Allegiance before the

Hon. Samuel Hughes before March 1, 1778 [Ref: O-33, J-1, which listed the name as "Adam Mony, Jr."].

MONG, Adam Sr. Second Sergeant, Militia, Capt. Samuel Hughes' Company, 1776/1777 [Ref: M-238, A-1146]. Took the Oath of Allegiance before the Hon. Joseph Sprigg before April 1, 1778 [Ref: O-53, J-16, which listed the name without the "Sr."]. His account of "clothing due to be delivered to William Simkins" was reported to the State on November 29, 1779 [Ref: P-250, which listed the name without the "Sr."]. G. N. Mong died testate before October 26, 1792 (date of balance book entry in Washington County) and one of his sons was Adam Mong [Ref: J-32].

MONG, Davolt. Private, Militia, 8th Class, Capt. Conrad Hogmire's Company, 1776/1777 [Ref: M-244, A-1146]. Took the Oath of Allegiance before September 1, 1780 [Ref: X-115, which listed the name as "Davalt Mank"].

MONG, G. N. See "Adam Mong" and "Jacob Mong," q.v.

MONG, Jacob. Private, Militia, 4th Class, Capt. Samuel Hughes' Company, 2nd Battalion, 1776/1777 [Ref: M-238, A-1146]. G. N. Mong died before October 26, 1792 (date of balance book entry in Washington County) and one of his sons was Adam Mong [Ref: J-32].

MONG, Nicholas. One of several patriots appointed by the Committee of Observation on December 30, 1776 "to form the county into companies (after the militia had marched) for the purpose of relieving the distressed inhabitants of said county and also to compel the Dunkards and Mennonists to give their assistance." [Ref: Q-346]. Took the Oath of Allegiance before the Hon. Joseph Sprigg before April 1, 1778 [Ref: O-53, J-16].

MONNINGER, Henry. Private, Militia, 5th Class, Capt. Michael Fackler's Company, 1776/1777 [Ref: M-245, A-1146].

MONNINGER, John. Third Corporal, Militia, Capt. Jacob Sharer's Company, 1776/1777 [Ref: M-248, A-1146].

MONOUGHAN, John. Took the Oath of Allegiance before the Hon. Henry Schnebley in 1778 [Ref: J-14, O-51, which latter source listed the name as "John Momoughan"]. Enrolled in the third militia company organized for the Revolutionary War in the Elizabeth Town District of Frederick County (now the Hagerstown area of Washington County), passed by the Committee of Observation on June 5, 1776, and assigned to Capt. John Reynolds' command [Ref: Q-273, which listed the name as "John Mauhgeman"].

MONROE, Barney. Took the Oath of Allegiance before the Hon. Samuel Hughes before March 1, 1778 [Ref: O-33, J-1].

MONTGOMERY, Charles. Private, Militia, 3rd Class, Capt. James Walling's Company, 2nd Battalion, 1776/1777 [Ref: M-238, A-1146, which listed the name as "Charles Mungomery"].

MONTGOMERY, John. Rendered patriotic service by providing "rashons" for the use of the military in July, 1775, as recorded by the Committee of Observation at Elizabeth Town on November 4, 1775 [Ref: Q-150].

MOODY, Balser. Second Lieutenant, Militia, by November 17, 1780 [Ref: M-105, which listed the name as "Balfour Moody"]. Appointed by the Committee of Observation to carry the Association of Freemen to male residents in his hundred (district) on March 4, 1776 "and present it for signing and make an exact account of those that sign and those that refuse with their reasons for refusing." [Ref: Q-153, L-82, which listed the name as "Balser Mudy"]. Also see "Balser Mondy," q.v.

MOORE, Christopher. Took the Oath of Allegiance before the Hon. John Barnes before February 28, 1778 [Ref: O-45, J-9].

MOORE, Daniel. Took the Oath of Allegiance before September 1, 1780 [Ref: X-116].

MOORE, Enoch (1758-   ). Private, Maryland Line, who applied for pension S5785 in Harrison County, Virginia on August 20, 1832, aged 74, stating he was born on June 18, 1758 in New Jersey and moved with his parents (not named) when a child to (now) Allegany County, Maryland. He enlisted there, served during the war, and in 1791 or 1792 moved to Virginia [Ref: V-II:2399].

MOORE, George. There were several men with this name who served in the Revolutionary War. Additional research will be necessary before drawing conclusions. (1) Private, Militia, 7th Class, Capt. Griffin Johnson's Company, 3rd Battalion, 1776/1777 [Ref: M-243]. (2) Third Corporal, Militia, Capt. Griffin Johnson's Company, 3rd Battalion, 1776/1777 [Ref: M-243]. (3) One took the Oath of Allegiance before the Hon. Richard Davis in 1778 [Ref: J-3, O-36, which latter source listed the name as "George Moone"]. (4) One George Moore was one of the persons appointed by the Committee of Observation on January 9, 1777 "to appraise the several wagons, horses, wagon cloths and blankets that can be procured for the use of Col. Joseph Smith's Battalion." [Ref: Q-33]. (5) One "George Moor" died in February, 1824, in his 84th year, and was a citizen of Cumberland [Ref: Z-1]. See "George Miller, Jr.," q.v.

MOORE, George Jr. Private, Militia, 3rd Class, Capt. Griffin Johnson's Company, 3rd Battalion, 1776/1777 [Ref: M-243]. One George Moore, son of George and Phoebe Moore, was born in Frederick County on October 14, 1749 and enlisted four times: once at Old Town or Shipton on the north branch of the Potomac in Maryland, once in New York, once in Washington County, Maryland as a susbtitute for his brother-in-law Obadiah Forshay, and lastly as a substitute for his brother William Moore. After the war he lived in Mason County, Kentucky (in 1793) and Champaign County, Ohio (in 1806) and Logan County, Ohio (in 1826) and Jasper County, Indiana (in 1842 with his son William). He applied for and received pension S33116 in Indiana on June 22, 1848 and died on July 18, 1848. He had married Nancy (Ann) Ball on October 24, 1780 and had 21 children, but the only ones named were William Moore, George Moore, John Moore, Mahala Woodfield, Nancy Dowden, Phoebe Moore, and Mary Standage. Nancy Moore died on February 26, 1854 [Ref: V-II:2399].

MOORE, John. Private, Militia, 1st Class, Capt. Griffin Johnson's Company, 3rd Battalion, 1776/1777 [Ref: M-243]. Took the Oath of Allegiance before the Hon. Richard Davis in 1778 [Ref: J-4, O-37].

MOORE, John. Private who was enrolled by Capt. Henry Hardman and passed on July 19, 1776 in Frederick (now Washington) County [Ref: D-51, which listed the name as "John Moor"]. Private, Militia, 4th Class, Capt. James Smith's Company, 2nd Battalion, 1776/1777 [Ref: M-240, A-1146]. See "George Moore, Jr.," q.v.

MOORE, Joseph. Private who was enlisted by Ensign Nathan Williams and passed on July 25, 1776 in Frederick (now Washington) County [Ref: D-51, which listed the name as "Joseph Moor"]. Private, Militia, 1st Class, Capt. John Bennet's Company, 1776/1777 [Ref: M-246, A-1146, which listed the name as "Joseph More"]. Took the Oath of Allegiance before the Hon. John Barnes before February 28, 1778 [Ref: O-44, J-9].

MOORE, Mahala and Mary. See "George Miller, Jr.," q.v.

MOORE, Nancy and Phoebe. See "George Miller, Jr.," q.v.

MOORE, Philip. Private, Militia, 8th Class, Capt. John Bennet's Company, 1776/1777 [Ref: M-246, A-1146, which listed the name as "Phillip More"] Took the Oath of Allegiance before the Hon. John Barnes before February 28, 1778 [Ref: O-44, J-9].

MOORE, Richard. Enrolled in the first militia company organized for the Revolutionary War in the Elizabeth Town District of Frederick County (now the Hagerstown area of Washington County) on January 6, 1776 [Ref: Q-270, W-1189, which listed the name as "Richard Moor"]. Private, Militia, 5th Class, Capt. John Rennolds' (Reynolds') Company, 2nd Battalion, 1776/1777 [Ref: M-240]. Took the Oath of Allegiance before September 1, 1780 [Ref: X-116].

MOORE, William. Ensign, Militia, Capt. Griffin Johnson's Company, by December 3, 1776 [Ref: M-105, M-243, B-501]. Ensign, Militia, Capt. Evan Baker's Company, 3rd Battalion, June 22, 1778 [Ref: M-105, E-

145, which listed the name as "William More"]. Took the Oath of Allegiance before the Hon. Lemuel Barritt before March 16, 1778 [Ref: O-43, J-8]. See "George Moore, Jr.," q.v.

MOOREHEAD, Joseph. Private, Militia, 7th Class, Capt. Henry Boteler's Company, 1776/1777 [Ref: M-237, A-1146, which listed the name as "Joseph Morehead"]. Took the Oath of Allegiance before the Hon. Christopher Cruse in Lower Antietam Hundred before March 2, 1778 [Ref: J-3, O-35, which latter source listed the name as "Joseph Moonhead"].

MORAN, Edmond. Rendered patriotic services by assisting to detect absenters (absconders or delinquents) from the militia in February, 1777 [Ref: Q-234].

MORFORD, Daniel. Took the Oath of Allegiance before the Hon. John Barnes before February 28, 1778 [Ref: O-44, J-9, which latter source listed the name as "Daniel Norford"].

MORGAN, David. See "David McCorgan," q.v.

MORGAN, Evan. Private, Maryland and Virginia Lines, who applied for pension S11098 in Monongalia County, Virginia on August 28, 1832, stating he enlisted in what is now Allegany County, Maryland at Tomlinson's Tavern and later served under Capt. Morgan Morgan (no relationship stated). [Ref: V-II:2416].

MORGAN, Morgan. See "Evan Morgan," q.v.

MORGAN, Moses. Private, Militia, 7th Class, Capt. Conrad Nichodemus' Company, 2nd Battalion, 1776/1777 [Ref: M-237, A-1146, which listed the name as "Moses Morgon"].

MORGAN, Nathaniel. Private, Militia, 1st Class, Capt. Peter Beall's Company, 1st Battalion, 1776/1777 [Ref: M-240]. Rendered patriotic service in Hagerstown by providing 17 shillings cash to Capt. John Nelson's Company, continental service (Maryland Line), April, 1776 [Ref: Q-161]. Took the Oath of Allegiance before the Hon. Joseph Sprigg before April 1, 1778 [Ref: O-53, J-16].

MORGAN, Peter. Private, Militia, 1st Class, Capt. Conrad Nichodemus' Company, 2nd Battalion, 1776/1777 [Ref: M-237, A-1146, which listed the name as "Peter Morgon"].

MORGAN, Richard. Private who was enrolled by Capt. Henry Hardman and passed on July 19, 1776 in Frederick (now Washington) County [Ref: D-51, which listed the name as "Richard Morgon"].

MORGON, William. Private, Militia, 7th Class, Capt. Conrad Nichodemus' Company, 2nd Battalion, 1776/1777 [Ref: M-237, A-1146].

MORRIS, Jonathan. Second Lieutenant, Upper District, Frederick County (now Washington County), August 7, 1776 [Ref: D-48].

MORRISON, George. Private who was enrolled by Capt. Henry Hardman and passed on July 19, 1776 in Frederick (now Washington) County [Ref: D-51].

MORRISON, James (1759-1824). Private, Maryland Line, 1782 [Ref: D-422]. "Died at Western-Port on December 6, 1824, after a lingering illness, James Morrison, in the 65th year of his age." [Ref: Z-3].

MORRISON, Joseph. Enrolled in the first militia company organized for the Revolutionary War in the Elizabeth Town District of Frederick County (now the Hagerstown area of Washington County) on January 6, 1776 [Ref: Q-270, W-1190]. Private, Militia, 6th Class, Capt. Joseph Chapline's Company, 2nd Battalion, 1776/1777 [Ref: M-241]. Took the Oath of Allegiance before the Hon. Joseph Chapline before April 17, 1779 [Ref: J-5, O-39].

MORRISON, William. Private, Militia, 2nd Class, Capt. Isaac Baker's Company, 1776/1777 [Ref: A-1146, M-247].

MOSS, Frederick. See "Frederick Mirs," q.v.

MOSSLEY, Jacob. Private, Militia, 8th Class, Capt. Charles Clinton's Company, 1776/1777 [Ref: M-245, A-1146].

MOTES, Davault. Took the Oath of Allegiance before the Hon. Joseph Chapline before April 17, 1779 [Ref: J-5, O-39].

MOTES, Henry. Took the Oath of Allegiance before September 1, 1780 [Ref: X-116, which listed the name as "Henry Moats"].

MOTHERSPAW, Philip. See "Philip Muterspaw," q.v.

MOUNCE, Joseph. Private, Militia, 5th Class, Capt. Daniel Cresap's Company, 3rd Battalion, 1776/1777 [Ref: M-241].

MOUNT, John. Private, Militia, 6th Class, Capt. Barnett Johnston's Company, 3rd Battalion, 1776/1777 [Ref: M-242]. Took the Oath of Allegiance before the Hon. William Yates in 1778 [Ref: O-48, J-12].

MOUNT, Samuel. Private, Militia, 1st Class, Capt. Barnett Johnston's Company, 3rd Battalion, 1776/1777 [Ref: M-242].

MOUNT, William. Private who enlisted in the militia on August 14, 1781 for service in the Continental Army [Ref: D-388]. Substitute, Maryland Line, discharged on October 30, 1781 [Ref: G-657, which listed the name as "William Mound"].

MOURER, Nicholas. First Lieutenant, Militia, Capt. George Swingle's (Swingley's) Company, 2nd Battalion, June 22, 1778 [Ref: M-106, E-145, N-1164, M-248, which latter source indicated he was Second Lieutenant in Capt. Peter Swingle's (Swingley's) Company, but no date was given]. Took the Oath of Allegiance before the Hon. Henry Schnebley in 1778 [Ref: O-50, J-14, which listed the name as "Nicholas Mower"]. Captain, 2nd Battalion, November 21, 1780 [Ref: G-220].

MOWING, Daniel. Private, Militia, 6th Class, Capt. Daniel Clapsaddle's Company, 1st Battalion, 1776/1777 [Ref: M-236, A-1146]. Took the Oath of Allegiance before the Hon. Henry Schnebley in 1778 [Ref: J-15, O-51, which listed the name as "Daniel Mowen"].

MOWING, John. Private, Militia, 1st Class, Capt. John Cellars' Company, 1776/1777 [Ref: A-1146, M-246]. Private who was enrolled by Capt. Henry Hardman and passed on July 19, 1776 in Frederick (now Washington) County [Ref: D-51, which listed the name as "John Mowen"].

MOWING, Ludwick. Private, Militia, 7th Class, Capt. Daniel Clapsaddle's Company, 1st Battalion, 1776/1777 [Ref: M-236, A-1146].

MOWING, Stephen. Private, Militia, 3rd Class, Capt. John Cellars' Company, 1776/1777 [Ref: A-1146, M-246].

MOXLEY, Daniel. Private who was enrolled by Capt. Aeneas Campbell and passed by Major Francis Deakins on July 18, 1776 [Ref: D-49].

MOXLEY, John. Private who was enrolled by Capt. Aeneas Campbell and passed by Major Francis Deakins on July 18, 1776 [Ref: D-49].

MOYER, Jonathan. Rendered patriotic service by supplying corn for the use of the military on February 17, 1780 [Ref: HH-73, and W-1190, which latter source listed the name as "Jonathon Mayer"]. "John Moyer" died at his residence near Hagerstown on January 6, 1826, in his 71st year [Ref: Z-79].

MOYER, Phelix. Private, Militia, 7th Class, Capt. Michael Fackler's Company, 1776/1777 [Ref: M-245, A-1146]. See "Felix Meyer," q.v.

MUFFETT, Daniel. Private, Militia, 5th Class, Capt. John Cellars' Company, 1776/1777 [Ref: A-1146, M-246].

MUFFETT, William. Private, Militia, 2nd Class, Capt. Peter Beall's Company, 1st Battalion, 1776/1777 [Ref: M-240, which listed the name as "William Muffett (Mussett?)"].

MUGG, Thomas. Private, Militia, 7th Class, Capt. Isaac Baker's Company, 1776/1777 [Ref: A-1146, M-247]. Took the Oath of Allegiance before the Hon. John Barnes before February 28, 1778 [Ref: O-44, J-9].

MUGGS, Thomas. Private, Militia, 2nd Class, Capt. Barnett Johnston's Company, 3rd Battalion, 1776/1777 [Ref: M-242].

MULHONEY, Daniel. Enrolled in the second militia company organized for the Revolutionary War in the Elizabeth Town District of Frederick County (now the Hagerstown area of Washington County) on March 9, 1776 [Ref: Q-272].

MULL, Henry. Private, Militia, 4th Class, Capt. Peter Beall's Company, 1st Battalion, 1776/1777 [Ref: M-240]. Took the Oath of Allegiance before the Hon. Henry Schnebley in 1778 [Ref: O-51, J-15, which listed the name as "Henry Mooll"].

MULLEN, Elenor. See "Thomas Bissett," q.v.

MULLEN, Michael. Private, Militia, 6th Class, Capt. Isaac Baker's Company, 1776/1777 [Ref: A-1146, M-247].

MULLENDORE, Joe. See "John Booth" and "Charles Swearingen," q.v.

MULLIHAN, Archibald. Private who was enlisted by Capt. John Reynolds and passed on July 18, 1776 in Frederick (now Washington) County [Ref: D-50].

MUNDLE (MONDLE), George. Private, Maryland Line, who applied for pension S41904 in Washington County, Pennsylvania on February 21, 1820, aged 61, stating he enlisted at Hagerstown, Maryland and had a wife aged about 62 (not named) and a daughter Margaret (aged 17). [Ref: V-II:2451].

MUNN, James. Private who was enrolled by Capt. Henry Hardman and passed on July 19, 1776 in Frederick (now Washington) County [Ref: D-51].

MUNOP(?), Moses. Took the Oath of Allegiance before the Hon. Lemuel Barritt before March 16, 1778 [Ref: O-42, J-7].

MUNROW, Bryan. Private, Militia, 4th Class, Capt. Daniel Clapsaddle's Company, 1st Battalion, 1776/1777 [Ref: M-236, A-1146].

MUNROW, Moses. Private, Militia, 2nd Class, Capt. Daniel Cresap's Company, 3rd Battalion, 1776/1777 [Ref: M-241].

MUNROW, Robert. Private, Militia, 8th Class, Capt. Daniel Cresap's Company, 3rd Battalion, 1776/1777 [Ref: M-241]. Took the Oath of Allegiance before the Hon. Lemuel Barritt before March 16, 1778 [Ref: O-42, J-7, which listed the name as "Robert Munroe"].

MURAKIN, Senica. Private, Militia, 6th Class, Capt. James Prather's Company, 3rd Battalion, 1776/1777 [Ref: M-243].

MURDOCK, Barbara. See "Andrew Bruce," q.v.

MURDOCK, Benjamin. Private, Militia, Capt. Charles Coulson's Company, enrolled August 28, 1776 [Ref: M-243, A-1146].

MURPHEY, Daniel. Private who was enlisted by Capt. John Reynolds and passed on July 18, 1776 in Frederick (now Washington) County [Ref: D-50].

MURPHY, Michael. Took the Oath of Allegiance before the Hon. Richard Davis in 1778 [Ref: J-4, O-37].

MURPHY, Susannah. See "Thomas Bissett," q.v.

MURRAY, James. See "Andrew Barringer" and "Richard Higgins" and "Joseph Martin" and "Adam Miller" and "Philip Nagal" and "Patrick Owens," q.v.

MURROW, Thomas. Enrolled in the first militia company organized for the Revolutionary War in the Elizabeth Town District of Frederick County (now the Hagerstown area of Washington County) on January 6, 1776 [Ref: Q-271, W-1190].

MUSE, Captain. See "Thomas McQuinny," q.v.

MUSGROVE, Henry. Enrolled in the second militia company organized for the Revolutionary War in the Elizabeth Town District of Frederick County (now the Hagerstown area of Washington County) on March 9, 1776 [Ref: Q-271]. Private, Militia, 3rd Class, Capt. Henry Boteler's Company, 1776/1777 [Ref: M-237, A-1146]. Took the Oath of Allegiance before the Hon. Christopher Cruse in Lower Antietam Hundred before March 2, 1778 [Ref: J-3, O-35, which listed the name as "Henry Musgraves"].

MUSSELMAN, Benjamin. Rendered patriotic service by providing a rifle for Capt. Daniel Cresap's Company in July, 1775, as recorded by the Committee of Observation at Elizabeth Town on November 4, 1775 [Ref: Q-149].

MUSSELMAN, Esther. See "Adam Troup," q.v.

MUSSETT, William. See "William Muffett," q.v.

MUTERSPAW, Philip (1744-c1840). Substitute, Maryland Militia, with Pennsylvania service; discharged on October 30, 1781 [Ref: N-39, G-656, which latter source listed the name as "Philip Motherspaw"]. Private who enlisted in the militia on August 14, 1781 for service in the Continental Army [Ref: D-387, which listed the name as "Philip Mustersbaugh"]. Private, Maryland and Pennsylvania Lines, who applied for pension S9435 in Rockbridge County, Virginia on August 5, 1833, stating he was born in 1744 in Germany and at age of 1 or 2 came to America with his parents (not named). He lived in Cumberland County, Pennsylvania at enlistment and later moved to Washington County, Maryland where he enlisted again. After the war he moved to Virginia [Ref: V-II:2464].

MYERS, Adam. See "Adam Meyer" and "Jeremiah Chapline," q.v.

MYERS, Elias. Took the Oath of Allegiance before the Hon. William Yates in 1778 [Ref: O-48, J-12].

MYERS, Elizabeth. See "Ludwick Myers," q.v.

MYERS, Francis. Private, Militia, Capt. William Heyser's Company, muster roll dated October 23, 1776, in continental service, and on duty in May, 1777 [Ref: D-264, W-1190, L-79, GG-98].

MYERS, Frederick. Private, Militia, 6th Class, Capt. Joseph Chapline's Company, 2nd Battalion, 1776/1777 [Ref: M-241, which listed the name as "Frederick Myres"].

MYERS, George. Enrolled in the first militia company organized for the Revolutionary War in the Elizabeth Town District of Frederick County (now the Hagerstown area of Washington County) on January 6, 1776 [Ref: Q-271, W-1190]. Private, Militia, 7th Class, Capt. Joseph Chapline's Company, 2nd Battalion, 1776/1777 [Ref: M-242, which listed the name as "George Myre"]. See "Ludwick Myers" and "George Miers," q.v.

MYERS, Jacob. See "Jacob Meyer (Myers)," q.v.

MYERS, John (1742-1836). Private, Flying Camp, who enlisted in Frederick County on August 5, 1776 [Ref: D-45, which listed the name as "John Myer"]. "John Myers" died on August 6, 1836, aged 94, and is buried in the Old Reformed Graveyard at Sharpsburg in Washington County, Maryland [Ref: JJ-I:27].

MYERS, Ludwick. Private, Militia, 7th Class, Capt. Basil Williams' Company, 1776/1777 [Ref: M-244, A-1146]. One Ludwick Myers died before September 28, 1780 (date of balance book entry in Washington County), leaving a widow (no name given in this account) and equal shares to George, Pegie, and Elizabeth Myers [Ref: J-22].

MYERS, Pegie. See "Ludwick Myers," q.v.

MYERS, Peter. Enrolled in the third militia company organized for the Revolutionary War in the Elizabeth Town District of Frederick County (now the Hagerstown area of Washington County), passed by the Committee of Observation on June 5, 1776, and assigned to Capt. John Reynolds' command [Ref: Q-273]. Private, Militia, 1st Class, Capt. Joseph Chapline's Company, 2nd Battalion, 1776/1777 [Ref: M-241, which listed the name as "Peter Myres"].

NADENBUSH, Thomas. Took the Oath of Allegiance before the Hon. Henry Schnebley in 1778 [Ref: O-49, J-13].

NAFFE, George. See "George Neff," q.v.

NAGAL, Philip. Substitute, Maryland Line, discharged from service on October 26, 1781 upon the recommendation of Dr. James Murray [Ref: G-653].

NAGEL, David. Took the Oath of Allegiance before the Hon. Henry Schnebley in 1778 [Ref: O-51, J-14].

NAGELEY, Peter. Took the Oath of Allegiance before the Hon. John Stull in 1778 [Ref: O-47, J-11, which latter source listed the name as "Peter Negeley"].

NANCE, Dianah. See "John Lynn," q.v.

NARRY, Martain. See "Martin Harry," q.v.

NAVE, Abraham. See "Abraham Neff" and "Leonard Bowers," q.v.

NAVE, Henry. Private, Militia, 5th Class, Capt. Basil Williams' Company, 1776/1777 [Ref: M-244, A-1146]. See "Henry Neff," q.v.
NAVE, John. See "John Neff" and "Leonard Bowers," q.v.
NAVE, Mark W. See "Leonard Bowers," q.v.
NAVE, Rebecca. See "Leonard Bowers," q.v.
NEAD, Charlotte. See "Matthias Nead," q.v.
NEAD, Daniel. Private, Militia, 2nd Class, Capt. Michael Fackler's Company, 1776/1777 [Ref: M-245, A-1146]. Sergeant, Select Militia, Capt. Adam Ott's Company, 1781 [Ref: M-238, A-1146, which listed the name as "Daniel Nied"]. See "Matthias Nead," q.v.
NEAD, Jacob. See "Matthias Nead," q.v.
NEAD, Matthias. Served on the Committee of Observation in February, 1777 [Ref: Q-228]. Took the Oath of Allegiance before the Hon. Henry Schnebley in 1778 [Ref: O-49, J-12]. Rendered patriotic service by supplying two blankets for the use of the military in March, 1776, as recorded by the Committee of Observation on April 12, 1776 [Ref: L-82, Q-157, which latter source listed the name as "Mathias Need"]. One of several patriots appointed by the Committee of Observation on December 30, 1776 "to form the county into companies (after the militia had marched) for the purpose of relieving the distressed inhabitants of said county and also to compel the Dunkards and Mennonists to give their assistance." [Ref: Q-345, which listed the name as "Matthias Neid"]. Appointed by the Committee of Observation on January 2, 1777 as one of the persons authorized "to appraise all the arms that Col. Stull's Battalion may take with them to camp." [Ref: Q-29, which listed the name as "Matthias Need"]. On January 6, 1777 he was appointed to serve on the Committee of Observation for Elizabeth Town District (now the Hagerstown area of Washington County) in the room of Capt. Bell who resigned [Ref: Q-32, which listed the name as "Matthias Neid"]. "Mathias Nead" died before March 19, 1791 (date of balance book entry in Washington County), leaving a widow (no name given in this account) and equal shares to Daniel Nead, Barbara Clinesmith, Jacob Nead, Charlotte Nead, and Uliana English [Ref: J-30].
NEAL, Christopher. Private who was enrolled by Capt. Henry Hardman and passed on July 19, 1776 in Frederick (now Washington) County [Ref: D-51, which listed the name as "Chr. Neal"].
NEALE, James. Private who was recruited and passed by County Lieutenant Thomas Sprigg on April 22, 1780 [Ref: D-336].
NEEDHAM, William. Took the Oath of Allegiance before September 1, 1780 [Ref: X-117].

NEFF (NAFF, NAVE, KNAVE), Abraham (c1740-1803). Private, Militia, 5th Class, Capt. Peter Swingle's (Swingley's) Company, 1776/1777 [Ref: A-1146, M-248, which listed the name as "Abraham Nave"]. One of several patriots appointed by the Committee of Observation on December 30, 1776 "to form the county into companies (after the militia had marched) for the purpose of relieving the distressed inhabitants of said county and also to compel the Dunkards and Mennonists to give their assistance." [Ref: Q-346]. On January 10, 1777 he was appointed to serve on the Committee of Observation for Elizabeth Town District in the room of Ludwick Young who had resigned [Ref: Q-35, Q-228, which listed the name as "Abraham Kneff"]. "Abraham Neff, an old inhabitant of Elizabeth Town" died on June 8, 1803, and was interred in the German Lutheran burying ground [Ref: LL-2:85]. See "Leonard Bowers," q.v.

NEFF (NAFF, NAVE, KNAVE), George. Took the Oath of Allegiance before the Hon. Henry Schnebley in 1778 [Ref: J-14, which listed the name as "George Naffe" and O-51, which listed the name as "George Haffe"].

NEFF (NAFF, NAVE, KNAVE), Henry. Private, Militia, 6th Class, Capt. James Walling's Company, 2nd Battalion, 1776/1777 [Ref: M-239, A-1146]. Private who was enlisted by Capt. John Reynolds and passed on July 18, 1776 in Frederick (now Washington) County [Ref: D-50].

NEFF (NAFF, NAVE, KNAVE), Jacob. Private, Militia, 3rd Class, Capt. Henry Boteler's Company, 1776/1777 [Ref: M-237, A-1146, which listed the name as "Jacob Nave"].

NEFF (NAFF, NAVE, KNAVE), Jacob. Private, Militia, 7th Class, Capt. Jeremiah Spires' Company, 2nd Battalion, 1776/1777 [Ref: M-239, A-1146].

NEFF (NAFF, NAVE, KNAVE), John. Private, Militia, 5th Class, Capt. James Walling's Company, 2nd Battalion, 1776/1777 [Ref: M-239, A-1146]. On September 23, 1780, Col. Lemuel Barritt recommended to Governor Lee that "John Naff" be commissioned as second lieutenant in the militia at Willstown since so many officers of the Western Battalion had moved out of Maryland to Kentucky and elsewhere [Ref: G-123]. It is interesting to note that when Francis Campble wrote his will at Shippensburg in Cumberland County, Pennsylvania in August, 1790 (probated in March, 1791) he mentioned, among other things, "land in tenure of John Neff." [Ref: Cumberland County, Pennsylvania Wills Book E, pp. 209-211]. See "Leonard Bowers," q.v.

NEFF (NAFF, NAVE, KNAVE), Leonard. Private, Militia, 6th Class, Capt. Michael Fackler's Company, 1776/1777 [Ref: M-245, A-1146, which listed the name as "Leonard Nave"]. Took the Oath of Allegiance before the Hon. Henry Schnebley in 1778 [Ref: O-51, J-15, which listed the name as "Leonard Naffe"].

NEFF (NAFF, NAVE, KNAVE), Michael. Private, Militia, 8th Class, Capt. Michael Fackler's Company, 1776/1777 [Ref: M-245, A-1146, which listed the name as "Michael Nave"].

NEFF (NAFF), Peter. Took the Oath of Allegiance before September 1, 1780 [Ref: X-117, which listed the name as "Peter Nanffs"].

NEIGHKIRK, Henry. See "James Chapline," q.v.

NEIMAN, Catharine and Conrad. See "Adam Weise," q.v.

NEITH, Thomas. Took the Oath of Allegiance before the Hon. Christopher Cruse in Sharpsburg Hundred before March 2, 1778 [Ref: O-34, J-2].

NELDIE, Christian. Private, Militia, 7th Class, Capt. James Smith's Company, 2nd Battalion, 1776/1777 [Ref: M-240, A-1146].

NELDIE, Jacob. Private, Militia, 3rd Class, Capt. James Smith's Company, 2nd Battalion, 1776/1777 [Ref: M-239, A-1146].

NELDIE, John. Private, Militia, 3rd Class, Capt. James Smith's Company, 2nd Battalion, 1776/1777 [Ref: M-239, A-1146].

NERVELL, William. Substitute, Maryland Line, discharged on October 30, 1781 [Ref: G-656].

NESBETT, Nathaniel. Took the Oath of Allegiance before the Hon. John Barnes before February 28, 1778 [Ref: O-44, J-9].

NEVIL, George. Took the Oath of Allegiance before the Hon. John Barnes before February 28, 1778 [Ref: O-45, J-9].

NEWCOMER, Barbara. See "Henry Newcomer," q.v.

NEWCOMER, Christopher. Private, Militia, 7th Class, Capt. James Walling's Company, 2nd Battalion, 1776/1777 [Ref: M-239, A-1146, which listed the name as "Christopher Newcommer"].

NEWCOMER, Henry. Private, Militia, 8th Class, Capt. James Walling's Company, 2nd Battalion, 1776/1777 [Ref: M-239, A-1146, which listed the name as "Henry Newcommer"]. Henry Newcomer and "---- Bleachy." [Yost Pleacker] of Washington County were among several persons apprehended in June, 1781 on the suspicion by Capt. Orendorff that they were "disaffected and dangerous persons whose going at large may be detrimental to the state." The captain stated he would interview them. A long transcript can be found in *Archives of Maryland, Volume 47*, which confirmed his suspicions about both men. It stated, in part, they "thought the King would over-come this country and we have raised a body of men for the service of the King." Henry Newcomer was tried, convicted, fined and imprisoned for his actions. Subsequently, on

January 27, 1783, upon the petition of a number of respectable citizens of Frederick and Washington Counties, plus the pleading of his wife Barbara in behalf of herself and their 11 children, the Council of Maryland remitted the balance of the imposed fines so that the family would not lose their property and be reduced to a state of begging and ruin [Ref: G-467, G-469, H-298, H-328, H-329, H-330, I-3, I-350, P-346, which latter source notes Christopher Orendorff's information about a conspiracy in Washington and Frederick Counties in 1781].

NEWCOMER, Peter (1753-1826). Private, Militia, 2nd Class, Capt. Conrad Hogmire's Company, 1776/1777 [Ref: M-244, A-1146]. "Rev. Peter Newcomer" died at his residence on Beaver Creek, 3 miles from Boonsborough, on January 4, 1826, aged about 73 [Ref: Z-52, Z-79].

NEWCOMER, Samuel. See "William Webb," q.v.

NEWELL, Joseph. Enrolled in the first militia company organized for the Revolutionary War in the Elizabeth Town District of Frederick County (now the Hagerstown area of Washington County) on January 6, 1776 [Ref: Q-270, W-1190, which listed the name as "Joseph Newel"]. Took the Oath of Allegiance before the Hon. Christopher Cruse in Sharpsburg Hundred before March 2, 1778 [Ref: O-34, J-2, which listed the name as "Joseph Newill"].

NEWELL, Thomas. Enrolled in the first militia company organized for the Revolutionary War in the Elizabeth Town District of Frederick County (now the Hagerstown area of Washington County) on January 6, 1776 [Ref: Q-271, W-1190, which listed the name as "Thomas Newel"]. Private, Militia, 7th Class, Capt. John Rennolds' (Reynolds') Company, 2nd Battalion, 1776/1777 [Ref: M-240].

NEWELL, William. Enrolled in the first militia company organized for the Revolutionary War in the Elizabeth Town District of Frederick County (now the Hagerstown area of Washington County) on January 6, 1776 [Ref: Q-270, W-1190, which listed the name as "William Newel"]. Private who enlisted in the militia on August 18, 1781 for service in the Continental Army [Ref: D-387].

NEWELL, William Jr. Took the Oath of Allegiance before the Hon. Christopher Cruse in Sharpsburg Hundred before March 2, 1778 [Ref: O-34, J-2, which listed the name as "William Newill, Jr."].

NEWEY, John. Enrolled in the second militia company organized for the Revolutionary War in the Elizabeth Town District of Frederick County (now the Hagerstown area of Washington County) on March 9, 1776 [Ref: Q-272].

NEWHOUSE, Elizabeth and John. See "Van Swearingen," q.v.

NEWMAN, John (1740-c1825). Private who was enrolled by Capt. Henry Hardman and passed on July 19, 1776 in Frederick (now Washington) County [Ref: D-51]. Took the Oath of Allegiance before the Hon. John Cellars in January, 1778 [Ref: K-1814, O-40, J-5]. Soldier who resided in Washington County and was granted a pension certificate in August, 1820, according to an Act of Congress of March 18, 1818, since he had proven that he was "in the enjoyment of a certain degree of poverty" as required by the Act as amended on May 1, 1820 [Ref: W-1190]. Private, Maryland Line, received pension S35008 at $96 per year effective March 5, 1819; aged 80 in 1820 with no family [Ref: R-43, V-III:2488].

NICEWONDER, Isaac. Private, Militia, 2nd Class, Capt. Daniel Clapsaddle's Company, 1st Battalion, 1776/1777 [Ref: M-236, A-1146].

NICEWONDER, John. Private, Militia, 1st Class, Capt. Martin Kershner's Company, 1776/1777 [Ref: A-1146, M-247].

NICEWONGER, John. Private, Militia, 3rd Class, Capt. Conrad Hogmire's Company, 1776/1777 [Ref: M-244, A-1146].

NICHODEMUS, Conrad. Fourth Corporal, Militia, Capt. Daniel Clapsaddle's Company, 1st Battalion, 1776/1777 [Ref: M-236, A-1146]. Took the Oath of Allegiance before the Hon. Christopher Cruse in Lower Antietam Hundred before March 2, 1778 [Ref: J-2, O-35, which latter source listed the name as "Conarad Nichodamus"].

NICHODEMUS (NICODEMUS), Conrad. Captain, Militia, 6th Company, 2nd Battalion, 1776/1777 [Ref: M-107, M-237, E-145]. Took the Oath of Allegiance before the Hon. Henry Schnebley in 1778 [Ref: O-50, J-13, which listed the name as "Conrad Nicodemus"]. Resigned his commission on October 28, 1780 [Ref: G-165, P-331].

NICHODEMUS (NICODEMUS), Frederick (1733-1816). First Lieutenant, Militia, Capt. Daniel Clapsaddle's Company, 1st Battalion, Flying Camp, commissioned September 26, 1776 [Ref: M-236, A-1146, D-73]. Took the Oath of Allegiance before the Hon. Andrew Rentch before March 7, 1778 [Ref: O-52, J-15, which listed the name as "Frederick Nicodemus"]. Born on February 26, 1733, married Margaret Ripple, served under Capt. Daniel Clapsaddle in Washington County, Maryland during the war, and died on October 26, 1816 in Franklin County, Pennsylvania. Their son John married Margaret Potter [Ref: BB-545, which listed the name as "Frederick Nicodemus"].

NICHOLAS, Joseph. Took the Oath of Allegiance before the Hon. Andrew Bruce before March 2, 1778 [Ref: O-41, J-6]. On September 23, 1780, Col. Lemuel Barritt recommended to Governor Lee that Joseph Nicholas be commissioned an ensign in the militia at Keystone since so many officers of the Western Battalion had moved out of Maryland to Kentucky and elsewhere [Ref: G-123].

NICHOL, Jacob. Private, Militia, 6th Class, Capt. Peter Beall's Company, 1st Battalion, 1776/1777 [Ref: M-240]. Rendered patriotic service by providing a coverlid for the use of the military in January, 1777, as recorded by the Committee of Observation on January 27, 1777 [Ref: Q-53]. Took the Oath of Allegiance before the Hon. Henry Schnebley in 1778 [Ref: O-49, J-13].

NICHOL, John. Enrolled in the second militia company organized for the Revolutionary War in the Elizabeth Town District of Frederick County (now the Hagerstown area of Washington County) on March 9, 1776 [Ref: Q-271]. Took the Oath of Allegiance before the Hon. Andrew Bruce before March 2, 1778 [Ref: O-41, J-6, which latter source listed the name as "John Nicole"].

NICHOLLS, Benjamin. Private, Militia, 6th Class, Capt. Charles Clinton's Company, 1776/1777 [Ref: M-245, A-1146].

NICHOLLS, John. Second Lieutenant, Militia, Capt. Henry Boteler's Company, 1776, and subsequently promoted to first lieutenant when Thomas Odel was promoted to captain in 1778 [Ref: M-237, A-1146]. Took the Oath of Allegiance before the Hon. Christopher Cruse in Lower Antietam Hundred before March 2, 1778 [Ref: J-3, O-35, which listed the name as "John Nichells"].

NICHOLLS, Joseph. Private, Militia, 6th Class, Capt. James Prather's Company, 3rd Battalion, 1776/1777 [Ref: M-243].

NICHOLLS, Trail. Fourth Sergeant, Militia, Capt. Henry Boteler's Company, 1776/1777 [Ref: M-237, A-1146].

NICHOLLS, William. Third Sergeant, Militia, Capt. Henry Boteler's Company, 1776/1777 [Ref: M-237, A-1146].

NICHOLS, Archibald. Enrolled in the second militia company organized for the Revolutionary War in the Elizabeth Town District of Frederick County (now the Hagerstown area of Washington County) on March 9, 1776 [Ref: Q-271].

NICHOLS, Flayl. Enrolled in the second militia company organized for the Revolutionary War in the Elizabeth Town District of Frederick County (now the Hagerstown area of Washington County) on March 9, 1776 [Ref: Q-271].

NICHOLS, Isaac. Took the Oath of Allegiance before the Hon. John Stull in 1778 [Ref: O-47, J-11].

NICHOLS, William. Enrolled in the second militia company organized for the Revolutionary War in the Elizabeth Town District of Frederick

County (now the Hagerstown area of Washington County) on March 9, 1776 [Ref: Q-272].

NIGH, Catherine. See "Christopher Burkett," q.v.

NIGH, George. Took the Oath of Allegiance before the Hon. Henry Schnebley in 1778 [Ref: O-50, J-14].

NIGHT, Thomas. Enrolled in the first militia company organized for the Revolutionary War in the Elizabeth Town District of Frederick County (now the Hagerstown area of Washington County) on January 6, 1776 [Ref: Q-271, W-1190].

NIHY, George. Took the Oath of Allegiance before the Hon. Henry Schnebley in 1778 [Ref: O-50, J-14, which latter source listed the name as "George Niky"].

NINOR, Christopher. Private who enlisted in the militia on August 23, 1781 for service in the Continental Army [Ref: D-388].

NISBITT, Nicholas. Private, Militia, 3rd Class, Capt. John Bennet's Company, 1776/1777 [Ref: M-246, A-1146].

NOGLE, Philip. Private who enlisted in the militia on August 18, 1781 for service in the Continental Army [Ref: D-388].

NOISE, Richard. See "Richard Noyse," q.v.

NON, Benjamin. Private, Militia, 2nd Class, Capt. Conrad Nichodemus' Company, 2nd Battalion, 1776/1777 [Ref: M-237, A-1146].

NORFORD, Daniel. See "Daniel Morford," q.v.

NORMAN, James. Private, Militia, 7th Class, Capt. Joseph Chapline's Company, 2nd Battalion, 1776/1777 [Ref: M-242]. Took the Oath of Allegiance before the Hon. Christopher Cruse in Sharpsburg Hundred before March 2, 1778 [Ref: O-34, J-2].

NORRIS, John. Enrolled in the third militia company organized for the Revolutionary War in the Elizabeth Town District of Frederick County (now the Hagerstown area of Washington County), passed by the Committee of Observation on June 5, 1776, and assigned to Capt. John Reynolds' command [Ref: Q-273].

NORRIS, John. Private, Militia, 1st Class, Capt. Joseph Chapline's Company, 2nd Battalion, 1776/1777 [Ref: M-241]. Took the Oath of Allegiance before the Hon. Joseph Chapline before April 17, 1779 [Ref: J-5, O-39].

NORRIS, Joseph. One of several patriots appointed by the Committee of Observation on January 7, 1777 "to form the county into companies (after the militia had marched) for the purpose of relieving the distressed inhabitants of said county and also to compel the Dunkards and Mennonists to give their assistance." [Ref: Q-31]. Took the Oath of

Allegiance before the Hon. Joseph Chapline before April 17, 1779 [Ref: J-5, O-39].

NORRIS, Patrick. Enrolled in the second militia company organized for the Revolutionary War in the Elizabeth Town District of Frederick County (now the Hagerstown area of Washington County) on March 9, 1776 [Ref: Q-272].

NORRISS, John. Private, Militia, 3rd Class, Capt. Barnett Johnston's Company, 3rd Battalion, 1776/1777 [Ref: M-242].

NORRISS, Thomas. Private, Militia, 4th Class, Capt. Barnett Johnston's Company, 3rd Battalion, 1776/1777 [Ref: M-242].

NORTHCRAFT, Edward (1758-c1840). Private, Maryland Line, who applied for pension S8020 in Allegany County, Maryland on December 14, 1835, stating he was born in Montgomery County, Maryland on August 18, 1758 and lived there at the time of his enlistment. In 1794 he moved to Sharpsburg, Maryland for 9 years, then to Pennsylvania for 5 years, and then moved near the line between Washington and Allegany Counties [Ref: V-III:2512].

NORWOOD, Belt. Took the Oath of Allegiance before the Hon. Samuel Hughes before March 1, 1778 [Ref: O-33, J-1].

NOSELAND, James. Private, Militia, Capt. Charles Coulson's Company, enrolled August 28, 1776 [Ref: A-1146, M-243, which listed the name as "James Noseland (Hogeland?)"].

NOWEL, James (c1755-1824). Private, Maryland Line, who received a disability pension in Washington County, Maryland on April 5, 1811, stating he had lived there many years. In 1811 he had 8 children of which 5 were very young (no names given). He later applied for and received pension S25331 and died in 1824 [Ref: V-III:2519]. See "James Nowles," q.v.

NOWELL, Joseph. Private, Militia, 4th Class, Capt. John Rennolds' (Reynolds') Company, 2nd Battalion, 1776/1777 [Ref: M-240].

NOWELL, William Jr. Private, Militia, 4th Class, Capt. John Rennolds' (Reynolds') Company, 2nd Battalion, 1776/1777 [Ref: M-240]. See "William Newell, Jr.," q.v.

NOWLES, Edward. Private who was enlisted by Lieut. Moses Chapline and passed on July 24, 1776 in Frederick (now Washington) County [Ref: D-50].

NOWLES, James. Private who was enlisted by Lieut. Moses Chapline and passed on July 24, 1776 in Frederick (now Washington) County [Ref: D-50, which listed the name as "James Nowles, D.S.T."]. See "James Nowel," q.v.

NOY, George. Private, Militia, 4th Class, Capt. Peter Swingle's (Swingley's) Company, 1776/1777 [Ref: A-1146, M-248].

NOYSE, Richard. Private who was enrolled by Capt. Henry Hardman and passed on July 19, 1776 in Frederick (now Washington) County [Ref: D-51, which listed the name as "Rhd. Noise"].

NOYSE, Thomas. Took the Oath of Allegiance before the Hon. William Yates in 1778 [Ref: O-48, J-12].

OAIR, John. Private, Militia, 3rd Class, Capt. James Walling's Company, 2nd Battalion, 1776/1777 [Ref: M-238, A-1146].

OATS, Matthias. Appointed by the Committee of Observation to carry the Association of Freemen to male residents in his hundred (district) on March 4, 1776 "and present it for signing and make an exact account of those that sign and those that refuse with their reasons for refusing." [Ref: Q-153, L-82].

OBINGER, Philip. See "George Troxel," q.v.

OBLENONER, George. Private, Militia, 5th Class, Capt. Martin Kershner's Company, 1776/1777 [Ref: A-1146, M-247].

ODEL, Thomas. Enrolled in the second militia company organized for the Revolutionary War in the Elizabeth Town District of Frederick County (now the Hagerstown area of Washington County) on March 9, 1776 [Ref: Q-271]. First Lieutenant, Militia, Capt. Henry Boteler's Company, 1776, and subsequently captain of that company upon the resignation of Capt. Boteler in 1778 [Ref: M-237, A-1146]. See "John Nicholls," q.v.

ODLEBERGER, Phillip. Private, Militia, 3rd Class, Capt. Samuel Hughes' Company, 2nd Battalion, 1776/1777 [Ref: M-238, A-1146].

ODLEBURGER, Phillip Jr. Private, Militia, 6th Class, Capt. Samuel Hughes' Company, 2nd Battalion, 1776/1777 [Ref: M-238, A-1146].

O'DONALD, John Jr. Enrolled in the first militia company organized for the Revolutionary War in the Elizabeth Town District of Frederick County (now the Hagerstown area of Washington County) on January 6, 1776 [Ref: Q-270, W-1190].

O'DONNELL, John. Private, Militia, 2nd Class, Capt. John Rennolds' (Reynolds') Company, 2nd Battalion, 1776/1777 [Ref: M-240, which listed the name as "John O. Doniel"]. Took the Oath of Allegiance before the Hon. Christopher Cruse in Lower Antietam Hundred before March 2, 1778 [Ref: J-3, O-35, which latter source listed the name as "John Odonel"].

OGLE, William. Private, Militia, 7th Class, Capt. Daniel Cresap's Company, 3rd Battalion, 1776/1777 [Ref: M-241]. Took the Oath of Allegiance before the Hon. Lemuel Barritt before March 16, 1778 [Ref: O-42, J-7].

O'HARA, Arthur. Private, Militia, 8th Class, Capt. James Smith's Company, 2nd Battalion, 1776/1777 [Ref: M-240, A-1146].

O'HARRA, Patrick. Took the Oath of Allegiance before the Hon. John Barnes before February 28, 1778 [Ref: J-9, O-40, which latter source listed the name as "Patrick Oharra"].

OLDWINE, Barney (1758-1823). Soldier who resided in Washington County and was granted a pension certificate in August, 1820, according to an Act of Congress of March 18, 1818, since he had proven that he was "in the enjoyment of a certain degree of poverty" as required by the Act as amended on May 1, 1820 [Ref: W-1190]. Private, Pennsylvania Line, pensioned at $96 per year effective October 29, 1818 and died in Washington County, Maryland on May 7, 1823, in his 64th year [Ref: R-43, Z-46].

OLDWINE (OHLWINE), Charles (1755-1830). Private, Pennsylvania Line, pensioned under the Act of March 18, 1818 in Washington County at $96 per year effective October 29, 1818, suspended September 5, 1820 under the Act of May 1, 1820, restored commencing July 23, 1823, and died November 19, 1830 [Ref: R-43]. Revolutionary soldier in the company of Capt. Pike of the 4th Regiment of Light Dragoons, served in the Battles of Monmouth and Bunker's Hill, "Charles Ohlwine died in Hagerstown, Maryland on Friday, November 19, 1830, aged 75 years, 3 months and 22 days, an old and respectable inhabitant of that place in which he lived for upwards of fifty years, among the few remaining Revolutionary Heroes. After the war he resumed his occupation, a stone mason. Being reduced in circumstances, he succeeded another Revolutionary patriot as crier of the Orphans' Court of his native county, where he was continued by the different courts until his decease." [Ref: Z-124, citing *The Torchlight* and *Maryland Herald* newspapers on November 25, 1830, and DD-14, citing *The Republican Banner* on November 27, 1830].

OLDWORT, Jacob. Took the Oath of Allegiance before the Hon. Lemuel Barritt before March 16, 1778 [Ref: O-42, J-8].

OLINGER, Christian. Private who was enrolled by Capt. Henry Hardman and passed on July 19, 1776 in Frederick (now Washington) County [Ref: D-51, which listed the name as "Chr. Alinger"].

OLINGER, Eustatious. Private, Militia, 7th Class, Capt. Peter Swingle's (Swingley's) Company, 1776/1777 [Ref: A-1146, M-249, which listed the name as "Eustatious Elinger"]. Took the Oath of Allegiance before the Hon. John Cellars in January, 1778 [Ref: K-1814, J-6, O-40, which latter source listed the name as "Eustations Olinger"].

OLINGER, Jacob. Private, Militia, Capt. Martin Kershner's Company, 32nd Battalion, December 27, 1776 [Ref: K-1814, Box 3]. Took the Oath of Allegiance before the Hon. Henry Schnebley in 1778 [Ref: O-50, J-14].

OLINGER, Philip. Private, Militia, 8th Class, Capt. Martin Kershner's Company, 1776/1777 [Ref: A-1146, M-248, which listed the name as "Phillip Alanger"]. Took the Oath of Allegiance before the Hon. John Cellars in January, 1778 [Ref: K-1814, O-40].

OLINGER, Stautius. Private, Militia, Capt. Martin Kershner's Company, 32nd Battalion, December 27, 1776 [Ref: K-1814, Box 3].

OMER, Henry. See "Henry Queer," q.v.

OPP, Nicholas. See "Nicholas Upp," q.v.

ORENDORFF (ORNDORFF), Christian (c1750-1824). Elected to serve on the Committee of Observation for the Elizabeth Town District of Frederick County (now the Hagerstown area of Washington County) on September 12, 1775 [Ref: Q-142, which listed the name as "Christian Orendurff"], and referred to as "Capt. Christian Orendoff" on February 19, 1776 [Ref: Q-152]. Enrolled in the third militia company organized for the Revolutionary War in the Elizabeth Town District, passed by the Committee of Observation on June 5, 1776, and assigned to Capt. John Reynolds' command [Ref: Q-273, which listed the name as "Christian Orindorf"]. Appointed to raise funds on January 24, 1775 for the Committee of Observation in Sharpsburg Hundred in Frederick (now Washington) County [Ref: L-75, which listed the name as "Christian Orndorff"]. Served on the Committee of Observation in April, 1776 [Ref: Q-155, which listed the name as "Christian Orandorff"]. Took the Oath of Allegiance before the Hon. Joseph Chapline before April 17, 1779 [Ref: J-5, O-39, which listed the name as "Christian Orendoff"]. Second Lieutenant, Upper District, Frederick County (now Washington County), July, 1776 [Ref: D-48, which listed the name as "Christian Orndorff"]. Lieutenant, Maryland Line, captured and later exchanged on October 25, 1780 [Ref: D-616, which listed the name as "Christian Orendorff"]. Captain, 1st Company, 3rd Maryland Line, 1781-1782 [Ref: D-448, N-41]. On February 19, 1819 the Treasurer of the Western Shore of Maryland was directed to pay to "Christian Orndorff" late a revolutionary officer, during life, the half pay of a captain [Ref: AA-379]. One "Christian Orndorff" died testate before December 3, 1799 (date of balance book entry in Washington County), but the distribution mentioned the daughters only [Ref: J-38]. However, Christian the soldier was still living in 1819. "Capt. Christian Orndorff died on the last Sunday in September, 1824 [another source states October 1, 1824], in his 67th year, at his residence near Martinsburg [now West Virginia]. A veteran of the Revolution, he entered the army in '76 as a lieutenant, advanced to captain in the 6th Regt. Maryland Line, which he held until close of the war. He was captured at Fort Washington. After exchange he joined the army at the South under Gen. Green." He married Anna Marie Stille [Ref: Z-69, citing *The Martinsburg Gazette*, September 30, 1824; and Y-II:2188]. Additional research may be necessary before drawing conclusions since there were two men named Christopher Orndorff who were also officers and it is possible that Christian could be confused with Christopher in some of the records (and vice-versa).

ORENDORFF (ORNDORFF), Christopher or Christian (1726-1797). Major, Militia, 2nd Battalion, June 22, 1778 [Ref: M-108. E-145]. Served on the Committee of Observation for the Elizabeth Town District (now the Hagerstown area of Washington County) in December, 1776 [Ref: Q-340, which listed the name as "Major Christr. Orindorf"]. Took the Oath of Allegiance before the Hon. Joseph Chapline before April 17, 1779 [Ref: J-5, O-39, which listed the name as "Christopher Ornduff"]. "Christian Orendorff, Sr." was born in Germany on November 15, 1726, married Elizabeth Hoffman, served as a major in the Revolution, and died in Maryland on December 10, 1797 [Ref: Y-II:2188]. "Elizabeth Ann Orndoff, widow of Major Christian Orndoff, formerly of this county, died at her granddaughter's [no name given] on Sunday night last [July 14, 1829] in the 97th year of her age. It is supposed that not less than 500 of her children's children are now living. Two of her children, one 60, the other 70 years of age, witnessed her interment. Up to the 6th generation followed her to the tomb." [Ref: Z-111, citing *The Torchlight and Public Advertiser* in Hagerstown on July 16, 1829]. See "Christian Orendorff" and "Christopher Orendorff, Jr.," q.v. Additional research may be necessary before drawing conclusions.

ORENDORFF (ORNDORFF), Christopher Jr. (1752-1823). Second Lieutenant, Militia, 1776. First Lieutenant, Militia, Capt. John Rennolds' (Reynolds') Company, 2nd Battalion, June 22, 1778 [Ref: M-108, M-240, E-145]. Captain, 2nd Battalion, November 21, 1780 [Ref: G-220, which listed the name as "Christo. Orndorff"]. Christopher Orndorff, formerly of Washington County, Maryland, died in Logan County, Kentucky on September 14, 1823, aged about 72. Mary Orndorff, relict of the late Christian *[sic]* Orndorff, died in Logan County on October 4, 1823, in her 68th year [Ref: Z-49]. "Christopher Orendorff" was born in Pennsylvania on November 23, 1752, married Mary Thomas, served as a captain in the Revolution, and died in Kentucky on September 14, 1823 [Ref: Y-II:2188]. See "Henry Newcomer" and "Christian Orendorff" and "Christopher Orendorff," q.v. Additional research may be necessary before drawing conclusions.

ORENDORFF, Elizabeth. See "Christian Orendorff," q.v.

ORENDORFF, Mary. See "Christopher Orendorff, Jr.," q.v.

ORN, John. Took the Oath of Allegiance before September 1, 1780 [Ref: X-117].

ORNEST, Henry. Private, Militia, 8th Class, Capt. Isaac Baker's Company, 1776/1777 [Ref: A-1146, M-247].

OSBURN, Benjamin. Private who was enrolled by Capt. Aeneas Campbell and passed by Major Francis Deakins on July 18, 1776 [Ref: D-49].

OSTER, Adam. Took the Oath of Allegiance before the Hon. Henry Schnebley in 1778 [Ref: O-50, J-13].

OSTER, Conrad. Private, Militia, 2nd Class, Capt. Martin Kershner's Company, 1776/1777 [Ref: A-1146, M-247]. Private, Militia, Capt. Martin Kershner's Company, 32nd Battalion, December 27, 1776 [Ref: K-1814, Box 3]. Took the Oath of Allegiance before the Hon. Henry Schnebley in 1778 [Ref: O-51, J-14]. See "Matthias Ridenour," q.v.

OSTER, Eve. See "Matthias Ridenour," q.v.

OSTER, Henry. See "Philip Oster," q.v.

OSTER, Jacob. Private, Militia, 2nd Class, Capt. John Bennet's Company, 1776/1777 [Ref: M-246, A-1146]. Took the Oath of Allegiance before the Hon. Henry Schnebley in 1778 [Ref: O-50, J-14].

OSTER, John. There were several men with this name who rendered service during the Revolutionary War. Additional research will be necessary before drawing conclusions. (1) Private, Militia, Capt. William Heyser's Company, 1776, in continental service [Ref: W-1190, L-79]. (2) Drummer, Militia, Capt. John Kershner's Company, on duty guarding prisoners of war at Fort Frederick on June 27, 1778 [Ref: D-328]. (3) Private, Militia, 3rd Class, Capt. Peter Beall's Company, 1st Battalion, 1776/1777 [Ref: M-240]. (4) Private, Militia, 5th Class, Capt. John Bennet's Company, 1776/1777 [Ref: M-246, A-1146]. (5) Took the Oath of Allegiance before the Hon. Joseph Sprigg before April 1, 1778 [Ref: O-53, J-15].

OSTER, Peter. Private, Militia, 3rd Class, Capt. John Bennet's Company, 1776/1777 [Ref: M-246, A-1146]. Private, Militia, Capt. John Kershner's Company, on duty guarding prisoners of war at Fort Frederick on June 27, 1778 [Ref: D-328].

OSTER, Phillip. Private, Militia, 6th Class, Capt. Peter Beall's Company, 1st Battalion, 1776/1777 [Ref: M-240]. Philip Oster died testate by December 22, 1804, naming his brother Henry Oster of Lancaster

County, Pennsylvania, and sister Elizabeth Lighter (wife of Christian) of Hagerstown, Maryland [Ref: MM-13:131, 132].

OTT, Adam (1753-1827). Private, Militia, 7th Class, Capt. Peter Beall's Company, 1st Battalion, 1776/1777 [Ref: M-240]. Took the Oath of Allegiance before the Hon. Joseph Sprigg before April 1, 1778 [Ref: O-53, J-16]. Served as a Recruiting Officer in 1779-1780 [Ref: F-54]. Rendered patriotic service by supplying corn for the use of the military on March 30, 1780 [Ref: W-1190, HH-73]. Captain, Select Militia, March 30, 1781 [Ref: M-238, M-109, G-368]. Lieutenant, Pennsylvania Line, pensioned under the Act of March 18, 1818 in Washington County at $240 per year effective July 30, 1821, suspended September 5, 1820 under the Act of May 1, 1820, restored commencing March 1, 1823 (resolution passed February 22, 1822). [Ref: R-43, AA-379]. "Col. Adam Ott" was born in 1754 and died on August 10, 1827, in his 74th year, an officer of merit in the Revolution, former Sheriff of Washington County, former member of the Maryland House of Delegates in 1789, and an electoral candidate for Thomas Jefferson in 1796 [Ref: Z-15, Z-93, Y-II:2197, KK-II:624, which contains more detailed information]. On March 12, 1828 the Treasurer of the Western Shore of Maryland was directed to pay to Julian Ott, of Washington County, during life, half quarterly, half pay of a lieutenant as further compensation for her husband Adam Ott's services during the Revolutionary War. On February 20, 1829 the Treasurer of the Western Shore of Maryland was directed to pay to Juliana Ott, widow of Adam Ott, a revolutionary soldier, such sum as may appear to be due him on the pension list of the State of Maryland at the time of his decease [Ref: AA-379, AA-380]. A bill of complaint filed in Washington County in 1828 indicated that Adam Ott died without lineal descent and his heirs at law were: John Ott (a brother); Jacob and Michael Ott (sons of Adam's brother Michael, deceased); Jacob, George, Polly, Catharine, Margaret, Julian, and Sally Ott (children of Adam's brother Jacob, deceased); and Peter Fisher, Adam Fisher, John Rigert and wife Catharine Rigert (nephews and niece of Adam Ott). [Ref: Z-99]. Julianna Ott, relict of the late Col. Adam Ott, died in Hagerstown on June 21, 1829, in her 69th year [Ref: Z-111]. See "Barnabas Coplar" and "Adam Weise" and "Michael Ott," q.v.

OTT, Catharine and George. See "Adam Ott," q.v.

OTT, Jacob. First Lieutenant, Militia, Capt. Peter Beall's Company, 2nd Battalion, January 15, 1777 through 1778 [Ref: M-240, A-1146, M-109, C-42, C-50]. Took the Oath of Allegiance before the Hon. Henry Schnebley in 1778 [Ref: O-49, J-12]. See "Michael Ott" and "Adam Ott," q.v.

OTT, John, Juliana, and Margaret. See "Adam Ott," q.v.
OTT, Mary. See "Peter Humrichouse," q.v.
OTT, Mathias. Rendered patriotic service by providing "rashons" for the use of the military in July, 1775, as recorded by the Committee of Observation at Elizabeth Town on November 4, 1775 [Ref: Q-150].
OTT, Michael. Rendered patriotic service by supplying a blanket for the use of the military in March, 1776, as recorded by the Committee of Observation on April 12, 1776 [Ref: L-82, Q-157, which latter source listed the name as "Michel Ott"]. Second Lieutenant, Militia, Capt. Peter Beall's Company, 1st Battalion, January 15, 1777 [Ref: M-240, C-42, C-50]. On September 27, 1776 the Committee of Observation for Elizabeth Town District (now the Hagerstown area of Washington County) recorded that Michael Ott had delivered to Capt. Clapsadle's Company "eighteen tomyhocks at 2 2/6 each." [Ref: Q-337]. One Michael Ott died before August 9, 1786 (date of balance book entry in Washington County), leaving a widow (no name given in this account) and sons Jacob and Michael Ott, with Adam Ott and John Miller as the administrators [Ref: J-26]. See "Adam Ott," q.v.
OTT, Polly and Sally. See "Adam Ott," q.v.
OTTER, George. Private, Militia, Capt. Charles Coulson's Company, enrolled August 28, 1776 [Ref: M-244, A-1146].
OTTO, Matthias. Private, Militia, 8th Class, Capt. Barnett Johnston's Company, 3rd Battalion, 1776/1777 [Ref: M-242, Q-48]. Took the Oath of Allegiance before the Hon. William Yates in 1778 [Ref: O-48, J-12].
OUSTEN, John. Rendered patriotic service in Hagerstown by providing "a rifle gun" to Capt. John Nelson's Company, continental service (Maryland Line), April, 1776 [Ref: Q-162].
OVERACRE, George. Private, Select Militia, Capt. Adam Ott's Company, 1781 [Ref: M-238, A-1146].
OWENS, Patrick. Private who enlisted in the militia on August 20, 1781 for service in the Continental Army [Ref: D-388]. Discharged upon the recommendation of Dr. James Murray on October 18, 1781. It appears he was a substitute for "Conrod Hogmires." [Ref: H-526, G-646, which latter source listed the name as "Patrick Owen"].
OWENS, Thomas. Enrolled in the second militia company organized for the Revolutionary War in the Elizabeth Town District of Frederick County (now the Hagerstown area of Washington County) on March 9, 1776 [Ref: Q-272]. Private, Militia, 7th Class, Capt. Jeremiah Spires' Company, 2nd Battalion, 1776/1777 [Ref: M-239, A-1146]. Took the Oath of Allegiance before the Hon. Richard Davis in 1778 [Ref: J-4, O-36, which listed the name as "Thomas Owen"].

OWSLEY, William. See "William Housley," q.v.

OX, William. Private, Militia, 3rd Class, Capt. Jacob Sharer's Company, 1776/1777 [Ref: A-1146, M-248, which listed the name as "William Ax(?)"]. Took the Oath of Allegiance before the Hon. John Stull in 1778 [Ref: O-47, J-11].

PAIN, Edward. Private who was enlisted by Capt. John Reynolds and passed on July 18, 1776 in Frederick (now Washington) County [Ref: D-50].

PAIN, Flayl. Enrolled in the second militia company organized for the Revolutionary War in the Elizabeth Town District of Frederick County (now the Hagerstown area of Washington County) on March 9, 1776 [Ref: Q-271].

PAINTER, George. Private, Militia, 7th Class, Capt. John Rennolds' (Reynolds') Company, 2nd Battalion, 1776/1777 [Ref: M-240].

PAINTER, Godfrey. Private, Militia, 5th Class, Capt. John Bennet's Company, 1776/1777 [Ref: M-246, A-1146, which listed the name as "Godfree Painter"]. "Godrey Paintor" recorded his animal brand in Washington County court on February 19, 1778, and "Godfrey Painter" recorded the same on February 23, 1778 [Ref: II]. Took the Oath of Allegiance before the Hon. John Barnes before February 28, 1778 [Ref: O-44, J-9].

PAINTER, Henry (1748-1827). Substitute, German Regiment, Maryland Line; discharged on December 10, 1781 [Ref: I-17, N-41]. He applied for pension in Nelson County, Virginia on July 10, 1818, aged 70, stating he was a German and enlisted for 3 years in Hagerstown, Maryland. He participated in the Battles of Trenton, Princeton, Germantown, Monmouth and the siege of York, and was discharged at Union Fort, Pennsylvania. When in the army he was described as "5 ft. 5 in., black hair, black eyes, dark complexion." He died on December 25, 1827 and his widow Sarah later applied for and received pension W5470 [Ref: U-20:4 (1932)]. See "Henry Benter," q.v.

PAINTER, John George. Enrolled in the third militia company organized for the Revolutionary War in the Elizabeth Town District of Frederick County (now the Hagerstown area of Washington County), passed by the Committee of Observation on June 5, 1776, and assigned to Capt. John Reynolds' command [Ref: Q-273].

PAINTER, Mary. See "Melchoir Painter," q.v.

PAINTER, Melchoir (1739 or 1755 - 1822). Soldier who resided in Washington County and was granted a pension certificate in August, 1820, according to an Act of Congress of March 18, 1818, since he had proven that he was "in the enjoyment of a certain degree of poverty" as required by the Act as amended on May 1, 1820 [Ref: W-1190]. Private, German Regiment, Maryland Line, pensioned at $96 per year effective June 16, 1818, and died December 15, 1822 [Ref: R-43]. Melchoir Painter married Ann Mary Miller in Washington County on December 7, 1779 [Ref: N-120, and N-41, which listed "Melcher Painter, born 1739" who served in the Maryland Line and "Michael Painter, born 1755" who served in the Maryland Militia. Additional research may be necessary before drawing conclusions]. On April 1, 1839 the Treasurer of the Western Shore of Maryland was directed to pay to Mary Painter, of Washington County, widow of Melchior Painter, a revolutionary soldier, or to her order, half pay of a private of the revolution during her life, quarterly, commencing January 1, 1839 [Ref: AA-380]. See "Melcher Benter," q.v.

PAINTER, Sarah. See "Henry Painter," q.v.

PAIRS, James. Took the Oath of Allegiance before the Hon. Lemuel Barritt before March 16, 1778 [Ref: O-43, J-8].

PALMER, Ann. See "Christian Welty," q.v.

PALMER, Peter. Took the Oath of Allegiance before September 1, 1780 [Ref: X-117]. Private, Militia, Capt. Martin Kershner's Company, 32nd Battalion, December 27, 1776 [Ref: K-1814, Box 3, which listed the name as "Peter Balmer"].

PALMORE (PALMOUR), Peter. Private, Militia, 5th Class, Capt. Jeremiah Spires' Company, 2nd Battalion, 1776/1777 [Ref: M-239, A-1146, which listed the name as "Peter Palmore"]. Private, Militia, 3rd Class, Capt. James Smith's Company, 2nd Battalion, 1776/1777 [Ref: M-239, A-1146, which listed the name as "Peter Palmour"]. Took the Oath of Allegiance before the Hon. John Cellars in January, 1778 [Ref: K-1814, O-40, J-5, which latter source listed the name as "Peter Pallmon"]. See "Peter Palmer," q.v.

PAPHENBERGER, Adam. See "Adam Poffenberger," q.v.

PARKER, Aaron. Private, Militia, 1st Class, Capt. Charles Clinton's Company, 1776/1777 [Ref: M-245, A-1146]. Third Sergeant, Militia, Capt. Charles Coulson's Company, enrolled August 28, 1776 [Ref: M-243, A-1146].

PARKER, Nathaniel. Took the Oath of Allegiance before the Hon. Lemuel Barritt before March 16, 1778 [Ref: O-43, J-8].

PARKER, Peter. Private, Militia, 2nd Class, Capt. James Prather's Company, 3rd Battalion, 1776/1777 [Ref: M-242].

PARKER, Robert. Private, Militia, Capt. Charles Coulson's Company, enrolled August 28, 1776 [Ref: M-244, A-1146, which listed the name as

"Robart Parker"]. Private, Militia, 1st Class, Capt. Charles Clinton's Company, 1776/1777 [Ref: M-245, A-1146].

PARKS, John. Private, Militia, 7th Class, Capt. Peter Beall's Company, 1st Battalion, 1776/1777 [Ref: M-240]. Rendered patriotic service by supplying a rug for the use of the military in March, 1776, as recorded by the Committee of Observation on April 12, 1776 [Ref: Q-156, L-82].

PARSONS, John. On February 2, 1781 the Council of Maryland proceedings noted a "pardon granted to John Parsons of Washington County convicted at Washington County August Court 1780, for Horse stealing, on Condition that he forthwith join the Regiment to which he belongs and do not desert there from during the present war, and further that he do not return to the said County of Washington during the term aforesaid." [Ref: G-297]. John Parsons had voluntarily enlisted in the 7th Maryland Regiment at Frederick Town on February 15, 1780, to serve three years [Ref: G-312, G-334].

PARVIN, Thomas. Private, Militia, 5th Class, Capt. James Prather's Company, 3rd Battalion, 1776/1777 [Ref: M-243].

PASSENBACK, Balsar. Private, Militia, 7th Class, Capt. Basil Williams' Company, 1776/1777 [Ref: M-244, A-1146].

PATRICK, William. Enrolled in the first militia company organized for the Revolutionary War in the Elizabeth Town District of Frederick County (now the Hagerstown area of Washington County) on January 6, 1776 [Ref: Q-270, W-1190]. Private, Militia, 3rd Class, Capt. Henry Boteler's Company, 1776/1777 [Ref: M-237, A-1146]. Private who was enlisted by Capt. John Reynolds and passed on July 18, 1776 in Frederick (now Washington) County [Ref: D-50]. Took the Oath of Allegiance before the Hon. Christopher Cruse in Lower Antietam Hundred before March 2, 1778 [Ref: J-3, O-35].

PATTERSON, Abigail and Ann. See "William Patterson," q.v.

PATTERSON, Charles. See "William Patterson," q.v.

PATTERSON, Elizabeth and Emsy. See "William Patterson," q.v.

PATTERSON, Hannah and Jane. See "William Patterson," q.v.

PATTERSON, James. First Lieutenant, Militia, Capt. James Walling's Company, 2nd Battalion, 1776/1777 [Ref: M-238, A-1146]. Recorded his animal brand in Washington County court on December 23, 1777 [Ref: II]. Took the Oath of Allegiance before the Hon. Henry Schnebley in 1778 [Ref: O-49, J-13]. Captain, 2nd Battalion, November 21, 1780 [Ref: G-220]. See "William Patterson," q.v.

PATTERSON, John. Private who was recruited and passed by County Lieutenant Thomas Sprigg on April 22, 1780 [Ref: D-336]. See "William Patterson," q.v.

PATTERSON, Joshua. See "William Patterson," q.v.
PATTERSON, Mary and Tece. See "William Patterson," q.v.
PATTERSON, William (1761-1835). Private, Maryland Line, who applied for pension in Scott County, Kentucky on October 21, 1834, stating he was born in Pennsylvania on October 26, 1761 and when just a child he moved with his father (not named) to Washington County, Maryland where he lived at the time of his enlistment. He married Abigail ---- in Loudoun County, Virginia on February 19, 1788 and had these children: Jane (born May 26, 1789), Mary (born September 13, 1790), Charles (born March 23, 1791), Hannah (born December 1, 1793), James (July 14, 1795), Tece (born April 13, 1797), Ann (born February 9, 1799), Emsy (born May 20, 1801), Elizabeth (born November 28, 1803), William (born February 15, 1804), Abigail (born February 3, 1806), Joshua (born March 9, 1807), and John (born February 17, 1809). William died on December 3, 1835 and his widow applied for and received pension W8509 in Scott County, Kentucky on August 16, 1838, aged 67 [Ref: V-III:2620]. There appears to have been more then one man with this name. Additional research may be necessary before drawing conclusions. (1) Enrolled in the first militia company organized for the Revolutionary War in the Elizabeth Town District of Frederick County (now the Hagerstown area of Washington County) on January 6, 1776 [Ref: Q-270, W-1190]. (2) Private, Militia, 2nd Class, Capt. Joseph Chapline's Company, 2nd Battalion, 1776/1777 [Ref: M-241]. (3) Rendered patriotic service by supplying corn for the use of the military on February 4, 1780 [Ref: W-1190 and HH-74, which both listed the name as "William Paterson"].
PATTON, Catharine and James. See "Adam Weise," q.v.
PATTON, Samuel (1755-   ). Sergeant, Maryland Line, who applied for and received pension S31901 in Hardin County, Kentucky on February 27, 1830, stating he was born on June 22, 1755 and enlisted at Sharpsburg, Maryland in 1776. He referred to his only son (no name given) who was supporting him and also referred to the loss of his wife (no name given). [Ref: V-III:2622, T-45].
PATTORF, David. See "David Pottorf," q.v.
PAUL, James. Took the Oath of Allegiance before the Hon. John Barnes before February 28, 1778 [Ref: J-9, O-44, which latter source listed the name as "James Paule"].
PAUL, William. Private, Militia, 1st Class, Capt. John Bennet's Company, 1776/1777 [Ref: M-246, A-1146]. Took the Oath of Allegiance before the Hon. John Stull in 1778 [Ref: O-47, J-11].

PAULES, John. Private, Militia, 8th Class, Capt. Conrad Nichodemus' Company, 2nd Battalion, 1776/1777 [Ref: M-237, A-1146].-

PAUPIN, James. Private who was recruited and passed by County Lieutenant Thomas Sprigg on April 22, 1780 [Ref: D-336].

PEACOCK, Neale. "Died near Cadiz, Harrison County, Ohio, on the 17th of August last [1827], Neale Peacock, formerly of Washington County, Maryland, many years a soldier of the Maryland Line. He fought with the gallant [Col. John Eager] Howard at the Eutaws and the Cowpens. He served also under Gen. [Nathaniel] Green and other illustrious chiefs." [Ref: Z-95].

PEARCE, Benjamin. Took the Oath of Allegiance before the Hon. William Yates in 1778 [Ref: J-12, O-48, which latter source listed the name as "Benjamin Paarce"].

PEARCE, Clement. Enrolled in the first militia company organized for the Revolutionary War in the Elizabeth Town District of Frederick County (now the Hagerstown area of Washington County) on January 6, 1776 [Ref: Q-270, W-1189]. Private, Militia, 6th Class, Capt. John Rennolds' (Reynolds') Company, 2nd Battalion, 1776/1777 [Ref: M-240].

PEARCE, Daniel. Private who enlisted in the militia on September 5, 1781 for service in the Continental Army [Ref: D-388].

PECK, Casper. Private, Militia, 6th Class, Capt. Henry Boteler's Company, 1776/1777 [Ref: M-237, A-1146]. "John Peck, of Sample's Manor" died testate in 1805 and among his heirs was a son Casper [Ref: MM-13:133, 134].

PECK, George. Took the Oath of Allegiance before the Hon. John Barnes before February 28, 1778 [Ref: O-44, J-9].

PECK, John. See "Casper Peck," q.v.

PEDDICORD (PETTICOAT), Nathan Jr. Took the Oath of Allegiance before the Hon. Richard Davis in 1778 [Ref: J-4, O-37, which listed the name as "Nathan Peddicort"]. Private, Militia, 7th Class, Capt. Jeremiah Spires' Company, 2nd Battalion, 1776/1777 [Ref: M-239, A-1146, which listed the name as "Nathan Petticord, Jr."]. See "Nathan Petticoat, Sr.," q.v.

PEDDICORD (PETTICOAT), Nathan Sr. Took the Oath of Allegiance before the Hon. Richard Davis in 1778 [Ref: J-5, O-37, which listed the name as "Nathan Peddicoart"]. Rendered patriotic service by supplying corn for the use of the military on January 27, 1780 [Ref: W-1190, which listed the name as "Nathan Petticoat" and HH-74, which listed the name as "Nathan Paticot"]. Private, Militia, 7th Class, Capt. Jeremiah Spires' Company, 2nd Battalion, 1776/1777 [Ref: M-239, A-1146, which listed the name as "Nathan Petticord, Sr."]. "Nathan Petticoat" died before

June 5, 1790 (date of balance book entry in Washington County), leaving a widow (not named, but Hannah Petticoat was the executrix) and equal shares to Nathan, William, Laken, Althea, and Rachel Petticoat [Ref: J-28].

PEDEN, Henry C. Jr. See "Abraham Lemaster," q.v.

PEEK, George. Took the Oath of Allegiance before the Hon. Christopher Cruse in Sharpsburg Hundred before March 2, 1778 [Ref: O-34, J-2].

PEIFER, Martin. Took the Oath of Allegiance before the Hon. Henry Schnebley in 1778 [Ref: O-49, J-12]. See "Martin Fifer," q.v.

PENCE, Christopher. Private, Militia, 7th Class, Capt. Daniel Clapsaddle's Company, 1st Battalion, 1776/1777 [Ref: M-236, A-1146].

PENCE, Jacob. Second Corporal, Militia, Capt. Jacob Sharer's Company, 1776/1777 [Ref: M-248, A-1146]. Took the Oath of Allegiance before the Hon. John Stull in 1778 [Ref: O-47, J-11]. Rendered patriotic service by supplying corn for the use of the military on February 25, 1780 [Ref: W-1190, HH-74].

PENDALL, Philip. See "Philip Pindell," q.v.

PENDERGRASS, Laurance. Private, Militia, 2nd Class, Capt. Griffin Johnson's Company, 3rd Battalion, 1776/1777 [Ref: M-243].

PENDERGRASS, Philip. Private, Militia, 1st Class, Capt. Griffin Johnson's Company, 3rd Battalion, 1776/1777 [Ref: M-243, which listed the name as "Phillip Pindergrass"].

PENDERGRASS, Robert. Private, Militia, 4th Class, Capt. Griffin Johnson's Company, 3rd Battalion, 1776/1777 [Ref: M-243].

PENN, Mary. See "Christopher Burkett," q.v.

PENNYBAKER, Benjamin. Private, Select Militia, Capt. Adam Ott's Company, 1781 [Ref: M-238, A-1146].

PERREN, Catherine, and others. See "Joseph Perrin," q.v.

PERRIN (PERREN), Joseph. Private, Militia, 8th Class, Capt. James Walling's Company, 2nd Battalion, 1776/1777 [Ref: M-239, A-1146]. One "Joseph Perren" died before August 20, 1785 (date of balance book entry in Washington County), leaving a widow (not named, but Rachel Perren was the administratrix) and equal shares to Deborah, Catherine, Rachel, John, Eleanor, and Joseph Perren [Ref: J-26].

PERRY, Daniel. Appointed by the Committee of Observation to carry the Association of Freemen to male residents in Upper Antietam Hundred on September 14, 1775 "and require their subscription to the same and make an exact account of those who sign and those that refuse with their reasons for refusing." [Ref: Q-143]. Third Sergeant, Militia, Capt. Conrad Hogmire's Company, 1776/1777 [Ref: M-244, A-1146]. Took the

Oath of Allegiance before the Hon. Samuel Hughes before March 1, 1778 [Ref: O-33, J-1].

PERRY, Joseph. Appointed to raise funds on January 24, 1775 for the Committee of Observation in Upper Antietam Hundred in Frederick (now Washington) County [Ref: L-75]. One of several patriots appointed by the Committee of Observation on December 30, 1776 "to form the county into companies (after the militia had marched) for the purpose of relieving the distressed inhabitants of said county and also to compel the Dunkards and Mennonists to give their assistance." [Ref: Q-346]. Took the Oath of Allegiance before the Hon. Andrew Rentch before March 7, 1778 [Ref: O-52, J-15, which listed the name as "Joseph Percy"].

PETER, Abraham. See "Michael Peter," q.v.

PETER, Balser. Private, Militia, 3rd Class, Capt. Martin Kershner's Company, 1776/1777 [Ref: A-1146, M-247]. Took the Oath of Allegiance before the Hon. John Cellars in January, 1778 [Ref: K-1814, O-40, J-6, which latter source listed the name as "Baltksor Peter"].

PETER, Elizabeth. See "Michael Peter," q.v.

PETER, Jacob. Rendered patriotic service by providing a rifle for Capt. Daniel Cresap's Company in July, 1775, as recorded by the Committee of Observation at Elizabeth Town on November 4, 1775 [Ref: Q-149]. See "Michael Peter," q.v.

PETER, Michael. Took the Oath of Allegiance before the Hon. Richard Davis in 1778 [Ref: J-4, O-37]. One Michael Peter died before September 10, 1791 (date of balance book entry in Washington County), leaving a widow (no name given in this account) and equal shares to Jacob, Elizabeth and Abraham Peter [Ref: J-31].

PETRY, Jacob (1735-1812). Took the Oath of Allegiance before the Hon. Henry Schnebley in 1778 [Ref: O-50, J-13]. Private, Militia, 7th Class, Capt. James Smith's Company, 2nd Battalion, 1776/1777 [Ref: M-240, A-1146, M-240, which listed the name as "Jacob Petay"]. "Jacob Petery" was born in 1735, died in 1812 (aged 76 years, 5 months), and was buried beside his wife Barbara (died in 1805) in Old St. John's Lutheran Churchyard [Ref: JJ-VII:105, which source noted that his stone was moved to Dunkard Church on Beaver Creek; others were moved to Rose Hill Cemetery in Hagerstown].

PETTERS, Abraham. Took the Oath of Allegiance before the Hon. Lemuel Barritt before March 16, 1778 [Ref: O-43, J-8].

PETTICOAT, Nathan, and others. See "Nathan Peddicord," q.v.

PFLENGER, Leonard. Took the Oath of Allegiance before the Hon. Henry Schnebley in 1778 [Ref: O-49, J-13].

PHELPS, John Jr. Took the Oath of Allegiance before the Hon. Richard Davis in 1778 [Ref: J-3, O-36]. Private, Militia, 4th Class, Capt. Basil Williams' Company, 1776/1777 [Ref: M-244, A-1146, which listed the name without the "Jr."].

PHELPS, John Sr. Took the Oath of Allegiance before the Hon. Richard Davis in 1778 [Ref: J-3, O-36].

PHELPS, Thomas. Private, Militia, 3rd Class, Capt. Barnett Johnston's Company, 3rd Battalion, 1776/1777 [Ref: M-242].

PHENIX, Matthew (c1752-   ). Private, New Jersey Line, who applied for and received pension S36225 in Washington County, Maryland on April 11, 1818, aged 66; still living in 1821 when he gave his age as 59 (69?). [Ref: V-III:2681].

PHIFER, Leonarhart. See "Leonard Piper (Pifer)," q.v.

PHIFER, Martin. See "Martin Piper (Pifer)," q.v.

PHILIPS, Thomas. Private, Militia, by January 22, 1777 when ordered by the Committee of Observation "to march with some company of militia to the reinforcement of his Excellency General Washington" or appear before the Committee and state his reason for not marching. He apparently marched since he never appeared to the contrary [Ref: Q-48]. Took the Oath of Allegiance before the Hon. William Yates in 1778 [Ref: O-48, J-12, which listed the name as "Thomas Phillips"].

PHILPOT, Bartin. Enrolled in the second militia company organized for the Revolutionary War in the Elizabeth Town District of Frederick County (now the Hagerstown area of Washington County) on March 9, 1776 [Ref: Q-271].

PHILPOT, Charles. Enrolled in the second militia company organized for the Revolutionary War in the Elizabeth Town District of Frederick County (now the Hagerstown area of Washington County) on March 9, 1776 [Ref: Q-272].

PHILPOT, Charles Thomas (1753-1836). Private who was enrolled by Lieut. Clement Hollyday and passed by Col. William Luckett on August 8, 1776 [Ref: D-49]. Charles T. Philpot was born in Maryland on November 20, 1753, married Elizabeth ----, served as a sergeant in the Revolution, and died before March 14, 1836 in Virginia [Ref: Y-III:2304].

PHILPOT, Elizabeth. See "Charles Thomas Philpot," q.v.

PHLEUGER, Peter. Took the Oath of Allegiance before the Hon. Henry Schnebley in 1778 [Ref: J-15, O-51, which latter source listed the name as "Peter Phlenger"]. Private, Militia, 1st Class, Capt. Daniel Clapsaddle's Company, 1st Battalion, 1776/1777 [Ref: M-236, A-1146, which listed the name as "Peter Fleger"].

PICKENPAW, Ruth. See "Gabriel Williams," q.v.

PICKELMAN, John. Private, Militia, 8th Class, Capt. John Cellars' Company, 1776/1777 [Ref: A-1146, M-247].

PICKLEHIMER, Jacob. Private, Militia, 7th Class, Capt. Henry Boteler's Company, 1776/1777 [Ref: M-237, A-1146].

PIERCE, Benjamin. Second Corporal, Militia, Capt. James Prather's Company, 3rd Battalion, 1776/1777 [Ref: M-242].

PIERCE, Daniel. Private, Militia, 6th Class, Capt. James Prather's Company, 3rd Battalion, 1776/1777 [Ref: M-243].

PIERCE, James. Private, Militia, 8th Class, Capt. James Prather's Company, 3rd Battalion, 1776/1777 [Ref: M-243].

PIFER, Jacob. See "Jacob Piper," q.v.

PIFER, Manuel. See "Manuel Piper," q.v.

PIFER, Martin. See "Martin Piper," q.v.

PIKE, Captain. See "Charles Oldwine," q.v.

PIMLEY, Elizabeth. See "Michael Weirick," q.v.

PINDELL, Eliza. See "Richard Pindell," q.v.

PINDELL, Jacob. Private, Militia, by January 22, 1777 when ordered by the Committee of Observation "to march with some company of militia to the reinforcement of his Excellency General Washington" or appear before the Committee and state his reason for not marching. He apparently marched since he never appeared to the contrary [Ref: Q-48, which listed the name as "Jacob Pendall"]. Took the Oath of Allegiance before the Hon. William Yates in 1778 [Ref: O-48, J-12, which listed the name as "Jacob Pindle"].

PINDELL, Philip. First Lieutenant, Militia, Capt. Barnett Johnston's Company, 1776. Captain, Militia, 3rd or Western Battalion, May 16, 1778 [Ref: M-111, M-242, E-86]. Ordered on January 22, 1777 by the Committee of Observation "to march with some company of militia to the reinforcement of his Excellency General Washington" or appear before the Committee and state his reason for not marching. He apparently marched since he never appeared to the contrary [Ref: Q-48, which listed the name as "Philip Pendall"].

PINDELL, Richard (1755-1833). Surgeon, Maryland Line [Ref: N-42, U-34:2 (1946)]. "Died in Lexington, Kentucky, on March 20, 1833, Doctor Richard Pindell in the 78th year of his age, formerly of Hagerstown in this [Washington] county, and well remembered here for his great private worth, professional ability and skill. His Revolutionary services endeared him to the public, as well as the private, social and benevolent qualities.." [Ref: DD-58, citing *The Republican Banner*, April 6, 1831]. Mrs. Eliza Pindell, wife of Dr. Richard Pindell and daughter of Col. Thomas Hart of Hagerstown, died after a long and painful indisposition on the Sunday before August 9, 1793 [Ref: LL-1:42]. See "Thomas Hart," q.v.

PINDELL, Thomas. Private, Militia, 1st Class, Capt. Barnett Johnston's Company, 3rd Battalion, 1776/1777 [Ref: M-242].

PINDLE, Mrs. Dr. See "Thomas Hart," q.v.

PINE, James. Took the Oath of Allegiance before the Hon. Henry Schnebley in 1778 [Ref: O-50, J-14].

PINKLEY, Nicholas. Private who was enlisted by Lieut. Christian Orndorff and passed on July 20, 1776 in Frederick (now Washington) County [Ref: D-50].

PINTS, James. Private, Militia, 7th Class, Capt. John Cellars' Company, 1776/1777 [Ref: A-1146, M-246].

PIPER (PIFER), Elizabeth. On February 24, 1777, Moyles Reiley was brought before the Committee of Observation for Elizabeth Town District (now the Hagerstown area of Washington County) "charged that he had abused Elizabeth Piper and family in her own house near Sharpsburgh during the absence of her husband at camp, ordered that the said Reiley be confined in the Tory Goal of this town, until he shall give bond and security in the penalty of 500 pounds conditioned that he shall behave quietly and peaceably for the future and pay expence of guard, etc." [Ref: Q-237]. See "William Fleck (Flick)," q.v.

PIPER (PIFER), Jacob (c1725-1813). Took the Oath of Allegiance before the Hon. Christopher Cruse in Sharpsburg Hundred before March 2, 1778 [Ref: O-35, J-2, which listed the name as "Jacob Piper, farmer"]. "Jacob Piper, Sr." died in 1813 and Elizabeth Flick, wife of Jacob Piper and daughter of William Flick, died in 1818. They are buried in the Old Reformed Graveyard at Sharpsburg, Maryland [Ref: JJ-I:28]. See "William Fleck (Flick)," q.v.

PIPER (PIFER), Jacob Jr. (1754-1837). Enrolled in the third militia company organized for the Revolutionary War in the Elizabeth Town District of Frederick County (now the Hagerstown area of Washington County), passed by the Committee of Observation on June 5, 1776, and was assigned to Capt. John Reynolds' command [Ref: Q-273, which listed the name as "Jacob Piper"]. Private, Militia, 1st Class, Capt. John Rennolds' (Reynolds') Company, 2nd Battalion, 1776/1777 [Ref: M-240]. Private, Maryland Line, Capt. William Heyser's Company, 1776, continental service, and on duty in May, 1777 [Ref: W-1190, L-79, which listed the name as "Jacob Pifer" and GG-98, which listed the name as "Jacob Piffer, Fifer"]. "Jacob Piper, Jr." died on October 3, 1837 and is buried in the Old Reformed Graveyard at Sharpsburg, Maryland [Ref: JJ-I:28]. See "William Fleck," q.v.

PIPER (PIFER), Joseph. Private, Militia, 4th Class, Capt. John Cellars' Company, 1776/1777 [Ref: A-1146, M-246].

PIPER (PIFER), Leonard. Private, Militia, 8th Class, Capt. Martin Kershner's Company, 1776/1777 [Ref: A-1146, M-248, which listed the name as "Leonarhart Phifer"]. Private, Militia, Capt. Martin Kershner's Company, 32nd Battalion, December 27, 1776 [Ref: K-1814 (Box 3), which listed the name as "Leonhard Piper"]. Took the Oath of Allegiance before the Hon. John Cellars in January, 1778 [Ref: O-40, J-5, K-1814, which latter source listed the name as "Lenoard Piper"].

PIPER (PIFER), Martin. There appears to have been more then one man with this name who served during the Revolutionary War. Additional research will be necessary before drawing conclusions. (1) Third Sergeant, Militia, Capt. Peter Beall's Company, 1st Battalion, 1776/1777 [Ref: M-240, which listed the name as "Martin Fifer"]. (2) Private, Militia, Capt. William Heyser's Company, muster roll dated October 23, 1776, in continental service, which stated he had deserted, yet he was on duty in May, 1777 [Ref: D-264, W-1190, L-79, which also listed the name as "Martin Pifer" and GG-99, which listed the name as "Martin Piffer"]. (3) Second Sergeant, Militia, Capt. John Kershner's Company, on duty guarding prisoners of war at Fort Frederick on June 27, 1778 [Ref: D-328, which listed the name as "Martain Phipher"]. (4) Private, Select Militia, Capt. Adam Ott's Company, 1781 [Ref: M-238, A-1146].

PIPER (PIFER), Manuel. Private, Militia, 4th Class, Capt. Michael Fackler's Company, 1776/1777 [Ref: M-245, A-1146]. Took the Oath of Allegiance before the Hon. Andrew Rentch before March 7, 1778 [Ref: O-52, J-15, which listed the name as "Manuell Pifer"].

PITCACH, Benjamin. Took the Oath of Allegiance before the Hon. William Yates in 1778 [Ref: O-48, J-12].

PITCHER, Thomas. Private who was enlisted by Capt. John Reynolds and passed on July 18, 1776 in Frederick (now Washington) County [Ref: D-50].

PITZER, Mary. See "Emery Altizer," q.v.

PLANK, Rebecca Elizabeth. See "Matthias Ringer," q.v.

PLAY, Rudolph. Rendered patriotic service in Hagerstown by "soaling one pair of shoes" for a soldier in Capt. John Nelson's Company, continental service (Maryland Line), April, 1776 [Ref: Q-161]. Private, Militia, 2nd Class, Capt. Peter Beall's Company, 1st Battalion, 1776/1777 [Ref: M-240, which listed the name as "Rudolph Pligh?"].

PLECKER, Jacob. Second Corporal, Militia, Capt. Griffin Johnson's Company, 3rd Battalion, 1776/1777 [Ref: M-243, which listed the name as "Jacob Flaker"].

PLECKER, Frederick. Private, Militia, 1st Class, Capt. Jacob Sharer's Company, 1776/1777 [Ref: A-1146, M-248, which listed the name as "Frederick Flaker"]. Took the Oath of Allegiance before the Hon. John Stull in 1778 [Ref: O-46, J-10, which listed the name as "Frederick Blacher"]. Ensign, Militia, Capt. Nicholas Mourer's Company, 2nd Battalion, November 21, 1780 [Ref: G-220, which listed the name as "Frederick Plecker"].

PLECKER, Peter. Private, Militia, 4th Class, Capt. Basil Williams' Company, 1776/1777 [Ref: A-1146, M-244, which listed the name as "Peter Plecher"].

PLECKER, Samuel. Took the Oath of Allegiance before the Hon. Christopher Cruse in Lower Antietam Hundred before March 2, 1778 [Ref: J-3, O-35, which listed the name as "Samuel Placker"].

PLECKER, Yost. Private, Militia, 6th Class, Capt. Basil Williams' Company, 1776/1777 [Ref: A-1146, M-244, which listed the name as "Jost Plecher"]. See "Henry Newcomer," q.v.

PLIGH, Rudolph. See "Rudolph Play," q.v

PLUMB, Henry. Private, Militia, 4th Class, Capt. Jacob Sharer's Company, 1776/1777 [Ref: A-1146, M-248].

PLUME, Henry. See "Henry Blume," q.v.

PLUMMER, John. Took the Oath of Allegiance before the Hon. Andrew Bruce before March 2, 1778 [Ref: O-41, J-7].

PLUMMER, Thomas. Private, Militia, 3rd Class, Capt. Charles Clinton's Company, 1776/1777 [Ref: M-245, A-1146]. Took the Oath of Allegiance before the Hon. Andrew Bruce before March 2, 1778 [Ref: O-41, J-6].

POENS, David. Took the Oath of Allegiance before the Hon. John Cellars in January, 1778 [Ref: O-40, J-5, K-1814, which latter source is the original record and the name looked like "Poens" or possibly even "Joens"].

POFFENBERGER, Adam. Private, Militia, 7th Class, Capt. John Rennolds' (Reynolds') Company, 2nd Battalion, 1776/1777 [Ref: M-240, which listed the name as "Adam Pashanbarger"]. Took the Oath of Allegiance before September 1, 1780 [Ref: X-118, which listed the name as "Adam Poughenberger"].

POFFENBERGER, Henry. Private, Militia, 7th Class, Capt. John Rennolds' (Reynolds') Company, 2nd Battalion, 1776/1777 [Ref: M-240, which listed the name as "Henry Pashanbarger"].

POFFENBERGER, John. Took the Oath of Allegiance before the Hon. Christopher Cruse in Sharpsburg Hundred before March 2, 1778 [Ref: O-35, J-2, which listed the name as "John Pofsenbarger"].

POFFENBERGER, Valentine. Private, Militia, 7th Class, Capt. James Smith's Company, 2nd Battalion, 1776/1777 [Ref: M-240, A-1146, which listed the name as "Valentine Paphenberger"]. Took the Oath of Allegiance before the Hon. Christopher Cruse in Sharpsburg Hundred before March 2, 1778 [Ref: O-35, J-2, which listed the name as "Valentine Pofsenbarger"].

POGSTON, Thomas. See "Thomas Logston," q.v.

POINTER, William. Private, German Regiment, Lt. Col. Ludwick Weltner's Company, continental service, 1779, and discharged on November 13, 1780 [Ref: D-265, GG-99].

POLAND, William. Private who was enrolled by Capt. Aeneas Campbell and passed by Major John Fulford on July 18, 1776 [Ref: D-49].

POORE, Benjamin. Private, Militia, 1st Class, Capt. James Prather's Company, 3rd Battalion, 1776/1777 [Ref: M-242].

POORE, Ersley. Private, Militia, 7th Class, Capt. James Prather's Company, 3rd Battalion, 1776/1777 [Ref: M-243].

POORE, James. Private, Militia, 3rd Class, Capt. James Prather's Company, 3rd Battalion, 1776/1777 [Ref: M-242].

POPE, William. Private, Militia, 6th Class, Capt. Michael Fackler's Company, 1776/1777 [Ref: M-245, A-1146].

PORTER, Henry. Fourth Corporal, Militia, Capt. Charles Coulson's Company, enrolled August 28, 1776 [Ref: M-243, A-1146]. Took the Oath of Allegiance before the Hon. Andrew Bruce before March 2, 1778 [Ref: O-41, J-6]. Michael Porter, Sr. died before June, 1827, and among his sons was Henry Porter [Ref: Z-14, citing an equity court case in Allegany County in 1827].

PORTER, Michael. See "Henry Porter," q.v.

POSSELWAITE, Samuel. Third Sergeant, Militia, Capt. James Prather's Company, 3rd Battalion, 1776/1777 [Ref: M-242].

POSSELWAITE, William. Private, Militia, 3rd Class, Capt. James Prather's Company, 3rd Battalion, 1776/1777 [Ref: M-242, which listed the name as "William Posselwait"]. Took the Oath of Allegiance before the Hon. Lemuel Barritt before March 16, 1778 [Ref: J-8, which listed the name as "William Postellwort" and O-43, which listed the name as "William Postlethwort"].

POSTATER, Andrew. Private, Militia, 6th Class, Capt. Martin Kershner's Company, 1776/1777 [Ref: A-1146, M-248].

POSTLE, Samuel. Took the Oath of Allegiance before the Hon. William Yates in 1778 [Ref: O-48, J-12].

POTH (POTE), Michael. Private who was enrolled by Capt. Henry Hardman and passed on July 19, 1776 in Frederick (now Washington)

County [Ref: D-51, which listed the name as "Michael Pote"]. Took the Oath of Allegiance before the Hon. Henry Schnebley in 1778 [Ref: O-51, which listed the name as "Michael Poth" and J-15, which listed the name as "Michael Foth"].

POTTENGER, John. Private, Militia, 5th Class, Capt. Basil Williams' Company, 1776/1777 [Ref: M-244, A-1146]. Took the Oath of Allegiance before the Hon. Richard Davis in 1778 [Ref: J-4, O-37, which listed the name as "John Pottinger"].

POTTER, Andrew. Ensign, Militia, Capt. Evan Baker's Company, 3rd Battalion, June 22, 1778 [Ref: M-112, E-145].

POTTER, Henry. Private, Militia, 3rd Class, Capt. Charles Clinton's Company, 1776/1777 [Ref: M-245, A-1146].

POTTER, Margaret. See "Frederick Nichodemus," q.v.

POTTORFF, Andrew. Second Sergeant, Militia, Capt. Isaac Baker's Company, 1776 (date not given). Second Lieutenant, Militia (date not given). [Ref: M-112, A-1146, M-247, which latter source listed the name as "Andrew Potterf"].

POTTORFF, Casper (1759-   ). Private, Militia, 5th Class, Capt. Michael Fackler's Company, 1776/1777 [Ref: A-1146, M-245, which listed the name as "Casper Potterff"]. Took the Oath of Allegiance before the Hon. John Cellars in January, 1778 [Ref: O-40, J-6, which listed the name as "Casper Potteroff" and K-1814, which listed the name as "Casper Potturf"]. Private, Maryland Militia, with Virginia service [Ref: N-42, which listed the name as "Casper Potterf"].

POTTORFF, David. Private, Militia, 7th Class, Capt. John Bennet's Company, 1776/1777 [Ref: M-246, A-1146, which listed the name as "David Pattorf"].

POTTORFF, Martin. Private, Militia, 1st Class, Capt. Isaac Baker's Company, 1776/1777 [Ref: A-1146, M-247, which listed the name as "Martin Pottarff"].

POTTORFF, Phillip. Private, Militia, 4th Class, Capt. John Bennet's Company, 1776/1777 [Ref: M-246, A-1146].

POTTORFF, Simon. Private, Militia, 8th Class, Capt. Isaac Baker's Company, 1776/1777 [Ref: A-1146, M-247, which listed the name as "Simon Pottarf"].

POTTS, Andrew. Private, Militia, 4th Class, Capt. Jacob Sharer's Company, 1776/1777 [Ref: A-1146, M-248].

POTTS, Jonathan. Took the Oath of Allegiance before the Hon. William Yates in 1778 [Ref: O-48, J-12].

POTTS, Richard (attorney). Took the Oath of Allegiance on July 26, 1777 [Ref: K-1814, Box 4].

POTTS, Samuel. Took the Oath of Allegiance before the Hon. William Yates in 1778 [Ref: O-48, J-12].

POTTS, Thomas. Private, Maryland Line [Ref: N-43].

POWEL, Joseph and Mary. See "Jacob Bishop," q.v.

POWELL, George. Private, Militia, 5th Class, Capt. James Smith's Company, 2nd Battalion, 1776/1777 [Ref: M-240, A-1146].

POWELL, John. Fourth Corporal, Militia, Capt. Barnett Johnston's Company, 3rd Battalion, 1776/1777 [Ref: M-242].

POWELL, John. Private who was enlisted by Ensign Nathan Williams and passed on July 25, 1776 in Frederick (now Washington) County [Ref: D-51]. Private, Militia, 4th Class, Capt. Barnett Johnston's Company, 3rd Battalion, 1776/1777 [Ref: M-242].

POWELL, Joseph and Mary. See "Jacob Bishop," q.v.

POWELL, Nathan. Took the Oath of Allegiance before the Hon. Joseph Sprigg before April 1, 1778 [Ref: O-53, J-15].

POWELL, Rachel. See "Moses Crossley," q.v.

POWELL, Thomas. Private, Militia, 3rd Class, Capt. James Smith's Company, 2nd Battalion, 1776/1777 [Ref: M-239, A-1146].

POWER, Benjamin (1753-   ). Private, Maryland Line, with Pennsylvania service [Ref: N-43]. Took the Oath of Allegiance before the Hon. Lemuel Barritt before March 16, 1778 [Ref: O-43, J-8].

POWER, Bostian. Private, Militia, 6th Class, Capt. Michael Fackler's Company, 1776/1777 [Ref: M-245, A-1146].

POWER, Edward. Enrolled in the first militia company organized for the Revolutionary War in the Elizabeth Town District of Frederick County (now the Hagerstown area of Washington County) on January 6, 1776 [Ref: Q-270, W-1190]. Private, Militia, 3rd Class, Capt. Joseph Chapline's Company, 2nd Battalion, 1776/1777 [Ref: M-241]. Took the Oath of Allegiance before the Hon. Christopher Cruse in Sharpsburg Hundred before March 2, 1778 [Ref: O-34, J-2].

POWER, Frederick. Private, Militia, 1776, who appeared before the Committee of Observation on January 20, 1777, and "made proof by Major Swearingen that his wife was in a very low state of health, therefor ordered that said Power be exempted from marching with the militia at this time." [Ref: Q-44].

POWER, James (1755-   ). Private, Maryland Militia [Ref: N-43].

POWER, Jesse (1761-   ). Private, Maryland Line [Ref: N-43].

POWER, Maurice. Fifer, Capt. William Heyser's Company, 1776, in continental service [Ref: W-1190, L-79].

POWERS, Peter. Private, Militia, 3rd Class, Capt. Conrad Nichodemus' Company, 2nd Battalion, 1776/1777 [Ref: M-237, A-1146].

POWETT, Michael. Private, Militia, 1st Class, Capt. Daniel Clapsaddle's Company, 1st Battalion, 1776/1777 [Ref: M-236, A-1146].

POWLESS, Henry. Second Corporal, Militia, Capt. Conrad Nichodemus' Company, 2nd Battalion, 1776/1777 [Ref: M-237, A-1146].

PRANNER, Philip. See "Philip Branner," q.v.

PRATHER, Basil. Took the Oath of Allegiance before the Hon. John Barnes before February 28, 1778 [Ref: O-44, J-9]. Recommended by the Committee of Observation in Elizabeth Town District (now the Hagerstown area of Washington County) to the Continental Congress on February 5, 1776 that he be commissioned a captain [Ref: Q-152]. One Basil Prather was born in Maryland in 1742, married Chloe or Clorender Robinson, served in the militia in North Carolina, and died in Indiana on October 7, 1822. Another Basil Prather was born in Maryland on May 10, 1740, married Frances or Fanny Merriwether, served as a lieutenant in Pennsylvania, and died on December 18, 1803 in Kentucky [Ref: Y-III:2358]. Additional research will be necessary before drawing conclusions. See "Thomas Prather," q.v.

PRATHER, Charles. Ensign, Militia, Capt. James Prather's Company, 3rd or Western Battalion, by May 16, 1778 [Ref: M-112, M-242, E-86]. Took the Oath of Allegiance before the Hon. Lemuel Barritt before March 16, 1778 [Ref: O-43, J-8]. Justice of the County Court, June 20, 1778 [Ref: E-141]. Justice of the Peace, January 30, 1781 [Ref: G-293].

PRATHER, Elizabeth. See "Thomas Prather," q.v.

PRATHER, Henry. Recommended by the Committee of Observation in Elizabeth Town District (now the Hagerstown area of Washington County) to the Continental Congress on February 5, 1776 that he be commissioned a lieutenant [Ref: Q-152]. See "Richard Prather," q.v.

PRATHER, James. Captain, Militia, 3rd or Western Battalion, May 16, 1778 [Ref: M-112, M-242, E-86]. Took the Oath of Allegiance before the Hon. Lemuel Barritt before March 16, 1778 [Ref: O-43, J-8]. See "Richard Prather," q.v.

PRATHER, James. Private, Militia, 4th Class, Capt. James Prather's Company, 3rd Battalion, 1776/1777 [Ref: M-242].

PRATHER, James. Private, Militia, 1st Class, Capt. John Bennet's Company, 1776/1777 [Ref: M-246, A-1146].

PRATHER, Jennett. See "Thomas Prather," q.v.

PRATHER, Rebecca. See "Richard Prather," q.v.

PRATHER, Richard. Took the Oath of Allegiance before the Hon. John Barnes before February 28, 1778 [Ref: O-44, J-9]. One Richard Prather died testate before February 8, 1794 (date of balance book entry in Washington County), leaving a widow (not named in this account) and equal shares to Thomas, James, Samuel, Henry and Rebecca Prather, and Elizabeth Pream [Ref: J-33].

PRATHER, Rignal. Third Corporal, Militia, Capt. Basil Williams' Company, 1776/1777 [Ref: M-244, A-1146]. Took the Oath of Allegiance before the Hon. Henry Schnebley in 1778 [Ref: O-50, J-14, which listed the name as "Reginal Brather"]. Rendered patriotic service by supplying corn for the use of the military on January 27, 1780 [Ref: W-1190, HH-74].

PRATHER, Samuel. Enrolled in the second militia company organized for the Revolutionary War in the Elizabeth Town District of Frederick County (now the Hagerstown area of Washington County) on March 9, 1776 [Ref: Q-271]. See "Richard Prather," q.v.

PRATHER, Thomas (1703/4-1785/7). Rendered patriotic service by supplying a blanket for the use of the military in March, 1776, as recorded by the Committee of Observation on April 12, 1776 [Ref: Q-156, L-82]. One of several patriots appointed by the Committee of Observation on January 7, 1777 "to form the county into companies (after the militia had marched) for the purpose of relieving the distressed inhabitants of said county and also to compel the Dunkards and Mennonists to give their assistance." [Ref: Q-31]. Took the Oath of Allegiance before the Hon. John Barnes before February 28, 1778 [Ref: O-44, J-9]. "Col. Thomas Prather" died before October 22, 1787 (date of balance book entry in Washington County), leaving a widow (not named, but Jennett Prather was one of the executors) and equal shares to Basil, Thomas, and Elizabeth Prather [Ref: J-27]. His first wife was Elizabeth Clagett and his second wife was Jeanette ----. [Ref: Y-III:2358]. See "Richard Prather" and the other "Thomas Prather," q.v.

PRATHER, Thomas. Private, Militia, 6th Class, Capt. John Bennet's Company, 1776/1777 [Ref: M-246, A-1146]. Took the Oath of Allegiance before the Hon. Richard Davis in 1778 [Ref: J-3, O-36]. Source Y-III:2358 lists seven men named Thomas Prather who were born in Maryland and rendered service in Maryland, North Carolina, and Pennsylvania. Additional research will be necessary before drawing conclusions. See "Richard Prather" and the other "Thomas Prather," q.v.

PREAM, Elizabeth. See "Richard Prather," q.v.

PRESTON, Stephen. Private who was enrolled by Capt. Henry Hardman and passed on July 19, 1776 in Frederick (now Washington) County [Ref: D-51].

PRICE, Joseph. First Sergeant, Militia, Capt. Jacob Sharer's Company, 1776/1777 [Ref: M-248, A-1146]. Took the Oath of Allegiance before the

Hon. John Stull in 1778 [Ref: O-47, J-11, which listed the name as "Joseph Prue"].

PRICE, Josiah (c1750-1825). First Sergeant, Militia, Capt. Isaac Baker's Company, 1776. First Lieutenant, Militia, Capt. Evan Baker's Company, 3rd Battalion, June 22, 1778 [Ref: M-112, E-145, M-247, A-1146]. Took the Oath of Allegiance before the Hon. Joseph Sprigg before April 1, 1778 [Ref: O-53, J-16]. "Mrs. Sarah Price, consort of Col. Josiah Price, died the week before January 9, 1808, after a painful illness, in the meridian of life." [Ref: LL-3:52]. "Col. Josiah Price died in Washington County on December 17, 1825, at an advanced age." [Ref: Z-79].

PRICE, Sarah. See "Josiah Price," q.v.

PRICE, Thomas. Captain of one of the two companies formed in Frederick County, which included Washington County, in 1776, who marched with his men to join Gen. George Washington in Boston and was subsequently promoted [Ref: L-78]. See "Otho Holland Williams," q.v.

PRICE, William. See "James Chapline," q.v.

PRIEST, Elizabeth and Hankey. See "Jacob Hefner," q.v.

PRIFHEN, Abraham. Private, Militia, 5th Class, Capt. John Cellars' Company, 1776/1777 [Ref: A-1146, M-246].

PRIGMORE, Jonathan. Took the Oath of Allegiance before the Hon. Richard Davis in 1778 [Ref: J-4, O-37, which latter source listed the name as "Jonathan Prigmone"].

PRIGMORE, Theodores Jr. Took the Oath of Allegiance before the Hon. Richard Davis in 1778 [Ref: J-4, O-37, which latter source listed the name as "Theodores Prigmone, Jr."].

PRIGMORE, Theodores Sr. Took the Oath of Allegiance before the Hon. Richard Davis in 1778 [Ref: J-4, O-37, which latter source listed the name as "Theodores Prigmone, Sr."].

PRIMM, James (c1754-1820). Private, Virginia Line, pensioned in Washington County at $96 per year effective May 9, 1818, and died May 1, 1820 [Ref: R-43].

PROHETH, William. Took the Oath of Allegiance before the Hon. Richard Davis in 1778 [Ref: J-5, O-38].

PROTZMAN, Nathaniel. Private who enlisted in the militia on August 22, 1781 for service in the Continental Army [Ref: D-388, which listed the name as "Nathaniel Prutzman"].

PRUNK, Jacob. Rendered patriotic service by supplying a blanket for the use of the military in March, 1776, as recorded by the Committee of Observation on April 12, 1776 [Ref: Q-156, L-82].

PRUSHELBAUGH, Michael. Private, Militia, 6th Class, Capt. John Cellars' Company, 1776/1777 [Ref: A-1146, M-246].

PRY, Jesse (1761-   ). Private, Maryland Line or Militia, who applied for pension (R8509) in Spencer County, Indiana on April 12, 1847, aged 80 (86?), stating he lived in Washington County, Maryland at the time of his enlistment and he was born on August 27, 1761 in Anne Arundel County, Maryland. He lived at Hagerstown, Maryland until 1810 and then moved to the Green River in Kentucky and in 1816 he moved to Indiana [Ref: V-III:2781, N-43].

PRY, John. Private, Militia, 8th Class, Capt. John Bennet's Company, 1776/1777 [Ref: M-246, A-1146]. Took the Oath of Allegiance before the Hon. John Barnes before February 28, 1778 [Ref: O-44, J-9].

PRY, Peter. Private, Maryland Line, discharged on November 29, 1781 [Ref: I-7]. See "Peter Fry," q.v.

PULLEN, William. Took the Oath of Allegiance before the Hon. Joseph Sprigg before April 1, 1778 [Ref: O-53, J-15]. Private, Militia, 2nd Class, Capt. Michael Fackler's Company, 1776/1777 [Ref: M-245, A-1146, which listed the name as "William Pullin"]. Private, Select Militia, Capt. Adam Ott's Company, 1781 [Ref: M-238, A-1146, which listed the name as "William Pulling"].

PURSELL, Basil. Private, Militia, 3rd Class, Capt. Griffin Johnson's Company, 3rd Battalion, 1776/1777 [Ref: M-243, which listed the name as "Basil Purill(?)"].

PURSELL, Daniel. Took the Oath of Allegiance before the Hon. Lemuel Barritt before March 16, 1778 [Ref: O-43, J-8].

PURSELL, David. Took the Oath of Allegiance before the Hon. Lemuel Barritt before March 16, 1778 [Ref: O-43, J-8].

PURSELL, John. Took the Oath of Allegiance before the Hon. Lemuel Barritt before March 16, 1778 [Ref: O-43, J-8]. Private, Militia, 6th Class, Capt. James Prather's Company, 3rd Battalion, 1776/1777 [Ref: M-243, which listed the name as "John Punsell"].

PURSELL, Thomas. Took the Oath of Allegiance before the Hon. Lemuel Barritt before March 16, 1778 [Ref: O-43, J-8].First Sergeant, Militia, Capt. James Prather's Company, 3rd Battalion, 1776/1777 [Ref: M-242, which listed the name as "Thomas Punsell"].

PURY, William. Private, Militia, 2nd Class, Capt. Griffin Johnson's Company, 3rd Battalion, 1776/1777 [Ref: M-243].

PUSETY, Dennis. First Lieutenant, Militia, Capt. Jacob Renblin's Company, July 27, 1777 [Ref: M-113].

PUTMAN, John. Private, Militia, 8th Class, Capt. Henry Boteler's Company, 1776/1777 [Ref: M-237, A-1146].

PUTMAN, John. Private, Militia, 8th Class, Capt. James Smith's Company, 2nd Battalion, 1776/1777 [Ref: M-240, A-1146].
PUTMAN, Peter. Private, Militia, 7th Class, Capt. Henry Boteler's Company, 1776/1777 [Ref: M-237, A-1146].
PUTTS, Samuel. Private, Militia, 1st Class, Capt. Barnett Johnston's Company, 3rd Battalion, 1776/1777 [Ref: M-242].
QUEER, Henry. Private, Militia, Capt. William Heyser's Company, enlisted July 18, 1776, muster roll dated October 23, 1776, in continental service [Ref: D-264, L-79, W-1190, which latter source mistakenly listed the name as "Henry Omer"]. Private, German Regiment, Lt. Col. Ludwick Weltner's Company, discharged on July 29, 1779 at Fort Wyoming, Pennsylvania [Ref: D-240, D-265, which listed the name as "Henry Quier" and GG-99, which listed the name as "Henry Queer, Quir"]. Private, Select Militia, Capt. Adam Ott's Company, 1781 [Ref: M-238, A-1146].
QUICK, Aaron. Took the Oath of Allegiance before the Hon. Lemuel Barritt before March 16, 1778 [Ref: O-42, J-7].
QUICK, Aaron Jr. Took the Oath of Allegiance before the Hon. Lemuel Barritt before March 16, 1778 [Ref: O-42, J-7].
QUICK, Andrew. Private, Militia, 6th Class, Capt. Charles Clinton's Company, 1776/1777 [Ref: M-245, A-1146]. Private, Militia, Capt. Charles Coulson's Company, enrolled August 28, 1776 [Ref: M-244, A-1146]. Took the Oath of Allegiance before the Hon. Lemuel Barritt before March 16, 1778 [Ref: O-42, J-7].
QUICK, Benjamin. Fourth Corporal, Militia, Capt. Daniel Cresap's Company, 3rd Battalion, 1776/1777 [Ref: M-241]. Took the Oath of Allegiance before the Hon. Lemuel Barritt before March 16, 1778 [Ref: O-42, J-7].
QUICK, Dennis. Private, Militia, 1st Class, Capt. Charles Clinton's Company, 1776/1777 [Ref: M-245, A-1146]. Second Corporal, Militia, Capt. Charles Coulson's Company, enrolled August 28, 1776 [Ref: M-243, A-1146]. Took the Oath of Allegiance before the Hon. Lemuel Barritt before March 16, 1778 [Ref: O-42, J-7].
QUICK, Jacob. Fourth Sergeant, Militia, Capt. Charles Clinton's Company, 1776/1777 [Ref: M-245, A-1146]. Fourth Sergeant, Militia, Capt. Charles Coulson's Company, enrolled August 28, 1776 [Ref: M-243, A-1146]. Took the Oath of Allegiance before the Hon. Lemuel Barritt before March 16, 1778 [Ref: O-42, J-7].
QUICK, Thomas. Private, Militia, 2nd Class, Capt. Daniel Cresap's Company, 3rd Battalion, 1776/1777 [Ref: M-241]. Private, Militia, Capt. Charles Coulson's Company, enrolled August 28, 1776 [Ref: M-244, A-

1146]. Took the Oath of Allegiance before the Hon. Lemuel Barritt before March 16, 1778 [Ref: O-42, J-7].

QUICKLE, Adam (c1749-c1844). Private, Maryland Line, whose son Peter applied for his father's pension (R8547) in Gallia County, Ohio on November 8, 1851, aged 69, stating Adam lived in Washington County, Maryland at the time of his enlistment and died about 1844 in Botetourt County, Virginia, aged 95, leaving no widow but left 6 children (no names given except Peter). Also see pension S11274 of Adam Quickel who was born in 1755 in York County, Pennsylvania, enlisted there and later moved to Botetourt County, Virginia. There are some similarities. Additional research will be necessary before drawing conclusions [Ref: V-III:2795].

QUIN, Mr. Private, Militia, by January 22, 1777 when ordered by the Committee of Observation "to march with some company of militia to the reinforcement of his Excellency General Washington" or appear before the Committee and state his reason for not marching. He apparently marched since he never appeared to the contrary [Ref: Q-48, which listed the name as "Mr. Quin, Clerk at Jacques's"].

QUINN, George. Took the Oath of Allegiance before the Hon. Joseph Sprigg before April 1, 1778 [Ref: O-53, J-16].

QUINTON, James. Private, Militia, 6th Class, Capt. Basil Williams' Company, 1776/1777 [Ref: M-244, A-1146].

RAGAN, John. Private, Militia, 3rd Class, Capt. Michael Fackler's Company, 1776/1777 [Ref: M-245, A-1146]. Rendered patriotic service by providing "rashons" for the use of the military in July, 1775, as recorded by the Committee of Observation at Elizabeth Town on November 4, 1775 [Ref: Q-150, which listed the name as "John Ragen"]. Rendered patriotic service in Hagerstown by providing sundries to Capt. John Nelson's Company, continental service (Maryland Line), April, 1776 [Ref: Q-161]. Rendered patriotic service by providing necessaries to Capt. John Reynolds' Company in the Flying Camp and belonging to the Maryland Service in July, 1776, as recorded by the Committee of Observation at Sharpsburg on August 6, 1776 [Ref: Q-333]. Took the Oath of Allegiance before the Hon. Henry Schnebley in 1778 [Ref: O-49, J-12].

RAGE, John. Private, Militia, 7th Class, Capt. Peter Beall's Company, 1st Battalion, 1776/1777 [Ref: M-240].

RAHAUSER, Mrs. See "Ludwick Young," q.v.

RAIDY, James. Private who was enrolled by Capt. Aeneas Campbell and passed by Major John Fulford on July 18, 1776 [Ref: D-49].

RALGLEZER, Henry. Rendered patriotic service by providing a rifle for Capt. Daniel Cresap's Company in July, 1775, as recorded by the Committee of Observation at Elizabeth Town on November 4, 1775 [Ref: Q-148].

RAMSEY, Allen (1764-   ). Private, Maryland or Pennsylvania Line, who applied for and received pension S32467 in Wabash County, Illinois on December 3, 1833, stating he was born on June 12, 1764 in (now) Harford County, Maryland and moved with his mother (not named) to Washington County, Maryland. There he enlisted and in 1784 moved to what became Vincennes County, Indiana. In 1792 he was taken prisoner by the Pottawatmie Indians and later released. He moved to Wabash County in 1819 [Ref: V-III:2804].

RANADAY, Charles. Took the Oath of Allegiance before the Hon. Lemuel Barritt before March 16, 1778 [Ref: O-42, J-8].

RANADY, John. Took the Oath of Allegiance before the Hon. Lemuel Barritt before March 16, 1778 [Ref: O-42, J-7, which latter source listed the name as "T--- Ranady"].

RANDLE, John. Private who was enlisted by Lieut. Christian Orndorff and passed on July 20, 1776 in Frederick (now Washington) County [Ref: D-50].

RANSBARGER, Stophel. Private, Militia, 3rd Class, Capt. Henry Boteler's Company, 1776/1777 [Ref: M-237, A-1146].

RAPE, John. Rendered patriotic service in Hagerstown by providing one pair of breeches to Capt. John Nelson's Company, continental service (Maryland Line), April, 1776 [Ref: Q-161].

RAPP, Matthias. Took the Oath of Allegiance before the Hon. Henry Schnebley in 1778 [Ref: O-50, J-14].

RASHR, William. See "William Busher," q.v.

RASMUSSEN, Tom N. See "Christopher Trovinger," q.v.

RATHERFORD, Allener. Private who was recruited and passed by County Lieutenant Thomas Sprigg on April 22, 1780 [Ref: D-336].

RAUGHLY, George. See "George Roughly," q.v.

RAVER, Chris. Private, German Regiment, Lt. Col. Ludwick Weltner's Company, continental service, discharged on July 26, 1779 [Ref: D-265].

RAWLINGS, Ann and Elizabeth. See "Solomon Rawlings," q.v.

RAWLINGS, Moses (1745-1809). Colonel, Maryland Line, 1776-1779 [Ref: D-77]. Assistant Commissary of Purchases for Washington County on September 10, 1779 [Ref: E-519]. The Council of Maryland noted the same day that "Col. Rawlings, we understand has resigned, he lives within a mile of Fort Frederick and, if he would undertake it, would be a proper person to have the Superintendance of the Prisoners." [Ref: E-

520]. On July 8, 1780, Col. Moses Rawlings was appointed Commissary for Purchases in Washington County [Ref: F-215]. Moses Rawlings was born in Maryland in 1745, married Elizabeth McMahon, and died in Virginia in May, 1809 [Ref: Y-III:2409]. See "Otho Holland Williams" and "Henry Ackart," q.v.

RAWLINGS, Solomon (c1743-1821). Soldier who resided in Washington County and was granted a pension certificate in August, 1820, according to an Act of Congress of March 18, 1818, since he had proven that he was "in the enjoyment of a certain degree of poverty" as required by the Act as amended on May 1, 1820 [Ref: W-1190]. Private, Maryland Line, who received pension S35039 at $96 per year effective May 26, 1818, and in 1820 was aged 77 with a wife (no name given) aged 67 and a daughter Elizabeth aged 30. Solomon died on July 3, 1821 [Ref: R-43, N-43, V-III:2818]. Ann Rawlings, relict of the late Solomon Rawlings, of Hagerstown, died on March 23, 1827 (age not given) after a lingering illness of many months, long a member of the Methodist Episcopal Church where she was interred [Ref: Z-89].

RAY, James. Private, Militia, 5th Class, Capt. Henry Boteler's Company, 1776/1777 [Ref: M-237, A-1146].

RAY, Jonathan (1759-   ). Private, Maryland line, who applied for and received pension S16513 in Marion County, Indiana on March 29, 1833, stating he was born in March, 1759 in Frederick County, Maryland and a cousin Samuel Davis in Ohio had his birth records. Jonathan lived at Hagerstown, Maryland at the time of his enlistment and a number of years after the war he moved to Huntington County, Pennsylvania. Four years later he moved to Ohio and in 1823 he moved to Marion County, Indiana [Ref: V-III:2821].

RAY, Michael. Private, Militia, 3rd Class, Capt. Samuel Hughes' Company, 2nd Battalion, 1776/1777 [Ref: M-238, A-1146].

RAY, William. Private, Militia, 2nd Class, Capt. Daniel Cresap's Company, 3rd Battalion, 1776/1777 [Ref: M-241]. Took the Oath of Allegiance before the Hon. Lemuel Barritt before March 16, 1778 [Ref: O-42, J-8].

RAY(?), William. Private, Militia, 3rd Class, Capt. James Prather's Company, 3rd Battalion, 1776/1777 [Ref: M-242].

RAYMER, Frederick. Private, Militia, 1st Class, Capt. John Bennet's Company, 1776/1777 [Ref: M-246, A-1146, which listed the name as "Frederick Raimer"]. Absconded (delinquent) and returned to duty by order of the Committee of Observation on February 8, 1777 [Ref: Q-232, Q-234, which listed the name as "Frederick Ramer"]. See "John Rayner," q.v.

RAYMER, John. Took the Oath of Allegiance before the Hon. Henry Schnebley in 1778 [Ref: O-50, J-14, which latter source listed the name as "John Rayomer"]. One "John Rayner" died testate before September 30, 1786 (date of balance book entry in Washington County), leaving a widow (no name given in this account) and sons Frederick, John, and Benjamin "Rayner." [Ref: J-27].

RAYNER, Benjamin, and others. See "John Raymer," q.v.

READ (REID), John. On April 22, 1780 the Council of Maryland ordered the Collector of Tax for Washington County to pay Capt. John Read of the Company of Infantry to be raised in virtue of the late Act of Assembly $7500 to be expended in the recruiting service. On July 4, 1780, Capt. John Reid was paid another $4000 for recruiting services at Fort Frederick [Ref: F-148, F-211].

READ, Samuel. Took the Oath of Allegiance before the Hon. John Barnes before February 28, 1778 [Ref: O-45, J-10].

REAM, Frederick. Private who was recruited and passed by County Lieutenant Thomas Sprigg on April 22, 1780 [Ref: D-336].

REAPLOGLE, Philip. Private, Militia, 8th Class, Capt. John Bennet's Company, 1776/1777 [Ref: A-1146, M-246, which listed the name as "Phillip Reaplogle (Reaylogle?)"]. On February 3, 1777 he was brought before the Committee of Observation for Elizabeth Town District (now the Hagerstown area of Washington County) "charged with being a deserter from Capt. John Bennet's Company of Militia in Col. Stull's Battalion, upon examination acknowledged the charge. Ordered that the said Reaplogle be confined in the Tory Goal for this county until a proper guard can be got to march him to join his respective company at camp." [Ref: Q-231]. Took the Oath of Allegiance before the Hon. John Barnes before February 28, 1778 [Ref: J-9, O-44, which listed the name as "Philop Replogh"].

REED, Casper. Private who enlisted in the militia on August 17, 1781 for service in the Continental Army [Ref: D-388].

REED, John. Private, Maryland Line. In November, 1812 the Treasurer of the Western Shore of Maryland was directed to pay to "John Reid" of Allegany County, $125, during life, quarterly, as a further remuneration for the services rendered his country during the Revolutionary War. "John Reed 2d" appeared on the rolls in January, 1820 [Ref: AA-384]. Additional research may be necessary before drawing conclusions. See "John Read (Reid)," q.v.

REED, Joseph. Second Lieutenant, Militia, Capt. James Prather's Company, 3rd or Western Battalion, May 16, 1778 [Ref: M-242, M-114, E-86, which latter source listed the name as "Joseph Read"]. Took the

Oath of Allegiance before the Hon. Lemuel Barritt before March 16, 1778 [Ref: O-43, J-8].

REED, Leonard. Private, Militia, 4th Class, Capt. Charles Clinton's Company, 1776/1777 [Ref: M-245, A-1146]. Private, Militia, Capt. Charles Coulson's Company, enrolled August 28, 1776 [Ref: M-244, A-1146].

REED, Peter. Private, Militia, 3rd Class, Capt. Peter Swingle's (Swingley's) Company, 1776/1777 [Ref: A-1146, M-248].

REED, Peter. Captain, by July, 1776, when he returned his list of non-enrollers and non-associators residing in his district to the Committee of Observation for Elizabeth Town District (now the Hagerstown area of Washington County). [Ref: Q-326]. Rendered patriotic service by supplying wheat for the use of the military on March 13, 1780 [Ref: W-1190, HH-73].

REED, Richard. Private, Militia, 6th Class, Capt. Griffin Johnson's Company, 3rd Battalion, 1776/1777 [Ref: M-243]. Took the Oath of Allegiance before the Hon. William Yates in 1778 [Ref: O-48, J-12].

REED, Samuel. Private, Militia, 4th Class, Capt. Isaac Baker's Company, 1776/1777 [Ref: A-1146, M-247]. Took the Oath of Allegiance before the Hon. Joseph Sprigg before April 1, 1778 [Ref: O-53, J-16].

REED, William. Private, Militia, 4th Class, Capt. Joseph Chapline's Company, 2nd Battalion, 1776/1777 [Ref: M-241]. Took the Oath of Allegiance before the Hon. Christopher Cruse in Sharpsburg Hundred before March 2, 1778 [Ref: O-34, J-2, which listed the name as "William Read"].

REEFNAUGH, Phillip. Private, Militia, 5th Class, Capt. Peter Beall's Company, 1st Battalion, 1776/1777 [Ref: M-240].

REEGER, Otzen. Private, Militia, Capt. William Heyser's Company, 1776, in continental service [Ref: W-1190, L-79].

REETER, Elias. Private, Militia, 3rd Class, Capt. Daniel Clapsaddle's Company, 1st Battalion, 1776/1777 [Ref: M-236, A-1146].

REEVER, Frederick. Private, Militia, 7th Class, Capt. Isaac Baker's Company, 1776/1777 [Ref: A-1146, M-247].

REEVER, Stuffle. Private, Militia, Capt. William Heyser's Company, enlisted July 27, 1776, muster roll dated October 23, 1776, in continental service, and discharged on July 29, 1779 at Fort Wyoming, Pennsylvania [Ref: D-264, W-1190, L-79, which latter source listed the name as "Stuffle Beever" and GG-99, which listed the name as "Christian/Stuffle Reaver, Reever, Raver, Raybert"].

REFNEH, Casper. Took the Oath of Allegiance before the Hon. John Stull in 1778 [Ref: O-47, J-11].

REHB, John. Took the Oath of Allegiance before the Hon. Henry Schnebley in 1778 [Ref: O-49, J-13, which latter source listed the name as "John Rebb"].
REICHEL, Adam. Took the Oath of Allegiance before the Hon. Henry Schnebley in 1778 [Ref: O-49, J-13].
REILEY, John. Took the Oath of Allegiance before the Hon. Samuel Hughes before March 1, 1778 [Ref: O-33, J-1].
REILEY, Moyles. See "Elizabeth Piper," q.v.
REINHART, George. Took the Oath of Allegiance before the Hon. Henry Schnebley in 1778 [Ref: O-50, J-13].
REINNHOLD, Fittus. Took the Oath of Allegiance before the Hon. Henry Schnebley in 1778 [Ref: J-14, O-51, which latter source listed the name as "Fittus Reihnhold"].
REIPS (REIFS?), John. Took the Oath of Allegiance before the Hon. John Barnes before February 28, 1778 [Ref: O-44, J-9].
REITENOWER, David, and others. See "David Ridenour," q.v.
RENBLIN, Jacob. Captain, Militia, July 27, 1777 [Ref: M-115].
RENNER, Phillip. Private, Militia, 1st Class, Capt. John Cellars' Company, 1776/1777 [Ref: A-1146, M-246].
RENTCH (RENCH), Andrew (1722-1782). Elected to serve on the Committee of Observation for the Elizabeth Town District (now the Hagerstown area of Washington County) on September 12, 1775 [Ref: Q-142, which listed the name as "Andrew Rench"] and referred to as "Major Andrew Rentch" on February 19, 1776 [Ref: Q-152]. Rendered patriotic service by supplying a blanket for the use of the military in March, 1776, as recorded by the Committee of Observation on April 12, 1776 [Ref: Q-156, L-82, which latter source listed the name as "Andrew Rench"]. Served on the Committee of Observation in April, 1776 [Ref: Q-154, Q-155]. Commissioned to be Lieutenant Colonel, 32nd Militia Battalion in (then) Frederick County, January 3, 1776 [Ref: AA-384]. Served on the Committee of Observation for the Elizabeth Town District in (now) Washington County in December, 1776 [Ref: Q-340, which referred to him as "Col. Andrew Rentch"]. Took the Oath of Allegiance on May 20, 1777 [Ref: K-1814, Box 4]. Justice who administered the Oath of Allegiance before March 7, 1778 [Ref: O-52, J-15]. Justice of the County Court, June 20, 1778 [Ref: E-141, which listed the name as "Andrew Rench"]. Justice of the Peace, January 30, 1781 [Ref: G-293]. "Andrew Rentch" died on October 7, 1782, aged 60, and is buried beside his wife Elizabeth Rentch (1739-1812) in the Salem Reformed Church Graveyard at Cearfoss in Washington County, Maryland [Ref: JJ-III:92].

RENTCH, Elizabeth. See "Andrew Rentch," q.v.

RENTCH (RENCH), John (1726-1794). Appointed to raise funds on January 24, 1775 for the Committee of Observation in Elizabeth Hundred in Frederick (now Washington) County [Ref: L-75, which listed the name as "John Rench"]. Appointed by the Committee of Observation to serve on a Committee for Licensing Suits on September 14, 1775 [Ref: Q-142, which listed the name as "John Rench"]. Elected to serve on the Committee of Observation for the Elizabeth Town District on September 12, 1775 [Ref: Q-142, which listed the name as "John Rench"], and referred to as "Mr. John Rench" on February 19, 1776 [Ref: Q-152]. Served on the Committee of Observation in April, 1776 [Ref: Q-154, Q-155]. Ensign, Upper District, Frederick County (now Washington County), July, 1776 [Ref: D-48, which listed the name as "John Rench"]. One of several patriots appointed by the Committee of Observation on December 30, 1776 "to form the county into companies (after the militia had marched) for the purpose of relieving the distressed inhabitants of said county and also to compel the Dunkards and Mennonists to give their assistance." [Ref: Q-345]. Appointed by the Committee of Observation to carry the Association of Freemen to male residents in his hundred (district) on March 4, 1776 "and present it for signing and make an exact account of those that sign and those that refuse with their reasons for refusing." [Ref: Q-153, L-82, which listed the name as "John Rench"]. Rendered patriotic service by supplying a blanket for the use of the military in March, 1776, as recorded by the Committee of Observation on April 12, 1776 [Ref: Q-157, L-82, which latter source listed the name as "John Rench"]. One of the persons appointed by the Committee of Observation for Elizabeth Town District on January 2, 1777 "to appraise the several wagons and horses that shall go with the militia in Col. John Stull's Battalion." [Ref: Q-29]. "John Rench" died on November 20, 1794, aged 68, and is buried beside his wife Margaret Rench (1731-1806) in the Salem Reformed Church Graveyard at Cearfoss in Washington County, Maryland [Ref: JJ-III:95].

RENTCH, John. Private, Militia, 6th Class, Capt. John Cellars' Company, 1776/1777 [Ref: A-1146, M-246].

RENTCH, John (of Joseph). Private, Militia, 1st Class, Capt. John Cellars' Company, 1776/1777 [Ref: A-1146, M-246].

RENTCH (RENCH), Joseph. Rendered patriotic service by supplying a blanket for the use of the military in March, 1776, as recorded by the Committee of Observation on April 12, 1776 [Ref: Q-157, L-82, which latter source listed the name as "Joseph Rench"]. On January 6, 1777 the Committee of Observation ordered that "a guard be sent immediately to fetch in Joseph Rentch's wagon and three horses, and also to bring Mr. Rentch with them, to shew cause why he has treated the authority of this committee with so much contempt, [and] if the horses can't be found, the guard is ordered to bring his oxen." [Ref: Q-32]. On January 10, 1777 Nicholas Martin and Joseph Rentch agreed "in partnership to furnish a team to draw the cannon for the use of Col. Stull's Battalion." [Ref: Q-35].

RENTCH (RENCH), Margaret. See "John Rentch," q.v.

RENTCH, Peter. Private, Militia, 1st Class, Capt. John Cellars' Company, 1776/1777 [Ref: A-1146, M-246]. "Peter Rench, merchant" died on September 29, 1796, about 4 miles from Hagerstown, after a short illness, leaving a wife and a numerous family [Ref: LL-1:64].

RENTCH (RENCH), Rebecca. See "Lodwick Young," q.v.

RENWICK, Robert. Private, Militia, 6th Class, Capt. Joseph Chapline's Company, 2nd Battalion, 1776/1777 [Ref: M-241].

RENWICK, William. Enrolled in the first militia company organized for the Revolutionary War in the Elizabeth Town District of Frederick County (now the Hagerstown area of Washington County) on January 6, 1776 [Ref: Q-271, W-1190, which listed the name as "William Renwicks"]. Private, Militia, 5th Class, Capt. Joseph Chapline's Company, 2nd Battalion, 1776/1777 [Ref: M-241]. Took the Oath of Allegiance before the Hon. Richard Davis in 1778 [Ref: J-4, O-36, which latter source listed the name as "William Benwick"].

RERLS, Frederick. Took the Oath of Allegiance before the Hon. John Barnes before February 28, 1778 [Ref: O-44, J-9, which latter source listed the name as "Frederick Reris"].

RESE, Nicholas. See "Nicholas Rose," q.v.

RESSE (REFFE), Mary. See "John Kibler," q.v.

RESLEY, Jeremiah. Enrolled in the second militia company organized for the Revolutionary War in the Elizabeth Town District of Frederick County (now the Hagerstown area of Washington County) on March 9, 1776 [Ref: Q-272].

REU, Isaac. Private, Militia, 5th Class, Capt. Michael Fackler's Company, 1776/1777 [Ref: M-245, A-1146].

REU, Matthew. See "Matthew Rice (Rue?)," q.v.

REUH, Mathias. Took the Oath of Allegiance before the Hon. Joseph Sprigg before April 1, 1778 [Ref: O-53, J-16].

REVENACHT, Phillip. Private, Militia, Capt. William Heyser's Company, 1776, in continental service [Ref: W-1190, L-79]. First Corporal, Militia, Capt. William Heyser's Company, muster roll dated October 23, 1776, in continental service [Ref: D-263, W-1190, which listed the name as

"Phillip Reevenach" and L-79, which listed the name as "P. Revenacht"]. Took the Oath of Allegiance before the Hon. Henry Schnebley in 1778 [Ref: O-51, J-14, which listed the name as "Philip Rieffennach"].

REYLER, Conrad. Private, Militia, 5th Class, Capt. Daniel Clapsaddle's Company, 1st Battalion, 1776/1777 [Ref: M-236, A-1146].

REYMER, Frederick. Took the Oath of Allegiance before the Hon. Henry Schnebley in 1778 [Ref: O-50, J-13].

REYNOLDS, Francis. Enrolled in the third militia company organized for the Revolutionary War in the Elizabeth Town District of Frederick County (now the Hagerstown area of Washington County), passed by the Committee of Observation on June 5, 1776, and assigned to Capt. John Reynolds' command [Ref: Q-272]. Private, Militia, 1st Class, Capt. John Rennolds' (Reynolds') Company, 2nd Battalion, 1776/1777 [Ref: M-240, which listed the name as "Francis Renold"]. Took the Oath of Allegiance before the Hon. Christopher Cruse in Sharpsburg Hundred before March 2, 1778 [Ref: O-34, J-2].

REYNOLDS, George. Private who was enlisted by Lieut. Moses Chapline and passed on July 24, 1776 in Frederick (now Washington) County [Ref: D-50].

REYNOLDS, Jeremiah. Took the Oath of Allegiance before the Hon. Richard Davis in 1778 [Ref: J-5, O-37, which listed the name as "Jeremiah Rennolds"].

REYNOLDS, John. Captain, Militia, Upper District, Frederick County, April 20, 1776. Captain, Militia, 2nd Battalion, Washington County, June 22, 1778 [Ref: M-115, A-356, E-145, which listed the name as "John Rennolds" and M-240, which listed the name as "John Renolds"]. Captain, Upper District, Frederick County (now Washington County), July, 1776 [Ref: D-48]. One of several patriots appointed by the Committee of Observation on January 19, 1777 "to form the county into companies (after the militia had marched) for the purpose of relieving the distressed inhabitants of said county and also to compel the Dunkards and Mennonists to give their assistance." [Ref: Q-43]. Appointed by the Committee of Observation to carry the Association of Freemen to male residents in his hundred (district) on March 4, 1776 "and present it for signing and make an exact account of those that sign and those that refuse with their reasons for refusing." [Ref: Q-153, L-82]. One John Reynolds died by June 11, 1782 (date of balance book entry in Washington County) with the administrator being Joseph Reynolds [Ref: J-23].

REYNOLDS, John Jr. Appointed by the Committee of Observation to carry the Association of Freemen to male residents in Sharpsburg

Hundred on September 14, 1775 "and require their subscription to the same and make an exact account of those who sign and those that refuse with their reasons for refusing." [Ref: Q-143]. Took the Oath of Allegiance before the Hon. Christopher Cruse in Sharpsburg Hundred before March 2, 1778 [Ref: O-34, J-1].

REYNOLDS, John Sr. One of the persons appointed by the Committee of Observation on January 9, 1777 "to appraise the several wagons, horses, wagon cloths and blankets that can be procured for the use of Col. Joseph Smith's Battalion." [Ref: Q-33]. Took the Oath of Allegiance before the Hon. Joseph Chapline before April 17, 1779 [Ref: J-5, O-39].

REYNOLDS, Joseph. Enrolled in the third militia company organized for the Revolutionary War in the Elizabeth Town District of Frederick County (now the Hagerstown area of Washington County), passed by the Committee of Observation on June 5, 1776, and assigned to Capt. John Reynolds' command [Ref: Q-273]. Enrolled in the third militia company organized for the Revolutionary War in the Elizabeth Town District of Frederick County (now the Hagerstown area of Washington County), passed by the Committee of Observation on June 5, 1776, and assigned to Capt. John Reynolds' command [Ref: Q-273, which listed the name as "Joseph Reynold"]. Took the Oath of Allegiance before the Hon. Joseph Chapline before April 17, 1779 [Ref: O-39, which listed the name as "Joseph Rennolds" and J-5, which listed the name as "Joseph Rennilds"].

REYNOLDS, Joseph (of John). Private, Militia, 2nd Class, Capt. John Rennolds' (Reynolds') Company, 2nd Battalion, 1776/1777 [Ref: M-240]. Ensign, Militia, Capt. John Rennolds' (Reynolds') Company, 2nd Battalion, by June 22, 1778 [Ref: M-115, B-145, which listed the name as "Joseph Rennolds, son of John"]. Took the Oath of Allegiance before the Hon. Christopher Cruse in Sharpsburg Hundred before March 2, 1778 [Ref: O-34, J-1]. Second Lieutenant, 2nd Battalion, November 21, 1780 [Ref: G-220]. See "John Reynolds," q.v.

REYNOLDS, Joseph (of William). Private, Militia, 6th Class, Capt. John Rennolds' (Reynolds') Company, 2nd Battalion, 1776/1777 [Ref: M-240].

REYNOLDS, William. Captain, Militia, 2nd Battalion, June 22, 1778 [Ref: M-115, E-145, which listed the name as "William Rennolds"].

RHODES, Basil. Private, Militia, 1st Class, Capt. Basil Williams' Company, 1776/1777 [Ref: M-244, A-1146, which listed the name as "Basil Roads"].

RHODES, Ezekiel. Private, Militia, 3rd Class, Capt. Basil Williams' Company, 1776/1777 [Ref: M-244, A-1146, which listed the name as "Ezekiel Roads"]. Rendered patriotic service by providing a coverlid for the use of the military in January, 1777, as recorded by the Committee of Observation on January 27, 1777 [Ref: Q-53].

RHODES, John. Private, Militia, Capt. William Heyser's Company, 1776, in continental service [Ref: W-1190, L-79, which listed the name as "John Rhods"].

RHODES, William. Private, Militia, 6th Class, Capt. Jeremiah Spires' Company, 2nd Battalion, 1776/1777 [Ref: M-239, A-1146, which listed the name as "William Roads"]. Took the Oath of Allegiance before the Hon. Richard Davis in 1778 [Ref: J-4, O-37].

RHODES, Zachariah (1756-   ). Private, Militia, 1st Class, Capt. Jeremiah Spires' Company, 2nd Battalion, 1776/1777 [Ref: M-239, A-1146]. Took the Oath of Allegiance before September 1, 1780 [Ref: X-119]. Applied for pension (R8735) in Jackson County, Virginia on November 19, 1833, stating he was born on July 13, 1756 in Washington County, Maryland and lived there at the time of his enlistment in the Maryland Line [Ref: V-III:2862].

RICE, Andrew. Took the Oath of Allegiance before the Hon. Andrew Bruce before March 2, 1778 [Ref: O-41, J-6].

RICE, Jacob. Private, Militia, 6th Class, Capt. James Walling's Company, 2nd Battalion, 1776/1777 [Ref: M-239, A-1146].

RICE, Matthew. Private, Militia, 8th Class, Capt. Griffin Johnson's Company, 3rd Battalion, 1776/1777 [Ref: M-243, which listed the name as "Matthew Rice (Rue?)"].

RICE, Nicholas. Took the Oath of Allegiance before the Hon. Joseph Sprigg before April 1, 1778 [Ref: O-53, J-16].

RICE, Solomon. See "Solomon Royse," q.v.

RICHARDS, Abraham. Enrolled in the second militia company organized for the Revolutionary War in the Elizabeth Town District of Frederick County (now the Hagerstown area of Washington County) on March 9, 1776 [Ref: Q-272].

RICHARDS, George Hall. Took the Oath of Allegiance before the Hon. Lemuel Barritt before March 16, 1778 [Ref: O-42, J-7, which listed the name as "George Hall Ritchards"].

RICHARDS, Godfrey. Private, Militia, 2nd Class, Capt. Charles Clinton's Company, 1776/1777 [Ref: M-245, A-1146]. Private, Militia, Capt. Charles Coulson's Company, enrolled August 28, 1776 [Ref: M-244, A-1146].

RICHARDS, Isaac. Private, Militia, Capt. Charles Coulson's Company, enrolled August 28, 1776 [Ref: M-244, A-1146].

RICHARDS, Richard. Private, Militia, by January 22, 1777 when ordered by the Committee of Observation "to march with some company of militia to the reinforcement of his Excellency General Washington" or appear before the Committee and state his reason for not marching. He apparently marched since he never appeared to the contrary [Ref: Q-48].

RICHARDSON, George. Private, Militia, 7th Class, Capt. Charles Clinton's Company, 1776/1777 [Ref: M-245, A-1146]. First Lieutenant, Militia, Capt. Charles Coulson's Company, by December 3, 1776 [Ref: M-243, M-115, B-501]. Took the Oath of Allegiance before the Hon. Andrew Bruce before March 2, 1778 [Ref: O-41, J-6].

RICHARDSON, Samuel (1753-   ). Private who was enrolled by Capt. Henry Hardman and passed on July 19, 1776 in Frederick (now Washington) County [Ref: D-51]. Private who was recruited and passed by County Lieutenant Thomas Sprigg on April 22, 1780 [Ref: D-336]. Applied for and received pension S40346 in Warren County, Ohio on June 16, 1818, aged 65, stating he had enlisted at Hagerstown, Maryland. In 1820 he states he had not had any family with him for 25 years [Ref: V-III:2878].

RICHIE, John. See "John Ritchie," q.v.

RICKENBAUGH, Martin. Private who was enrolled by Capt. Henry Hardman and passed on July 19, 1776 in Frederick (now Washington) County [Ref: D-51]. Took the Oath of Allegiance before the Hon. Henry Schnebley in 1778 [Ref: O-51, J-14, which listed the name as "Martin Rickenback" and "Martin Rickenbach"]. Private, Militia, 5th Class, Capt. Martin Kershner's Company, 1776/1777 [Ref: A-1146, M-247, which listed the name as "Martin Rigenbough"].

RICKOLD, Maynard. Took the Oath of Allegiance before the Hon. William Yates in 1778 [Ref: O-48, J-12, which latter source listed the name as "Matnard Rickold"].

RIDENOUR, Barbara and Benjamin. See "Martin Ridenour," q.v.

RIDENOUR, Catherine. See "Martin Ridenour," q.v.

RIDENOUR, Daniel. See "Matthias, David, Nicholas, Henry and Jacob Ridenour," q.v.

RIDENOUR (REITENOWER), David (1749-1804). First Sergeant, Militia, Capt. Martin Kershner's Company, 1776/1777 [Ref: M-247, A-1146]. Third Sergeant, Militia, Capt. Martin Kershner's Company, 32nd Battalion, December 27, 1776 [Ref: K-1814, Box 3]. David Ridenour, of Elizabeth Town, died after a short indisposition on the Saturday before October 3, 1804, in his 55th year [Ref: LL-2:100]. See the other "David Ridenour," q.v.

RIDENOUR, David (c1725-c1800). Took the Oath of Allegiance before the Hon. Henry Schnebley in 1778 [Ref: O-49, J-13, which listed the name as "David Reitenower"]. Rendered patriotic service by supplying wheat for the use of the military on March 10, 1780 [Ref: W-1190, which listed the name as "David Rittenower" and HH-72, which listed the name as "David Reitenower"]. Daniel Ridenour died before December 9, 1800 (date of balance book entry in Washington County), leaving an equal share of his estate to David Ridenour [Ref: J-39].

RIDENOUR, Elizabeth. See "Martin Ridenour," q.v.

RIDENOUR, Eve. See "Mathias Ridenour," q.v.

RIDENOUR (REITENOWER), George. Took the Oath of Allegiance before the Hon. Henry Schnebley in 1778 [Ref: J-15, O-51, which latter source listed the name as "George Reitenower"]. Second Sergeant, Militia, Capt. Conrad Hogmire's Company, 1776/1777 [Ref: M-244, A-1146, which listed the name as "George Ridnour"].

RIDENOUR (REITENOWER), Henry. One of several patriots appointed by the Committee of Observation on December 30, 1776 "to form the county into companies (after the militia had marched) for the purpose of relieving the distressed inhabitants of said county and also to compel the Dunkards and Mennonists to give their assistance." [Ref: Q-345]. Rendered patriotic service by supplying rye for the use of the military on February 14, 1780 [Ref: W-1190, which listed the name as "Henry Rittenower" and HH-72, which listed the name as "Henry Reitenower"]. Took the Oath of Allegiance before the Hon. Henry Schnebley in 1778 [Ref: O-49, J-13, which listed the name as "Henry Reitenower"]. Daniel Ridenour died before December 9, 1800 (date of balance book entry in Washington County), leaving an equal share of his estate to Henry Ridenour [Ref: J-39]. See "Matthias Ridenour" and the other Henry Ridneour," q.v.

RIDENOUR (REITENOWER), Henry. Private, Militia, 1st Class, Capt. John Cellars' Company, 1776/1777 [Ref: A-1146, M-246]. Took the Oath of Allegiance before the Hon. Henry Schnebley in 1778 [Ref: O-49, J-12, which listed the name as "Henry Reitenower"]. See the other "Henry Ridenour," q.v.

RIDENOUR (REITENOWER), Henry Jr. Private, Militia, 3rd Class, Capt. Martin Kershner's Company, 1776/1777 [Ref: A-1146, M-247, which listed the name without the "Jr."]. Took the Oath of Allegiance before the Hon. Henry Schnebley in 1778 [Ref: O-51, J-14, which listed the name as "Henry Reitenower, Jr."].

RIDENOUR (REITENOWER), Jacob (c1755-1827). Private, Militia, 8th Class, Capt. Martin Kershner's Company, 1776/1777 [Ref: A-1146, M-248]. Private, Militia, Capt. Martin Kershner's Company, 32nd Battalion, December 27, 1776 [Ref: K-1814 (Box 3), which listed the name as

"Jacob Ridenouer"]. Private, Militia, Capt. John Kershner's Company, on duty guarding prisoners of war at Fort Frederick on June 27, 1778 [Ref: D-328]. Took the Oath of Allegiance before the Hon. Henry Schnebley [Ref: J-13, which listed the name as "Jacob Reitenower" and O-50, which listed the name as "Jacob Reitenswer"]. Private, Maryland Line, and invalid (disabled) soldier [Ref: N-44]. Jacob Ridenour, a soldier of the Revolution, died at his residence near Cave-town on September 21, 1827 [Ref: Z-94]. Daniel Ridenour died before December 9, 1800 (date of balance book entry in Washington County), leaving an equal share of his estate to Jacob Ridenour [Ref: J-39]. Since there were two men named Jacob Ridenour who rendered service during the Revolutionary War, additional research will be necessary before drawing conclusions. See "Matthias Ridenour," q.v.

RIDENOUR (REITENOWER), Jacob. Took the Oath of Allegiance in January, 1778 before the Hon. John Cellars [Ref: K-1814, O-40, J-6]. The widow (no name given) of the late Jacob Reidenour died on November 4, 1821 in Washington County [Ref: Z-56]. See the other "Jacob Ridenour," q.v.

RIDENOUR, John. See "Matthias Ridenour," q.v.

RIDENOUR (REITENOWER), Ludwick. Private, Militia, 7th Class, Capt. Martin Kershner's Company, 1776/1777 [Ref: A-1146, M-248, which listed the name as "Lodwick Ridenour"]. Private, Militia, Capt. Martin Kershner's Company, 32nd Battalion, December 27, 1776 [Ref: K-1814 (Box 3), which listed the name as "Ludwig Ridenouer"]. Took the Oath of Allegiance before the Hon. John Cellars in January, 1778 [Ref: K-1814, O-40, J-6]. Rendered patriotic service by supplying wheat for the use of the military on April 11, 1780 [Ref: W-1190, and HH-73, which latter source listed the name as "Ludk. Rydenouer"].

RIDENOUR (REITENOWER), Martin (c1746-1821). Private, Militia, 2nd Class, Capt. Martin Kershner's Company, 1776/1777 [Ref: A-1146, M-247]. Ensign, Militia, Capt. Martin Kershner's Company, 32nd Battalion, December 27, 1776 [Ref: K-1814, Box 3]. Second Lieutenant, Militia, Capt. Conrad Hogmire's Company, and subsequently Captain, Militia (date not given). [Ref: M-116, M-244, A-1146]. Took the Oath of Allegiance in 1778 before the Hon. Henry Schnebley [Ref: O-51, J-15, which listed the name as "Martin Reitenower"]. "Capt. Martin Ridenour" died in Hagerstown, after a lingering illness, on August 18, 1821, in his 75th year [Ref: Z-55].

RIDENOUR (REITENOWER), Martin (c1720-c1798). Took the Oath of Allegiance before the Hon, Andrew Rentch before March 7, 1778 [Ref: O-52, J-15, which latter source listed the name as "Martain Redenour"].

Rendered patriotic service by supplying wheat and rye for the use of the military on March 3, 1780 [Ref: W-1190, which listed the name as "Martin Rittenower" and HH-72, which listed the name as "Martin Reitenower"]. Martin Ridenour died before October 9, 1798 (date of balance book entry in Washington County), leaving a widow (no name given in this account) and equal shares to Elizabeth, Martin, Catherine, Benjamin, Susanne, and Barbara Ridenour, Margaret Adult, and Dorothy Koogle [Ref: J-36]. Source Y-III:2465 states that one Martin Ridenour was born in Maryland in 1754, married (name not given), rendered patriotic service, and died before October 9, 1794. Additional research will be necessary before drawing conclusions.

RIDENOUR (REITENOWER), Matthias (c1732-c1792). One of several patriots appointed by the Committee of Observation for Elizabeth Town District (now the Hagerstown area of Washington County) on December 30, 1776 "to form the county into companies (after the militia had marched) for the purpose of relieving the distressed inhabitants of said county and also to compel the Dunkards and Mennonists to give their assistance." [Ref: Q-345]. On January 2, 1777 the Committee of Observation for Elizabeth Town District appointed Matthias Ridenour as one of the persons authorized "to appraise the several wagons and horses that shall go with the militia in Col. John Stull's Battalion and make return thereof to this Committee." [Ref: Q-29, Q-53]. Elected to serve on the Committee of Observation on January 8, 1777 in the room of Capt. John Cellar who had resigned [Ref: Q-33, Q-228]. Two men by this name took the Oath of Allegiance in 1778: one before the Hon. Joseph Sprigg before April 1, 1778 [Ref: J-16, O-53, which latter source listed the name as "Matthias Ridenowo (Reitenower)"], and one before the Hon. Henry Schnebley [Ref: O-50, J-14, which listed the name as "Matthias Reitenower"]. One "Mathias Ridenour" died testate before February 14, 1795 (date of balance book entry in Washington County), leaving equal shares to Nicholas, Henry, Jacob, John, Mathias Ridenour, and Daniel Ridenour, Eve Oster, and Rosena Eichelberger or Echelberger [Ref: J-34]. A Daniel Ridenour died before December 9, 1800 (date of balance book entry in Washington County), leaving a widow (no name given in this account) and equal shares of his estate to Nicholas, Henry, Jacob, Matthias, and David Ridenour, Conrad Oster, and Valentine Ackenberger [Ref: J-39]. Mathias Ridenour was born in France before 1732, married Eve ----, and died in Maryland before March 3, 1792 [Ref: Y-III:2465].

RIDENOUR (REITENOWER), Nicholas (1755-1823). One of several patriots appointed by the Committee of Observation on December 30,

1776 "to form the county into companies (after the militia had marched) for the purpose of relieving the distressed inhabitants of said county and also to compel the Dunkards and Mennonists to give their assistance." [Ref: Q-345]. Second Corporal, Militia, Capt. Martin Kershner's Company, 32nd Battalion, December 27, 1776 [Ref: K-1814, Box 3]. First Corporal, Militia, Capt. Martin Kershner's Company, 1776/1777 [Ref: M-247, A-1146]. Took the Oath of Allegiance before the Hon. Henry Schnebley in 1778 [Ref: O-49, J-13, which listed the name as "Nicholas Reitenower"]. Daniel Ridenour died before December 9, 1800 (date of balance book entry in Washington County), leaving an equal share of his estate to Nicholas Ridenour [Ref: J-39]. Nicholas Ridenour died at his residence about 6 miles from Hagerstown on January 25, 1823, in his 68th year; interred in Lutheran burial ground at Williamsport; discourse delivered by Rev. Kurtz [Ref: Z-44]. See the other "Nicholas Ridenour," q.v.

RIDENOUR (REITENOWER), Nicholas (1755-1823). Took the Oath of Allegiance in 1778 before the Hon. Henry Schnebley [Ref: O-50, which listed the name as "Nicholas Rietenower"]. Nicholas Ridenour was born on February 25, 1755, married Catherine Tackler, rendered patriotic service in Maryland, and died on April 2, 1823 [Ref: Y-III:2465]. There were two men with this name who were born in 1755, took the Oath of Allegiance in 1778, and died in 1823. Additional research may be necessary before drawing conclusions. See "Matthias Ridenour" and the other "Nicholas Ridenour," q.v.

RIDENOUR (REITENOWER), Peter. One of several patriots appointed by the Committee of Observation on December 30, 1776 "to form the county into companies (after the militia had marched) for the purpose of relieving the distressed inhabitants of said county and also to compel the Dunkards and Mennonists to give their assistance." [Ref: Q-345]. Took the Oath of Allegiance (affirmed) before the Hon. Henry Schnebley in 1778 [Ref: J-15, which listed the name as "Peter Reitenower" and O-51, which listed the name as "Peter Rictenawer"].

RIDENOUR, Susanne. See "Martin Ridenour," q.v.

RIDGELY, Frederick. Took the Oath of Allegiance before the Hon. Joseph Sprigg before April 1, 1778 [Ref: O-53, J-16, which latter source listed the name as "Frederick Ridgeley"].

RIDGELY, Isaac. Took the Oath of Allegiance before the Hon. Richard Davis in 1778 [Ref: J-3, O-36, which latter source listed the name as "Isaac Ridgeley"]. Private, Militia, 6th Class, Capt. Jeremiah Spires' Company, 2nd Battalion, 1776/1777 [Ref: M-239, A-1146].

RIECHART (RIGGER), Casper. Private, Militia, 4th Class, Capt. Peter Swingle's (Swingley's) Company, 1776/1777 [Ref: A-1146, M-248]. Took the Oath of Allegiance before the Hon. Henry Schnebley in 1778 [Ref: O-51, J-14, which listed the name as "Casper Rigger"].

RIECHART (RIGGER), John. Private, Militia, 8th Class, Capt. Peter Swingle's (Swingley's) Company, 1776/1777 [Ref: A-1146, M-249]. Took the Oath of Allegiance before the Hon. Henry Schnebley in 1778 [Ref: O-51, J-14, which listed the name as "John Rigger"]. On September 23, 1780, Col. Lemuel Barritt recommended to Governor Lee that "John Ruggard" be commissioned a captain in the militia at Willstown since so many officers of the Western Battalion had moved to Kentucky and elsewhere [Ref: G-123]. See "Adam Ott," q.v.

RIECHART (RIGGER), Peter. Private, Militia, 3rd Class, Capt. Peter Swingle's (Swingley's) Company, 1776/1777 [Ref: A-1146, M-248]. Took the Oath of Allegiance before the Hon. Joseph Sprigg before April 1, 1778 [Ref: O-53, J-16, which listed the name as "Peter Rigger"].

RIEFFENNACH, Philip. See "Philip Revenacht," q.v.

RIGGER, Casper. See "Casper Riechart," q.v.

RIGGLEMAN, George. Private, Militia, Capt. William Heyser's Company, enlisted August 18, 1776, muster roll dated October 23, 1776, which mistakenly stated he had deserted [Ref: D-264, W-1190, L-79, which latter source listed the name as "George Biggleman"]. Private, German Regiment, Lt. Col. Ludwick Weltner's Company, continental service, 1776, and discharged on October 12, 1779 [Ref: GG-99, D-265, which listed the name as "George Regliman" and D-243, which listed the name as "George Regalman"].

RIGERT, Catharine and John. See "Adam Ott," q.v.

RIGHDOUT, Thomas. Private, Militia, 7th Class, Capt. Barnett Johnston's Company, 3rd Battalion, 1776/1777 [Ref: M-242].

RIGHTER, John. Private, Select Militia, Capt. Adam Ott's Company, 1781 [Ref: M-238, A-1146].

RILEY, Barney. Private who was enrolled by Capt. Henry Hardman and passed on July 19, 1776 in Frederick (now Washington) County [Ref: D-51, which listed the name as "Barny Riely"]. Private, Militia, 8th Class, Capt. Michael Fackler's Company, 1776/1777 [Ref: M-245, A-1146, which listed the name as "---- Riley"].

RILEY, Patrick. Private who was enrolled by Capt. Henry Hardman and passed on July 19, 1776 in Frederick (now Washington) County [Ref: D-51, which listed the name as "Patrick Ryley"].

RIMELY, Philip. Rendered patriotic service by supplying four coverlids for the use of the military in March, 1776, as recorded by the Committee of Observation on April 12, 1776 [Ref: Q-156, which listed the name as "Philip Rymely" and L-82, which listed the name as "Philip Rymeby"]. Private, Militia, 8th Class, Capt. Daniel Clapsaddle's Company, 1st Battalion, 1776/1777 [Ref: M-236, A-1146, which listed the name as "Phillip Rimely"]. Took the Oath of Allegiance before the Hon. Andrew Rentch before March 7, 1778 [Ref: O-52, J-15, which listed the name as "Phillip Rimill" or Rimile?].

RINE, Patrick. Private who was enrolled by Lieut. Clement Hollyday and passed by Major Francis Deakins on July 25, 1776 [Ref: D-49].

RINEHART, George. Private, Militia, 8th Class, Capt. Peter Beall's Company, 1st Battalion, 1776/1777 [Ref: M-240].

RINEHART, Thomas. Private, Militia, 6th Class, Capt. Peter Beall's Company, 1st Battalion, 1776/1777 [Ref: M-240]. Took the Oath of Allegiance before the Hon. Joseph Sprigg before April 1, 1778 [Ref: O-53, J-16].

RINGER, Conrad. Private, Militia, 7th Class, Capt. Conrad Nichodemus' Company, 2nd Battalion, 1776/1777 [Ref: M-237, A-1146].

RINGER, John (1752-1827). Private, Militia, 1st Class, Capt. Conrad Nichodemus' Company, 2nd Battalion, 1776/1777 [Ref: M-237, A-1146, D-261]. John Ringer was born in 1752, married Anne Bordenheimer, served as a private in the Revolution, and died on July 7, 1287 [Ref: Y-III:2471]. See "John Rinkar," q.v.

RINGER, Matthias (c1763-1843). Applied for pension (R8831) in Washington County, Maryland on April 12, 1836, aged 73, stating he served in the Maryland Line [Ref: V-III:2893]. "Matthias Ringer, Jr." was born between 1760 and 1763, married Rebecca Elizabeth Plank, served as a private in Maryland during the Revolution, and died on February 11, 1843 [Ref: Y-III:2471]. It must be noted, however, that his pension was rejected and he is not listed in the rolls in *Archives of Maryland, Volume 18*. Additional research will be necessary before drawing conclusions.

RINGER, Matthias Sr. (c1734-1810). Rendered patriotic service (not specified) in Maryland, married Susanna ----, and died before March 17, 1810 [Ref: Y-III:2471].

RINGER, Susanna. See "Matthias Ringer, Sr.," q.v.

RINKAR, John. Enrolled in the second militia company organized for the Revolutionary War in the Elizabeth Town District of Frederick County (now the Hagerstown area of Washington County) on March 9, 1776 [Ref: Q-272]. See "John Ringer," q.v.

RIPLE, Ludwick. Third Corporal, Militia, Capt. Conrad Hogmire's Company, 1776/1777 [Ref: M-244, A-1146].

RIPPLE, Margaret. See "Frederick Nichodemus," q.v.

RISLEY, Daniel. Private, Militia, 5th Class, Capt. Henry Boteler's Company, 1776/1777 [Ref: M-237, A-1146].

RISMEL, George. Private who was enrolled by Capt. Henry Hardman and passed on July 19, 1776 in Frederick (now Washington) County [Ref: D-51].

RITCHIE, John (c1742-1807). Private, 5th Maryland Line, December 5, 1776 to at least January 1, 1780 [Ref: D-240, which listed the name as "John Richie"]. "John Ritchie" died on the Friday before April 10, 1807, "supposed to be age 65," and for many years manager of the Antietam Iron Works. He is buried in the Old Reformed Graveyard at Sharpsburg, Maryland and his son Archibald Ritchie (1795-1828) is buried beside him [Ref: JJ-I:27, LL-3:56].

RITTER, ----. Rendered patriotic service by providing a rifle for Capt. Daniel Cresap's Company in July, 1775, as recorded by the Committee of Observation at Elizabeth Town on November 4, 1775 [Ref: Q-149].

RITTER, Abraham. Private, Militia, Capt. Martin Kershner's Company, 32nd Battalion, December 27, 1776 [Ref: K-1814, Box 3].

RITTER, Conrad. Private, Militia, Capt. Martin Kershner's Company, 32nd Battalion, December 27, 1776 [Ref: K-1814 (Box 3), which listed the name as "Conroad Ritter"].

RITTER, Elias. Private, Militia, Capt. John Kershner's Company, on duty guarding prisoners of war at Fort Frederick on June 27, 1778 [Ref: D-328, which listed the name as "Elias Reeter"]. Took the Oath of Allegiance before the Hon. Henry Schnebley in 1778 [Ref: O-50, J-13].

RITTER, Jacob. One of several patriots appointed by the Committee of Observation on December 30, 1776 "to form the county into companies (after the militia had marched) for the purpose of relieving the distressed inhabitants of said county and also to compel the Dunkards and Mennonists to give their assistance." [Ref: Q-345]. Took the Oath of Allegiance before the Hon. Henry Schnebley in 1778 [Ref: O-50, J-13].

RITTER, Valentine. Enrolled in the third militia company organized for the Revolutionary War in the Elizabeth Town District of Frederick County (now the Hagerstown area of Washington County), passed by the Committee of Observation on June 5, 1776, and assigned to Capt. John Reynolds' command [Ref: Q-273].

ROACH, Jesse and Mary Ann. See "Jeremiah Chapline," q.v.

ROADS, Zachariah. See "Zachariah Rhodes," q.v.

ROAM, Adam. Took the Oath of Allegiance before September 1, 1780 [Ref: X-119].

ROAM, Conrad. Took the Oath of Allegiance before September 1, 1780 [Ref: X-119].

ROAM, Henry. Took the Oath of Allegiance before September 1, 1780 [Ref: X-119]. "Henry Rome" died before May 17, 1799 (date of balance book entry in Washington County), leaving a widow (not named, but Mary Rome was the administratrix) and equal shares to Susanna, Elizabeth, Jacob, Catherine, and David Rome [Ref: J-37].

ROARER, Frederick. See "Frederick Rohrer," q.v.

ROBERTS, Christena. See "Edward Roberts," q.v.

ROBERTS, Edward. Private, Virginia Line, who enlisted at Fort Pleasant, Virginia on August 20, 1776 and lived in (now) Allegany County, Maryland during the war. He married Christena Bray on July 5, 1784 in Maryland and moved to Jessamine County, Kentucky, then to Clinton County, Ohio, and then to Montgomery County, Kentucky in 1792. He applied for pension in Montgomery County on October 7, 1819, aged 65. Date of death not stated, but his widow Christena Roberts applied for and received pension W8569 in Clinton County, Ohio in 1844 and later moved to Jefferson County, Iowa [Ref: T-58].

ROBERTS, Jane and Mary. See "William Roberts," q.v.

ROBERTS, William (c1753-c1834). Enrolled in the first militia company organized for the Revolutionary War in the Elizabeth Town District of Frederick County (now the Hagerstown area of Washington County) on January 6, 1776 [Ref: Q-270, W-1189]. Private, Militia, 2nd Class, Capt. Joseph Chapline's Company, 2nd Battalion, 1776/1777 [Ref: M-241]. Took the Oath of Allegiance before the Hon. Joseph Chapline before April 17, 1779 [Ref: J-5, O-39]. Applied for and received pension S35053 in Allegany County, Maryland on April 27, 1818, stating he served in the Maryland Line. In 1820 he was aged 67 with a wife aged 57, a son aged 22, and two daughters aged 17 and 15 who lived with him (no names given). [Ref: V-III:2911]. In December, 1815 the Treasurer of the Western Shore of Maryland was directed to pay to William Roberts, of Allegany County, a private in the Revolutionary War, half pay of a private, "as a further remuneration to him for those services by which his country has been so essentially benefitted." On March 4, 1834 the Treasurer of the Western Shore of Maryland was directed to pay to Jane Roberts, of Allegany County, during life, quarterly, half pay of a private for the services rendered by her husband during the war. On March 26, 1839 the Treasurer of the Western Shore of Maryland was directed to pay to Mary Roberts, of Allegany County, $9.89, for 2 months and 29 days' pension due Jane Roberts, of Allegany County, at the time of her death as a Revolutionary pensioner [Ref: AA-386].

ROBERTSON, John. Private, Militia, Capt. William Heyser's Company, muster roll dated October 23, 1776, in continental service and on duty in May, 1777 [Ref: D-264, W-1190, L-79, which listed the name as "John Roberston" and GG-99, which listed the name as "John Robertson, Robinson"].

ROBINETT, Elisha. Private, Militia, 1st Class, Capt. Griffin Johnson's Company, 3rd Battalion, 1776/1777 [Ref: M-243, which listed the name as "Elisha Robinitt"].

ROBINETT, Ezekiel. Private, Militia, 7th Class, Capt. Griffin Johnson's Company, 3rd Battalion, 1776/1777 [Ref: M-243].

ROBINETT, Joseph. Private, Militia, 2nd Class, Capt. Griffin Johnson's Company, 3rd Battalion, 1776/1777 [Ref: M-243].

ROBINETT, Moses. Fourth Corporal, Militia, Capt. Griffin Johnson's Company, 3rd Battalion, 1776/1777 [Ref: M-243, which listed the name as "Moses Robonitt"].

ROBINETT, Moses. Private, Militia, 2nd Class, Capt. Griffin Johnson's Company, 3rd Battalion, 1776/1777 [Ref: M-243].

ROBINETT, Moses. Private, Militia, 3rd Class, Capt. Griffin Johnson's Company, 3rd Battalion, 1776/1777 [Ref: M-243].

ROBINETT, Samuel. Private, Militia, 7th Class, Capt. Griffin Johnson's Company, 3rd Battalion, 1776/1777 [Ref: M-243].

ROBINETT, Samuel. Third Sergeant, Militia, Capt. Griffin Johnson's Company, 3rd Battalion, 1776/1777 [Ref: M-243, which listed the name as "Samuel Robonitt"].

ROBINSON, Charles (c1753-   ). Private, Maryland Line, pensioned in Washington County under the Act of June 7, 1832 at the annual allowance of $40 retroactive to March 4, 1831 [Ref: R-51].

ROBINSON, Chloe or Clorender. See "Basil Prather," q.v.

ROBINSON, Elisha. Private who was recruited on November 10, 1780 [Ref: D-346].

ROBINSON, John. Private, Militia, 3rd Class, Capt. Michael Fackler's Company, 1776/1777 [Ref: M-245, A-1146]. Private, Militia, Capt. John Kershner's Company, on duty guarding prisoners of war at Fort Frederick on June 27, 1778 [Ref: D-328].

ROBISON, Thomas. Private who was enrolled by Capt. Henry Hardman and passed on July 19, 1776 in Frederick (now Washington) County [Ref: D-51].

ROBY, Arthur John. Private, Militia, 7th Class, Capt. Peter Swingle's (Swingley's) Company, 1776/1777 [Ref: A-1146, M-249].

ROBY, Benjamin. Took the Oath of Allegiance before the Hon. Richard Davis in 1778 [Ref: J-4, O-37].

ROBY, Lawrance. Took the Oath of Allegiance before the Hon. Richard Davis in 1778 [Ref: J-4, O-37]. Private, Militia, 1st Class, Capt. Peter Swingle's (Swingley's) Company, 1776/1777 [Ref: A-1146, M-248, which listed the name as "Laurance Robey"].

ROBY, Michael. Took the Oath of Allegiance before the Hon. Richard Davis in 1778 [Ref: J-3, O-36].

ROBY, Michael Hains. Private, Militia, 5th Class, Capt. Jeremiah Spires' Company, 2nd Battalion, 1776/1777 [Ref: M-239, A-1146, which listed the name as "Michael Hains Ruby"].

ROBY, Owen (c1750-1799). Took the Oath of Allegiance before the Hon. Richard Davis in 1778 [Ref: J-4, O-37]. Private, Militia, 3rd Class, Capt. Peter Swingle's (Swingley's) Company, 1776/1777 [Ref: A-1146, M-248, which listed the name as "Owen Robey"]. An Owen Roby died in 1799 and among his nine heirs was a son William Roby and a daughter Statia Roby who married Martin Engle and no longer reside in Maryland [Ref: Z-12, citing an equity court case in Allegany County in 1827].

ROBY, Statia. See "Owen Roby," q.v.

ROBY, Thomas. Took the Oath of Allegiance before the Hon. Richard Davis in 1778 [Ref: J-4, O-36].

ROBY, William. Private, Militia, 3rd Class, Capt. Jeremiah Spires' Company, 2nd Battalion, 1776/1777 [Ref: M-239, A-1146]. Took the Oath of Allegiance before the Hon. Richard Davis in 1778 [Ref: J-4, O-37]. See "Owen Roby," q.v.

ROCHESTER, Nathaniel (1751-1831). Appeared in court and qualified as Sheriff of Washington County in February, 1804 [Ref: II-59]. "Died at Rochester, New York on May 17, 1831 in the 80th year of his age, Colonel Nathaniel Rochester, formerly of Hagerstown." [Ref: DD-23, citing *The Republican Banner* on May 28, 1831]. His service in the Revolutionary War was not stated. Additional research will be necessary before drawing conclusions.

ROCKENBACK, Jacob. Took the Oath of Allegiance before the Hon. Christopher Cruse in Sharpsburg Hundred before March 2, 1778 [Ref: O-35, J-2]. Private, Militia, 1st Class, Capt. Jacob Sharer's Company, 1776/1777 [Ref: A-1146, M-248, which listed the name as "Jacob Rockenbaugh"].

ROCKWELL, Mainyard. Private, Militia, 6th Class, Capt. Barnett Johnston's Company, 3rd Battalion, 1776/1777 [Ref: M-242].

ROD, Frederick. Private, Militia, 1st Class, Capt. Conrad Nichodemus' Company, 2nd Battalion, 1776/1777 [Ref: M-237, A-1146].

RODES, Barbara. See "Jacob Martin," q.v.

RODGERS, Alexander. Enrolled in the third militia company organized for the Revolutionary War in the Elizabeth Town District of Frederick County (now the Hagerstown area of Washington County), passed by the Committee of Observation on June 5, 1776, and assigned to Capt. John Reynolds' command [Ref: Q-273].

RODRICK, Jacob. Private, Militia, 7th Class, Capt. Henry Boteler's Company, 1776/1777 [Ref: M-237, A-1146].

RODRICK, John. Private, Militia, 4th Class, Capt. Henry Boteler's Company, 1776/1777 [Ref: M-237, A-1146].

ROGERS, Isabella and John. See "George Calmes," q.v.

ROHRBACK, William. See "Henry Young," q.v.

ROHRER, Anna. See "Jacob Bower," q.v.

ROHRER, Barbara. See "Jacob Rohrer" and "Christian Rohrer," q.v.

ROHRER, Christian. Private, Militia, 5th Class, Capt. Michael Fackler's Company, 1776/1777 [Ref: M-245, A-1146, which listed the name as "Christian Rorer"]. Rendered patriotic service by supplying a blanket for the use of the military in March, 1776, as recorded by the Committee of Observation on April 12, 1776 [Ref: Q-156, which listed the name as "Christian Rhour" and L-82, which listed the name as "Ch'n. Rohrer"]. "Christian Rohrer" died testate by September 14, 1805, leaving a wife Fronica and seven children (names not given). [Ref: MM-13:176].

ROHRER, Frederick. There were two men with this name who rendered service during the Revolutionary War. Additional research may be necessary before drawing conclusions. (1) "Frederick Rohrer, Esq., died at Greensburgh, Pennsylvania, of dropsy in the chest, on Sunday evening, September 21, 1823, at half past 9 o'clock, in the 82nd year of his age. He was a native of France, born July 28, 1742. He came to America during the war between France and Britain. He married Catherine Deemer in 1766 in York County and shortly after removed to Hagerstown. In that year he first visited the Western Country, as far as Pittsburgh, then composed of a few Indian huts. He brought a number of cattle with him which he exchanged to General St. Clair for a tract of land in Ligonier Valley. He still left his family in Hagerstown and in 1767 brought the first wheat over the mountains ever imported into the Western Country. He cultivated it, together with other grain on his farm in the Valley, and prepared for his family, whom he removed there in the following fall. He took out a warrant for all that tract of land on the Connemaugh River, on which the salt is now made, and was the first to discover those immense springs of salt water. In 1771 he returned with his family to Hagerstown, being unable to live any longer amongst the Indians. [*Note:* It is indeed strange that this long obituary would omit his military service during the Revolutionary War]. In 1793 he removed to Greensburgh, from Hagerstown, where he remained until the time of his death. Some time after his removal there he was appointed a Justice of the Peace by Governor McKean. He was interred in the German burying ground. He had 9 children, 42 grandchildren, and 17 great-grandchildren" (no names were given). [Ref: Z-48, Z-49]. (2) "Frederick Rohrer, Sr." was born on March 20, 1755, died on February 12, 1832, and is buried beside his wife Magdalena Rohrer (1761-1812) and daughter Mary Ann Rohrer (1820-1830) in a graveyard on the Diamond King Farm below the old marble quarry near Boonsboro in Washington County, Maryland [Ref: JJ-III:54]. The following patriotic service could apply to one or both of these men: Second Corporal, Militia, Capt. Henry Boteler's Company, 1776/1777 [Ref: M-237, A-1146, which listed the name as "Frederick Rorer"]. Rendered patriotic service by providing a rifle for Capt. Daniel Cresap's Company and by providing "rashons" and a gun for the use of the military in July, 1775, as recorded by the Committee of Observation at Elizabeth Town on November 4, 1775. Rendered patriotic service in Hagerstown by providing sundry necessaries to Capt. John Nelson's Company, continental service (Maryland Line), April, 1776 [Ref: Q-148, Q-150, Q-161, which listed the name as "Fred. Roarer"]. Rendered patriotic service by supplying wheat for the use of the military on April 6, 1780 [Ref: W-1190, which listed the name as "Frederick Rohrer" and HH-73, which listed the name as "Fredk. Rohra"]. First Sergeant, Militia, Capt. Peter Beall's Company, 1st Battalion, 1776/1777 [Ref: M-240, which listed the name as "Frederick Roser" or Rorer?].

ROHRER, George. Enrolled in the third militia company organized for the Revolutionary War in the Elizabeth Town District of Frederick County (now the Hagerstown area of Washington County), passed by the Committee of Observation on June 5, 1776, and assigned to Capt. John Reynolds' command [Ref: Q-273, which listed the name as "George Boahrer"]. Took the Oath of Allegiance before the Hon. Christopher Cruse in Sharpsburg Hundred before March 2, 1778 [Ref: O-34, J-2, which listed the name as "George Bohrer" or Rohrer?].

ROHRER, Jacob (1741-1804). Rendered patriotic service by providing a rifle for Capt. Daniel Cresap's Company in July, 1775, as recorded by the Committee of Observation at Elizabeth Town on November 4, 1775 [Ref: Q-148, which listed the name as "Jacob Roarer"]. Rendered patriotic service by supplying a blanket for the use of the military in March, 1776, as recorded by the Committee of Observation on April 12, 1776 [Ref: Q-156, which listed the name as "Jacob Rhour" and L-82, which listed the name as "Jacob Rohrer"]. Jacob Rohrer died at his residence near Hagerstown on the Saturday before October 17, 1804, in his 63rd year, and was interred in the family burying ground [Ref: LL-2:100]. "Jacob Rohrer, brewer" died testate in 1804, leaving a wife Barbara anda very lengthy will [Ref: MM-13:89-90]. "Jacob Rohrer, Sr." operated a brewery near Hagerstown prior to 1800 [Ref: LL-2:49]. "Barbara Rohrer, wife of Jacob Rohrer, Sr." died on March 5, 1822 in her 70th year [Ref: Z-40].

ROHRER, Jacob (1746-1822). Private, Militia, Capt. John Kershner's Company, on duty guarding prisoners of war at Fort Frederick until discharged on May 20, 1778 [Ref: D-328, which listed the name as "Jacob Rorer"]. "Jacob Rohrer, Sr.," an old inhabitant of Washington County, died at his residence about 4 miles from Hagerstown on April 9, 1822, in his 76th year. He was born on the farm on which he died." [Ref: Z-58].

ROHRER, John. Rendered patriotic service by providing a rifle for Capt. Daniel Cresap's Company in July, 1775, as recorded by the Committee of Observation at Elizabeth Town on November 4, 1775 [Ref: Q-149, which listed the name as "John Roarer"]. Private, Militia, 8th Class, Capt. Henry Boteler's Company, 1776/1777 [Ref: M-237, A-1146, which listed the name as "John Rorer"]. Rendered patriotic service by supplying two blankets for the use of the military in March, 1776, as recorded by the Committee of Observation on April 12, 1776 [Ref: Q-157, which listed the name as "John Rhora" and L-82, which listed the name as "John Rolter" ?]. Private, Militia, 8th Class, Capt. Samuel Hughes' Company, 2nd Battalion, 1776/1777 [Ref: A-1146, M-238, which listed the name as "John Roser" or Rorer?]. See "Jacob Bower," q.v.

ROHRER, Magdalena and Mary Ann. See "Frederick Rohrer," q.v.

ROHRER, Martin. Private, Militia, 5th Class, Capt. Samuel Hughes' Company, 2nd Battalion, 1776/1777 [Ref: M-238, A-1146, which listed the name as "Martin Rorer"].

ROHRER, Samuel. On July 25, 1776 the Committee of Observation for Elizabeth Town District (now the Hagerstown area of Washington County) remitted the fine imposed on Samuel Rohrer for not enrolling due to his being an invalid [Ref: Q-333].

ROLAND, Henry. Rendered patriotic service by providing a rifle for Capt. Daniel Cresap's Company in July, 1775, as recorded by the Committee of Observation at Elizabeth Town on November 4, 1775 [Ref: Q-149]. On March 4, 1776 the Committee of Observation "ordered that Henry Roland be kept under guard of six men until sent to the Council of Safety for trial, but in case he shall sign the Association, enroll into some company, ask pardon of this Committee, and give good security for his good behavior for the future, to be released." [Ref: Q-154]. Private, Militia, 4th Class, Capt. Jacob Sharer's Company, 1776/1777 [Ref: A-1146, M-248]. See "Henry Rowland," q.v.

ROMAN, Reynon. See "Reynon Bowman," q.v.

ROME, Henry, and others. See "Henry Roam," q.v.

ROOF, Anthony. Took the Oath of Allegiance before the Hon. Henry Schnebley in 1778 [Ref: O-49, J-13, which listed the name as "Anthony Rouff"].

ROOF, Matthias. Private, Militia, 6th Class, Capt. John Bennet's Company, 1776/1777 [Ref: M-246, A-1146, which listed the name as "Mathias Rufe"]. Deserted and returned to duty in Capt. Evan Baker's Company by order of the Committee of Observation on February 8, 1777 [Ref: Q-232, Q-234, which listed the name as "Matthias Roof"]. Took the Oath of Allegiance before the Hon. Henry Schnebley in 1778 [Ref: O-49, J-13, which listed the name as "Mathias Rouff"].

ROOF, Michael. One of several patriots appointed by the Committee of Observation on December 30, 1776 "to form the county into companies (after the militia had marched) for the purpose of relieving the distressed inhabitants of said county and also to compel the Dunkards and Mennonists to give their assistance." [Ref: Q-346]. Took the Oath of Allegiance before the Hon. Henry Schnebley in 1778 [Ref: O-49, J-13, which listed the name as "Michael Rouff"].

ROOF, Nicholas. Private, Militia, 4th Class, Capt. John Bennet's Company, 1776/1777 [Ref: M-246, A-1146, which listed the name as "Nicholas Rufe"]. Deserted and returned to duty in Capt. Evan Baker's Company of Militia by order of the Committee of Observation on February 8, 1777 [Ref: Q-232, Q-234]. Took the Oath of Allegiance before the Hon. John Barnes before February 28, 1778 [Ref: O-45, J-10, which listed the name as "Nicholas Rouff"].

ROOF, Rudolph. Rendered patriotic service by providing necessaries to Capt. John Reynolds' Company in the Flying Camp and belonging to the Maryland Service in July, 1776, as recorded by the Committee of Observation at Sharpsburg on August 6, 1776 [Ref: Q-332]. Took the Oath of Allegiance before the Hon. Andrew Rentch before March 7, 1778 [Ref: O-52, J-15, which listed the name as "Rudey Roof"]. Private, Militia, 5th Class, Capt. John Cellars' Company, 1776/1777 [Ref: A-1146, M-246, which listed the name as "Rudoph Roof" or Rufe?].

ROOK, Thomas James. Took the Oath of Allegiance before the Hon. Lemuel Barritt before March 16, 1778 [Ref: O-42, J-7].

ROOT, Jacob. Private, Militia, 6th Class, Capt. Jacob Sharer's Company, 1776/1777 [Ref: A-1146, M-248]. One Jacob Root died testate by December 17, 1805, leaving a wife Barbara, and among his heirs was one son Jacob (and seven daughters). [Ref: MM-13:176].

RORDAM, Jacob. See "Jacob Bordam," q.v.

ROSE, David. Took the Oath of Allegiance before the Hon. Christopher Cruse in Lower Antietam Hundred before March 2, 1778 [Ref: J-3, O-35, which latter source listed the name as "David Ross"].

ROSE, Jonathan. Took the Oath of Allegiance before the Hon. William Yates in 1778 [Ref: O-48, J-12].

ROSE, Nicholas. Private, Militia, 6th Class, Capt. James Smith's Company, 2nd Battalion, 1776/1777 [Ref: A-1146, M-240, which listed the name as "Nicholas Rose (Rese)"].

ROSS, David. See "David Rose," q.v.

ROSS, Henry. Private who was recruited and passed by County Lieutenant Thomas Sprigg on April 22, 1780 [Ref: D-336].

ROSSE, David. See "David Bosse," q.v.

ROTHE, John. Private, Militia, Capt. William Heyser's Company, muster roll dated October 23, 1776, in continental service and on duty in May, 1777 [Ref: D-264, GG-99, which listed the name as "John Roth, Rothe"].

ROUGH, George. Private, Militia, 1st Class, Capt. John Bennet's Company, 1776/1777 [Ref: M-246, A-1146]. Took the Oath of Allegiance before the Hon. John Barnes before February 28, 1778 [Ref: O-44, J-9].

ROUGH, John. Took the Oath of Allegiance before the Hon. John Barnes before February 28, 1778 [Ref: O-44, J-9].

ROUGH, Peter. Private, Militia, 3rd Class, Capt. John Bennet's Company, 1776/1777 [Ref: M-246, A-1146]. Private, Militia, Capt. John Kershner's Company, on duty guarding prisoners of war at Fort Frederick on June 27, 1778 [Ref: D-328]. Took the Oath of Allegiance before the Hon. John Barnes before February 28, 1778 [Ref: O-44, J-9].

ROUGHLY, George. Took the Oath of Allegiance before the Hon. John Barnes before February 28, 1778 [Ref: J-9, O-44, which latter source listed the name as "George Raughly"].

ROUGHSLOUGH, Peter. Took the Oath of Allegiance before the Hon. John Barnes before February 28, 1778 [Ref: J-9, O-45, which latter source listed the name as "Peter Boughslough"].

ROUNER, Michael and Sarah. See "Peter Ham," q.v.

ROUSH, George (1760-   ). Private, Pennsylvania and Virginia Lines, who applied for and received pension S7401 in Mason County, Virginia on November 18, 1833, stating he was born in 1760 about 4 miles from

Hagerstown, Maryland and lived in Hampshire County, Virginia at the time of his enlistment. His oldest sister Mrs. Mary Hinkle, whom he had not seen for 40 years, lived in Greenbrier County, Virginia and had his birth record [Ref: V-III:2963].

ROUSSER, John. See "John Bousser," q.v.

ROUTZEN, John. See "Henry Franks," q.v.

ROVER, Jacob. Private, Militia, 3rd Class, Capt. Samuel Hughes' Company, 2nd Battalion, 1776/1777 [Ref: M-238, A-1146].

ROW, E. See "Dewald Shaffer," q.v.

ROW, John. Private who was recruited and passed by County Lieutenant Thomas Sprigg on April 22, 1780 [Ref: D-336].

ROWLAND, Abraham (1757-1821). Private, Militia, 4th Class, Capt. Peter Swingle's (Swingley's) Company, 1776/1777 [Ref: A-1146, M-248]. Abraham Rowland, an old inhabitant of Hagerstown, died on October 21, 1821, aged 64, and his widow Barbara died on October 11, 1841, aged 86. They were buried in Old St. John's Lutheran Churchyard and subsequently reinterred in Rose Hill Cemetery in Hagerstown [Ref: JJ-VII:105, Z-56].

ROWLAND, Barbara. See "Abraham Rowland," q.v.

ROWLAND, Christian. Private, Militia, 6th Class, Capt. Peter Swingle's (Swingley's) Company, 1776/1777 [Ref: A-1146, M-248].

ROWLAND, David. Private, Militia, 4th Class, Capt. Peter Swingle's (Swingley's) Company, 1776/1777 [Ref: A-1146, M-248].

ROWLAND, Henry. Private, Militia, 7th Class, Capt. Peter Swingle's (Swingley's) Company, 1776/1777 [Ref: A-1146, M-249]. See "Henry Roland," q.v.

ROWLAND, Jacob Jr. Private, Militia, 7th Class, Capt. Peter Swingle's (Swingley's) Company, 1776/1777 [Ref: A-1146, M-249].

ROWLAND, John. Private, Militia, 1st Class, Capt. Isaac Baker's Company, 1776/1777 [Ref: A-1146, M-247].

ROYSE, Solomon (1763-1858). Private, Maryland Line, who applied for pension in Adair County, Kentucky in February 4, 1833, stating he was born on September 11, 1763 in Orange County, New York and moved with his father (not named) to Maryland when 6 or 7 years old. He lived in Washington County, Maryland at the time of his enlistment and lived there for some time after the war. He then moved to Hampshire County, Virginia and in 1792 he moved to Bourbon County, Kentucky. He married Sarah Stotts on November 3, 1796 in Green County, Kentucky (marriage bond dated October 31, 1796 gave his name as "Solomon Rice") and in 1798 they moved to Adair County. Solomon Royse died on April 14, 1858 and his widow applied for and received pension W3598 on October 29, 1858, aged 87. She also received bounty land #26476-160-55 [Ref: V-III-2970, T-1].

ROZER, Jacob. Private, Militia, 7th Class, Capt. Peter Beall's Company, 1st Battalion, 1776/1777 [Ref: M-240].

RUBART, John. Third Sergeant, Militia, Capt. Daniel Cresap's Company, 3rd Battalion, 1776/1777 [Ref: M-241].

RUCKER, Philip. Took the Oath of Allegiance before the Hon. Christopher Cruse in Lower Antietam Hundred before March 2, 1778 [Ref: J-3, O-35, which latter source listed the name as "Phillip Bucker"].

RUDE, Andrew. Private who enlisted in the militia on September 5, 1781 for service in the Continental Army [Ref: D-388].

RUE, Isaac. See "Isaac Reu," q.v.

RUE, Isaac. Took the Oath of Allegiance before the Hon. Henry Schnebley in 1778 [Ref: O-49, J-13].

RUE, Mathew. See "Matthew Rice," q.v.

RUGGARD, John. See "John Riechart (Rigger)," q.v.

RUGGLES, James. Applied for pension (R9067) in 1836, aged 73, stating he enlisted in 1777 under Capt. Bell and Lt. Cresap in Maryland. "It was stated he must have served in the regiment under Col. Rawlings, but that he was not on the rolls of that regiment or of the line of the State of Maryland, therefore his claim was rejected on account of lack of roof." [Ref: T-43].

RUGGLES, William. Private, Militia, 5th Class, Capt. Charles Clinton's Company, 1776/1777 [Ref: M-245, A-1146]. Private who enlisted in the militia on September 5, 1781 for service in the Continental Army [Ref: D-388, which listed the name as "William Rugles"].

RUPLE, Jacob. Private, Militia, Capt. Charles Coulson's Company, enrolled August 28, 1776 [Ref: M-243, A-1146].

RUSH, John. Private, Militia, 4th Class, Capt. Martin Kershner's Company, 1776/1777 [Ref: A-1146, M-247].

RUSSELL, Caleb. Private, Militia, 6th Class, Capt. James Prather's Company, 3rd Battalion, 1776/1777 [Ref: M-243]. Took the Oath of Allegiance before the Hon. Lemuel Barritt before March 16, 1778 [Ref: O-43, J-8, which listed the name as "Callob Russell"].

RUSSELL, Eve. See "Jacob Russell, Jr.," q.v.

RUSSELL, George. Private, Militia, 8th Class, Capt. John Rennolds' (Reynolds') Company, 2nd Battalion, 1776/1777 [Ref: M-240]. See "Jacob Russell, Jr.," q.v.

RUSSELL, Henry and Jacob. See "Jacob Russell, Jr.," q.v.

RUSSELL, Jacob Jr. (1753-1837). Fourth Corporal, Militia, Capt. John Rennolds' (Reynolds') Company, 2nd Battalion, 1776/1777 [Ref: M-240].

Jacob Russell died on June 2, 1837, age 83 years, 6 months, 22 days, and is buried beside his wife Eve Russell (1754-1833) in a graveyard at the Geeting Meeting House, 1st U. B. Church at Mt. Hebron, Eakle's Mill, in Washington County [Ref: JJ-V:64, which listed the name as "Jacob Russell, Sr."]. His father "Jacob Russell" died on February 7, 1798, aged 71, and is also buried there. A balance book entry in Washington County on December 19, 1801 indicates he left a widow (no name given in this account) and equal shares of his estate to Jacob Russell, George Russell, John Russell, Henry Russell, Peter Barkman, John Fluke, Henry Fluke, Christian Middlecof, and Peter Thomas [Ref: J-39].

RUSSELL, John. Private who enlisted in the militia on September 5, 1781 for service in the Continental Army [Ref: D-388]. See "Jacob Russell, Jr.," q.v.

RUTH, Richard. Private, Militia, 4th Class, Capt. Daniel Cresap's Company, 3rd Battalion, 1776/1777 [Ref: M-241]. See "Richard Huth," q.v.

RUTHERFORD, Allener. See "Allener Ratherford," q.v.

RUTLIDGE, Stephen. Private who was enrolled by Capt. Henry Hardman and passed on July 19, 1776 in Frederick (now Washington) County [Ref: D-51].

RUTTER, Abraham. Took the Oath of Allegiance before the Hon. John Cellars in January, 1778 [Ref: K-1814, O-40, J-5].

RUTTER, Alexander. Private, Militia, 6th Class, Capt. James Walling's Company, 2nd Battalion, 1776/1777 [Ref: M-239, A-1146]. Took the Oath of Allegiance before the Hon. John Stull in 1778 [Ref: O-47, J-11].

RUTTER, Cunard. Took the Oath of Allegiance before the Hon. John Cellars in January, 1778 [Ref: K-1814, O-40, J-5, which latter source listed the name as "Canard Rutter"].

RUTTER, Edmond. Took the Oath of Allegiance before the Hon. John Stull in 1778 [Ref: O-47, J-11]. Rendered patriotic service by providing clothing for the use of the military on July 5, 1778 [Ref: CC-106]. "Edmund Rutter (no dates) and Margaret Rutter (1754-1797) were married on August 8, 1772, had 12 children (9 sons and 3 daughters), and are buried in a graveyard on the Earl Horst farm near Funkstown, east, near Dual Highway" in Washington County, Maryland [Ref: JJ-IV:20].

RUTTER, Edmond Jr. Private, Militia, 5th Class, Capt. James Walling's Company, 2nd Battalion, 1776/1777 [Ref: M-239, A-1146]. Fourth Sergeant, Militia, Capt. Jacob Sharer's Company, 1776/1777 [Ref: M-248, A-1146].

RUTTER, Edward. Took the Oath of Allegiance before the Hon. John Stull in 1778 [Ref: O-47, J-11].

RUTTER, John. Second Lieutenant, Militia, 1776, Capt. James Walling's Company, 2nd Battalion, June 22, 1778 [Ref: M-118, M-238, E-145, M-238, A-1146]. Took the Oath of Allegiance on July 27, 1777 [Ref: K-1814, Box 4].

RUTTER, Margaret. See "Edmond Rutter," q.v.

RUTTER, Thomas. Took the Oath of Allegiance before the Hon. John Cellars in January, 1778 [Ref: O-40, J-6, K-1814, which latter source listed the name as "Thos. Ruter"]. Private, Militia, 2nd Class, Capt. John Cellars' Company, 1776/1777 [Ref: A-1146, M-246, which listed the name as "Thomas Ruten"].

RUTTER, William. Fourth Sergeant, Militia, Capt. James Walling's Company, 2nd Battalion, 1776/1777 [Ref: M-238, A-1146]. Took the Oath of Allegiance before the Hon. John Stull in 1778 [Ref: O-47, J-11].

RYE, Mathias. Private, Militia, 8th Class, Capt. Jacob Sharer's Company, 1776/1777 [Ref: A-1146, M-248].

SABATOR, William. Enrolled in the second militia company organized for the Revolutionary War in the Elizabeth Town District of Frederick County (now the Hagerstown area of Washington County) on March 9, 1776 [Ref: Q-272].

SABBOTH, Maria. See "Thomas Crampton," q.v.

SAFETY, Fulty. Rendered patriotic service by supplying a blanket for the use of the military in March, 1776, as recorded by the Committee of Observation on April 12, 1776 [Ref: Q-156, L-82, which latter source listed the name as "Felty Safety"].

SAFLEY, Henry (1759-   ). Private, Maryland Militia, with Virginia service [Ref: N-45]. Private who was enlisted by Lieut. Moses Chapline and passed on July 24, 1776 in Frederick (now Washington) County [Ref: D-50, which listed the name as "Henry Saftly"].

SAILER, Alexander. Private, Militia, Capt. William Heyser's Company, enlisted July 28, 1776, muster roll dated October 23, 1776 [Ref: D-264, which listed the name as "Alex. Sailor" and W-1190 and L-79, which listed the name as "Alexander Seller"]. Private, German Regiment, discharged on July 9 or August 9, 1779 [Ref: D-250, which listed the name as "Alexander Sealors" and GG-99, which listed the name as "Alexander Saylor, Sailor, Taylor"].

SAILER, John. Private, Militia, 4th Class, Capt. Peter Beall's Company, 1st Battalion, 1776/1777 [Ref: M-240]. Took the Oath of Allegiance before the Hon. Henry Schnebley in 1778 [Ref: O-51, which listed the name as "John Sailler" and J-15, which listed the name as "John Miller"?]. See "John Adam Grime," q.v.

SAILER, Mathias. Took the Oath of Allegiance before the Hon. Joseph Sprigg before April 1, 1778 [Ref: O-53, J-16, which listed the name as "Mathias Sailor"]. One of several patriots appointed by the Committee of Observation on December 30, 1776 "to form the county into companies (after the militia had marched) for the purpose of relieving the distressed inhabitants of said county and also to compel the Dunkards and Mennonists to give their assistance." [Ref: Q-346].

SAILER, Peter (c1753-1836). Fourth Sergeant, Militia, Capt. Peter Beall's Company, 1st Battalion, 1776/1777 [Ref: M-240]. Took the Oath of Allegiance before the Hon. Henry Schnebley in 1778 [Ref: O-51, J-15, which listed the name as "Peter Sailler"]. Peter Sailer, Sr. died on February 15, 1836, aged about 83 years, and is buried in Zion Reformed Church cemetery in Hagerstown [Ref: JJ-VI:15].

SAILOR, Samuel and John. See "John Adam Grime," q.v.

SAINTAMAN, Jacob. Private, Militia, 5th Class, Capt. Joseph Chapline's Company, 2nd Battalion, 1776/1777 [Ref: M-241].

SALLADAY, Frederick. Took the Oath of Allegiance before the Hon. Richard Davis in 1778 [Ref: J-4, O-37, which listed the name as "Frederick Sallerday"].

SALLADAY, John. Private, Militia, 6th Class, Capt. Basil Williams' Company, 1776/1777 [Ref: M-244, A-1146]. Took the Oath of Allegiance before the Hon. Richard Davis in 1778 [Ref: J-4, O-37, which listed the name as "John Sallerday"].

SALLADAY, Melchar. Private, Militia, 3rd Class, Capt. Daniel Clapsaddle's Company, 1st Battalion, 1776/1777 [Ref: M-236, A-1146].

SALLADAY, Phillip. Private, Militia, 1st Class, Capt. Basil Williams' Company, 1776/1777 [Ref: M-244, A-1146]. Took the Oath of Allegiance before the Hon. Richard Davis in 1778 [Ref: J-4, O-37, which listed the name as "Phillip Sallerday"]. Philip Solladay married Anna Christiana Flick in Sharpsburg, Washington County, Maryland circa 1779 [Ref: N-49, N-123]. See "William Fleck," q.v.

SALLOTT, Nicholas. See "Nicholas Serlott," q.v.

SALMON, Christopher. Took the Oath of Allegiance before the Hon. Andrew Bruce before March 2, 1778 [Ref: O-41, J-7].

SALMON, Daniel. Took the Oath of Allegiance before the Hon. Andrew Bruce before March 2, 1778 [Ref: O-41, J-7].

SALTER, Samuel. Took the Oath of Allegiance before the Hon. Henry Schnebley in 1778 [Ref: O-50, J-14].

SAM, Nicholas. Took the Oath of Allegiance before the Hon. Christopher Cruse in Sharpsburg Hundred before March 2, 1778 [Ref: O-34, J-2]. Enrolled in the third militia company organized for the Revolutionary War in the Elizabeth Town District of Frederick County (now the Hagerstown area of Washington County), passed by the Committee of Observation on June 5, 1776, and assigned to Capt. John Reynolds' command [Ref: Q-273, which listed the name as "Nicholas Saums"].

SAMPSON, William. Private, Militia, by January 22, 1777 when ordered by the Committee of Observation "to march with some company of militia to the reinforcement of his Excellency General Washington" or appear before the Committee and state his reason for not marching. He apparently marched since he never appeared to the contrary [Ref: Q-48].

SAMPY, Daniel. Soldier who married Peggy Hinnys in Washington County in 1785 [Ref: N-122]. It should be noted, however, that he is not listed on the rolls in *Archives of Maryland, Volume 18*.

SANDERS, Samuel. Private, Militia, 7th Class, Capt. Conrad Hogmire's Company, 1776/1777 [Ref: M-244, A-1146].

SANDMAN, Jacob. Took the Oath of Allegiance before the Hon. Christopher Cruse in Sharpsburg Hundred before March 2, 1778 [Ref: O-35, J-2].

SANDS, Thomas. Private who was enlisted by Lieut. Moses Chapline and passed on July 24, 1776 in Frederick (now Washington) County [Ref: D-50]. Took the Oath of Allegiance before the Hon. William Yates in 1778 [Ref: O-48, J-12].

SANFORD, Sidney. See "Joseph Cresap," q.v.

SAPP, George. Took the Oath of Allegiance before the Hon. Henry Schnebley in 1778 [Ref: O-51, J-15, which listed the name as "George Zapp"].

SAPP, John. Private, Militia, Capt. Charles Coulson's Company, enrolled August 28, 1776 [Ref: M-244, A-1146, which listed the name as "John Sap"].

SAPORT, George. See "George Laport," q.v.

SARADEHAM, Simon. Private, Militia, 1st Class, Capt. Barnett Johnston's Company, 3rd Battalion, 1776/1777 [Ref: M-242].

SARER, George. See "George Sharer," q.v.

SARJEANT, Richard Jr. Private who was enrolled by Lieut. Clement Hollyday and passed by Col. William Luckett on August 8, 1776 [Ref: D-49].

SAULGIBER, Jacob. Private, Militia, 8th Class, Capt. James Smith's Company, 2nd Battalion, 1776/1777 [Ref: M-240, A-1146].

SAVAGE, John. Took the Oath of Allegiance before the Hon. Joseph Sprigg before April 1, 1778 [Ref: O-53, J-16].

SAVETY, Frederick. Private, Militia, 6th Class, Capt. Basil Williams' Company, 1776/1777 [Ref: M-244, A-1146].

SAYES, Samuel. Private, Militia, 6th Class, Capt. Barnett Johnston's Company, 3rd Battalion, 1776/1777 [Ref: M-242].

SCHLOSSER, Henry. Took the Oath of Allegiance before the Hon. Christopher Cruse in Lower Antietam Hundred before March 2, 1778 [Ref: O-35, J-3, which listed the name as "Henry Schloser" and "Henry Schlaser"]. A Susan Schlosser was born on September 28, 1749, died on October 30, 1830, and is buried in a graveyard on the Daniel Foltz farm at Iron Bridge, Antietam Creek, near Monroe in Washington County [Ref: JJ-V:50]. This plot also contains only one other grave, but it has no stone; perhaps it is the grave of Henry Schlosser. Additional research will be necessary before drawing conclusions.

SCHLOSSER, Peter. Private, Militia, 4th Class, Capt. James Smith's Company, 2nd Battalion, 1776/1777 [Ref: M-240, A-1146, which listed the name as "Peter Schloser" and "Peter Slouser"]. One "Peter Schloszer" was born in 1710, died in 1790, and is buried in the Old Reformed Graveyard at Sharpsburg, Maryland [Ref: JJ-I:27].

SCHLOSSER, Susan. See "Henry Schlosser," q.v.

SCHNEBLEY, Conrad. Appointed by the Committee of Observation to carry the Association of Freemen to male residents in Lower Antietam Hundred on September 14, 1775 "and require their subscription to the same and make an exact account of those who sign and those that refuse with their reasons for refusing." [Ref: Q-143].

SCHNEBLEY, Elizabeth. See "Henry Schnebley," q.v.

SCHNEBLEY, Henry (1726-1805). Appointed by the Committee of Observation to carry the Association of Freemen to male residents in Salisbury Hundred on September 14, 1775 "and require their subscription to the same and make an exact account of those who sign and those that refuse with their reasons for refusing." [Ref: Q-143, which listed the name as "Doctor Schnebly"]. Served on the Committee of Observation for the Elizabeth Town District (now the Hagerstown area of Washington County) in December, 1776 [Ref: Q-340, which referred to him as "Dr. Henry Schnebley"]. Took the Oath of Allegiance on May 20, 1777 [Ref: K-1814 (Box 4), which listed the name as "Henry Shnebely"]. Justice of the Orphans Court, June 4, 1777 [Ref: C-275, which listed the name as "Henry Schnoboly"]. Justice of the County Court, June 20, 1778 [Ref: E-141, which listed the name as "Henry Schnebely"]. Justice who administered the Oath of Allegiance in 1778

[Ref: O-49, O-50, O-51, J-13, J-14, J-15]. Rendered patriotic service by supplying wheat for the use of the military on March 27, 1780 and wheat and rye on April 19, 1780 [Ref: P-280, P-284, HH-72, W-1190, which listed the name as "Henry Schnebly" and "Henry Schnebely"]. Rendered patriotic service by hauling flour to the mill for the use of the military on April 24, 1780 [Ref: HH-72]. Contractor for Wagons and Teams by September 2, 1780 when paid by the Collector of the Tax for Washington County [Ref: G-137, F-274, which listed the name as "Henry Schnebely, Esq." and G-214, which listed the name as "Dr. Henry Schnebely"]. Justice of the Peace and Judge of the Orphans Court, January 30, 1781 [Ref: G-293, which listed the name as "Henry Schnebely"]. Purchased grain for the use of the military in 1780 and filed his report on April 16, 1780 [Ref: HH-72]. "Henry Schnebeley" served in the Maryland House of Delegates, 1777-1778, and was medical purveyor for the army in 1780 in Washington County [Ref: KK-I:76-80, KK-II:712-713, which contains more detailed information]. "Dr. Henry Schnebly" died testate on July 24, 1805, aged 79. He is buried in Zion Reformed Church cemetery in Hagerstown with other family members, including his wife Catharine (1739-1804) and another whose tombstone has been transcribed to read as follows: *"Hier Rubet Elizabetha Schnebly, Ehegattin Des Doctor Heinty Schnebly, Gebohren Im Jahr, 1735, Gestorben 10 Sep 1795, Ihr Abyter Etrwan 18 Jahr, Lebte In Der Ehe 10 Jahr 1y 4m."* [Ref: JJ-VI:17, MM-13:171, 172]. See "Henry Schnebley, Jr.," q.v.

SCHNEBLEY, Henry. Private, Militia, 4th Class, Capt. John Cellars' Company, 1776/1777 [Ref: A-1146, M-246, which listed the name as "Henry Shnebley"]. Private, Select Militia, Capt. Adam Ott's Company, 1781 [Ref: M-238, A-1146]. It is unclear whether this service pertains to Dr. Henry Schnebley or Henry Schnebley, Jr. Additional research will be necessary before drawing conclusions.

SCHNEBLEY, Henry Jr. (1756-1787). Private, Militia, 4th Class, Capt. John Cellars' Company, 1776/1777 [Ref: A-1146, M-246, which listed the name as "Henry Shnebley Junr"]. Took the Oath of Allegiance before the Hon. Henry Schnebley in 1778 [Ref: O-51, J-14]. "Henry Schnebly, son of Dr. Henry and Mary Schnebly" died on July 15, 1787, aged 31 years, 5 months, 13 days, and is buried in Zion Reformed Church cemetery in Hagerstown [Ref: JJ-VI:17].

SCHNEBLEY, John (1750-1838). Private, Militia, 8th Class, Capt. John Cellars' Company, 1776/1777 [Ref: A-1146, M-246]. Took the Oath of Allegiance before the Hon. Henry Schnebley in 1778 [Ref: O-51, J-15]. Private, Select Militia, Capt. Adam Ott's Company, 1781 [Ref: M-238,

A-1146, which listed the name as "John Schnebly"]. "John Schnebly" was born on February 3, 1750, died on January 17, 1838, and is buried in St. Paul's Lutheran Reformed Church cemetery on Route 40 near Clearspring in Washington County [Ref: JJ-V:90].

SCHNEBLEY, Mary. See "Henry Schnebley, Jr.," q.v.

SCHNEGENBERGER, Christian. Took the Oath of Allegiance before the Hon. Henry Schnebley in 1778 [Ref: O-49, J-12].

SCHNEIDER, Casper. Rendered patriotic service by supplying flour for the use of the military on February 17, 1780 [Ref: W-1190, HH-72]. Took the Oath of Allegiance before the Hon. Henry Schnebley in 1778 [Ref: O-50, J-14, which listed the name as "Casper Shneider"]. See "Casper Snyder," q.v.

SCHNEIDER, Daniel. Took the Oath of Allegiance before the Hon. Henry Schnebley in 1778 [Ref: O-50, J-14, which listed the name as "Daniel Shneider"].

SCHNEIDER, John. Took the Oath of Allegiance before the Hon. Henry Schnebley in 1778 [Ref: O-49, J-13, which listed the name as "John Shneider"]. See "John Snyder," q.v.

SCHNELL, Henry. Took the Oath of Allegiance before the Hon. Henry Schnebley in 1778 [Ref: O-51, J-15]. "Phillip Shnell" died before June 14, 1791 (date of balance book entry in Washington County) and one of his sons was "Henry Shnell." [Ref: J-31].

SCHOFF, Jacob. Private, Militia, 2nd Class, Capt. John Rennolds' (Reynolds') Company, 2nd Battalion, 1776/1777 [Ref: M-240].

SCHUHMAN, John. See "John Shuman (Shoeman)," q.v.

SCHULTZ, George. Took the Oath of Allegiance (affirmed) before the Hon. Henry Schnebley in 1778 [Ref: O-51, J-15]. See "George Shultz," q.v.

SCHULTZ, Jacob. Took the Oath of Allegiance before the Hon. Andrew Bruce before March 2, 1778 [Ref: O-41, J-6, which latter source mistakenly listed the name as "Jacob Achultz"].

SCHULTZ, Martin. Private, Militia, 3rd Class, Capt. Jacob Sharer's Company, 1776/1777 [Ref: A-1146, M-248, which listed the name as "Martin Shultz"].

SCHWEITZER, Frederick. Private, Militia, Capt. William Heyser's Company, muster roll dated October 23, 1776, missing at Bonumtown, New Jersey on May 10, 1777, returned, reenlisted on July 16, 1778 [Ref: GG-99, D-264, W-1190, L-79, which also listed the name as "Frederick Switzer"]. Private, German Regiment, Lt. Col. Ludwick Weltner's Company, discharged on July 16, 1779 at Fort Wyoming, Pennsylvania [Ref: D-265, which listed the name as "Frederick Schwidzer" and D-251, which listed the name as "Frederick Switzer" and GG-99, which listed the name as "Frederick Sweitzer, Switzer, Schwidzer"].

SCHWEITZER, John. Took the Oath of Allegiance before the Hon. Henry Schnebley in 1778 [Ref: O-50, J-14]. Rendered patriotic service by supplying wheat for the use of the military on April 3, 1780 [Ref: W-1190, HH-72, which both listed the name as "John Shweitzer"].

SCHWENGEL, George Jr. Took the Oath of Allegiance before the Hon. Henry Schnebley in 1778 [Ref: O-50, J-14].

SCHWENGEL, Nicholas. Took the Oath of Allegiance before the Hon. Henry Schnebley in 1778 [Ref: O-50, J-14].

SCOFIELD, John. Took the Oath of Allegiance before the Hon. Richard Davis in 1778 [Ref: J-4, O-37].

SCOTT, David. Private, Militia, 2nd Class, Capt. Daniel Clapsaddle's Company, 1st Battalion, 1776/1777 [Ref: M-236, A-1146]. Took the Oath of Allegiance before the Hon. Joseph Sprigg before April 1, 1778 [Ref: O-53, J-16].

SCOTT, James. Private, Militia, 8th Class, Capt. Daniel Clapsaddle's Company, 1st Battalion, 1776/1777 [Ref: M-236, A-1146]. Took the Oath of Allegiance before the Hon. Richard Davis in 1778 [Ref: J-5, O-37]. See "Joseph Cresap," q.v.

SCOTT, John. Private, Militia, 3rd Class, Capt. James Prather's Company, 3rd Battalion, 1776/1777 [Ref: M-242]. Took the Oath of Allegiance before the Hon. Joseph Sprigg before April 1, 1778 [Ref: O-53, J-16].

SCOTT, John. Rendered patriotic service in Hagerstown by providing 60 yards of linen to Capt. John Nelson's Company, continental service (Maryland Line), April, 1776 [Ref: Q-162]. Took the Oath of Allegiance before the Hon. Lemuel Barritt before March 16, 1778 [Ref: O-43, J-8].

SCOTT, Levi (1762-   ). Private, North Carolina Line, who applied for and received pension S30690 in Henry County, Kentucky on October 11, 1843, stating he was born in 1762 near Hagerstown, Maryland and lived in Burke County, North Carolina at the time of his enlistment. He later moved to Mercer County, Kentucky, then to Fayette County, Kentucky and in 1800 to Henry County, Kentucky [Ref: V-III:3047].

SCOTT, William. There were several men with this name who rendered service during the Revolutionary War. Additional research may be necessary before drawing conclusions. (1) First Sergeant, Militia, Capt. Daniel Clapsaddle's Company, 1st Battalion, 1776/1777 [Ref: M-236, A-1146]. (2) Private, Militia, 7th Class, Capt. Peter Beall's Company, 1st Battalion, 1776/1777 [Ref: M-240]. (3) One rendered patriotic service in Hagerstown by providing sundries to Capt. John Nelson's Company, continental service (Maryland Line), April, 1776 [Ref: Q-161]. (4) One rendered patriotic service by providing a blanket for the use of the military in January, 1777, as recorded by the Committee of Observation on January 27, 1777 [Ref: Q-53]. (5) One served on the Committee of Observation for Elizabeth Town District (now the Hagerstown area of Washington County) on February 22, 1777 [Ref: Q-237]. () One took the Oath of Allegiance before the Hon. Joseph Sprigg before April 1, 1778 [Ref: O-53, J-16].

SEABURN, Peter. Private who was enlisted by Lieut. Moses Chapline and passed on July 24, 1776 in Frederick (now Washington) County [Ref: D-50].

SEAGRIEST, Esther. See "John Wolf," q.v.

SEAVNER, Conrad. Private, Militia, 5th Class, Capt. James Smith's Company, 2nd Battalion, 1776/1777 [Ref: M-240, A-1146].

SECTTNER, John Conrad. Took the Oath of Allegiance before the Hon. Henry Schnebley in 1778 [Ref: O-51, J-14].

SEIBERT, David. See "David Seybert," q.v.

SEIBERT (SYBERT, SIBERT), Jacob. Second Corporal, Militia, Capt. Isaac Baker's Company, 1776/1777 [Ref: M-247, A-1146, which listed the name as "Jacob Syvert"]. Two men by this name took the Oath of Allegiance before the Hon. John Barnes before February 28, 1778 [Ref: O-44, J-9, which listed the name as "Jacob Sibert"]. One rendered patriotic service by supplying wheat for the use of the military on February 16, 1780 [Ref: W-1190, HH-72]. One Jacob Seibert died suddenly at his residence near West Conococheague on February 15, 1810, an old inhabitant of Washington County [Ref: LL-3:83].

SEIBERT (SYBERT, SIBERT), John. First Sergeant, Militia, Capt. Samuel Hughes' Company, 1776/1777 [Ref: M-238, A-1146, which listed the name as "John Sibert"]. Took the Oath of Allegiance before the Hon. John Stull in 1778 [Ref: O-47, J-11, which listed the name as "John Sibird"]. Ensign, Militia, Capt. Samuel Hughes' Company, 1st Battalion, June 22, 1778. Second Lieutenant, Capt. David Gillespie's Company, 1st Battalion, November 21, 1780. Captain, 1781 [Ref: M-127, E-147, H-34, G-220, which listed the name as "John Sybert"]. "John Seibert" was born on February 14, 1744, married Margaret Knode on September 13, 1766 [which listed his name as "John Seybert"] and died on October 5, 1794. He is buried beside his wife Margaret and son John Seibert (1770-1799) in a graveyard on the Ralph B. Wyand farm at Mt. Atna, northwest side of Cross Road, in Washington County, Maryland [Ref: JJ-IV:104].

SEIBERT (SYVERT, SIBERT), John Jacob. Private, Militia, 8th Class, Capt. Isaac Baker's Company, 1776/1777 [Ref: A-1146, M-247, which listed the name as "John Jacob Syvert"].
SEIBERT, Margaret. See "John Seibert," q.v.
SEIBERT (SYBERT, SIBERT), Peter. Private, Militia, 3rd Class, Capt. Samuel Hughes' Company, 2nd Battalion, 1776/1777 [Ref: M-238, A-1146, which listed the name as "Peter Sibert"]. Took the Oath of Allegiance before the Hon. John Stull in 1778 [Ref: O-47, J-11, which listed the name as "Peter Sibird"]. Private, Militia, Capt. John Kershner's Company, on duty guarding prisoners of war at Fort Frederick on June 27, 1778 [Ref: D-328, which listed the name as "Peter Sybert"].
SEIGEART, John. Took the Oath of Allegiance before the Hon. John Barnes before February 28, 1778 [Ref: O-45, J-9].
SEITZLER, William. On January 25, 1777 the Committee of Observation ordered Capt. Lynck to pay William Seitzler 2 pounds 5 shillings for attending Garret Glasson, a sick soldier. Paid 20 shillings by Capt. Linck for boarding and attending Garret Glasson, a sick soldier in the Flying Camp of this State on February 22, 1777 [Ref: Q-51, Q-236]. Took the Oath of Allegiance before the Hon. Henry Schnebley in 1778 [Ref: O-49, J-13].
SELBY, William. Private, Militia, 3rd Class, Capt. Jeremiah Spires' Company, 2nd Battalion, 1776/1777 [Ref: M-239, A-1146, which listed the name as "William Silby"]. Took the Oath of Allegiance before the Hon. Richard Davis in 1778 [Ref: J-3, O-36].
SELETY, Christian. See "William Fleck," q.v.
SELHART, Godfrey. Took the Oath of Allegiance before the Hon. Joseph Sprigg before April 1, 1778 [Ref: O-53, J-16].
SELLER, Alexander. See "Alexander Sailer," q.v.
SELLERS, John. See "John Cellar," q.v.
SENNIS, Thomas. Rendered patriotic service by providing dry goods for the use of the military in July, 1775, as recorded by the Committee of Observation at Elizabeth Town on November 4, 1775 [Ref: Q-150].
SERLOTT, Nicholas. Private, Militia, 1st Class, Capt. Conrad Nichodemus' Company, 2nd Battalion, 1776/1777 [Ref: M-237, A-1146, which listed the name as "Nicholas Sallott"]. Took the Oath of Allegiance before the Hon. Christopher Cruse in Lower Antietam Hundred before March 2, 1778 [Ref: J-2, O-35, which listed the name as "Nicholas Serlott"]. Took the Oath of Allegiance before the Hon. Joseph Sprigg before April 1, 1778 [Ref: O-53, J-16, which listed the name as "Nicholas Sirlott"].

SEWELL, William. Private, Militia, 4th Class, Capt. Barnett Johnston's Company, 3rd Battalion, 1776/1777 [Ref: M-242]. Third Corporal, Militia, Capt. Barnett Johnston's Company, 3rd Battalion, 1776/1777 [Ref: M-242].

SEYBERT, David (1760-1836). Private, Pennsylvania Militia, who pensioned in Allegany County, Maryland at $80 per year under the Act of June 7, 1832, retroactive to March 4, 1831 [Ref: R-45]. David Seybert was born in Pennsylvania in 1760, married Susannah Stall, and died in Maryland in October, 1836 [Ref: Y-III:2616].

SHACKLER, Frederick. Private, Militia, 3rd Class, Capt. Isaac Baker's Company, 1776/1777 [Ref: A-1146, M-247]. Private, Militia, Capt. John Kershner's Company, on duty guarding prisoners of war at Fort Frederick on June 27, 1778 [Ref: D-328].

SHACKLEY, Martin. Private, Militia, 7th Class, Capt. Jacob Sharer's Company, 1776/1777 [Ref: A-1146, M-248].

SHACKLEY, Michael. Private, Militia, 5th Class, Capt. Samuel Hughes' Company, 2nd Battalion, 1776/1777 [Ref: M-238, A-1146].

SHAE (SHAD?), John. Private, Militia, 6th Class, Capt. Conrad Nichodemus' Company, 2nd Battalion, 1776/1777 [Ref: A-1146, M-237].

SHAFER, A., and others. See "Dewald Shaffer," q.v.

SHAFER, Barbara, and others. See "John Shafer," q.v.

SHAFER, John. Took the Oath of Allegiance before September 1, 1780 [Ref: X-119]. One John Shafer died before December 18, 1781 (date of balance book entry in Washington County), leaving a widow Barbara Shafer and equal shares to John, Henry, Catherine, Elizabeth, Mary, George, and Leonard Shafer [Ref: J-22].

SHAFFER, Dewald. Took the Oath of Allegiance before the Hon. Henry Schnebley in 1778 [Ref: J-14, O-51, which latter source listed the name as "Dewald Shoffer"]. "Davoll Shafer" died testate before April 29, 1787 (date of balance book entry in Washington County), leaving a widow (no name given in this account), and equal shares to D. Shafer, C. Winter, M. Bumgarner, A. Shafer, G. Shafer, P. Hassen, E. Row, A. Shafer, S. Yost, B. Shafer, and M. Shafer [Ref: J-27].

SHAFFER, George. Rendered patriotic service by supplying wheat for the use of the military on March 28, 1780 [Ref: W-1190, HH-72]. See "John Shafer," q.v.

SHAFLER, Margarete. See "John Kenistrick," q.v.

SHAHAN, Edward. Second Corporal, Militia, Capt. Jeremiah Spires' Company, 2nd Battalion, 1776/1777 [Ref: M-239, A-1146].

SHAILER, Michael. Took the Oath of Allegiance before the Hon. John Stull in 1778 [Ref: O-47, J-11].

SHAILER, Peter. Took the Oath of Allegiance before the Hon. John Stull in 1778 [Ref: O-47, J-11].

SHALL (SHAUL), George (c1757-1837). Private, Pennsylvania Militia or Line, pensioned in Washington County under the Act of June 7, 1832 at the annual allowance of $30 retroactive to March 4, 1831, stating he was aged 75 and lived at York, Pennsylvania during the war [Ref: R-51, V-III:3079]. "Margaret Shall, wife of George" died on December 17, 1827 at her residence near Hagerstown, in her 67th year [Ref: Z-96]. "George Shaul died at the residence of Jacob Kausler, Esq., on December 6, 1837, in the 81st year of his age, an old and respectable inhabitant of Hagerstown, and a soldier in the Revolution." [Ref: DD-130, citing *The Republican Banner*, December 23, 1837].

SHALL, Margaret. See "George Shall," q.v.

SHALLEY, Peter. See "Peter Sholley," q.v.

SHANEFIR (SHANEFIN, SHANIFERT), Frederick. Private, Militia, 5th Class, Capt. Martin Kershner's Company, 1776/1777 [Ref: A-1146, M-247]. "Frederick Shanifert" died testate before April 9, 1785 (date of balance book entry in Washington County), leaving a widow (no name given in this account) and equal shares to Elizabeth, John, Frederick, Mary, Catherine, Margaret, and Eve "Shanifert." [Ref: J-25]. The final account of the estate of "Frederick Shanifelt" was recorded on May 17, 1799 in Washington County and the balance was divided between Frederick, Mary, Catherine, Margaret and Eve, with William Shanifelt as the administrator [Ref: J-37].

SHANEFIR (SHANEFIN), William. Private, Militia, 1st Class, Capt. Daniel Clapsaddle's Company, 1st Battalion, 1776/1777 [Ref: M-236, A-1146]. See "Frederick Shanefir," q.v.

SHANIFELT, Frederick, and others. See "Frederick Shanefir," q.v.

SHANIFERT, Frederick, and others. See "Frederick Shanefir," q.v.

SHANGLER, Matthias. On July 2, 1776, Capt. John Reynolds reported to the Committee of Observation for the Elizabeth Town District (now the Hagerstown area of Washington County) that "Matthias Shangler, invalid non effective, has signed the Association." [Ref: Q-325].

SHANIFERT, Frederick. See "Frederick Shanefir," q.v.

SHANK, Christian Jr. Private, Militia, 4th Class, Capt. John Cellars' Company, 1776/1777 [Ref: A-1146, M-246].

SHANK, Christian Sr. One of several patriots appointed by the Committee of Observation on December 30, 1776 "to form the county into companies (after the militia had marched) for the purpose of relieving the distressed inhabitants of said county and also to compel the Dunkards and Mennonists to give their assistance." [Ref: Q-345].

Private, Militia, 8th Class, Capt. John Cellars' Company, 1776/1777 [Ref: A-1146, M-246].

SHANK, Jacob. Private, Militia, 5th Class, Capt. Samuel Hughes' Company, 2nd Battalion, 1776/1777 [Ref: M-238, A-1146].

SHANK, Michael. Private, Militia, 2nd Class, Capt. John Cellars' Company, 1776/1777 [Ref: A-1146, M-246].

SHANK, Peter. First Sergeant, Militia, Capt. Conrad Nichodemus' Company, 2nd Battalion, 1776/1777 [Ref: M-237, A-1146]. Two men by this name took the Oath of Allegiance before the Hon. John Stull in 1778 [Ref: O-47, J-11].

SHANTON, Raymon. Private, Militia, 5th Class, Capt. Joseph Chapline's Company, 2nd Battalion, 1776/1777 [Ref: M-241]. Took the Oath of Allegiance before the Hon. Joseph Chapline before April 17, 1779 [Ref: J-5, O-39, which listed the name as "Ramon Shanton"].

SHARER, George. Second Lieutenant, Militia, Capt. John Funk's Company, 2nd Battalion, by June 22, 1778. First Lieutenant, Militia, June 22, 1778 through March 26, 1781 (resigned). [Ref: M-119, E-145, H-34, H-150, A-1146, M-248, which latter source listed the name as "George Sarer"]. Took the Oath of Allegiance before the Hon. John Stull in 1778 [Ref: O-47, J-11].

SHARER, Isaac. Second Sergeant, Militia, Capt. Jacob Sharer's Company, 1776/1777 [Ref: M-248, A-1146]. Took the Oath of Allegiance before the Hon. John Stull in 1778 [Ref: O-47, J-11].

SHARER, Jacob. Captain, Militia, 1776 [Ref: A-1146, M-248, which listed the name as "Jacob Sarer"]. Took the Oath of Allegiance before the Hon. John Stull in 1778 [Ref: O-47, J-11]. "Jacob Sherer" died suddenly at his residence about 3 miles from Hagerstown on the Sunday before July 15, 1808, an old and respectable inhabitant of Washington County [Ref: LL-3:69].

SHARER, Peter. Private, Militia, 7th Class, Capt. Jacob Sharer's Company, 1776/1777 [Ref: A-1146, M-248]. Took the Oath of Allegiance before the Hon. John Stull in 1778 [Ref: O-47, J-11].

SHAT, Melcher. Private, Militia, 7th Class, Capt. Peter Swingle's (Swingley's) Company, 1776/1777 [Ref: A-1146, M-249].

SHAUL, George. See "George Shall," q.v.

SHAVER, David. Private, Militia, 1st Class, Capt. Samuel Hughes' Company, 2nd Battalion, 1776/1777 [Ref: M-238, A-1146].

SHAVER, George. One of several patriots appointed by the Committee of Observation on December 30, 1776 "to form the county into companies (after the militia had marched) for the purpose of relieving the distressed inhabitants of said county and also to compel the

Dunkards and Mennonists to give their assistance." [Ref: Q-346]. Took the Oath of Allegiance before the Hon. John Barnes before February 28, 1778 [Ref: O-45, J-9]. Private who enlisted in the militia on August 22, 1781 for service in the Continental Army [Ref: D-388]. Substitute, Maryland Line, discharged on October 30, 1781 [Ref: G-657]. See "Peter Shaver," q.v.

SHAVER, Jacob. There were several men with this name who rendered service during the Revolutionary War. Additional research will be necessary before drawing conclusions. (1) Private, Militia, 1st Class, Capt. Samuel Hughes' Company, 2nd Battalion, 1776/1777 [Ref: M-238, A-1146]. (2) Private, Militia, 7th Class, Capt. Samuel Hughes' Company, 2nd Battalion, 1776/1777 [Ref: M-238, A-1146]. (3) Private, Militia, 5th Class, Capt. Conrad Hogmire's Company, 1776/1777 [Ref: M-244, A-1146]. (4) Rendered patriotic service by supplying wheat for the use of the military on April 6, 1780 [Ref: W-1190, HH-73].

SHAVER, John. Private, Militia, 6th Class, Capt. James Smith's Company, 2nd Battalion, 1776/1777 [Ref: M-240, A-1146]. Took the Oath of Allegiance before the Hon. John Stull in 1778 [Ref: O-47, J-11].

SHAVER, Paul. Private, Militia, 6th Class, Capt. Isaac Baker's Company, 1776/1777 [Ref: A-1146, M-247].

SHAVER, Peter. Private, Militia, 5th Class, Capt. Isaac Baker's Company, 1776/1777 [Ref: A-1146, M-247]. First Corporal, Militia, Capt. Conrad Hogmire's Company, 1776/1777 [Ref: M-244, A-1146]. Took the Oath of Allegiance before the Hon. John Barnes before February 28, 1778 [Ref: O-45, J-10]. Gave a deposition on August 11, 1779 regarding the non-receipt of his clothing allowance [Ref: O-234]. One Peter Shaver died before July 25, 1795 (date of balance book entry in Washington County), leaving a widow (no name given in this account) and equal shares to Phillip, George, and Polly Shaver [Ref: J-34].

SHAVER, Phillip and Polly. See "Peter Shaver," q.v.

SHAVER, Powell. Took the Oath of Allegiance before the Hon. John Barnes before February 28, 1778 [Ref: O-45, J-9].

SHAW, David. Private, Militia, 4th Class, Capt. Samuel Hughes' Company, 2nd Battalion, 1776/1777 [Ref: M-238, A-1146].

SHAW, Henry. Private who was recruited and passed by County Lieutenant Thomas Sprigg on April 22, 1780 [Ref: D-336].

SHAW, Thomas. Private, Militia, 6th Class, Capt. Griffin Johnson's Company, 3rd Battalion, 1776/1777 [Ref: M-243, which listed the name as "Thomas Shaws"].

SHAW, William. See "Rezin Simpson," q.v.

SHEESE, Peter. One of several patriots appointed by the Committee of Observation on December 30, 1776 "to form the county into companies (after the militia had marched) for the purpose of relieving the distressed inhabitants of said county and also to compel the Dunkards and Mennonists to give their assistance." [Ref: Q-345, which listed the name as "Peter Shees"]. Private, Militia, Capt. William Heyser's Company, muster roll dated October 23, 1776, in continental service, which mistakenly stated he had deserted, yet he was on duty in May, 1777 [Ref: D-264, L-79, GG-99, W-1190, which latter source listed the name as "Peter Shuse"]. One "Peter Shees" died testate before April 10, 1790 (date of balance book entry in Washington County) and one of his heirs was Peter "Shees." [Ref: J-29].

SHEETS, Adam. Private, 3rd Maryland Line, recruited in Baltimore on March 2, 1780 [Ref: D-334]. An "Adam Sheetz" died intestate in Allegany County in 1821 [Ref: Z-11, citing an equity case in 1826]. Additional research may be necessary before drawing conclusions.

SHEETS, Conrad. Private, Militia, 2nd Class, Capt. Michael Fackler's Company, 1776/1777 [Ref: M-245, A-1146, which listed the name as "Conroad Sheets"].

SHEETS, Daniel. See "Jacob Kuhn," q.v.

SHEGTEN, Wendle. Private, Militia, 3rd Class, Capt. Conrad Nichodemus' Company, 2nd Battalion, 1776/1777 [Ref: M-237, A-1146].

SHEHAN, Jeremiah. Private who was recruited and passed by County Lieutenant Thomas Sprigg on April 22, 1780 [Ref: D-336].

SHEHAN, William. Took the Oath of Allegiance before the Hon. Richard Davis in 1778 [Ref: J-5, O-38].

SHEIMER, John. Private, Select Militia, Capt. Adam Ott's Company, 1781 [Ref: M-238, A-1146].

SHEKLY, Michael. Fourth Corporal, Militia, Capt. James Walling's Company, 2nd Battalion, 1776/1777 [Ref: M-238, A-1146].

SHELL, John. First Sergeant, Militia, Capt. Peter Swingle's (Swingley's) Company, 2nd Battalion, 1776/1777 [Ref: M-248, A-1146].

SHELLERS, William. Private, Militia, 8th Class, Capt. James Smith's Company, 2nd Battalion, 1776/1777 [Ref: M-240, A-1146].

SHEPHERD, Henry. Private who was recruited and passed by County Lieutenant Thomas Sprigg on April 22, 1780 [Ref: D-336].

SHEPHERD, James. Private, Militia, 8th Class, Capt. James Prather's Company, 3rd Battalion, 1776/1777 [Ref: M-243, which listed the name as "James Shepheard"].

SHEPHERD, John. Private, Militia, 6th Class, Capt. James Prather's Company, 3rd Battalion, 1776/1777 [Ref: M-243, which listed the name as "John Shephard"].

SHEPHERD, Robert. Private, Militia, 2nd Class, Capt. James Prather's Company, 3rd Battalion, 1776/1777 [Ref: M-242, which listed the name as "Robert Shephard"].

SHEPHERD, Samuel. Private, Militia, 4th Class, Capt. James Prather's Company, 3rd Battalion, 1776/1777 [Ref: M-242, which listed the name as "Samuel Shephard"].

SHEPHERD, Thomas. Enrolled in the first militia company organized for the Revolutionary War in the Elizabeth Town District of Frederick County (now the Hagerstown area of Washington County) on January 6, 1776 [Ref: Q-270, W-1190]. Private, Militia, 7th Class, Capt. Joseph Chapline's Company, 2nd Battalion, 1776/1777 [Ref: M-242, which listed the name as "Thomas Sheapheard"]. Took the Oath of Allegiance before the Hon. Christopher Cruse in Sharpsburg Hundred before March 2, 1778 [Ref: O-34, J-1, which listed the name as "Thomas Shepard"].

SHETLER, William. Took the Oath of Allegiance before the Hon. Richard Davis in 1778 [Ref: J-5, O-37, which latter source listed the name as "William Shetter"].

SHEW, Peter (of Peter). Private, Militia, 2nd Class, Capt. Daniel Clapsaddle's Company, 1st Battalion, 1776/1777 [Ref: M-236, A-1146].

SHEWALL, William. See "William Shule," q.v.

SHIFLER, Nicholas. Fourth Corporal, Militia, Capt. Conrad Nichodemus' Company, 2nd Battalion, 1776/1777 [Ref: M-237, A-1146]. Third Corporal, Militia, Capt. Henry Boteler's Company, 1776/1777 [Ref: M-237, A-1146].

SHILLING, Catey. See "Frederick Knockel," q.v.

SHILLING, Phillip. Private, Militia, 1st Class, Capt. Jacob Sharer's Company, 1776/1777 [Ref: A-1146, M-248]. Took the Oath of Allegiance before the Hon. John Stull in 1778 [Ref: O-47, J-11]. See "Frederick Knockel," q.v.

SHIRLEY, John. Enrolled in the first militia company organized for the Revolutionary War in the Elizabeth Town District of Frederick County (now the Hagerstown area of Washington County) on January 6, 1776 [Ref: Q-270, W-1189].

SHIRTZER, Casper (c1756-   ). Soldier who resided in Washington County and was granted a pension certificate in August, 1820, according to an Act of Congress of March 18, 1818, since he had proven that he was "in the enjoyment of a certain degree of poverty" as required by the

Act as amended on May 1, 1820 [Ref: W-1190]. Private, Pennsylvania Line, pensioned at $96 per year effective May 7, 1818 [Ref: R-43].

SHIVELY, Catherine. See "Adam Troup," q.v.

SHIVELY, Jacob. Rendered patriotic service by providing a rifle for Capt. Daniel Cresap's Company in July, 1775, as recorded by the Committee of Observation at Elizabeth Town on November 4, 1775 [Ref: Q-149].

SHLEY, Paul. Private who was enrolled by Capt. Henry Hardman and passed on July 19, 1776 in Frederick (now Washington) County [Ref: D-51].

SHOCK, Christian. Private, Militia, 3rd Class, Capt. Michael Fackler's Company, 1776/1777 [Ref: M-245, A-1146]. Took the Oath of Allegiance before the Hon. Andrew Rentch before March 7, 1778 [Ref: O-52, J-15]. Private, Militia, Capt. John Kershner's Company, on duty guarding prisoners of war at Fort Frederick until discharged on June 19, 1778 [Ref: D-328].

SHOCK, Frederick. Took the Oath of Allegiance before the Hon. John Stull in 1778 [Ref: O-47, J-11].

SHOCKEY, Abraham. Private, 6th Maryland Line, 1777, who died on November 1, 1782 [Ref: Y-III:2654, D-290, D-445, D-557, which also listed the name as "Abraham Shockee" and "Abram Stockee"].

SHOCKEY, Isaac and Christian. See "David Harry," q.v.

SHOCKEY, Nicholas. See "Nicholas Hockey," q.v.

SHOCKEY, Valentine. Private, Militia, 4th Class, Capt. Conrad Hogmire's Company, 1776/1777 [Ref: M-244, A-1146].

SHOEMAKER, John. See "John Shumaker," q.v.

SHOFFER, Dewald. See "Dewald Shaffer," q.v.

SHOLLEY, Adam. Took the Oath of Allegiance before the Hon. Christopher Cruse in Lower Antietam Hundred before March 2, 1778 [Ref: J-2, O-35, which listed the name as "Adam Sholly"]. Private, Militia, 4th Class, Capt. Conrad Nichodemus' Company, 2nd Battalion, 1776/1777 [Ref: M-237, A-1146, which listed the name as "Adam Shally"].

SHOLLEY, Luke. First Sergeant, Militia, Capt. John Cellars' Company, 1776/1777 [Ref: M-246, A-1146, which listed the name as Luke Sholey"]. First Sergeant, Militia, Capt. John Kershner's Company, on duty guarding prisoners of war at Fort Frederick, June 27, 1778 [Ref: D-328]. Took the Oath of Allegiance before the Hon. John Cellars in January, 1778 [Ref: K-1814, O-40, J-6, which latter sources listed the name as "Lake Sholley"].

SHOLLEY, Peter. Enrolled in the third militia company organized for the Revolutionary War in the Elizabeth Town District of Frederick County (now the Hagerstown area of Washington County), passed by the

Committee of Observation on June 5, 1776, and assigned to Capt. John Reynolds' command [Ref: Q-273, which listed the name as "Peter Shelley"]. Appointed by the Committee of Observation on July 7, 1776 "to take the number of inhabitants within Lower Antietam Hundred, both whites and blacks, distinguishing respectively the age and sex of each, to be transmitted to the Council of Safety immediately." [Ref: Q-331, which listed the name as "Peter Shalley"]. Appointed by the Committee of Observation to carry the Association of Freemen to male residents in his hundred (district) on March 4, 1776 "and present it for signing and make an exact account of those that sign and those that refuse with their reasons for refusing." [Ref: Q-153, which listed the name as "Peter Molley" and L-82, which listed the name as "Peter Shelley"]. Took the Oath of Allegiance before the Hon. Christopher Cruse in Lower Antietam Hundred before March 2, 1778 [Ref: J-3, O-35, which listed the name as "Peter Shally"].

SHONECEY, Edward. Took the Oath of Allegiance before the Hon. Richard Davis in 1778 [Ref: J-3, O-36]. Private, Militia, 5th Class, Capt. Basil Williams' Company, 1776/1777 [Ref: A-1146, M-244, which listed the name as "Edward Shawness"].

SHOOP, Adam. See "Adam Shupe," q.v.

SHOOP, Agnes. See "Jacob Shupe," q.v.

SHOOTS, Conrad. See "Conrad Shutz," q.v.

SHOWENFIELD, Frederick. Rendered patriotic service by supplying wheat for the use of the military on February 10, 1780 [Ref: W-1190, HH-72, which latter source listed the name as "Frederick Shuwenfeld" or possibly "Frederick Shumenfeld"].

SHOWMAN, John. See "John Shoeman," q.v.

SHRAWDER, Philip. Captain, German Regiment, Lt. Col. Ludwick Weltner's Company, continental service, 1779 pay roll [Ref: D-264].

SHRINEHART, Frederick. Private, Militia, 5th Class, Capt. Samuel Hughes' Company, 2nd Battalion, 1776/1777 [Ref: M-238, A-1146].

SHRIVER, Henry. Private, Militia, 3rd Class, Capt. Daniel Clapsaddle's Company, 1st Battalion, 1776/1777 [Ref: M-236, A-1146]. Took the Oath of Allegiance before the Hon. Andrew Rentch before March 7, 1778 [Ref: O-52, J-15].

SHRIVER, John. Took the Oath of Allegiance before the Hon. Andrew Rentch before March 7, 1778 [Ref: O-52, J-15]. Private, Militia, Capt. John Kershner's Company, on duty guarding prisoners of war at Fort Frederick on June 27, 1778 [Ref: D-328, which listed the name as "John Shriber"].

SHRYER, Mary C. See "Michael Kershner," q.v.

SHRYHAWK (SHRYOCK), Colonel. See "Thomas Bartley," q.v.
SHRYOCK, George. See "Polly Lewis" and "William Lewis," q.v.
SHRYOCK, Catherine and Elizabeth. See "Leonard Shryock," q.v.
SHRYOCK, Henry. Rendered patriotic service by providing "rashons & caps" for the use of the military in July, 1775, as recorded by the Committee of Observation at Elizabeth Town on November 4, 1775 [Ref: Q-150, which listed him as "Capt. Shriock"]. First Major, Militia, 32nd Battalion, Frederick (now Washington) County, January 6, 1776 [Ref: M-121]. Rendered patriotic service in Hagerstown by providing rifles and boarding and dieting the officers and men of Capt. John Nelson's Company, continental service (Maryland Line), April, 1776 [Ref: Q-160]. Referred to as "Col. Henry Shryock" in February, 1777 [Ref: Q-234]. Served on the Committee of Observation in April, 1776 [Ref: Q-154, Q-155]. Took the Oath of Allegiance before the Hon. Joseph Sprigg before April 1, 1778 [Ref: O-53, J-16, which listed the name as "Henry Shryoch"]. Appointed the Assistant Deputy Quartermaster General of the Army of the United States in Washington County on June 2, 1778 and licensed to act by the Council of Maryland on September 17, 1778 [Ref: E-529]. Still in service as a purchaser in Hagerstown in April, 1780 and October, 1780 [Ref: G-153, P-280, P-284, HH-73]. Justice of the Peace, January 30, 1781 [Ref: G-293]. Elected Sheriff of Washington County, November 22, 1782 [Ref: I-307]. See "Leonard Shryock," q.v.
SHRYOCK, Jacob. Rendered patriotic service by providing "rashons" for the use of the military in July, 1775, as recorded by the Committee of Observation at Elizabeth Town on November 4, 1775 [Ref: Q-150, which listed the name as "Jacob Shriock"]. Rendered patriotic service by providing necessaries to Capt. John Reynolds' Company in the Flying Camp and belonging to the Maryland Service in July, 1776, as recorded by the Committee of Observation at Sharpsburg on August 6, 1776 [Ref: Q-332].
SHRYOCK, John. First Lieutenant, Militia, Capt. Michael Fackler's Company, 1776/1777 (succeeded, but date not given). [Ref: M-121, M-245, A-1146, Q-268]. Took the Oath of Allegiance before the Hon. Henry Schnebley in 1778 [Ref: O-49, J-12, which listed the name as "John Shryach"]. See "John Swan" and "Leonard Shryock," q.v.
SHRYOCK, John (1752-   ). Private, German Regiment, continental service, 1776. Private, Third Vacant Company, under Capt. Philip Graybell and Col. Lewis Weltner at Valley Forge in March, 1778. Discharged on July 20, 1779 [Ref: N-47, which listed the name as "John Shryock" and D-250, which listed the name as "John Shrayock" and FF-

222, which listed the name as "John Schryock"]. See "Leonard Shryock," q.v.

SHRYOCK, Leonard. Rendered patriotic service by supplying a blanket for the use of the military in March, 1776, as recorded by the Committee of Observation on April 12, 1776 [Ref: Q-156, L-82]. Second Lieutenant, Militia, Capt. Michael Fackler's Company, by January 15, 1777 [Ref: M-121, C-42, C-50, M-245, A-1146]. Took the Oath of Allegiance before the Hon. Henry Schnebley in 1778 [Ref: O-49, J-12, which listed the name as "Leonard Shryach"]. "Leonard Shyock" died before October 29, 1791 (date of balance book entry in Washington County), leaving a widow (no name given in this account) and equal shares to Henry, John, Catherine, Mary, Michael, Elizabeth and Susannah "Shyock." [Ref: J-31]. A subsequent entry on May 26, 1798 listed the same heirs and spelled all their names as "Shryock." [Ref: J-36].

SHRYOCK, Mary, Michael and Susannah. See "Leonard Shryock," q.v.

SHUFF, Jacob. Enrolled in the first militia company organized for the Revolutionary War in the Elizabeth Town District of Frederick County (now the Hagerstown area of Washington County) on January 6, 1776 [Ref: Q-271, W-1190]. Private, Militia, 6th Class, Capt. Charles Clinton's Company, 1776/1777 [Ref: M-245, A-1146, which listed the name as "Jacob South"].

SHUG, Jacob. Took the Oath of Allegiance before the Hon. Henry Schnebley in 1778 [Ref: O-51, J-15].

SHUGANS, James. Private, Militia, 3rd Class, Capt. Griffin Johnson's Company, 3rd Battalion, 1776/1777 [Ref: M-243].

SHULE, William. Private, Militia, by January 22, 1777 when ordered by the Committee of Observation "to march with some company of militia to the reinforcement of his Excellency General Washington" or appear before the Committee and state his reason for not marching. He apparently marched since he never appeared to the contrary [Ref: Q-48, which listed the name as "Wm. Shewall"]. Took the Oath of Allegiance before the Hon. John Barnes before February 28, 1778 [Ref: O-44, J-9].

SHULTZ, George. Fourth Corporal, Militia, Capt. Martin Kershner's Company, 32nd Battalion, December 27, 1776 [Ref: K-1814 (Box 3), which listed the name as "George Shulz"]. "George Schultz" took the Oath of Allegiance before the Hon. Henry Schnebley in 1778 [Ref: O-50, J-13]. "George Shultz" died testate before December 15, 1784 (date of balance book entry in Washington County), leaving a widow, two sons and four daughters, but naming only daughter Mary [Ref: J-25].

SHUMAKER (SHOUMAKER), Balser. Private, Militia, 1st Class, Capt. Daniel Clapsaddle's Company, 1st Battalion, 1776/1777 [Ref: M-236, A-1146, which listed the name as "Bolcher Shomaker"]. Took the Oath of Allegiance before the Hon. Andrew Rentch before March 7, 1778 [Ref: O-52, J-15, which listed the name as "Balser Shoumaker"].

SHUMAKER (SHOEMAKER), John. Private, Militia, Capt. William Heyser's Company, muster roll dated October 23, 1776, in continental service, which stated he had deserted, yet he was on duty in May, 1777 [Ref: D-264, L-79, GG-99].

SHUMAKER (SHOEMAKER), Michael. Private, German Regiment, continental service, 1776, and discharged on July 24, 1779 [Ref: D-250].

SHUMAN, George. Private, Militia, 2nd Class, Capt. John Rennolds' (Reynolds') Company, 2nd Battalion, 1776/1777 [Ref: M-240].

SHUMAN (SHOWMAN), John (c1735-1821). Took the Oath of Allegiance before the Hon. Henry Schnebley in 1778 [Ref: O-50, J-13, which listed the name as "John Shuhman"]. "John Showman" died at Pleasant Valley in Washington County on March 6, 1821, at an advanced age [Ref: Z-57].

SHUMAN, John Jr. Private, Militia, 8th Class, Capt. John Rennolds' (Reynolds') Company, 2nd Battalion, 1776/1777 [Ref: M-240].

SHUMAN, Thomas (1759-1824). Private, Militia, 8th Class, Capt. Peter Beall's Company, 1st Battalion, 1776/1777 [Ref: M-240]. Thomas Shuman was born on July 18, 1759, died on May 25, 1824, was buried in Old St. John's Lutheran Churchyard, and subsequently reinterred in Rose Hill Cemetery in Hagerstown [Ref: JJ-VII:104].

SHUNFORD, Mary. See "John Kibler," q.v.

SHUPE (SHOOP), Adam (1744-1820). Private, Militia, 5th Class, Capt. Jacob Sharer's Company, 1776/1777 [Ref: A-1146, M-248, which listed the name as "Adam Shoop"]. "Adam Shupe" was born on January 24, 1744, died on June 2, 1820, and is buried in the Shang Graveyard near Boonsboro, Maryland [Ref: JJ-II:91].

SHUPE (SHOOP), Jacob (c1750-1802). Private, Militia, 5th Class, Capt. Martin Kershner's Company, 1776/1777 [Ref: A-1146, M-247, which listed the name as "Jacob Shup"]. Took the Oath of Allegiance before the Hon. Christopher Cruse in Sharpsburg Hundred before March 2, 1778 [Ref: O-34, J-2, which listed the name as "Jacob Shop"]. "Jacob Shupe" died in Elizabeth Town on the Tuesday before September 2, 1802, after a painful illness, leaving a large family [Ref: LL-2:76]. "Mrs. Shupe, widow of late Jacob Shupe" died in Hagerstown on January 23, 1829, at an advanced age [Ref: Z-106]. "Jacob Shoop" died testate in 1802, leaving a wife Agnes and several children [Ref: MM-12:80, 81].

SHUROCK, George. See "William Lewis," q.v.

SHUSE, Peter. See "Peter Sheese," q.v.

SHUTZ, Conrad. Took the Oath of Allegiance before the Hon. Henry Schnebley in 1778 [Ref: O-51, J-15]. "Conrad Shoots" recorded his animal brand in Washington County court on March 25, 1778 [Ref: II].

SICKLEY, John. Private who was recruited and passed by County Lieutenant Thomas Sprigg on April 22, 1780 [Ref: D-336].

SIDENER, Christian. Third Corporal, Militia, Capt. James Prather's Company, 3rd Battalion, 1776/1777 [Ref: M-242, which listed the name as "Christian Snidwar"]. See "Crosteon B. Sneker(?)," q.v.

SIDENER, Christopher. Private, Militia, 1st Class, Capt. James Smith's Company, 2nd Battalion, 1776/1777 [Ref: M-239, A-1146, which listed the name as "Christopher Sidner"]. Took the Oath of Allegiance before the Hon. Joseph Sprigg before April 1, 1778 [Ref: J-16, O-53, which latter source listed the name as "Christopher Sidenor"].

SIDENER, Frederick. Private, Militia, 7th Class, Capt. James Smith's Company, 2nd Battalion, 1776/1777 [Ref: M-240, A-1146, which listed the name as "Frederick Sidner"]. Took the Oath of Allegiance before the Hon. Joseph Sprigg before April 1, 1778 [Ref: J-16, O-53, which latter source listed the name as "Frederick Sidenor"].

SIDENER, Martin. Took the Oath of Allegiance before the Hon. Henry Schnebley in 1778 [Ref: O-50, J-13, which listed the name as Martin Sceittner"]. Rendered patriotic service by supplying wheat and corn for the use of the military on March 3, 1780 [Ref: W-1190, which listed the name as "Martin Seider" and HH-72, which listed the name as "Martin Seidner"].

SIDES (SIDER), Christian. Private, Militia, 1st Class, Capt. Daniel Clapsaddle's Company, 1st Battalion, 1776/1777 [Ref: M-236, A-1146]. Private, Militia, Capt. William Heyser's Company, muster roll dated October 23, 1776, in continental service, which stated he had reportedly "deserted." [Ref: D-264, W-1190, L-79].

SIDES (SIDER), John. Private, Militia, 8th Class, Capt. Conrad Hogmire's Company, 1776/1777 [Ref: M-244, A-1146].

SILWELL, Jeremiah. See "Jeremiah Stillwell," q.v.

SIMKINS (SIMPKINS), Dickenson Sr. Took the Oath of Allegiance before the Hon. Andrew Bruce before March 2, 1778 [Ref: O-41, which listed the name as "Dickenson Simkins Snr." and J-6, which listed the name as "Dickinson Simkins, Sr."].

SIMKINS (SIMPKINS), Dickerson. First Lieutenant, Militia, Frederick County, July 27, 1776. First Lieutenant, Militia, Capt. Charles Clinton's Company, 3rd Battalion, Washington County, June 22, 1778 [Ref: M-

121, B-127, E-145, M-245, A-1146, which also listed the name as "Dickson Simpkins" and "Dickenson Simpkins"].
SIMKINS (SIMPKINS), Dickinson. Took the Oath of Allegiance before the Hon. Andrew Bruce before March 2, 1778 [Ref: O-41, J-6, which listed the name as "Dickinson Simpkins"].
SIMKINS (SIMPKINS), George. Private, Select Militia, Capt. Adam Ott's Company, 1781 [Ref: M-238, A-1146].
SIMKINS (SIMPKINS), John. Ensign, Militia, Capt. James Walling's Company, 2nd Battalion, 1776. Ensign, Select Militia, Capt. Adam Ott's Company, March 30, 1781 [Ref: M-238, M-121, G-368, which also listed the name as "John Simpkins"].
SIMKINS (SIMPKINS), Silas. Second Sergeant, Militia, Capt. Charles Clinton's Company, 1776/1777 [Ref: M-245, A-1146, which listed the name as "Silas Simpkins"]. Paid on May 16 1778 for riding express from Old Town to Washington County [Ref: E-86].
SIMKINS (SIMPKINS), William. Took the Oath of Allegiance before the Hon. Samuel Hughes before March 1, 1778 [Ref: O-33, J-1]. See "Boston Baker" and "Adam Mong," q.v.
SIMMONS, Jonathan. Fourth Sergeant, Militia, Capt. Basil Williams' Company, 1776/1777 [Ref: M-244, A-1146]. Took the Oath of Allegiance before the Hon. Richard Davis in 1778 [Ref: J-3, O-36]. "Jonathan Simmonds" died testate before September 9, 1804 [Ref: MM-13:88]. See "Levy Simmons," q.v.
SIMMONS, Levy. Private, Militia, 8th Class, Capt. Basil Williams' Company, 1776/1777 [Ref: M-244, A-1146]. Took the Oath of Allegiance before the Hon. Richard Davis in 1778 [Ref: J-3, O-36]. One "Levi Simmonds" was a son of Jonathan Simmonds who died in 1804 [Ref: MM-13:88].
SIMMONS, Richard. Private, Militia, 8th Class, Capt. Basil Williams' Company, 1776/1777 [Ref: M-244, A-1146].
SIMON, John. Private, Militia, 2nd Class, Capt. Michael Fackler's Company, 1776/1777 [Ref: M-245, A-1146].
SIMON, Peter. Private, Militia, 4th Class, Capt. Daniel Clapsaddle's Company, 1st Battalion, 1776/1777 [Ref: M-236, A-1146]. Took the Oath of Allegiance before the Hon. Joseph Sprigg before April 1, 1778 [Ref: O-53, J-16, which listed the name as "Peter Sunon"].
SIMPSON, Mary. See "Rezin Simpson," q.v.
SIMPSON, Rezin (1755-1828). Private and sergeant, Maryland Line (Dragoons), who received payment from the Treasurer of the Western Shore of Maryland by resolutions passed in November, 1812 and December, 1815. On February 18, 1830 the Treasurer of the Western

Shore of Maryland was directed to pay to "Robert Swan, for use of Mary Simpson, widow of the late Rezin Simpson, a pensioner of the State of Maryland, $27.50 balance due said Simpson at time of his decease." On February 24, 1830 the Treasurer of the Western Shore of Maryland was directed to pay to "William Shaw, for use of Mary Simpson, of Allegany County, during widowhood, quarterly, half pay of sergeant for the services of her late husband, Rezin Simpson, who was a soldier of the Revolutionary War." [Ref: AA-392]. "Died at Western-Port in Allegany County on July 20, 1828, Rezin Simpson, a Revolutionary soldier, in his 73rd year." [Ref: Z-20]. However, Source Y-III:2675 states that a Rezin Simpson was born in 1758 in Maryland, married Jane Burgess, served as a sergeant in Maryland during the Revolution, and died in Virginia in 1816. Therefore, additional research may be necessary before drawing conclusions.

SIMPSON (SIMSON), William. Private who was recruited and passed by County Lieutenant Thomas Sprigg on April 22, 1780 [Ref: D-336].

SIMS, Ignatius. Appointed by the Committee of Observation to carry the Association of Freemen to male residents in Marsh Hundred on September 14, 1775 "and require their subscription to the same and make an exact account of those who sign and those that refuse with their reasons for refusing." [Ref: Q-143]. Private, Militia, 2nd Class, Capt. James Smith's Company, 2nd Battalion, 1776/1777 [Ref: M-239, A-1146, which listed the name as "Ignatius Simms"]. Rendered patriotic service by providing necessaries to Capt. John Reynolds' Company in the Flying Camp and belonging to the Maryland Service in July, 1776, as recorded by the Committee of Observation at Sharpsburg on August 6, 1776 [Ref: Q-333]. Took the Oath of Allegiance before the Hon. Richard Davis in 1778 [Ref: J-4, O-36, which listed the named as "Ignatius Semms"]. See "John McKey," q.v.

SIMS, Richard. Took the Oath of Allegiance before the Hon. Richard Davis in 1778 [Ref: J-3, O-36].

SIMS, Thomas. Rendered patriotic service by providing a rifle for Capt. Daniel Cresap's Company in July, 1775, as recorded by the Committee of Observation at Elizabeth Town on November 4, 1775 [Ref: Q-149]. On January 2, 1777 the Committee of Observation for Elizabeth Town District (now the Hagerstown area of Washington County) ordered the Treasurer to "pay to Mr. Thomas Simms the sum of fifty pounds to be appropriated in order to complete the Tory Goal, and to lay the several accounts before this Committee for Inspection." [Ref: Q-29].

SINN, George. Rendered patriotic service by providing caps for the use of the military in July, 1775, as recorded by the Committee of

Observation at Elizabeth Town on November 4, 1775 [Ref: Q-150, which listed the name as "George Zin"].
SINN, John. Private, Militia, 8th Class, Capt. Barnett Johnston's Company, 3rd Battalion, 1776/1777 [Ref: M-242].
SISLER, Thomas. Took the Oath of Allegiance before September 1, 1780 [Ref: X-120].
SISTNORT, Valentine. Took the Oath of Allegiance before the Hon. John Barnes before February 28, 1778 [Ref: O-44, J-9, which latter source listed the name as "Valentine Sistnoort"].
SITES, Wendal. One of several patriots appointed by the Committee of Observation on December 30, 1776 "to form the county into companies (after the militia had marched) for the purpose of relieving the distressed inhabitants of said county and also to compel the Dunkards and Mennonists to give their assistance." [Ref: Q-346].
SKILES, Ephraim. Private who was enlisted by Ensign Nathan Williams and passed on July 25, 1776 in Frederick (now Washington) County [Ref: D-51]. Took the Oath of Allegiance before the Hon. Richard Davis in 1778 [Ref: J-4, O-36, which listed the name as "Ephraim Skeles"].
SKILES, Ephraim Jr. Private, Militia, 1st Class, Capt. James Smith's Company, 2nd Battalion, 1776/1777 [Ref: M-239, A-1146, which listed the name as "Ephraim Shiles, Jr."].
SKILES, William. Private, Militia, 4th Class, Capt. James Smith's Company, 2nd Battalion, 1776/1777 [Ref: M-240, A-1146, which listed the name as "William Skeles"]. Took the Oath of Allegiance before the Hon. Richard Davis in 1778 [Ref: J-4, O-36, which listed the name as "William Skeles"].
SKILES, William Jr. Took the Oath of Allegiance before the Hon. Richard Davis in 1778 [Ref: J-4, O-36, which listed the name as "William Skeles, Jr."].
SKINNER, James (1755-   ). Soldier and pensioner of the Revolution who resided in the 2nd Division of Allegany County in 1840, aged 85 [Ref: EE-28:4 (p. 445), containing an article by Elba Anthony Dardeau, Jr.].
SKINNER, William. Private, Militia, 7th Class, Capt. Barnett Johnston's Company, 3rd Battalion, 1776/1777 [Ref: M-242, Q-48]. Two men by this name took the Oath of Allegiance in 1778: one before the Hon. William Yates [Ref: O-48, J-12], and one before the Hon. Henry Schnebley [Ref: O-50, J-13].
SLACK, Martin. Took the Oath of Allegiance before the Hon. Henry Schnebley in 1778 [Ref: O-49, J-13].
SLAGLE, John (1746-1812). Private, Flying Camp, enlisted in Frederick County on July 20, 1776 [Ref: D-46, which listed the name as "John

Slagel"]. "John Slagle" died on December 3, 1812, aged 66 years, 5 months, 15 days, and is buried in a graveyard on the R. S. Dillon farm, west of Hancock, south of Packing House on Oliver farm in Washington County. This cemetery also includes other family members with the surname spelled "Shlageal" [Ref: JJ-II:48].

SLATER, William. See "William Staler," q.v.

SMISAR, Mathias. Private, Militia, 1st Class, Capt. John Bennet's Company, 1776/1777 [Ref: M-246, A-1146]. "Mathias Smyser" died before August 13, 1782 (date of balance book entry in Washington County), leaving a widow and seven children (no names were given). [Ref: J-23]. See "George Berger," q.v.

SMITH, Adam (c1753-1831). Private, Militia, 2nd Class, Capt. Michael Fackler's Company, 1776/1777 [Ref: M-245, A-1146]. Second Lieutenant, Militia, Capt. William Heyser's Company, muster roll dated October 23, 1776, in continental service [Ref: D-263]. Took the Oath of Allegiance before the Hon. Joseph Sprigg before April 1, 1778 [Ref: O-53, J-15]. Soldier of the Revolution who died in Huntingdon County, Pennsylvania on May 20, 1831, aged 77, formerly of Hagerstown [Ref: DD-23, citing *The Republican Banner*, May 28, 1831]. He applied for and received pension S40455 in Huntington County, Pennsylvania on June 11, 1819, aged 66, stating he lived at Hagerstown, Maryland at the time of his enlistment. In 1820 his children (no names given) were all "of age." [Ref: V-III:3169].

SMITH, Catharine. See "Adam Smith," q.v.

SMITH, Christian. Soldier and pensioner of the Revolution who resided in the 1st Division of Allegany in 1840, aged 88 [Ref: EE-28:4 (p. 445), containing an article by Elba Anthony Dardeau, Jr.]. One Christian Smith was born in Maryland in 1755, married Catherine Fress, served as a lieutenant in Maryland during the Revolution, and died after 1804 in Pennsylvania [Ref: Y-III:2700]. Additional research will be necessary before drawing conclusions.

SMITH, Christopher (1750-1820). Private, Maryland Line, 1777-1780 [Ref: D-354, D-392, D-447, D-498]. Christopher Smith, founder of Smithsburg, was born in 1750, died in 1820, and is buried in the Trinity Evangelical Lutheran Church Graveyard at Smithsburg in Washington County, Maryland [Ref: JJ-III:28].

SMITH, David. There were three men with this name who rendered service during the Revolutionary War. (1) Private, Militia, 2nd Class, Capt. Jacob Sharer's Company, 1776/1777 [Ref: A-1146, M-248]. Took the Oath of Allegiance before the Hon. John Cellars in January, 1778 [Ref: K-1814, O-40, J-5]. (2) Private, Militia, 5th Class, Capt. Daniel

Cresap's Company, 3rd Battalion, 1776/1777 [Ref: M-241]. Took the Oath of Allegiance before the Hon. Lemuel Barritt before March 16, 1778 [Ref: O-42, J-8]. (3) Took the Oath of Allegiance before the Hon. John Stull in 1778 [Ref: O-47, J-11]. One David Smith rendered patriotic service by supplying wheat for the use of the military on February 7, 1780 [Ref: W-1190, HH-73].

SMITH, Everheart. Private, Militia, Capt. William Heyser's Company, muster roll dated October 23, 1776, in continental service and on duty in May, 1777 [Ref: D-264, W-1190, L-79, which listed the name as "Everhearet Smith" and GG-99, which listed the name as "Eberhart Smith"].

SMITH, George. Enrolled in the third militia company organized for the Revolutionary War in the Elizabeth Town District of Frederick County (now the Hagerstown area of Washington County), passed by the Committee of Observation on June 5, 1776, and assigned to Capt. John Reynolds' command [Ref: Q-273]. Private, Militia, 7th Class, Capt. Michael Fackler's Company, 1776/1777 [Ref: M-245, A-1146]. Took the Oath of Allegiance before the Hon. John Stull in 1778 [Ref: O-47, J-11].

SMITH, George. Private, Militia, 4th Class, Capt. Jacob Sharer's Company, 1776/1777 [Ref: A-1146, M-248]. Took the Oath of Allegiance before the Hon. Christopher Cruse in Sharpsburg Hundred before March 2, 1778 [Ref: O-34, J-2]. See "Michael Smith," q.v.

SMITH, Henry. There were three men with this name who rendered service during the Revolutionary War. (1) Private, Militia, 4th Class, Capt. Daniel Clapsaddle's Company, 1st Battalion, 1776/1777 [Ref: M-236, A-1146]. (2) Private, Militia, 4th Class, Capt. John Rennolds' (Reynolds') Company, 2nd Battalion, 1776/1777 [Ref: M-240]. (3) Private, Militia, 3rd Class, Capt. John Rennolds' (Reynolds') Company, 2nd Battalion, 1776/1777 [Ref: M-240].

SMITH, Jachabod. Took the Oath of Allegiance before the Hon. William Yates in 1778 [Ref: O-48, J-12].

SMITH, Jacob (1758-1834). Private, Militia, 8th Class, Capt. Jacob Sharer's Company, 1776/1777 [Ref: A-1146, M-248]. Took the Oath of Allegiance before the Hon. John Stull in 1778 [Ref: O-47, J-11]. He applied for pension in Morgan County, Virginia on May 27, 1833, stating he was born in 1758 and lived at Sharpsburg, Maryland at the time of his enlistment. After the war he moved near Boonesborough, Maryland and married Catharine French around 1814 at Sandy Creek about 15 miles from Morgantown, Virginia. Around 1818 they moved to Monongalia County, Virginia and in 1829 to Morgan County, Virginia, where he died on July 26, 1834. Catharine Smith applied for and received pension W7186 on October 8, 1853 and also bounty land warrant #39337-160-55 in 1856, aged near 70 years [Ref: V-III:3192]. Jacob French was born in Germany in 1758, married first to Christena Iseminger and second to Catharine French, served in Maryland as a private during the Revolution, and died on July 26, 1834 in Virginia [Ref: Y-III:2708].

SMITH, James. Elected to serve on the Committee of Observation for the Elizabeth Town District (now the Hagerstown area of Washington County) on September 12, 1775 [Ref: Q-142]. Appointed by the Committee of Observation to serve on a Committee for Licensing Suits on September 14, 1775 [Ref: Q-142]. Captain, Militia, 2nd Battalion, 1776-1780 [Ref: M-122, M-239, E-145, A-1146, G-220]. Took the Oath of Allegiance before the Hon. Richard Davis in 1778 [Ref: J-5, O-38]. See "John Leiter (Lighter)," q.v.

SMITH, James. Private, Militia, Capt. Charles Coulson's Company, enrolled August 28, 1776 [Ref: M-243, A-1146]. Took the Oath of Allegiance before the Hon. Lemuel Barritt before March 16, 1778 [Ref: O-43, J-8]. Corporal, German Regiment, Lt. Col. Ludwick Weltner's Company, continental service, promoted August 1, 1779 [Ref: D-264].

SMITH, James. Private who was recruited in Washington County on October 19, 1780 [Ref: D-346].

SMITH, John. There were several men by this name who rendered service during the Revolutionary War. Additional research will be necessary before drawing conclusions. (1) Private, Militia, Capt. Martin Kershner's Company, 32nd Battalion, December 27, 1776 [Ref: K-1814, Box 3]. (2) Private, Militia, 7th Class, Capt. Michael Fackler's Company, 1776/1777 [Ref: M-245, A-1146]. (3) Private, Capt. William Heyser's Company, enlisted July 27, 1776, muster roll dated October 23, 1776, in continental service [Ref: D-264, W-1190, L-79]. (4) Private who was recruited and passed by County Lieutenant Thomas Sprigg on April 22, 1780 [Ref: D-336]. (5) Private, German Regiment, Lt. Col. Ludwick Weltner's Company, discharged October 12, 1779 at Tioga, Pennsylvania [Ref: D-265, GG-99]. (6) One John Smith took the Oath of Allegiance before the Hon. Richard Davis in 1778 [Ref: J-3, O-36], one took the Oath of Allegiance before the Hon. John Stull in 1778 [Ref: O-47, J-11], and two took the Oath of Allegiance before the Hon. John Stull in 1778 [Ref: O-47, J-11]. (7) One John Smith rendered patriotic service by providing clothing for the use of the military on July 5, 1778 [Ref: CC-106]. (8) Pension S6117 concerns a John Smith who was born in Prince George's County, Maryland in 1760 and moved (with his father, no name given) to Frederick County where he served in the war. He later lived in Washington and Allegany Counties, Maryland and then moved to Harrison County, Virginia where he died prior to January 2, 1840 [Ref: V-III:3198]. See "Michael Smith," q.v.

SMITH, Joseph. There were several men by this name who rendered service during the Revolutionary War. Additional research may be necessary before drawing conclusions. (1) Elected to serve on the Committee of Observation for the Elizabeth Town District (now the Hagerstown area of Washington County) on September 12, 1775 [Ref: Q-142]. Referred to as "Major Joseph Smith, chairman" on February 19, 1776 [Ref: Q-152]. Lieutenant Colonel, Militia, 36th Battalion, Frederick County, 1776, and Colonel, April 20, 1776. Colonel, Militia, 2nd Battalion, Washington County, June 22, 1778 [Ref: M-122, A-356, E-145]. Appointed by the Maryland Convention on November 8, 1776 to be one of the three judges of elections for Washington County [Ref: CC-55]. Took the Oath of Allegiance before the Hon. Henry Schnebley in 1778 [Ref: O-50, J-14]. (2) Private, Militia, 5th Class, Capt. John Bennet's Company, 1776/1777 [Ref: M-246, A-1146]. Took the Oath of Allegiance before the Hon. Henry Schnebley in 1778 [Ref: O-50, J-14]. (3) Private who was recruited and passed by County Lieutenant Thomas Sprigg on April 22, 1780 [Ref: D-336]. Took the Oath of Allegiance before September 1, 1780 [Ref: X-120]. (4) Took the Oath of Allegiance before the Hon. Christopher Cruse in Sharpsburg Hundred before March 2, 1778 [Ref: O-34, J-1].

SMITH, Joshua. See "Jacob Kuhn," q.v.

SMITH, Lodowick. Private who enlisted in the militia on August 24, 1781 for service in the Continental Army [Ref: D-388, D-412].

SMITH, Lorance. Took the Oath of Allegiance before the Hon. Christopher Cruse in Sharpsburg Hundred before March 2, 1778 [Ref: O-34, J-1].

SMITH, Marian. See "Lodwick Young," q.v.

SMITH, Martin. Two men by this name were listed as recruited and passed by County Lieutenant Thomas Sprigg on April 22, 1780 [Ref: D-336].

SMITH, Mary. See "Otho Holland Williams," q.v.

SMITH, Michael (1752-1842). Private, Maryland and Pennsylvania Lines, who applied for pension in Harrison County, Kentucky in September 18, 1832, stating he was born in 1752 in Washington County, Maryland, lived there at the time of his enlistment in June, 1776 under Capt. Cresap and Col. Rawlings, and participated in the Battle of Long Island. He reenlisted at Little York, Pennsylvania, served under Col. Swope, was captured by the Hessians, and released after 2 or 3 months (no dates given). He married Nancy Levite (widow) after September 18, 1797 (date of bond) in Montgomery County, Kentucky and died there on November 24, 1842. His widow Nancy Smith later moved to Rush County, Indiana where she received pension W6088 and died on December 28, 1850. The surviving children in 1856 were George W. Smith (of Bath County, Kentucky), Amanda McConnell, wife of James R. McConnell (of Rush County, Indiana), Elizabeth Carpenter, wife of Squire C. Carpenter (of Bath County, Kentucky), and John Smith (of Pike County, Missouri). In 1841 Michael Smith had referred to his son Peter Smith (of Bourbon County, Kentucky). [Ref: V-III:3211, T-11, T-12].

SMITH, Nancy. See "Michael Smith," q.v.

SMITH, Nicholas. Private, Militia, 8th Class, Capt. John Cellars' Company, 1776/1777 [Ref: A-1146, M-246]. One of the persons appointed by the Committee of Observation for Elizabeth Town District (now the Hagerstown area of Washington County) on January 2, 1777 "to appraise the several wagons and horses that shall go with the militia in Col. John Stull's Battalion." [Ref: Q-29]. Served on the Committee of Observation in February, 1777 [Ref: Q-228]. Took the Oath of Allegiance before the Hon. John Cellars in January, 1778 [Ref: K-1814, O-40, J-6].

SMITH, Peter. Private, Militia, 1st Class, Capt. Peter Beall's Company, 1st Battalion, 1776/1777 [Ref: M-240].

SMITH, Peter. Private, Militia, 1st Class, Capt. Jacob Sharer's Company, 1776/1777 [Ref: A-1146, M-248].

SMITH, Peter. See "Michael Smith," q.v.

SMITH, Philip. Enrolled in the third militia company organized for the Revolutionary War in the Elizabeth Town District of Frederick County (now the Hagerstown area of Washington County), passed by the Committee of Observation on June 5, 1776, and assigned to Capt. John Reynolds' command [Ref: Q-273]. Private, Militia, 6th Class, Capt. Joseph Chapline's Company, 2nd Battalion, 1776/1777 [Ref: M-241]. Took the Oath of Allegiance before the Hon. Joseph Chapline before April 17, 1779 [Ref: J-5, O-39]. See "Philip D. Smyth," q.v.

SMITH, Robert. Private, Militia, 4th Class, Capt. Barnett Johnston's Company, 3rd Battalion, 1776/1777 [Ref: M-242].

SMITH, Robert. First Lieutenant, Militia, Capt. James Smith's Company, 2nd Battalion, June 22, 1778 [Ref: M-122, M-239, E-145, A-1146]. Took the Oath of Allegiance before the Hon. Richard Davis in 1778 [Ref: J-4, O-37]. Captain, 2nd Battalion, November 21, 1780 [Ref: G-220].

SMITH, Samuel. Private who was enrolled by Capt. Henry Hardman and passed on July 19, 1776 in Frederick (now Washington) County [Ref: D-51].

SMITH, Thomas. One of several patriots appointed by the Committee of Observation on January 7, 1777 "to form the county into companies (after the militia had marched) for the purpose of relieving the distressed inhabitants of said county and also to compel the Dunkards and Mennonists to give their assistance." [Ref: Q-31]. Elected by the Committee of Observation on January 14, 1777 to serve in the room of Col. Samuel Beall who had resigned [Ref: Q-38]. Took the Oath of Allegiance before the Hon. Richard Davis in 1778 [Ref: J-5, O-38]. Rendered patriotic service by supplying rye for the use of the military on January 31, 1780 [Ref: W-1190, HH-74].

SMITH, Thomas. Private who was enrolled by Capt. Henry Hardman and passed on July 19, 1776 in Frederick (now Washington) County [Ref: D-51]. Private, Militia, 2nd Class, Capt. John Rennolds' (Reynolds') Company, 2nd Battalion, 1776/1777 [Ref: M-240].

SMITH, William. Private, Militia, 8th Class, Capt. Basil Williams' Company, 1776/1777 [Ref: M-244, A-1146]. See "Otho Holland Williams," q.v.

SMITH, William Mercer. Enrolled in the first militia company organized for the Revolutionary War in the Elizabeth Town District of Frederick County (now the Hagerstown area of Washington County) on January 6, 1776 [Ref: Q-271, W-1190]. See "William Messersmith," q.v.

SMITHLY, John. Private, Militia, Capt. William Heyser's Company, enlisted August 2, 1776, muster roll dated October 23, 1776, which mistakenly reported him as "deserted." [Ref: D-264, W-1190, L-79, which listed the name as "John Smithley"]. Private, German Regiment, Lt. Col. Ludwick Weltner's Company, continental service, discharged on October 12, 1779 at Fort Wyoming, Pennsylvania [Ref: GG-99, D-265, D-251, which latter source listed the name as "John Smithly or Smith"].

SMITHLY, Phillip. Private, Militia, Capt. William Heyser's Company, enlisted August 2, 1776, muster roll dated October 23, 1776, which mistakenly reported him as "deserted." [Ref: D-264]. Private, German Regiment, Lt. Col. Ludwick Weltner's Company, continental service, discharged on October 12, 1779 at Fort Wyoming, Pennsylvania [Ref: GG-99, D-265, D-250, which latter source listed the name as "Philip Smithly or Smith"].

SMITHSON, Daniel. Took the Oath of Allegiance before the Hon. William Yates in 1778 [Ref: O-48, J-12].

SMYSER, Mathias. See "Mathias Smisar," q.v.

SMYTH, Philip D. (1759-   ). Private, Maryland Line, who applied for and received pension S40466 in Switzerland County, Indiana on October 19, 1825, stating he was born on April 26, 1759 at Hagerstown, Maryland and served in the Maryland Line. After living in Indiana for some time he moved to Cincinnati, Ohio on March 10, 1828 [Ref: V-III:3237, which listed the name as "Philip D. Smyth or Philip D. Smith or Philip Smith"]. See "Philip Smith," q.v.

SNAVELY, Henry. Appointed to raise funds on January 24, 1775 for the Committee of Observation in Salisbury Hundred in Frederick (now Washington) County [Ref: L-75]. One Henry Snavely was a son of Conrad Snavely who died testate in 1804 [Ref: MM-13:88, 89].

SNEKER(?), Crosteon B(?). Took the Oath of Allegiance before the Hon. Lemuel Barritt before March 16, 1778 [Ref: J-8, O-43, which latter source listed the name as "Crosteon Bsnedker"]. Perhaps this is actually "Christian Sidener," q.v.

SNELL, Margaret. See "Christopher Burkett," q.v.

SNIDER, Frederick. See "Frederick Snyder," q.v.

SNIDER, Henry. Took the Oath of Allegiance before the Hon. John Stull in 1778 [Ref: J-11, O-47].

SNIDER, Jacob. Private, Militia, 3rd Class, Capt. John Bennet's Company, 1776/1777 [Ref: M-246, A-1146].

SNIDER, John. Private, German Regiment, continental service, 1776, and discharged on July 24, 1779 [Ref: D-251, Q-48]. Took the Oath of Allegiance before the Hon. Henry Schnebley in 1778 [Ref: J-15, O-51, which listed the name as "John Snheder"].

SNIDWAR, Christian. See "Christian Sidener," q.v.

SNIVELY, Casper (1761-1839). Captain, Revolutionary War, died on October 16, 1839, aged 77 years, 11 months, 2 days, and is buried beside his wife Mary Snively (1770-1832), daughter of J. and Catharine Snively, in a graveyard at the Geeting Meeting House, 1st U. B. Church at Mt. Hebron, Eakle's Mill, in Washington County [Ref: JJ-V:63].

SNIVELY, Catharine, J., and Mary. See "Casper Snively," q.v.

SNIVELY, Michael. Private, Militia, 3rd Class, Capt. Griffin Johnson's Company, 3rd Battalion, 1776/1777 [Ref: M-243].

SNOAK, Mathias. Private, Militia, 4th Class, Capt. Martin Kershner's Company, 1776/1777 [Ref: A-1146, M-247].

SNYDER, Adam. Took the Oath of Allegiance before the Hon. William Yates in 1778 [Ref: O-48, J-12]. Private, Militia, 8th Class, Capt. Conrad Nichodemus' Company, 2nd Battalion, 1776/1777 [Ref: M-237, A-1146, which listed the name as "Adam Snider"].

SNYDER, Ann. See "Jacob Snyder," q.v.

SNYDER, Anthony. Took the Oath of Allegiance before the Hon. John Barnes before February 28, 1778 [Ref: O-44, J-9].

SNYDER, Casper. Private, Militia, 3rd Class, Capt. John Bennet's Company, 1776/1777 [Ref: M-246, A-1146, which listed the name as "Casper Snider"]. Deserted and returned to duty on February 8, 1777 by order of the Committee of Observation [Ref: Q-232, Q-234, which listed the name as "Gasper Snyder"]. Private, Militia, Capt. John Kershner's Company, on duty guarding prisoners of war at Fort Frederick on June 27, 1778 [Ref: D-328, which listed the name as "Casper Snider"]. See "Casper Schneider," q.v.

SNYDER, Daniel. See "Daniel Schneider" and "John Snyder," q.v.

SNYDER, David. See "John Snyder," q.v.

SNYDER, Felix. Private who was recruited and passed by County Lieutenant Thomas Sprigg on April 22, 1780 [Ref: D-336, which listed the name as "Felix Snider"].

SNYDER, Frederick. Private, Militia, by January 22, 1777 when ordered by the Committee of Observation "to march with some company of militia to the reinforcement of his Excellency General Washington" or appear before the Committee and state his reason for not marching. He apparently marched since he never appeared to the contrary [Ref: Q-48, which listed the name as "Fredk. Snider"]. Took the Oath of Allegiance before the Hon. John Stull in 1778 [Ref: O-47, J-11, which listed the name as "Frederick Snyder"]. Private who was recruited and passed by County Lieutenant Thomas Sprigg on April 22, 1780 [Ref: D-336]. Private who enlisted in the militia on August 18, 1781 for service in the Continental Army [Ref: D-388, D-412]. Substitute, Maryland Line, discharged on October 30, 1781 [Ref: G-656, which listed the name as "Frederick Snider"].

SNYDER, Henry. Private, Militia, 5th Class, Capt. Daniel Clapsaddle's Company, 1st Battalion, 1776/1777 [Ref: M-236, A-1146]. See "Henry Snider," q.v.

SNYDER, Henry. Private, Militia, 3rd Class, Capt. James Walling's Company, 2nd Battalion, 1776/1777 [Ref: M-238, A-1146].

SNYDER, Henry John. Private, Militia, 5th Class, Capt. John Cellars' Company, 1776/1777 [Ref: A-1146, M-246].

SNYDER, Jacob (1745-1829). Private, Militia, 5th Class, Capt. Isaac Baker's Company, 1776/1777 [Ref: A-1146, M-247]. "Jacob Snyder, Sr." died on June 11, 1829, aged 83 years, 8 months, 12 days and is buried beside Anna Snyder (1749-1818) in a graveyard on a farm owned by Samuel Snyder near Mt. Carmel Church in Boonsboro, Maryland [Ref: JJ-III:55].

SNYDER, John. There were several men with this name who rendered services during the Revolutionary War. Additional research will be necessary before drawing conclusions. (1) Private, Militia, 6th Class, Capt. Peter Beall's Company, 1st Battalion, 1776/1777 [Ref: M-240]. (2) Private, Militia, 5th Class, Capt. Isaac Baker's Company, 1776/1777 [Ref: A-1146, M-247]. (3) Took the Oath of Allegiance before the Hon. John Barnes before February 28, 1778 [Ref: O-45, J-10]. (4) Private, Select Militia, Capt. Adam Ott's Company, 1781 [Ref: M-238, A-1146, which listed the name as "John Snider"]. (5) Private, Militia, 8th Class, Capt. Barnett Johnston's Company, 3rd Battalion, 1776/1777 [Ref: M-242, which listed the name as "John Snider"]. (6) Private who was recruited and passed by County Lieutenant Thomas Sprigg on April 22, 1780 [Ref: D-336, which listed the name as "John Snider"]. (7) First Corporal, Militia, Capt. John Bennet's Company, 1776/1777 [Ref: M-246, A-1146, which listed the name as "John Shnider"]. (8) One John Snyder died testate in or by 1792 (exact date not given in balance book entry in Washington County), leaving equal shares to Elizabeth Gillium, John Snyder, and David Snyder [Ref: J-31]. (9) Another John Snyder died testate between September and November, 1802, and among his heirs were natural sons Daniel and Peter [Ref: MM-12:81, 82]. See "John Schneider," q.v.

SNYDER, Martin. Private, Militia, 8th Class, Capt. Samuel Hughes' Company, 2nd Battalion, 1776/1777 [Ref: M-238, A-1146, which listed the name as "Martin Snider"]. Took the Oath of Allegiance before the Hon. John Stull in 1778 [Ref: O-47, J-11, which listed the name as "Martin Snider"].

SNYDER, Peter. There appears to have been several men by this name who rendered service during the Revolutionary War. Additional research will be necessary before drawing conclusions. (1) Private, Militia, 1st Class, Capt. Griffin Johnson's Company, 3rd Battalion, 1776/1777 [Ref: M-243, which listed the name as "Peter Snider"]. (2) Private, Militia, 8th Class, Capt. Barnett Johnston's Company, 3rd Battalion, 1776/1777 [Ref: M-242, which listed the name as "Peter Snider"]. (3) One took the Oath of Allegiance before the Hon. William Yates in 1778 [Ref: O-48, J-12]. (4) One Peter Snyder applied for and received pension S3947 in Richland County, Ohio on October 31, 1832, aged 73, stating he was born in 1759 and lived in Washington County, Maryland at the time of his enlistment. In 1803 or 1804 he moved to Bedford County, Pennsylvania for 3 or 4 years and then to Washington County, Pennsylvania for 15 or 20 years and then to Ohio. He died on August 22, 1842 [Ref: V-III:3247]. See "John Snyder," q.v.

SOLLADAY, Philip. See "Phillip Salladay," q.v.

SOLOMON, Samuel. On March 1, 1777 the Committee of Observation ordered that he be paid "the sum of 12/6 [12 shillings, 6 pence] for his services and expences in apprehending delinquents in Capt. Abraham Baker's Company of Militia." [Ref: Q-238, Q-247].

SOOK, Henry. Private, Militia, 5th Class, Capt. John Rennolds' (Reynolds') Company, 2nd Battalion, 1776/1777 [Ref: M-240]. On January 20, 1777 the Committee of Observation resolved "that Henry Sook be exempted from marching with the militia as it appears he is unfit for that service." [Ref: Q-44].

SOOKEY, Martain. Took the Oath of Allegiance before the Hon. John Stull in 1778 [Ref: O-47, J-11].

SOTSSER, Henry. Private, Militia, 2nd Class, Capt. Conrad Nichodemus' Company, 2nd Battalion, 1776/1777 [Ref: M-237, A-1146].

SOUTH, Benjamin. First Sergeant, Militia, Capt. James Smith's Company, 2nd Battalion, 1776/1777 [Ref: M-239, A-1146]. Took the Oath of Allegiance before the Hon. Richard Davis in 1778 [Ref: J-4, O-37]. Ensign, Capt. James Patterson's Company, 2nd Battalion, November 21, 1780 [Ref: G-220].

SOUTH, Hannah and James. See "William South," q.v.

SOUTH, Thomas. Took the Oath of Allegiance before the Hon. Richard Davis in 1778 [Ref: J-3, O-36].

SOUTH, William. Officer, New Jersey Line, who married Hannah ---- in Washington County, Maryland in 1780 or 1782 (she was born there on August 22, 1765) and lived near Hagerstown, Maryland for ten years before moving to Kentucky. Five or six years later they moved to Clermont County, Ohio where he died on June 27, 1811 or June 13, 1812 (both dates were given). Hannah South received pension W4077 and died on October 6, 1843. In 1840 James South, brother of William, made affidavit in Clermont County, Ohio that he served under William South [Ref: V-III:3251]. The Souths were from Middlesex County, New Jersey.

SOUTTER, Felix. Took the Oath of Allegiance before the Hon. Henry Schnebley in 1778 [Ref: O-50, J-13].

SOWER (SOUER), Henry. Rendered patriotic service in Hagerstown by providing "a rifle gun" to Capt. John Nelson's Company, continental service (Maryland Line), April, 1776 [Ref: Q-162].

SOWERS, Michael. Private, Maryland Line, who applied for and received pension S46548 in Fayette County, Pennsylvania on June 18, 1828, a resident of Brownsville, stating he was a German (no age given) and had enlisted at Hagerstown, Maryland [Ref: V-III:3254].

SPACE, Daniel. Took the Oath of Allegiance before the Hon. John Stull in 1778 [Ref: O-47, J-11]. Private, Militia, 4th Class, Capt. James Walling's Company, 2nd Battalion, 1776/1777 [Ref: M-239, A-1146, which listed the name as "Daniel Speace"].

SPANG, Leonard. Enrolled in the third militia company organized for the Revolutionary War in the Elizabeth Town District of Frederick County (now the Hagerstown area of Washington County), passed by the Committee of Observation on June 5, 1776, and assigned to Capt. John Reynolds' command [Ref: Q-273]. Private, Militia, 8th Class, Capt. Joseph Chapline's Company, 2nd Battalion, 1776/1777 [Ref: M-242, which listed the name as "Leonard Spong"]. Took the Oath of Allegiance before the Hon. Christopher Cruse in Sharpsburg Hundred before March 2, 1778 [Ref: O-34, J-2].

SPANGLE, Henry. Private, Militia, 4th Class, Capt. Basil Williams' Company, 1776/1777 [Ref: M-244, A-1146].

SPANGLER, Matthew. Took the Oath of Allegiance before the Hon. Christopher Cruse in Sharpsburg Hundred before March 2, 1778 [Ref: O-34, J-2].

SPANGLER, Matthias. One of several patriots appointed by the Committee of Observation on January 19, 1777 "to form the county into companies (after the militia had marched) for the purpose of relieving the distressed inhabitants of said county and also to compel the Dunkards and Mennonists to give their assistance." [Ref: Q-43].

SPANKAN, Edward. Took the Oath of Allegiance before the Hon. Richard Davis in 1778 [Ref: J-5, O-37].

SPARLING, Andrew. Private, Militia, 4th Class, Capt. John Bennet's Company, 1776/1777 [Ref: M-246, A-1146]. Took the Oath of Allegiance before the Hon. John Barnes before February 28, 1778 [Ref: O-45, J-10].

SPARROW, Alexander. Private who was enlisted by Lieut. Moses Chapline and passed on July 24, 1776 in Frederick (now Washington) County [Ref: D-50].

SPARROW, Jacob. One of several patriots appointed by the Committee of Observation on January 9, 1777 "to procure as many blankets as may be wanting to supply Col. Smith's Battalion." [Ref: Q-34].

SPENCER, Elizabeth and Mary, see "William Groves," q.v.

SPENGLER, Casper. See "Yost Harbaugh," q.v.

SPESSARD (SPESSER), Michael (1750-1825). Private, Militia, 3rd Class, Capt. Samuel Hughes' Company, 2nd Battalion, 1776/1777 [Ref: M-238, A-1146, which listed the name as "Michael Specer"]. Private, Militia, Capt. John Kershner's Company, on duty guarding prisoners of war at

Fort Frederick on June 27, 1778 [Ref: D-328, which listed the name as "Michael Spesser"]. "Michael Spessard" was born in December, 1750, died in April, 1825, and is buried beside Christeanna Spessard (1755-1831) in the Bethel United Brethren Church Graveyard at Chewsville in Washington County, Maryland [Ref: JJ-IV:98].

SPIRES, Ezekiel. Lieutenant, by July, 1776, when Capt. Peter Reed agreed to be his security for collecting fines from non-enrollers and non-associators in his district [Ref: Q-326].

SPIRES, Jeremiah. Captain, Militia, 8th Company, 2nd Battalion, 1776-1778 [Ref: M-124, E-145, M-239]. Took the Oath of Allegiance before the Hon. Richard Davis in 1778 [Ref: J-3, O-36, which listed the name as "Jeramiah Spiers"].

SPIRES, Zachariah. Private, Militia, 1st Class, Capt. Peter Swingle's (Swingley's) Company, 1776/1777 [Ref: A-1146, M-248]. Rendered patriotic service by supplying a blanket for the use of the military in March, 1776, as recorded by the Committee of Observation on April 12, 1776 [Ref: Q-157, L-82].

SPIRES, Zephaniah. Second Lieutenant, Militia, Capt. Basil Williams' Company, 2nd Battalion, June 22, 1778 [Ref: M-124, M-244, E-145].

SPLISE, Peter. Private who was enrolled by Capt. Henry Hardman and passed on July 19, 1776 in Frederick (now Washington) County [Ref: D-51].

SPRIGG, Joseph (1736-1800). Served on the Committee of Observation for the Elizabeth Town District (now the Hagerstown area of Washington County) in December, 1776 [Ref: Q-340]. Took the Oath of Allegiance on May 20, 1777 [Ref: K-1814, Box 4]. Justice of the Orphans Court, June 4, 1777 [Ref: C-275]. Justice of the County Court, June 20, 1778 [Ref: E-141]. Justice of the Peace, January 30, 1781 [Ref: G-293]. Served in the Maryland House of Delegates, 1777-1780, and subsequently relocated to Calvert County, Maryland by 1791 [Ref: KK-I:76-82, KK-II:762-763, which contains more detailed information].

SPRIGG, Joseph. Private, Militia, 4th Class, Capt. Michael Fackler's Company, 1776/1777 [Ref: M-245, A-1146]. Took the Oath of Allegiance before the Hon. Joseph Sprigg before April 1, 1778 [Ref: O-53, O-54, J-15, J-16].

SPRIGG, M. C. See "Philip Strider," q.v.

SPRIGG, Osborn. Private, Militia, 4th Class, Capt. Daniel Clapsaddle's Company, 1st Battalion, 1776/1777 [Ref: M-236, A-1146]. Took the Oath of Allegiance before the Hon. Samuel Hughes before March 1, 1778 [Ref: O-33, J-1].

SPRIGG, Samuel. Private who was enrolled by Capt. Henry Hardman and passed on July 19, 1776 in Frederick (now Washington) County [Ref: D-51]. Took the Oath of Allegiance before the Hon. Richard Davis in 1778 [Ref: J-4, O-37].

SPRIGG, Thomas, of Osborn (c1747-1809). Served on the Committee of Observation in February, 1777 [Ref: Q-228]. Took the Oath of Allegiance on June 7, 1777 [Ref: K-1814, Box 4]. County Lieutenant from December 21, 1779 to at least January 23, 1781 [Ref: M-124, F-39, H-34, D-336, G-179, P-257]. Resigned from serving as Register of Wills on November 25, 1780, and served in the Maryland House of Delegates, 1780-1782 [Ref: G-224, KK-I:84-86, KK-II:766-767, which contains more detailed information].

SPRIGG, Thomas. Private, Militia, 8th Class, Capt. Michael Fackler's Company, 1776/1777 [Ref: M-245, A-1146].

SPROUTS, William. Private, Militia, 8th Class, Capt. John Cellars' Company, 1776/1777 [Ref: A-1146, M-247].

SPURRINGER, George. Private, Militia, 4th Class, Capt. James Smith's Company, 2nd Battalion, 1776/1777 [Ref: M-240, A-1146].

STACK, John. Private, Select Militia, Capt. Adam Ott's Company, 1781 [Ref: M-238, A-1146].

STADDERT, James. Took the Oath of Allegiance before the Hon. Lemuel Barritt on February 25, 1778 [Ref: O-43, J-8].

STADLER, Henry. See "Henry Statler," q.v.

STAIR, Casper. Private, Militia, 4th Class, Capt. Samuel Hughes' Company, 2nd Battalion, 1776/1777 [Ref: M-238, A-1146].

STAIR, Christian. Took the Oath of Allegiance before the Hon. Joseph Sprigg before April 1, 1778 [Ref: O-54, J-16, which listed the name as "Christian Stare"].

STAIR, Frederick. Private, Militia, 4th Class, Capt. Samuel Hughes' Company, 2nd Battalion, 1776/1777 [Ref: M-238, A-1146].

STAIR, Frederick. Private, Militia, 8th Class, Capt. Samuel Hughes' Company, 2nd Battalion, 1776/1777 [Ref: M-238, A-1146].

STAIR, John. Took the Oath of Allegiance before the Hon. Henry Schnebley in 1778 [Ref: O-51, J-14, which listed the name as "John Stare"].

STAKE, George (c1765-1837). Private, Maryland Militia. "Departed this life on Tuesday evening last in this town [Williamsport] in the 72nd year of his age. He was employed at the close of our Revolutionary struggle in the defense of his county and composed one of the guard detailed for the securing the prisoners at Fort Frederick." [Ref: DD-122, citing *The Republican Banner*, February 18, 1837].

STAKE, Martin. Private, Militia, 5th Class, Capt. Peter Beall's Company, 1st Battalion, 1776/1777 [Ref: M-240].
STALE (STAB?), John. Private, Militia, 4th Class, Capt. Conrad Nichodemus' Company, 2nd Battalion, 1776/1777 [Ref: A-1146, M-237].
STALER, William. Took the Oath of Allegiance before the Hon. John Stull in 1778 [Ref: O-47, J-11, which latter source listed the name as "William Slater"].
STALL, Susannah. See "David Seybert," q.v.
STALLINGS, William. Private who was enrolled by Capt. Aeneas Campbell and passed by Major Francis Deakins on July 18, 1776 [Ref: D-49].
STAMBURGH, Phillip. See "Phillip Strumbaugh," q.v.
STANDAGE, Mary. See "George Miller," q.v.
STANDERSON, Gerard. Took the Oath of Allegiance before the Hon. Henry Schnebley in 1778 [Ref: O-51, J-15].
STANTON, Benjamin. Private, Militia, 3rd Class, Capt. Charles Clinton's Company, 1776/1777 [Ref: M-245, A-1146].
STANTON, Michael. Private, Militia, 4th Class, Capt. Charles Clinton's Company, 1776/1777 [Ref: M-245, A-1146].
STAR, William. Took the Oath of Allegiance before the Hon. John Stull in 1778 [Ref: O-47, J-11].
STARE, Christian. See "Christian Stair," q.v.
START, John G. (1745-1811). John G. Start died on March 16, 1811, aged 66 years, 3 months, 6 days, and is buried in the cemetery at St. Paul's Lutheran Reformed Church on Route 40 near Clearspring in Washington County [Ref: JJ-V:92]. Although no military service has been found under this name, there was a John Start who served in the 4th Battalion of Talbot County, Maryland Militia, in 1776 [Ref: D-67]. Additional research will be necessary before drawing conclusions.
STARTZMAN, Adam. Private, Militia, 7th Class, Capt. Michael Fackler's Company, 1776/1777 [Ref: M-245, A-1146, which listed the name as "Adam Stasman"]. Private, Select Militia, Capt. Adam Ott's Company, 1781 [Ref: M-238, A-1146, which listed the name as "Adam Stertzman"].
STARTZMAN, Daniel. Private, Militia, 1st Class, Capt. Isaac Baker's Company, 1776/1777 [Ref: A-1146, M-247, which listed the name as "Daniel Statsman"]. Rendered patriotic service by providing a rifle for Capt. Daniel Cresap's Company in July, 1775, as recorded by the Committee of Observation at Elizabeth Town on November 4, 1775 [Ref: Q-149, which listed the name as "Daniel Stutsman"].

STARTZMAN, David. Private, Militia, 1st Class, Capt. Isaac Baker's Company, 1776/1777 [Ref: A-1146, M-247, which listed the name as "David Statsman"].

STARTZMAN, Eve. See "Henry Startzman," q.v.

STARTZMAN, Henry (1748-1811). One of several patriots appointed by the Committee of Observation on December 30, 1776 "to form the county into companies (after the militia had marched) for the purpose of relieving the distressed inhabitants of said county and also to compel the Dunkards and Mennonists to give their assistance." [Ref: Q-345, which listed the name as "Henry Stertzman"]. Rendered patriotic service by supplying a blanket for the use of the military in March, 1776, as recorded by the Committee of Observation on April 12, 1776 [Ref: L-82, Q-157, which latter source listed the name as "Henry Stertsman"]. Took the Oath of Allegiance before the Hon. Henry Schnebley in 1778 [Ref: O-49, J-13]. Rendered patriotic service by supplying wheat and corn for the use of the military on March 14, 1780 [Ref: W-1190, and HH-73, which listed the name as "Henry Startzman, Sr."]. Henry Startzman was born on May 5, 1749, died on April 23, 1811, was buried in Old St. John's Lutheran Churchyard, and subsequently reinterred in Rose Hill Cemetery in Hagerstown [Ref: JJ-VII:104]. Eve Startzman, relict of the late Henry Startzman, died at the residence of her son-in-law Jacob Firey, about 4 miles from Hagerstown on June 7, 1825, in her 83rd year, and was interred in the Lutheran burial ground. She was the mother of 9 children (of whom four are dead) and lived to see 64 grand children and 8 great-grandchildren [Ref: Z-74, Z-75].

STARTZMAN, Henry Jr. Private, Militia, 8th Class, Capt. Martin Kershner's Company, 1776/1777 [Ref: A-1146, M-248, which listed the name as "Henry Statsman, Jr."]. Took the Oath of Allegiance before the Hon. Henry Schnebley in 1778 [Ref: O-49, which listed the name without the "Jr." and J-13, which listed the name as "Henry Startman"]. Rendered patriotic service by supplying corn for the use of the military on March 14, 1780 [Ref: W-1190, HH-73, which both listed the name with the "Jr."].

STARTZMAN, John George. Took the Oath of Allegiance before the Hon. Joseph Sprigg before April 1, 1778 [Ref: O-53, J-16, which listed the name as "John George Stortzman"].

STATLER, Henry. See "Henry Stotler," q.v.

STAUFER, Mathias. Private, Militia, 3rd Class, Capt. Conrad Nichodemus' Company, 2nd Battalion, 1776/1777 [Ref: M-237, A-1146].

STEEL, John. Private who was enrolled by Capt. Aeneas Campbell and passed by Major Francis Deakins on July 18, 1776 [Ref: D-49].

363

STEER, Michael. Private, Militia, 2nd Class, Capt. Samuel Hughes' Company, 2nd Battalion, 1776/1777 [Ref: M-238, A-1146].

STEFFEE (STIFFER), Andrew. Private, Militia, 8th Class, Capt. Samuel Hughes' Company, 2nd Battalion, 1776/1777 [Ref: M-238, A-1146]. One "Andrew Steffee" died before November 14, 1801 (date of balance book entry in Washington County), leaving a widow (no name given in this account) and equal shares to Andrew, Nicholas, George, Michael, Peter, and Elizabeth Steffee, and Catherine Augustine [Ref: J-39].

STEFFEE, Elizabeth. See "Andrew Steffee," q.v.

STEFFEE (STIFFER), George. Third Sergeant, Militia, Capt. Samuel Hughes' Company, 1776/1777 [Ref: A-1146, M-238, which listed the name as "George Stiffer (Stiffee?)"]. See "Andrew Steffee," q.v.

STEFFEE, Michael, Nicholas and Peter. See "Andrew Steffee," q.v.

STEIN, Jacob. Private, Militia, 3rd Class, Capt. Barnett Johnston's Company, 3rd Battalion, 1776/1777 [Ref: M-242].

STEINVAUFFER, John. Took the Oath of Allegiance before the Hon. Henry Schnebley in 1778 [Ref: O-51, J-14].

STEMPLE, Godfreit. One of several patriots appointed by the Committee of Observation on December 30, 1776 "to form the county into companies (after the militia had marched) for the purpose of relieving the distressed inhabitants of said county and also to compel the Dunkards and Mennonists to give their assistance." [Ref: Q-346]. Took the Oath of Allegiance before the Hon. Henry Schnebley in 1778 [Ref: O-49, J-12, which listed the name as "Godfries Stampel"].

STERRONTON, George. Private, Militia, 2nd Class, Capt. Barnett Johnston's Company, 3rd Battalion, 1776/1777 [Ref: M-242].

STEVENS, James and Mary. See "John Burk," q.v.

STEWARD, Thomas. Took the Oath of Allegiance before the Hon. Christopher Cruse in Sharpsburg Hundred before March 2, 1778 [Ref: O-34, J-2].

STEWART, George. Took the Oath of Allegiance before the Hon. Joseph Sprigg before April 1, 1778 [Ref: O-53, J-16].

STEWART, Harrietta. See "Zadock Williams," q.v.

STEWART, James. Ensign, Militia, Capt. Joseph Chapline's Company, 2nd Battalion, June 22, 1778 [Ref: M-125, E-145]. Took the Oath of Allegiance before the Hon. Joseph Sprigg before April 1, 1778 [Ref: O-53, J-16].

STEWART, James. Private who was enlisted by Ensign Nathan Williams and passed on July 25, 1776 in Frederick (now Washington) County [Ref: D-51]. Took the Oath of Allegiance before the Hon. Christopher Cruse in Sharpsburg Hundred before March 2, 1778 [Ref: O-34, J-1].

STEWART, Jeremiah. See "William Stewart," q.v.

STEWART, John (1755-c1840). Sergeant, Maryland and Pennsylvania Lines, who applied for pension (S14585) in Clermont County, Ohio on November 8, 1832, stating he was born on February 1, 1755 in Lancaster County, Pennsylvania, moved to Hagerstown, Maryland in 1775, and was drafted on December 26, 1776. He served his time and then returned to his father's home (no name given) in Lancaster County. He enlisted in York County in October, 1779 and was still in service in 1781 or 1782. He moved from Pennsylvania to Fayette County, Kentucky, near Lexington, and then to Clermont County, Ohio to live with his nephew William Boyds. In 1833 he moved back to Kentucky to be with his friends and was still there in 1835 [Ref: U-23:2 (1935) and V-III:3336, which latter source had inadvertently omitted the pension application number].

STEWART, William (c1761-1831). Soldier who resided in Washington County and was granted a pension certificate in August, 1820, according to an Act of Congress of March 18, 1818, since he had proven that he was "in the enjoyment of a certain degree of poverty" as required by the Act as amended on May 1, 1820 [Ref: W-1190]. Private, Pennsylvania Line, who received pension S35089 at $96 per year effective August 1, 1820, aged 58, and referred to his son Jeremiah Stewart, aged 4, but did not mention his wife [Ref: R-43, V-III:3330]. There were several men named William Stewart who served in the Revolutionary War, including one who was born in Maryland circa 1760, married Elizabeth Clinton, served as a lieutenant and adjutant in Pennsylvania, and died on February 5, 1831 in New York [Ref: Y-III:2809]. Additional research will be necessary before drawing conclusions.

STEYER, John. See "John Tobias Stoyer," q.v.

STIFFER, Andrew. See "Andrew Steffee," q.v.

STILDIBRAN, Philip. Rendered patriotic service by providing a rifle for Capt. Daniel Cresap's Company in July, 1775, as recorded by the Committee of Observation at Elizabeth Town on November 4, 1775 [Ref: Q-148].

STILLE, Anna Maria. See "Christian Orendorff, Jr.," q.v.

STILLWELL, Jeremiah. Second Corporal, Militia, Capt. Barnett Johnston's Company, 3rd Battalion, 1776/1777 [Ref: M-242, which listed the name as "Jeremiah Silwell"]. Took the Oath of Allegiance before the Hon. William Yates in 1778 [Ref: O-48, J-12].

STILLWELL, Stephen. Private, Militia, 5th Class, Capt. Peter Swingle's (Swingley's) Company, 1776/1777 [Ref: A-1146, M-248]. Took the Oath of Allegiance before the Hon. Henry Schnebley in 1778 [Ref: O-50, J-14, which listed the name as "Stephen Stettwell"].

STOCK, John. Private, Militia, 3rd Class, Capt. Peter Swingle's (Swingley's) Company, 1776/1777 [Ref: A-1146, M-248].

STOCKEY, Jacob. See "Jacob Stuckey," q.v.

STOCKWELL, James. Took the Oath of Allegiance before September 1, 1780 [Ref: X-121].

STOCKWELL, Michael. Private, Militia, 6th Class, Capt. Griffin Johnson's Company, 3rd Battalion, 1776/1777 [Ref: M-243].

STOCKWELL, William. Private, Militia, 2nd Class, Capt. John Rennolds' (Reynolds') Company, 2nd Battalion, 1776/1777 [Ref: M-240].

STOCKWELL, William. Private, Militia, 7th Class, Capt. Barnett Johnston's Company, 3rd Battalion, 1776/1777 [Ref: M-242].

STOGDON, Thomas. Private who was enlisted by Capt. John Reynolds and passed on July 18, 1776 in Frederick (now Washington) County [Ref: D-50].

STOLL, Henry. See "Henry Stull," q.v.

STONE, Thomas. See "James Gillespie," q.v.

STONE, William. Private, Militia, 3rd Class, Capt. Conrad Hogmire's Company, 1776/1777 [Ref: M-244, A-1146].

STONEBRAKER, Adam. Private, Militia, Capt. William Heyser's Company, enlisted August 22, 1776, muster roll dated October 23, 1776, in continental service [Ref: D-264, which listed the name as "Adam Stonebreaker" and W-1190, which listed the name as "Adam Stonebraker" and L-79, which listed the name as "Adam Stonebrake"]. Corporal, German Regiment, Lt. Col. Ludwick Weltner's Company, after May 22, 1777, and discharged on July 26, 1779 [Ref: D-264, D-251, GG-99, which latter source listed him as "Adam Stonebreaker, of Hagerstown"].

STONEBRAKER, Gerrett. Private, Militia, 6th Class, Capt. Jacob Sharer's Company, 1776/1777 [Ref: A-1146, M-248].

STONEBRAKER, Michael. Private, Militia, 2nd Class, Capt. Jeremiah Spires' Company, 2nd Battalion, 1776/1777 [Ref: M-239, A-1146].

STONEBRAKER, Valentine. Private, Militia, 5th Class, Capt. James Smith's Company, 2nd Battalion, 1776/1777 [Ref: M-240, A-1146].

STONEKING, Henry. Private, Militia, 3rd Class, Capt. John Cellars' Company, 1776/1777 [Ref: A-1146, M-246].

STONER, John. Private who was enrolled by Capt. Henry Hardman and passed on July 19, 1776 in Frederick (now Washington) County [Ref: D-51].

STONESIFER, Daniel. Private, Militia, 1st Class, Capt. Conrad Nichodemus' Company, 2nd Battalion, 1776/1777 [Ref: M-237, A-1146].

STONESIFER, John. Second Sergeant, Militia, Capt. Peter Beall's Company, 1st Battalion, 1776/1777 [Ref: M-240, which listed the name as "John Stonecyfer"].

STOOKEY, Peter. See "Peter Stuckey," q.v.

STORAM, Jacob. See "Jacob Stroam," q.v.

STORMS, Abraham (1755-1842). "Died at Lebanon, Ohio, on May 4, 1842, in his 87th year, Abraham Storms, a Revolutionary soldier." [Ref: EE-10:2 (p. 55), containing Robert W. Barnes' article citing the *Baltimore Sun*, May 11, 1842].

STOSSER, George. Private, Militia, 2nd Class, Capt. Conrad Nichodemus' Company, 2nd Battalion, 1776/1777 [Ref: M-237, A-1146].

STOTHERD, James. Private, Militia, 1st Class, Capt. James Prather's Company, 3rd Battalion, 1776/1777 [Ref: M-242].

STOTLER, Betsey and Christiana. See "Henry Stotler," q.v.

STOTLER, Esther. See "Henry Funk," q.v.

STOTLER (STATLER), Henry (1757-1837). Private, Militia, Capt. William Heyser's Company, enlisted August 4, 1776, muster roll dated October 23, 1776, which mistakenly stated he had deserted [Ref: D-264, W-1190, L-79, which latter source listed the name as "Henry Stadler"]. Private, German Regiment, Lt. Col. Ludwick Weltner's Company, continental service, discharged on October 12, 1779 at Fort Wyoming, Pennsylvania [Ref: D-265, GG-99, which listed the name as "Henry Statler, Stotler, Stalter"]. A pension was applied for by his widow (no name given) and children (W15803) on May 18, 1841 in Washington County, Maryland, stating Henry had died between April 25 and May 2, 1837, aged about 81, leaving three children: John (aged 41 in 1841), Nancy, and Betsey [Ref: GG-99, N-50, V-III:3364, which latter sources listed the name as "Henry Stotler"]. "Henry Stotler" was born on January 15, 1757, died on April 30, 1757, and is buried beside Christiana Stotler (1759-1825) in a graveyard on the Charles Clopper farm near Bagtown in Washington County, Maryland [Ref: JJ-IV:97].

STOTLER (STATLER), John. Took the Oath of Allegiance before the Hon. John Cellars in January, 1778 [Ref: K-1814, O-40, J-5, which latter source listed the name as "John Statlen"]. See "Henry Funk" and "Henry Stotler," q.v.

STOTLER, Nancy. See "Henry Stotler," q.v.

STOTTS, Sarah. See "Solomon Royse," q.v.

STOVER, Catherine. See "Michael Stover," q.v.

STOVER, Christopher. Private, Militia, 7th Class, Capt. Conrad Hogmire's Company, 1776/1777 [Ref: M-244, A-1146].
STOVER, Frederick and George. See "Michael Stover," q.v.
STOVER, Jacob. Private, Militia, 2nd Class, Capt. James Walling's Company, 2nd Battalion, 1776/1777 [Ref: M-238, A-1146]. See "Michael Stover," q.v.
STOVER, John and Margaret. See "Michael Stover," q.v.
STOVER, Mathias. See "Mathias Staufer," q.v.
STOVER, Michael. Third Sergeant, Militia, Capt. Peter Swingle's (Swingley's) Company, 2nd Battalion, 1776/1777 [Ref: M-248, A-1146]. Took the Oath of Allegiance before the Hon. Richard Davis in 1778 [Ref: J-4, O-36, which latter source listed the name as "Michael Stower"]. Second Lieutenant, Capt. Nicholas Mourer's Company, 2nd Battalion, November 21, 1778 [Ref: G-220]. Michael Stover died by 1801 (exact date not given in the balance book in Washington County), leaving a widow (no name given, but Catherine Stover was the administratrix) and equal shares to John, George, Jacob, Frederick, Margaret, and Catherine Stover [Ref: J-39].
STOYER (STEYER), John Tobias (1762-1854). Private, Pennsylvania Militia, applied for and received pension (S7633) in Allegany County, Maryland at $33.33 per year under the Act of June 7, 1832 retroactive to March 4, 1831, stating he was born on June 20, 1762 about 15 miles from Little York, Pennsylvania, lived there at the time of his enlistment, and moved to Allegany County, Maryland after the war [Ref: R-45, V-III:3369]. "John Tobias Steyer" was born in Pennsylvania on June 20, 1762, married Elizabeth Eckert, and died on April 6, 1854 in Maryland [Ref: Y-III:2809].
STRATFORD, Joshua. Private, Militia, 8th Class, Capt. James Prather's Company, 3rd Battalion, 1776/1777 [Ref: M-243]. Took the Oath of Allegiance before the Hon. Lemuel Barritt before March 16, 1778 [Ref: O-43, J-8].
STRAYLY, Wentle. Private, Militia, Capt. William Heyser's Company, muster roll dated October 23, 1776, in continental service, died on January 15, 1777 [Ref: D-264, W-1190, L-79, which also listed the name as "Wentle Strayly" and G-99, which listed the name as "Wendel Strayley"].
STRICKER, Edney. See "John Ferguson," q.v.
STRIDER, Killian. Enrolled in the third militia company organized for the Revolutionary War in the Elizabeth Town District of Frederick County (now the Hagerstown area of Washington County), passed by the Committee of Observation on June 5, 1776, and assigned to Capt. John

Reynolds' command [Ref: Q-272]. Took the Oath of Allegiance before the Hon. Christopher Cruse in Sharpsburg Hundred before March 2, 1778 [Ref: O-35, J-2, which listed the name as "Kilian Strider"].

STRIDER, Philip (c1750-1840/1). Enrolled in the first militia company organized for the Revolutionary War in the Elizabeth Town District of Frederick County (now the Hagerstown area of Washington County) on January 6, 1776 [Ref: Q-271, W-1190]. Took the Oath of Allegiance before the Hon. John Stull in 1778 [Ref: O-47, J-11]. On April 6, 1841 the Treasurer of the Western Shore of Maryland was directed to pay to "M. C. Sprigg, for legal representative of Philip Strider, late of Bedford County, Pennsylvania and pensioner of the State of Maryland, who died January 6, 1840 [sic], $12.93, amount of arrears due him from September 10, 1840 [sic] to day of his death." [Ref: AA-397].

STRIDER, William. Private, Militia, 6th Class, Capt. Joseph Chapline's Company, 2nd Battalion, 1776/1777 [Ref: M-241].

STROAM, Henry. Private, Militia, Capt. William Heyser's Company, enlisted July 17, 1776, muster roll dated October 23, 1776, in continental service, which mistakenly reported he had deserted [Ref: D-264, W-1190, L-79]. Private, German Regiment, Lt. Col. Ludwick Weltner's Company, discharged on July 17, 1779 at Fort Wyoming, Pennsylvania [Ref: D-265, GG-99, which listed the name as "Henry Stroam, Straam"].

STROAM, Jacob. Private who was enrolled by Capt. Henry Hardman and passed on July 19, 1776 in Frederick (now Washington) County [Ref: D-51, which listed the name as "Jacob Storam"].

STRONG, James. Private, Militia, 8th Class, Capt. John Bennet's Company, 1776/1777 [Ref: M-246, A-1146]. Took the Oath of Allegiance before the Hon. John Barnes before February 28, 1778 [Ref: O-45, J-9].

STRUMBAUGH, George and Magdelena. See "Phillip Strumbaugh," q.v.

STRUMBAUGH, Phillip. Private, Militia, 1st Class, Capt. Conrad Hogmire's Company, 1776/1777 [Ref: M-244, A-1146, which listed the name as "Phillip Stamburgh"]. "Phillip Strumbaugh" died before April 18, 1801 (date of balance book entry in Washington County), leaving a widow (no name given, but Magdelena Strumbaugh and Matthias Young were administrators) and equal shares to George Strumbaugh and Magdelena Young [Ref: J-39].

STUART, George. Private, Militia, 3rd Class, Capt. Daniel Clapsaddle's Company, 1st Battalion, 1776/1777 [Ref: M-236, A-1146].

STUART, George. Private, Militia, 7th Class, Capt. Peter Swingle's (Swingley's) Company, 1776/1777 [Ref: A-1146, M-249].

STUART, George. Private, Militia, Capt. John Kershner's Company, on duty guarding prisoners of war at Fort Frederick on June 27, 1778 [Ref: D-328].
STUART, James. Enrolled in the first militia company organized for the Revolutionary War in the Elizabeth Town District of Frederick County (now the Hagerstown area of Washington County) on January 6, 1776 [Ref: Q-270, W-1189].
STUART, Thomas. Enrolled in the first militia company organized for the Revolutionary War in the Elizabeth Town District of Frederick County (now the Hagerstown area of Washington County) on January 6, 1776 [Ref: Q-270, W-1190]. Private, Militia, 6th Class, Capt. Peter Swingle's (Swingley's) Company, 1776/1777 [Ref: A-1146, M-248].
STUART, Thomas. Fourth Sergeant, Militia, Capt. John Rennolds' (Reynolds') Company, 2nd Battalion, 1776/1777 [Ref: M-240].
STUCKEY, Jacob. Private, Militia, 7th Class, Capt. Isaac Baker's Company, 1776/1777 [Ref: A-1146, M-247, which listed the name as "Jacob Stockey"]. Simon Stuckey died testate by March 19, 1796 (date of balance book entry in Washington County) and one of his sons was Jacob Stuckey [Ref: J-35].
STUCKEY, Peter. Private, Militia, 7th Class, Capt. Daniel Clapsaddle's Company, 1st Battalion, 1776/1777 [Ref: M-236, A-1146]. Took the Oath of Allegiance before September 1, 1780 [Ref: X-121, which listed the name as "Peter Stookey"].
STUCKEY, Simon. See "Jacob Stuckey," q.v.
STUDANBAKER, Mary. See "John Miller," q.v.
STUDEBAKER, Jacob. Private, Militia, 2nd Class, Capt. John Cellars' Company, 1776/1777 [Ref: A-1146, M-246].
STUDER, Philip. Soldier who resided in Washington County and was granted a pension certificate in August, 1820, according to an Act of Congress of March 18, 1818, since he had proven that he was "in the enjoyment of a certain degree of poverty" as required by the Act as amended on May 1, 1820 [Ref: W-1190].
STULL, Daniel, of John (1755-   ). First Lieutenant, Upper District, Frederick County (now Washington County), July, 1776, and captain, 7th Maryland Line, 1776-1778 (resigned). [Ref: D-48, KK-II:792].
STULL, Henry. Took the Oath of Allegiance before the Hon. John Barnes before February 28, 1778 [Ref: O-44, J-9, which listed the name as "Henry Stoll"].
STULL, John (1733-1791). Appointed to raise funds on January 24, 1775 for the Committee of Observation in Elizabeth Hundred in Frederick (now Washington) County [Ref: L-75]. Elected to serve as president of

the Committee of Observation for the Elizabeth Town District on September 12, 1775 [Ref: Q-142], and which referred to as "Coll. John Stull" on February 19, 1776 [Ref: Q-152]. Appointed by the Committee of Observation to carry the Association of Freemen to male residents in his hundred (district) on March 4, 1776 "and present it for signing and make an exact account of those that sign and those that refuse with their reasons for refusing." [Ref: Q-153, L-82]. Rendered patriotic service by supplying a blanket for the use of the military in March, 1776, as recorded by the Committee of Observation on April 12, 1776 [Ref: Q-157, L-82]. Served on the Committee of Observation in April, 1776 [Ref: Q-154, Q-155]. Served on the Committee of Observation for the Elizabeth Town District in December, 1776 [Ref: Q-340]. Reimbursed by the Committee for money advanced from the publick fines on April 24, 1777 [Ref: Q-248]. Justice of the Orphans Court, June 4, 1777 [Ref: C-275]. Justice who administered the Oath of Allegiance in 1778 [Ref: O-47, O-47, J-10, J-11]. Justice of the County Court, June 20, 1778 [Ref: E-141]. Rendered patriotic service by supplying rye and corn for the use of the military on April 11, 1780 [Ref: W-1190, HH-72, which both listed the name as "Col. John Stull"] and supplying wheat on February 23, 1780 [Ref: HH-73, which listed the name as "John Stull"]. Justice of the Peace and Judge of the Orphans Court, January 30, 1781, and served in the Maryland House of Delegates, 1779-1785 [Ref: G-293, K-I:82-90, K-II:792-793, which contains more detailed information]. "John Stull, of Hagerstown, was of German birth and his speech was broken English. He was a man of remarkable force of character, of excellent judgment, and a strict sense of justice. He became so accustomed to deciding causes and the people became so accustomed to looking up to him for guidance with firm confidence in his ability and rectitude, that it seemed the most natural thing that he should be a member of the Court which under the first constitution was composed of a law Judge and the Justices of the Peace, as soon as the County was organized." [Ref: L-76]. Col. John Stull, late President of the Washington County Court, died on the Saturday before April 13, 1791, at an advanced age [Ref: LL-1:30]. See "Mark Hardin," q.v.

STULL, Mary. On January 18, 1777 the Committee of Observation "ordered that Capt. Henry Butler obtain an order on Mrs. Mary Stull for two hundred dollars to enable him to march his company to camp." [Ref: Q-43].

STULL, Susannah. See "Mark Hardin," q.v.

STUP, Joseph. Private, Militia, 2nd Class, Capt. Martin Kershner's Company, 1776/1777 [Ref: A-1146, M-247].

STUTTS, Henry. Private, Militia, 5th Class, Capt. John Bennet's Company, 1776/1777 [Ref: M-246, A-1146].

STYDINGER (STEIDINGER), Frederick (1727-1790). One of several patriots appointed by the Committee of Observation on December 30, 1776 "to form the county into companies (after the militia had marched) for the purpose of relieving the distressed inhabitants of said county and also to compel the Dunkards and Mennonists to give their assistance." [Ref: Q-345]. Appointed by the Committee of Observation on January 1, 1777 to act as quartermaster in Elizabeth Town and "to provide quarters for recruits or soldiers belonging to the United States." [Ref: Q-28]. Elected to the Committee of Observation on January 7, 1777 in the room of Capt. Michael Fackler whose seat was vacated by his being in actual service [Ref: Q-33, Q-228]. Took the Oath of Allegiance before the Hon. Joseph Sprigg before April 1, 1778 [Ref: O-53, which listed the name as "Frederick Stidinger" and J-15, which listed the name as "Frederick Stiginger"]. Rendered patriotic service by supplying wheat for the use of the military on March 22, 1780 [Ref: W-1190, which listed the name as "Frederick Stydenger" and HH-73, which listed the name as "Fredk. Stydinger"]. Frederick and wife Magdalena were buried in Old St. John's Lutheran Churchyard and subsequently reinterred in Rose Hill Cemetery in Hagerstown. His tombstone has been transcribed as follows: *"Got Freidrich Steidinger, Gebohvan in Jahr 1727, d. 2 April im Deitland in Hertzoctum Wirtenbreg im Weittershaus sem er Drat in die ehmit Marlamaedelean Schauerim A 1751, d. 10 May und Zeygter 8 kinder Nerilich 3 sons und 5 tegter ?? storb im iar Christ 1790 d. a4 Decem."* His wife's tombstone has been transcribed as follows: *"Magdalena Steidinger, siemar beg 1724 im April starb 27 fen Non 1801 u ist Hftmon eir 77y 7m."* [Ref: JJ-VII:104 (which tombstone transcriptions contained some spelling errors, but were copied verbatim herein), and LL-1:29].

STYER, George. Private, Militia, 4th Class, Capt. Basil Williams' Company, 1776/1777 [Ref: M-244, A-1146]. On January 25, 1777 the Committee of Observation ordered "that Mr. George Styer deliver unto Thomas Brooke all the powder left in his care." [Ref: Q-51].

STYER, John. See "John Tobias Stoyer," q.v.

SUDER, Peter. See "Peter Suter," q.v.

SUGART, John. Private, Militia, 4th Class, Capt. Barnett Johnston's Company, 3rd Battalion, 1776/1777 [Ref: M-242].

SULF, Jacob. Private, Militia, 5th Class, Capt. Joseph Chapline's Company, 2nd Battalion, 1776/1777 [Ref: M-241].

SULIVANE, Philip. Private who was enrolled by Lieut. Clement Hollyday and passed by Major Francis Deakins on July 25, 1776 [Ref: D-49].

SULLEMS, Henry. Private, Militia, 3rd Class, Capt. James Walling's Company, 2nd Battalion, 1776/1777 [Ref: M-238, A-1146].

SUNON, Peter. See "Peter Simon," q.v.

SUTER, Philip (1748-1818). Enrolled in the third militia company organized for the Revolutionary War in the Elizabeth Town District of Frederick County (now the Hagerstown area of Washington County), passed by the Committee of Observation on June 5, 1776, and assigned to Capt. John Reynolds' command [Ref: Q-273, which listed the name as "Peter Suder"]. "Peter Suter" died on April 4, 1818, aged 70, was buried in Old St. John's Lutheran Churchyard, and subsequently reinterred in Rose Hill Cemetery in Hagerstown [Ref: JJ-VII:104].

SUTHERLAND, Catharine and Nancy. See "William Sutherland," q.v.

SUTHERLAND, William (c1748-1843). Private, Maryland Line, who applied for pension in Casey County, Kentucky on April 19, 1833, aged 85, stating he lived at Hagerstown, Maryland at the time of his enlistment in the fall of 1776. He married Catharine Ensminger in Rockbridge County, Virginia on August 6, 1789 (by Rev. John Brown). William died on July 20, 1843, at which time he had 2 children (not named) over age 50. His widow applied for and received pension W8771 in Boyle County, Kentucky (just inside the Casey County line) on November 9, 1843, aged 76, and mentioned her children but only named Nancy Sutherland [Ref: V-III:3393, T-21].

SWALES, William. Private, Militia, 6th Class, Capt. Griffin Johnson's Company, 3rd Battalion, 1776/1777 [Ref: M-243]. Took the Oath of Allegiance before the Hon. William Yates in 1778 [Ref: O-48, J-12, which listed the name as "William Swails"].

SWAN, James. Took the Oath of Allegiance before the Hon. Lemuel Barritt before March 16, 1778 [Ref: O-42, J-8].

SWAN, John. Appointed to raise funds on January 24, 1775 for the Committee of Observation in Elizabeth Hundred in Frederick (now Washington) County [Ref: L-75]. Rendered patriotic service by providing store goods for the use of the military in July, 1775, as recorded by the Committee of Observation at Elizabeth Town on November 4, 1775 [Ref: Q-150]. In November, 1775, John Shryack made accusations that John Swan was "an enemy to America" and the matter was brought before the Committee of Observation. They found no basis for the charges and Swan was acquitted [Ref: Q-147].

SWAN, Robert. See "Rezin Simpson," q.v.

SWANK, David. Ensign, Militia, Capt. Charles Clinton's Company, 3rd or Western Battalion, May 16, 1778 [Ref: M-127, E-86, M-245, A-1146]. Took the Oath of Allegiance before the Hon. Andrew Bruce before March 2, 1778 [Ref: O-41, J-6, which latter source listed the name as "David Wank"].
SWANK, Jacob. Private, Militia, 5th Class, Capt. Jacob Sharer's Company, 1776/1777 [Ref: A-1146, M-248]. Took the Oath of Allegiance before the Hon. John Stull in 1778 [Ref: O-47, J-11].
SWANK, John. Private, Militia, 6th Class, Capt. Jacob Sharer's Company, 1776/1777 [Ref: A-1146, M-248].
SWANK, Peter. Ensign, Militia, Capt. Conrad Nichodemus' Company, 2nd Battalion, June 22, 1778 [Ref: M-127, E-145].
SWATZEL, Christian. Private, Militia, 1st Class, Capt. Peter Swingle's (Swingley's) Company, 1776/1777 [Ref: A-1146, M-248].
SWATZELL, John. Private, Militia, 8th Class, Capt. Peter Swingle's (Swingley's) Company, 1776/1777 [Ref: A-1146, M-249].
SWEARINGEN, Benoni. Private, Militia, 4th Class, Capt. Joseph Chapline's Company, 2nd Battalion, 1776/1777 [Ref: M-241, which listed the name as "Bennona Swearengan"]. Ensign, Select Militia, Capt. Joseph Chapline's Company, June 4, 1781 [Ref: M-127, G-459, which listed the name as "Benone Swearingan"].
SWEARINGEN, Charles (1733-1818). Elected to serve on the Committee of Observation for the Elizabeth Town District (now the Hagerstown area of Washington County) on September 12, 1775 [Ref: Q-142, which listed the name as "Charles Sweringen"], and referred to as "Major Charles Swearingen" on February 19, 1776 [Ref: Q-152]. Appointed by the Committee of Observation to serve on a Committee for Licensing Suits on September 14, 1775 [Ref: Q-142, which listed the name as "Charles Sweringen"]. Rendered patriotic service by supplying a blanket for the use of the military in March, 1776, as recorded by the Committee of Observation on April 12, 1776 [Ref: Q-156, L-82]. Served on the Committee of Observation in April, 1776 [Ref: Q-154, Q-155]. Second Major, Militia, 36th Battalion, Frederick County, January 6, 1776, and First Major, April 20, 1776. Lieutenant Colonel, Militia, 2nd Battalion, Washington County, June 22, 1778 [Ref: M-127, A-356, E-145, G-220]. Took the Oath of Allegiance before the Hon. John Stull in 1778 [Ref: O-47, J-11, which latter source listed the name as "Charles Swearinger"]. On January 20, 1777 the Committee of Observation resolved "that Samuel Swearingen, son of Major Charles Swearingen, be exempted from Marching with the militia as it appears to Committee that he is not 16 years of age." [Ref: Q-44]. "Died Friday morning

October 27, 1820 at her residence on Conococheague Manor [Washington County], Mrs. Susanna Swearingen, relict of the late Col. Charles Swearingen, in the 82nd year of her age, married for upwards of 59 years, raised a large family, several of whom and their branches are now to be found in Maryland, Virginia, Kentucky and Illinois." [Ref: Z-33]. Col. Charles Swearingen died on June 27, 1818, aged 85, and is buried beside his wife Susanna ("died age 83 years, lived together 61 years") in a graveyard on the Joe Mullendore farm at Antietam Creek and Devil's Backbone in Washington County [Ref: JJ-V:49].

SWEARINGEN, Drusilla. See "John Booth," q.v.

SWEARINGEN, Elizabeth. See "Van Swearingen," q.v.

SWEARINGEN, Major. See "Frederick Power," q.v.

SWEARINGEN, Samuel. Appointed by the Committee of Observation on July 7, 1776 "to take the number of inhabitants within Marsh Hundred, both whites and blacks, distinguishing respectively the age and sex of each, to be transmitted to the Council of Safety immediately." [Ref: Q-331]. Took the Oath of Allegiance before the Hon. Richard Davis in 1778 [Ref: J-4, O-37]. See "Charles Swearingen," q.v.

SWEARINGEN, Samuel Jr. Private, Militia, 8th Class, Capt. Peter Swingle's (Swingley's) Company, 1776/1777 [Ref: A-1146, M-249, which listed the name as "Samuel Swereingen Junr"].

SWEARINGEN, Sarah. See "Van Swearingen," q.v.

SWEARINGEN, Susannah. See "Charles Swearingen," q.v.

SWEARINGEN, Thomas. Appointed by the Committee of Observation to carry the Association of Freemen to male residents in Conococheague Hundred on September 14, 1775 "and require their subscription to the same and make an exact account of those who sign and those that refuse with their reasons for refusing." [Ref: Q-143, which listed the name as "Thomas Sweringen"]. One of several patriots appointed by the Committee of Observation on December 30, 1776 "to form the county into companies (after the militia had marched) for the purpose of relieving the distressed inhabitants of said county and also to compel the Dunkards and Mennonists to give their assistance." [Ref: Q-345, which listed the name as "Thomas Swearengen"].

SWEARINGEN, Van. Took the Oath of Allegiance before the Hon. Richard Davis in 1778 [Ref: J-4, which listed the name as "Van Sweringen" and O-37, which listed the name as "Van Swaringen"]. Rendered patriotic service by providing clothing for the use of the military on July 5, 1778 [Ref: CC-106, which listed the name as "Van Sweringen, Sr."]. Also see pension application S31401 about one Van Swearingen who was born on November 3, 1754 about 10 miles from

Hagerstown, Maryland, in 1770 moved to what is now Fayette County, Pennsylvania, served in the Maryland and Pennsylvania Lines, married Sarah ----, moved to Virginia and then to Kentucky, and applied for pension in Shelby County, Kentucky in 1832. He died on July 28, 1839. Another Van Swearingen also served in the Pennsylvania Line and later to Virginia where he died in 1793. His widow Elizabeth married John Newhouse in 1799, moved to Kentucky and then to Hamilton County, Ohio and received pension W5415 [Ref: V-III:3401]. Additional research may be necessary before drawing conclusions.

SWINGLEY (SWINGLE), George (1724-   ). Elected to serve on the Committee of Observation for the Elizabeth Town District (now the Hagerstown area of Washington County) on September 12, 1775 [Ref: Q-142, which listed the name as "George Zwingly"], and referred to as "Mr. George Swingler" on March 4, 1776 [Ref: Q-153]. Served on the Committee of Observation in April, 1776 [Ref: Q-154, Q-155, which listed the name as "George Swingley"]. One of several patriots appointed by the Committee of Observation on December 30, 1776 "to form the county into companies (after the militia had marched) for the purpose of relieving the distressed inhabitants of said county and also to compel the Dunkards and Mennonists to give their assistance." [Ref: Q-346, which listed the name as "George Swingley"]. One of the persons appointed by the Committee of Observation on January 9, 1777 "to appraise the several wagons, horses, gears, wagon cloths, blankets, etc. that can be procured for the use of Col. Smith's Battalion." [Ref: Q-40, Q-41, which listed the name as "George Swingley"]. Rendered patriotic service by supplying a blanket for the use of the military in March, 1776, as recorded by the Committee of Observation on April 12, 1776 [Ref: Q-157, which listed the name as "George Swengle" and L-82, which listed the name as "George Swingly"]. Captain, Militia, June 22, 1778 [Ref: M-127, E-145, A-1146, M-249, which latter source indicated that "George Swingley Junr" was recommended for captain of Peter Swingle's company]. Took the Oath of Allegiance before the Hon. John Stull in 1778 [Ref: O-47, J-11, which listed the name as "George Swingly"]. Major, 2nd Battalion, November 21, 1780 [Ref: G-220, which listed the name as "George Swingle"]. He might have been the George Swingle born in 1724 and brother of Nicholas Swingle born in 1720. Additional research will be necessary before drawing conclusions [Ref: KK-II:796]. See "George Swingley, Jr.," q.v.

SWINGLEY (SWINGLE), George Jr. (1757-1840). Private, Militia, 6th Class, Capt. Peter Swingle's (Swingley's) Company, 1776/1777 [Ref: A-1146, M-248, which listed the name as "George Swingle, Jr."]. Took the

Oath of Allegiance before the Hon. John Stull in 1778 [Ref: O-47, J-11, which listed the name as "George Swingly"]. George Swingle applied for and received pension S4914 in Lewis County, Kentucky on April 9, 1833, stating he was born on December 11, 1757 in Lancaster County, Pennsylvania and lived in Washington County, Maryland at the time of his enlistment. About 15 years after the war he moved to Jefferson County, Tennessee for 10 or 12 years, then to Montgomery County, Kentucky around 1807 or 1808, and then to Lewis County, Kentucky. In 1833 a son George Swingle, Jr. was aged 53, and George, the soldier, moved to Greenup County, Kentucky in 1838. He had his pension transferred to Cincinnati or Chilicothe, Ohio and was on the Franklin County, Kentucky list on July 23, 1838. He died on November 15, 1840 [Ref: V-III:3407, T-39]. "George Swingle, born 1757, Major, Maryland Militia." [Ref: N-51]. See the other "George Swingley," q.v. Additional research may be necessary before drawing conclusions.

SWINGLEY (SWINGLE), Leonard. Private, Militia, 3rd Class, Capt. Peter Swingle's (Swingley's) Company, 1776/1777 [Ref: A-1146, M-248, which listed the name as "Leonard Swingle"]. Rendered patriotic service by supplying wheat for the use of the military on April 15, 1780 [Ref: W-1190, and HH-73, which listed the name as "Leonard Swingle"]. Took the Oath of Allegiance before the Hon. John Stull in 1778 [Ref: O-47, J-11, which listed the name as "Leonard Swingley"].

SWINGLEY (SWINGLE), Michael. Private, Militia, 8th Class, Capt. Peter Swingle's (Swingley's) Company, 1776/1777 [Ref: A-1146, M-249, which listed the name as "Michael Swingly"]. Took the Oath of Allegiance before the Hon. John Stull in 1778 [Ref: J-11, O-47, which latter source listed the name as "Michael Swingley"].

SWINGLEY (SWINGLE), Nicholas (1749-1843). Private, Militia, 5th Class, Capt. Peter Swingle's (Swingley's) Company, 1776/1777 [Ref: A-1146, M-248, which listed the name as "Nicholas Swingley" and KK-II:796, which listed the name as "Nicholas Swingle"]. It should be noted that he was not a son of the Nicholas Swingle or Swingley who died in 1785, but was probably a cousin [Ref: KK-II:796].

SWINGLEY (SWINGLE), Nicholas (1720-1785). Took the Oath of Allegiance before the Hon. John Stull in 1778 [Ref: O-47, J-11, which listed the name as "Nicholas Swingly"]. Recruiting Officer, 1779-1780 [Ref: F-54]. Served in the Maryland House of Delegates, 1783 [Ref: KK-I:90, KK:II-796, which contains more detailed information]. See "George Swingley," q.v.

SWINGLEY (SWINGLE), Peter. Captain, Militia, 3rd Company, 2nd Battalion, 1776/1777 [Ref: M-248, A-1146, which listed the name as

"Peter Swingle"]. One of several patriots appointed by the Committee of Observation on January 9, 1777 "to procure as many blankets as may be wanting to supply Col. Smith's Battalion." [Ref: Q-34, which listed the name as "Mr. Peter Swingley"].

SWISHER, John. One of several patriots appointed by the Committee of Observation on December 30, 1776 "to form the county into companies (after the militia had marched) for the purpose of relieving the distressed inhabitants of said county and also to compel the Dunkards and Mennonists to give their assistance." [Ref: Q-345].

SWITCHFIELD, Joshua. First Sergeant, Militia, Capt. Charles Clinton's Company, 1776/1777 [Ref: M-245, A-1146].

SWITZER, Daniel. Private who enrolled in Capt. William Heyser's Company prior to June, 1776, at which time the Committee of Observation remitted the fine he had previously paid for not enrolling [Ref: Q-267].

SWITZER, Frederick. See "Frederick Schweitzer," q.v.

SWOP, Barnet. See "Adam Miller," q.v.

SWOPE, Catharine. See "Peter Swope," q.v.

SWOPE, Colonel. See "Michael Smith," q.v.

SWOPE, Peter (1750-1811). Private, Select Militia, Capt. Adam Ott's Company, 1781 [Ref: M-238, A-1146, which listed the name as "Peter Swoop"]. Peter Swope was born on December 20, 1750, died on July 15, 1811, and is buried in the St. Paul's Lutheran Reformed Church cemetery on Route 40 near Clearspring in Washington County [Ref: JJ-V:91]. "Died on Friday, September 28, 1832, of a lingering illness, at the residence of James H. Bowles, Esq., near Hancock, Mrs. Catharine Swope, aged 75 years [born October 1, 1757], relict of the late Peter Swope of Washington County; buried in the Hancock Public Cemetery on High Street, West Section." [Ref: JJ-II:26, and DD-46, citing *The Republican Banner*, October 6, 1832].

SYBERT, John. See "John Seibert," q.v.

SYLASTER, Michael. Took the Oath of Allegiance before the Hon. Christopher Cruse in Lower Antietam Hundred before March 2, 1778 [Ref: J-3, O-35, which latter source listed the name as "Michael Sylaser"].

TACKLER, Catherine. See "Nicholas Ridenour," q.v.

TACKLER, Michael. See "Adam Weise," q.v.

TALBARD, Thomas. Took the Oath of Allegiance before the Hon. Lemuel Barritt before March 16, 1778 [Ref: O-43, J-8].

TALBERT, James. Private, Militia, 2nd Class, Capt. Jeremiah Spires' Company, 2nd Battalion, 1776/1777 [Ref: M-239, A-1146].

TALBOT, Notley. Private who was enrolled by Capt. Aeneas Campbell and passed by Major Francis Deakins on July 18, 1776 [Ref: D-49].

TAMER, Michael. Ensign, Militia, January 15, 1777 [Ref: M-127, C-50, C-42, which latter source listed the name as "Michael Tomer"].

TAMIN, Ambroce. Took the Oath of Allegiance before the Hon. Christopher Cruse in Sharpsburg Hundred before March 2, 1778 [Ref: O-34, J-2, which latter source listed the name as "Ambrace Tamin"].

TAMLANE, Grove. See "Grove Tomlin," q.v.

TANGLER, George. Private, Select Militia, Capt. Adam Ott's Company, 1781 [Ref: M-238, A-1146]. Private, Militia, 3rd Class, Capt. John Cellars' Company, 1776/1777 [Ref: A-1146, M-246, which listed the name as "George Tenglen"].

TANNEHILL, Adamson. On March 8, 1826 the Treasurer of the Western Shore of Maryland was directed to pay to "Mrs. Agnes M. Tannehill, of Allegany County in the State of Pennsylvania, during life, the half pay of a captain, as a further remuneration for her late husband's services [no name given] during the Revolutionary War." [Ref: AA-397]. Adamson Tannehill was a lieutenant and then captain in the 4th Maryland Line from 1777 through 1781 [Ref: D-301, D-350, D-365].

TANNER, Abraham. Private, Militia, 4th Class, Capt. John Bennet's Company, 1776/1777 [Ref: A-1146, M-246, which listed the name as "Abraham Tonner"].

TANNER, John. Private, Militia, 4th Class, Capt. Henry Boteler's Company, 1776/1777 [Ref: M-237, A-1146].

TANT, Bearnhard. See "Bernhard Faut," q.v.

TARR, Phillip. Private, Militia, 3rd Class, Capt. Basil Williams' Company, 1776/1777 [Ref: M-244, A-1146].

TARTER, Nathaniel. Private, Militia, 5th Class, Capt. Barnett Johnston's Company, 3rd Battalion, 1776/1777 [Ref: M-242].

TARWALTER, Jacob. Took the Oath of Allegiance before the Hon. Andrew Bruce before March 2, 1778 [Ref: O-41, J-6].

TASKER, Richard R. Private, Maryland Line. On February 12, 1820 the Treasurer of the Western Shore of Maryland was directed to pay to Richard R. Tasker, of Allegany County, for life, quarterly, half pay of a private, for his services during the Revolutionary War [Ref: AA-398].

TAWCH(?), Robert. Private, Militia, 8th Class, Capt. Barnett Johnston's Company, 3rd Battalion, 1776/1777 [Ref: M-242].

TAYLOR, Alexander. Private, German Regiment, Lt. Col. Ludwick Weltner's Company, continental service, discharged August 9, 1779 [Ref: D-265].

TAYLOR, John. Took the Oath of Allegiance before the Hon. John Barnes before February 28, 1778 [Ref: O-45, J-10].

TAYLOR, Thomas. On February 23, 1780 the Council of Maryland proceedings noted "pardon granted to Thomas Taylor condemned in Washington County Court for horse stealing on condition that he forthwith enlist himself into some one of the regiments of the quota of this state in the Continental Army and that he do not desert therefrom." [Ref: F-94]. Another entry by the Council on February 24, 1780 indicated that the sheriff and recruiting officer were instructed that any bounty money that Thomas Taylor might be entitled to should be paid "to his wife who lives in Harford County and who with several children are in extreme indigent circumstances." [Ref: F-96]. Apparently, Taylor did not enlist because on October 19, 1780 the Council issued a warrant for "the execution of Thomas Taylor, condemned at Washington County Court 22nd August last for felony." [Ref: F-333]. However, on April 28 [1781] John Stull, Washington County, wrote to Governor Thomas Sim Lee and stated "I aske the Liberty to Inform you that Thomas Taylor a Greable to your Reprive Did inList in the Service of the United States, has since Deserted with Two others Stole three horses they are a Gain apprehended and now in Gaol. I wd be Glad your Excelency wd Take order with the said Tayler as he is an Extraordinary felow and prehaps Get a way." [Ref: F-483]. There were two men named Thomas Taylor in the Maryland Line in 1781 and several others between 1776 and 1780 as well [Ref: D-169, D-170, D-412].

TEACHLER, John. Took the Oath of Allegiance before the Hon. Joseph Sprigg before April 1, 1778 [Ref: O-53, J-16, which latter source listed the name as "John Teacher"].

TECKERHOOF, Barbara. See "Christian Welty," q.v.

TEDRE (TUDERO), Reuben. Private, Militia, 3rd Class, Capt. Daniel Clapsaddle's Company, 1st Battalion, 1776/1777 [Ref: M-236, A-1146, which listed the name as "Ruben Tudero"]. Private who was recruited and passed by County Lieutenant Thomas Sprigg on April 22, 1780 [Ref: D-336, which listed the name as "Reuben Tedre"].

TEETER, Abraham. Private, Militia, Capt. John Kershner's Company, on duty guarding prisoners of war at Fort Frederick on June 27, 1778 [Ref: D-328, which listed the name as "Abraham Feeter"]. Rendered patriotic service in Hagerstown by providing a rifle to Capt. John Nelson's Company, continental service (Maryland Line), April, 1776 [Ref: Q-162, which listed the name as "Abraham Teetes"]. Private, Militia, 3rd Class, Capt. Samuel Hughes' Company, 2nd Battalion, 1776/1777 [Ref: M-238, A-1146, which listed the name as "Abraham Deeder"].

TEETER, Isaac. Private, Militia, 4th Class, Capt. Isaac Baker's Company, 1776/1777 [Ref: A-1146, M-247].

TEETER, Jacob. Private, Militia, 8th Class, Capt. Isaac Baker's Company, 1776/1777 [Ref: A-1146, M-247]. Private who was enlisted by Ensign Nathan Williams and passed on July 25, 1776 in Frederick (now Washington) County [Ref: D-51]. Took the Oath of Allegiance before the Hon. Christopher Cruse in Lower Antietam Hundred before March 2, 1778 [Ref: J-3, O-35, which listed the name as "Jacob Teter"].

TEETER, John. Private who was enlisted by Ensign Nathan Williams and passed on July 25, 1776 in Frederick (now Washington) County [Ref: D-51].

TEISHER, John and Mary. See "John Tisher," q.v.

TERUSH, Abraham. Private, Militia, 5th Class, Capt. Daniel Clapsaddle's Company, 1st Battalion, 1776/1777 [Ref: M-236, A-1146].

TESERN, Frederick. Took the Oath of Allegiance before the Hon. John Barnes before February 28, 1778 [Ref: O-44, J-9].

TETWILER, Catherine. See "John Kenistrick," q.v.

THAIRMAN, Thomas. First Corporal, Militia, Capt. Charles Clinton's Company, 1776/1777 [Ref: M-245, A-1146].

THAIRMAN, Thomas. Private, Militia, 4th Class, Capt. Charles Clinton's Company, 1776/1777 [Ref: M-245, A-1146].

THAMAN, Phillip. Private, Militia, 3rd Class, Capt. John Rennolds' (Reynolds') Company, 2nd Battalion, 1776/1777 [Ref: M-240].

THEIR, Michael. Took the Oath of Allegiance before the Hon. Henry Schnebley in 1778 [Ref: O-49, J-13].

THOMAS, Amos (1749-1808). Died on February 19, 1809, between 5 and 6 a.m., after a short warning, Amos Thomas, in the 59th year of his age; served as an officer in the Revolutionary War [Ref: LL-3:122].

THOMAS, Andrew. Private, Militia, 7th Class, Capt. John Rennolds' (Reynolds') Company, 2nd Battalion, 1776/1777 [Ref: M-240].

THOMAS, Catharine. See "John Ferguson," q.v.

THOMAS, Catherine. See "Martin Bilmire," q.v.

THOMAS, Christian. Private, Militia, 1st Class, Capt. Conrad Nichodemus' Company, 2nd Battalion, 1776/1777 [Ref: M-237, A-1146].

THOMAS, Christopher. Private, Militia, 5th Class, Capt. Isaac Baker's Company, 1776/1777 [Ref: A-1146, M-247].

THOMAS, Elizabeth. See "William Tongue" and "Griffin (Griffith) Johnson," q.v.

THOMAS, Francis. See "John Ferguson," q.v.

THOMAS, George. See "John Wagner," q.v.

THOMAS, Governor. See "John Ferguson," q.v.

THOMAS, Jacob (1747-1811). Private, Militia, 8th Class, Capt. Conrad Nichodemus' Company, 2nd Battalion, 1776/1777 [Ref: M-237, A-1146]. Took the Oath of Allegiance before the Hon. Henry Schnebley in 1778 [Ref: O-50, J-14]. Jacob Thomas died on September 10, 1811, aged 64 years, 3 months, and is buried beside his wife Susannah Thomas (1755-1824) in the graveyard at the Geeting Meeting House, 1st U. B. Church at Mt. Hebron, Eakle's Mill, in Washington County [Ref: JJ-V:64].

THOMAS, John. Private, Militia, 1st Class, Capt. Conrad Nichodemus' Company, 2nd Battalion, 1776/1777 [Ref: M-237, A-1146]. One John Thomas (1735-1802) is buried in a graveyard on the Henry Dorier farm north of Hancock, Maryland [Ref: JJ-II:47]. See "John Ferguson," q.v.

THOMAS, Mary. See "Christopher Orendorff," q.v.

THOMAS, Michael. One of several patriots appointed by the Committee of Observation on January 19, 1777 "to form the county into companies (after the militia had marched) for the purpose of relieving the distressed inhabitants of said county and also to compel the Dunkards and Mennonists to give their assistance." [Ref: Q-43].

THOMAS, Michael Jr. Private, Militia, 2nd Class, Capt. Conrad Nichodemus' Company, 2nd Battalion, 1776/1777 [Ref: M-237, A-1146].

THOMAS, Peter. Private, Militia, 4th Class, Capt. Conrad Nichodemus' Company, 2nd Battalion, 1776/1777 [Ref: M-237, A-1146]. See "Jacob Russell, Jr.," q.v.

THOMAS, Susannah. See "Jacob Thomas," q.v.

THOMER, Ludwig. Took the Oath of Allegiance before the Hon. Henry Schnebley in 1778 [Ref: O-51, J-14].

THOMPSON, Benjamin. See "Benjamin Tomson," q.v.

THOMPSON, Ignatious. Private, Militia, 7th Class, Capt. Joseph Chapline's Company, 2nd Battalion, 1776/1777 [Ref: M-242].

THOMPSON, James. Private who was enlisted by Lieut. Moses Chapline and passed on July 24, 1776 in Frederick (now Washington) County [Ref: D-50].

THOMPSON, John. Private, Militia, 4th Class, Capt. Daniel Clapsaddle's Company, 1st Battalion, 1776/1777 [Ref: M-236, A-1146]. Took the Oath of Allegiance before the Hon. Samuel Hughes before March 1, 1778 [Ref: O-33, J-1].

THOMPSON, Joseph. Private, Militia, 7th Class, Capt. John Bennet's Company, 1776/1777 [Ref: M-246, A-1146, Q-48]. Took the Oath of Allegiance before the Hon. John Barnes before February 28, 1778 [Ref: O-45, J-10].

THOMPSON, Martha. See "Henry Franks," q.v.

THOMPSON, William. Private, Militia, 5th Class, Capt. Peter Swingle's (Swingley's) Company, 1776/1777 [Ref: A-1146, M-248]. Took the Oath of Allegiance before the Hon. Richard Davis in 1778 [Ref: J-4, O-37].

THORNBOURGH, Francis. Private who was enlisted by Lieut. Moses Chapline and passed on July 24, 1776 in Frederick (now Washington) County [Ref: D-50].

THORMAN, George. Took the Oath of Allegiance before September 1, 1780 [Ref: X-121].

THORNIN, Alworth. Took the Oath of Allegiance before the Hon. Lemuel Barritt before March 16, 1778 [Ref: O-42, J-8].

TICE, Henry. Private, Militia, 3rd Class, Capt. Martin Kershner's Company, 1776/1777 [Ref: A-1146, M-247]. Private, Militia, Capt. Martin Kershner's Company, 32nd Battalion, December 27, 1776 [Ref: K-1814 (Box 3), which listed the name as "Henery Tice"]. Private, Militia, Capt. John Kershner's Company, on duty guarding prisoners of war at Fort Frederick on June 27, 1778 [Ref: D-328, which listed the name as "Henry Tyce"].

TICE, Michael. Private, Militia, Capt. Martin Kershner's Company, 32nd Battalion, December 27, 1776 [Ref: K-1814 (Box 3), which listed the name as "Michel Tice"].

TILHART, Christopher. First Corporal, Militia, Capt. Jacob Sharer's Company, 1776/1777 [Ref: M-248, A-1146].

TILLER, Jacob. Private, Militia, 8th Class, Capt. Martin Kershner's Company, 1776/1777 [Ref: A-1146, M-248].

TINSLEY, James. Private, Militia, 8th Class, Capt. Barnett Johnston's Company, 3rd Battalion, 1776/1777 [Ref: M-242].

TISHER (TEISHER), Daniel. Private, Militia, 1st Class, Capt. Martin Kershner's Company, 1776/1777 [Ref: A-1146, M-247].

TISHER (TEISHER), Jacob. Fourth Corporal, Militia, Capt. Martin Kershner's Company, 1776/1777 [Ref: M-247, A-1146]. Private, Militia, Capt. John Kershner's Company, on duty guarding prisoners of war at Fort Frederick on June 27, 1778 [Ref: D-328, which listed the name as "Jacob Tysher"].

TISHER (TEISHER), John (1747-1820). Private, Militia, 7th Class, Capt. Martin Kershner's Company, 1776/1777 [Ref: A-1146, M-248]. "John Teisher" died at his residence near Hagerstown on January 14, 1820, in his 73rd year. "Mary Teisher, relict of the late John Teisher" died at her residence about 3 miles from Hagerstown on September 26, 1822, in her 55th year, leaving several children (names not given). [Ref: Z-42, Z-52].

TITER, Jacob. Private, Militia, 5th Class, Capt. Henry Boteler's Company, 1776/1777 [Ref: M-237, A-1146].

TITSWORD(?), Isaac. Private, Militia, 8th Class, Capt. Daniel Cresap's Company, 3rd Battalion, 1776/1777 [Ref: M-241].

TITTLE, James. Private, Militia, Capt. Charles Coulson's Company, enrolled August 28, 1776 [Ref: M-244, A-1146].

TITTLE, Sarah. See "Lemuel Barritt," q.v.

TOBE, Michael. Third Sergeant, Militia, Capt. Conrad Nichodemus' Company, 2nd Battalion, 1776/1777 [Ref: M-237, A-1146].

TOICE, George. See "George Joice," q.v.

TOMER, Michael. See "Michael Tamer," q.v.

TOMKINS, Silas. Private who was enlisted by Capt. John Reynolds and passed on July 18, 1776 in Frederick (now Washington) County [Ref: D-50].

TOMLIN, Grove. Private who was enrolled by Capt. Aeneas Campbell and passed by Major Francis Deakins on July 18, 1776 [Ref: D-49, which listed the name as "Grove Tomlin (Tamlane)"].

TOMLINSON (TOMSON?), Benjamin. Took the Oath of Allegiance before the Hon. John Cellars in January, 1778 [Ref: K-1814, which is the original record and the name appeared to be "Benjamin Tomson," yet O-40 listed the name as "Benja. Tomlinson" and J-6 listed the name as "Benjamin Tomlison"].

TOMLINSON, James. Private, Militia, Capt. Charles Coulson's Company, enrolled August 28, 1776 [Ref: M-243, A-1146]. Private, Militia, 2nd Class, Capt. Daniel Cresap's Company, 3rd Battalion, 1776/1777 [Ref: M-241].

TOMLINSON, Jessy. Private, Militia, Capt. Charles Coulson's Company, enrolled August 28, 1776 [Ref: M-243, A-1146].

TOMLINSON, John. Took the Oath of Allegiance before the Hon. Andrew Bruce before March 2, 1778 [Ref: O-41, J-6]. Rendered patriotic service by providing a rifle for Capt. Daniel Cresap's Company in July, 1775, as recorded by the Committee of Observation at Elizabeth Town on November 4, 1775 [Ref: Q-148, which listed the name as "John Tombleson"].

TOMM, Adam. Private, Militia, 2nd Class, Capt. Samuel Hughes' Company, 2nd Battalion, 1776/1777 [Ref: M-238, A-1146, which listed the name as "Adam Tom"].

TOMM, George. Private, Militia, 4th Class, Capt. Conrad Hogmire's Company, 1776/1777 [Ref: M-244, A-1146, which listed the name as "George Tom"].

TOMM, Henry (c1750-1829). Private, Militia, Capt. William Heyser's Company, muster roll dated October 23, 1776, in continental service [Ref: D-264, W-1190, L-79]. Wounded in the arm at the Battle of

Germantown in August, 1777 and in hospital at Reading Courthouse, Pennsylvania on November 17, 1777; subsequently transferred to Invalid Corps [Ref: U-39:1 (1951), and GG-99, which listed the name as "Henry Tomm or Tom"]. Resided in Washington County and was granted a pension certificate in August, 1820, according to an Act of Congress of March 18, 1818, since he had proven that he was "in the enjoyment of a certain degree of poverty" as required by the Act as amended on May 1, 1820 [Ref: W-1190]. He received pension S35103 of $20 per year from March 4, 1794, $48 per year from April 24, 1816, $96 per year from March 30, 1818. In 1820 he was aged 70 with a wife aged 63 (no name given), a daughter Nancy (aged 20 with an infant child), and a son John (aged 16) living with him. Henry Tomm died on June 13, 1829 [Ref: GG-100, R-19, R-43, V-III:3514].

TOMM, John. See "Henry Tomm," q.v.

TOMM, Mathias. Private, Militia, 7th Class, Capt. Samuel Hughes' Company, 2nd Battalion, 1776/1777 [Ref: M-238, A-1146, which listed the name as "Mathias Tom"].

TOMM, Michael. Private, Militia, 2nd Class, Capt. Conrad Nichodemus' Company, 2nd Battalion, 1776/1777 [Ref: M-237, A-1146, which listed the name as "Michael Tom"].

TOMM, Nancy. See "Henry Tomm," q.v.

TONGUE, John. Took the Oath of Allegiance before the Hon. John Barnes before February 28, 1778 [Ref: J-9, O-44 which latter source listed the name as "John Longue"].

TONGUE, William (1756-   ). Private, Maryland Militia; married Elizabeth Thomas in Washington County in May, 1794 [Ref: N-52, N-124].

TOOTWILER, Henry. See "Henry Tutwiler," q.v.

TRACY, Timothy. Private, Militia, 4th Class, Capt. Daniel Cresap's Company, 3rd Battalion, 1776/1777 [Ref: M-241, which listed the name as "Timothy Trasey"]. Took the Oath of Allegiance before the Hon. Lemuel Barritt before March 16, 1778 [Ref: O-42, which listed the name as "Timothy Tracy" and J-7, which listed the name as "Timothy Trach"].

TRAMELL, Philip. Took the Oath of Allegiance before the Hon. Lemuel Barritt before March 16, 1778 [Ref: O-43, J-8]. Private, Militia, 5th Class, Capt. James Prather's Company, 3rd Battalion, 1776/1777 [Ref: M-243, which listed the name as "Phillip Tramill"].

TRANTLE, Samuel. Private, Militia, 2nd Class, Capt. James Walling's Company, 2nd Battalion, 1776/1777 [Ref: M-238, A-1146].

TRAPP (TROPP), Christian. Took the Oath of Allegiance before the Hon. Henry Schnebley in 1778 [Ref: O-49, J-13].

TRAPP (TRUPP), Christopher. Private, Militia, 5th Class, Capt. Michael Fackler's Company, 1776/1777 [Ref: M-245, A-1146].

TRESAL, Goodhart. Took the Oath of Allegiance before the Hon. Andrew Rentch before March 7, 1778 [Ref: O-52, J-15]. Private, Militia, Capt. John Kershner's Company, on duty guarding prisoners of war at Fort Frederick, 1778, and who reportedly "deserted" on June 2, 1778 [Ref: D-328, which listed the name as "Goodhert Tressel"].

TRESLER, Frederick (1759-   ). Private, Maryland Militia, with Pennsylvania service [Ref: N-52]. Took the Oath of Allegiance before September 1, 1780 [Ref: X-122]. A John Tresler died before November 17, 1798 (date of balance book entry in Washington County) and one of his sons was "Fredk. Tresler." [Ref: J-36].

TRESSLER, Peter. Appeared before the Committee of Observation on June 28, 1776, having been accused of "expressing sentiments inimical to the liberties of America and advising Capt. Keller's Company to lay down their arms, [and] upon hearing the evidence the Committee was of the opinion they ought to be discharged, on promising good behaviour for the future." [Ref: Q-324]. First Corporal, Militia, Capt. Conrad Nichodemus' Company, 2nd Battalion, 1776/1777 [Ref: M-237, A-1146, which listed the name as "Peter Treslen"].

TRIDLE, Jacob. Private, Militia, 5th Class, Capt. James Walling's Company, 2nd Battalion, 1776/1777 [Ref: M-239, A-1146].

TROTTER, Loudon. Took the Oath of Allegiance before the Hon. Andrew Bruce before March 2, 1778 [Ref: O-41, J-6]. Private, Militia, 2nd Class, Capt. Charles Clinton's Company, 1776/1777 [Ref: M-245, A-1146, which listed the name as "Lowden Trotter"].

TROTTER, Richard. Private, Militia, Capt. Charles Coulson's Company, enrolled August 28, 1776 [Ref: M-244, A-1146].

TROUP, Adam. Private, Militia, 6th Class, Capt. Isaac Baker's Company, 1776/1777 [Ref: A-1146, M-247]. One Adam Troup died before November 6, 1790 (date of balance book entry in Washington County), leaving a widow (no name given in this account) and equal shares to David Troup, Adam Troup, Henry Troup, Jacob Troup (son of Henry), Esther Musselman, Catherine Shively, and Mary Brewore [Ref: J-30].

TROUP, David, Henry, and Jacob. See "Adam Troup," q.v.

TROUT, Christian (1753-1847). Private, Maryland Line, who applied for pension in Pike County, Kentucky on October 6, 1834, stating he was born in 1753 at Sharpsburg, Maryland, lived there at the time of his enlistment, and later moved to Virginia. He married Elizabeth Geerhart on September 15, 1795 in Rockbridge County, Virginia and moved to Kentucky in 1822. Christian died in Pike County on June 16, 1847 and his widow applied for and received pension W7326 in Greene County, Indiana on May 7, 1850, aged 75. She also received bounty land warrant #35685-160-55. A son, Lewis Trout, lived in Indiana in 1853 [Ref: V-III:3540].

TROUT, Elizabeth and Lewis. See "Christian Trout," q.v.

TROUTMAN, John. Private, Militia, 3rd Class, Capt. Jacob Sharer's Company, 1776/1777 [Ref: A-1146, M-248].

TROVINGER, Christopher (c1753-1820). Private, Militia, Lancaster County, Pennsylvania, who married Barbara Kimmel (1763-1809) in 1778 and a son Joseph was born in Washington County, Maryland on December 11, 1790. Christopher died on December 17, 1820 at his residence about 3 miles from Hagerstown, after a lingering illness, in the 64th year of his age [Ref: Z-33, Y-III:2978, and S-3071, being the SAR application of Tom N. Rasmussen, of Taneytown, Maryland, approved on March 29, 1990 (National No. 134691) and citing DAR National No. 547526 as a reference].

TROXEL, Abraham. Private who was enrolled by Capt. Henry Hardman and passed on July 19, 1776 in Frederick (now Washington) County [Ref: D-51]. Appointed to serve on the Committee of Observation on February 1, 1777 [Ref: Q-229, which listed the name as "Abraham Troxall"]. Took the Oath of Allegiance before the Hon. Andrew Rentch before March 7, 1778 [Ref: O-52, J-15]. One "Abraham Troxell" died before January 15, 1791 (date of balance book entry in Washington County), leaving a widow (no name given in this account) and equal shares to David, Catherine, Magdalena, Anna, Sarah and Susannah Troxel [Ref: J-30]. A subsequent account on June 22, 1793 mentioned the widow (no name given) and heirs as David Troxell, Catherine Sevilar, Magdalena Troxell, Anna Troxell, Susannah Troxell, and Salome Troxell [Ref: J-33]. See "George Troxel," q.v.

TROXEL, Abraham Jr. Private, Militia, 3rd Class, Capt. Martin Kershner's Company, 1776/1777 [Ref: A-1146, M-247, which listed the name as "Abraham Troxell, Jr."]. Private, Militia, Capt. John Kershner's Company, on duty guarding prisoners of war at Fort Frederick on June 27, 1778 [Ref: D-328, which listed the name as "Abraham Troxal, Jr."]. Took the Oath of Allegiance before the Hon. Henry Schnebley in 1778 [Ref: J-13, which listed the name as "Abraham Troxel" and O-49, which listed the name as "Abraham Troxal"].

TROXEL, Anna. See "Abraham Troxel," q.v.

TROXEL, Catherine. See "George Troxel" and "Abraham Troxel," q.v.

TROXEL, Christian. Rendered patriotic service by providing clothing for the use of the military on July 5, 1778 [Ref: CC-106].

TROXEL, Daniel. See "George Troxel," q.v.

TROXEL, David. See "Abraham Troxel," q.v.

TROXEL, George. Took the Oath of Allegiance before the Hon. John Cellars in January, 1778 [Ref: K-1814, O-40, J-5, which latter source listed the name as "George Trossel"]. Private, Militia, 4th Class, Capt. Martin Kershner's Company, 1776/1777 [Ref: A-1146, M-247, which listed the name as "George Troxell"]. "George Troxell" died testate before June 18, 1785 (date of balance book entry in Washington County), leaving a widow (no name given in this account) and heirs as Peter, Abraham, Daniel, and Catherine Troxell, and Philip Obinger (of Philadelphia). [Ref: J-25].

TROXEL, John. Private who was enrolled by Capt. Henry Hardman and passed on July 19, 1776 in Frederick (now Washington) County [Ref: D-51].

TROXEL, Magdalena. See "Abraham Troxel," q.v.

TROXEL, Peter. See "George Troxel," q.v.

TROXEL, Salome, Sarah, and Susannah. See "Abraham Troxel," q.v.

TROY, Timothy. Private who was recruited and passed by County Lieutenant Thomas Sprigg on April 22, 1780 [Ref: D-336].

TRULING, John. Rendered patriotic service by providing clothing for the use of the military on July 5, 1778 [Ref: CC-106].

TRUMPOUR, Leonard. Private, Militia, 2nd Class, Capt. John Bennet's Company, 1776/1777 [Ref: M-246, A-1146]. Took the Oath of Allegiance before the Hon. John Barnes before February 28, 1778 [Ref: O-45, J-9, which listed the name as "Leonard Trumpower"].

TUCKER, Tempest. Private, Militia, 6th Class, Capt. Samuel Hughes' Company, 2nd Battalion, 1776/1777 [Ref: M-238, A-1146].

TUDERO, Reuben. See "Reuben Tedre (Tudero)," q.v.

TURNER, James. Private, Militia, 8th Class, Capt. Henry Boteler's Company, 1776/1777 [Ref: M-237, A-1146]. Took the Oath of Allegiance before the Hon. Christopher Cruse in Lower Antietam Hundred before March 2, 1778 [Ref: J-3, O-35]. Applied for and received pension S3841 in Allen County, Ohio on August 18, 1832, stating he was born in Baltimore, Maryland on October 27, 1755 and lived at Hagerstown, Maryland at the time of his enlistment. He married in 1777 (wife's name not given), lived in Washington County, Maryland for 4 years and then moved to Washington County, Pennsylvania for 2 years. He then moved to Mason County, Kentucky for 20 years, then to Champaign County, Ohio for 16 years, and then to Allen County, Kentucky [Ref: V-III:3557].

TUSSY, Jacob. Enrolled in the first militia company organized for the Revolutionary War in the Elizabeth Town District of Frederick County (now the Hagerstown area of Washington County) on January 6, 1776 [Ref: Q-271, W-1190]. Private, Militia, 3rd Class, Capt. Joseph Chapline's Company, 2nd Battalion, 1776/1777 [Ref: M-241]. Took the Oath of Allegiance before the Hon. Christopher Cruse in Sharpsburg Hundred before March 2, 1778 [Ref: O-35, J-2].

TUTER, Francis. Private, Militia, 4th Class, Capt. Basil Williams' Company, 1776/1777 [Ref: M-244, A-1146].

TUTER, Jacob. Private, Militia, 2nd Class, Capt. Basil Williams' Company, 1776/1777 [Ref: M-244, A-1146].

TUTER, John. Private, Militia, 2nd Class, Capt. Basil Williams' Company, 1776/1777 [Ref: M-244, A-1146].

TUTER, Peter Jr. Private, Militia, 1st Class, Capt. Basil Williams' Company, 1776/1777 [Ref: M-244, A-1146].

TUTWILER, Catherine. See "Jacob Tutwiler" and "John Kenistrick," q.v.

TUTWILER, Henry (1744-1793). Rendered patriotic service by providing two deer skins and making one pair of breeches for the use of the military in July, 1775, as recorded by the Committee of Observation at Elizabeth Town on November 4, 1775 [Ref: Q-150, which listed the name as "Henry Turtwiler"]. Rendered patriotic service in Hagerstown by providing sundries to Capt. John Nelson's Company, continental service (Maryland Line), April, 1776 [Ref: Q-161, which listed the name as "Henry Tootwiler"]. Private, Militia, 7th Class, Capt. Peter Beall's Company, 1st Battalion, 1776/1777 [Ref: M-240, which listed the name as "Henry Tootwiler"]. Took the Oath of Allegiance before the Hon. Joseph Sprigg before April 1, 1778 [Ref: O-53, J-16]. "Henry Tutwiler" died testate before September 27, 1794 (date of balance book entry in Washington County). [Ref: J-33]. "Henry Tutweiler" died on June 14, 1793, aged 48 years, 6 months, and is buried in Zion Reformed Church cemetery in Hagerstown [Ref: JJ-VI:18].

TUTWILER, Jacob. Private, Militia, 1st Class, Capt. James Walling's Company, 2nd Battalion, 1776/1777 [Ref: A-1146, M-238, which listed the name as "Jacob Tudewiler"]. "Catharine Tutweiler, wife of Jacob" died in December, 1820 in her 75th year [Ref: Z-34]. "Jacob Tutweiler" died in Hagerstown on January 30, 1828, of an advanced age, after a long illness [Ref: Z-97].

TUTWILER, Jonathan (1753-1819). Private, Maryland Line, who applied for and received pension S35105 in Washington County at $96 per year effective March 31, 1818. He was born on August 22, 1753, married Barbara Wagner, and died on July 20, 1819 [Ref: N-52, V-III:3565, Y-III:2999, and R-43, which latter source listed the name as "Jonathan Tutwiller"].

TWIGG, Charles. See "Griffin Johnson," q.v.
TWIGG, Francis (1750-1829). Private, Militia, 6th Class, Capt. Griffin Johnson's Company, 3rd Battalion, 1776/1777 [Ref: M-243]. "Died at his residence about 6 miles from Cumberland on Sat. last [prior to April 25, 1829], Francis Twigg, Sr., in the 79th year of his age, after a severe affliction of upwards of four years." [Ref: Z-24]. Francis Twigg was born in England in 1750, married Mary Leasure, served in Maryland during the Revolution, and died before July 1, 1829 [Ref: Y-III:2999].
TWIGG, John. Private, Militia, 7th Class, Capt. Griffin Johnson's Company, 3rd Battalion, 1776/1777 [Ref: M-243]. See "Griffin Johnson," q.v.
TWIGG, Lewis M. W. See "Griffin Johnson," q.v.
TWIGG, Mary. See "Robert Twigg," q.v.
TWIGG, Robert (c1745-1805). Private, Militia, 4th Class, Capt. Griffin Johnson's Company, 3rd Battalion, 1776/1777 [Ref: M-243]. Robert Twigg was born circa 1745 in Maryland, married Mary ----, and died before May 25, 1805 [Ref: Y-III:2999].
TYLER, John. Private who was recruited and passed by County Lieutenant Thomas Sprigg on April 22, 1780 [Ref: D-336].
TYSHER, Peter. Took the Oath of Allegiance before the Hon. Joseph Sprigg before April 1, 1778 [Ref: O-54, J-16].
UHRENBAN, Jacob. Took the Oath of Allegiance before the Hon. Henry Schnebley in 1778 [Ref: O-49, J-13, which latter source listed the name as "Jacob Uranban"].
ULERY, Stephen. Rendered patriotic service by providing a rifle for Capt. Daniel Cresap's Company in July, 1775, as recorded by the Committee of Observation at Elizabeth Town on November 4, 1775 [Ref: Q-149].
ULTHEART, Lawrance. Took the Oath of Allegiance before the Hon. Joseph Sprigg before April 1, 1778 [Ref: O-53, J-16].
UNSELL, John. Took the Oath of Allegiance before the Hon. Joseph Sprigg before April 1, 1778 [Ref: O-53, J-16]. Private, Militia, 8th Class, Capt. Peter Beall's Company, 1st Battalion, 1776/1777 [Ref: M-240, which listed the name as "John Onsell"]. On September 6, 1776 William Hyser reported to the Committee of Observation that he had "received of John Uncel the quantity of sixteen musketts and bonyonetts with wipers for the German Battalion." [Ref: Q-336]. See "Francis Wagoner" and "Nicholas Hockey," q.v.
UPP, Nicholas. Private, Militia, 4th Class, Capt. Michael Fackler's Company, 1776/1777 [Ref: M-245, A-1146]. Took the Oath of Allegiance before the Hon. Henry Schnebley in 1778 [Ref: O-49, J-13, which listed the name as "Nicholas Opp"].

URANBAN, Jacob. See "Jacob Uhrenban," q.v.

URVIN, James. Private, Militia, 3rd Class, Capt. James Smith's Company, 2nd Battalion, 1776/1777 [Ref: M-239, A-1146].

VALENTINE, Frederick. Private, Militia, 2nd Class, Capt. Charles Clinton's Company, 1776/1777 [Ref: M-245, A-1146]. Took the Oath of Allegiance before the Hon. Andrew Bruce before March 2, 1778 [Ref: O-41, J-6].

VALENTINE, George (1752-1839). Private, Maryland and Pennsylvania Lines, who applied for and received pension S17171 in Fairfield County, Ohio, stating he was born on January 2, 1752 in Lancaster County, Pennsylvania, lived there at the time of his first enlistment, and later enlisted at Hagerstown, Maryland. In 1803 he moved to Ohio and died in Fairfield County on November 27, 1839 [Ref: V-III:3578, which also listed the name as "George Vallentine"]. Private who enlisted in the militia on August 15, 1781 for service in the Continental Army [Ref: D-388, D-412]. Substitute, Maryland Line, discharged on October 30, 1781 [Ref: G-657].

VANDIKE, John W. See "John Jeremiah Jacob," q.v.

VANSWERINGIN, Thomas. Took the Oath of Allegiance before the Hon. John Cellars in January, 1778 [Ref: K-1814, O-40, J-6, which latter source listed the name as "Thomas Vansweringer"].

VEATCH, William. Private who was enrolled by Capt. Aeneas Campbell and passed by Major Francis Deakins on July 18, 1776 [Ref: D-49].

VERNER, Nicholas. Rendered patriotic service by providing a rifle for Capt. Daniel Cresap's Company in July, 1775, as recorded by the Committee of Observation at Elizabeth Town on November 4, 1775 [Ref: Q-149].

VICKERS, J. W. See "John Grove," q.v.

VOLGAMETT, Joseph. See "Joseph Wolgamot," q.v.

WADDELL, Mary, and others. See "Joseph Lemaster," q.v.

WADDLE, George (1757-   ). Private, Maryland Militia [Ref: N-53].

WADDLE, James. Private who was recruited and passed by County Lieutenant Thomas Sprigg on April 22, 1780 [Ref: D-336].

WADE, Augustine. On October 1, 1783 the Council of Maryland proceedings noted that Augustine Wade had produced satisfactory proof that he was a private in the Maryland Line and that he was disabled by a wound received at the Battle of Brandywine on September 11, 1777. They directed the Treasurer of the Western Shore to pay "such pension as he thought sufficient for his support, not exceeding his half pay, to commence from the time his whole pay ceased, which appears to us was in August, 1778." [Ref: I-458].

WADE, Henry. Private, Militia, 5th Class, Capt. Jeremiah Spires' Company, 2nd Battalion, 1776/1777 [Ref: M-239, A-1146].

WADE, John. Private who was enlisted by Capt. John Reynolds and passed on July 18, 1776 in Frederick (now Washington) County [Ref: D-50]. Fourth Corporal, Militia, Capt. Jeremiah Spires' Company, 2nd Battalion, 1776/1777 [Ref: M-239, A-1146]. Took the Oath of Allegiance before the Hon. Richard Davis in 1778 [Ref: J-3, O-36].

WADSWORTH, Elizabeth. See "John Byrnes," q.v.

WAEFF, Daniel. See "Yost Harbaugh," q.v.

WAGELEY, John. Private, Militia, 7th Class, Capt. Jacob Sharer's Company, 1776/1777 [Ref: A-1146, M-248].

WAGNER, Barbara. See "Jonathan Tutwiler," q.v.

WAGNER, Elizabeth. See "John Wagner," q.v.

WAGNER, John (1760-1837). Took the Oath of Allegiance before the Hon. Henry Schnebley in 1778 [Ref: O-49, J-13]. John Wagner died on February 5, 1837, aged 77, and is buried beside his wife Elizabeth Wagner (1763-1836) and another Elizabeth Wagner (1820-1838) in a graveyard on the George Thomas farm near Boonsboro, Maryland, on Monroe Road going to Antietam Creek [Ref: JJ-II:92]. See "John Wagoner," q.v.

WAGONER, Christopher. Private, German Regiment, Lt. Col. Ludwick Weltner's Company, continental service, enlisted August 10, 1776, and discharged on October 12, 1779 at Fort Wyoming, Pennsylvania [Ref: D-265, which listed the name as "Christopher Waggoner" and D-259, which listed the name as "Chrisr. Waggoner" and GG-100, which listed the name as "Christopher/Stuffle Wagner"]. Discharged on October 30, 1781, from Frederick County [Ref: G-657].

WAGONER, Francis. Private, Militia, 6th Class, Capt. Peter Beall's Company, 1st Battalion, 1776/1777 [Ref: M-240]. Rendered patriotic service by providing a rifle for Capt. Daniel Cresap's Company in July, 1775, as recorded by the Committee of Observation at Elizabeth Town on November 4, 1775 [Ref: Q-149, which listed the name as "Francis Waggoner"]. Rendered patriotic service in Hagerstown by providing three rifles to Capt. John Nelson's Company, continental service (Maryland Line), April, 1776 [Ref: Q-161, which listed the name as "Francis Waggoner"]. On September 17, 1776 he and Euness Deets [Ernst Deitz] "delivered unto Col. Henry Shriock thirty-one muskets and thirty bonyenetts all with iron ramrods for the use of the Flying Camp and made for John Uncel." [Ref: Q-336]. Took the Oath of Allegiance before the Hon. Joseph Sprigg before April 1, 1778 [Ref: O-53, J-16, which listed the name as "Francis Waggoner"].

WAGONER, Henry. Private, Militia, Capt. William Heyser's Company, muster roll dated October 23, 1776, in continental service, and severely wounded in the leg at the Battle of Germantown on October 4, 1777; reenlisted on August 5, 1778 [Ref: GG-100, W-1190, L-79, D-264, which latter source listed the name as "Henry Wagner"]. Applied for a pension [Ref: GG-100, which listed the name as "Henry Wagner, Waggoner"].

WAGONER, Jacob (1754-   ). Private, German Regiment, continental service, 1776, and discharged on July 24, 1779 [Ref: D-259, N-53, which latter source listed the name as "Jacob Waggoner"].

WAGONER, John. There were several men named John Wagoner who rendered patriotic service during the Revolutionary War. Additional research will be necessary before drawing conclusions. One was a private in the militia, 2nd Class, Capt. Daniel Clapsaddle's Company, 1st Battalion, 1776/1777 [Ref: M-236, A-1146]. One was a private in the militia, 1st Class, Capt. Peter Swingle's (Swingley's) Company, 1776/1777 [Ref: A-1146, M-248]. One was a private in the militia, 3rd Class, Capt. Jacob Sharer's Company, 1776/1777 [Ref: A-1146, M-248]. One was an ensign in the militia, Capt. John Funk's Company, 2nd Battalion, June 22, 1778 [Ref: M-132, E-145]. One "John Waggoner" died on December 15, 1842, at Frederick County, a soldier of the Revolution, one of Washington's bodyguards [Ref: EE-10:2 (p. 55), containing Robert W. Barnes' article which cited the *Baltimore Sun* on January 13, 1840, but should have read 1843]. See "John Wagner," q.v.

WAGONER, Martin. Private, Militia, 6th Class, Capt. Daniel Clapsaddle's Company, 1st Battalion, 1776/1777 [Ref: M-236, A-1146].

WAGONER, Peter. Private, Militia, 1st Class, Capt. Joseph Chapline's Company, 2nd Battalion, 1776/1777 [Ref: M-241].

WAGONER, Peter. Private, Militia, 2nd Class, Capt. Michael Fackler's Company, 1776/1777 [Ref: M-245, A-1146].

WAGONER, Peter. Took the Oath of Allegiance before the Hon. John Stull in 1778 [Ref: O-47, J-11, which latter source listed the name as "Peter Waggoner"].

WAGONER, Phillip. Took the Oath of Allegiance before the Hon. Christopher Cruse in Sharpsburg Hundred before March 2, 1778 [Ref: O-34, J-2, which listed the name as "Phillip Waggoner"]. One Phillip Wagoner died testate before December 27, 1788 (date of balance book entry in Washington County), leaving a widow (not named, but Regana Wagoner was the executrix) and equal shares to ten heirs (no names were given in this account). [Ref: J-29].

WAGONER, Regana. See "Phillip Wagoner," q.v.

WAGONER, Stuffle. Private, Militia, Capt. William Heyser's Company, muster roll dated October 23, 1776, in continental service [Ref: D-264, W-1190, L-79, which listed the name as "Stuffle Waggner"].
WAHLAGER, Jacob. Second Lieutenant, Militia (date not given). [Ref: M-132].
WAITENBERGER, Frederick. Enrolled in the first militia company organized for the Revolutionary War in the Elizabeth Town District of Frederick County (now the Hagerstown area of Washington County) on January 6, 1776 [Ref: Q-270, W-1189].
WALCH, William. Took the Oath of Allegiance before the Hon. William Yates in 1778 [Ref: O-48, J-12].
WALFORD, Adam. Took the Oath of Allegiance before the Hon. Joseph Sprigg before April 1, 1778 [Ref: O-53, J-16].
WALKER, Christopher. Private who was enrolled by Capt. Henry Hardman and passed on July 19, 1776 in Frederick (now Washington) County [Ref: D-51, which listed the name as "Chr. Walker"]. Private, Militia, 7th Class, Capt. Jacob Sharer's Company, 1776/1777 [Ref: A-1146, M-248].
WALKER, Gedeon. Private who was recruited and passed by County Lieutenant Thomas Sprigg on April 22, 1780 [Ref: D-336].
WALKER, Jacob. Private, Militia, 3rd Class, Capt. Basil Williams' Company, 1776/1777 [Ref: M-244, A-1146].
WALKER, John. Private who was enlisted by Lieut. Christian Orndorff and passed on July 20, 1776 in Frederick (now Washington) County [Ref: D-50]. Took the Oath of Allegiance before the Hon. John Stull in 1778 [Ref: O-47, J-11].
WALKER, Nicholas. Private, Militia, 8th Class, Capt. John Rennolds' (Reynolds') Company, 2nd Battalion, 1776/1777 [Ref: M-240].
WALKER, William. Private, enlisted by Capt. John Reynolds and passed on July 18, 1776 in Frederick (now Washington) County [Ref: D-50]. Ensign, Militia, 2nd Battalion, 1776. Second Lieutenant, Militia, Capt. John Rennolds' (Reynolds') Company, June 22, 1778 [Re: M-132, E-145, M-240]. Took the Oath of Allegiance before the Hon. Christopher Cruse in Sharpsburg Hundred before March 2, 1778 [Ref: O-34, J-1]. First Lieutenant, Capt. Christopher Orendorff's Company, 2nd Battalion, November 21, 1780 [Ref: G-220].
WALLACE, Alitha. See "James Chapline," q.v.
WALLACE, Samuel. Private, Militia, 1st Class, Capt. Isaac Baker's Company, 1776/1777 [Ref: A-1146, M-247].
WALLACE, William. See "James Chapline," q.v.
WALLBACK, Godfry. See "Godfry Woolback," q.v.

WALLING, Delashmut. Appointed by the Committee of Observation on July 7, 1776 "to take the number of inhabitants within Upper Antietam Hundred, both whites and blacks, distinguishing respectively the age and sex of each, to be transmitted to the Council of Safety immediately." [Ref: Q-331, which listed the name as "Delashmut Wallen"]. Private, Militia, 8th Class, Capt. James Walling's Company, 2nd Battalion, 1776/1777 [Ref: M-239, A-1146, which listed the name as "Delashmett Walling"]. Took the Oath of Allegiance before the Hon. Joseph Sprigg before April 1, 1778 [Ref: O-53, J-15].

WALLING, James. Captain, Militia, 5th Company, 2nd Battalion, 1776-1778 [Ref: M-132, M-238, E-145]. Appointed by the Committee of Observation to carry the Association of Freemen to male residents in his hundred (district) on March 4, 1776 "and present it for signing and make an exact account of those that sign and those that refuse with their reasons for refusing." [Ref: Q-153, L-82]. One of several patriots appointed by the Committee of Observation on January 9, 1777 "to procure as many blankets as may be wanting to supply Col. Smith's Battalion." [Ref: Q-34, which listed the name as "James Wallen"]. Took the Oath of Allegiance before the Hon. Joseph Sprigg before April 1, 1778 [Ref: O-53, J-15]. Lieutenant Colonel, 2nd Battalion, November 21, 1780 [Ref: G-220]. Mary Walling, wife of the late Col. James Walling, of Washington County, died Tuesday last [before August 23, 1825] in her 64th year [Ref: Z-75].

WALLING, James Sr. Took the Oath of Allegiance before the Hon. Samuel Hughes before March 1, 1778 [Ref: O-33, J-1].

WALLING, Mary. See "James Walling," q.v.

WALLINGSFORD, Elizabeth. See "Michael Hargan," q.v.

WALLIS, William. Private who was enrolled by Capt. Henry Hardman and passed on July 19, 1776 in Frederick (now Washington) County [Ref: D-51].

WALLS, Elizabeth. See "Henry Franks," q.v.

WALLS, Nathan. Took the Oath of Allegiance before the Hon. William Yates in 1778 [Ref: J-12, O-48, which latter source listed the name as "Hathan Walls"].

WALMORE, Michael. Private, Militia, 5th Class, Capt. Jeremiah Spires' Company, 2nd Battalion, 1776/1777 [Ref: M-239, A-1146].

WALTENBACK, Teeter. Private who was enlisted by Lieut. Moses Chapline and passed on July 24, 1776 in Frederick (now Washington) County [Ref: D-50].

WALTER, Jacob. Enrolled in the third militia company organized for the Revolutionary War in the Elizabeth Town District of Frederick County (now the Hagerstown area of Washington County), passed by the Committee of Observation on June 5, 1776, and assigned to Capt. John Reynolds' command [Ref: Q-273]. Private, Militia, 4th Class, Capt. Joseph Chapline's Company, 2nd Battalion, 1776/1777 [Ref: M-241]. Took the Oath of Allegiance before the Hon. Joseph Chapline before April 17, 1779 [Ref: J-5, O-39].

WALTER, John. Private, Militia, 6th Class, Capt. Henry Boteler's Company, 1776/1777 [Ref: M-237, A-1146].

WALTER, Nicholas. Enrolled in the third militia company organized for the Revolutionary War in the Elizabeth Town District of Frederick County (now the Hagerstown area of Washington County), passed by the Committee of Observation on June 5, 1776, and assigned to Capt. John Reynolds' command [Ref: Q-273]. Took the Oath of Allegiance before September 1, 1780 [Ref: X-122].

WALTER, William. Took the Oath of Allegiance before the Hon. Christopher Cruse in Sharpsburg Hundred before March 2, 1778 [Ref: O-34, J-2].

WALTERS, Levi. Private who was enrolled by Capt. Aeneas Campbell and passed by Major Francis Deakins on July 18, 1776 [Ref: D-49].

WALTZ, George. See "George Woltz," q.v.

WAMPOLE, Peter. Private, Militia, Capt. Charles Coulson's Company, enrolled August 28, 1776 [Ref: M-243, A-1146].

WANK, David. See "David Swank," q.v.

WARBLE, Molly. See "Jacob Fisher," q.v.

WARD, Cornelious. Private, Militia, 6th Class, Capt. Daniel Cresap's Company, 3rd Battalion, 1776/1777 [Ref: M-241]. Took the Oath of Allegiance before the Hon. Lemuel Barritt before March 16, 1778 [Ref: O-42, J-7, which sources mistakenly listed the name as "Cosnealne Ward" and "Cosnealve Ward"].

WARD, Edward. Took the Oath of Allegiance before the Hon. Andrew Bruce before March 2, 1778 [Ref: O-41, J-7].

WARD, Edward. Took the Oath of Allegiance before the Hon. Lemuel Barritt before March 16, 1778 [Ref: O-43, J-8].

WARD, Henry. Took the Oath of Allegiance before the Hon. Richard Davis in 1778 [Ref: J-4, O-36].

WARD, Jacob. Took the Oath of Allegiance before the Hon. John Barnes before February 28, 1778 [Ref: O-44, J-9].

WARD, John. Private who was enrolled by Capt. Henry Hardman and passed on July 19, 1776 in Frederick (now Washington) County [Ref: D-51].

WARD, Philip. Private who enlisted in the militia on September 5, 1781 for service in the Continental Army [Ref: D-388].

WARDEN, Larin. See "Larin Hardin," q.v.

WARE, Frederick. Private, Militia, 4th Class, Capt. Michael Fackler's Company, 1776/1777 [Ref: M-245, A-1146].

WARE, Martin. Took the Oath of Allegiance before the Hon. Joseph Sprigg before April 1, 1778 [Ref: O-53, J-16].

WAREMAN, Francis. Private, Militia, 7th Class, Capt. Barnett Johnston's Company, 3rd Battalion, 1776/1777 [Ref: M-242].

WARKIN, Peter. Took the Oath of Allegiance before the Hon. Samuel Hughes before March 1, 1778 [Ref: O-33, J-1].

WARLEY, Thomas. See "Thomas Worley," q.v.

WARMAN, Henry. Private, Militia, 2nd Class, Capt. Griffin Johnson's Company, 3rd Battalion, 1776/1777 [Ref: M-243].

WARMAN, Thomas. Lieutenant, Maryland Line, Rawlings' Regiment, captured and later exchanged on October 25, 1780 [Ref: D-616].

WARNER, Jacob. Private, Militia, 1st Class, Capt. James Walling's Company, 2nd Battalion, 1776/1777 [Ref: M-238, A-1146].

WARREN, Thomas. Lieutenant in Capt. Michael Cresap's Company in 1776 [Ref: L-78]. Took the Oath of Allegiance before the Hon. Andrew Bruce before March 2, 1778 [Ref: O-41, J-6, which listed the name as "Thomas Warring"].

WARTSBARGER, George Frederick. Private, Militia, 8th Class, Capt. Joseph Chapline's Company, 2nd Battalion, 1776/1777 [Ref: M-242, which listed the name as "George Frederick Waterbager"]. Rendered patriotic service by supplying wheat for the use of the military on January 28, 1780 [Ref: W-1190, HH-74, which both listed the name as "George Frederick Wartsbarger"].

WASHERBAUGH, John. Private, Militia, 2nd Class, Capt. Martin Kershner's Company, 1776/1777 [Ref: A-1146, M-247].

WASHINGTON, George. See "William Adams" and "Robert Andrews" and "John Bear" and "Archibald Brown" and Michael Byrne" and "Jacob Cloward" and "Robert Compton" and "Michael Cresap" and "Daniel Donovan" and "Samuel Forsythe" and "Edmond Guire" and "Patrick Kelly" and "John Lynn" and "William Matthews" and "Charles McColough" and "George McDonald" and "Barnaby McMackin" and "Elijah Mills" and "Jacob Mills" and "Michael Mills" and "Adam Myer" and "Thomas Philips" and "Jacob Pindell" and "Philip Pindell" and "Thomas Price" and "Mr. Quin" and "Richard Richards" and "William Sampson" and "William Shule" and "Frederick Snyder" and "John Wagoner" and "William Welch" and "Otho Holland Williams," q.v.

WATERS, George. Enrolled in the second militia company organized for the Revolutionary War in the Elizabeth Town District of Frederick County (now the Hagerstown area of Washington County) on March 9, 1776 [Ref: Q-272, which listed the name as "George Warters"]. Took the Oath of Allegiance before the Hon. Christopher Cruse in Lower Antietam Hundred before March 2, 1778 [Ref: J-3, O-35].

WATERS, Joseph. Private, Militia, 6th Class, Capt. Jeremiah Spires' Company, 2nd Battalion, 1776/1777 [Ref: M-239, A-1146]. Took the Oath of Allegiance before the Hon. Richard Davis in 1778 [Ref: J-4, O-37].

WATSON, James. Private, Militia, 4th Class, Capt. John Cellars' Company, 1776/1777 [Ref: A-1146, M-246]. Took the Oath of Allegiance before the Hon. Henry Schnebley in 1778 [Ref: O-50, J-14].

WATTSTEIN, John. Took the Oath of Allegiance before the Hon. Henry Schnebley in 1778 [Ref: O-50, J-14].

WAYES, Andrew. See "Andrew Mayes," q.v.

WAYNE, General. See "William Lewis" and "Robert Marshall," q.v.

WEAKLEY, James. Private who was enrolled by Lieut. Clement Hollyday and passed by Col. William Luckett on August 8, 1776 [Ref: D-49].

WEALE, George. Took the Oath of Allegiance before the Hon. Richard Davis in 1778 [Ref: J-5, O-37, which latter source listed the name as "George Weele"].

WEAVER, Jacob. Private who enlisted in the militia on August 24, 1781 for service in the Continental Army [Ref: D-388]. Private, Maryland Line, discharged on November 29, 1781 [Ref: I-7].

WEAVER, Michael (1751-1821). Private, Militia, Capt. William Heyser's Company, enlisted July 19, 1776, muster roll dated October 23, 1776 [Ref: D-264, W-1190, L-79, which listed the name as "Michael Weever"]. Private, German Regiment, Lt. Col. Ludwick Weltner's Company, discharged on July 26, 1779 at Fort Wyoming, Pennsylvania [Ref: GG-100, D-265, D-259]. He applied for and received pension S40660 at Shippensburg in Cumberland County, Pennsylvania on September 25, 1818, stating he had enlisted at Hagerstown, Maryland. In 1820 he moved to Franklin County, Pennsylvania and stated he had no family. He died on May 21, 1821 [Ref: GG-100, V-III:3714].

WEBB, John. One of several patriots appointed by the Committee of Observation on December 30, 1776 "to form the county into companies (after the militia had marched) for the purpose of relieving the distressed inhabitants of said county and also to compel the Dunkards and Mennonists to give their assistance." [Ref: Q-346]. Took the Oath of Allegiance before the Hon. William Yates in 1778 [Ref: O-48, J-12].

WEBB, John Jr. Second Corporal, Militia, Capt. Conrad Hogmire's Company, 1776/1777 [Ref: M-244, A-1146]. Took the Oath of Allegiance before the Hon. Joseph Sprigg before April 1, 1778 [Ref: O-53, J-16]. Ensign, Militia, Capt. Philip Pindell's Company, 3rd or Western Battalion, May 16, 1778 [Ref: E-86, which listed the name without the "Jr."].

WEBB, John Sr. Took the Oath of Allegiance before the Hon. Joseph Sprigg before April 1, 1778 [Ref: O-53, J-16].

WEBB, William (1755-1807). Fourth Sergeant, Militia, Capt. Conrad Hogmire's Company, 1776/1777 [Ref: M-244, A-1146]. Took the Oath of Allegiance before the Hon. Joseph Sprigg before April 1, 1778 [Ref: O-53, J-16]. "William Webb, Esq." died on January 21, 1807, aged 52, and is buried in one of the graveyards on the Samuel Newcomer farm near Leitersburg in Washington County [Ref: JJ-V:23].

WEBER, Engell. Took the Oath of Allegiance before the Hon. Henry Schnebley in 1778 [Ref: O-50, J-14].

WEBSTER, Mathias. Took the Oath of Allegiance before the Hon. Richard Davis in 1778 [Ref: J-4, O-37].

WEGG, John. Private, Militia, 7th Class, Capt. Barnett Johnston's Company, 3rd Battalion, 1776/1777 [Ref: M-242].

WEIGLE, George Adam. Enrolled in the third militia company organized for the Revolutionary War in the Elizabeth Town District of Frederick County (now the Hagerstown area of Washington County), passed by the Committee of Observation on June 5, 1776, and assigned to Capt. John Reynolds' command [Ref: Q-273].

WEINNAND, Philip (1754-   ). Private, Maryland Line, who applied for and received pension S1267 in Jefferson County, Kentucky on May 6, 1833, aged 79, stating he was born on March 10, 1754 near Reading, Pennsylvania and lived near Little York, Pennsylvania when he went to Hagerstown, Maryland to enlist in 1776. He lived in Pennsylvania until 1797 when he moved to Kentucky [Ref: V-III:3730, T-52, which latter source listed the name as "Philip Weinnard"].

WEIRICK, Christian. Enrolled in the third militia company organized for the Revolutionary War in the Elizabeth Town District of Frederick County (now the Hagerstown area of Washington County), passed by the Committee of Observation on June 5, 1776, and assigned to Capt. John Reynolds' command [Ref: Q-273]. Private who was enlisted by Lieut. Christian Orndorff and passed on July 20, 1776 in Frederick (now Washington) County [Ref: D-50].

WEIRICK, Elizabeth. See "Michael Weirick," q.v.

WEIRICK, Jacob. Took the Oath of Allegiance before the Hon. Henry Schnebley in 1778 [Ref: J-13, which listed the name as "Jacob Weisrich" and O-50, which listed the name as "Jacob Weiarich"].

WEIRICK, Michael (1754-1825). Fifer, Maryland Line, who applied for pension in York County, Pennsylvania on November 3, 1818. In 1820 he was aged 66 with a wife Elizabeth and a daughter (not named) who lived with them. His widow applied for and received pension W3321 in June, 1839, aged 78 and upwards, stating she was Elizabeth Pimley before marrying Michael Weirick or Weirich on November 16, 1784. A son Nicholas was born on August 12, 1785. Michael died on August 23, 1825 in York County and Elizabeth died on December 29, 1843. The only surviving child in 1851 was Catharine Baum, wife of George S. Baum, of York County, and she was administratrix of her mother's estate on February 22, 1853 [Ref: V-III:3731, N-53].

WEIRICK, Nicholas. Enrolled in the third militia company organized for the Revolutionary War in the Elizabeth Town District of Frederick County (now the Hagerstown area of Washington County), passed by the Committee of Observation on June 5, 1776, and assigned to Capt. John Reynolds' command [Ref: Q-273]. Private who was enlisted by Lieut. Christian Orndorff and passed on July 20, 1776 in Frederick (now Washington) County [Ref: D-50]. See "Michael Weirick," q.v.

WEISE (WISE), Adam (1751-1833). Ensign, Militia (date not given). [Ref: M-139]. Took the Oath of Allegiance before the Hon. Joseph Sprigg before April 1, 1778 [Ref: O-53, J-16, N-53, which latter source listed the name as "Adam Weise"]. Adam Wise or Weise applied for a pension in Dauphin County, Pennsylvania on August 31, 1833, stating he was born on December 23, 1751 at New Goshen in the part of Philadelphia County, Pennsylvania that later became Montgomery County. In 1774 he moved to Hagerstown in Washington County, Maryland, lived there at the time of his enlistment in December, 1776. He was promoted to First Corporal by Capt. Michael Tackler [sic] in 1777, promoted to First Sergeant by Capt. Adam Ott, and in 1780 was commissioned an Ensign in the Washington County Militia. In May, 1783 he moved to Millersburg in Upper Paxton Township, Dauphin County, Pennsylvania. Adam was married three times: (1) ---- (no name given); (2) Mariah ----; and, (4) Catharine Neiman Patton (born November 10, 1785), daughter of Conrad and Catharine Nieman of Montgomery County, Pennsylvania, and widow of James Patton, married on December 10, 1820. Adam died on October 5, 1833 at Millersburg, Pennsylvania and Catharine applied for and received pension W26072 on September 6, 1853 [Ref: V-III:3731, U-25:1 (1937)].

WEISONG, Jacob. Private who was enlisted by Lieut. Moses Chapline and passed on July 24, 1776 in Frederick (now Washington) County [Ref: D-50].

WEISS, Adam. See "Adam Weise," q.v.

WEISS, George. Took the Oath of Allegiance before the Hon. Henry Schnebley in 1778 [Ref: O-49, J-13]. See "George Wise," q.v.

WEISS, John George. Took the Oath of Allegiance before the Hon. Henry Schnebley in 1778 [Ref: O-50, J-13].

WELABERGER, Mathias. See "Matthias Wellberger," q.v.

WELCH, Ossias. Private, Militia, 6th Class, Capt. Isaac Baker's Company, 1776/1777 [Ref: A-1146, M-247].

WELCH, William. Private, Militia, by January 22, 1777 when ordered by the Committee of Observation "to march with some company of militia to the reinforcement of his Excellency General Washington" or appear before the Committee and state his reason for not marching. He apparently marched since he never appeared to the contrary [Ref: Q-48]. Took the Oath of Allegiance before the Hon. John Barnes before February 28, 1778 [Ref: O-44, J-9, which latter source listed the name as "William Welsh"].

WELDAY, Christian. See "Christian Welty," q.v.

WELKER, Andrew. Private, Militia, Capt. Charles Coulson's Company, enrolled August 28, 1776 [Ref: M-244, A-1146].

WELKER, Pall(?). Private, Militia, Capt. Charles Coulson's Company, enrolled August 28, 1776 [Ref: M-244, A-1146].

WELLBARGER, Mathias. Private, Militia, 3rd Class, Capt. John Bennet's Company, 1776/1777 [Ref: M-246, A-1146].

WELLBERGER, Matthias. Private, Militia, 8th Class, Capt. Isaac Baker's Company, 1776/1777 [Ref: A-1146, M-247, which listed the name as "Mathias Willberger"]. Private, Militia, Capt. Martin Kershner's Company, 32nd Battalion, December 27, 1776 [Ref: K-1814 (Box 3), which listed the name as "Matthias Wheelberger"]. Took the Oath of Allegiance before the Hon. John Cellars in January, 1778 [Ref: K-1814, which listed the name as "Matthias Welaberger" and O-40, which listed the name as "Mathias Welabergen"].

WELLINGER, Valentine. See "Wallentine Wollinger," q.v.

WELLS, Jeremiah. Private, Militia, 5th Class, Capt. Basil Williams' Company, 1776/1777 [Ref: M-244, A-1146]. Rendered patriotic service by supplying a blanket for the use of the military in March, 1776, as recorded by the Committee of Observation on April 12, 1776 [Ref: L-82, Q-157, which listed the name as "Jeremiah Wels"]. Took the Oath of

Allegiance before the Hon. Richard Davis in 1778 [Ref: J-4, O-37]. Jeremiah Wells died testate by June 5, 1804 [Ref: MM-13:40, 41].

WELLS, Robert. Private, Militia, 6th Class, Capt. Griffin Johnson's Company, 3rd Battalion, 1776/1777 [Ref: M-243]. Private who was enlisted by Lieut. Christian Orndorff and passed on July 20, 1776 in Frederick (now Washington) County [Ref: D-50].

WELSH, John. Private who was enrolled by Capt. Henry Hardman and passed on July 19, 1776 in Frederick (now Washington) County [Ref: D-51].

WELSH, John Peirce. Private who was enlisted by Ensign Nathan Williams and passed on July 25, 1776 in Frederick (now Washington) County [Ref: D-51].

WELSH, William. Private, Militia, 1st Class, Capt. Barnett Johnston's Company, 3rd Battalion, 1776/1777 [Ref: M-242]. Took the Oath of Allegiance before the Hon. John Barnes before February 28, 1778 [Ref: O-44, J-9].

WELTNER, Ludwick. Lieutenant Colonel, German Regiment, 1777-1781 [Ref: D-264, GG-96]. Colonel, German Regiment, Pennsylvania and Maryland Lines, at Valley Forge in March, 1778 [Ref: FF-222].

WELTY, Christian. Took the Oath of Allegiance before September 1, 1780 [Ref: X-123, which listed the name as "Christian Welday"]. Christian Welty died before October 21, 1797 (date of balance book entry in Washington County), leaving a widow (name not given in this account) and equal shares to Barbara Teckerhoof, Magdalena Boster, and Christly, Mary, Henny, Catha, John, Susanna, and Joseph Welty [Ref: J-35].

WELTY, Catha, Henny, and others. See "Christian Welty," q.v.

WENGER, Leonard. Took the Oath of Allegiance before the Hon. Henry Schnebley in 1778 [Ref: O-49, J-13].

WENTRE, George. Took the Oath of Allegiance before the Hon. Richard Davis in 1778 [Ref: J-4, O-36]. One "George Witner" died suddenly in May, 1824, at his farm about 8 miles west of Cumberland while repairing one of the cog wheels in his mill, leaving a numerous family [Ref: Z-2]. Additional research will be necessary before drawing conclusions.

WERMER, Jacob (reverend). Took the Oath of Allegiance before the Hon. Henry Schnebley in 1778 [Ref: O-50, J-14].

WERT, Jacob. Took the Oath of Allegiance before the Hon. Andrew Rentch before March 7, 1778 [Ref: O-52, J-15].

WERTZ, George (1752-   ). Private, Maryland Militia, with Pennsylvania service [Ref: N-54].

WERTZ, Jacob. Took the Oath of Allegiance before the Hon. Joseph Sprigg before April 1, 1778 [Ref: O-53, J-16, which listed the name as "Jacob Wetz"].

WERTZ, Peter. Rendered patriotic service by providing a rifle for Capt. Daniel Cresap's Company in July, 1775, as recorded by the Committee of Observation at Elizabeth Town on November 4, 1775 [Ref: Q-149]. Private, Militia, 2nd Class, Capt. John Bennet's Company, 1776/1777 [Ref: M-246, A-1146, which listed the name as "Peter Wart"].

WESSA, Jacob. Took the Oath of Allegiance before the Hon. John Stull in 1778 [Ref: O-47, J-11].

WEST, Thomas. Private who was enrolled by Capt. Henry Hardman and passed on July 19, 1776 in Frederick (now Washington) County [Ref: D-51].

WESTERBARGER, John. Private, Militia, 3rd Class, Capt. Jacob Sharer's Company, 1776/1777 [Ref: A-1146, M-248].

WESTERBERGER, Paul. Rendered patriotic service by supplying wheat for the use of the military on March 7, 1780 [Ref: W-1190, which listed the name as "Paul Wertzberger" and HH-73, which listed the name as "Paull Westeberger"].

WEYMER, Jacob. Rendered patriotic service by supplying wheat for the use of the military on April 18, 1780 [Ref: W-1190, HH-72].

WHEAT, Joseph. Took the Oath of Allegiance before the Hon. Richard Davis in 1778 [Ref: J-5, O-37].

WHEAT, Zadock. Took the Oath of Allegiance before the Hon. Richard Davis in 1778 [Ref: J-4, O-37].

WHEELBERGER, Matthias. See "Matthias Wellberger," q.v.

WHEELER, Henry. Private, Militia, Capt. Charles Coulson's Company, enrolled August 28, 1776 [Ref: M-244, A-1146].

WHEETMORE, Christian. Appeared before the Committee of Observation on June 5, 1776 and, stating that he had not enrolled because he was upward of fifty years of age, the Committee remitted his fine (four pounds) for not enrolling due to his age [Ref: Q-269].

WHELAN, Elizabeth. See "John Johnson," q.v.

WHELAND, Peter. Rendered patriotic service by providing a rifle for Capt. Daniel Cresap's Company in July, 1775, as recorded by the Committee of Observation at Elizabeth Town on November 4, 1775 [Ref: Q-148].

WHETSTONE, Balser. Took the Oath of Allegiance before the Hon. John Stull in 1778 [Ref: J-11, O-47, which latter source listed the name as "Bolser Whitstone"].

WHETSTONE, Christopher. Private, Militia, 1st Class, Capt. Isaac Baker's Company, 1776/1777 [Ref: A-1146, M-247, which listed the name as "Christr. Whetstone"].

WHETSTONE, Daniel (1750-   ). Private, Militia, 2nd Class, Capt. Jacob Sharer's Company, 1776, with North Carolina service [Ref: A-1146, M-248, N-54].

WHETSTONE, David. Private, Select Militia, Capt. Adam Ott's Company, 1781 [Ref: M-238, A-1146].

WHETSTONE, John. Third Corporal, Militia, Capt. Martin Kershner's Company, 32nd Battalion, December 27, 1776 [Ref: K-1814 (Box 3), which listed the name as "John Wetchstone"].

WHETSTONE, Matthias. Private, Militia, Capt. Martin Kershner's Company, 32nd Battalion, December 27, 1776 [Ref: K-1814 (Box 3), which listed the name as "Matthias Wetchstone"].

WHETSTONE, Peter. Took the Oath of Allegiance before the Hon. Joseph Sprigg before April 1, 1778 [Ref: O-53, J-16, which listed the name as "Peter Wetstone"].

WHITE, Abraham (1762-1853). Private, Pennsylvania Line, who applied for a pension in Vermillion County, Indiana in September, 1833, stating he was born on June 21, 1762 in Washington County, Maryland and lived at the Redstone Settlement on the Monongahela River in what later became Fayette County, Pennsylvania. There he enlisted in the war and 16 or 17 years later he moved to Shelby County, Kentucky. He married Milly Hopewell, daughter of John, in Bullitt County, Kentucky on January 10, 1808. Milly White applied for and received pension W6473 on 1855, aged 72, stating Abraham had died on June 22, 1853 [Ref: V-III:3783].

WHITE, Chs. Private who was enrolled by Capt. Henry Hardman and passed on July 19, 1776 in Frederick (now Washington) County [Ref: D-51].

WHITE, Isaac S. See "Jeremiah Chapline," q.v.

WHITE, John. Private, Militia, 5th Class, Capt. James Smith's Company, 2nd Battalion, 1776/1777 [Ref: M-240, A-1146].

WHITE, John. Private, Militia, 8th Class, Capt. Michael Fackler's Company, 1776/1777 [Ref: M-245, A-1146].

WHITE, Milly. See "Abraham White," q.v.

WHITE, Peter. One of several patriots appointed by the Committee of Observation on December 30, 1776 "to form the county into companies (after the militia had marched) for the purpose of relieving the distressed inhabitants of said county and also to compel the Dunkards and Mennonists to give their assistance." [Ref: Q-345]. Appointed by the

Committee of Observation to carry the Association of Freemen to male residents in Marsh Hundred on September 14, 1775 "and require their subscription to the same and make an exact account of those who sign and those that refuse with their reasons for refusing." [Ref: Q-143]. Took the Oath of Allegiance before the Hon. Joseph Chapline before April 17, 1779 [Ref: J-5, O-39].

WHITEHEAD, Deborah. See "Joseph Cresap," q.v.

WHITEHEAD, Elizabeth and Mary. See "Michael Cresap," q.v.

WHITEHEAD, Sarah. See "Joseph Cresap," q.v.

WHITEMAN, Jacob. Took the Oath of Allegiance before the Hon. Henry Schnebley in 1778 [Ref: O-50, J-14].

WHITEMIRE, George. Private, Militia, 2nd Class, Capt. James Walling's Company, 2nd Battalion, 1776/1777 [Ref: M-238, A-1146].

WHITEMIRE, William. Private, Militia, 2nd Class, Capt. Joseph Chapline's Company, 2nd Battalion, 1776/1777 [Ref: M-241].

WHITSTONE, Bolser. See "Balser Whetstone," q.v.

WIART, Joseph. See "Joseph Wyand," q.v.

WICKART, Melchor. Private who enlisted in the militia on August 10, 1781 for service in the Continental Army [Ref: D-388]. Substitute, Maryland Line, discharged on October 30, 1781 [Ref: G-656, which listed the name as "Michl. Wickert"].

WICKLE, George. Private, Militia, 3rd Class, Capt. John Rennolds' (Reynolds') Company, 2nd Battalion, 1776/1777 [Ref: M-240, which listed the name as "George Wukle (Wickle?)"].

WICKLE, Henry. Took the Oath of Allegiance before the Hon. John Stull in 1778 [Ref: O-47, J-11, which listed the name as "Henry Wikel"]. Private, Militia, 2nd Class, Capt. Peter Beall's Company, 1st Battalion, 1776/1777 [Ref: M-240, which listed the name as "Henry Wykell"].

WICKS, Daniel. Private who was enrolled by Capt. Henry Hardman and passed on July 19, 1776 in Frederick (now Washington) County [Ref: D-51].

WIDDOWS, Abraham. Private, Pennsylvania Line, who enlisted at Lancaster, Pennsylvania. His brother, Isaac Widdows, aged 68, stated on October 25, 1822 in Washington County, Maryland, that Abraham had served in the Revolutionary War and a few years after the revolution again enlisted and was killed on the Wabash River [Ref: V-III:3821].

WIDMIRE, William. Enrolled in the third militia company organized for the Revolutionary War in the Elizabeth Town District of Frederick County (now the Hagerstown area of Washington County), passed by the Committee of Observation on June 5, 1776, and assigned to Capt. John Reynolds' command [Ref: Q-272]. Took the Oath of Allegiance before the Hon. Christopher Cruse in Sharpsburg Hundred before March 2, 1778 [Ref: O-34, J-2, which listed the name as "William Widmyer"]. See "William Whitemire," q.v.

WIGGINS, John. Private, Militia, 4th Class, Capt. Barnett Johnston's Company, 3rd Battalion, 1776/1777 [Ref: M-242]. Took the Oath of Allegiance before the Hon. William Yates in 1778 [Ref: O-48, J-12, which listed the name as "John Wiggons"].

WIGGINS, Philip. Took the Oath of Allegiance before the Hon. Lemuel Barritt before March 16, 1778 [Ref: O-43, J-8].

WIGGINS, Thomas. Private, Militia, 1st Class, Capt. James Prather's Company, 3rd Battalion, 1776/1777 [Ref: M-242].

WIGGINS, Uriah. Private, Militia, 2nd Class, Capt. Barnett Johnston's Company, 3rd Battalion, 1776/1777 [Ref: M-242]. Took the Oath of Allegiance before the Hon. William Yates in 1778 [Ref: O-48, J-12, which listed the name as "Uriah Wiggons"].

WIGGINS, William. Private, Militia, 1st Class, Capt. Barnett Johnston's Company, 3rd Battalion, 1776/1777 [Ref: M-242]. Took the Oath of Allegiance before the Hon. William Yates in 1778 [Ref: O-48, J-12, which listed the name as "William Wiggons"].

WILAN, Peter. Private, Militia, 1st Class, Capt. John Bennet's Company, 1776/1777 [Ref: M-246, A-1146].

WILD, William. Rendered patriotic service in Hagerstown by providing a rifle to Capt. John Nelson's Company, continental service (Maryland Line), April, 1776 [Ref: Q-162].

WILES, Thomas. Private, Militia, 2nd Class, Capt. John Rennolds' (Reynolds') Company, 2nd Battalion, 1776/1777 [Ref: M-240].

WILES, Thomas Jr. Enrolled in the first militia company organized for the Revolutionary War in the Elizabeth Town District of Frederick County (now the Hagerstown area of Washington County) on January 6, 1776 [Ref: Q-270, W-1190].

WILES, William. Took the Oath of Allegiance before the Hon. John Stull in 1778 [Ref: O-47, J-11].

WILHELM, George (c1755-c1821). Private, Militia, Capt. William Heyser's Company, enlisted July 17, 1777, muster roll dated October 23, 1776, in continental service [Ref: D-264, W-1190, L-79]. Private, German Regiment, Lt. Col. Ludwick Weltner's Company, discharged on July 17, 1779 at Fort Wyoming, Pennsylvania [Ref: D-265]. "George Willhelm" applied for and received pension S40700 in Fayette County, Pennsylvania on September 8, 1818, aged 65; however, on July 7, 1819 he gave his age as 63 and on June 6, 1820 he again gave his age as 65. In 1820 he stated he had wife aged about 60 (no name given) and these children at home: George (age 14), Jacob (age 9), and Priscilla (age 7). [Ref: V-III:3847]. He died in Fayette County, Pennsylvania, age 66 [Ref: GG-100].

WILHELM, Jacob and Priscilla. See "George Wilhelm," q.v.

WILKINS, John. Enrolled in the first militia company organized for the Revolutionary War in the Elizabeth Town District of Frederick County (now the Hagerstown area of Washington County) on January 6, 1776 [Ref: Q-270, W-1190]. Private, Militia, 7th Class, Capt. Joseph Chapline's Company, 2nd Battalion, 1776/1777 [Ref: M-242]. Took the Oath of Allegiance before the Hon. Christopher Cruse in Sharpsburg Hundred before March 2, 1778 [Ref: O-34, J-1].

WILKINS, Thomas. Private who was enlisted by Lieut. Christian Orndorff and passed on July 20, 1776 in Frederick (now Washington) County [Ref: D-50].

WILLBERGER, Mathias. See "Matthias Wellberger," q.v.

WILLERSON, Jeremiah. Took the Oath of Allegiance before the Hon. Lemuel Barritt before March 16, 1778 [Ref: O-43, J-8].

WILLIAMS, Abigail and Albert. See "Gabriel Williams," q.v.

WILLIAMS, Anarah and Archabald. See "Lawrence Williams," q.v.

WILLIAMS, Basil. Captain, Militia, 2nd Battalion, by January 25, 1777 and to at least June 22, 1778 [Ref: Q-51, M-137, M-244, E-145]. One of several patriots appointed by the Committee of Observation on January 9, 1777 "to procure as many blankets as may be wanting to supply Col. Smith's Battalion." [Ref: Q-34, which listed the name as "Capt. Bazil Williams"]. Took the Oath of Allegiance before the Hon. Richard Davis in 1778 [Ref: J-3, O-36]. See "Lawrence Williams" and "Jarratt Williams," q.v.

WILLIAMS, Basil. Private who was enlisted by Ensign Nathan Williams and passed on July 25, 1776 in Frederick (now Washington) County [Ref: D-51]. Fourth Corporal, Militia, Capt. Basil Williams' Company, 1776/1777 [Ref: M-244, A-1146].

WILLIAMS, Benjamin and Bettey. See "Lawrence Williams," q.v.

WILLIAMS, Cassandra. Rendered patriotic service by making hunting shirts for the use of the military in July, 1775, as recorded by the Committee of Observation at Elizabeth Town on November 4, 1775 [Ref: Q-150].

WILLIAMS, Clark. See "Gabriel Williams," q.v.

WILLIAMS, Edward Green. See "Otho Holland Williams," q.v.

WILLIAMS, Eleven. Private, Militia, 8th Class, Capt. Basil Williams' Company, 1776/1777 [Ref: M-244, A-1146].

WILLIAMS, Eli. See "Lawrence Williams," q.v.

WILLIAMS, Elie or Ely (1750-1823). Private, Militia, 4th Class, Capt. Peter Swingle's (Swingley's) Company, 1776/1777 [Ref: A-1146, M-248]. Appointed by the Maryland Convention on November 8, 1776 to be one of the three judges of elections for Washington County [Ref: CC-55, which listed the name as "Ely Williams"]. Took the Oath of Allegiance on May 28, 1777 [Ref: K-1814 (Box 4), which listed the name as "Elie Williams, clerk"]. Appointed Auctioneer of Washington County on March 2, 1781 and Purchaser of Cloathing on June 5, 1781 [Ref: G-334, which listed the name as "Elie Williams" and G-462, which listed the name as "Ely Williams"]. "Colonel Elie Williams, of Washington County, died at Georgetown, D. C. on Sunday last [December 29, 1822], in his 73rd year, a patriot of '76, occasioned by long and severe bilious disorder." [Ref: Z-44, citing the *Hagerstown Weekly Advertiser*, December 31, 1822, and EE-10:2 (p. 57), containing Robert W. Barnes' article citing the *Frederick Herald*, January 4, 1823]. "Eli Williams, whose name appears so frequently among those patriots who were endeavoring to promote the independence was a younger brother of Gen. Otho Holland Williams. He was a soldier in the Revolutionary War, and attained the rank of colonel. He was for many years after the war the Clerk of the Circuit Court for Washington County, a position in which his son, Otho Holland Williams, succeeded him. One of his daughters became the wife of Chief Justice John Buchanan." [Ref: L-76, Z-12, which latter source cited an equity court case in 1827 involving the estate of the late Elie Williams of Allegany County, Maryland].

WILLIAMS, Elisha. See "David Lynn," q.v.

WILLIAMS, Elizabeth. See "Gabriel Williams," q.v.

WILLIAMS, Gabriel (1756-1827). Private, Flying Camp, who applied for pension in Monongalia County, Virginia on April 26, 1818, aged 62, stating he had lived there for 17 years and previously lived in Berkeley County, Virginia and Washington County, Maryland. He married Margaret Lytton (born in March, 1764) in Washington County on June 22, 1784. Their children were: Clark (born December 3, 1784), Abigail (born December 10, 1786), Elizabeth (born September 9, 1788), Ruth (born December 15, 1790 and married ---- Pickenpaw), John (born December 6, 1792 and died December 18, 1806), Gabriel (born December 21, 1795), Mark (born January 18, 1797), Sinthy or Sintha (born March 9, 1799 and died February 4, 1831), Margaret (born November 10, 1801 and died March 1, 1809), Otho L. (born November 4, 1803, married Ruth S. Hale on August 23, 1831 in Greene County, Pennsylvania, and had a son Albert born October 25, 1832), and ---- ("last son" born July 8, 1808). Gabriel died on November 20, 1827 and his widow applied for and received pension W9896 on May 1, 1840 in Henry County, Indiana [Ref: V-III:3853, N-55, N-125]. One Gabriel Williams was a sergeant in the 7th Maryland Line in 1780 [Ref: D-258].

WILLIAMS, Green. See "Lawrence Williams," q.v.

WILLIAMS, Harriet. See "David Lynn," q.v.

WILLIAMS, Harrison. See "Lawrence Williams," q.v.

WILLIAMS, Harry Lee. See "Otho Holland Williams," q.v.

WILLIAMS, James. Private, Militia, 4th Class, Capt. Samuel Hughes' Company, 2nd Battalion, 1776/1777 [Ref: M-238, A-1146]. Took the Oath of Allegiance before the Hon. Samuel Hughes before March 1, 1778 [Ref: O-33, J-1].

WILLIAMS, James. Private, Militia, 8th Class, Capt. Daniel Cresap's Company, 3rd Battalion, 1776/1777 [Ref: M-241]. Private who was enrolled by Capt. Aeneas Campbell and passed by Major Francis Deakins on July 18, 1776 [Ref: D-49]. Took the Oath of Allegiance before the Hon. Lemuel Barritt before March 16, 1778 [Ref: O-42, J-7].

WILLIAMS, James. Private, Select Militia, Capt. Adam Ott's Company, 1781 [Ref: M-238, A-1146].

WILLIAMS, Jarratt or Gerard (1759-1833). Private, Militia, 1st Class, Capt. Basil Williams' Company, 1776/1777 [Ref: M-244, A-1146, which listed the name as "Tarott Williams"]. Took the Oath of Allegiance before the Hon. Richard Davis in 1778 [Ref: J-5, O-38, which listed the name as "Jarrot Williams"]. "Jarratt or Gerard Williams" applied for pension in Fleming County, Kentucky on August 6, 1832, aged 73, stating he had volunteered in February, 1777 at Hagerstown in Washington County, Maryland, and served under his father, Capt. Basil Williams. "Ruth Ann Williams, widow of Gerard" applied for and received pension W298 in Kentucky, stating she was married to him in Pittsburgh, Pennsylvania on February 2, 1792 and her name then was Ruth Clemmons. "Jarrett Williams" made affidavit for his brother Lawrence's pension application and died on June 20, 1833 [Ref: T-35, T-36]. See "Lawrence Williams," q.v.

WILLIAMS, John. Private who was enrolled by Capt. Aeneas Campbell and passed by Major John Fulford on July 18, 1776 [Ref: D-49]. See "Gabriel Williams," q.v.

WILLIAMS, Joseph. Private, Militia, 2nd Class, Capt. Samuel Hughes' Company, 2nd Battalion, 1776/1777 [Ref: M-238, A-1146].

WILLIAMS, Joseph. Private, Militia, 6th Class, Capt. Samuel Hughes' Company, 2nd Battalion, 1776/1777 [Ref: M-238, A-1146].

WILLIAMS, Joseph. Took the Oath of Allegiance before the Hon. John Barnes before February 28, 1778 [Ref: O-44, J-9].

WILLIAMS, Juty or Duty. See "Lawrence Williams," q.v.

WILLIAMS, Lawrence (1758-1834). Private who was enlisted by Ensign Nathan Williams and passed on July 25, 1776 in Frederick (now Washington) County [Ref: D-51]. Private, Militia, 8th Class, Capt. Basil Williams' Company, 1776/1777 [Ref: M-244, A-1146]. Took the Oath of Allegiance before the Hon. Richard Davis in 1778 [Ref: J-4, O-36]. Lawrence Williams applied for pension in Fleming County, Kentucky (in which vicinity he had lived since 1787) on August 6, 1832, stating he was born on February 28, 1758, enlisted in Washington County, Maryland, later enlisted near Hagerstown, Maryland, and also served under his brother Capt. Nathan Williams who was killed at the Battle of Camden in South Carolina. After this tour of duty he moved to Catfish Camp in what later became Washington County, Pennsylvania and also enlisted there in 1779. He moved to Stockton's Station, Kentucky in May, 1787 and married Polly ---- some time between 1787 and 1789 at the home of her brother-in-law Mr. Downing at Kentucky Station (which later was in Mason County) and they immediately went to Stockton's Station to live. Their children were Eli (born March 6, 1790 and still living in 1838 in Fleming County, Kentucky), Basil (born June 20, 1791), Bettey (born August 2, 1794), Anarah (born March 10, 1797), Nancy (born March 22, 1799), Green (born February 7, 1801), Benjamin (born January 22, 1803), Leaven (born March 22, 1805), Reasen (born February 15, 1807), and Samuel (born September 5, 1810). The children of Eli Williams, son of Lawrence, were Sally (born January 11, 1819), Marah (born August 18, 1823), Lawrence (born February 18, 1825), and Harrison (born November 11, 1826). Also shown were Archabald Williams (born November 26, 1826) and Juty or Duty Williams (birth date illegible). In 1832 Jarrett Williams (brother of Lawrence the soldier) lived in Fleming County, Kentucky. Polly Williams applied for and received pension W9018 in Fleming County on September 6, 1838, aged 67, stating that Lawrence had died on September 14, 1834 [Ref: V-III:3862, T-36]. See "Jarratt Williams," q.v.

WILLIAMS, Leaven. See "Lawrence Williams," q.v.

WILLIAMS, Mark and Margaret. See "Gabriel Williams," q.v.

WILLIAMS, Mary. See "William Williams," q.v.

WILLIAMS, Matthew. Private, Militia, 3rd Class, Capt. Samuel Hughes' Company, 2nd Battalion, 1776/1777 [Ref: M-238, A-1146]. Private, Militia, Capt. John Kershner's Company, on duty guarding prisoners of war at Fort Frederick on June 27, 1778 [Ref: D-328].

WILLIAMS, Nathan. Ensign, Upper District, Frederick County (now Washington County), July, 1776 [Ref: D-48]. Captain, Maryland Line, killed at the Battle of Camden in South Carolina [Ref: V-III:3862, V-III:3863]. See "Lawrence Williams" and "Zadock Williams," q.v.

WILLIAMS, Otho Holland (1749-1794). Born on March 1, 1749, son of Joseph Williams and Prudence Holland, in Prince George's County. Otho was appointed to raise funds on January 24, 1775 for the Committee of Observation in Elizabeth Hundred in Frederick (now Washington) County [Ref: L-75]. He served as a lieutenant under Capt. Thomas Price in the Flying Camp and after his company joined Gen. George Washington in Boston, Price was promoted and Otho took command of the company in 1776. At the fall of Fort Washington, Lt. Col. Rawlings was wounded and the command of the regiment fell upon him. Otho was also wounded and compelled to surrender after a desperate struggle. He was a prisoner of war for 15 months in New York until exchanged in 1778. He was then given command of the 6th Maryland Line and was Deputy Adjutant General under Gen. Horatio Gates. He took part in the Battle of Camden in 1780 and was appointed Adjutant General under Gen. Nathaniel Green. Near the close of the war he was promoted to brigadier general. He settled in Baltimore after the war and was appointed Collector of the Port. He subsequently purchased a farm in Washington County and plus a tract at the mouth of the Conococheague, where he laid out the town of Williamsport in 1787. Otho Holland Williams married Mary Smith, daughter of William Smith, and had these children: Robert Smith Williams (died in childhood), William Eli Williams (married Susan F. Cooke), Edward Green Williams (married Anne Gilmor), Harry Lee Williams (died unmarried), and Otho Holland Williams, Jr. (who was thrown from a horse and killed). Gen. Otho Holland Williams died at Woodstock, Virginia on his way to Sweet Springs on July 15, 1794. He is buried in Williamsport, Maryland [Ref: L-78, L-79, D-77, D-255, D-616]. See "Eli Williams," q.v.

WILLIAMS, Otho L. See "Gabriel Williams," q.v.

WILLIAMS, Peter. Private, Militia, 1st Class, Capt. Charles Clinton's Company, 1776/1777 [Ref: M-245, A-1146]. Ensign, Militia, Capt. Charles Coulson's Company, by December 3, 1776 [Ref: M-137, M-243, B-501].

WILLIAMS, Polly. See "Lawrence Williams," q.v.

WILLIAMS, Robert. See "Zadock Williams" and "Otho Holland Williams," q.v.

WILLIAMS, Ruth. See "Gabriel Williams" and "Jarratt (Gerard) Williams," q.v.

WILLIAMS, Sally and Samuel. See "Lawrence Williams," q.v.

WILLIAMS, Shadrack. Private, Militia, 5th Class, Capt. Isaac Baker's Company, 1776/1777 [Ref: A-1146, M-247, which listed the name as "Shaderick Williams"]. Took the Oath of Allegiance before the Hon. Richard Davis in 1778 [Ref: J-4, O-36].

WILLIAMS, Sinthy or Syntha. See "Gabriel Williams," q.v.

WILLIAMS, William (1761-c1840). Private, Maryland and Virginia Lines, who applied for and received pension S11627 in Clermont County, Ohio on September 18, 1835, having lived there over 33 years. He was born on April 24, 1761 in Washington County, Maryland and enlisted there during the war. In the fall of 1778 he moved with his father (no name given) to Washington County, Pennsylvania, then to Brooke County, Virginia, and in 1781 to Ohio County, Virginia, where he also enlisted. He later moved to Newtown in Hamilton County, Ohio and then to Clermont County. William's brother James was born in 1759 and was a Justice of the Peace in Adams County, Ohio in 1835. Zebina Williams (no relationship given) was a Justice of the Peace in Clermont County in 1835. William's widow Mary was living in Gallipolis, Ohio in 1850 [Ref: V-III:3870].

WILLIAMS, William Eli. See "Otho Holland Williams," q.v.

WILLIAMS, Zadock. Ensign, Militia, Capt. Basil Williams' Company, June 22, 1778 [Ref: M-138, M-244, E-145]. Took the Oath of Allegiance before the Hon. Richard Davis in 1778 [Ref: J-3, O-36]. "Zadock Williams, nephew of Nathan Williams, applied for bounty land (#1666-200) on June 15, 1830 in Clarke County, Kentucky, stating his brother Nathan or Nathaniel Williams was killed in battle. On July 8, 1828 the following children of the soldier's deceased brother Zadock Williams were shown as heirs, to wit: Prudence Banfield, Harrietta Stewart, Robert Williams and Zadock Williams (affidavit made in Fleming County, Kentucky). On August 9, 1830 it was stated the soldier's two younger brothers Robert and Jarrett Williams applied in Jefferson County, Kentucky and stated their brother Nathan Williams was killed in battle and that their older brother was named Zedekiah and not Zadock Williams and he was killed by the Indians about 1790 leaving the five above named children." [Ref: V-III:3863].

WILLIAMS, Zebina. See "William Williams," q.v.

WILLIAMSON, Thomas. Private who was recruited and passed by County Lieutenant Thomas Sprigg on April 22, 1780 [Ref: D-336].

WILLIS, Andrew (1752-1823). Soldier who resided in Washington County and was granted a pension certificate in August, 1820, according to an Act of Congress of March 18, 1818, since he had proven that he was "in the enjoyment of a certain degree of poverty" as required by the Act as amended on May 1, 1820 [Ref: W-1190]. Private, Maryland Line, who applied for and received pension S35141 at $96 per year effective March 31, 1818. In 1820 he was aged 68 and had an "old and frail" wife (not named). They lived with a son (not named). Andrew died on December 4, 1823 [Ref: R-43, V-III:3875]. In December, 1817 the Treasurer of the Western Shore of Maryland was directed to pay to Andrew Willis, of Washington County, a private in the Revolutionary War, quarterly, the half pay of a private "as a further remuneration to him for those services by which his country has been so essentially benefitted." On February 18, 1825 the Treasurer of the Western Shore of Maryland was directed to pay to Lettie Willis, of Washington County, half pay of a private "as further compensation for her husband Andrew Willis' services during the Revolutionary War, beginning from date to which husband's pension has been paid." [Ref: AA-409].

WILLIS, Lettie. See "Andrew Willis," q.v.

WILLISON, Cornelious. Private, Militia, 2nd Class, Capt. Griffin Johnson's Company, 3rd Battalion, 1776/1777 [Ref: M-243].

WILLISON, Cornelius. First Lieutenant, Militia, Capt. Griffin Johnson's Company, by December 3, 1776 [Ref: M-138, B-501].

WILLISON, Edward. Private, Militia, 1st Class, Capt. Griffin Johnson's Company, 3rd Battalion, 1776/1777 [Ref: M-243].

WILLISON, Jeremiah. First Lieutenant, Militia, Capt. Griffin Johnson's Company, 3rd Battalion, June 22, 1778 [Ref: M-138, M-243, E-145].

WILLISON, John Jr. Private, Militia, 7th Class, Capt. Griffin Johnson's Company, 3rd Battalion, 1776/1777 [Ref: M-243].

WILLISON, John Sr. Private, Militia, 8th Class, Capt. Griffin Johnson's Company, 3rd Battalion, 1776/1777 [Ref: M-243].

WILLISON, Richard Jr. Private, Militia, 7th Class, Capt. Griffin Johnson's Company, 3rd Battalion, 1776/1777 [Ref: M-243].

WILLISON, Richard Sr. Private, Militia, 8th Class, Capt. Griffin Johnson's Company, 3rd Battalion, 1776/1777 [Ref: M-243].

WILLSON, Gilbreath. Private, Militia, 6th Class, Capt. Charles Clinton's Company, 1776/1777 [Ref: M-245, A-1146].

WILLSON, John Ennees. Took the Oath of Allegiance before the Hon. Richard Davis in 1778 [Ref: J-4, O-36].

WILLSON, Walter. See "Walter Wilson," q.v.

WILLSON, William. Private, Militia, 5th Class, Capt. Jeremiah Spires' Company, 2nd Battalion, 1776/1777 [Ref: M-239, A-1146].

WILSHAP, Delman. The "son-in-law of Delman Wilshap" (name not given) rendered patriotic service by providing a rifle for Capt. Daniel Cresap's

Company in July, 1775, as recorded by the Committee of Observation at Elizabeth Town on November 4, 1775 [Ref: Q-149].

WILSON, David (c1746-1828). Soldier who resided in Washington County and was granted a pension certificate in August, 1820, according to an Act of Congress of March 18, 1818, since he had proven that he was "in the enjoyment of a certain degree of poverty" as required by the Act as amended on May 1, 1820 [Ref: W-1190]. Private, Maryland Line, pensioned at $96 per year effective March 28, 1818 (half pay of a private; resolution passed February 16, 1820). He died on December 21, 1828 [Ref: R-43, AA-410]. On February 20, 1829 the Treasurer of the Western Shore of Maryland was directed to pay to "Rachel Wilson, widow of the late David Wilson, whatever sum appears to have been due to her said husband David Wilson, at time of his decease, on account of his services during the Revolutionary War." [Ref: AA-410].

WILSON, Edward. Took the Oath of Allegiance before the Hon. Andrew Bruce before March 2, 1778 [Ref: O-41, J-7].

WILSON, Lewis. Private, Militia, 1st Class, Capt. Joseph Chapline's Company, 2nd Battalion, 1776/1777 [Ref: M-241]. Took the Oath of Allegiance before September 1, 1780 [Ref: X-123].

WILSON, Rachel. See "David Wilson," q.v.

WILSON, Walter. One of several patriots appointed by the Committee of Observation on January 19, 1777 "to form the county into companies (after the militia had marched) for the purpose of relieving the distressed inhabitants of said county and also to compel the Dunkards and Mennonists to give their assistance." [Ref: Q-43]. Rendered patriotic service by providing necessaries to Capt. John Reynolds' Company in the Flying Camp and belonging to the Maryland Service in July, 1776, as recorded by the Committee of Observation at Sharpsburg on August 6, 1776 [Ref: Q-333]. Took the Oath of Allegiance before the Hon. Christopher Cruse in Sharpsburg Hundred before March 2, 1778 [Ref: O-34, J-2]. "Walter Willson" died before September 6, 1783 (date of balance book entry in Washington County), balance and heirs were not given, but James Chapline and Walter Willson were the executors [Ref: J-24]. See "David Meek," q.v.

WINDER, Alexander. See "James Winder," q.v.

WINDER, Daniel. Took the Oath of Allegiance before the Hon. John Stull in 1778 [Ref: O-47, J-11].

WINDER, George. Took the Oath of Allegiance before the Hon. Andrew Rentch before March 7, 1778 [Ref: O-52, J-15].

WINDER, Jacob. Took the Oath of Allegiance before the Hon. John Stull in 1778 [Ref: O-47, J-11].

WINDER, James (c1735-1782). Took the Oath of Allegiance before the Hon. John Stull in 1778 [Ref: O-47, J-11]. Rendered patriotic service by supplying wheat for the use of the military on March 25, 1780 [Ref: W-1190, HH-73, which both listed the name as "James Winders"]. "James Winder" died on July 4, 1782 (age not given) and is buried beside Alexander Winder (1765-1789) in the Funkstown Public Cemetery in Washington County, Maryland [Ref: J-IV:7].

WINDER, James (c1758-   ). Private, Militia, 2nd Class, Capt. Jacob Sharer's Company, 1776/1777 [Ref: A-1146, M-248, which listed the name as "James Winders"]. Took the Oath of Allegiance before the Hon. John Stull in 1778 [Ref: O-47, J-11].

WINDER, John. Private, Militia, 3rd Class, Capt. James Walling's Company, 2nd Battalion, 1776/1777 [Ref: M-238, A-1146, which listed the name as "John Winders"].

WINDER, Thomas. Third Sergeant, Militia, Capt. James Walling's Company, 2nd Battalion, 1776/1777 [Ref: M-238, A-1146]. Rendered patriotic service by providing clothing for the use of the military on July 5, 1778 [Ref: CC-106, which listed the name as "Thomas Winders"]. Took the Oath of Allegiance before the Hon. John Stull in 1778 [Ref: O-47, J-11].

WINDLESS, Daniel. Private, Militia, 8th Class, Capt. James Walling's Company, 2nd Battalion, 1776/1777 [Ref: M-239, A-1146].

WINFIELD, William. Took the Oath of Allegiance before the Hon. Andrew Bruce before March 2, 1778 [Ref: O-41, J-7].

WINGER, Catherine and John. See "Henry Funk," q.v.

WINKENCOME, John. Private, Militia, 2nd Class, Capt. Michael Fackler's Company, 1776/1777 [Ref: M-245, A-1146].

WINLING, Peter. Private, Militia, 4th Class, Capt. Conrad Hogmire's Company, 1776/1777 [Ref: M-244, A-1146].

WINN, John (c1746-c1825). Soldier who resided in Washington County and was granted a pension certificate in August, 1820, according to an Act of Congress of March 18, 1818, since he had proven that he was "in the enjoyment of a certain degree of poverty" as required by the Act as amended on May 1, 1820 [Ref: W-1190]. Private, Pennsylvania Line, pensioned (S35140) at $96 per year effective April 20, 1818. He had enlisted at Shippensburg in Cumberland County, Pennsylvania, applied for pension in Franklin County, and moved to Washington County, Maryland in 1820. He stated he "had no home, no wife, or child." In 1821 he returned to Franklin County, Pennsylvania [Ref: R-43, V-III:3907, R-43, which latter source stated he served in the Maryland Line].

WINN, Sampson. Private, Militia, Capt. Charles Coulson's Company, enrolled August 28, 1776 [Ref: M-244, A-1146].

WINSEN, Richard. Took the Oath of Allegiance before the Hon. John Barnes before February 28, 1778 [Ref: O-44, J-9, which latter source listed the name as "Richard Wiser"].

WINTER, C. See "Dewald Shaffer," q.v.

WINTERS, George. Private, Militia, 8th Class, Capt. Samuel Hughes' Company, 2nd Battalion, 1776/1777 [Ref: M-238, A-1146].

WINTERS, James. Private, Militia, 3rd Class, Capt. Charles Clinton's Company, 1776/1777 [Ref: M-245, A-1146]. Took the Oath of Allegiance before the Hon. Lemuel Barritt before March 16, 1778 [Ref: O-43, J-8, which listed the name as "James Wintors"].

WIREY, Adam. Third Corporal, Militia, Capt. Michael Fackler's Company, 1776/1777 [Ref: M-245, A-1146].

WIREY, Jacob. Private, Militia, 8th Class, Capt. Peter Beall's Company, 1st Battalion, 1776/1777 [Ref: M-240].

WIRLEY, David. Private, Militia, Capt. John Kershner's Company, on duty guarding prisoners of war at Fort Frederick until discharged on June 5, 1778 [Ref: D-328].

WIRTMAN, John. Private, Militia, 4th Class, Capt. Martin Kershner's Company, 1776/1777 [Ref: A-1146, M-247].

WISE, Adam (blacksmith). Rendered patriotic service and was paid by the Committee of Observation on January 14, 1777 for work done to the carriage of artillery in Col. Stull's Battalion [Ref: Q-39]. See "Adam Weise," q.v.

WISE, Catharine. See "Adam Weise," q.v.

WISE, Deater (Teter). Enrolled in the third militia company organized for the Revolutionary War in the Elizabeth Town District of Frederick County (now the Hagerstown area of Washington County), passed by the Committee of Observation on June 5, 1776, and assigned to Capt. John Reynolds' command [Ref: Q-273, which listed the name as "Deater Wise"]. Private, Militia, 8th Class, Capt. Joseph Chapline's Company, 2nd Battalion, 1776/1777 [Ref: M-242, which listed the name as "Teter Wise"].

WISE, George. Private, Militia, 4th Class, Capt. Michael Fackler's Company, 1776/1777 [Ref: M-245, A-1146]. Private, Capt. William Heyser's Company, muster roll dated October 23, 1776, in continental service and on duty in May, 1777 [Ref: D-264, W-1190, L-79, GG-100]. See "George Weiss," q.v.

WISE, John. Private, Militia, 8th Class, Capt. Peter Beall's Company, 1st Battalion, 1776/1777 [Ref: M-240].

WISE, Peter. Enrolled in the first militia company organized for the Revolutionary War in the Elizabeth Town District of Frederick County (now the Hagerstown area of Washington County) on January 6, 1776 [Ref: Q-271, W-1190]. Private, Militia, 4th Class, Capt. Joseph Chapline's Company, 2nd Battalion, 1776/1777 [Ref: M-241]. Took the Oath of Allegiance before the Hon. Christopher Cruse in Sharpsburg Hundred before March 2, 1778 [Ref: O-35, J-2].

WISE, Valentine. Private, Militia, 5th Class, Capt. Conrad Nichodemus' Company, 2nd Battalion, 1776/1777 [Ref: M-237, A-1146].

WISER, Richard. See "Richard Winsen," q.v.

WISNER, Jacob. There appears to have been two men with this name who served in the Revolutionary War. Additional research may be necessary before drawing conclusions. (1) Private, Militia, 5th Class, Capt. Daniel Clapsaddle's Company, 1st Battalion, 1776/1777 [Ref: M-236, A-1146]. (2) Private, Militia, 2nd Class, Capt. Michael Fackler's Company, 1776/1777 [Ref: M-245, A-1146]. One Jacob Wisner was born in January, 1759 in Lancaster County, Pennsylvania and served in the Maryland Line. He applied for pension (R11743) in Brown County, Ohio on September 1, 1835, stating he had lived in Washington County, Maryland at the time of his enlistment and that he had lived in Ohio for 21 years [Ref: N-55, V-III:3914].

WISNER, Judith. See "George Miller," q.v.

WISOGER, Henry. Private, Militia, 4th Class, Capt. Martin Kershner's Company, 1776/1777 [Ref: A-1146, M-247].

WISSINGER, Susannah. See "John Miller," q.v.

WITNER, George. See "George Wentre," q.v.

WITRICK, Jacob. Private, Militia, 1st Class, Capt. James Smith's Company, 2nd Battalion, 1776/1777 [Ref: M-239, A-1146]. Took the Oath of Allegiance before the Hon. Henry Schnebley in 1778 [Ref: O-51, J-14, which listed the name as "Jacob Witterich"].

WITZELL, Peter. Private, Militia, 2nd Class, Capt. Daniel Clapsaddle's Company, 1st Battalion, 1776/1777 [Ref: M-236, A-1146].

WITZELL, Peter. Private, Militia, 4th Class, Capt. James Walling's Company, 2nd Battalion, 1776/1777 [Ref: M-239, A-1146].

WOBREY, Stephen Jr. Private, Militia, 3rd Class, Capt. Isaac Baker's Company, 1776/1777 [Ref: A-1146, M-247].

WOLF (WOOLF), Jacob (c1763-1839). Private, Militia, 7th Class, Capt. Samuel Hughes' Company, 2nd Battalion, 1776/1777 [Ref: M-238, A-1146]. One "Jacob Wolf married Chaterina Zug, born April 27, 1760." [Ref: *Bible Records of Washington County, Maryland* by the Washington County Historical Society (Family Line Publications, 1992),

p. 94]. Jacob Wolf died on March 7, 1839, aged 76 years and 22 days. He is buried beside his wife Catharine Wolf (March 3, 1756 - December 18, 1815), daughter of Jacob Zuck, in a graveyard walled in with concrete blocks on a farm southeast of Manor Church near Tilghmanton in Washington County [Ref: JJ-V:50]. Since there appears to have been two men named Jacob Wolf or Woolf, additional research will be necessary before drawing conclusions. See "Jacob Woolf" and "John Wolf," q.v.

WOLF (WOOLF), John. Private, Militia, 6th Class, Capt. Samuel Hughes' Company, 2nd Battalion, 1776/1777 [Ref: M-238, A-1146]. John Woolf died testate before December 22, 1792 (date of balance book entry in Washington County), leaving equal shares to Jonathan, Jacob, Daniel, Joseph, Susannah, Hannah, and Elizabeth Woolf, and Esther Seagriest [Ref: J-32].

WOOLF, Jonathan and Joseph. See "Jacob Wolf," q.v.

WOLF (WOOLF), Leonard. Private, Militia, 2nd Class, Capt. James Smith's Company, 2nd Battalion, 1776/1777 [Ref: M-239, A-1146].

WOLF, Mathias. Private who was enlisted by Lieut. Christian Orndorff and passed on July 20, 1776 in Frederick (now Washington) County [Ref: D-50].

WOLFHART, Goodfree. Private, Militia, Capt. Charles Coulson's Company, enrolled August 28, 1776 [Ref: M-244, A-1146].

WOLFKILL, Conrad. Private, Militia, 3rd Class, Capt. Conrad Nichodemus' Company, 2nd Battalion, 1776/1777 [Ref: M-237, A-1146, which listed the name as "Conrod Woolfhill"].

WOLFKILL, Jacob. Private, Select Militia, Capt. Adam Ott's Company, 1781 [Ref: M-238, A-1146].

WOLFORD, John (1763-c1850). Private, Maryland Line, who applied for a pension (R11027) in Hampshire County, Virginia on November 24, 1845, stating he was born in 1763 in Washington County, Maryland, lived there at the time of his enlistment, and moved to Virginia around 1805 [Ref: V-III:3923].

WOLGAMOT, David. Appointed by the Committee of Observation on July 7, 1776 "to take the number of inhabitants within Salisbury Hundred, both whites and blacks, distinguishing respectively the age and sex of each, to be transmitted to the Council of Safety immediately." [Ref: Q-331, which listed the name as David Wolgamet"]. Fourth Sergeant, Militia, Capt. Martin Kershner's Company, 1776/1777 [Ref: M-247, A-1146, which listed the name as "David Wolgamaot"]. Third Sergeant, Militia, Capt. John Kershner's Company, on duty guarding prisoners of war at Fort Frederick, June 27, 1778 [Ref: D-328]. Took the Oath of

Allegiance before the Hon. John Cellars in January, 1778 [Ref: K-1814, O-40, which listed the name as "David Woulgemot" and J-5, which listed the name as "David Woulgamet"].

WOLGAMOT, John. Took the Oath of Allegiance before September 1, 1780 [Ref: X-122, which listed the name as "John Volgamett"].

WOLGAMOT, Joseph. First Lieutenant, Militia, Capt. Martin Kershner's Company, 32nd Battalion, December 27, 1776 [Ref: K-1814, Box 3]. Took the Oath of Allegiance before the Hon. John Barnes before February 28, 1778 [Ref: O-44, J-9, which latter source listed the name as "Joseph Wolgomot"].

WOLGAMOT, Joseph. Private, Militia, 7th Class, Capt. Barnett Johnston's Company, 3rd Battalion, 1776/1777 [Ref: M-242, which listed the name as "Joseph Valganote(?)"].

WOLGAMOT, Samuel Jr. Private, Militia, 7th Class, Capt. John Rennolds' (Reynolds') Company, 2nd Battalion, 1776/1777 [Ref: M-240].

WOLLINGER, Wallentine. Took the Oath of Allegiance before the Hon. John Stull in 1778 [Ref: O-47, J-11, which latter source listed the name as "Wallentine Wellinger"].

WOLTZ, George. Took the Oath of Allegiance before the Hon. Henry Schnebley in 1778 [Ref: O-49, J-12, which latter source listed the name as "George Waltz"].

WOLTZ, Mary. See "Dr. Peter Woltz," q.v.

WOLTZ, Peter (doctor). Served on the Committee of Observation in February, 1777 [Ref: Q-228]. Took the Oath of Allegiance before the Hon. Henry Schnebley in 1778 [Ref: O-49, J-12]. Mary Woltz, relict of the late Dr. Peter Woltz, formerly of Hagerstown, died at the house of her son-in-law Capt. Ent in Fredericktown on April 3, 1824, in her 71st year [Ref: Z-51]. See "Garret Glasson," q.v.

WOLTZ, Peter. Private, Militia, 5th Class, Capt. Peter Beall's Company, 1st Battalion, 1776/1777 [Ref: M-240].

WOLTZLAGER, Valentine. Private, Militia, 5th Class, Capt. Jacob Sharer's Company, 1776/1777 [Ref: A-1146, M-248].

WOLVERTON, Charles. Enrolled in the second militia company organized for the Revolutionary War in the Elizabeth Town District of Frederick County (now the Hagerstown area of Washington County) on March 9, 1776 [Ref: Q-271].

WOODCOCK, John. Private, Militia, 7th Class, Capt. Michael Fackler's Company, 1776/1777 [Ref: M-245, A-1146].

WOODFIELD, Mahala. See "George Miller, Jr." q.v.

WOODHOUSE, David. Private, Militia, 7th Class, Capt. Basil Williams' Company, 1776/1777 [Ref: M-244, A-1146]. Took the Oath of Allegiance before the Hon. Richard Davis in 1778 [Ref: J-3, O-36].

WOODS, Edward. Private, Militia, 2nd Class, Capt. Michael Fackler's Company, 1776/1777 [Ref: M-245, A-1146].

WOOLBACK, Adam. Took the Oath of Allegiance before the Hon. Andrew Bruce before March 2, 1778 [Ref: O-41, J-6].

WOOLBACK, Godfry. Took the Oath of Allegiance before the Hon. Andrew Bruce before March 2, 1778 [Ref: O-41, J-7, which latter source listed the name as "Godfry Wallback"].

WOOLF, Daniel, Elizabeth, and Hannah. See "Jacob Wolf," q.v.

WOOLF, Jacob. Private, Militia, 8th Class, Capt. James Smith's Company, 2nd Battalion, 1776/1777 [Ref: M-240, A-1146]. See "Jacob Wolf," q.v.

WOOLF, Susannah. See "John Woolf," q.v.

WOOLFORD, Godfrey. Private, Militia, 3rd Class, Capt. Charles Clinton's Company, 1776/1777 [Ref: M-245, A-1146].

WOOLHEADER, Adam. Private, Militia, 2nd Class, Capt. Conrad Hogmire's Company, 1776/1777 [Ref: M-244, A-1146].

WOOLSLAYER, Jacob. Second Corporal, Militia, Capt. Michael Fackler's Company, 1776/1777 [Ref: M-245, A-1146].

WORK, Robert. Enrolled in the first militia company organized for the Revolutionary War in the Elizabeth Town District of Frederick County (now the Hagerstown area of Washington County) on January 6, 1776 [Ref: Q-270, W-1190].

WORKMAN, Andrew. Private, Militia, Capt. Charles Coulson's Company, enrolled August 28, 1776 [Ref: M-243, A-1146]. Private, Militia, 7th Class, Capt. Charles Clinton's Company, 1776/1777 [Ref: M-245, A-1146]. Took the Oath of Allegiance before the Hon. Andrew Bruce before March 2, 1778 [Ref: O-41, J-7].

WORKMAN, Isaac. Private, Militia, Capt. Charles Coulson's Company, enrolled August 28, 1776 [Ref: M-243, A-1146]. Private, Militia, 5th Class, Capt. Charles Clinton's Company, 1776/1777 [Ref: M-245, A-1146]. Took the Oath of Allegiance before the Hon. Andrew Bruce before March 2, 1778 [Ref: O-41, J-7].

WORKMAN, Jacob. Private, Militia, 4th Class, Capt. Charles Clinton's Company, 1776/1777 [Ref: M-245, A-1146]. Private, Militia, Capt. Charles Coulson's Company, enrolled August 28, 1776 [Ref: M-243, A-1146].

WORKMAN, John. Private, Militia, 2nd Class, Capt. Charles Clinton's Company, 1776/1777 [Ref: M-245, A-1146]. Private, Militia, Capt.

Charles Coulson's Company, enrolled August 28, 1776 [Ref: M-243, A-1146]. Took the Oath of Allegiance before the Hon. Andrew Bruce before March 2, 1778 [Ref: O-41, J-7].

WORKMAN, John. Took the Oath of Allegiance before the Hon. John Cellars in January, 1778 [Ref: K-1814, O-40, J-6].

WORKMAN, Joseph. Private, Militia, Capt. Charles Coulson's Company, enrolled August 28, 1776 [Ref: M-243, A-1146]. Took the Oath of Allegiance before the Hon. Andrew Bruce before March 2, 1778 [Ref: O-41, J-7].

WORKMAN, Stephen. Private, Militia, Capt. Charles Coulson's Company, enrolled August 28, 1776 [Ref: M-243, A-1146]. Third Sergeant, Militia, Capt. Charles Clinton's Company, 1776/1777 [Ref: M-245, A-1146]. Took the Oath of Allegiance before the Hon. Andrew Bruce before March 2, 1778 [Ref: O-41, J-7]. On September 23, 1780, Col. Lemuel Barritt recommended to Governor Lee that Stephen Workman be commissioned an ensign in the militia at Willstown since so many officers of the Western Battalion had moved out of Maryland to Kentucky and elsewhere [Ref: G-123].

WORKMAN, William. Private, Militia, 5th Class, Capt. Charles Clinton's Company, 1776/1777 [Ref: M-245, A-1146].

WORLEY, David (1759-   ). Private, Maryland Line, who applied for a pension (R11870) in Union County, Ohio, a resident of Millcreek Township, on April 5, 1833, stating he was born in 1759 in Frederick County, Maryland, enlisted at Fort Frederick in Washington County, Maryland, and also served as a substitute for Thomas Worley (no relationship stated). [Ref: V-III:3961].

WORLEY, Francis. Enrolled in the second militia company organized for the Revolutionary War in the Elizabeth Town District of Frederick County (now the Hagerstown area of Washington County) on March 9, 1776 [Ref: Q-272, which listed the name as "Francis Worldley"]. Private, Militia, 5th Class, Capt. Henry Boteler's Company, 1776/1777 [Ref: M-237, A-1146]. Took the Oath of Allegiance before the Hon. Christopher Cruse in Lower Antietam Hundred before March 2, 1778 [Ref: J-3, O-35].

WORLEY, Thomas. Fourth Sergeant, Militia, Capt. Isaac Baker's Company, 1776 (date not given). [Ref: M-247, A-1146]. Second Lieutenant, Militia, Capt. Evan Baker's Company, 3rd Battalion, June 22, 1778 [Ref: M-134, E-145, which listed the name as "Thomas Warley"]. First Lieutenant, Militia (date not given). [Ref: M-140]. Took the Oath of Allegiance before the Hon. John Barnes before February 28, 1778 [Ref: O-44, J-9]. See "David Worley," q.v.

WORLEY, William. Private, Militia, 7th Class, Capt. Isaac Baker's Company, 1776/1777 [Ref: A-1146, M-247].

WORMAN, Francis. Private, Militia, 6th Class, Capt. Griffin Johnson's Company, 3rd Battalion, 1776/1777 [Ref: M-243].

WORTH, Peter. Took the Oath of Allegiance before the Hon. John Barnes before February 28, 1778 [Ref: O-44, J-9].

WOTH, Christopher. Took the Oath of Allegiance before the Hon. John Barnes before February 28, 1778 [Ref: O-44, J-9].

WOULF, ---- (blank). Private, Militia, 1st Class, Capt. James Walling's Company, 2nd Battalion, 1776/1777 [Ref: M-238, A-1146].

WRIGHT, Bazzell (1764-1853). Private, Maryland Line, who applied for and received pension S15966 in Jackson County, Virginia in November, 1833, stating he was born in 1764 in Prince George's County, Maryland and lived in Washington County, Maryland at the time of his enlistment. After the war he lived in Wood County, Virginia and married Nancy Jones, daughter of John Jones, on February 13, 1804 and raised seven children (3 boys and 4 girls, no names given). He died on December 6, 1853 in Jackson County, Virginia and his widow Nancy Right applied for a pension. "Widow's application too dim to read on microcopy, see National Archives Series M804, #2048." [Ref: V-III:2889].

WRIGHT, Elijah (1756-c1840). Private who enlisted in the militia on August 20, 1781 for service in the Continental Army [Ref: D-388]. Substitute, Maryland Line, discharged on October 30, 1781 [Ref: G-656, which listed the name as "Elijah Right"]. He applied for and received pension S1273 in Bullitt County, Kentucky on July 15, 1833, aged 77, stating that he had served three tours of duty during the war: (1) Entered the service in Warrington Township, York County, Pennsylvania in July, 1776; (2) Enlisted in Cumberland County, Pennsylvania in 1777 and served three years; and, (3) Removed to Washington County, Maryland and joined the militia in August, 1781. Elijah was born in York County on February 7, 1756 and ultimately settled in Kentucky. One James Wright was mentioned as his only surviving heir, but no dates or relationship were given [Ref: T-17].

WRIGHT, Henry. Private, Militia, 6th Class, Capt. Barnett Johnston's Company, 3rd Battalion, 1776/1777 [Ref: M-242, which listed the name as "Henry Right"].

WRIGHT, James. See "Elijah Wright," q.v.

WRIGHT, Nancy. See "Bazzell Wright," q.v.

WRIGHT, Samuel. Private, Militia, 4th Class, Capt. Daniel Cresap's Company, 3rd Battalion, 1776/1777 [Ref: M-241, which listed the name as "Samuel Right"]. Took the Oath of Allegiance before the Hon. Lemuel Barritt before March 16, 1778 [Ref: O-42, J-8].

WRIGHT, Thomas. Private who enlisted in the militia on August 17, 1781 for service in the Continental Army [Ref: D-388, D-412]. Substitute, Maryland Line, discharged on October 30, 1781 [Ref: G-656].

WULLENSHLEGER, Jacob. Took the Oath of Allegiance before the Hon. Henry Schnebley in 1778 [Ref: O-49, J-13].

WYAND (WYANT, WIART), Joseph. Took the Oath of Allegiance before the Hon. Henry Schnebley in 1778 [Ref: O-50, J-14]. "Jost Wyant" was a private in the militia, 2nd Class, Capt. Peter Beall's Company, 1st Battalion, 1776/1777 [Ref: M-240]. "Joseph Wiart" died testate before March 17, 1787 (date of balance book entry in Washington County), leaving a widow (not named, but Catherine Wiart was the executrix), and heirs: Elizabeth Forney and her 6 children, Susan Brown and her 5 children, and Sary Angel and her 4 children [Ref: J-27].

WYAND, Ralph B. See "John Seibert," q.v.

WYCKOFF (WYCOFF), Samuel Jr. (1760-   ). Private who enlisted in the militia on September 5, 1781 for service in the Continental Army [Ref: D-388]. He applied for and received pension S4736 in Licking County, Ohio on October 29, 1832, stating he was born on June 10, 1760 in Hunterdon County, New Jersey and lived in (now) Allegany County, Maryland at the time of his enlistment. He later lived in Loudoun and Hardy Counties, Virginia and then moved to Ohio. He also stated his youngest son (no name given) had the family Bible [Ref: V-III:3979].

WYONGE, Philip. Private who was enlisted by Lieut. Moses Chapline and passed on July 24, 1776 in Frederick (now Washington) County [Ref: D-50].

WYORY, Jacob. Private, Select Militia, Capt. Adam Ott's Company, 1781 [Ref: M-238, A-1146].

YAKLY, Barbara and Henry. See "Jacob Yakly (Yakle)," q.v.

YAKLY (YAKLE), Jacob. Rendered patriotic service by supplying wheat and rye for the use of the military on March 13, 1780 [Ref: W-1190, HH-73, which listed the name as Jacob Yakle"]. "Jacob Yakly" died before October 21, 1786 (date of balance book entry in Washington County), leaving a widow (not named, but Barbara Yakly was the administratrix), and equal shares to Tobias Ritter, Leonard Knave, Isaac Aley, Henry Yakly, and Jacob Yakly [Ref: J-27].

YANDERS, Eve. See "Christian Foglesong," q.v.

YARE, Henry. Rendered patriotic service on September 17, 1776 when he "delivered unto Col. Henry Shriock fifty-nine musketts with iron ramrods and wipers and thirteen boyenetts for the use of the flying camp." [Ref: Q-335].

YATES, Amos. See "William Yates," q.v.

YATES, John. Private, Militia, 8th Class, Capt. Peter Swingle's (Swingley's) Company, 1776/1777 [Ref: A-1146, M-249]. Took the Oath of Allegiance before the Hon. Christopher Cruse in Sharpsburg Hundred before March 2, 1778 [Ref: O-35, J-2, which listed the name as "John Yeats"]. Thomas Yates, Sr. died before February 21, 1789 (date of balance book entry in Washington County) and one of his heirs was John Yates [Ref: J-29].

YATES, Joseph and Joshua. See "William Yates," q.v.

YATES, Mary and Sarah. See "William Yates," q.v.

YATES, Thomas. See "John Yates" and "William Yates," q.v.

YATES, William. Elected to serve on the Committee of Observation for the Elizabeth Town District (now the Hagerstown area of Washington County) on September 12, 1775 [Ref: Q-142]. Took the Oath of Allegiance on June 7, 1777 [Ref: K-1814, Box 4]. Justice who administered the Oath of Allegiance in 1778 [Ref: O-48, J-11, J-12]. Justice of the County Court, June 20, 1778 [Ref: E-141, which listed the name as "William Yeates"]. Justice of the Peace, January 30, 1781 [Ref: G-293, which listed the name as "William Yeates"]. One William Yates died testate before October 12, 1790 (date of balance book entry in Washington County), leaving a widow (no name given in this account) and equal shares to Sarah, Mary, Joseph, Joshua, William, and Amos Yates [Ref: J-29, J-30].

YATES, William. Private, Militia, 1st Class, Capt. Barnett Johnston's Company, 3rd Battalion, 1776/1777 [Ref: M-242]. Thomas Yates, Sr. died before February 21, 1789 (date of balance book entry in Washington County) and one of his heirs was William Yates [Ref: J-29]. Also see the other "William Yates," q.v.

YEAKLEY, Michael. Private, Militia, Capt. William Heyser's Company, enlisted July 22, 1776, muster roll dated October 23, 1776, in continental service [Ref: D-264, W-1190, L-79, which listed the name as "Michael Yeakly"]. Private, German Regiment, Lt. Col. Ludwick Weltner's Company, discharged on July 17, 1779 at Fort Wyoming, Pennsylvania [Ref: GG-100, D-265, which listed the name as "Michael Yockley"]. Applied for depreciation pay by March, 1785 [Ref: GG-100, which listed the name as "Michael Yeakly, Yakely, Yockley, Jackell"].

YEATES, William. See "William Yates," q.v.

YERTEE, Peter (1740-1824). Private, Militia, 1st Class, Capt. Henry Boteler's Company, 1776/1777 [Ref: M-237, A-1146, which listed the name as "Peter Yosty"]. "Peter Yertee" was born in 1740, died in 1824, and is buried beside Magdalene Yertee (1738-1820) in a graveyard on the Wilbur Jennings farm at the north end of Brownville in Washington County, Maryland [Ref: JJ-III:55].

YOCKLEY, Michael. See "Michael Yeakley," q.v.

YOST, Henry. Private, Militia, 3rd Class, Capt. Jacob Sharer's Company, 1776/1777 [Ref: A-1146, M-248, which listed the name as Henry Youst"]. First Lieutenant, Militia, Capt. John Funk's Company, 2nd Battalion, June 22, 1778 [Ref: M-140, E-145]. Rendered patriotic service by providing a rifle for Capt. Daniel Cresap's Company in July, 1775, as recorded by the Committee of Observation at Elizabeth Town on November 4, 1775 [Ref: Q-149]. In January, 1776, the Committee of Observation ordered that Henry Yost "be supplied with six pounds of powder to prove his muskets with." [Ref: Q-152]. Took the Oath of Allegiance before the Hon. John Stull in 1778 [Ref: O-47, J-11].

YOST, S. See "Dewald Shaffer," q.v.

YOSTY, Peter. See "Peter Yertee," q.v.

YOUNG, Balser. Private, Militia, 3rd Class, Capt. Isaac Baker's Company, 1776/1777 [Ref: A-1146, M-247]. Private who enlisted in the militia on August 15, 1781 for service in the Continental Army [Ref: D-388].

YOUNG, Catharine. See "Ludwick Young," q.v.

YOUNG, Eustachius. Took the Oath of Allegiance before the Hon. Henry Schnebley in 1778 [Ref: O-50, J-13].

YOUNG, George (reverend). Took the Oath of Allegiance before the Hon. Henry Schnebley in 1778 [Ref: O-49, J-13].

YOUNG, George. Private, Militia, 6th Class, Capt. Charles Clinton's Company, 1776/1777 [Ref: M-245, A-1146]. Private, Militia, 8th Class, Capt. John Bennet's Company, 1776/1777 [Ref: M-246, A-1146]. Took the Oath of Allegiance before the Hon. Henry Schnebley in 1778 [Ref: O-49, J-13]. Ensign, Militia, by November 17, 1780 [Ref: M-140].

YOUNG, Godfrey. Private, Militia, Capt. William Heyser's Company, muster roll dated October 23, 1776, in continental service and on duty in May, 1777 [Ref: D-264, W-1190, L-79, GG-100, which latter source listed the name as "Godfried Young"].

YOUNG, Henry (1732-1829). Soldier who resided in Washington County and was granted a pension certificate in August, 1820, according to an Act of Congress of March 18, 1818, since he had proven that he was "in the enjoyment of a certain degree of poverty" as required by the Act as amended on May 1, 1820 [Ref: W-1190]. Private, Pennsylvania Line, pensioned at $96 per year effective June 16, 1818 [Ref: R-43]. "Henry Young died in Sharpsburg on February 6, 1829 in his 97th year, an old

Revolutionary soldier; served as a teacher in the German and English language. He has been an inhabitant of Sharpsburg for upwards of 30 years. He was a U. S. pensioner for several years; resided in the family of William Rohrback for last 5 years; interred in German Lutheran burying ground; discourse delivered by Rev. Defenbaugh of this place [Hagerstown]." [Ref: Z-107].

YOUNG, Isaac. See "Lodwick Young," q.v.

YOUNG, Jacob. Private, Militia, 5th Class, Capt. John Cellars' Company, 1776/1777 [Ref: A-1146, M-246]. See "Lodwick Young," q.v.

YOUNG, John. Private, Militia, 6th Class, Capt. Samuel Hughes' Company, 2nd Battalion, 1776/1777 [Ref: M-238, A-1146]. Took the Oath of Allegiance before the Hon. Henry Schnebley in 1778 [Ref: O-51, J-14].

YOUNG, Ludwick. Appointed by the Committee of Observation to carry the Association of Freemen to male residents in Elizabeth Town Hundred on September 14, 1775 "and require their subscription to the same and make an exact account of those who sign and those that refuse with their reasons for refusing." [Ref: Q-143]. Second Lieutenant, Militia, Capt. John Cellars' Company, 1776/1777 [Ref: M-246, A-1146]. Served on the Committee of Observation for the Elizabeth Town District (now the Hagerstown area of Washington County) in December, 1776 [Ref: Q-340]. Took the Oath of Allegiance before the Hon. Henry Schnebley in 1778 [Ref: O-49, J-12, which listed the name as "Ludwig Young"]. "Lodwick Young" died testate before June 4, 1799 (date of balance book entry in Washington County), leaving equal shares to Jacob Young, Marian Smith, Rebecca Rench, Isaac Young, and Lodwick Young [Ref: J-37]. Catharine Young, widow of the late Ludwick Young, formerly of Washington County, died at the house of her sister Mrs. Rahauser in Hagerstown on October 27, 1825, in her 58th year [Ref: Z-78].

YOUNG, Magdelena and Matthias. See "Phillip Strumbaugh," q.v.

YOUNG, Michael. Private, Militia, 7th Class, Capt. Martin Kershner's Company, 1776/1777 [Ref: A-1146, M-248]. Private, Militia, Capt. Martin Kershner's Company, 32nd Battalion, December 27, 1776 [Ref: K-1814 (Box 3), which listed the name as "Michel Young"]. Took the Oath of Allegiance before the Hon. John Cellars in January, 1778 [Ref: K-1814, O-40, J-5].

YOUNG, Samuel. Private, Militia, 2nd Class, Capt. Michael Fackler's Company, 1776/1777 [Ref: M-245, A-1146]. Rendered patriotic service in Hagerstown by providing sundries to Capt. John Nelson's Company, continental service (Maryland Line), April, 1776 [Ref: Q-161]. Took the

Oath of Allegiance before the Hon. John Cellars in January, 1778 [Ref: K-1814, O-40, J-6]. "Samuel Young, M. D." was born in County Down, Ireland in May, 1739, died on July 23, 1838, was buried in Old St. John's Lutheran Churchyard, and subsequently reinterred in Rose Hill Cemetery in Hagerstown [Ref: JJ-VII:106].

YOUNGER, Tiller. Private, Militia, 7th Class, Capt. Henry Boteler's Company, 1776/1777 [Ref: M-237, A-1146]. Private, Militia, 3rd Class, Capt. John Rennolds' (Reynolds') Company, 2nd Battalion, 1776/1777 [Ref: M-240]. Private who enlisted in the militia on August 18, 1781 for service in the Continental Army [Ref: D-387].

ZACHARIAH, Jacob. Private, Militia, 6th Class, Capt. Jacob Sharer's Company, 1776/1777 [Ref: A-1146, M-248, which listed the name as "Jacob Zacharias"]. Took the Oath of Allegiance before the Hon. John Stull in 1778 [Ref: O-47, J-11].

ZAPP, George. See "George Sapp," q.v.

ZELLER, Jacob. Rendered patriotic service by supplying wheat for the use of the military on February 11, 1780 [Ref: W-1190, HH-72]. Elizabeth Zeller, wife of Capt. Jacob Zeller, of Washington County, died on September 27, 1823 after a short illness, aged about 57, leaving a husband and 5 children [Ref: Z-48]. See "Jacob Cellar," q.v.

ZIMMERMAN, Yoest. Took the Oath of Allegiance before the Hon. John Cellars in January, 1778 [Ref: K-1814, O-40, J-6, which latter source listed the name as "Joest Simerman"].

ZINN, George. See "George Sinn," q.v.

ZOTT, Michael. Took the Oath of Allegiance before the Hon. Henry Schnebley in 1778 [Ref: O-49, J-12].

ZUCK (ZUG), Catherine (Chaterina). See "Jacob Wolf," q.v.

ZWINGLY, George. See "George Swingley," q.v.

OTHER BOOKS BY THE AUTHOR:

A Closer Look at St. John's Parish Registers [Baltimore County, Maryland], 1701-1801

A Collection of Maryland Church Records

A Guide to Genealogical Research in Maryland: 5th Edition, Revised and Enlarged

Abstracts of the Ledgers and Accounts of the Bush Store and Rock Run Store, 1759-1771

Abstracts of the Orphans Court Proceedings of Harford County, 1778-1800

Abstracts of Wills, Harford County, Maryland, 1800-1805

Baltimore City [Maryland] Deaths and Burials, 1834-1840

Baltimore County, Maryland, Overseers of Roads, 1693-1793

Bastardy Cases in Baltimore County, Maryland, 1673-1783

Bastardy Cases in Harford County, Maryland, 1774-1844

Bible and Family Records of Harford County, Maryland, Families: Volume V

Children of Harford County: Indentures and Guardianships, 1801-1830

Colonial Delaware Soldiers and Sailors, 1638-1776

Colonial Families of the Eastern Shore of Maryland
Volumes 5, 6, 7, 8, 9, 11, 12, 13, 14, and 16

Colonial Maryland Soldiers and Sailors, 1634-1734

Dr. John Archer's First Medical Ledger, 1767-1769, Annotated Abstracts

Early Anglican Records of Cecil County

Early Harford Countians, Individuals Living in Harford County, Maryland in Its Formative Years
Volume 1: A to K, Volume 2: L to Z, and Volume 3: Supplement

Harford County Taxpayers in 1870, 1872 and 1883

Harford County, Maryland, Divorce Cases, 1827-1912: An Annotated Index

Heirs and Legatees of Harford County, Maryland, 1774-1802

Heirs and Legatees of Harford County, Maryland, 1802-1846

Inhabitants of Baltimore County, Maryland, 1763-1774

Inhabitants of Cecil County, Maryland, 1649-1774

Inhabitants of Harford County, Maryland, 1791-1800

Inhabitants of Kent County, Maryland, 1637-1787

Joseph A. Pennington & Co., Havre De Grace, Maryland, Funeral Home Records:
Volume II, 1877-1882, 1893-1900

Maryland Bible Records, Volume 1: Baltimore and Harford Counties

Maryland Bible Records, Volume 2: Baltimore and Harford Counties

Maryland Bible Records: Volume 3, Carroll County

Maryland Bible Records: Volume 4, Eastern Shore

Maryland Deponents, 1634-1799

Maryland Deponents: Volume 3, 1634-1776

Maryland Public Service Records, 1775-1783: A Compendium of Men and Women of Maryland Who Rendered Aid in Support of the American Cause against Great Britain during the Revolutionary War

Marylanders to Carolina: Migration of Marylanders to North Carolina and South Carolina prior to 1800

Marylanders to Kentucky, 1775-1825

Methodist Records of Baltimore City, Maryland: Volume 1, 1799-1829
Methodist Records of Baltimore City, Maryland: Volume 2, 1830-1839
Methodist Records of Baltimore City, Maryland: Volume 3, 1840-1850 (East City Station)
More Maryland Deponents, 1716-1799
More Marylanders to Carolina: Migration of Marylanders to North Carolina and South Carolina prior to 1800
More Marylanders to Kentucky, 1778-1828
Presbyterian Records of Baltimore City, Maryland, 1765-1840
Quaker Records of Baltimore and Harford Counties, Maryland, 1801-1825
Quaker Records of Northern Maryland, 1716-1800
Quaker Records of Southern Maryland, 1658-1800
Revolutionary Patriots of Anne Arundel County, Maryland
Revolutionary Patriots of Baltimore Town and Baltimore County, 1775-1783
Revolutionary Patriots of Calvert and St. Mary's Counties, Maryland, 1775-1783
Revolutionary Patriots of Caroline County, Maryland, 1775-1783
Revolutionary Patriots of Cecil County, Maryland
Revolutionary Patriots of Charles County, Maryland, 1775-1783
Revolutionary Patriots of Delaware, 1775-1783
Revolutionary Patriots of Dorchester County, Maryland 1775-1783
Revolutionary Patriots of Frederick County, Maryland, 1775-1783
Revolutionary Patriots of Harford County, Maryland, 1775-1783
Revolutionary Patriots of Kent and Queen Anne's Counties
Revolutionary Patriots of Lancaster County, Pennsylvania
Revolutionary Patriots of Maryland, 1775-1783: A Supplement
Revolutionary Patriots of Maryland, 1775-1783: Second Supplement
Revolutionary Patriots of Montgomery County, Maryland, 1776-1783
Revolutionary Patriots of Prince George's County, Maryland, 1775-1783
Revolutionary Patriots of Talbot County, Maryland, 1775-1783
Revolutionary Patriots of Worcester and Somerset Counties, Maryland, 1775-1783
St. George's (Old Spesutia) Parish, Harford County, Maryland: Church and Cemetery Records, 1820-1920
St. John's and St. George's Parish Registers, 1696-1851
Survey Field Book of David and William Clark in Harford County, Maryland, 1770-1812
The Crenshaws of Kentucky, 1800-1995
The Delaware Militia in the War of 1812
Union Chapel United Methodist Church Cemetery Tombstone Inscriptions, Wilna, Harford County, Maryland

www.ingramcontent.com/pod-product-compliance
Lightning Source LLC
Chambersburg PA
CBHW050326230426
43663CB00010B/1754